I0762239

Leonardo, Frida and the Others

The History of Art
800 Years — 100 Artists

CAMILLE JOUNEAUX

Leonardo, Frida and the Others

The History of Art
800 Years — 100 Artists

PRESTEL
MUNICH • LONDON • NEW YORK

Foreword

When I began to take a serious interest in the history of art, I sought to find my own path, as I visited venues, read, and watched documentaries. I gradually acquired a jumbled collection of knowledge, which I then needed to organise, articulate, and sometimes deconstruct. Above all, I became aware that there was an unspoken foundation of essential notions that were only explained to us on rare occasions. Had I been aware of these fundamentals from the beginning, the learning process, for me, would have been faster and easier. This is the first observation that guided the writing of this book: gathering the fundamentals, the essential knowledge that can enable one to decode a painting containing a wealth of references.

These fundamentals are also the artists presented in this book, in 'chrono-thematic' order, i.e. by period, then by school or by movement. Of course, this process required some arbitration. Some choices were difficult indeed, whereas some were more obvious. Who could imagine this book without the presence of Leonardo da Vinci or Vincent Van Gogh? However, alongside these ineffable monuments of painting (and the comforting landmarks that they represent), this book introduces new faces, particularly those of women artists – not because they have remained unknown until this day, far from it. However, their works are less often cited in books like this one, as if they were simply embedded in a global history, however legitimate they may be.

Similarly, the history of painting is often narrated with a capital *H*, as if it were universal. It isn't, however; the history taught is that of Western painting. For this reason, I wanted to evoke other continents and cultures, even if only briefly. The alternative would have required me to write an encyclopaedia spanning multiple volumes, which was not my purpose. My aim is to show that, alongside the history that we know and believe to be that of all humans, a thousand other equally captivating histories unfurled. And this is the second axis that structures this book: the desire to offer a more balanced vision of eight centuries of painting.

These two approaches come together to offer a history of painting told through artists and their works, deciphered step by step.
A history punctuated by instructive parentheses and delightful parallels, inviting readers to understand how this great uninterrupted fresco, from Giotto to Banksy, came into existence.

From Giotto to Banksy
An uninterrupted fresco

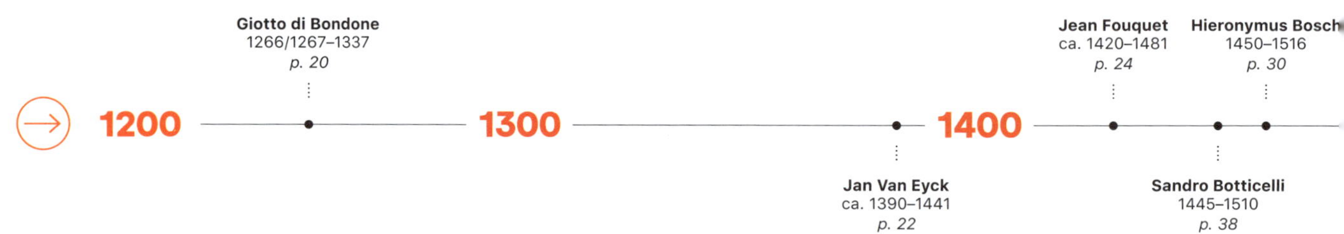

Rachel Ruysch
1664–1750
p. 108

Antoine Watteau
1684–1721
p. 138

Giambattista Tiepolo
1696–1770
p. 150

William Hogarth
1697–1764
p. 148

Jean Siméon Chardin
1699–1779
p. 144

1700

François Boucher
1703–1770
p. 154

Jean-Honoré Fragonard
1732–1806
p. 158

Francisco de Goya
1746–1828
p. 174

Jacques-Louis David
1748–1825
p. 170

Adelaide Labille-Guiard
1749–1803
p. 164

Élisabeth Vigée Le Brun
1755–1842
p. 168

Marie-Guillemine Benoist
1768–1826
p. 172

Caspar David Friedrich
1774–1840
p. 176

J. M. W. Turner
1775–1851
p. 178

Jean-Auguste-Dominique Ingres
1780–1867
p. 180

Théodore Géricault
1791–1824
p. 184

Eugène Delacroix
1798–1863
p. 190

1800

Jean-François Millet
1814–1875
p. 202

Gustave Courbet
1819–1877
p. 198

Rosa Bonheur
1822–1899
p. 206

William Bouguereau
1825–1905
p. 210

Gustave Moreau
1826–1898
p. 212

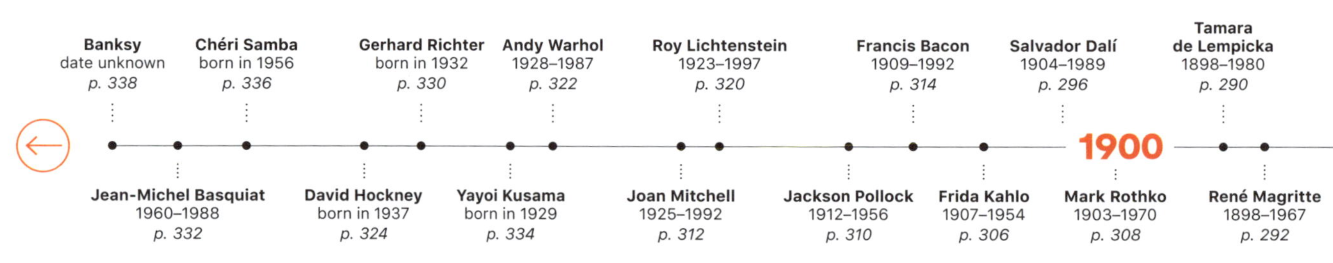

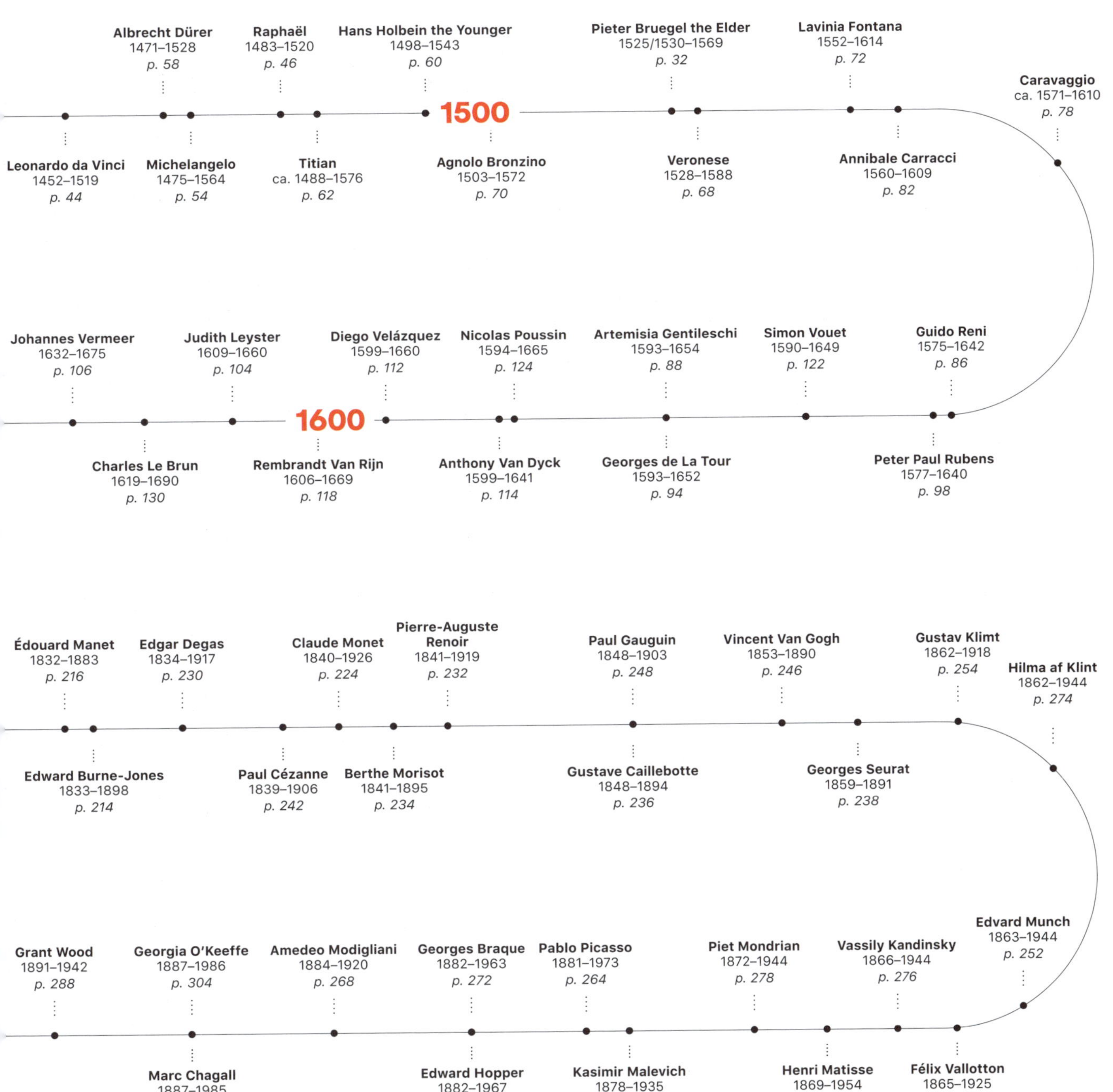

Albrecht Dürer
1471–1528
p. 58
Raphaël
1483–1520
p. 46
Hans Holbein the Younger
1498–1543
p. 60
Pieter Bruegel the Elder
1525/1530–1569
p. 32
Lavinia Fontana
1552–1614
p. 72
Caravaggio
ca. 1571–1610
p. 78
1500
Leonardo da Vinci
1452–1519
p. 44
Michelangelo
1475–1564
p. 54
Titian
ca. 1488–1576
p. 62
Agnolo Bronzino
1503–1572
p. 70
Veronese
1528–1588
p. 68
Annibale Carracci
1560–1609
p. 82
Johannes Vermeer
1632–1675
p. 106
Judith Leyster
1609–1660
p. 104
Diego Velázquez
1599–1660
p. 112
Nicolas Poussin
1594–1665
p. 124
Artemisia Gentileschi
1593–1654
p. 88
Simon Vouet
1590–1649
p. 122
Guido Reni
1575–1642
p. 86
1600
Charles Le Brun
1619–1690
p. 130
Rembrandt Van Rijn
1606–1669
p. 118
Anthony Van Dyck
1599–1641
p. 114
Georges de La Tour
1593–1652
p. 94
Peter Paul Rubens
1577–1640
p. 98
Édouard Manet
1832–1883
p. 216
Edgar Degas
1834–1917
p. 230
Claude Monet
1840–1926
p. 224
Pierre-Auguste Renoir
1841–1919
p. 232
Paul Gauguin
1848–1903
p. 248
Vincent Van Gogh
1853–1890
p. 246
Gustav Klimt
1862–1918
p. 254
Hilma af Klint
1862–1944
p. 274
Edward Burne-Jones
1833–1898
p. 214
Paul Cézanne
1839–1906
p. 242
Berthe Morisot
1841–1895
p. 234
Gustave Caillebotte
1848–1894
p. 236
Georges Seurat
1859–1891
p. 238
Grant Wood
1891–1942
p. 288
Georgia O'Keeffe
1887–1986
p. 304
Amedeo Modigliani
1884–1920
p. 268
Georges Braque
1882–1963
p. 272
Pablo Picasso
1881–1973
p. 264
Piet Mondrian
1872–1944
p. 278
Vassily Kandinsky
1866–1944
p. 276
Edvard Munch
1863–1944
p. 252
Marc Chagall
1887–1985
p. 270
Edward Hopper
1882–1967
p. 302
Kasimir Malevich
1878–1935
p. 280
Henri Matisse
1869–1954
p. 262
Félix Vallotton
1865–1925
p. 250

Contents

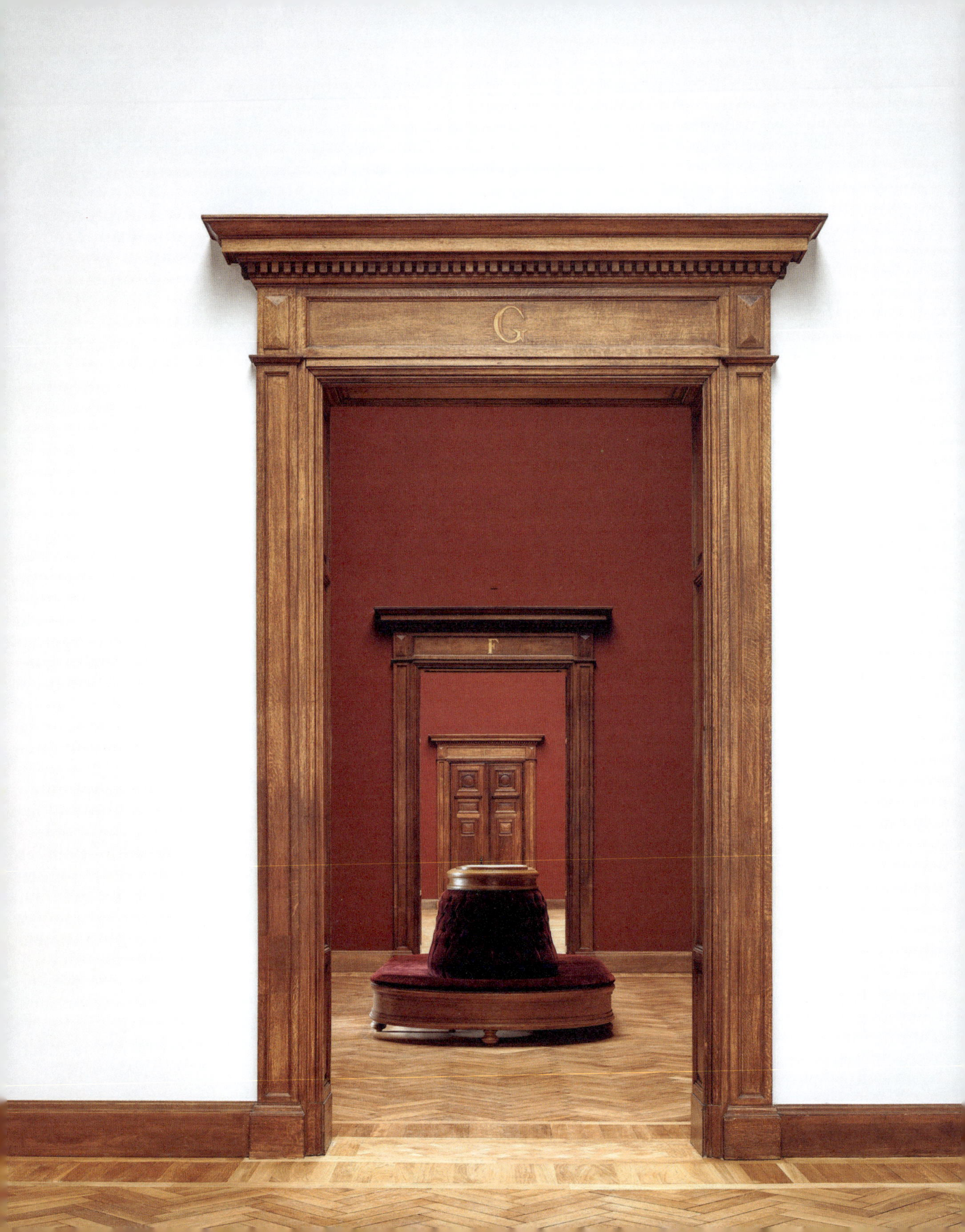
G
F

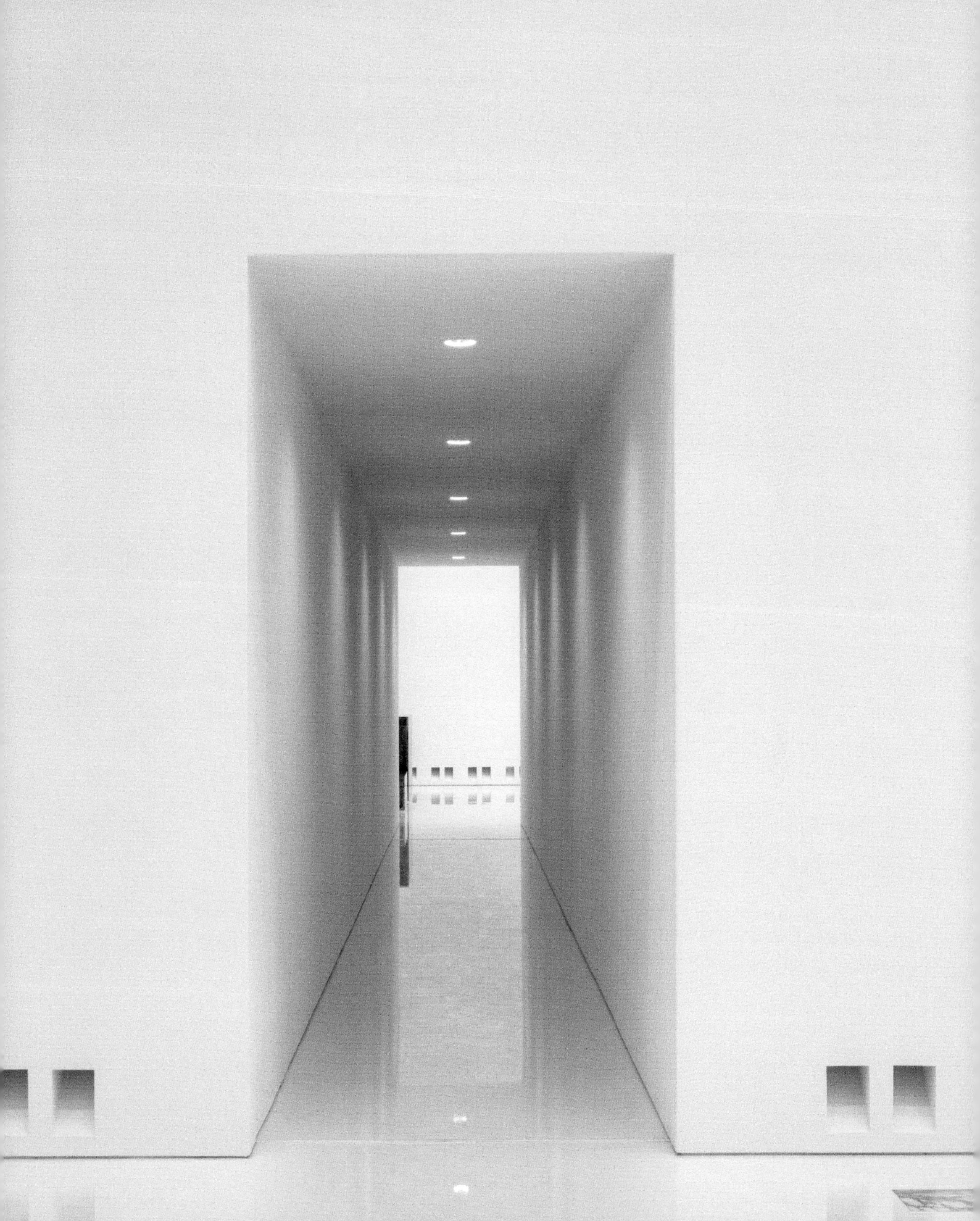

An ideal museum to learn to find your way around

You are here

All museums are different: each institution is organised around the collections that it hosts, which vary from one location to another. However, there is a typical organisation within traditional museums of fine arts, presented here in the form of an ideal museum. When a visitor becomes aware of this, they are able to find their way around easily, and better understand what they are looking at.

A walk through the ages

Routes are generally chronological, i.e. works are presented according to their date of creation. This allows visitors within a single room to capture a view of an entire century, or any given period, at a glance. If you are following a traditional tour route, you will very likely start with the oldest paintings and finish with modern and contemporary art.

By painting schools

When a collection contains a substantial number of works, these are organised according to countries and movements.

When works are organised both according to the date and the subject, the museum is said to offer a 'chrono-thematic' tour.

If you are admiring a work by Botticelli, the Italian painter of the Renaissance, you are unlikely to see it presented next to a work by Renoir, the French painter of the 19th century.

Ground floor

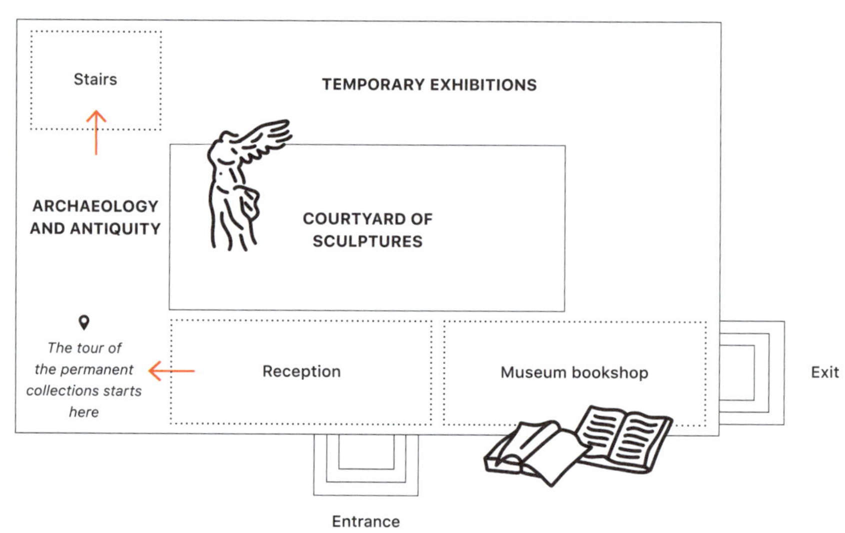

First floor

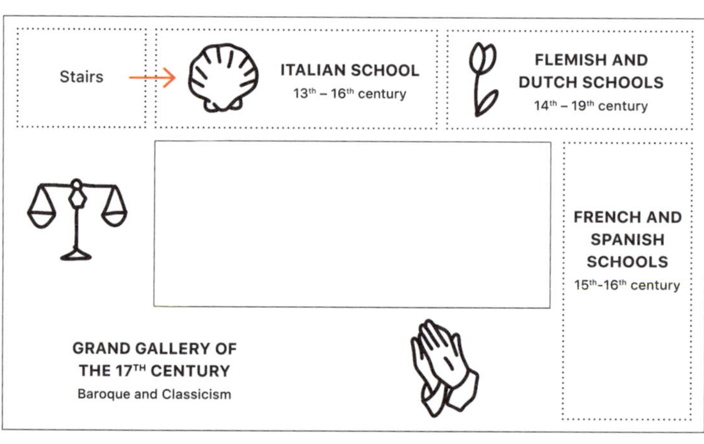

THE PRECIOUS CAPTION

While the location and context where a work is exhibited provide useful information, nothing beats reading the museum label (also referred to as a caption) to learn all about it. The caption is the painting's identity card. It provides the visitor with information about the main characteristics of the work: title, artist, date or period of production, creation technique, size, etc.

Second floor

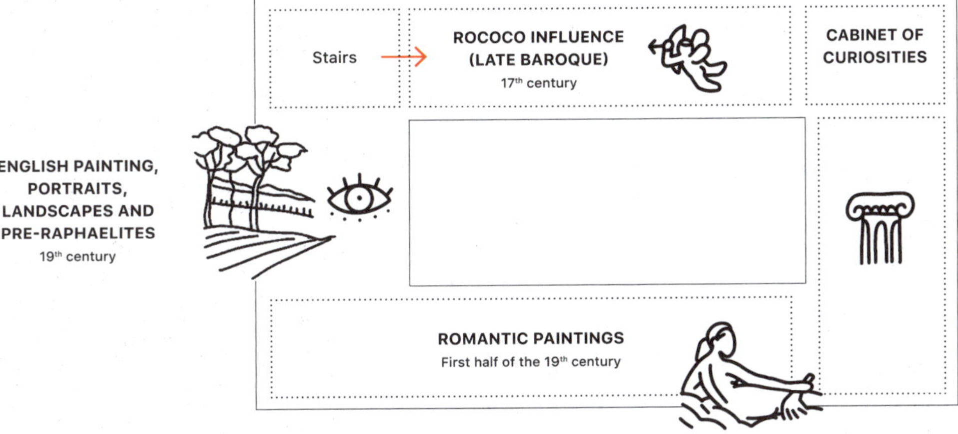

Third floor

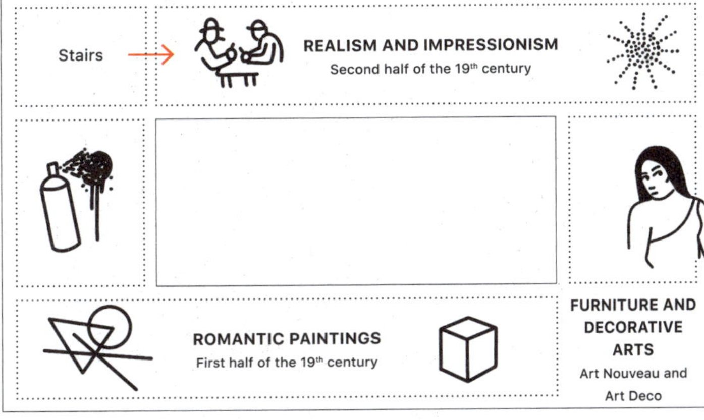

BEHIND THE SCENES

This ideal museum could also feature additional rooms, where young visitors might attend creative workshops. Today, institutions are promoting initiatives to encourage the public to visit these venues regularly. And let's not forget that every museum features spaces that are not accessible to visitors, such as storage rooms, where they keep works that are currently not exhibited.

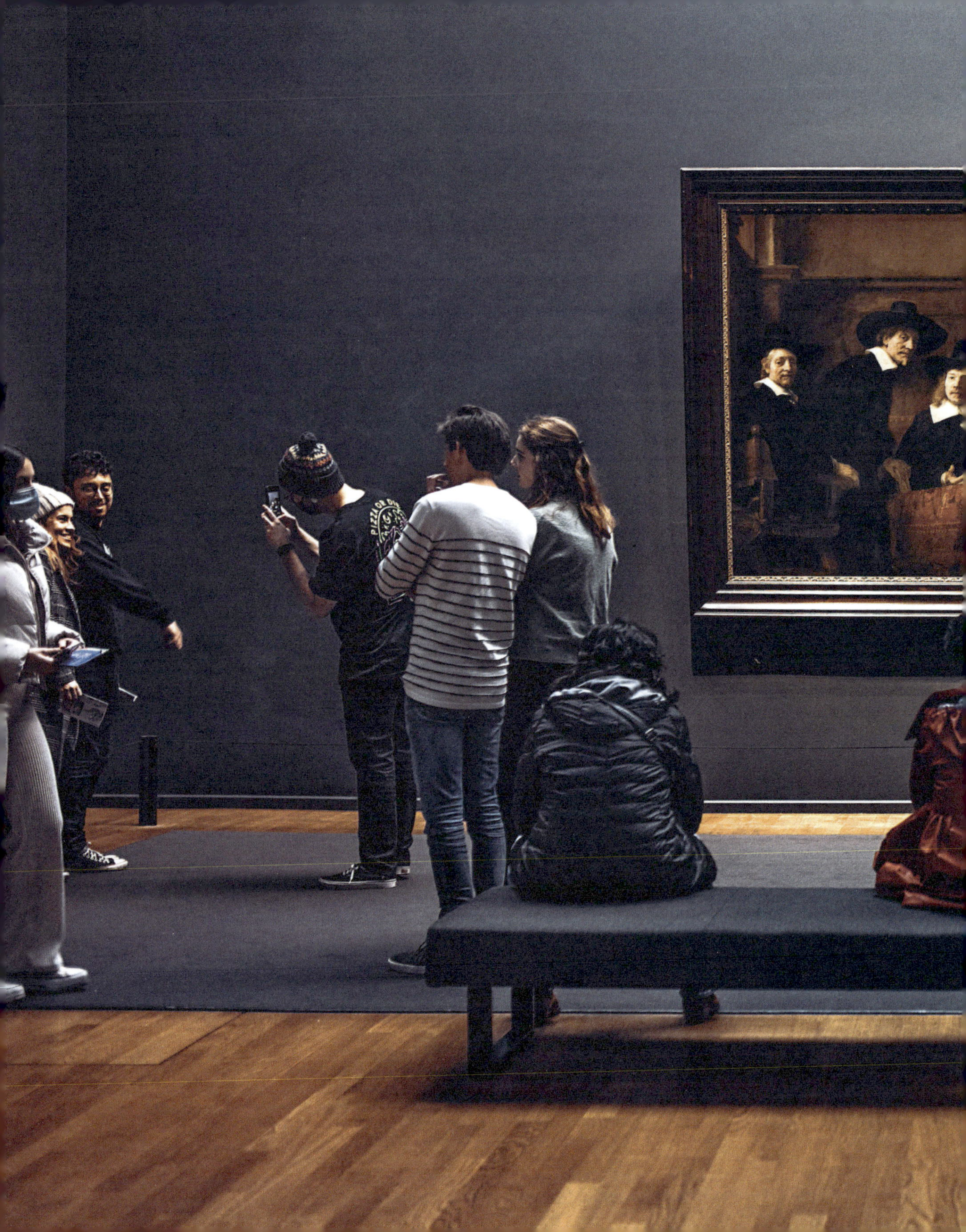

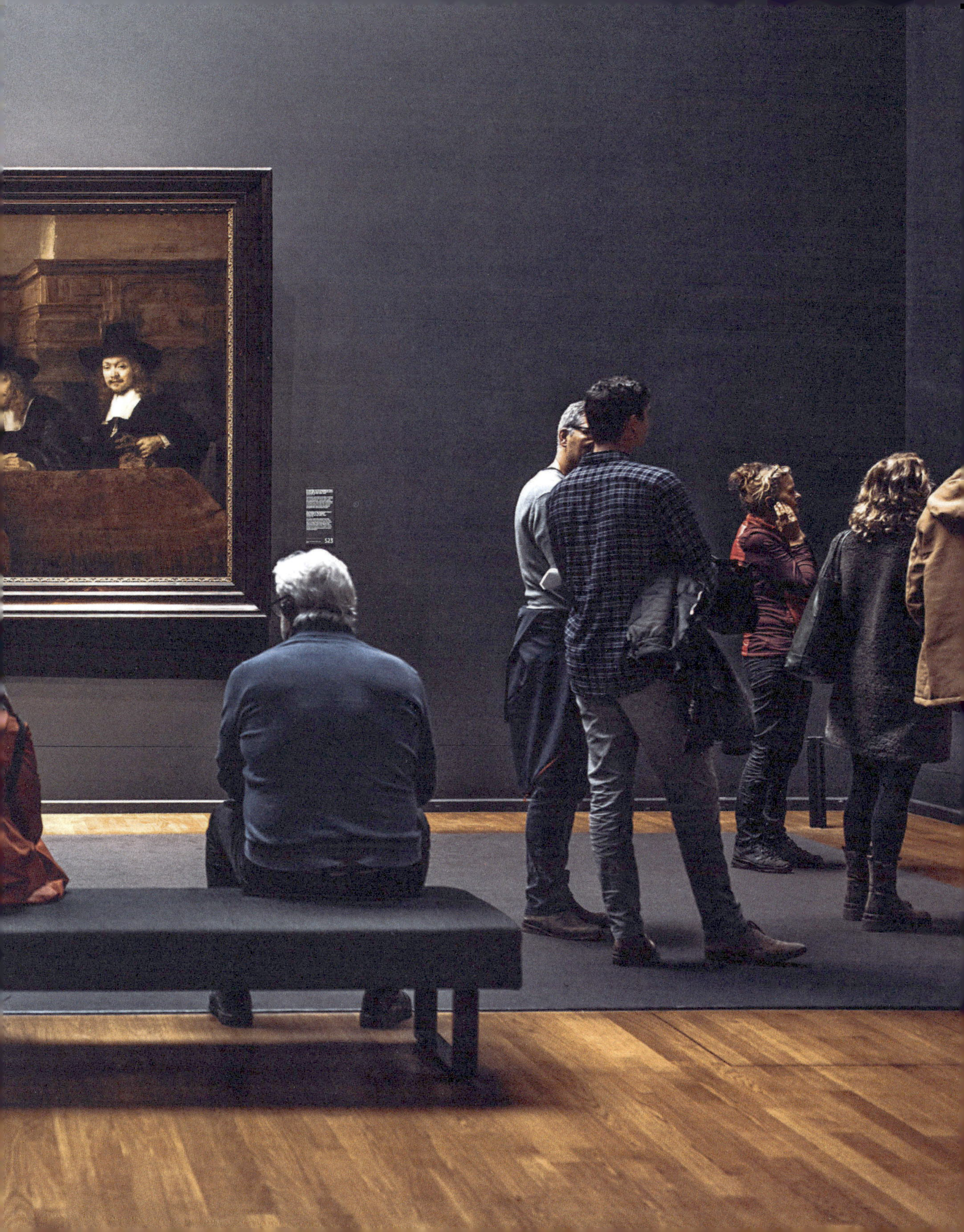

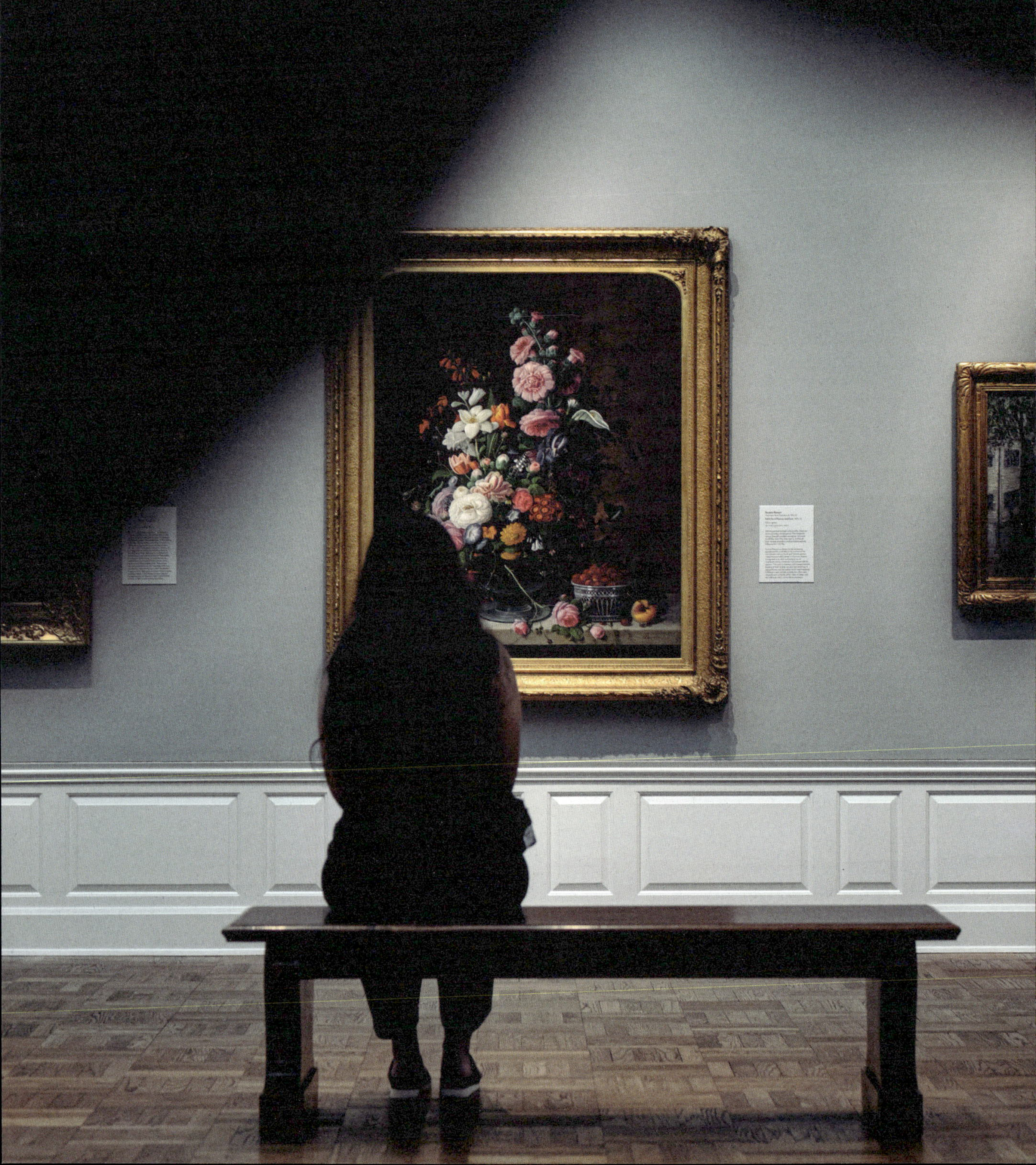

A few useful concepts

A short glossary of technical terms

Technical? Indeed. Difficult? No. These words aren't as scary as you think. You have certainly already come across most of them. It isn't essential that you remember them, and you can refer to this page whenever you like.

- **Abstraction:** this term refers to the fact of not representing reality. An abstract painting features no elements that the viewer can associate with an object, a person or an animal – in short, no shape pertaining to their world. 'Abstraction' is the opposite of 'figuration'.

- **Easel:** this is the accessory, mostly made of wood, on which an artist places the painting that they are working on. Because of an easel's relatively small size, 'easel painting' involves works of a similarly reasonable size.

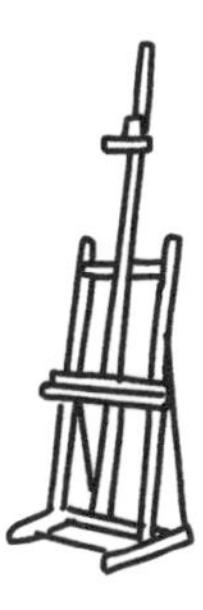

- **Colour:** this general term characterises all the colours in a painting. It is synonymous with the term 'palette'.

- **Composition:** this term refers to the way the various elements, shapes and colours are arranged on the painting – the overall structure of what the viewer sees.

- **Figuration:** a figurative painting is a work that offers a representation of the real world, whether it is scrupulously realistic or based on the artist's free interpretation. All or part of the elements composing it are representations of people or objects that the eye is able to identify. 'Figuration' is the opposite of 'abstraction'.

- **Glaze:** extremely diluted paint, allowing the artist to produce transparency and gradation effects (p. 22).

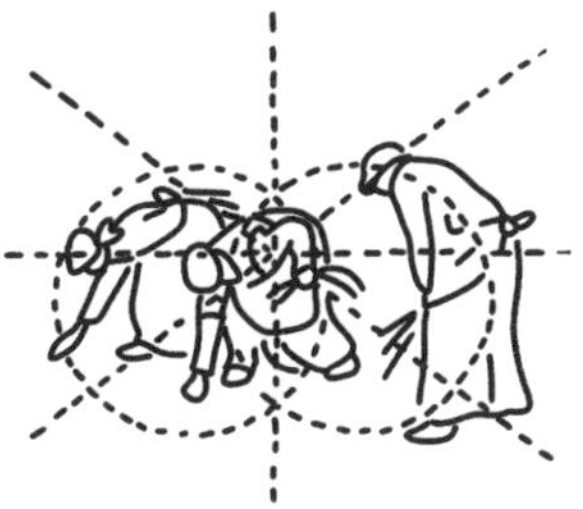

- **Lines:** the manner in which elements of a composition are arranged can create imaginary lines that create a sense of movement in the work or, on the contrary, contribute to its stability.

- **Monumentality:** monumentality can refer to the scale of a large painting, or to the place and power of a figure within a given frame. A painting can be small, yet feature a monumental figure.

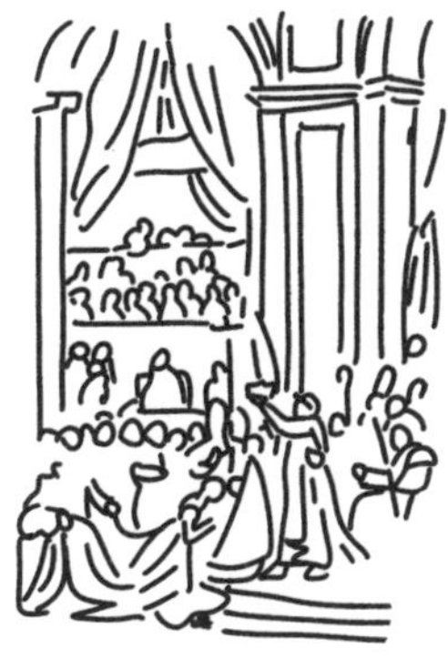

- **Motif:** this refers to a subject or a theme presented in an image. Some motifs appear consistently throughout the history of art, such as the Virgin and Child or Saint John the Baptist.

- **Palette:** the palette is the object on which a painter mixes their colours before applying them to the canvas. By extension, this term also refers to colour.

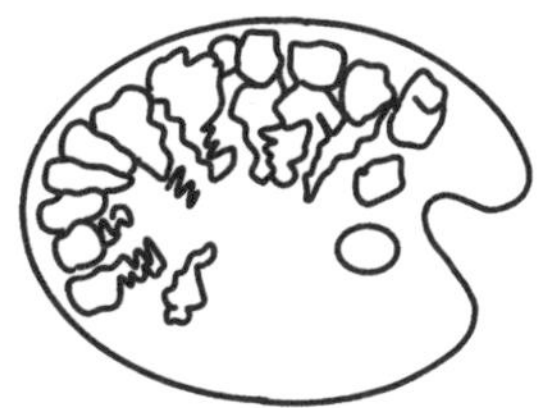

- **Perspective:** this term refers to the geometric use of the surface of the work to produce a sense of depth (pp. 34–35).

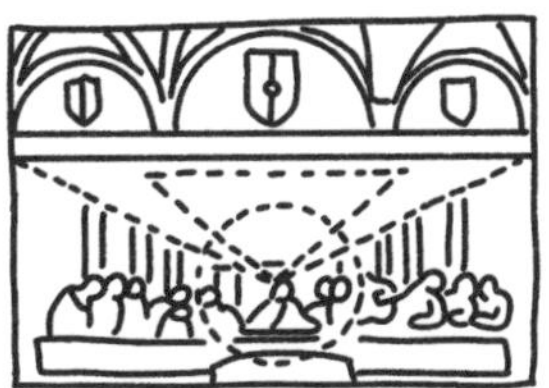

- **Pigment:** this is a natural or artificial material from which a colour is produced. Traditionally, artists would grind their pigments, then mix them with a binder to obtain a fluid material that could then be applied to the support. Techniques vary according to the binder used, from oil paint to watercolour.

- **Plane:** in a painting, planes are successive surfaces producing an impression of depth. This technique is referred to as the 'layering of planes'. One generally distinguishes the foreground, presenting elements located at the front, as close as possible to the viewer, from the background, which defines objects located further away.

- **Altarpiece:** the decorated upper part of a church altar. The altarpiece is frequently carved or painted. When it is a painting, it is always produced in a large format that matches the size of the altar and is visible from a distance, for all the faithful attending mass.

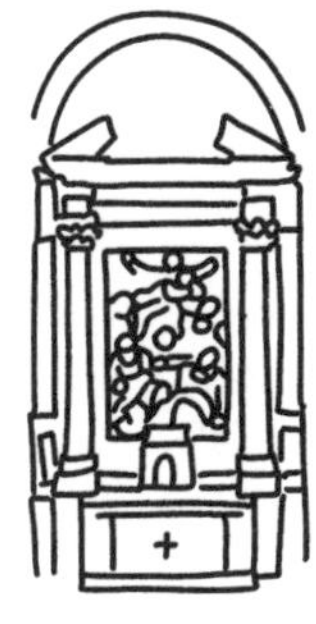

- **Support:** this refers to the material on which the artist paints (wood, canvas, copper, etc.). This surface is prepared prior to the application of paint (pp. 240–241).

- **Tempera:** also called 'distemper', this technique consists in mixing pigments with a water-based binder and a substance capable of agglutinating them. The most commonly used additives include vegetable gum, glue or egg.

- **Touch:** this refers to the application of paint to the support. By extension, an artist's touch refers to their brush strokes and their unique manner of painting.

The pioneers

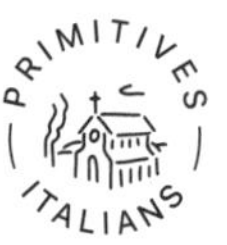

13TH-14TH CENTURY

Mobile supports, golden backgrounds, increasingly naturalistic decorations

Giotto di Bondone
p. 20

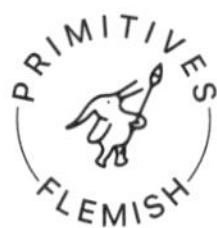

15TH CENTURY

Perfecting the technique of oil painting, realism and precision

Jan Van Eyck
p. 22

Hieronymus Bosch
p. 30

The masters of the Renaissance

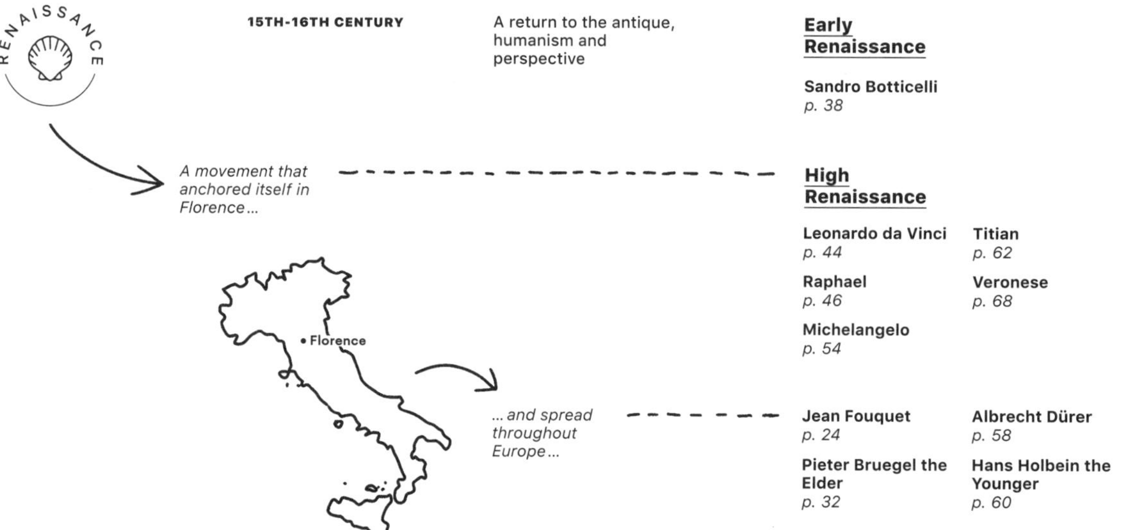

15TH-16TH CENTURY

A return to the antique, humanism and perspective

Early Renaissance

Sandro Botticelli
p. 38

A movement that anchored itself in Florence…

High Renaissance

Leonardo da Vinci
p. 44

Raphael
p. 46

Michelangelo
p. 54

Titian
p. 62

Veronese
p. 68

… and spread throughout Europe…

Jean Fouquet
p. 24

Pieter Bruegel the Elder
p. 32

Albrecht Dürer
p. 58

Hans Holbein the Younger
p. 60

The masters of Mannerism

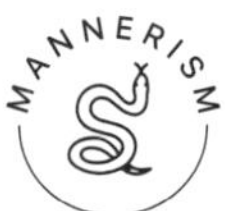

16TH CENTURY

Exaggeration of the Renaissance masters' approach, serpentine figures, shimmering colours

Agnolo Bronzino
p. 70

Lavinia Fontana
p. 72

PART

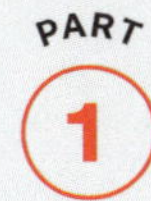

From Giotto di Bondone to Lavinia Fontana

Eternal painting

From the “early painters” to the excesses of Mannerism

Having laid the foundations of easel painting, the Italian primitives are regarded as pioneers in the history of Western painting. In their wake, painters of the Renaissance produced a repertoire of works that influenced and inspired artists throughout time.

Giotto di Bondone

Square one in the history of painting

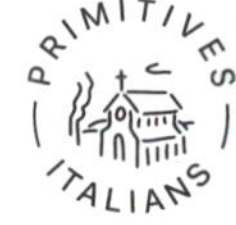

In Italy, in the 14th century, artists began to emerge from the medieval Gothic style. The works of Giotto di Bondone would be among the first to sow the seeds of a true revolution: the Renaissance.

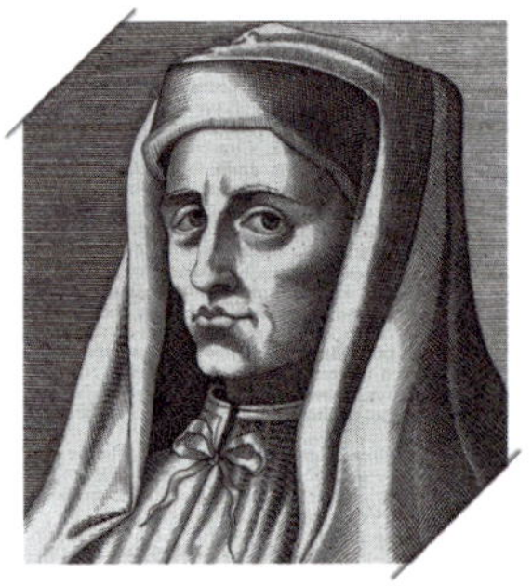

A farewell to the Byzantine pomp

Gradually abandoning the influence of Byzantine icons, Giotto evolved towards a new, more realistic sensibility, driven by his sense of detail and the humanity he managed to instil in his characters.

First successful trials

Although his perspectives remained awkward, Giotto already displayed a certain perception of space. He had the ability to imagine three-dimensional architectures, and organised his compositions to tell real stories.

Myth or reality?

Giotto's standing as the "first artist" made him the subject of many anecdotes. Today, it is difficult to disentangle the truth from the false. However, it is believed that he was a pupil of the great painter Cimabue, who was said to have noticed him, as a child, drawing a sheep from his flock.

THE ARTIST AND HIS TIMES

1230
One "Robin Hood" was declared an outlaw

1266
(or 1267)
Birth in Colle di Vespignano or in Florence

Circa
1298
Painted *Saint Francis of Assisi Receiving the Stigmata of Christ*

1337
Died in Florence

1347
The Black Death epidemic swept across Europe

Jan Van Eyck
Page 22

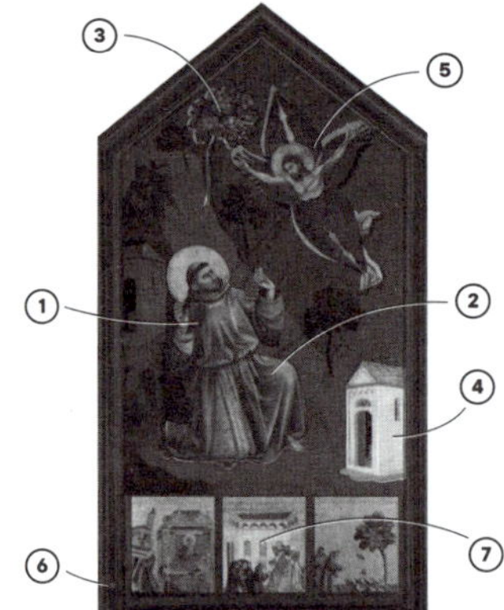

SAINT FRANCIS OF ASSISI RECEIVING THE STIGMATA OF CHRIST

Circa 1298
Gold ground and tempera on wood
313 × 163 cm
Louvre Museum, Paris

WHAT ARE WE LOOKING AT?

Francis had taken a vow of poverty and lived in a hermitage when he received the stigmata from Christ – the marks of his suffering, symbolising the saint's commitment to his life as a follower of Jesus.

① Copy and paste

The saint is receiving the same wounds as Christ: the marks of crucifixion on his hands and feet, and the wound in his side caused by the lance of the Roman soldier Longinus.

② Back to basics

Having taken a vow of poverty, Francis is depicted wearing a simple outfit, consisting of a robe and a rope. This outfit is still worn by some monks today.

③ Nature lover

A lover all of God's creations, Francis lived close to nature, which Giotto represents here with subtle details.

④ Vocational retraining

The buildings remind us that the saint became a mason and dedicated himself to repairing ruined churches; they also display Giotto's perception of space in volume.

⑤ The wings of an angel

The transmission of the stigmata is represented by the lines connecting the angel to the saint. The six wings indicate that the angel is a seraph. Its face is that of Christ, represented in a very humanised way.

⑥ Customer relations

It is thought that this depicts the coat of arms of the Cinquini, powerful merchants from Pisa, who commissioned this work.

⑦ In following episodes

The bottom of an altarpiece is called a predella. Here, Giotto has adorned it with other scenes from the life of Saint Francis.

④ +

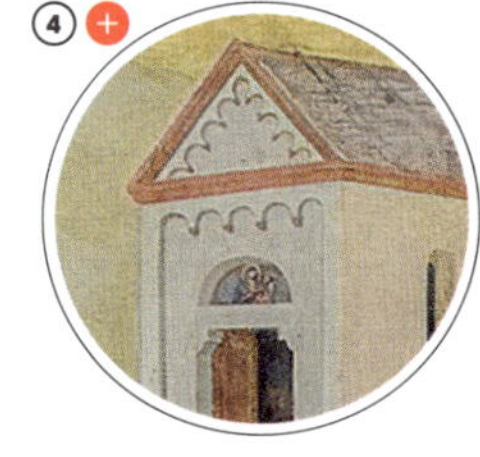

GIOTTO'S ART IN A NUTSHELL

- A perception of space that enabled him to tell stories.
- Religious scenes rooted in reality.
- A markedly sensitive representation of the human figure.

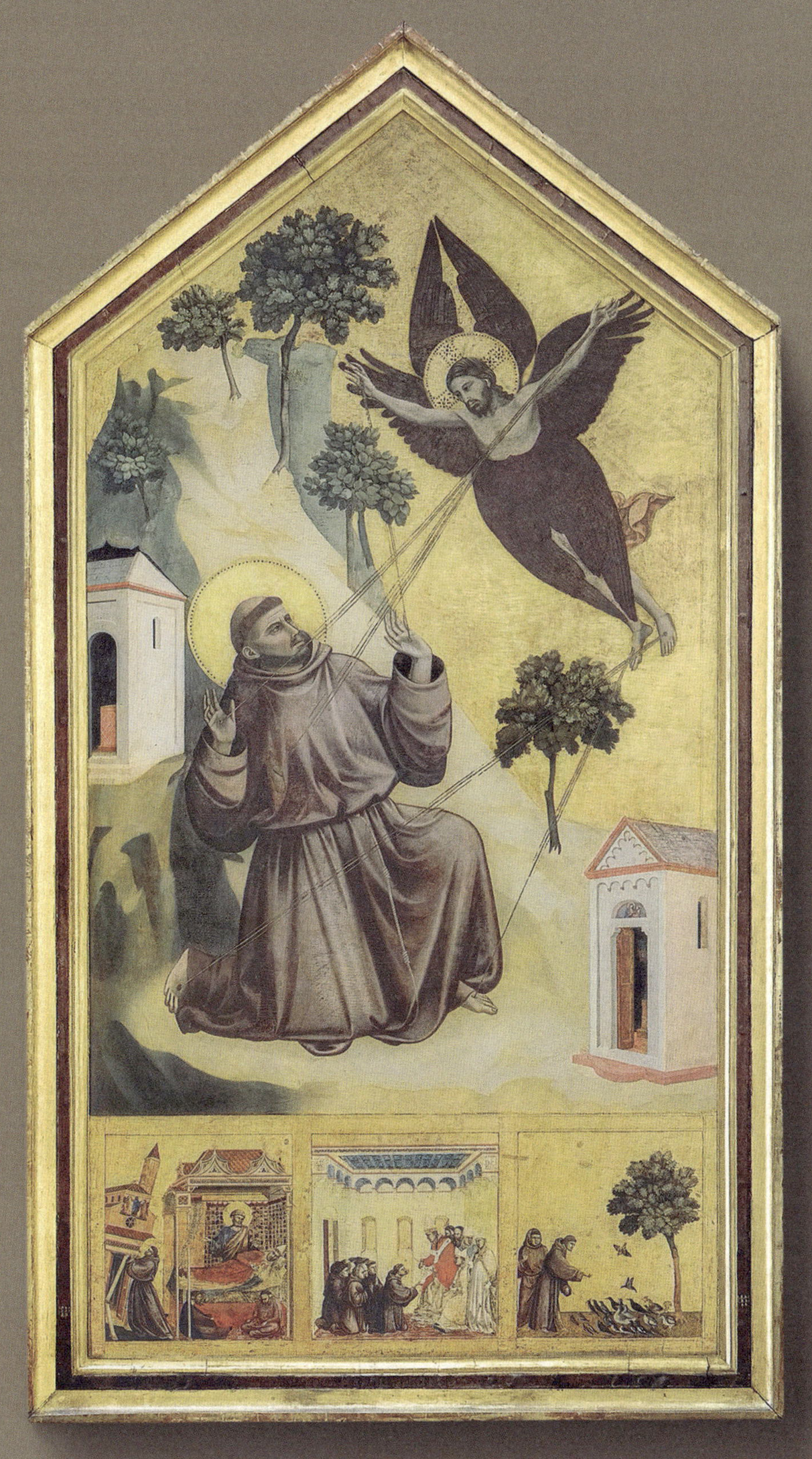

Jan Van Eyck
The Flemish Primitives' headline act

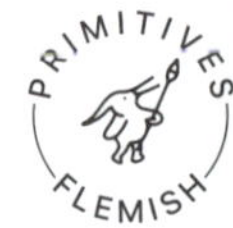

In the 15th century, Flemish artists perfected the technique of oil painting – a turning point in the history of art. Van Eyck is considered to be the most talented among them.

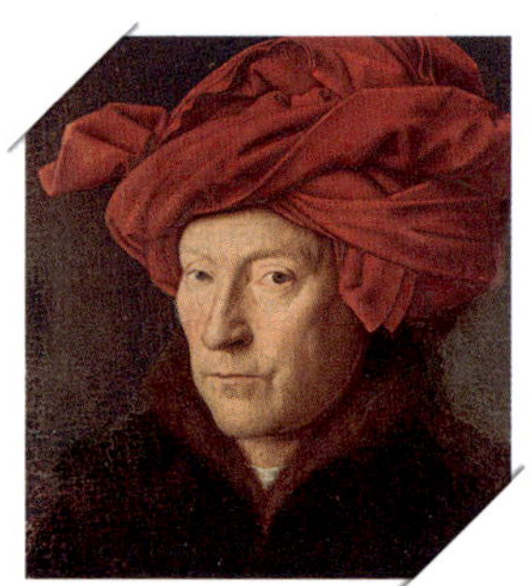

Watch out for wrinkles!

Van Eyck's remarkable talent lies in the virtuosity of his oil painting technique. He applied the highly diluted pigments in transparent layers called glazes (p. 17). He achieved refined detail and great realism, particularly in the modelling of faces.

False modesty

The artist's motto was "To the best of my ability" *("Als ich can")*. However, the altarpiece *The Adoration of the Mystic Lamb*, bears the following inscription: "The painter Hubert van Eyck, than whom none was greater, began this work. Jan [his brother], second in art, completed it at the request of Joos Vijd on the sixth of May." With Hubert dead, Jan became the best ...

Good status

Van Eyck lived in comfort. He was supported by patrons, among which were important personalities such as Philip the Good, Duke of Burgundy. The sovereign would also entrust him with unofficial diplomatic missions, which were generously paid.

FASHIONABLE PAINTERS

Between Gothic influences and pictorial innovations, the Flemish Primitives were highly sought after by the new bourgeois elite.

Giotto di Bondone
Page 20

Circa
1390
Born in Maaseik?

1431
Joan of Arc died at the stake

1434
Painted *The Arnolfini Portrait*

1441
Died in Bruges

1492
Christopher Columbus set foot in the Bahamas

Jean Fouquet
Page 24

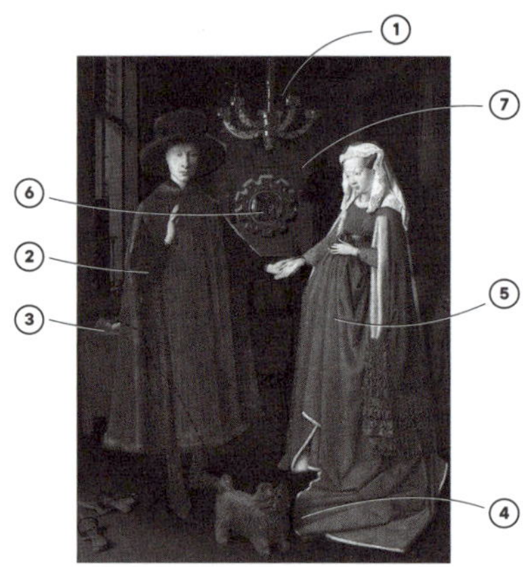

THE ARNOLFINI PORTRAIT ↗

1434
Oil on wood (oak)
82.6 × 60 cm
National Gallery, London

WHAT ARE WE LOOKING AT?

Maybe a secret marriage, or a posthumous tribute: the woman is said to have passed before the painting was finished. However, this might also be a simple portrait – one of the first in history that is not religious.

① Remember that you are mortal ...

The candle evokes the transience of existence: it is a vanitas (p. 110). There is only one candle; while it may therefore symbolise the presence of God, it could also be a nuptial sign. However, it may also merely be a way of saving money, by lighting only one candle at a time.

② A touch of Italian chic

In 1516, the painting is known as *Hernoul le Fin with his Wife in a Chamber*. "Hernoul le Fin" is the distorted name of Arnolfini, a family of Italian merchants.

③ Discreet luxury

Hard to come by in northern Europe, oranges imply a certain affluence; however, the brick wall, visible through the window, means that the scene is set in a simple house.

④ Faithful companion

The dog is likely a symbol of loyalty, while the bed, another sign of prosperity, evokes marital bliss.

⑤ Pregnant?

No! This is the way that women held their dresses. This detail is misleading; indeed, Van Eyck would often paint women with protruding bellies.

⑥ Surprise guests

The intriguing, eye-catching mirror is adorned with ten scenes depicting the passion of Christ. It also reveals the presence of guests. Could these be Van Eyck and his brother Hubert?

⑦ I was there

The inscription *Van Eyck fuit hic* translates to "Van Eyck was there." Painters would normally use the words *"Fecit"* (made) or *"Pinxit"* (painted). Did the scene really take place?

⑥ +

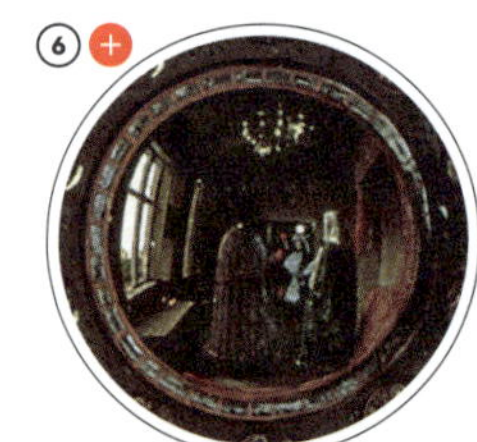

THE FLEMISH PRIMITIVES IN A NUTSHELL

- Realism: meticulous details and unflattering portraits. The Flemish were in search of truth.
- Perspective: well-studied vanishing lines, sense of depth and layering of planes.
- A mixture of genres: religious scenes were often transposed into household interiors.

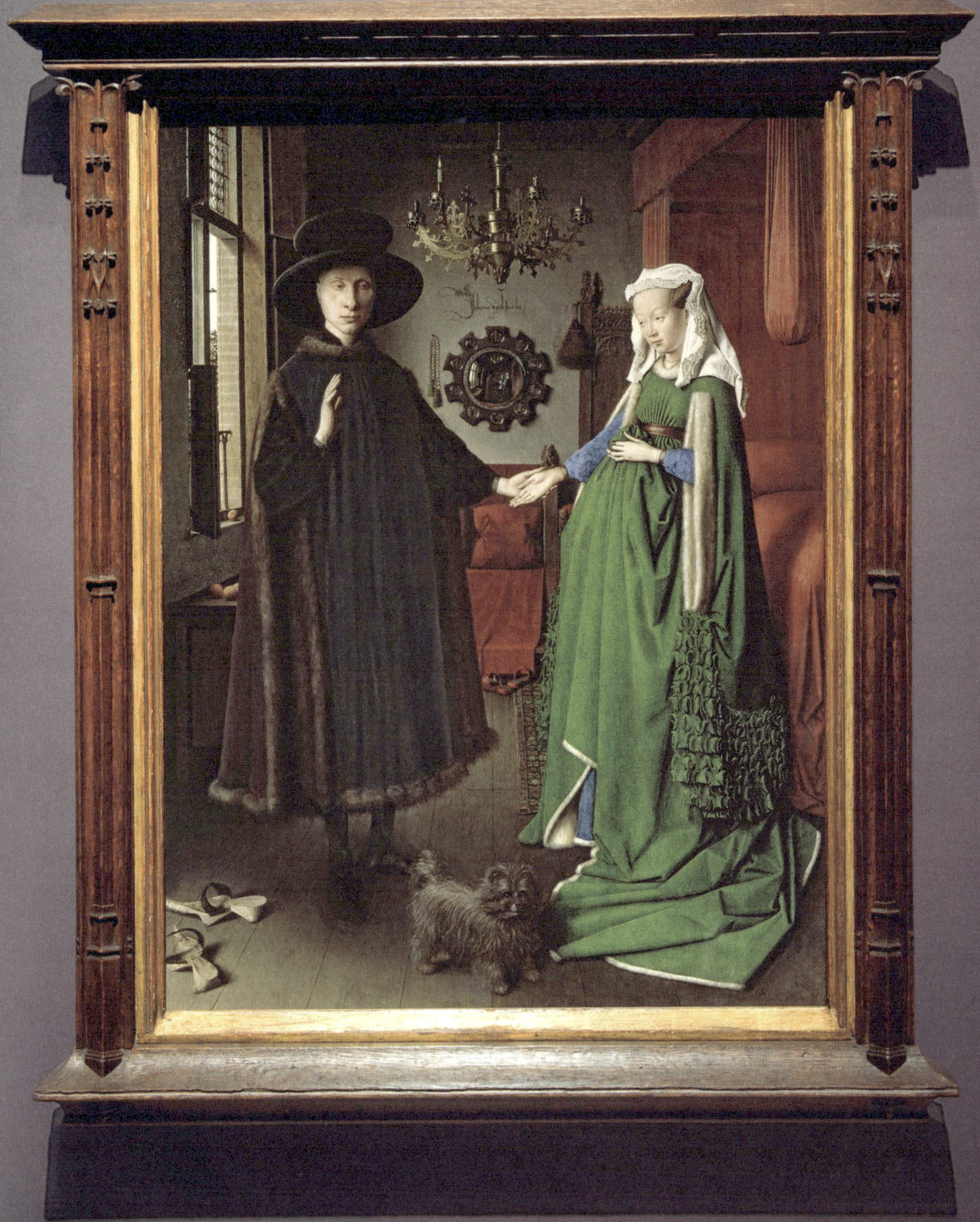

Jean Fouquet
A sophisticated clientele

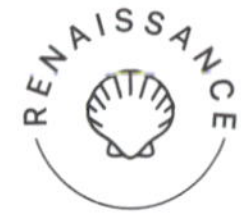

Compared to Jan Van Eyck and his talented Italian contemporaries, Jean Fouquet was one of the greatest French artists of his time. Attentive to innovation, he was particularly renowned for the quality of his portraits.

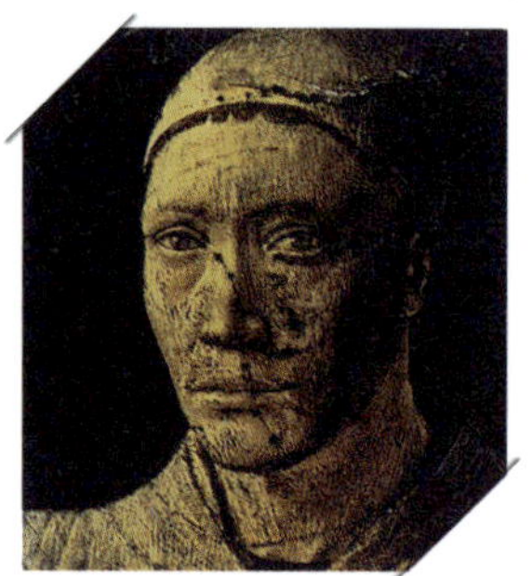

Overbooked

Fouquet was known as a painter, in particular for his portraits. He also excelled as an illuminator, and designed models for other media, such as sculptures, stained glass and tapestries. Associated with the French Court, he was tasked with organising ceremonies and shows.

An artist under influence

At the time, France was a crossroads of influences between Northern Europe and Italy. Fouquet fused these varied artistic cultures in his paintings: he was well acquainted with the innovations of the Flemish primitives, and possessed thorough knowledge of the codes of Italian painting.

Prestigious services

Pope, kings, high dignitaries and more: the cream of the crop flocked to the artist to have their portrait painted. His work as a portraitist was renowned as far away as Italy. He knew how to render nature and instilled life into his conscientiously individualised models.

GOLDEN BOOK OF HOURS

When he illustrated a famous prayer book, the *Book of Hours* by Étienne Chevalier, Fouquet produced one of the greatest French masterpieces of illumination.

Jan Van Eyck
Page 22

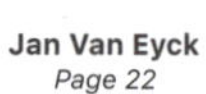

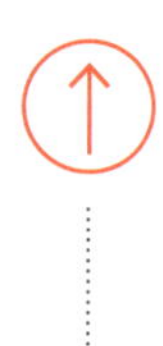

Circa
1420
Born in Tours

1421
Beijing became the capital of the Ming Empire

1452 to **1455**
Painted *Madonna Surrounded by Seraphim and Cherubim*

1498
Vasco da Gama found his way to India

1481
Died in Tours

Hieronymus Bosch
Page 30

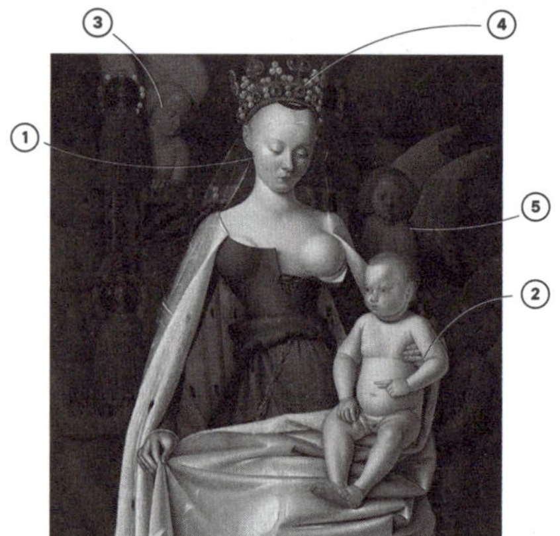

MADONNA SURROUNDED BY SERAPHIM AND CHERUBIM

1452–1455
Oil on wood
92 × 83.5 cm
Royal Museum of Fine Arts Antwerp, Belgium

WHAT ARE WE LOOKING AT?

This depiction of the Virgin Mary with Jesus is unusual in its artistic choices, which remains surprising, even today.
The work is the right panel of a diptych, known as the *Melun Diptych*.

① The not-so-Holy Virgin

Under the features of Mary holding Jesus on her lap, one recognises Agnes Sorel, mistress of King Charles VII. This bold and controversial choice caused much discussion.

② Follow the guide

Jesus appears to be pointing to something, but nothing is to be seen. And with good reason: this painting is the right panel of a diptych. The left panel, which Christ is pointing at, depicts the patron who commissioned the work: Étienne Chevalier. The two panels are now kept in different museums.

③ *Mamma mia!*

The image of the Virgin surrounded by angels is reminiscent of Italian Virgins in majesty (*Maestà*); the painter knew his classics well. Here, the figures are depicted in three-quarter view, but the impression of frontality is reinforced by the throne and the angels; the one placed above Christ is facing viewers, while another, to the lower left, is painted in profile.

④ Melting pot

In addition to the codes of Italian iconography, this painting displays the influence of the Flemish primitives. Smooth skin tones, realism and meticulous details are reminiscent of the art of Van Eyck.

⑤ Colour coding

The angels are depicted using different colours, which is not without meaning: the blue ones are cherubim, while the red ones are seraphim. This alternation contributes to the singularity of the work and plays on warm and cold tones, conveying the icy eroticism of this sensual Virgin.

④ +

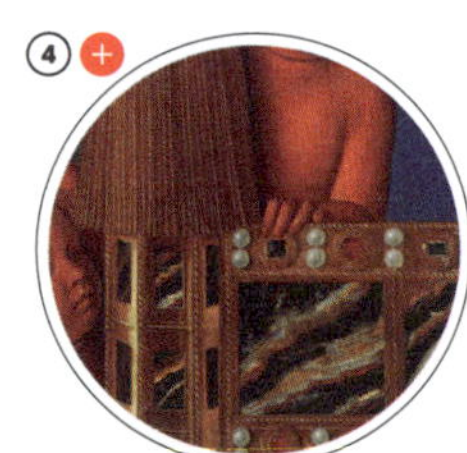

A COVETED VIRGIN

Henry IV attempted to acquire this already famous painting for 10,000 livres, in vain. In 1608, the future king Louis XIII also fell under the spell of the portrait. He was struck by its good state of preservation, is rumoured to have said: "Il semble estre tout frais faict." (It appears to be freshly painted.)

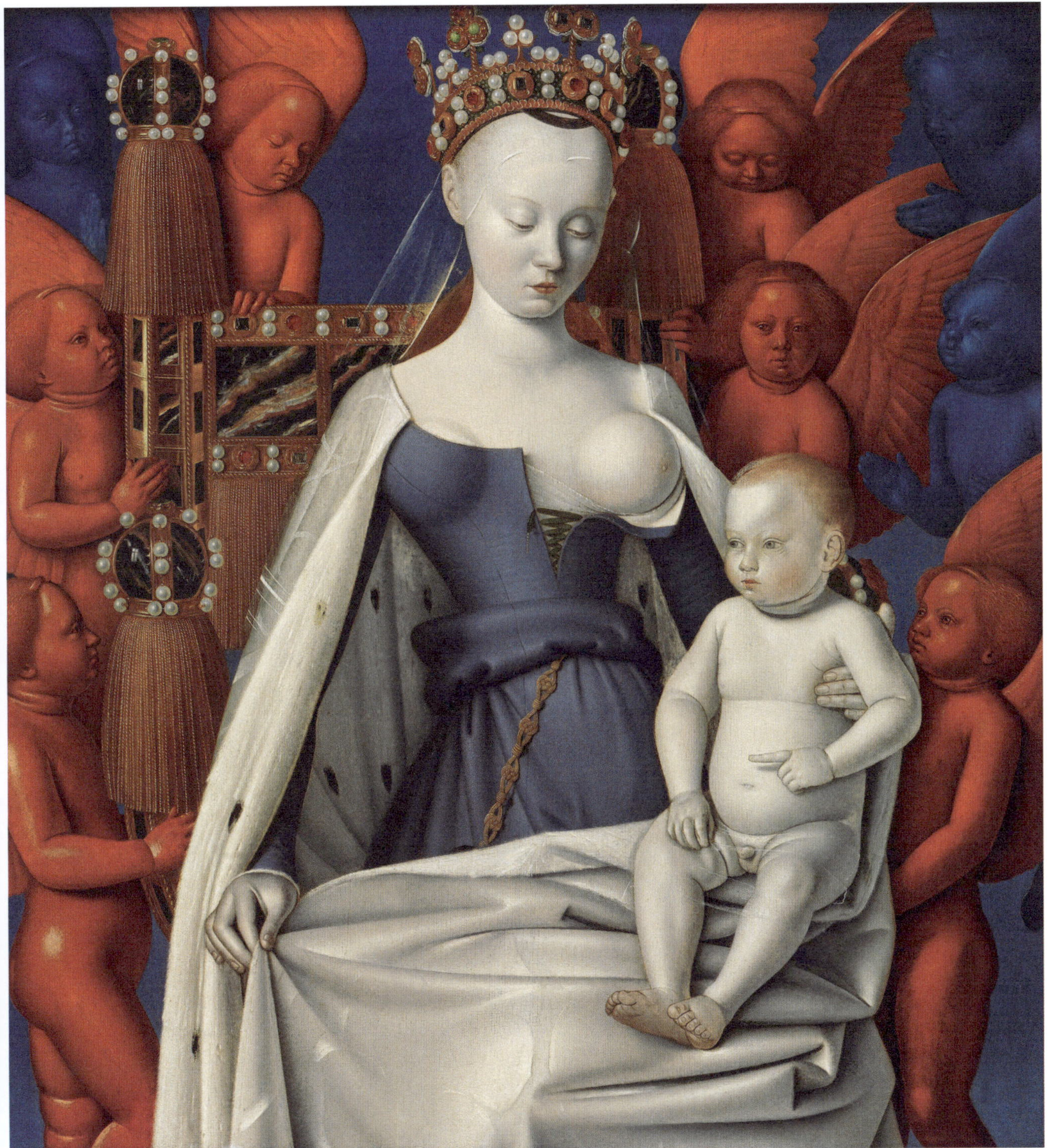

A head of its own

According to early descriptions, the setting of the *Melun Diptych* was decorated with medallions. Among them was a self-portrait of the artist, now kept in the Louvre Museum. This small work is believed to be the first known isolated self-portrait in Western painting.

Official portraits
Kings seen in paintings

The tradition of the official portrait was well established. While presidents have replaced kings and photography has replaced painting, in the great course of history, one immutable fact remains: every detail counts to convey the right message.

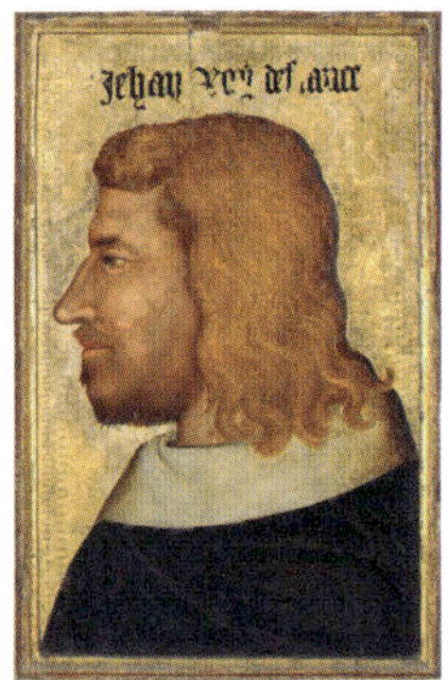

JOHN II THE GOOD

This is one of the first easel portraits ever produced. The king's profile is reminiscent of coins; far from being idealised, however, this representation strives for resemblance. The background is gold, as on medieval icons. Royal insignia are not yet featured in this work.

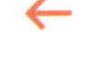

Anonymous of the French school
Louvre Museum, Paris.

ca. 1350–1370

HENRY IV

Henry IV wears the cross of the Order of the Holy Spirit. He stands upright, in front of a red drapery revealing the architecture of an official palace, a symbol of stable and solid power. Both a warrior and peacemaker, the king stands in armour, wearing the white scarf of the Protestant soldiers. Politics thus makes its way into the picture.

Frans Pourbus the Younger
Louvre Museum, Paris.

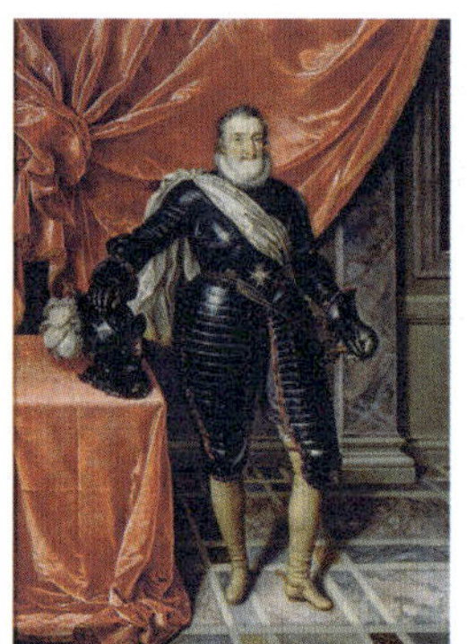

ca. 1600

ca. 1440–1460

CHARLES VII

This emblematic painting is highly representative of its time. Wider framing is applied, and the monarch is depicted as a gentleman of the Court. However, his presence is imposing: the fundamentals of the royal portrait are apparent. The king is framed by drapery, highlighting his majesty and charisma.

Jean Fouquet
Louvre Museum, Paris

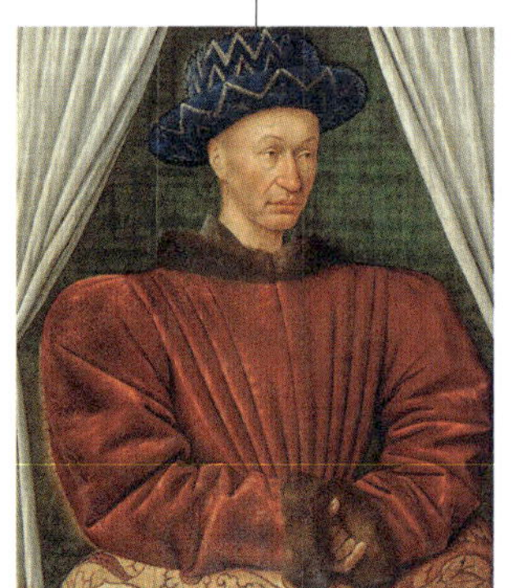

ca. 1525–1550

FRANCIS I OF FRANCE

This portrait, which displays the same composition as the portrait of Charles VII, is also remembered as a classic of this genre. The drapery has been replaced by a patterned decoration featuring crowns, while the king's hand rests on the hilt of his sword.

Jean Clouet
Louvre Museum, Paris

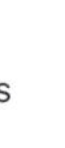

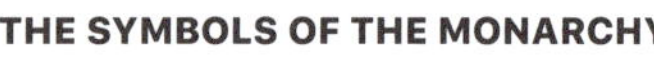

THE SYMBOLS OF THE MONARCHY

Crown
Royalty

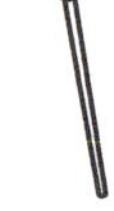

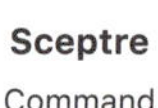

Sceptre
Command

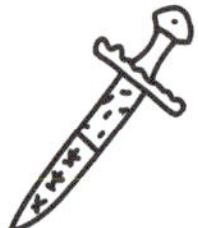

Sword
Military power

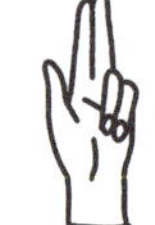

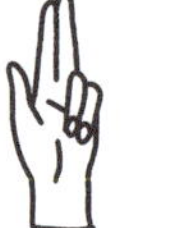

Hand of justice
Judiciary power

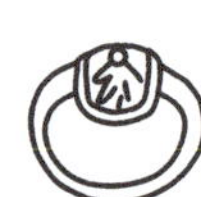

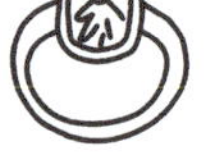

Ring
Connection to the Church

Fleur de Lys
French royalty

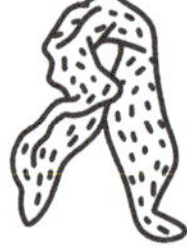

Ermine fur
Moral purity

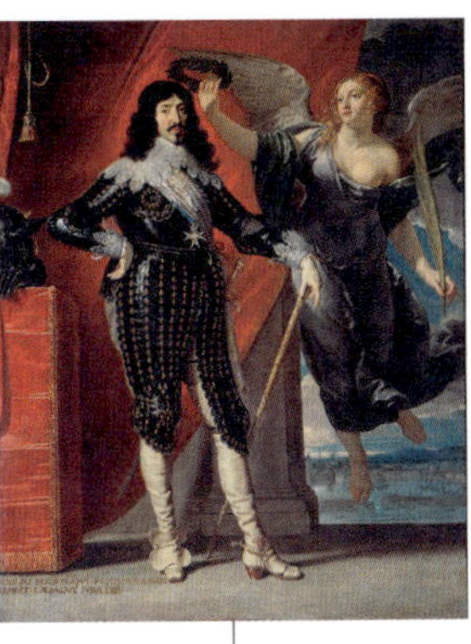

LOUIS XIII

The most prominent painter of his time, Champaigne would represent Louis XIII on many occasions. Here, the king stands in armour, leaning on a cane, heralding the sceptres that he is destined to hold. His victories in war are represented by an allegory of victory.

←

Philippe de Champaigne
Musée du Louvre, Paris.

1635

LOUIS XV

Rigaud's portrait of Louis XIV became a "hit", so to speak. Here, the painter used all of its components to portray Louis XV in all his majesty, on several occasions.

→

Hyacinthe Rigaud
Musée National des Châteaux de Versailles et de Trianon.

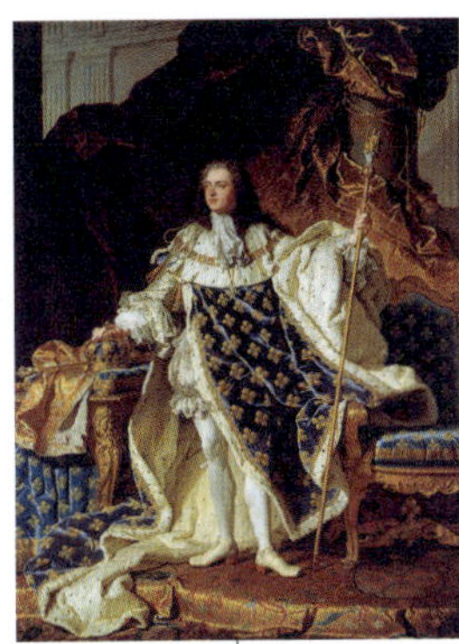

1730

1701

LOUIS XIV

Although the art of the royal portrait never ceased to evolve since John II, Hyacinthe Rigaud set the codes once and for all with his portrait of Louis XIV. Here, the drapery is spectacular, and the architecture imposing. All the markers of the monarchy appear in this portrait, in which Rigaud graces the king with unprecedented grandeur. The realistic features of Louis XIV are imbued with impressive majesty.

→

Hyacinthe Rigaud
Louvre Museum, Paris.

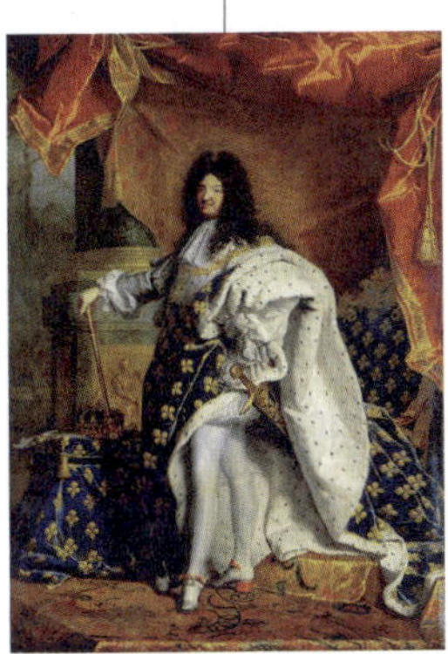

ROYAL TOUCH-UP

In his portrait of Louis XIV, Rigaud allowed himself to bend reality somewhat; he portrayed the monarch standing on two beautiful legs, much more youthful than his own.

A GOLDEN DESTINY

It was in 1530 that Francis I of France founded the collection named "Joyaux de la Couronne de France"(the French Crown Jewels). Among the first stones that were added to it was the sublime Côte-de-Bretagne red spinel. Over time, the treasure was enriched with precious jewels such as the Regent Diamond, a 140.6 carat diamond acquired by Philippe d'Orléans. Following a theft in 1792, the treasure was partially restored, before part of it was sold by the state in 1887. Some of the pieces are now kept in the Muséum National d'Histoire Naturelle, in Paris, and the Louvre Museum, where Louis XV's crown is kept.

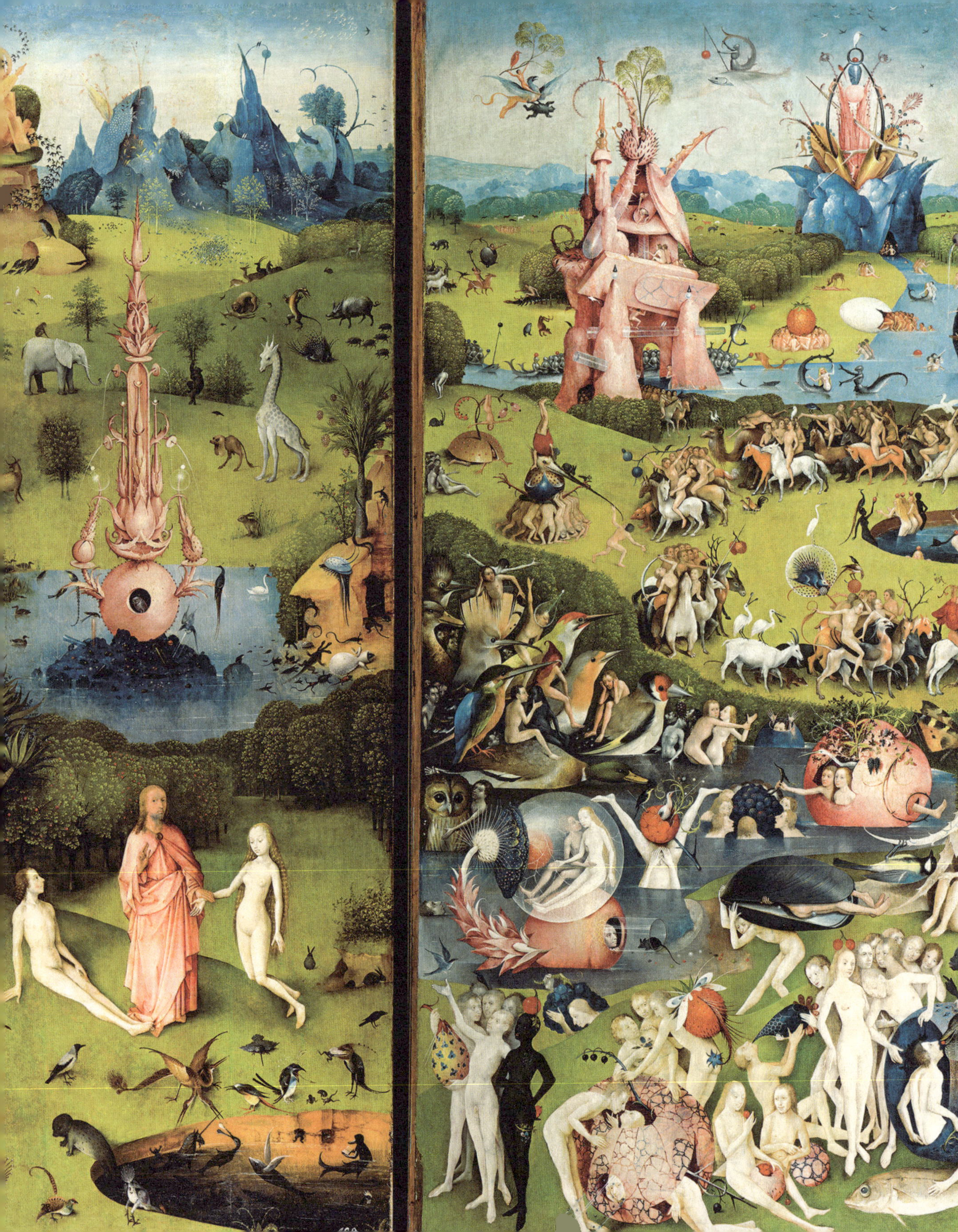

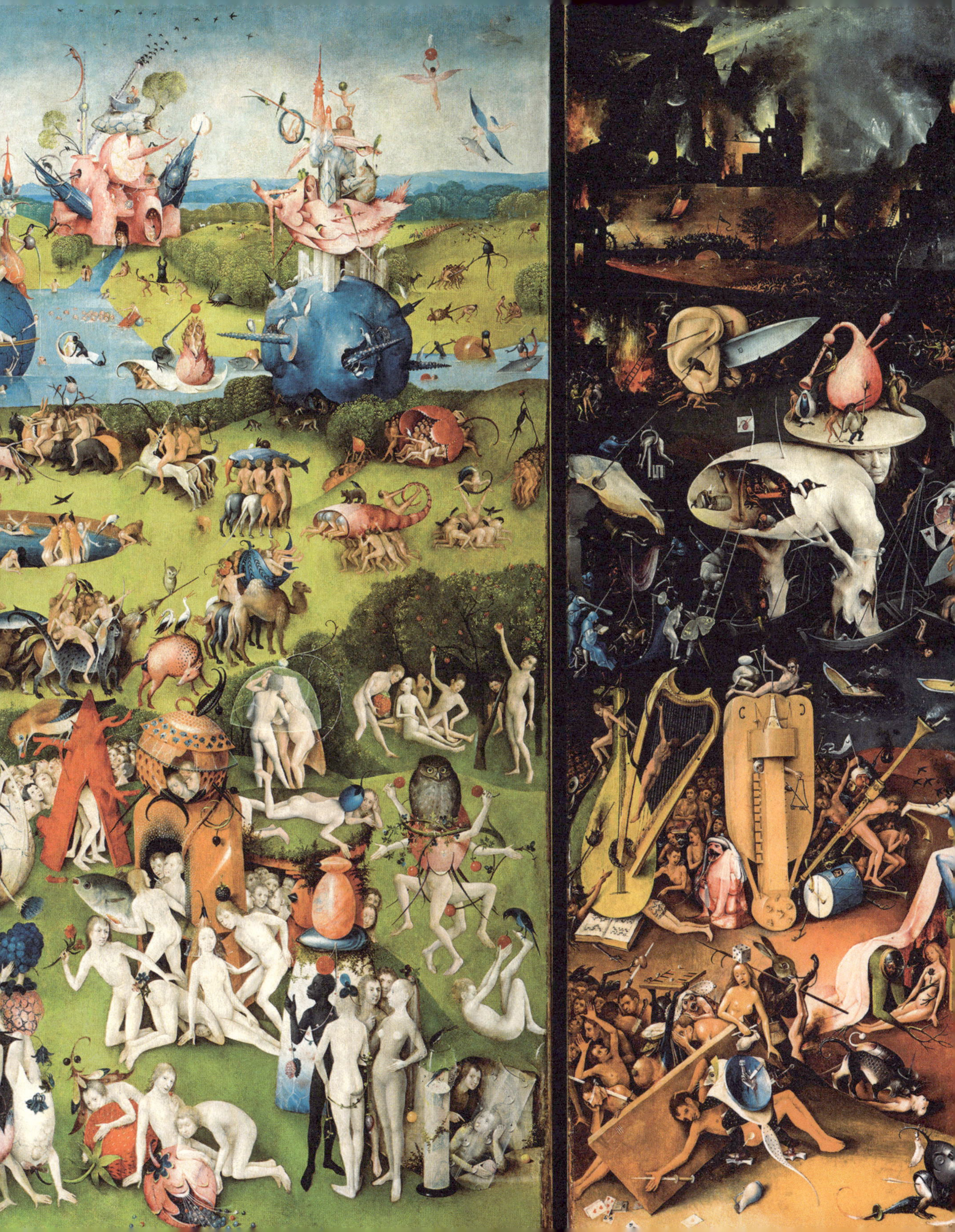

Hieronymus Bosch
A painter in Wonderland

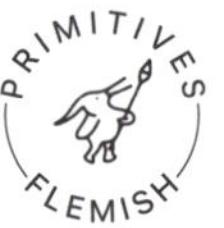

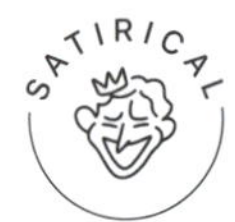

Jheronimus Van Aken is known as Hieronymus Bosch, after his birthplace, Den Bosch (*'s-Hertogenbosch* in Dutch). He is famous for his creative fantasy world, which resulted in a body of work that strays far from the beaten track.

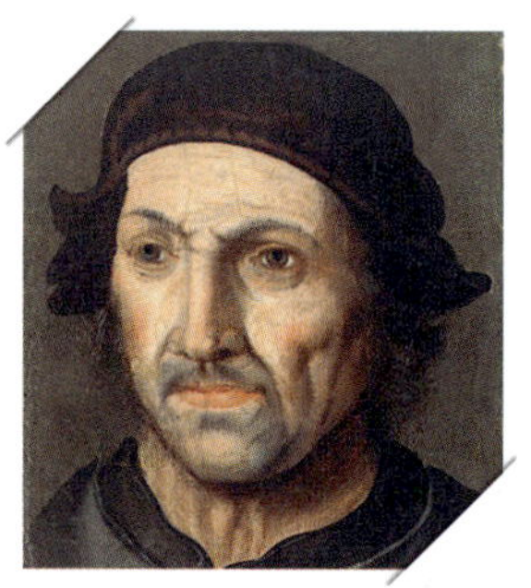

Art that leaves no one indifferent

An undoubtedly erudite Flemish painter, Bosch mainly painted moralising religious scenes, brimming with references. Unique, mysterious and avant-garde, his work is renowned for its wild creativity, and has been met with both rejection and admiration.

An ideal context

Born into a family of painters, Bosch was a popular and wealthy artist. He married well, enabling him to forge social links that were beneficial to his career in peaceful and flourishing Flanders.

Beliefs and reality

While at times, he was likened to a drug addict or a Satanist, owing to his eccentricities, he was most likely a man who sought to be a part of his community. His brush strokes were guided by a religion that viewed humans through the prism of sin.

SOURCES OF INSPIRATION

Bosch's abundant work was undoubtedly inspired by the hustle and bustle of the construction sites in his town, as well as the sculpted reliefs of churches. His infernal visions may also have originated in the fires that broke out in Den Bosch, in 1463, and in his grandfather's foundry.

Jean Fouquet
Page 24

1435
Alberti wrote his best-selling work, *"De Pictura"*

Circa
1450
Born in Den Bosch

1454
Gutenberg printed his first Bible

1490 to **1500**
Painted *The Garden of Delights*

1516
Died in Den Bosch

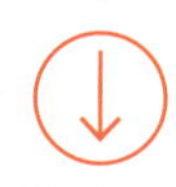

Pieter Bruegel the Elder
Page 32

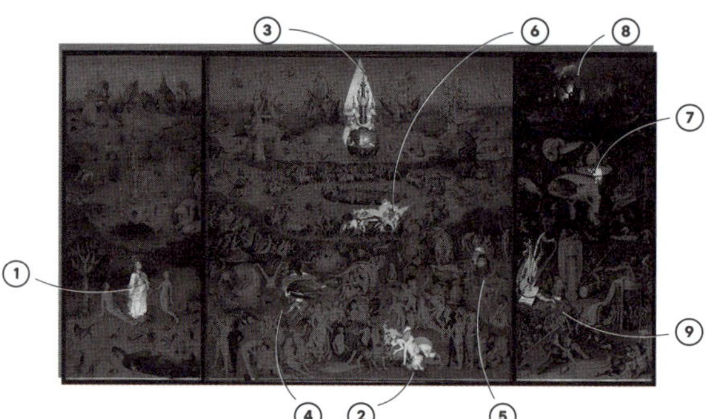

THE GARDEN OF DELIGHTS

1490–1500
Oil on oak
205.5 × 384.9 cm
(open with frame)
Prado Museum, Madrid

WHAT ARE WE LOOKING AT?

This work is a triptych. Inside, paintings can be read as chapters of a story about sin. On the left, a depiction of a lush Garden of Eden, where original sin will occur; in the middle, an overcrowded paradise, corrupted by debauchery, and on the right, sinners in hell.

① When Eve met Adam

After creating Eve, God (represented here as a young man with a beard) presents her to Adam. The shadow of original sin looms.

② Tainted strawberries

The work is strewn with fruit, particularly strawberries, symbols of fleeting earthly pleasures. Their taste vanishes as soon as they are consumed.

③ Source of trouble

This fountain is the source of the four rivers that flow into Eden. Its sphere features a broken surface, another allusion to the ephemeral nature of earthly pleasures. It echoes the fountain on the left panel.

④ Timeless innuendos

Lust transpires everywhere in the picture, and is notably suggested by a mussel shell. If there ever was a hint that stood the test of time …

⑤ These owls aren't a hoot

Two sinister owls evoke evil. They appear to be staring at the viewer …

⑥ Bizarre riders

These men ride strange creatures, which may be the artist's way of telling that mankind is driven by irrational desires.

⑦ Yes, that's Hieronymus …

This very characteristic figure may be a self-portrait. He is looking at us, as if to indicate that this work contains a message intended for the viewer.

⑧ A very real nightmare

The infernal flames may have been inspired by the fire that consumed the painter's home town, Den Bosch, when he was still a teenager.

⑨ Game over

While the central panel mainly denounces lust, hell depicts other vices that were condemned in Bosch's time, such as gambling or profane music.

② +

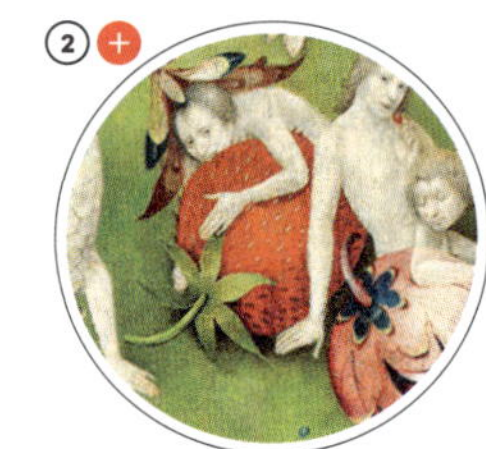

AN AERIAL VIEW

When the triptych is closed, it depicts the world at the time of its creation: a crystal sphere, inside which Earth appears as a rough draft. The luminous reflection on the glass could indicate the presence of the Sun, beyond the frame. Top left, God can be seen contemplating his creation. Two Latin sentences appear on top of the scene: *Ipse dixit et facta sunt* ("For he spoke, and they were made. He spoke, and all things were done") and *Ipse mandavit et creata sunt* ("He commanded, and they were created").

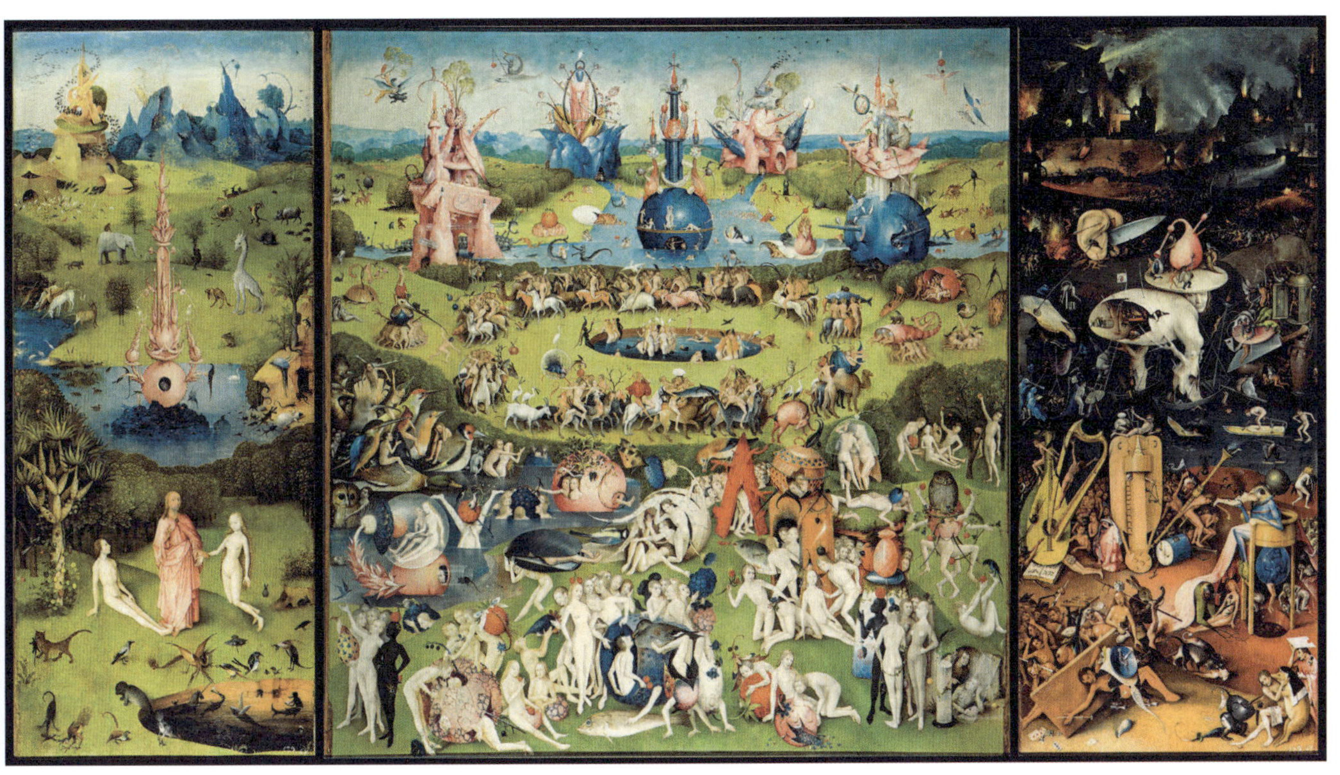

A travelling triptych

The Garden of Delights was in Brussels in 1517. It then became the property of William of Orange, before being taken to Spain by the Duke of Alba in 1570. Twenty years later, the triptych joined the collections of the Spanish Crown in the Escorial Palace. In 1939, the work was moved to the Prado Museum.

Pieter Bruegel the Elder
A daring Fleming

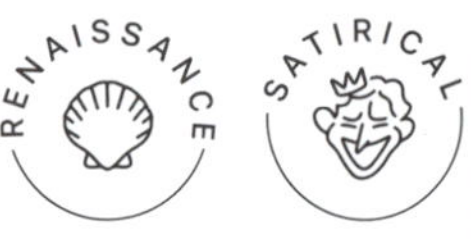

Bruegel was an inventive artist. His work balances great inventiveness in the interpretation of classical subjects and the desire to join the pictorial tradition of his artistic home.

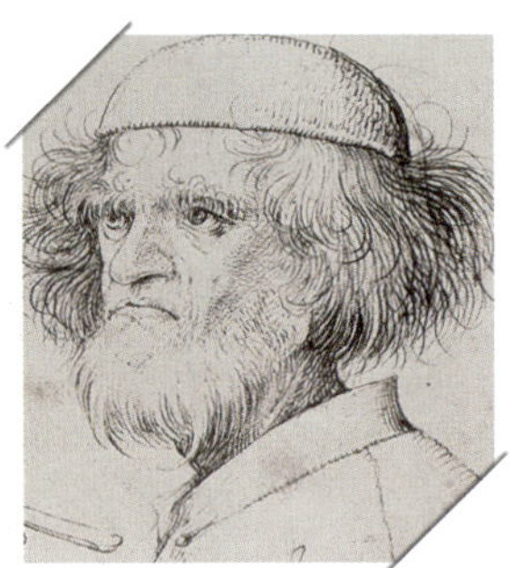

A career in details

Bruegel was likely taught by the painter Coecke Van Aelst and his wife, the miniaturist Mayken Verhulst, who may have influenced Bruegel's penchant for detail. And throughout his life, the artist worked in collaboration with the print publisher Hieronymus Cock.

The soul of a nature lover

Bruegel travelled to Italy. There, with great interest, he drew many landscapes, balancing the grandeur and intensity of nature with the insignificance of man.

Best laugh about it

Bruegel was greatly influenced by the work of Hieronymus Bosch. He enjoyed his "drolleries", which can also be observed in his works, to the extent that he was nicknamed "Pier den Drole". He was an imaginative artist, regardless of supports or subjects. He commented on human nature, pinpointing its weaknesses with humour. His humanist work is an invitation to self-mockery.

WITH OR WITHOUT AN 'H'?

The name Brueghel was written with an *h*, but the painter started to sign his works as 'Bruegel'. His descendants reverted to the original spelling.

Hieronymus Bosch
Page 30

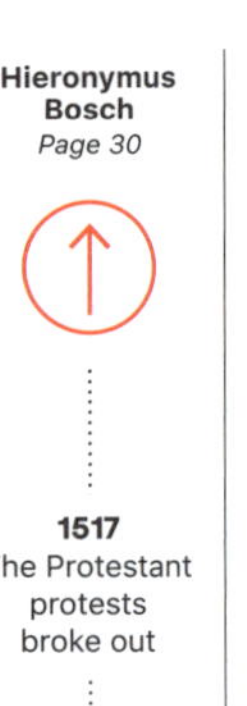

1517
The Protestant protests broke out

Circa
1525
Born near Breda

1534
Jacques Cartier took up residence in Canada

1565
Painted *The Harvesters*

1569
Died in Brussels

Sandro Botticelli
Page 38

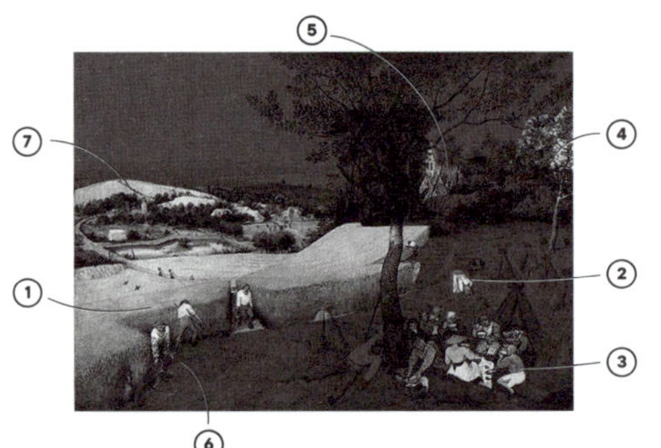

THE HARVESTERS

1565
Oil on wood
119 × 162 cm
Metropolitan Museum of Art, New York

WHAT ARE WE LOOKING AT?

This work is part of a cycle of six paintings (one of which has been lost) representing the months of the year. Here, Bruegel offers a picturesque depiction of life in the countryside, at the time of harvests. This work may also have a religious meaning.

① A well-deserved reward

The gently undulating landscape conveys a sense of harmony between man and nature. The scene is set in August or September, and the farmers are reaping the fruits of what they have sown.

② One with nature

Bruegel evokes this idea with humour, with the position in which this woman is depicted: as she bends over, her body takes on the same shape as the bales of hay that she is gathering.

③ Lunch break

In the foreground, the farmers are resting. Feeling hungry after work, they appear to be eating and drinking with a touching appetite. Pears can be seen on the knees of the woman who is turning her back to us.

④ The source of pleasure

The pear tree stands here. A man is shaking it, perched in its branches. One can see pears suspended in the air as they fall, while others, already lying on the ground, are being picked up by farmers.

⑤ A symbol of pleasure

The gathering of fruit may refer to original sin. A church is seen in the distance, not far from the pear tree. This arrangement supports the hypothesis that this painting bears a religious interpretation.

⑥ Cheers!

Bruegel's taste for mockery is also evident in this man's face. If one follows his gaze, he is looking at the amphora, covered with a hat, which probably contains beer.

⑦ A journey in several parts

Our gaze is drawn towards the background of the painting; it falls upon the cart, the pond, then the villagers enjoying themselves, before losing itself in the distance, on the horizon.

THE BRUEGHEL, A DYNASTY OF ARTISTS

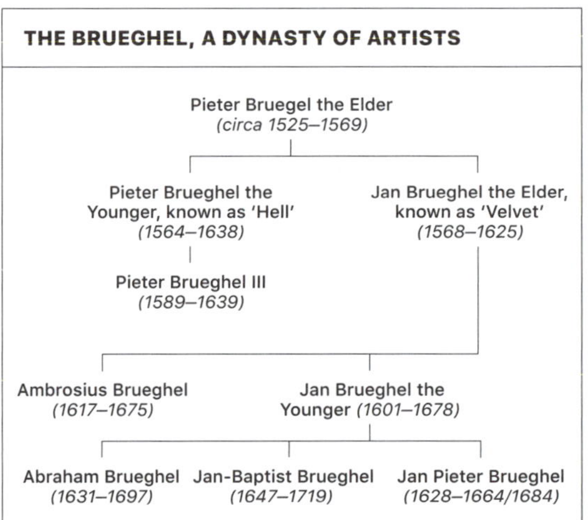

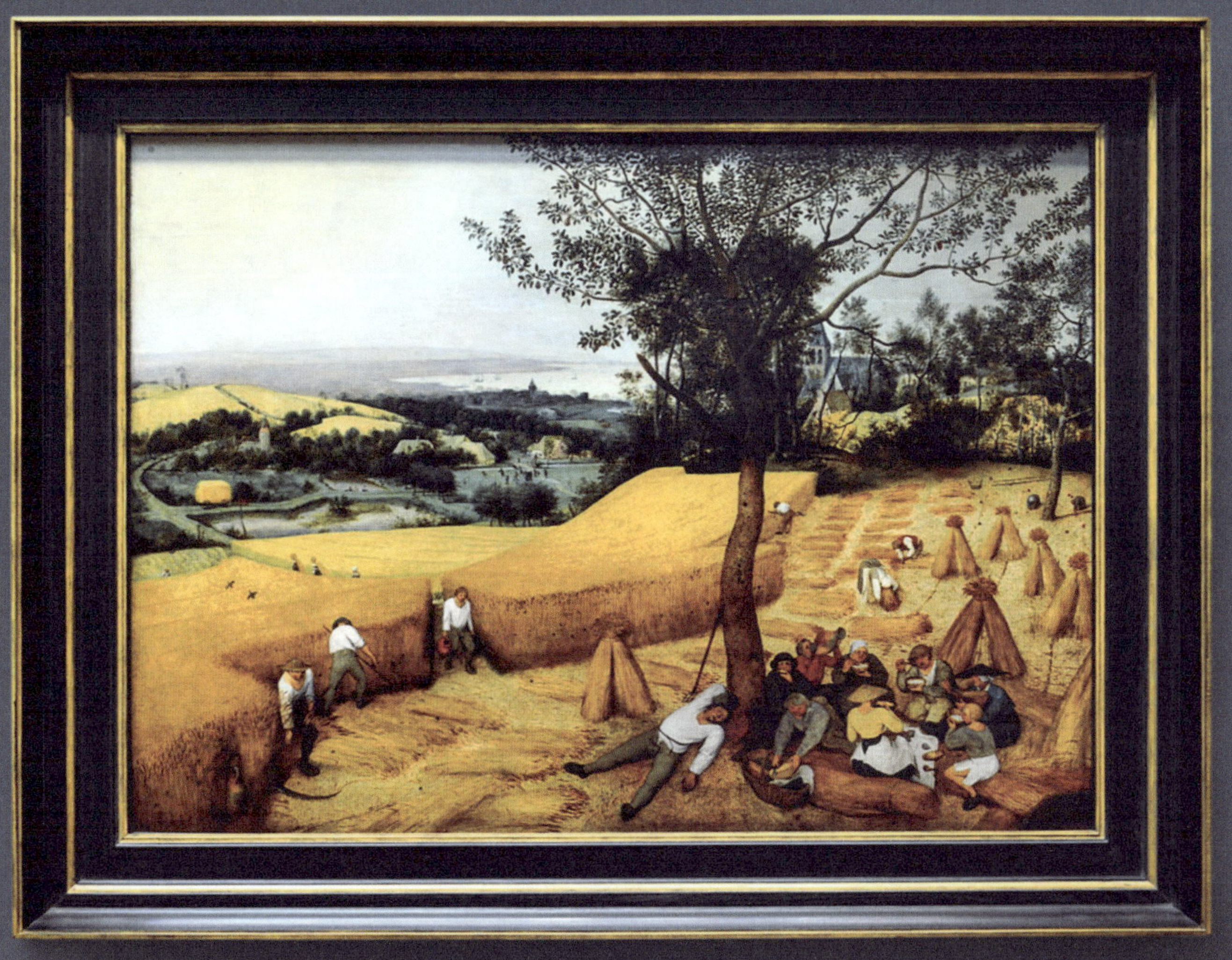

Proportion and perspective

Two obsessions of artists

During the Renaissance, artists sought to attain an ideal of harmony, balance and proportion in all things. To achieve this, they would base their compositions on tangible knowledge.

The quest for perfection

300 BC

THE GOLDEN RATIO

Also called phi (ϕ), the golden ratio is a proportion. Its application offers results so harmonious and so balanced that it seems to possess magical properties. The first precise definition of the golden ratio can be found in antiquity, in Euclid's *Elements*. Renaissance thinkers would be inspired by this ideal of harmony. However interesting the properties of the golden ratio may be, research today tends to argue against its excessive application in the analysis of classical works.

1435

THE QUEST FOR A PERFECT BODY

The art theorist Leon Battista Alberti wrote a treatise in which he established the ideal proportions of the human body. He recommended observing nature, and outlined the characteristics of the ideal painting. His approach provided advice on how to represent hair and draperies floating in the wind, or on the proper use of black and white.

1471

DIVINE INTERVENTION

Alberti met the monk and mathematician Luca Pacioli, who associated the aesthetics of the Renaissance with the golden ratio and spoke of "divine proportion". This is how the ratio acquired its mystical character; it appeared to find its origins in God, allowing artists to reach a sacred ideal. Leonardo da Vinci, who illustrated Pacioli's treatise, applied the golden ratio to the anatomy, deemed perfect, of his *Vitruvian Man* (p. 43).

PERFECT URBAN UTOPIA

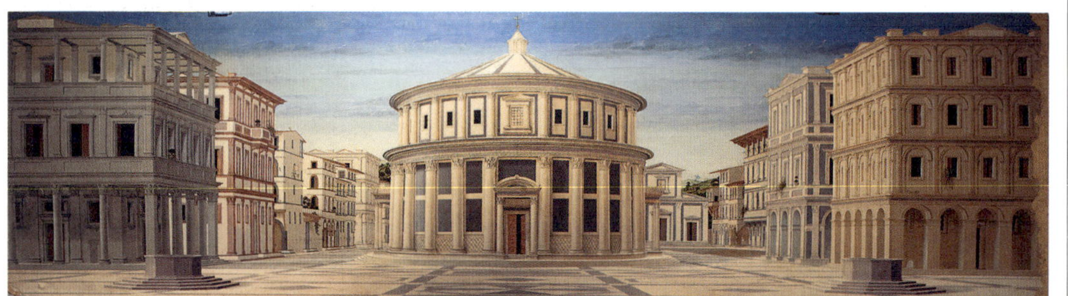

The quest for perfect harmony is embodied in "ideal cities", cleverly ordered according to a central perspective.

Attributed to Luciano Laurana, The Ideal City (circa 1470) Galleria nazionale delle Marche, Urbino.

Perspective systems

①

HIERARCHICAL PROPORTION

The most important elements are the largest; their size does not take reality into account, nor do their proportions relate to those of other elements.

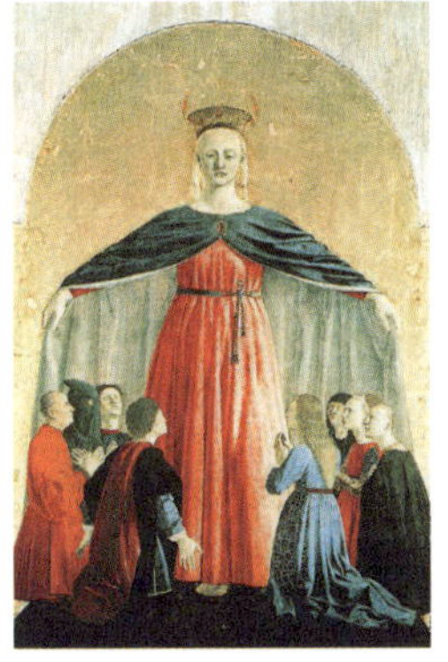

↑

Piero della Francesca Madonna della Misericordia (from the Polyptych of the Misericordia) 1445–1462, Museo Civico, Sansepolcro

②

OBLIQUE PROJECTION

Elements in the background are the same size as the elements in the foreground. Edges that convey the impression of depth run parallel to each other.

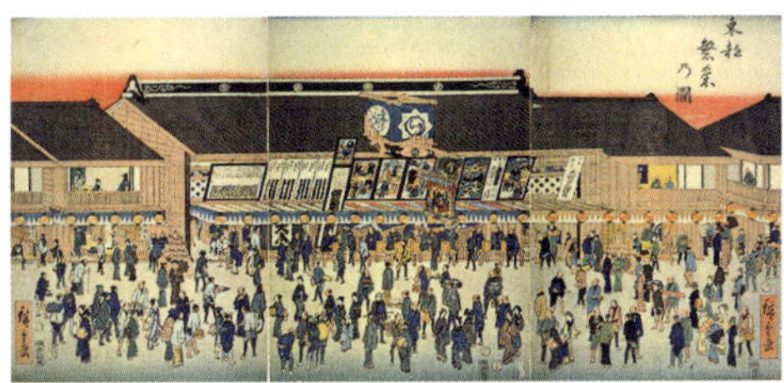

↑

Hiroshige
Kawarazaki-za 1854,
Los Angeles County Museum of Art

③

LINEAR OR POINT-PROJECTION PERSPECTIVE

This perspective is the most frequently used in the Renaissance and in Western painting. The image's lines converge towards a vanishing point; the closer the elements are to the vanishing point, the smaller they become.

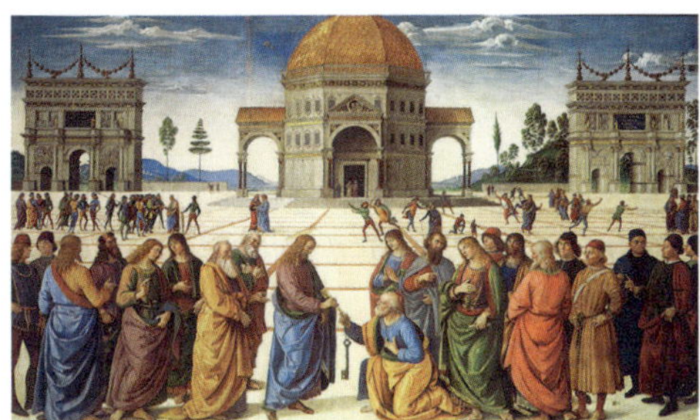

↑

Perugino
The Delivery of the Keys to Saint Peter
1481–1482,
Sistine Chapel, Rome

④

ATMOSPHERIC PERSPECTIVE

Also called aerial perspective, this form of perspective is rather an optical illusion that plays on colours to accentuate the idea of depth. Warm colours indicate proximity, while cold colours indicate distance.

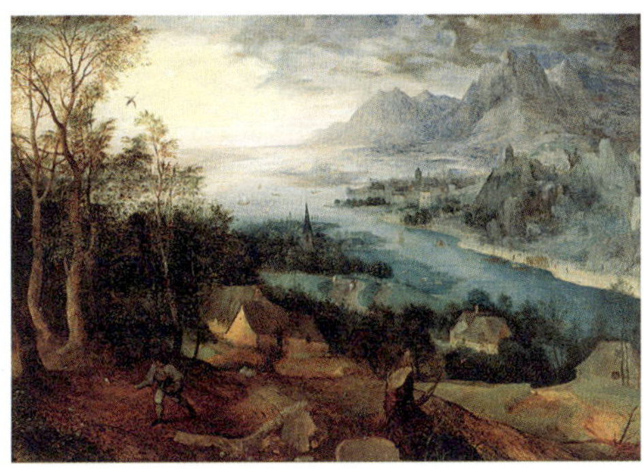

↑

Pieter Bruegel the Elder
Parable of the Sower 1557,
Timken Museum of Art, San Diego

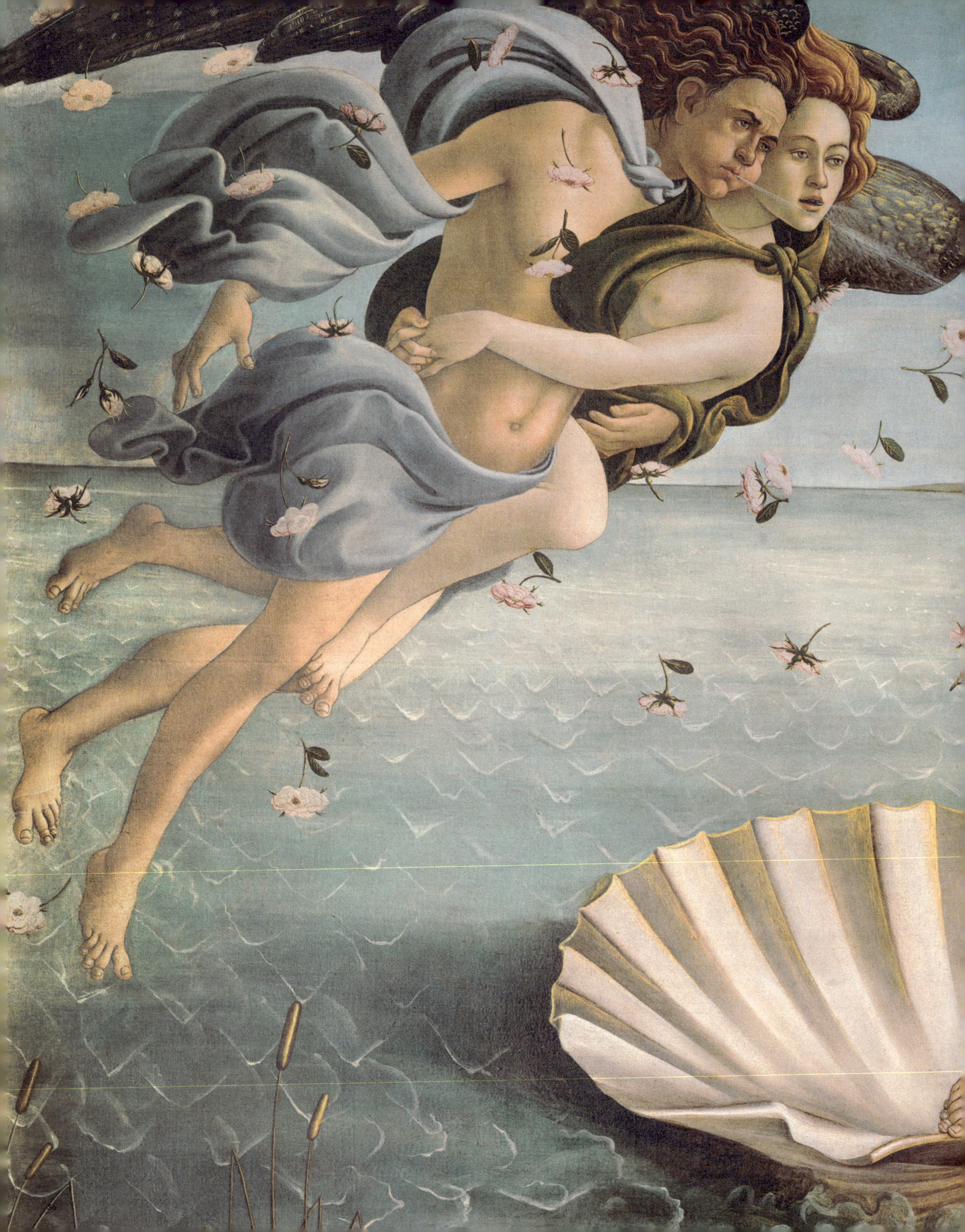

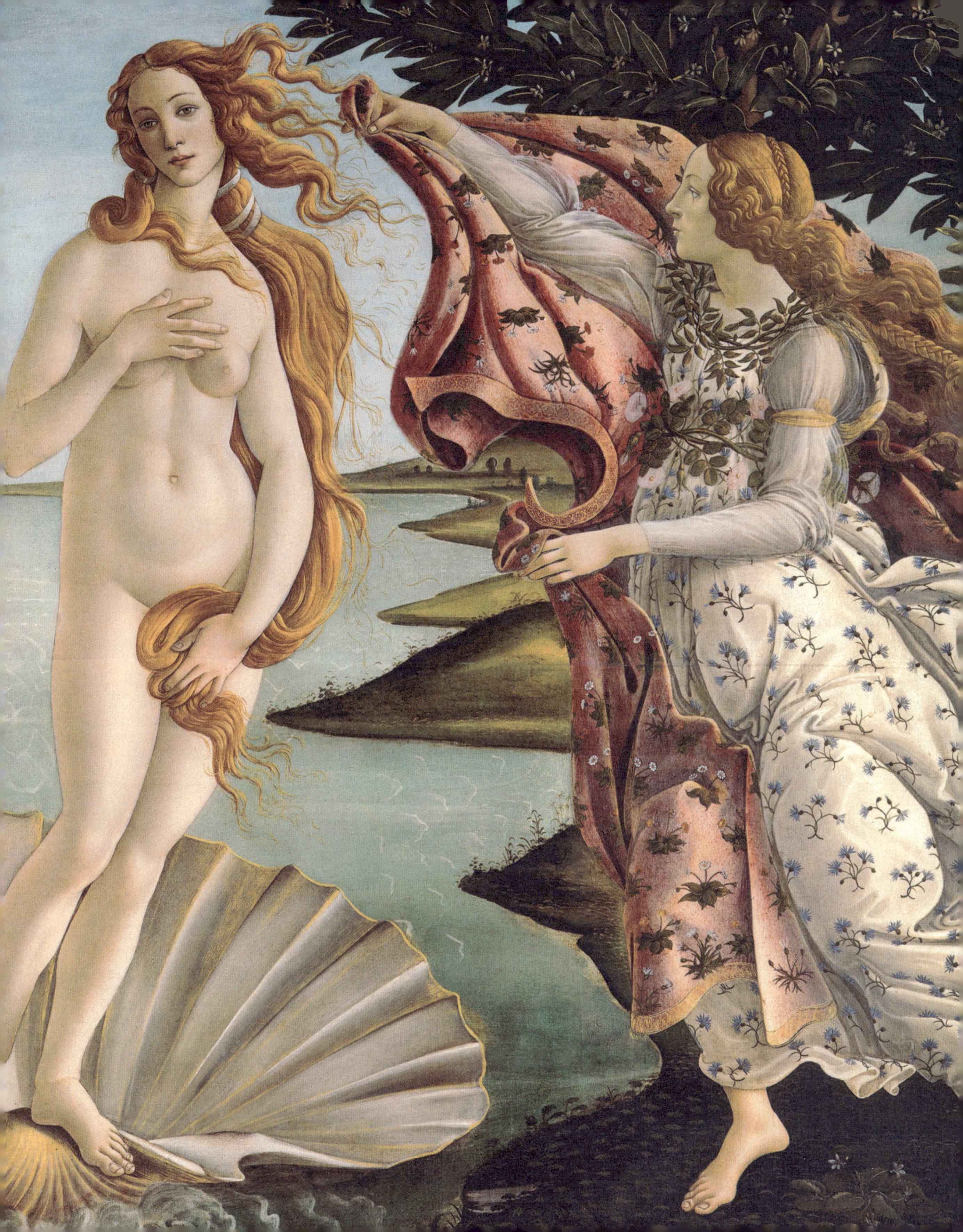

Sandro Botticelli

The Renaissance takes its course

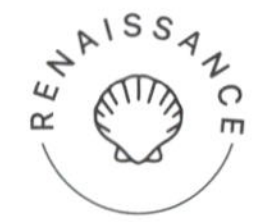

Botticelli is said to have begun his training with a goldsmith, before continuing under the supervision of Filippo Lippi, who introduced him to the painting of Madonnas and religious scenes. From these years, the artist would retain a meticulous approach to drawing and a taste for precise lines outlining his subjects.

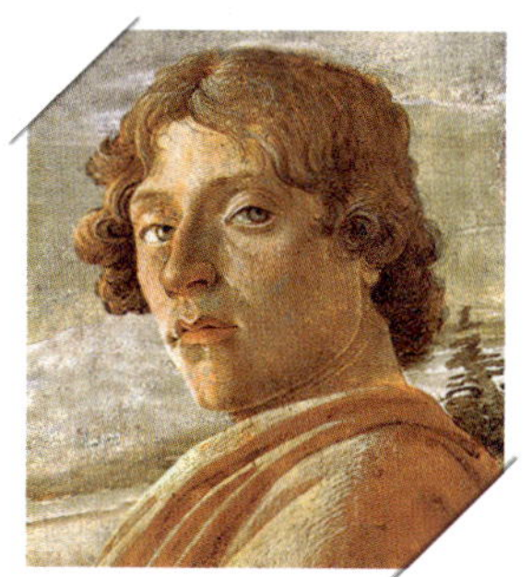

He knew his classics

A pleasant and cultured man, Botticelli was associated with local powers, then in the hands of the Medici. His paintings feature antique, literary and philosophical references of his time. He produced intellectually complex, but accessible works in the taste of the Renaissance.

Like a boss!

Botticelli owned a prosperous studio. Supervising a large team of assistants and apprentices, Botticelli ran a tight ship, producing works to meet the needs of a large clientele. As he grew older, tired and ill, he entrusted an increasing part of the production process to his studio.

A change in plans

After arriving in Florence, the monk Savonarola rose to power. The Medici culture disappeared, and was promptly replaced by religious rigorism. Botticelli adapted to this new demand: he dressed his sensual Venuses, turning them into saints absorbed by their faith.

DON'T JUDGE A PAINTER BY THEIR BRUSHES

The creator of these serene figures is a sociable and approachable painter. Botticelli was even reputed to be a prankster, and would play tricks on his apprentices.

Pieter Bruegel the Elder
Page 32

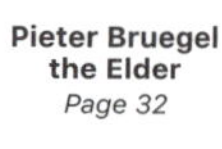

1445
Born in Florence

1453
The Byzantine Empire fell

Circa
1485
Painted *The Birth of Venus*

1510
Died in Florence

1519
Magellan and Elcano first attempted to circumnavigate the Earth under sail

Leonardo da Vinci
Page 44

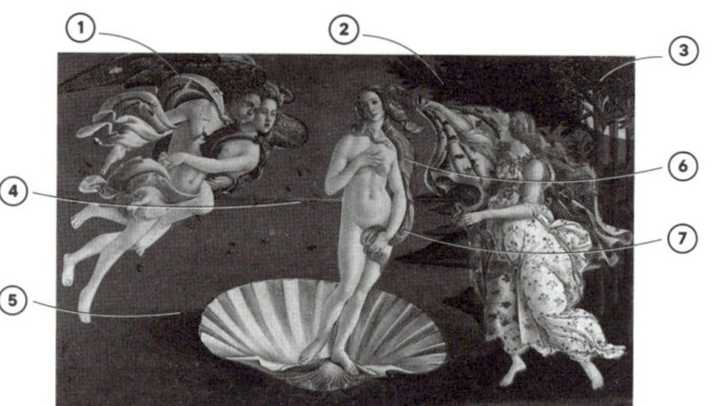

THE BIRTH OF VENUS ↗

Circa 1485
Tempera on canvas
172.5 × 278.5 cm
Uffizi Gallery, Florence

WHAT ARE WE LOOKING AT?

Botticelli graced the Renaissance with one of its icons and the history of art with one of its greatest masterpieces. The painting does not illustrate the birth of the goddess, but the moment after, when she is about to set foot on land.

① Weather report

Zephyr, the gentle west wind, is pushing the goddess towards the earth. The character at his side is sometimes identified as Chloris, his wife, or Aura, the sea breeze.

② A warm welcome

Flora, goddess of flowers, or perhaps Eiar, the embodiment of spring, is preparing to cover the goddess; however, the shape of the drape, borne by the wind, echoes Venus's curves, highlighting her sensuality, rather than hiding it.

③ The patron lurks amidst the trees

Laurel or orange trees? The vegetation refers to the Medici, by pronunciation. The orange tree, called *"mala medica"*, is said to be an emblem of the family. If it were a laurel, it could refer to Lorenzo de Medici.

④ A flat country ...

Perspectives are still basic. Landscapes would acquire more importance with the rise of the next generation of artists, such as Leonardo da Vinci.

⑤ Seashells and antiquity

By placing his Venus in a seashell, Botticelli is following in the footsteps of Apelles, the greatest painter of antiquity. While Apelles' original work was lost, it has been copied many times.

⑥ Cover up that bosom, which we would endure to look on

The pose evokes a "hit" from the statuary of antiquity: the *Venus Pudica*, who tries in vain to hide her nakedness. The Medici owned a statue of her. A coincidence? Most likely not.

⑦ Saint or goddess?

In addition to these references, Venus's long hair, which covers her body, is inspired by religion, reminiscent of the Christian saint Mary Magdalene.

①

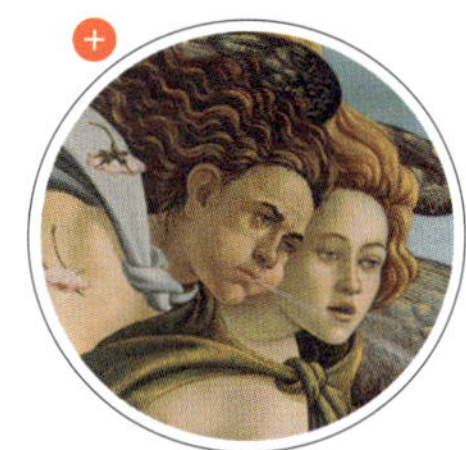

BOTTICELLI'S ART IN A NUTSHELL

- A symbolic language inherited from antiquity.
- A reflection on beauty and ideal.
- Melancholic and contemplative characters.

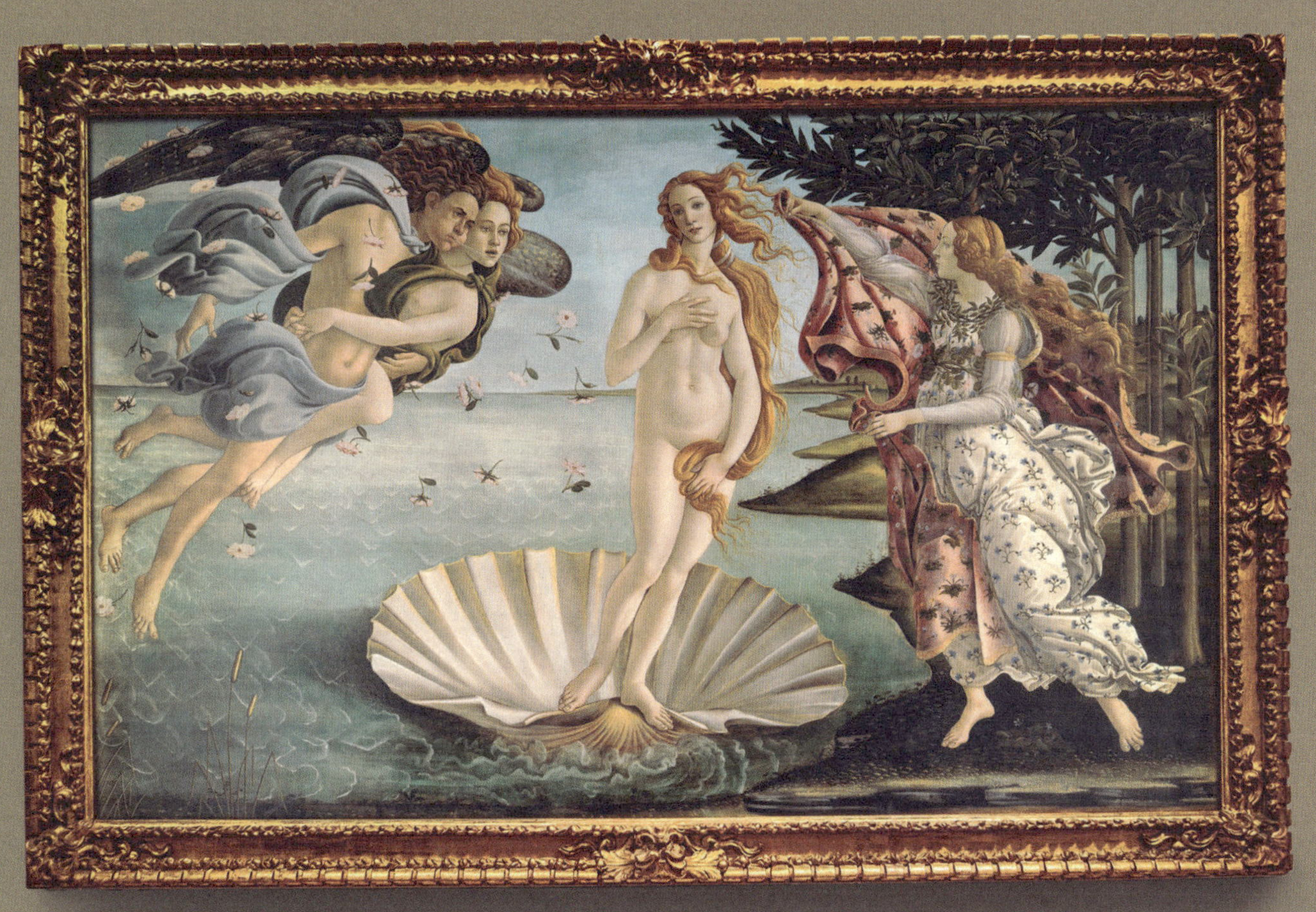

Botticelli and Cassatt

In the name of the mother

The theme of motherly love moved Renaissance artists to paint holy figures with humanity, engaging the viewer. The subject is so universal that it is a recurring theme in the history of art, stripped of any religious interpretation.

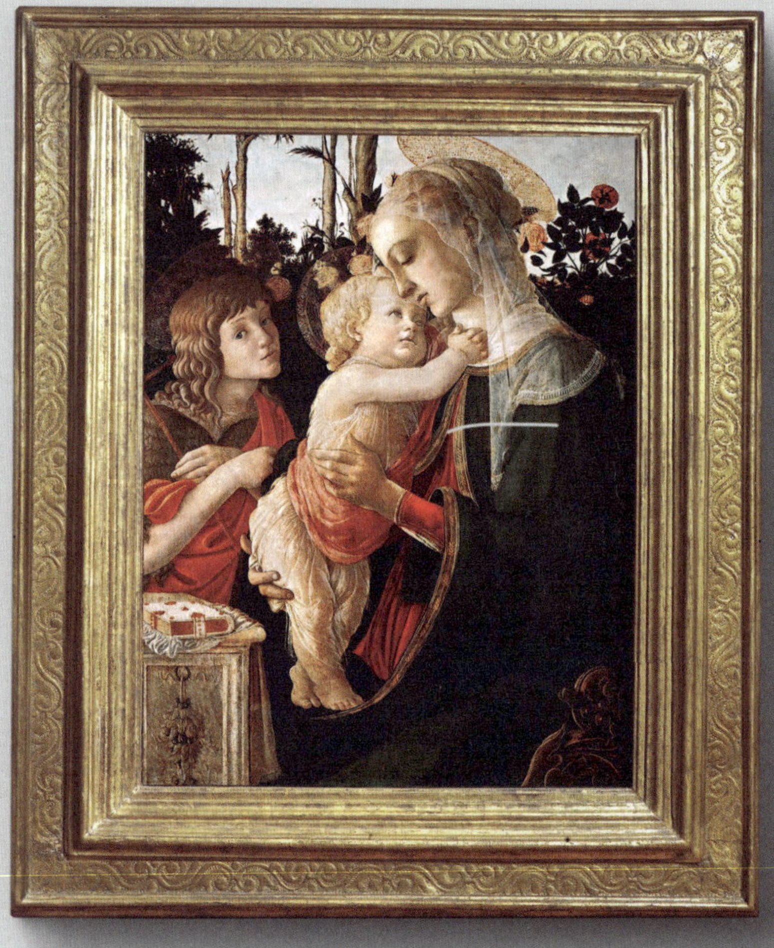

VIRGIN AND CHILD WITH THE YOUNG SAINT JOHN THE BAPTIST
BY SANDRO BOTTICELLI AND HIS STUDIO
1450–1475

The halos leave no doubt as to the identity of the characters, and the melancholy of the Virgin heralds the fate of the Child. The tender gesture of Christ and the way he seeks his mother's gaze for comfort are moving.

Tempera on poplar wood, 90.7 × 67 cm
Louvre Museum, Paris

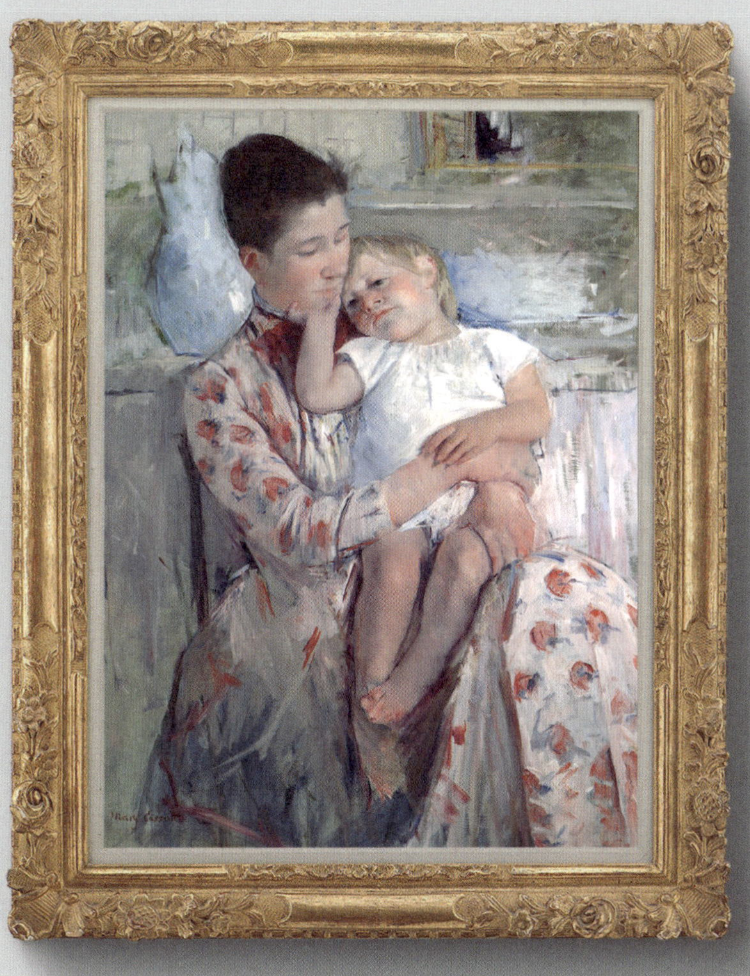

***MOTHER AND CHILD* BY MARY CASSATT**
Circa 1890

The painting is not religious, but it does display the same intimacy as Botticelli's work, reinforced by the gaze of the figures, which are looking away from the viewer. Their unbreakable bond is expressed by the meticulous depiction of the figures, in contrast to the hastily treated background.

Oil on canvas, 90.17 × 64.44 cm
Wichita Art Museum, Wichita

The Renaissance
Antiquity returns in force

From the 15th century onwards, a great movement was born in Florence: the Renaissance. Arts, sciences, philosophy… This major turning point in Western history had repercussions in many areas, and soon spread to the whole of Europe.

Two key events

The figures of Leonardo and Botticelli are easily associated with the Renaissance; however, the movement drew its roots in architecture and sculpture. As early as the 14th century, the first signs of the Renaissance could be observed on the building sites that appeared throughout Florence.

1401

A landmark tender

Lorenzo Ghiberti and Filippo Brunelleschi were competing for the creation of the northern doors of the Baptistery of San Giovanni. In their bas-reliefs, the draperies still feature somewhat stiff gothic influences, but the two artists recycle classic ancient motifs.

1420

A site to behold

Ghiberti was responsible for the doors of the Baptistery, but Brunelleschi was not left out. He began work on an exceptional project that would require 16 years: the creation of the dome of the Cathedral of Santa Maria del Fiore.

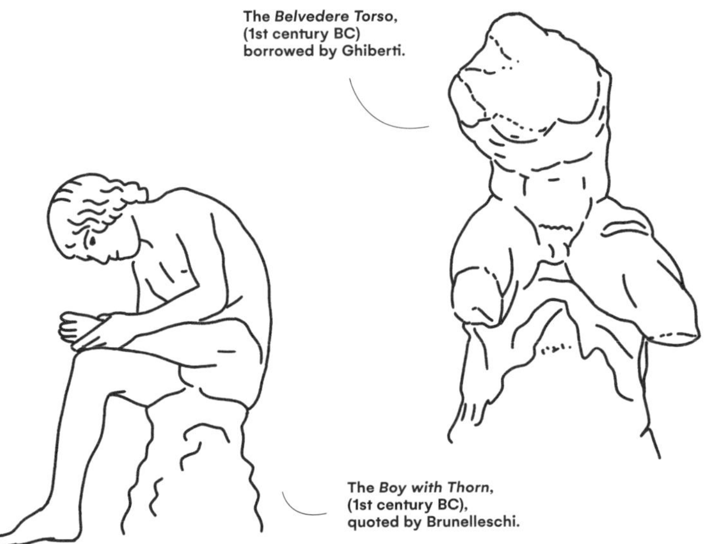

The *Belvedere Torso*, (1st century BC) borrowed by Ghiberti.

The *Boy with Thorn*, (1st century BC), quoted by Brunelleschi.

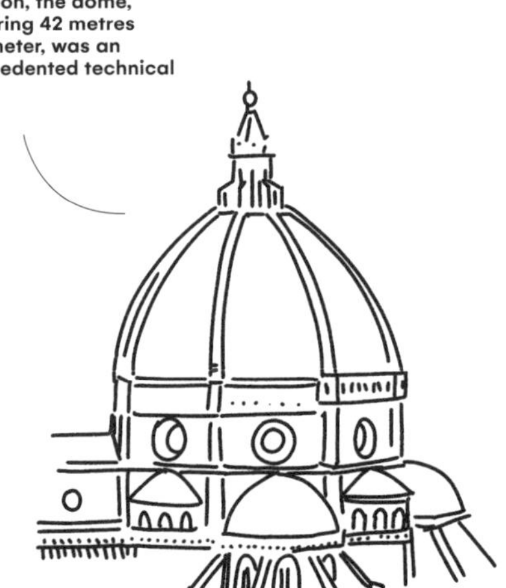

Inspired by the ancient Pantheon, the dome, measuring 42 metres in diameter, was an unprecedented technical feat.

FROM ARTISAN TO ARTIST

Artists became aware of their status as early as the Late Middle Ages, when creators first began signing their works. The Renaissance drove the point home, and the poet Dante, in *The Divine Comedy*, defined an artist as follows: one "who has the skill of his art, but a trembling hand" – in other words, one who is responsible for both the idea and the gesture.

A human-centric era

In the Middle Ages, humans were shrouded in their faith. In the Renaissance, however, they reclaimed their importance. In their quest for knowledge, thinkers honoured Plato and Aristotle. Inspired by the Roman architect Vitruvius, Leonardo da Vinci propagated this humanistic vision in a famous image.

In itself, the *Vitruvian Man* compiles a rigorous anatomical study, an inventory of proportions, an observation of movement, a lesson in mathematics, an aesthetic proposal and more. A drawing worth a thousand words, indeed!

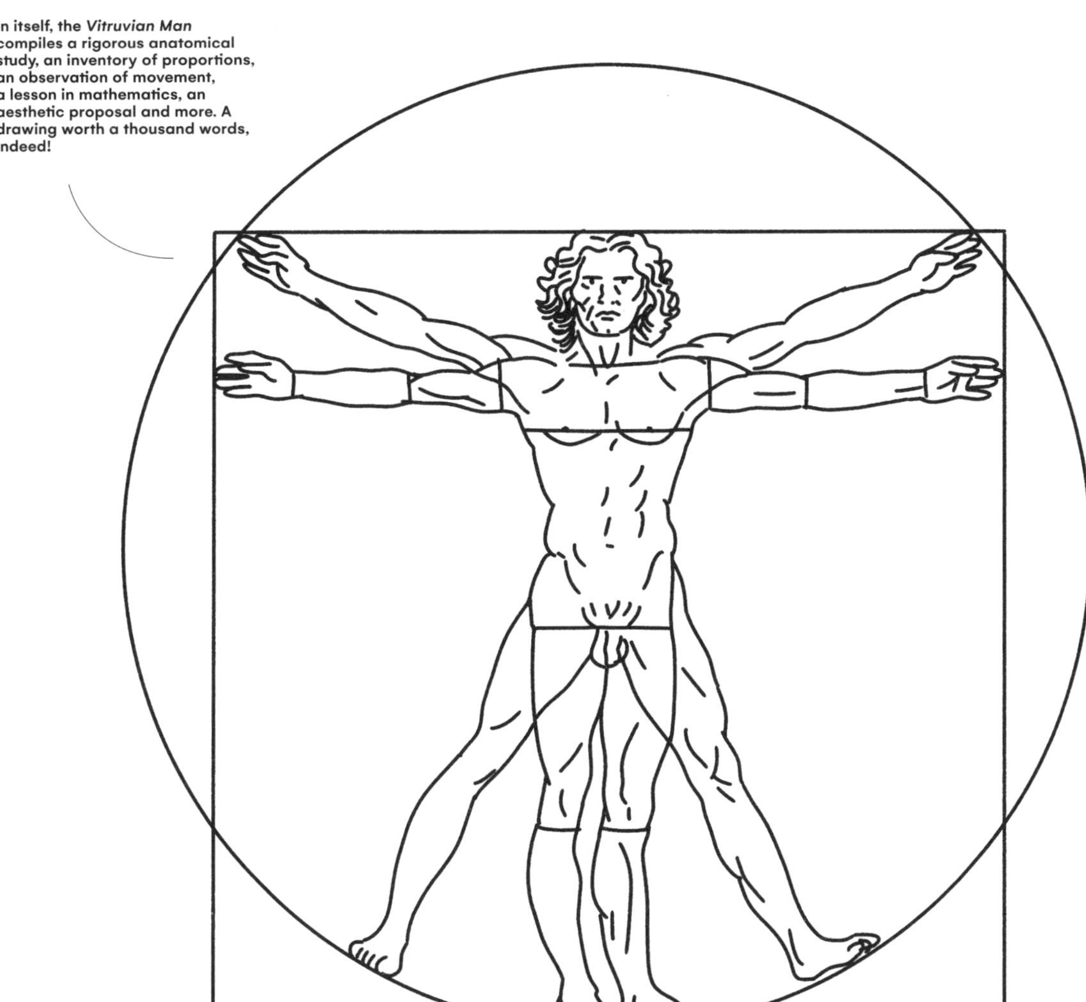

A BREATH OF FRESH AIR

The Renaissance also paid tribute to the perfection of nature – another way of celebrating God, creator of all things. Landscapes became further developed in religious scenes. In 1348, Ambrogio Lorenzetti painted one of the first panoramic landscapes in his fresco *The Allegory of Good and Bad Government*, at the Palazzo Pubblico in Siena.

Leonardo da Vinci

A genius at playing hooky from school

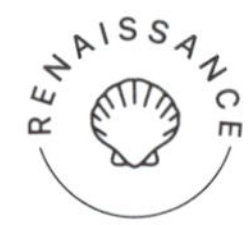

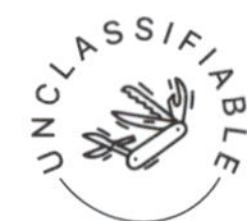

Leonardo's first school was nature. The artist learned much from observing it, and throughout his life, he sought to imitate and let himself be inspired by it, whether in his paintings or his inventions. This is what is known today as "biomimicry".

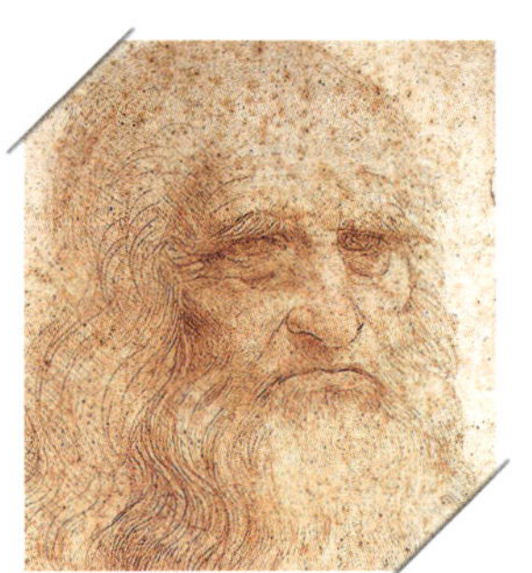

The king of contouring

Leonardo honed his skills in Verrocchio's studio. Inspired by the master's trade as a sculptor, he learned to render light and shadow in drawing. Later, he mastered the technique called sfumato, which he applied to model contours using subtle gradations.

Food for thought

While he considered sculpture to be a manual task, Leonardo saw painting as a *cosa mentale*, a "mind thing" – an arduous science, which aimed to recreate the three dimensions of nature on a flat surface.

Jack of all trades

Leonardo wasn't just a painter; he was also a sculptor, an architect, a war strategist, an engineer and more. All his work is recorded in codices, notebooks which he sometimes filled using specular writing, which can be read using a mirror.

AN IMPORTED MASTERPIECE

Who is the Mona Lisa? Behind the world's most famous smile is Lisa Gherardini, wife of Florentine entrepreneur Francesco del Giocondo. The patron would never take possession of the portrait. Leonardo, invited by Francis I of France, left for France, taking his painting with him.

Sandro Botticelli
Page 38

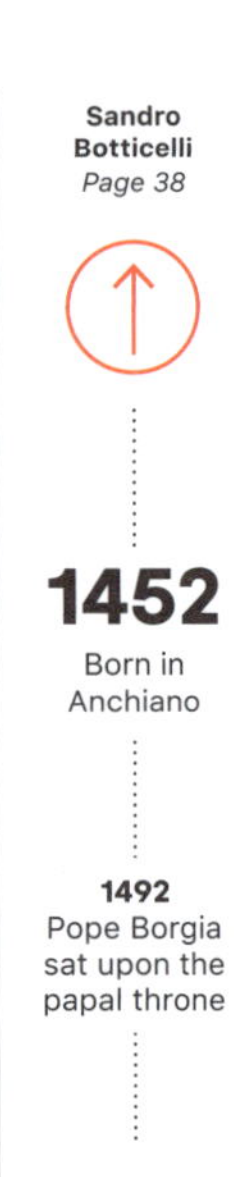

1452
Born in Anchiano

1492
Pope Borgia sat upon the papal throne

1503 to **1519**
Painted *The Virgin and Child with Saint Anne*

1509
Erasmus wrote *In Praise of Folly*

1519
Died in Amboise

Raphael
Page 46

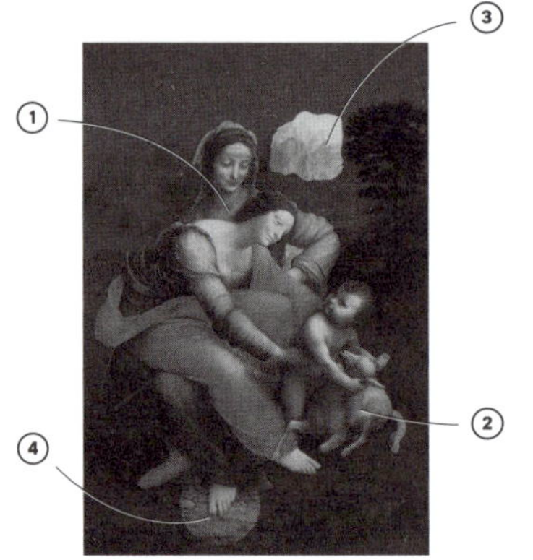

THE VIRGIN AND CHILD WITH SAINT ANNE

1503–1519
Oil on wood
168.4 × 113 cm
Louvre Museum, Paris

WHAT ARE WE LOOKING AT?

This work shows Saint Anne, mother of the Virgin Mary, with her daughter Mary and the Child Jesus, who is playing with a lamb.

① Anachronism and miracles

According to the texts, Anne died before the birth of Jesus. This work therefore requires a spiritual perspective. As Anne was sterile and Mary was a virgin, the child is the result of two miraculous pregnancies. The trinity depicted here – Jesus with his mother and grandmother – echoes the Holy Trinity formed by the Child with God the Father and the Holy Spirit. This symbolic image explains why the two women appear to be about the same age.

② It's destiny

Christ is playing with a lamb, a symbol of his forthcoming sacrifice. The Virgin, leaning towards him, appears to be in an ambiguous situation: it is hard to say whether she is attempting to hold him back or if, on the contrary, letting him go to embrace his destiny.

In preparatory drawings, Saint Anne's hand delicately prevented the Virgin from holding on to her son, but Leonardo removed this detail in the painted version.

③ Colours for perspective

In this painting, Leonardo uses atmospheric perspective to produce an impression of depth. The foreground, painted in warm tones, appears close to us, while the landscape in the background is composed of icy blue tones suggesting distance.

④ Proprietary technique

The painter applied his mastery of sfumato to model the faces. Leonardo used light glazes to render the veils on Saint Anne's forehead and the water at her feet.

② +

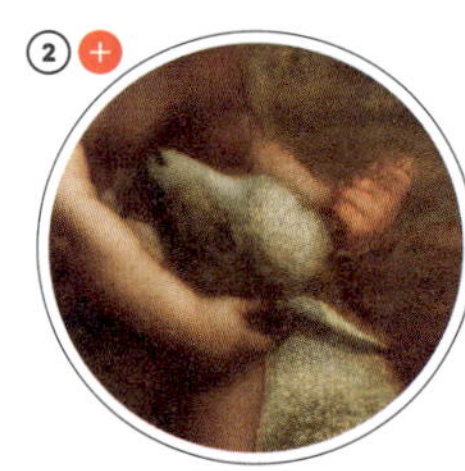

WHO'S THE STRONGEST OF THEM ALL?

Painting and sculpture culminated during the Italian Renaissance, but a fierce debate opposed the two disciplines, with each side defending the superiority of its craft over the other. This debate was named "Paragone", and Leonardo da Vinci made a major contribution to it through his painted works, which he placed above all other works.

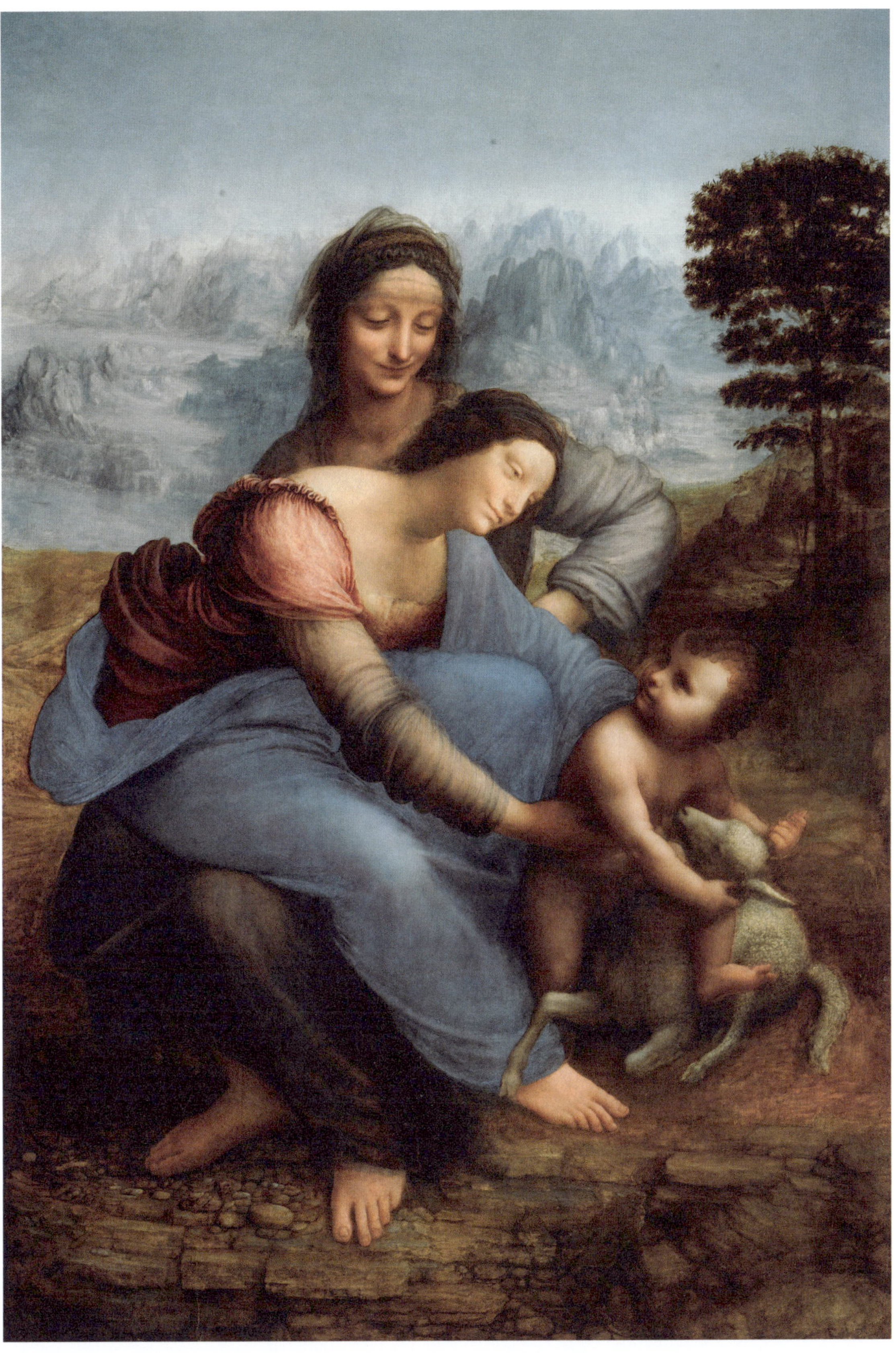

Raphael

A wholly divine artist

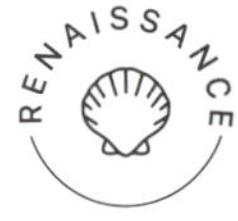

Raffaello Sanzio is as renowned for his human qualities as for his artistic proficiency. His painting displays great intelligence, shaping complex ideas with a grace and balance never before attained.

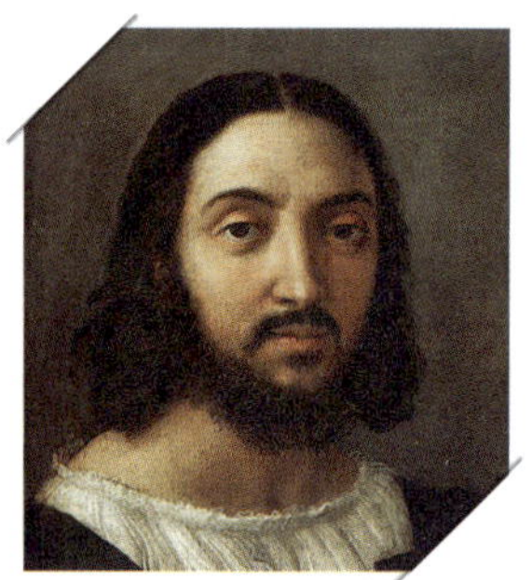

Amen to the man

Raphael was closely linked to the Christian religion; he contributed to renewing its image, as he sought to achieve an ideal of grace and humanity. Born and deceased on Good Friday, the artist himself possessed a mystical aura; his formidable human, almost Christlike qualities were the subject of praise.

Conceptual art before it was a thing

Raphael's great talent was his ability to represent ideas as scenes. He knew how to materialise a story, while his perfect mastery of the technical aspects of drawing and colour enabled him to imitate nature with virtuosity.

Sehnsucht

He was attracted to antiquity, from which he drew forms and ideas, and took a close interest in the archaeological discoveries of his time. Shortly before his premature death, he had written a letter to Pope Leo X, in which he reflected on a project to reconstruct ancient Rome.

IT WAS SAID OF HIM

"His second life, that of fame which fears neither time nor death, will be eternal both by his works and by the learned men who will praise it." Giovanni Pico della Mirandola, Italian philosopher and theologian of the 16th century.

Leonardo da Vinci
Page 44

1483
Born in Urbino

1501
Michelangelo sculpted his *Pietà*

1516 to **1520**
Raphael painted *The Transfiguration*

1519
Charles V was elected to lead the Holy Roman Empire

1520
Died in Rome

Michelangelo
Page 54

THE TRANSFIGURATION

1516–1520
Fatty paint with tempera on wood
410 × 279 cm
Vatican Museums, Rome

WHAT ARE WE LOOKING AT?

***The Transfiguration* represents a scene from the life of Christ, as told in the Gospel according to Matthew; it depicts Jesus, illuminated by the light of the Holy Spirit and surrounded by the prophets Moses and Elijah.**

Two in one

This painting juxtaposes two scenes from the Gospel of Matthew. The Transfiguration of Christ is represented at the top. Raised in the air, he is surrounded by Moses, on the left, and Elijah, on the right. At their feet, the apostles James, Peter and John are overwhelmed by this sight.

A crisis of faith and an epileptic seizure

At the bottom of the painting, the apostles are confronted with a child possessed by a demon; the child is most likely epileptic, but their lack of faith prevents him from healing. Two of them, pointing their fingers towards Christ, appear to comprehend the solution; the group, however, remains blinded by its emotions. Raphael depicted the coexistence of these episodes in order to illustrate a single idea: the belief in the existence of Christ on Earth.

A chaotic scene

With its brown tones, the earthly world displays a realistic consistency, reinforced by the materiality of the scene's muscular protagonists; however, it is also disordered. The distribution of colours – blue, red and green – sets the viewer's gaze on a disorderly path.

An old trick

This chaos contrasts with the spherical, perfect organisation of the upper section. The light of the Christ stands in contrast to the dark void below him; he appears to blend with the clouds. The supernatural character of the scene is reinforced by the difference in scale between the characters, reminiscent of the art of the Middle Ages, disorienting the viewer.

SEPARATE ROOMS

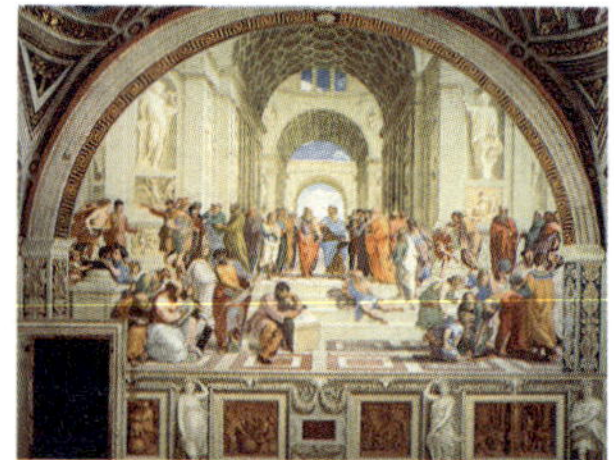

The School of Athens, 1508–1512, Vatican Palace

The Vatican Palace contains four rooms known as the "Raphael Rooms". Their decoration was created by the painter and his studio, for Pope Julius II. The Room of the Signatura houses, among others, *The School of Athens*, one of the master's greatest masterpieces.

A GRAND EXIT

Raphael's ultimate masterpiece and pictorial testament, the *Transfiguration* was found in his studio at the time of his death. At his funeral, it would be carried in procession, preceding his coffin.

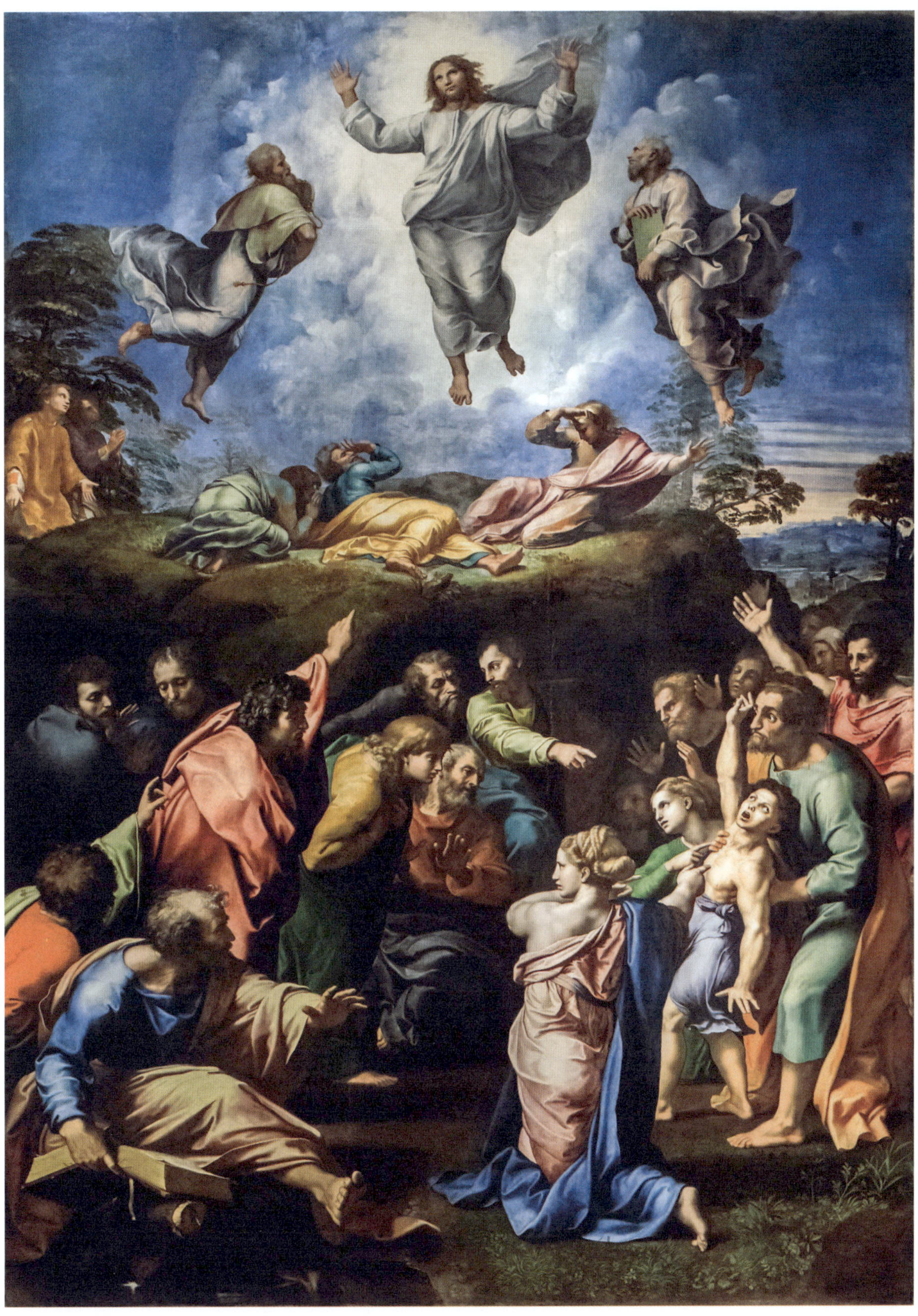

In the midst of saints
Drawings by design

The subject can be recognised through the iconography, i.e. the study of the motifs identifying the theme or the characters. In religious painting, saints can be identified by their attributes. However, caution is required, as the use of attributes is not systematic, and a saint can be represented without his attribute. Also, one same attribute can also be shared among several saints.

The Four Evangelists

WHO ARE THE EVANGELISTS?

- The Four Evangelists are considered to be the authors of the Gospels, the texts that recount the story of Jesus's life in the New Testament.
- Alongside these texts, some gospels, called "Apocrypha", have not been accepted by the Church.
- In paintings, the Evangelists are sometimes depicted writing, or holding a book in their hands.

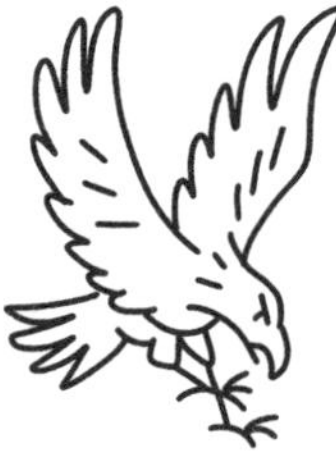

John

John is the youngest of the Twelve Apostles, and is often depicted as a young man.

Totem creature:
an eagle

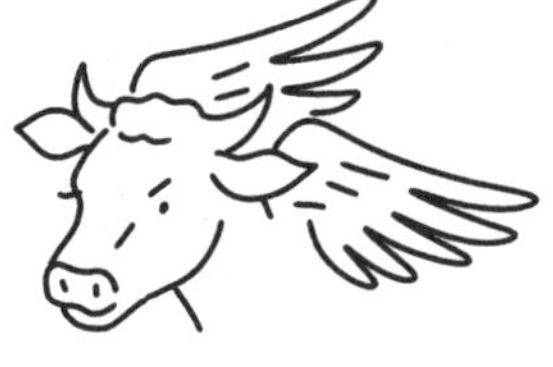

Luke

Luke is the patron saint of painters.

Totem creature:
an ox (sometimes winged)

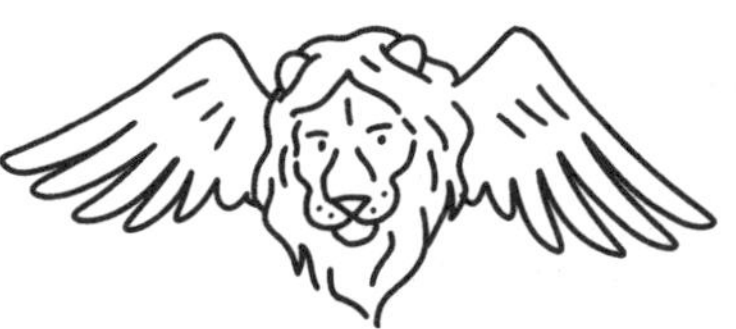

Mark

Mark is the symbol of the city of Venice.

Totem creature:
a lion (sometimes winged, and wearing a halo)

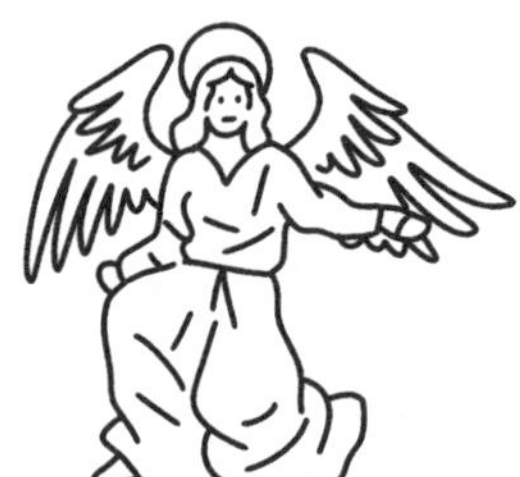

Matthew

Matthew is a tax collector. He is also associated with the sword, the instrument of his martyrdom.

Totem creature:
a winged man (mistaken for an angel)

The twelve apostles of Christ

WHAT IS AN APOSTLE?

Generally speaking, an apostle is a person entrusted with spreading a doctrine or opinion. The Twelve Apostles were the disciples chosen by Jesus in the early days of the Church. Their number refers to the twelve tribes of Israel, which Jesus intended to unite.

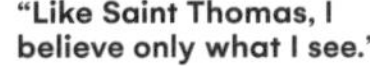

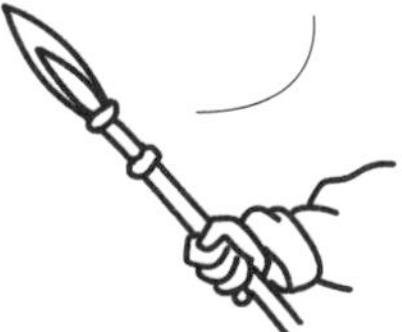

Thomas

The lance is the symbol of Thomas's martyrdom, and is also the weapon used to wound Christ. In disbelief, Thomas would thrust his hand into Christ's wound.

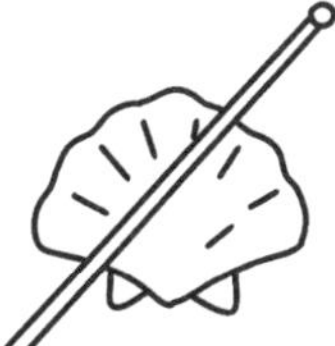

James the Greater or James of Zebedee

The pilgrim's staff and the seashell are references to the Way of St. James (Camino de Santiago). Pilgrims would sow a seashell collected in Galicia to their garments, as a mark of completing the journey.

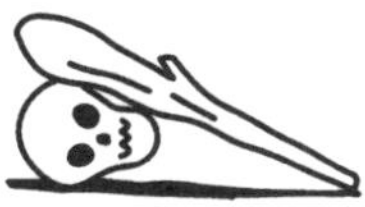

James the Less or James of Alpheus

James was thrown off a cliff, but survived his fall; his skull was then smashed with a club.

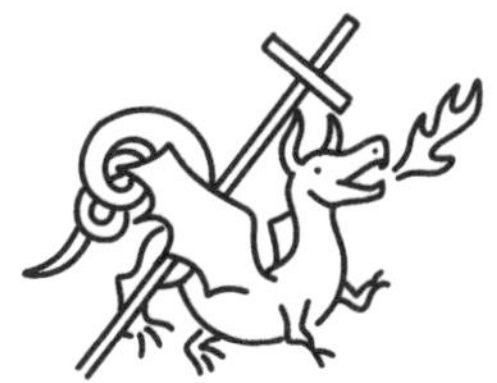

Philip

Philip was crucified upside down. Sometimes, he is depicted holding a long stick adorned with a cross or a dragon – the one that he defeated.

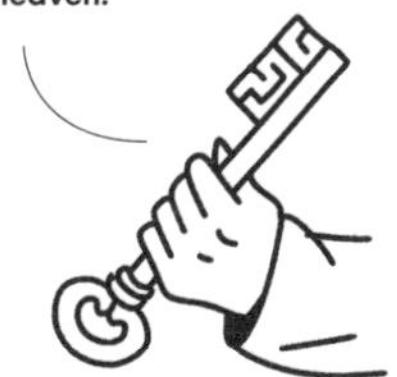

Peter

First bishop of Rome, Peter is often represented holding the key symbolising the promise made by Jesus.

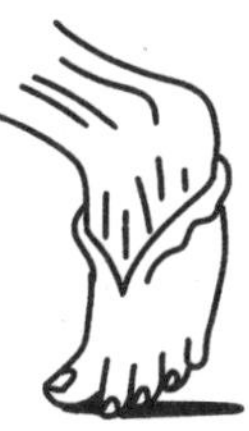

Bartholomew

Accounts of Bartholomew's death differ. In some versions, he was flayed alive. He is often depicted holding a knife, or holding his skin in his hand.

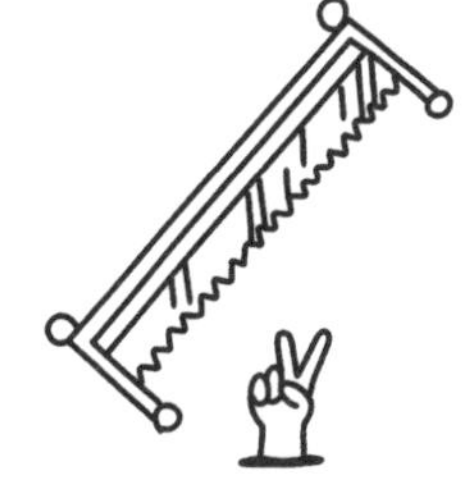

Simon

Simon was cut into pieces with a saw. This martyrdom alludes to the martyrdom suffered by the prophet Isaiah in the Old Testament.

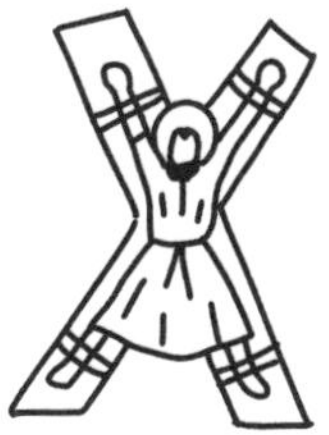

Andrew

Andrew was crucified on an X-shaped cross. A fisherman by trade before meeting with Christ, he is sometimes depicted with nets.

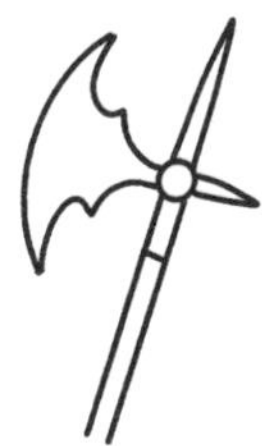

Jude or Thaddeus

Beaten to death with a club, he is also sometimes represented with a halberd or an axe.

Matthias

Absent at the Last Supper, Matthias became an apostle after the death of Judas. He died by decapitation; the axe is sometimes replaced by a sword.

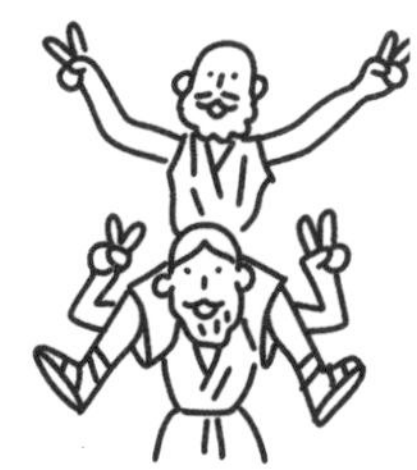

John and Matthew

They are part of the Four Evangelists (see box opposite).

Ingres and Chardin
The myth of the artist

The history of art has created the myth of the brilliant and solitary artist. In reality, however, most painters were supported by studios, apprentices and assistants. They were both entrepreneurs and painters.

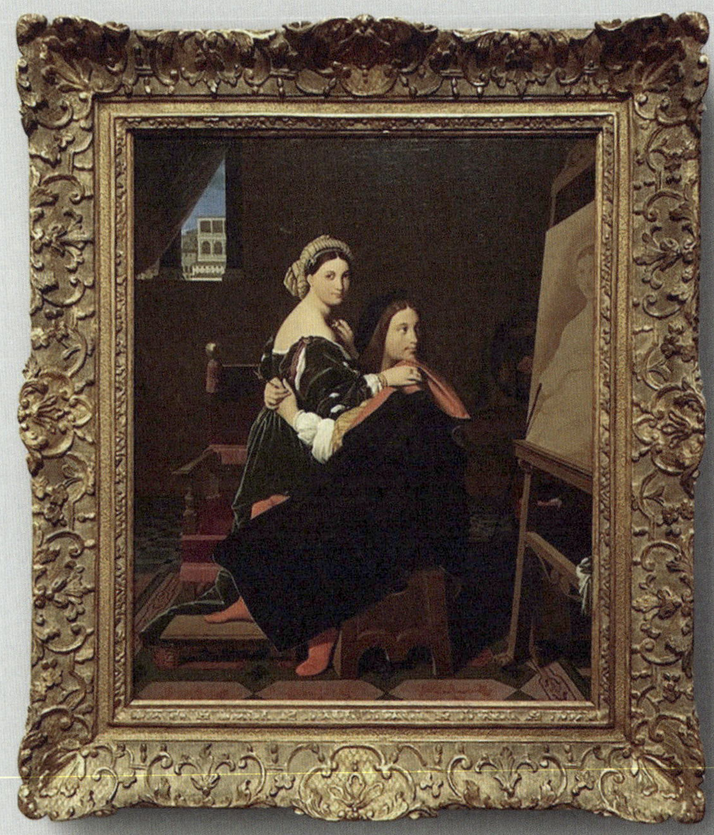

***RAPHAEL AND LA FORNARINA* BY JEAN-AUGUSTE-DOMINIQUE INGRES**
1814

A lovable character in every sense of the word, Raphael has been remembered as the perfect son-in-law in the history of art. Ingres fuels this legend by depicting him as a seducer and a genius contemplating his work. In the background appears Rome, the theatre of his glory.

Oil on canvas, 66 × 54 cm
Fogg Art Museum, Cambridge

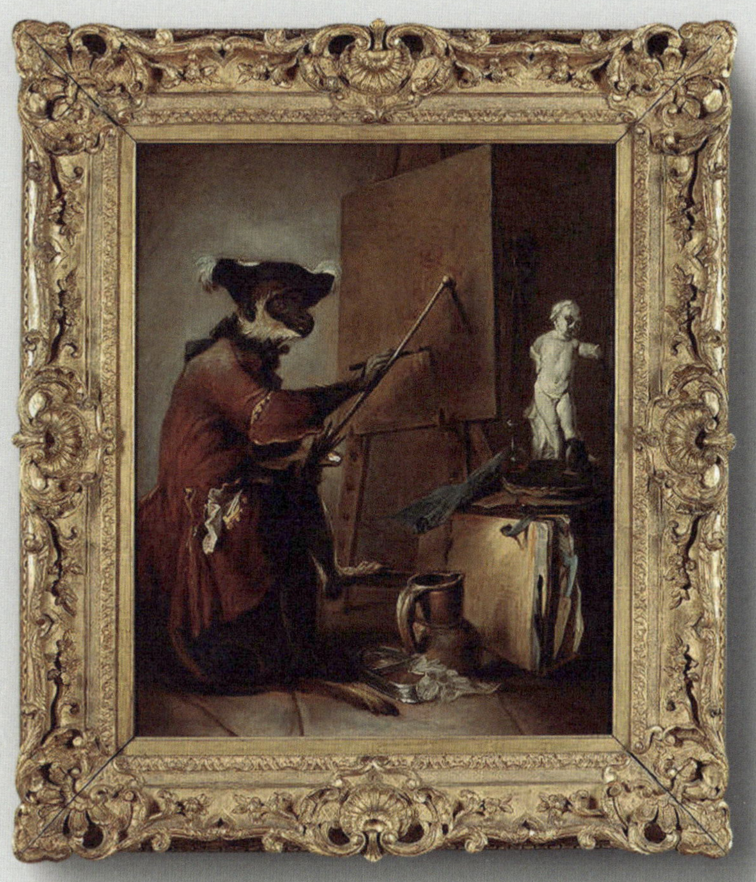

***THE MONKEY PAINTER* BY JEAN SIMÉON CHARDIN**
1739–1740

With crossed legs, wearing a jacket with stripes, this monkey is adopting a human attitude, producing a comical scene. Chardin used a playful approach to knock the mythical artist off their pedestal and mock those who aspire to be beheld as geniuses, too diligent and unable to think beyond the tip of their brush.

Oil on canvas, 73 × 59.5 cm
Louvre Museum, Paris

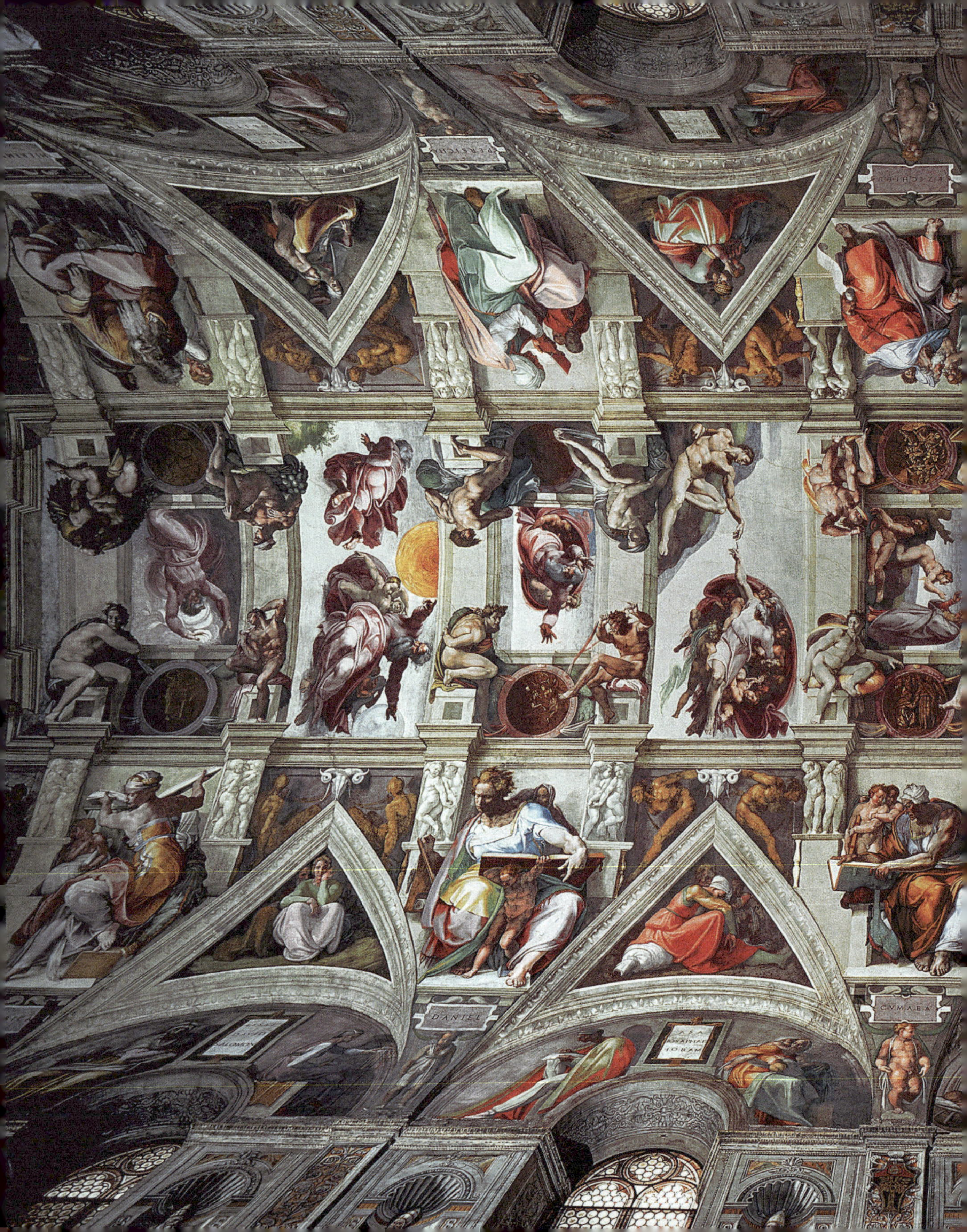

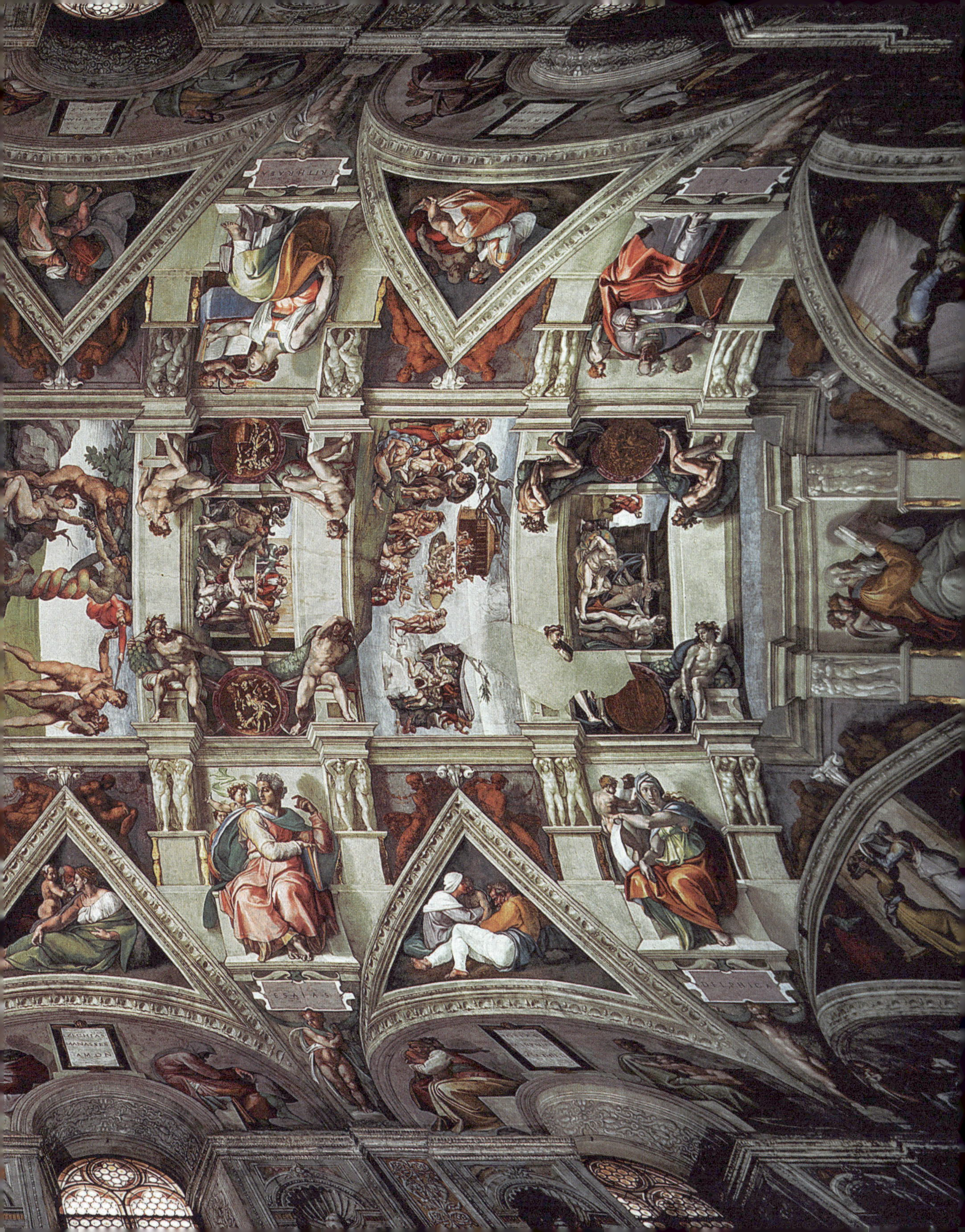

Michelangelo

Painting enters the realm of the third dimension

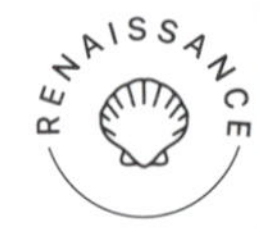

Mythologised as a genius by the history of art, Michelangelo Buonarroti was one of the greatest painters and sculptors of his time. The decorative programme of the Sistine Chapel influenced generations of artists after his time.

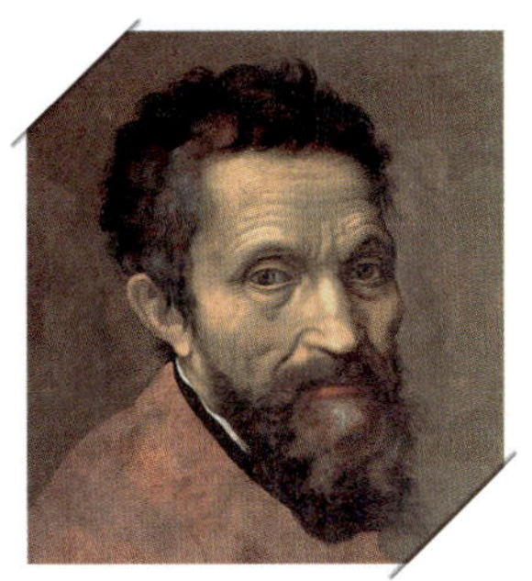

Consuming jealousy

Michelangelo was trained in painting and sculpture. His talents were noticed by Lorenzo the Magnificent, who offered him wages and a room in his palace. This preference would earn Michelangelo a punch from a rival, breaking his nose.

With sculpture in his soul

Preferring the chisel to the paintbrush, Michelangelo used painting as another means of sculpting. His palette was vivid, and the muscular and dynamic silhouettes that he created produced an illusion of relief and depth.

Unseen sponsor

The artist's greatest patron was Pope Julius II. The head of the Church entrusted him with the creation of his tomb – a genuine masterpiece... that would, in fact, never see the light of day! Its execution was endlessly delayed by constant renegotiations of the contract, before being entirely superseded by other assignments.

MICHELANGELO SAID

"My beard is pointing at heaven, my brain is crushed in a casket, my breast twists like a harpy's. My brush, above me all the time, dribbles paint so my face makes a fine floor for droppings!" he would complain while painting the Sistine Chapel.

Raphael
Page 46

1453
The Hundred Years' War finally came to an end

1475
Born in Caprese

1508 to **1512**
Painted the ceiling of the Sistine Chapel

1515
Francis I of France became known by schoolchildren

1564
Died in Rome

Albrecht Dürer
Page 58

THE CEILING OF THE SISTINE CHAPEL

1508–1512
Fresco
4,000 × 1,400 cm
St. Peter's Basilica in Rome, Vatican

WHAT ARE WE LOOKING AT?

Created by Michelangelo himself, in connection with the scenes from the Old and New Testaments that already existed in the chapel, the decorative scene adorning the ceiling heralds the arrival of a messiah: Jesus Christ.

A start to everything

The nine central scenes narrate the story of the Genesis, the tale of the origins of the world. The gift of life is symbolised by God's hand approaching Adam's, without touching it, thus marking the distance between man and his creator. *The Creation of Adam* is one of the most famous images in the world.

The rule of three

Framed by *Ignudis*, masculine nudes, the nine scenes can be read in sets of three: 1. God proceeds to create the world. 2. God and humans in heaven. 3. Humans on Earth with Noah. The cycle ends with Noah's discovery of the vine, which may evoke the blood of Christ.

Visionaries

Monumental figures seated on thrones surround the scenes from the Genesis. They are prophets and sibyls, alternately. Their gifts of divination suggest that their purpose here is to announce the arrival of a messiah.

Jesus returns

In the corners, the Hebrews are freed by the intervention of saviours in the image of the one that Christ will become. To establish a link between the Old Testament and the New Testament, which tells the story of Jesus's life, his ancestors are depicted on the triangular vaults located above the windows.

Timeless beauty

Restored in the 1980s, the fresco revealed the bright, shimmering colours that influenced Mannerist artists (p. 70). The monumentality of its characters, with their powerful physical stature, would leave a lasting impression for many more years.

THREE FAMOUS SCULPTURES BY MICHELANGELO

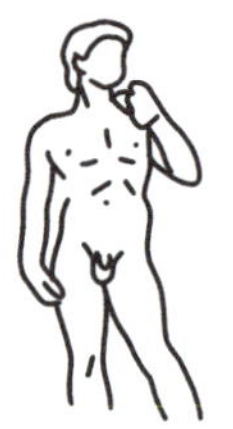

David
1504, Accademia Gallery in Florence

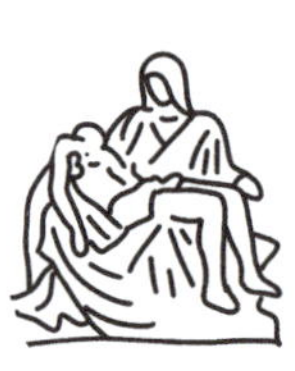

Pietà
1497, Saint Peter's Basilica, Vatican

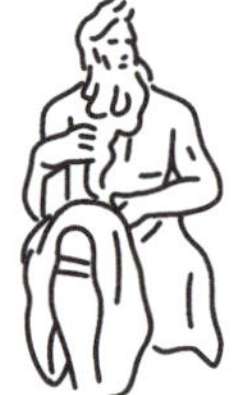

Moses
1515, Basilica of Saint Peter in Chains

MICHELANGELO'S ART IN A NUT-SHELL

- Monumental characters.
- A shimmering palette.
- Bodies painted like sculptures.
- A grandiose inspiration referred to as *terribilità*.

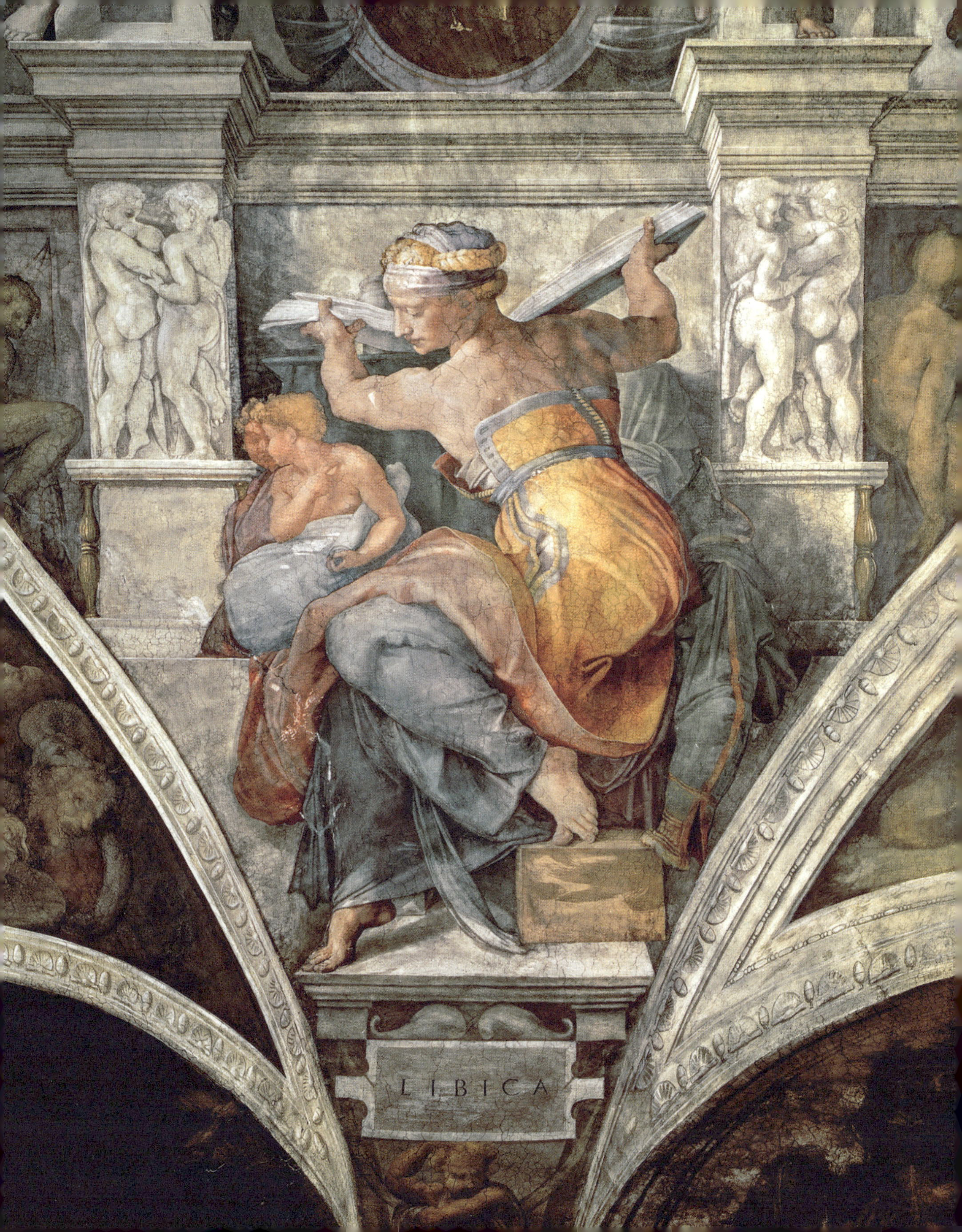
LIBICA

Meanwhile in America

The Mexica calendar makes history

In the 16th century, the flourishing Mesoamerican culture was devastated by the Spanish colonists. Precious testimonies from this period have reached us through codices, illustrated manuscripts, among which the Codex Borbonicus.

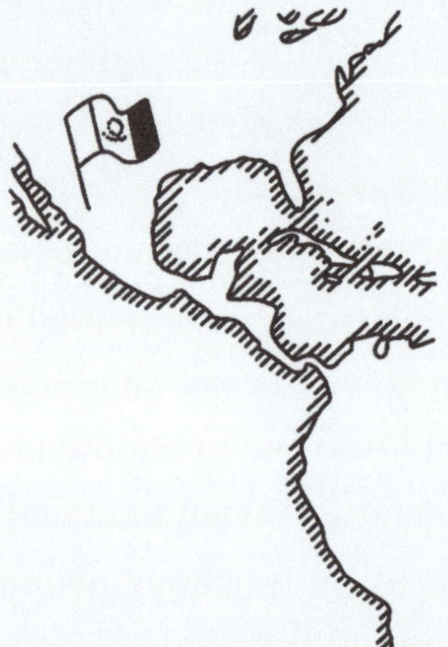

Setting the scene

In the 16th century, the Mesoamerican culture dominated southern Mexico and Central America. It formed a cultural area, i.e. an area whose inhabitants shared common cultural traits. In this case, for instance, they were united by the same calendar, the same deities and the same agricultural practices.

The most important city was Tenochtitlán. Between 1519 and 1521, in the wake of Christopher Columbus, the Spanish armies conquered this territory, destroying the Aztec civilisation (also called *Mexica*), and founded Mexico City on the ruins of its capital.

The masterpiece

- The Codex Borbonicus is a traditional *Mexica* manuscript, containing three calendars with different functions (divinatory or ritualistic, for instance). The *Xiuhmolpilli* calendar forms a 52-year cycle.
- The sheet presented here is the second page. The perimeter features 26 boxes, each containing a symbol: a rabbit, a reed, a flint or a house. This sign is associated with a number, from 1 to 13, represented by red circles. Each association corresponds to a year, and each sign serves to identify the divine forces at work at that time.
- The centre of the sheet confronts two gods of the *Mexica*. On the left, the god Quetzalcoatl can be recognised in numerous attributes, including religious accessories such as the snake-shaped censer, which refers to his nickname – the Feathered Serpent. On the right, his brother, the fearsome Tezcatlipoca, also called the Smoking Mirror, can be recognised by his yellow-striped face and his circular chest.

WHO ARE THE MEXICA-AZTECS?

The *Mexica* are better known as "Aztecs", a term which refers to Aztlán, the mythological place from which this people is said to have immigrated. However, "Aztec" is a name propagated by Westerners. Today, the name *Mexica* is preferred – a name chosen by the people themselves, referring to the god Mexi.

The *Mexica* are believed to have settled in the Valley of Mexico around 1300, among other populations, but their name was then generalised to include all the peoples of the region.

The empire known as the "Aztec" empire was founded at the time of the alliance formed between Tenochtitlán, Texcoco and Tlacopán around 1428. Its downfall occurred at the hands of the Spaniards, in the 16th century.

The *Mexica* society was divided into two social classes: nobles and commoners. Nobles owned the land and ruled, while commoners worked in their service, with varying degrees of hierarchy and wealth. They were peasants, merchants, craftsmen, and more.

SOME DOUBTS ABOUT THE DATE ...

Although it is established that the codex dates back to the beginning of the 16th century, there is still some uncertainty regarding the precise date of its creation. Today, we still do not know whether it is an authentic Aztec manuscript from the pre-Columbian era (i.e. prior to the arrival of Christopher Columbus), or whether it was created under colonial influence.

OTHER FAMOUS MESOAMERICAN CODICES

A distinction is generally made between the pre-Columbian codices (1, 2, 3), which predate the arrival of the Spaniards in America, and the so-called colonial codices (4), which were produced under European influence.

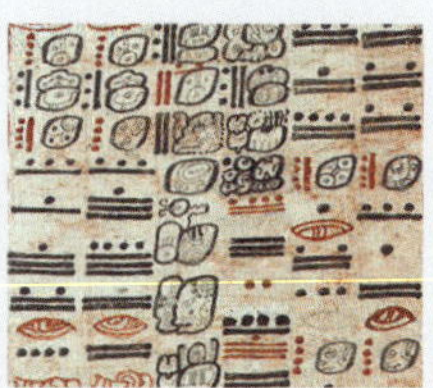

① **Dresden Codex**
1200–1250
SLUB, Dresden

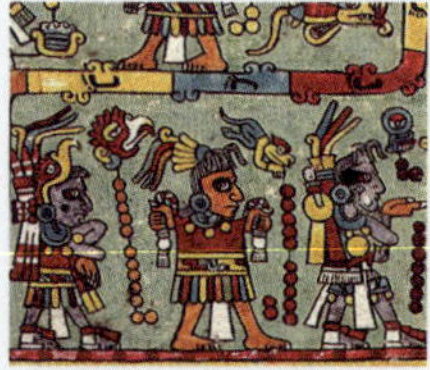

② **Zouche-Nuttall Codex**
1200–1521
British Museum, London

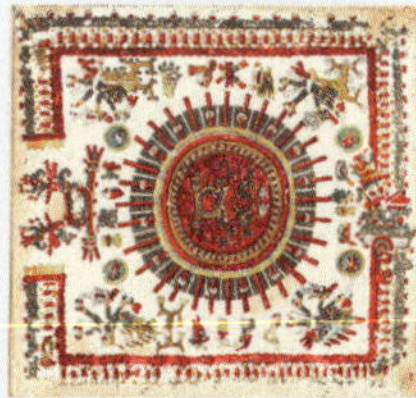

③ **Codex Borgia**
Circa 1500
Vatican Apostolic Library, Vatican

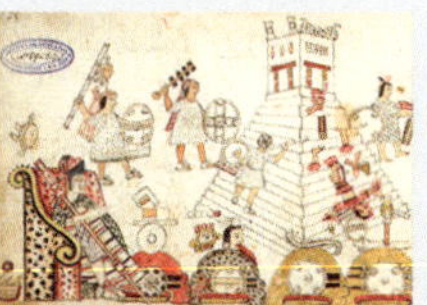

④ **Azcatitlan Codex**
16th century
Bibliothèque Nationale de France, Paris

Collective work
CODEX BORBONICUS
Folio 22
First half of the 16th century
Painting on beaten ficus fibre, covered with gypsum
Facsimile of the document kept in the library of the French National Assembly, Paris

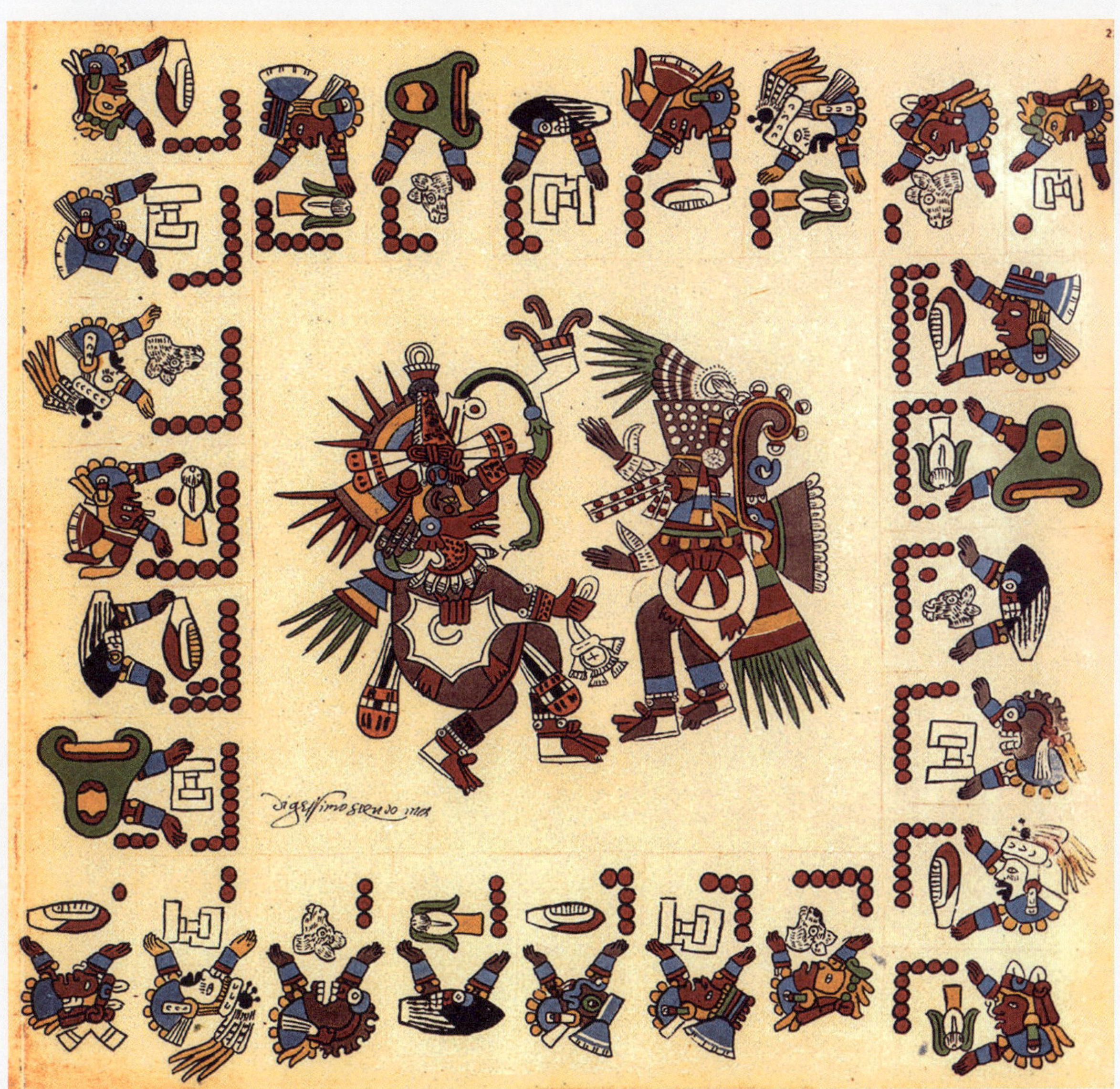

Albrecht Dürer

The surgeon of lines

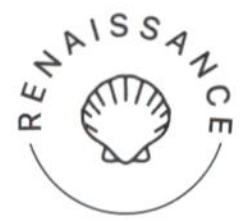

Dürer, whose father was a goldsmith, was no stranger to meticulous work. He acquired a sense of decorative drawing before being trained in the studio of the painter Michael Wolgemut. Throughout his career, the "surgeon of lines" would produce a repertoire of motifs, with drawings inspired from nature.

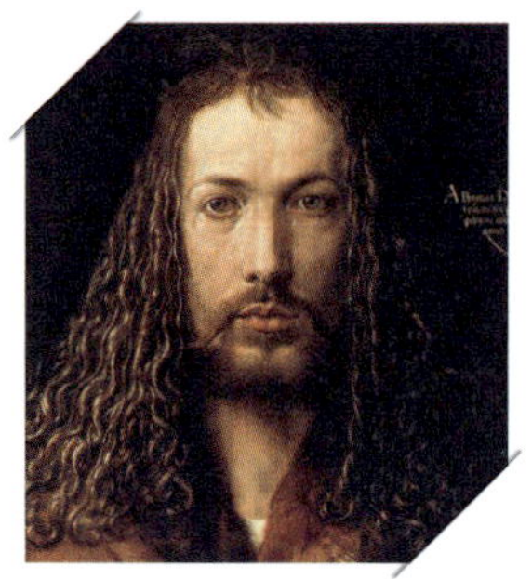

Travel broadens the artist's mind

Dürer's art was influenced by his Flemish neighbours, whom he would visit, but he also spent time in Italy, on two separate occasions – the first time as an obscure celebrity, the second time as a famous artist. He became acquainted with Italian art, discovered the trending scientific theories at the time and acquired a taste for beauty, proportions and colour – in other words, the very essence of the Renaissance.

Engraving: photocopying the past

Dürer was not only a formidable painter, he was also known in his time for his talents as an engraver – an activity that contributed to his fame. Engraved works were designed to be reproduced and circulated in large numbers.

The invention of the copyright?

Dürer left his mark on history, both literally and figuratively. He invented a monogram for himself, consisting of an "A" crowned by a "D", with which he signed his works to spread his name and to protect himself from copiers.

A FINE STROKE OF THE PEN

Dürer was as talented at drawing as he was at painting. He mastered many techniques, and some of his drawings are true masterpieces.

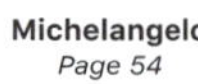
Michelangelo
Page 54

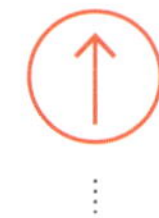

1455
The Wars of the Roses broke out: a prickly bouquet for the English

1471
Born in Nuremberg

1493
Painted *Portrait of the Artist Holding a Thistle*

1522
Suleiman the Magnificent conquered the island of Rhodes

1528
Died in Nuremberg

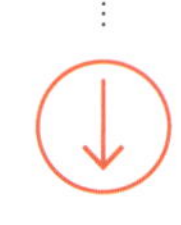

Hans Holbein
Page 60

PORTRAIT OF THE ARTIST HOLDING A THISTLE

1493
Oil on parchment pasted on canvas
56.5 × 44.5 cm
Louvre Museum, Paris

WHAT ARE WE LOOKING AT?

Before Dürer, artists would sometimes represent themselves as extras in ensemble paintings. Dürer produced one of the first self-portraits in the history of Western painting. While the painter did not apply his famous monogram to this work, it is an affirmation of his status as an artist. "I paint myself; therefore I am", he could have signed.

Unfiltered realism

Dürer painted a self-portrait with uncompromising realism. The meticulous care with which he treated the details of the face and hands testifies to his interest in drawing.

A wedding gift ...

The artist is holding a thistle. This flower is said to be a symbol of marital fidelity: Dürer is rumoured to have painted this portrait as a gift for Agnes Frey, whom he married the following year.

...Or a sign of passion?

The thistle can also refer to the passion of Christ. The flower's thorns symbolise the thorns of the crown that Jesus wore on the way of the cross. Did the painter feel that he was invested with a divine mission?

Profession of faith

Next to the date, the inscription in German reads: "My affairs follow the course allotted to them on high." Dürer may be referring to the divine nature of his art, as well as to his resignation to marry the woman chosen for him by his father.

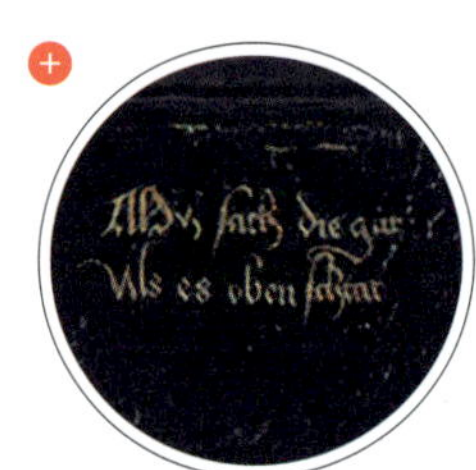

1,000 DRAWINGS
70 PAINTINGS
300 ENGRAVINGS
3 BOOKS PRINTED
7 SELF-PORTRAIT

DÜRER'S ART IN A NUTSHELL

- A combination of Flemish realism and Italian ideal.
- Incomparable drawings and engravings.
- An emblematic monogram.

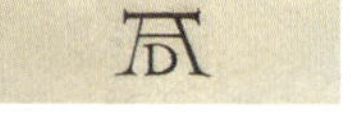

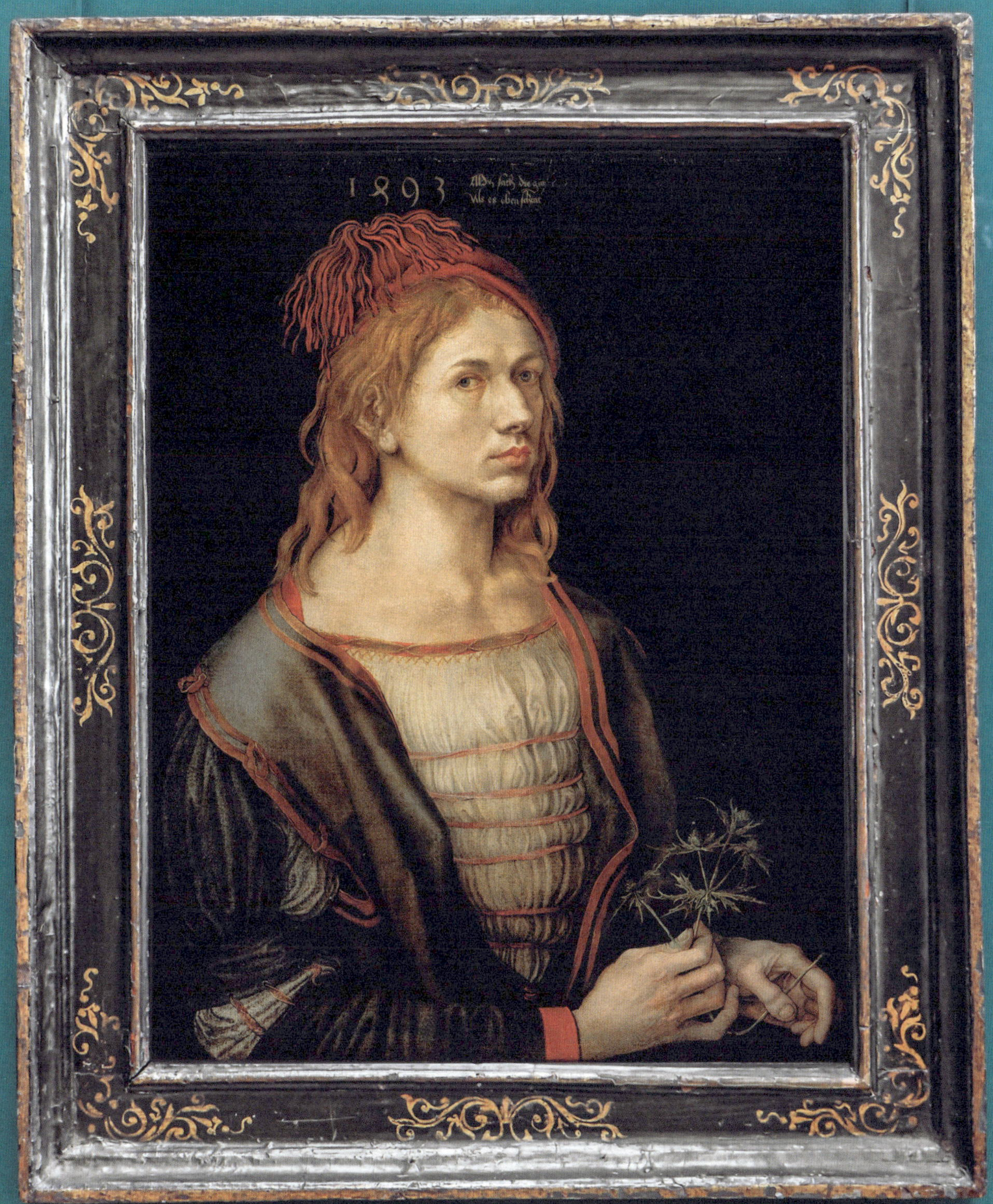
1493

Hans Holbein the Younger

London's most popular German

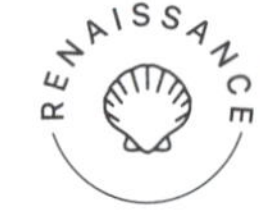

**Holbein was one of the greatest portraitists of his time.
He enjoyed a successful career in Basel, but his art, at the crossroads of European influences, was particularly sought after in England.**

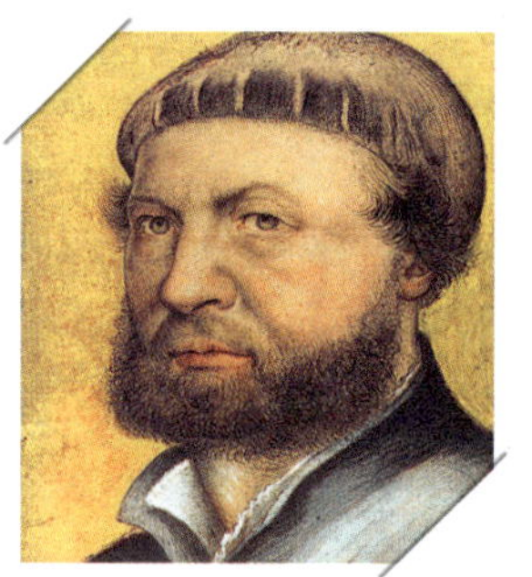

London calling

Holbein had a successful career in Basel, but soon sought to escape the pressures of the Reformation and iconoclasm. After staying in France, where he found no patrons, he met with success in London, becoming the official painter to King Henry VIII.

The best of both worlds

The German painter admired his compatriot Dürer (p. 58), but was also inspired by Italian art in France at the court of King Francis I of France. He was influenced by a new ideal of beauty, which he sought to combine with his own demands for verisimilitude.

Spatial effects performed by a professional

He was intrigued by the representation of volumes on a flat surface, and excelled at producing effects of relief and depth to create illusions. His perception of space graced his works with formidable narrative power.

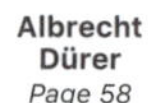

Albrecht Dürer
Page 58

1498
Born in Augsburg

1501
Beginning of the Sefevid dynasty, which ruled over Persia until 1736

1533
Painted *The Ambassadors*

1543
Died in London

1547
Ivan the Terrible became the first Tsar of Russia

Titian
Page 62

THE AMBASSADORS
(JEAN DE DINTEVILLE AND GEORGES DE SELVE)

1533
Oil on wood (oak)
207 × 209.5 cm
National Gallery, London

WHAT ARE WE LOOKING AT?

This is both a double portrait and a commission produced in a sensitive political and religious context. Every accessory contains a message, right down to the strange, deformed skull in the foreground.

① Rising tensions

Jean de Dinteville was the ambassador of Francis I of France to the English court, on the occasion of the marriage of Henry VIII to Anne Boleyn. This event required the sovereign to divorce, creating a schism with the Vatican amidst the already tense context of the Lutheran Reformation.

② A youngster

Georges de Selve was a bishop, but was, however, too young to be consecrated. He was 24 years old, as stated on the book under his elbow.

③ Noble materials

The play of textures and meticulously painted fabrics allowed Holbein to display the full extent of his talent.

④ Braggarts

The many astronomical instruments demonstrate the wealth of their owners and their understanding of the sciences.

⑤ False notes

One of the lute's strings is broken, and a flute is missing from a case. The open book next to it shows Lutheran songs. This still life is a metaphor of religious disharmony.

⑥ A matter of perspective

This is an anamorphosis. When viewed from the right angle, it reveals a skull. It embodies the message delivered by this work: appearance is but vanity (p. 110). While men look away, they fail to see that death lurks around them.

⑦ It's a sin

This crucifix, practically hidden by a curtain, strengthens the message delivered by the skull: God's message is shrouded by the veil of appearances.

② +

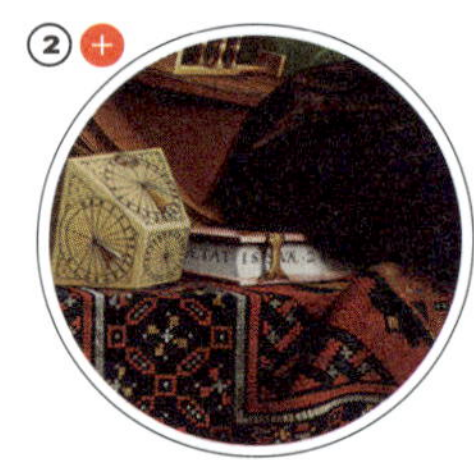

A TRUE REVELATION

The anamorphosis works as follows: when one stands to the left of the painting, one can observe a perfectly proportioned human skull.

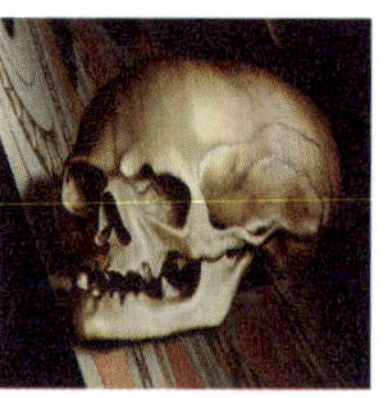

WELL-SHARPENED

It was in France that Holbein learned the three-pencil technique, which consists of drawing with three colours: black stone, sanguine (red) and chalk (white).

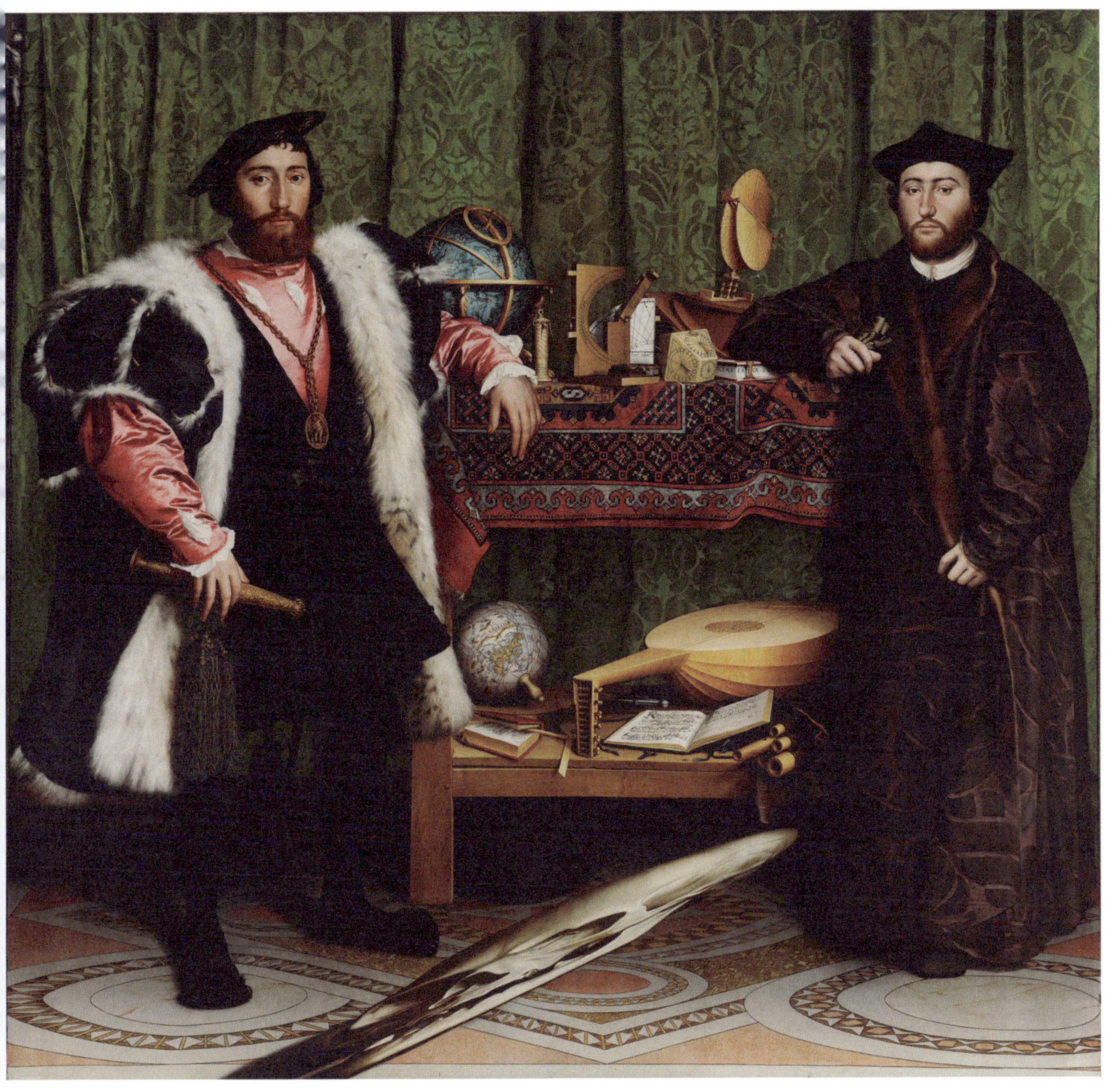

IOANNES HOLBEIN PINGEBAT. 1533

The painter meticulously dated his work and drew a sophisticated signature in Latin on the marble floor, in the shadow of Jean de Dinteville (this inscription is not visible in the reproduction). This practice was unusual for Holbein. On this occasion, he was likely particularly proud of his work.

Titian

No need to sort through his colours

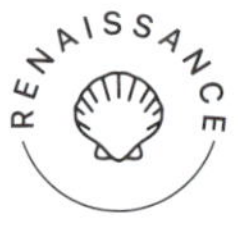

At the time of Tiziano Vecellio, known as Titian, Venice imported precious pigments from all over the world by sea. The artist was a genius of colour and the leader of the Venetian school. He influenced artists throughout the centuries.

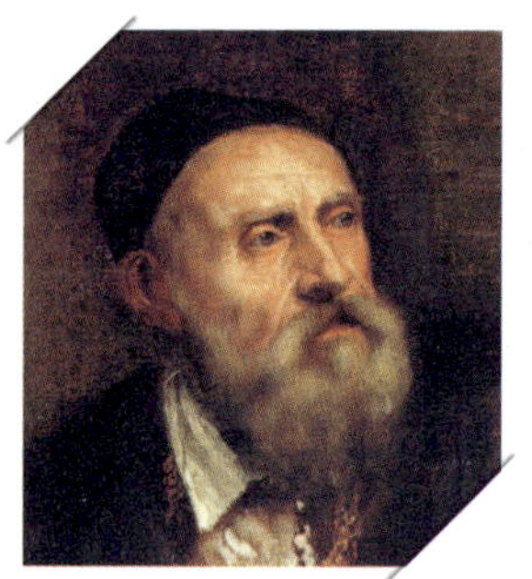

Influential references

Throughout his extensive career, he would brush shoulders with the greatest. His work for Italian rulers made him popular with Emperor Charles V and Pope Paul III. He devoted most of the remainder of his career to working for Spanish King Philip II.

Setting the tones

Titian was one of the greatest colourists in the history of art. He combined colours with virtuosity, and expressed contrasts with nuance. Towards the end of his life, his palette grew smaller; he would use his fingers to mix colours, directly on the canvas.

With painting in his soul

Akin to all great painters, he excelled in many disciplines; his portraits, however, were particularly praised for their liveliness. His knowledge of colour enabled him to perfectly render skin tones, an ability that he used to masterfully depict female nudes.

LIVES THAT MATTER

Giorgio Vasari narrated the life of Titian, among other artists, in *The Lives of the Most Excellent Painters, Sculptors, and Architects*, a founding text of the history of Western art.

Hans Holbein
Page 60

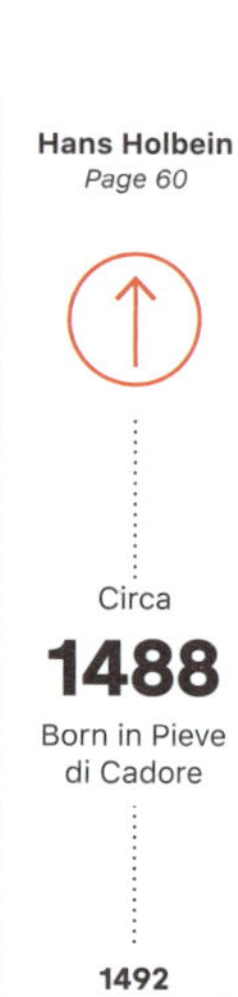

Circa
1488
Born in Pieve di Cadore

1492
A 280-pound meteorite fell in Alsace

1559 to **1562**
Painted *The Rape of Europa*

1567
Birth of Claudio Monteverdi, pioneer of opera

1576
Died in Venice

Veronese
Page 68

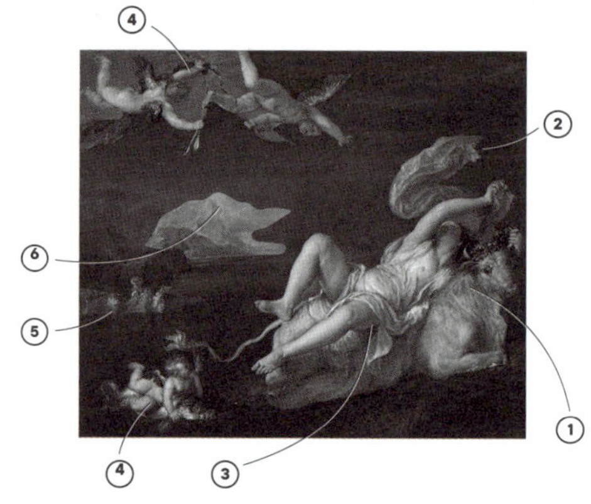

THE RAPE OF EUROPA

1559–1562
Oil on canvas
178 × 205 cm
Isabella Stewart Gardner Museum, Boston

WHAT ARE WE LOOKING AT?

This is a myth told by Ovid in *Metamorphoses*. To kidnap the beautiful Europa, Jupiter transformed into a bull. This painting is part of *Poesie*, a cycle comprising six works, produced for Philip II.

① A treacherous bull

Beneath this bovine guise lies Jupiter (p. 156). He has transformed to approach the princess on the shore, before fleeing with her across the sea. He is wearing the flowers with which Europe has naively adorned his horns.

② An area of turbulence

The young woman's position expresses her distress. She has no choice but to cling to the god's horns, or she will fall into the water. The position of her legs seems to indicate that she is sliding off the animal's back.

③ By hook or crook

The young woman's sensuality is highlighted by the drape of her tunic, revealing her breasts and clinging to her stomach under the effect of the water. The soaring red drape accentuates the impression of movement and the dramatic momentum.

④ Casting error

Although there is nothing consensual about this rape, amoretti are seen filling the sky. In the water, a third amoretto is riding a dolphin, an attribute of Venus (p. 156).

⑤ A devilish beast

Europe's maids, in despair, are calling her from the shore. With them is the herd amidst which the god hid.

⑥ Sea view

The viewer's gaze drifts towards the landscape, which is a fine example of the atmosphere rendered by Venetian painting. The horizon appears to merge with the sky, in a mixture of intense azure and fire.

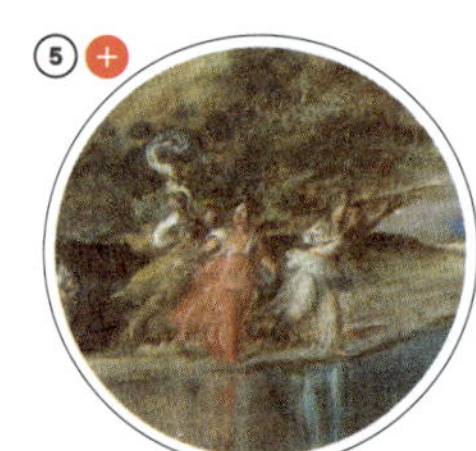

THE VENETIAN SCHOOL IN A NUTSHELL

- An exceptional palette.
- A sensual approach to painting, which contrasts with the moral rigour of the Renaissance.
- Blended, slightly blurred contours.
- An intense atmospheric ambience.

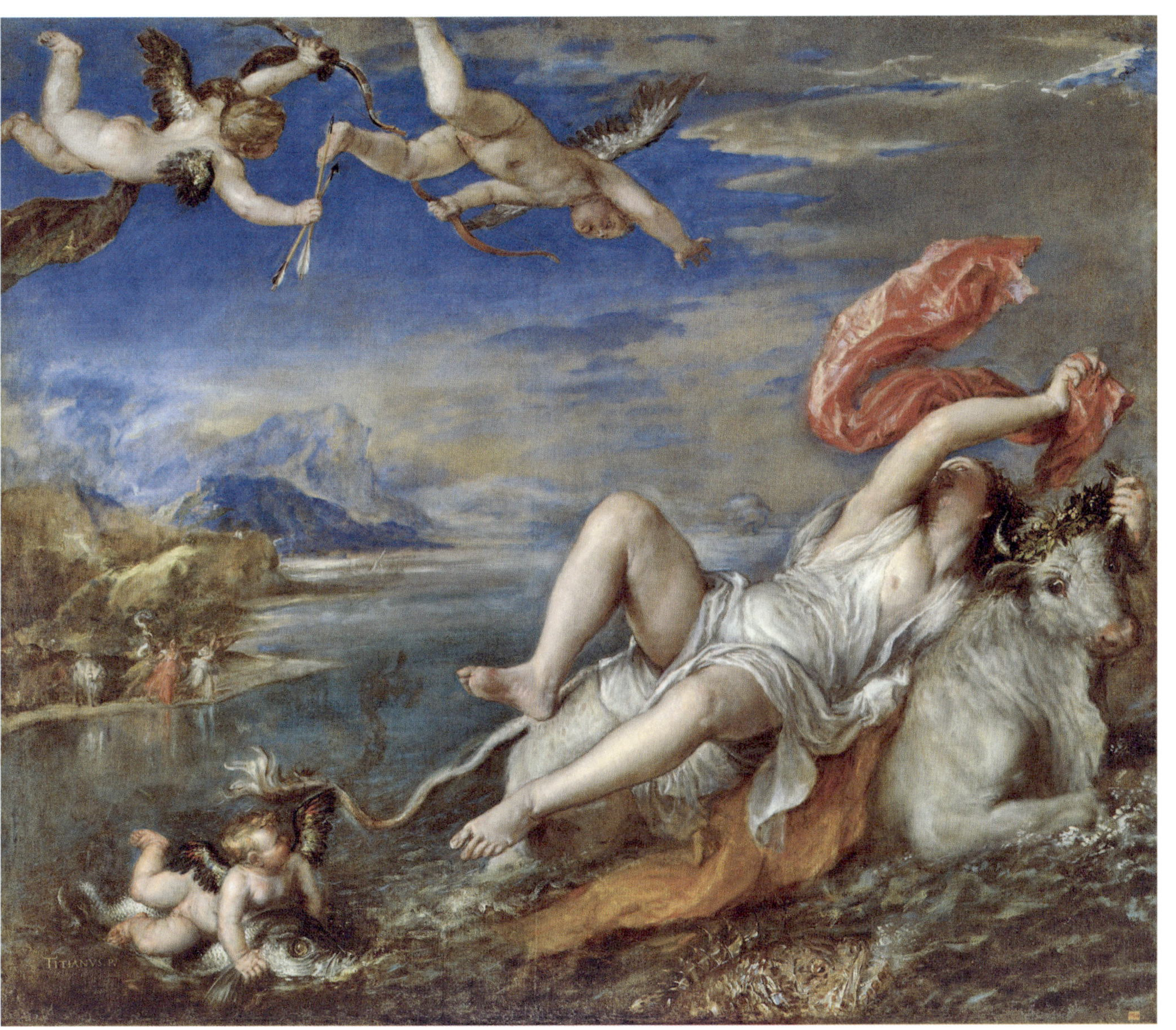

Deceptive appearances

In *Metamorphoses*, Ovid recounts the various transformations that occur in Greco-Roman mythology. The god Jupiter is well acquainted with this practice. To abuse young people, he successively transformed into a bull, a goddess, a golden rain, a swan, an eagle, etc.

Titian and Goya

The naked truth

For many years, artists used the pretext of mythology to paint sensual bodies, which aimed to captivate the viewer's gaze. When one dispels this pretext, however, a paradox remains: that of barely respectable honesty and the inability to let one's gaze settle on the subject.

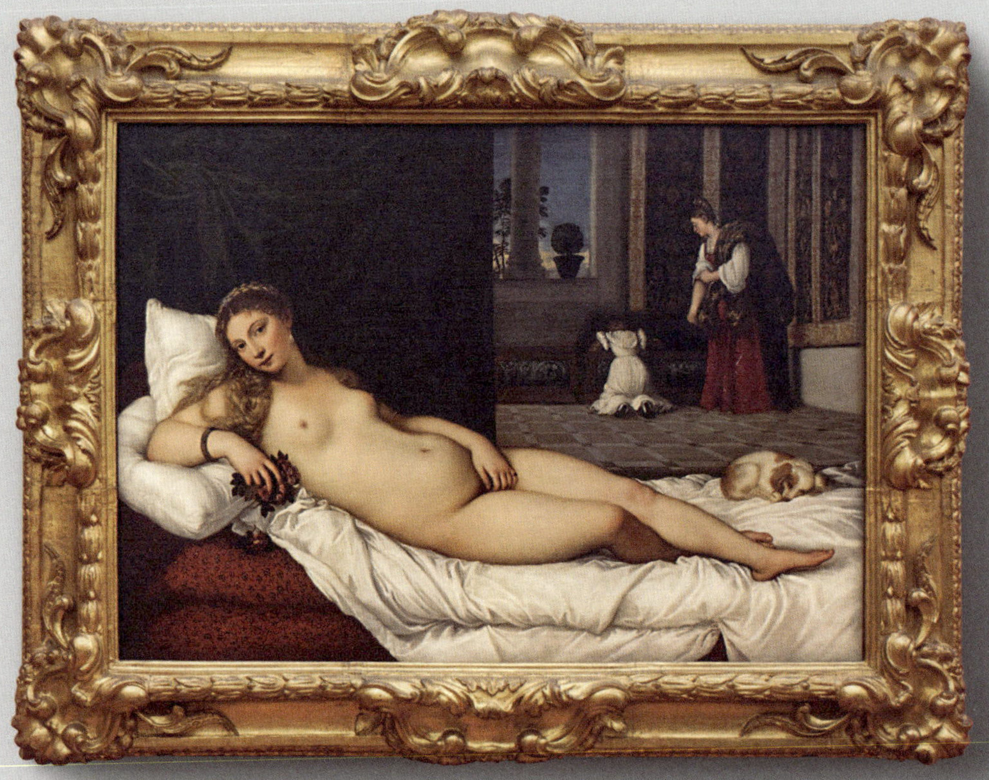

***VENUS OF URBINO* BY TITIAN**
1538

Titian depicted a particularly sensual Venus. She is gazing straight at the viewer, and her hand, placed on her genitalia, is both modest and allusive; however, the dog lying at her feet and the busy maids evoke a nuptial context. The goddess is a promise of marital happiness.

Oil on canvas, 119 × 165 cm
Uffizi Gallery, Florence

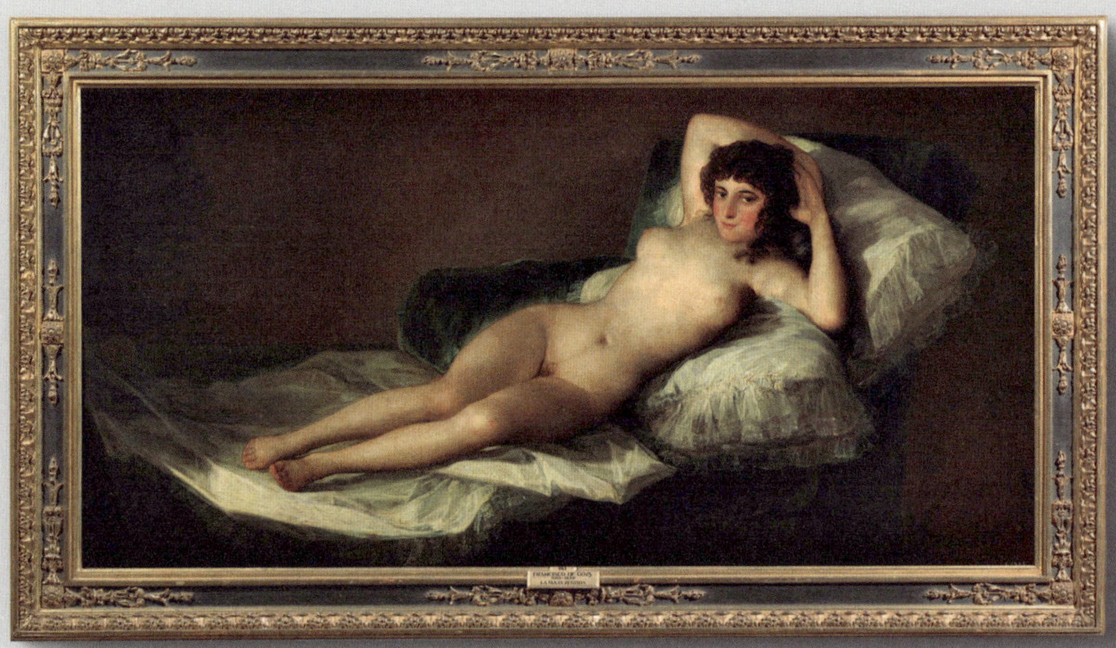

THE NAKED MAJA BY GOYA
1795–1800

This work features no mythological pretext nor goddess. The indoor premise, devoid of any luxury, the realistic face and the hairy genitalia highlight the profane dimension of this nude. Depicted in a harsh light, eroticism gives way to an audacity, designed to bewilder the viewer.

Oil on canvas, 97.3 × 190.6 cm
Prado Museum, Madrid

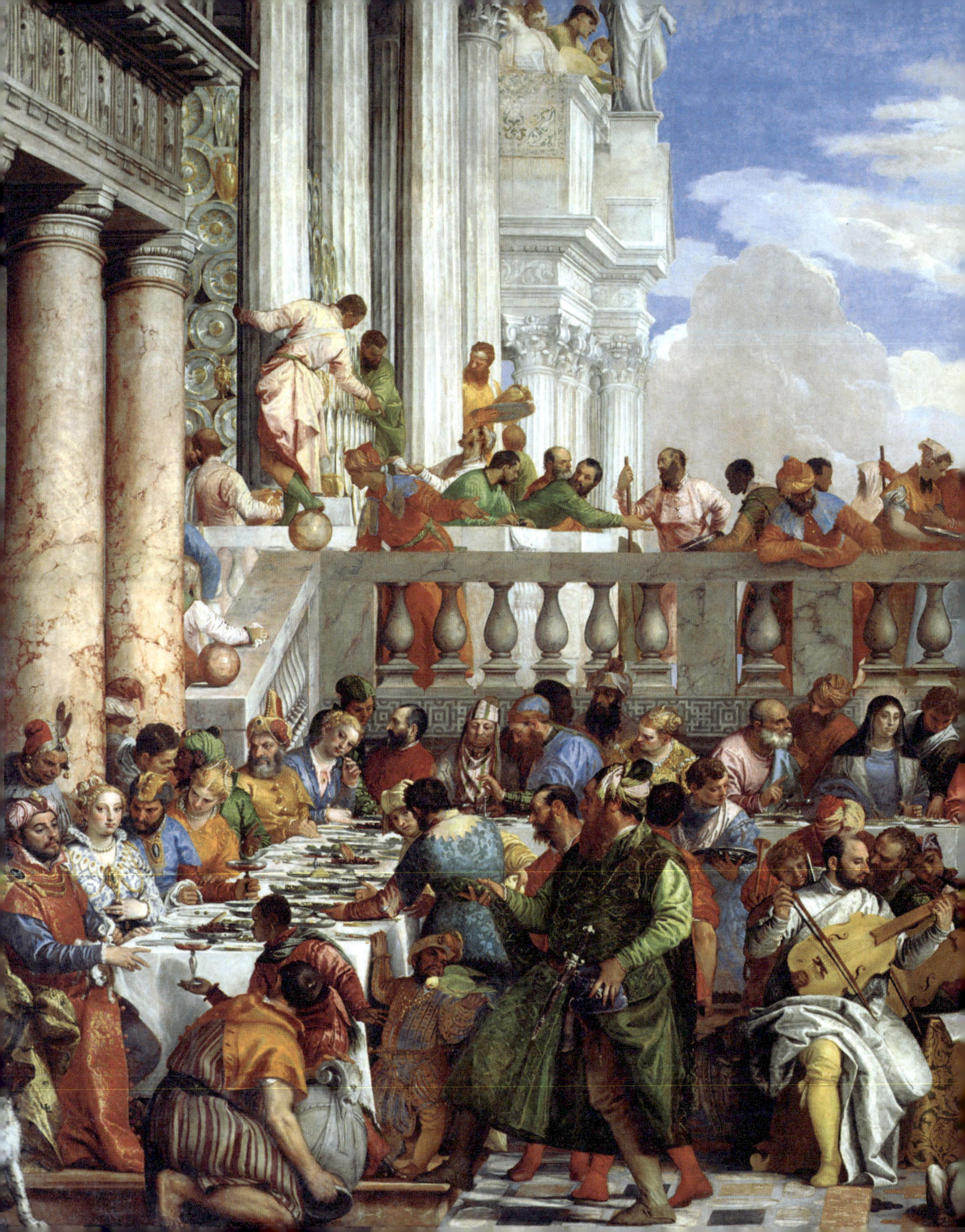

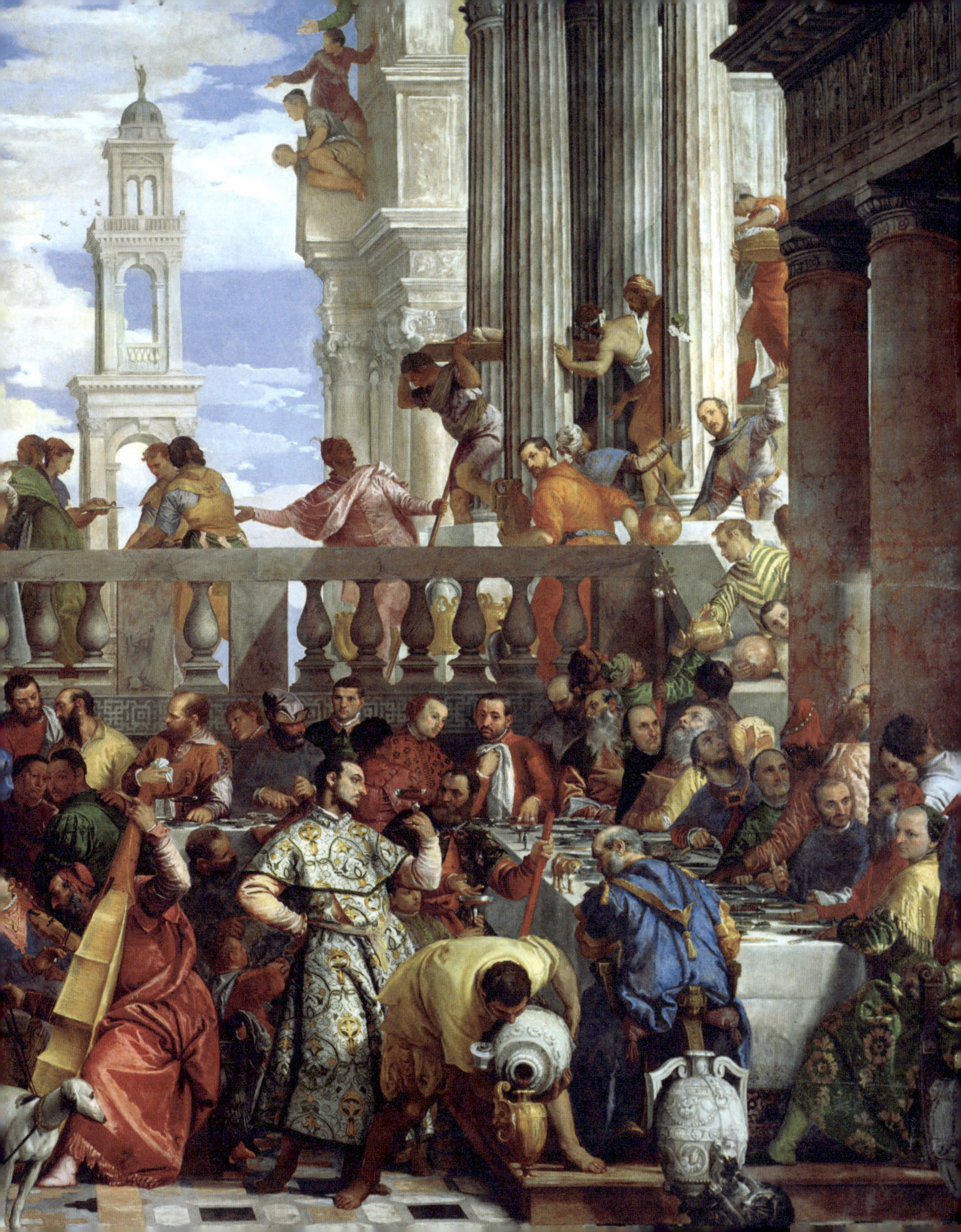

Veronese

Navigating the Venetian maze with skill

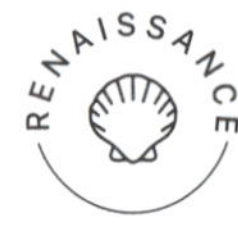

Paolo Caliari, known as Veronese, is one of the great names of the Venetian school. Celebrated for his use of colour, he produced many official works, whilst benefiting from the support of Venetian patricians.

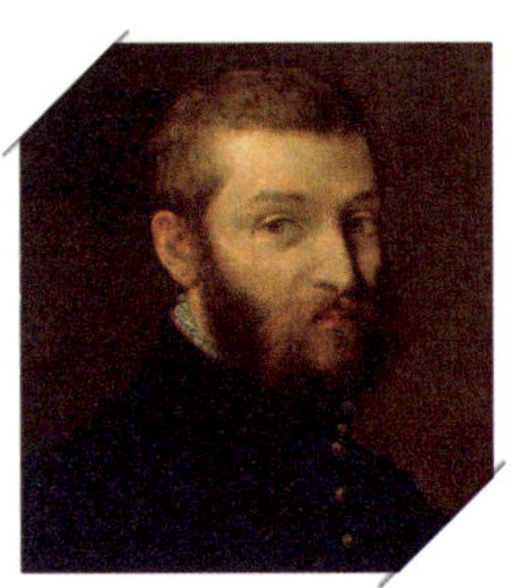

Masters by the mile

The son of a stonemason, who presumably taught him the art of modelling, Veronese was likely a pupil of Sanmicheli, to whom he owed his taste for architecture. However, his training is also attributed to the painters Badile and Caroto. At an early age, he learned the art of fresco, in which he excelled.

A clean sweep

As a painter of altarpieces and official decorations, he enjoyed a spectacular career in Venice. He benefited from the support of the local aristocracy, and produced portraits that conveyed their status with a sense of intimacy. After Titian's death (p. 62), he drew the attention of the rulers of Europe.

Simply too classy

The art of Veronese relied on drawing as much as it did on colour. One can admire his luminous palette, which grew darker over time, his elegant colour combinations and his sensual textures. He staged majestic architectures like no other.

MAKING A NAME FOR HIMSELF

While his father gave him the name Bazaro, Veronese preferred Caliari – the name of his mother, the illegitimate daughter of a family of aristocrats; this choice spoke about the painter's ambitions.

Titian
Page 62

1528
Born in Verona

1543
Copernicus publishes his theory of heliocentrism

1562 to **1563**
Painted *The Wedding at Cana*

1588
Died in Venice

1600
The British founded the first East India Company

Agnolo Bronzino
Page 70

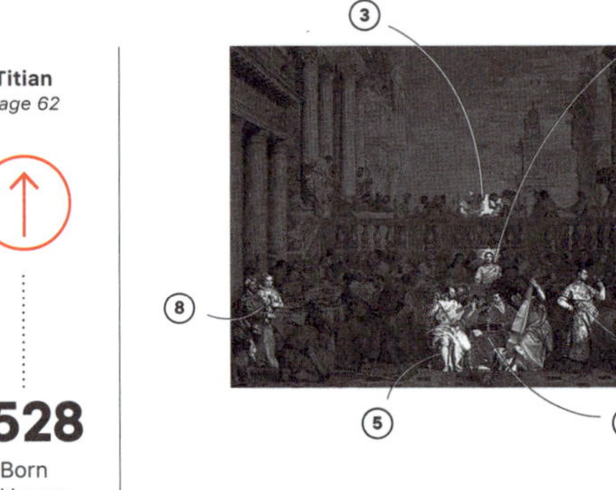

THE WEDDING AT CANA

1562–1563
Oil on canvas
677 × 994 cm
Louvre Museum, Paris

WHAT ARE WE LOOKING AT?

Here, Veronese depicts the famous biblical episode in which Jesus turned water into wine at a wedding in Cana, Galilee. This would be the first miracle that he performed.

① A special inscription

The wedding at Cana is told in the Gospel according to St John; however, Veronese was likely inspired by the version narrated by the writer Aretinus, who might be depicted as the old man raising his eyes to the heavens.

② In a world of his own

Jesus is seated in the place of honour. Preoccupied with the miracle that he accomplished, he appears indifferent to the tumult that surrounds him.

③ Bad omen

In the centre of the canvas, a scene is unfolding just above Jesus's head: servants are cutting up lamb meat, no doubt alluding to his forthcoming sacrifice.

④ Tick-tock

Immediately below Christ, an hourglass placed on the musicians' table is a sign that his days are numbered.

⑤ Painters lead the dance

Veronese can be identified among the musicians, clothed in white, while the ageing Titian appears in red.

⑥ He can't believe it

The steward is fascinated by the miracle of the wine, while a servant in the foreground pours the beverage from a precious jar.

⑦ A last-minute guest

The painting features over 150 figures. The detailed physiognomies suggest that these are portraits – a hypothesis supported by the fact that the figure to the left of Aretinus was painted separately, then pasted onto the canvas.

⑧ High-end

The colours are rich, as required by the contract for this work: Veronese used the most precious pigments to produce this painting.

② +

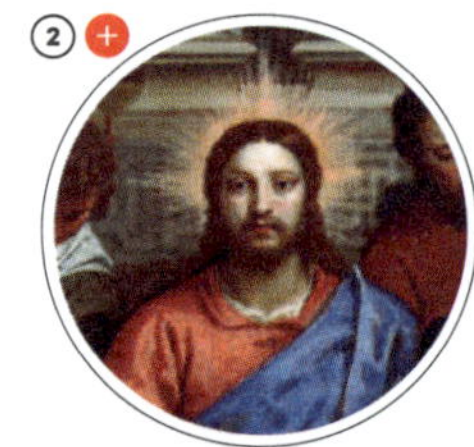

HEADLINERS OF THE VENETIAN SCHOOL IN THE 16TH CENTURY

- Veronese
- Titian (p. 62)
- Tintoretto (1518–1594)
- Jacopo Bassano (1510–1592)
- Lorenzo Lotto (1480–1556)
- Sebastiano del Piombo (1485–1547)

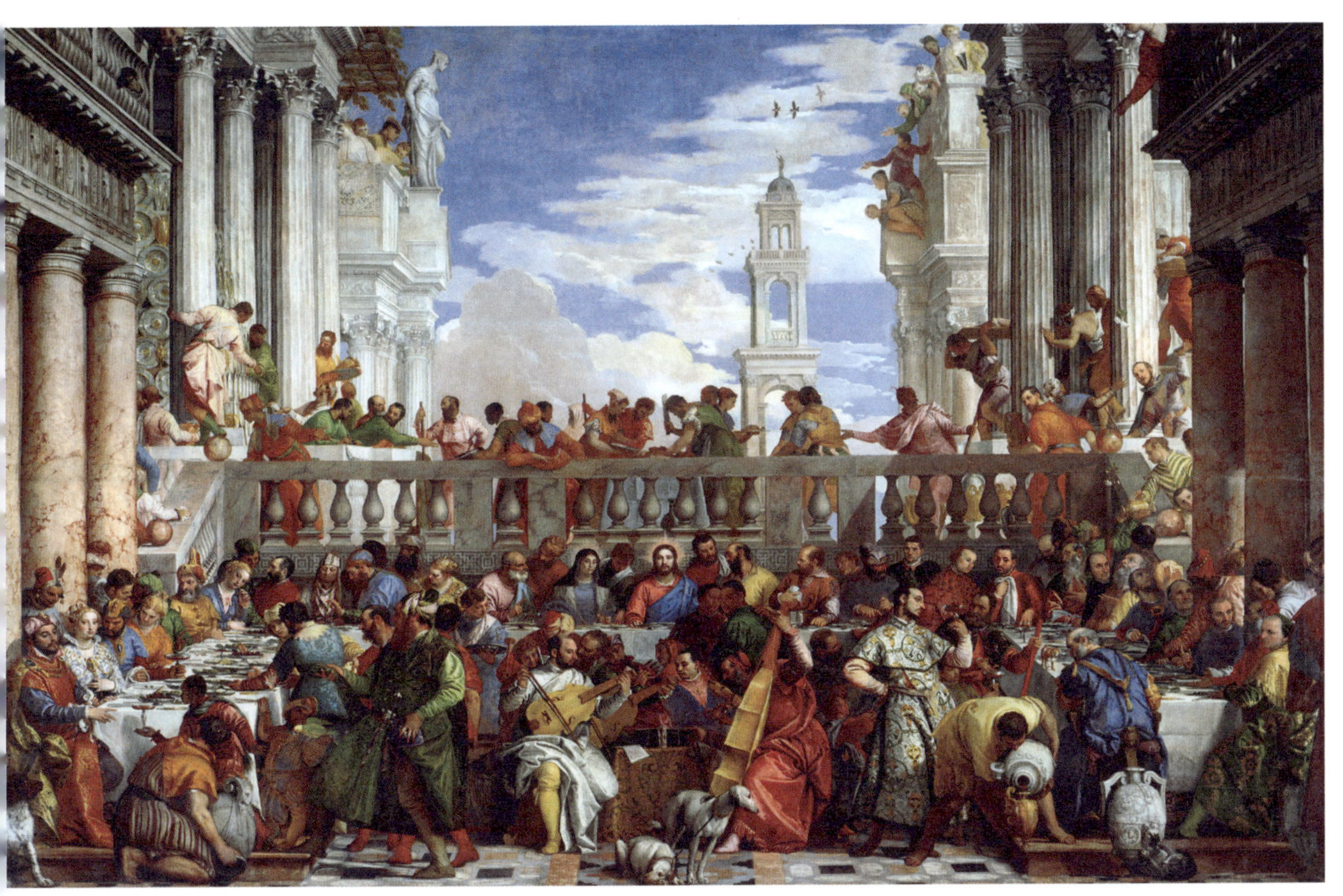

A grand wedding

The Wedding at Cana is the largest painting in the Louvre; yet it is easy to miss. This work is exhibited facing another monument of the museum: *Mona Lisa*.
Only a work of this magnitude could compete with the 753 square feet painted by Veronese.

Agnolo Bronzino

When the Renaissance exaggerates

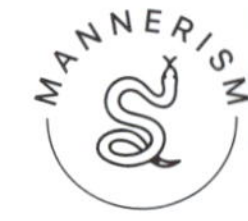

Agnolo di Cosimo di Mariano, known as Bronzino, was one of the most sought-after painters of Mannerism. In this art that pushed the Renaissance to its limits, he had become a master, depicting figures that are as strange as they are sublime.

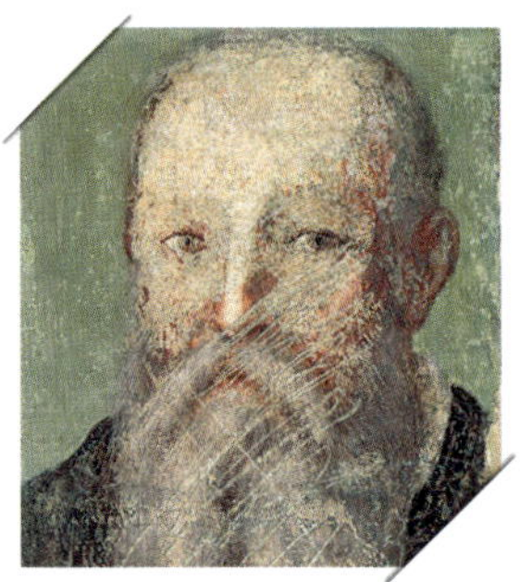

An exemplary career

Born into a modest family, Bronzino trained with Pontormo. He became a scholarly painter, emblematic of Mannerism, who drew from the history of art to fill his paintings with references, ranging from Michelangelo (p. 54) to Dürer (p. 58).

Better than real life

Bronzino particularly excelled in the art of portraiture. His refined paintings express his models' social status, rather than their identity. They are idealised masks that attract the viewer's gaze, just as much as they create distance.

Political colour

In 1540, Bronzino became the official painter to the Medici. Appointed Duke of Florence, Cosimo I de' Medici called upon Bronzino's talent for the purpose of propaganda. He aspired to legitimise his family's newfound greatness.

A NICKNAME WITH A SHINE TO IT

Bronzino means "little bronze". It may have been a nickname given to him because of his red hair.

Paolo Veronese
Page 68

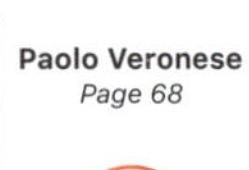

1503
Born in Florence

1534
Barbarossa became the Sultan of Tunis

Circa
1545
Painted *An allegory with Venus and Cupid*

1550
The Spanish justified the colonisation of the Americas with the Valladolid controversy

1572
Died in Florence

Lavinia Fontana
Page 72

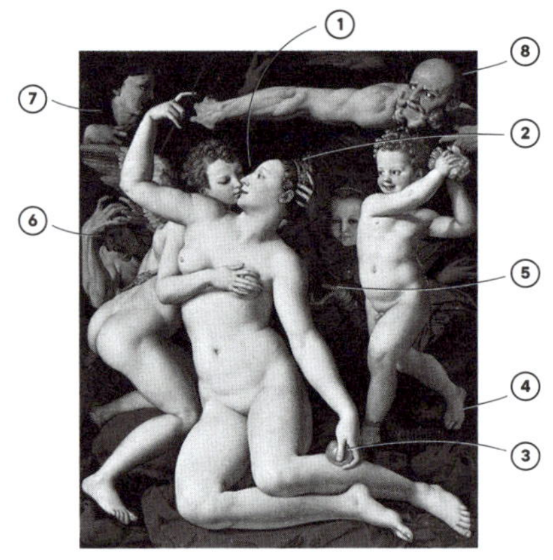

AN ALLEGORY WITH VENUS AND CUPID

Circa 1545
Oil on wood
146.1 × 116.2 cm
National Gallery, London

WHAT ARE WE LOOKING AT?

This strange painting features Venus and her son Cupid, but its meaning is ambiguous. Bronzino may be warning viewers of the pitfalls of carnal love or, on the contrary, celebrating its triumph in the face of peril.

① An incestuous kiss?

Mother and son, Venus and Cupid are divine incarnations of love. They are therefore not subject to the laws of mortals.

② It's a scam!

The characters are seducing each other to better betray each other. Cupid is attempting to strip Venus of her crown, while she is stealing one of his famous arrows.

③ In war as in love

In her hand, Venus holds the trophy for her beauty: the apple that Paris gave her in exchange for the love of Helen of Troy, the fruit that caused the war to break out.

④ Careful, prickly!

This foot belongs to a cheerful-faced allegory of pleasure, that is, however, about to experience the pain of stepping on a thorn.

⑤ Almost keeping up appearances

The young girl in the background is offering sweet honey, but her body extends into the tail of a snake: she is the incarnation of deceit.

⑥ It's an ugly affair

This ugly and angry woman embodies suffering or jealousy, or maybe sickness – in any event, a bad omen.

⑦ Let's forget everything

This figure, with the back of her head missing, is undoubtedly oblivion. Is she maybe trying to shroud the action under the sheet?

⑧ Time at work

The man over which an hourglass stands embodies time. He is either helping oblivion to hide the characters, or preventing her from doing so.

⑥ +

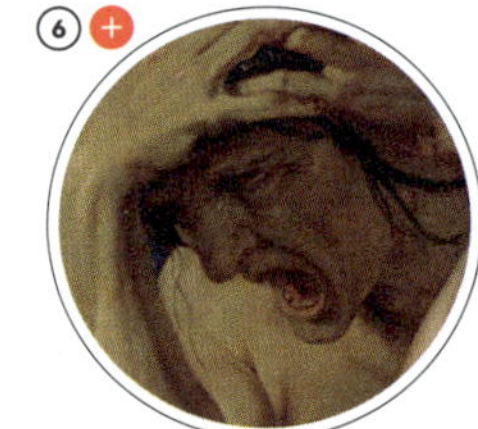

MANNERISM IN A NUTSHELL

- Serpentine silhouettes, bodies contorted in strange and unstable positions.
- Bright, acidic, almost fluorescent and shimmering colours. They are described using an Italian term: *"cangiante"*.
- A complex form of symbolism that is sometimes difficult to decipher.

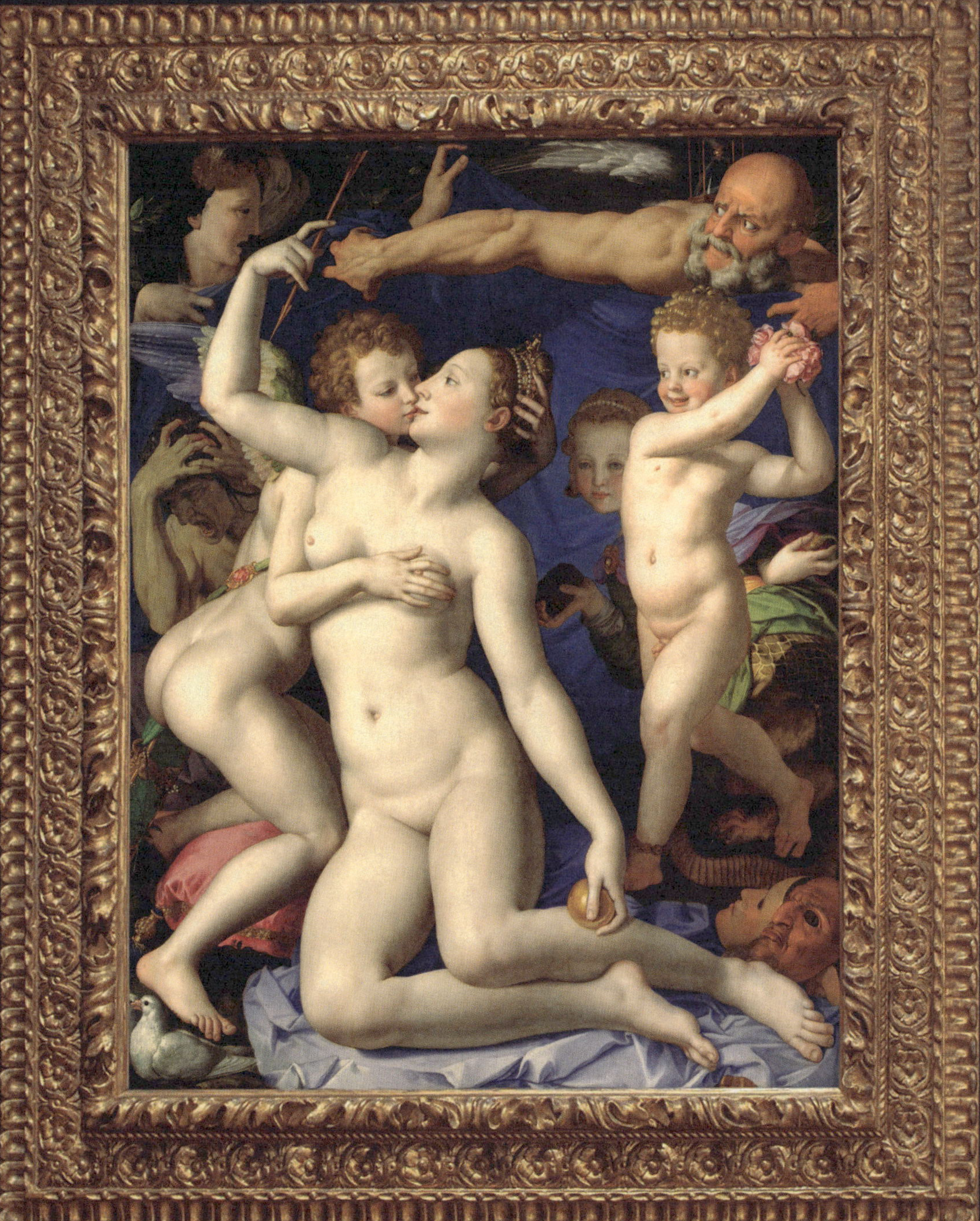

Lavinia Fontana

Leading a studio and a family

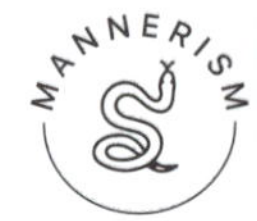

She would be one of the first women painters to be remembered in the history of art. Fontana was sought after for her portraits, but also distinguished herself in other forms of art.

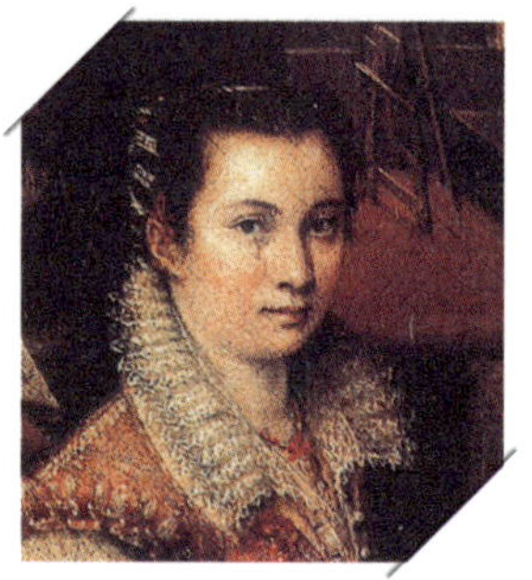

A solid CV

Fontana studied with her father, also a painter. She acquired a solid reputation in Bologna. A protégée of the pope, she then moved to Rome with her family to serve him. There, she was admitted to the Accademia di San Luca, which was normally open to men only.

A fusion of genres

A sought-after portraitist, she excelled at reproducing the richness and diversity of fabrics, as well as the refinement of jewellery. She embraced historical and religious painting, and did not shy away from representing the naked female body.

A practical arranged marriage

Fontana would become the first woman painter in Europe to achieve critical and commercial success in direct competition with men. Thanks to her income, she was able to marry, without need for a dowry, the painter Zappi, who became her assistant. She supported their family of eleven children.

IT WAS SAID OF HER

"She was coveted by Roman ladies, whom she painted better than men would." Luigi Lanzi, Italian intellectual of the 18th century.

Agnolo Bronzino
Page 70

1552
Born in Bologna

1598
Henri IV brought the French Wars of Religion to an end with the Edict of Nantes

1613
Painted *Portrait of Bianca degli Utili Maselli*

1614
Died in Rome

1623
The construction of the first Château de Versailles began

Caravaggio
Page 78

PORTRAIT OF BIANCA DEGLI UTILI MASELLI WITH SIX OF HER CHILDREN ↗

1613
Oil on canvas
99 × 133.5 cm,
Private collection

WHAT ARE WE LOOKING AT?

With this portrait of a noble Roman family, Fontana displayed all her talent in the refined representation of hair, accessories and clothes adorned with intricate patterns.

A forest of children

This group portrait is that of the Maselli family, of Rome, as stated by the inscription in the upper right-hand corner. In the centre, the mother, Bianca, died at the age of 37 after giving birth to her nineteenth child. This portrait is therefore quite a few children shy of the truth!

Impeccable behaviour

The composition is stable. The mother ensures the symmetrical distribution of space, but the atmospheres differ. On the left, the well-behaved children are looking at the viewer. They are disciplined, to the extent that their arrangement echoes their mother's hairstyle. On the right, the other three children are somewhat more unruly. Two of the boys are looking at each other, excluding the viewer from their game. The third boy seems to be planning something silly: his hands are hidden by his mother's back.

Unisex wardrobe

Despite the general harmony of the clothes, subtle differences can be found. The five boys are wearing clothes featuring the same pattern, while the motifs on the mother's and daughter's clothes differ. They are also distinguishable by their jewellery.

Very telling details

The figures' solemn faces are counterbalanced by their attitudes. The little girl is tenderly holding her mother's finger and the dog's paw. On her elder brother's shoulder, a bird is a perched in a comical position. On the other side of the painting, a boy is holding a medallion, while another holds a quill and ink, symbols of the future that is envisioned for them.

PRICES THAT RISE AND RISE ...

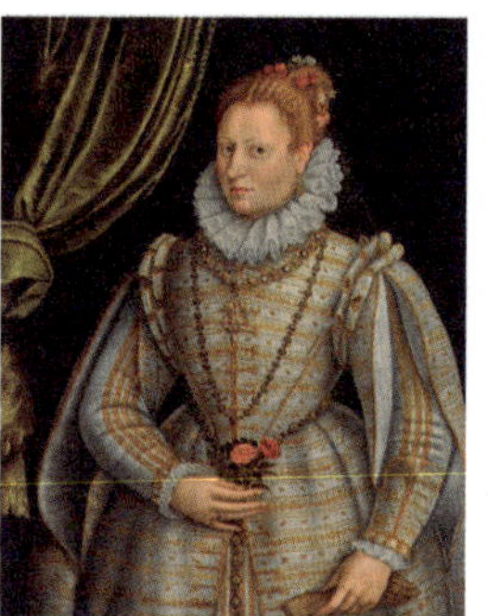

Portrait of a Lady, 1605–1615, private collection

As the general public begins to rediscover and appreciate women artists, the value of their works is surging in auction rooms, and Lavinia Fontana is no exception. This trend is exemplified by this Portrait of a Lady, *painted circa 1605–1615.*

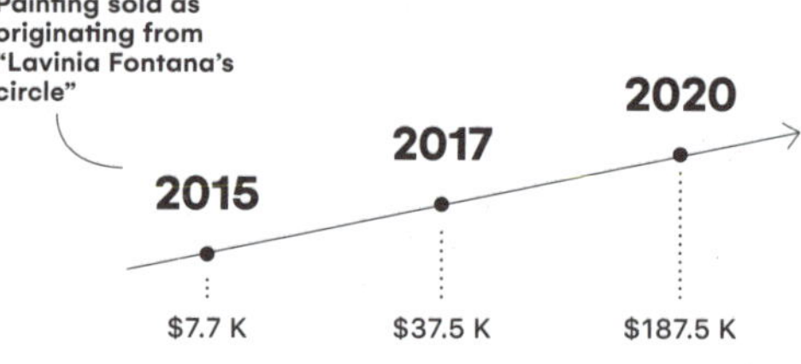

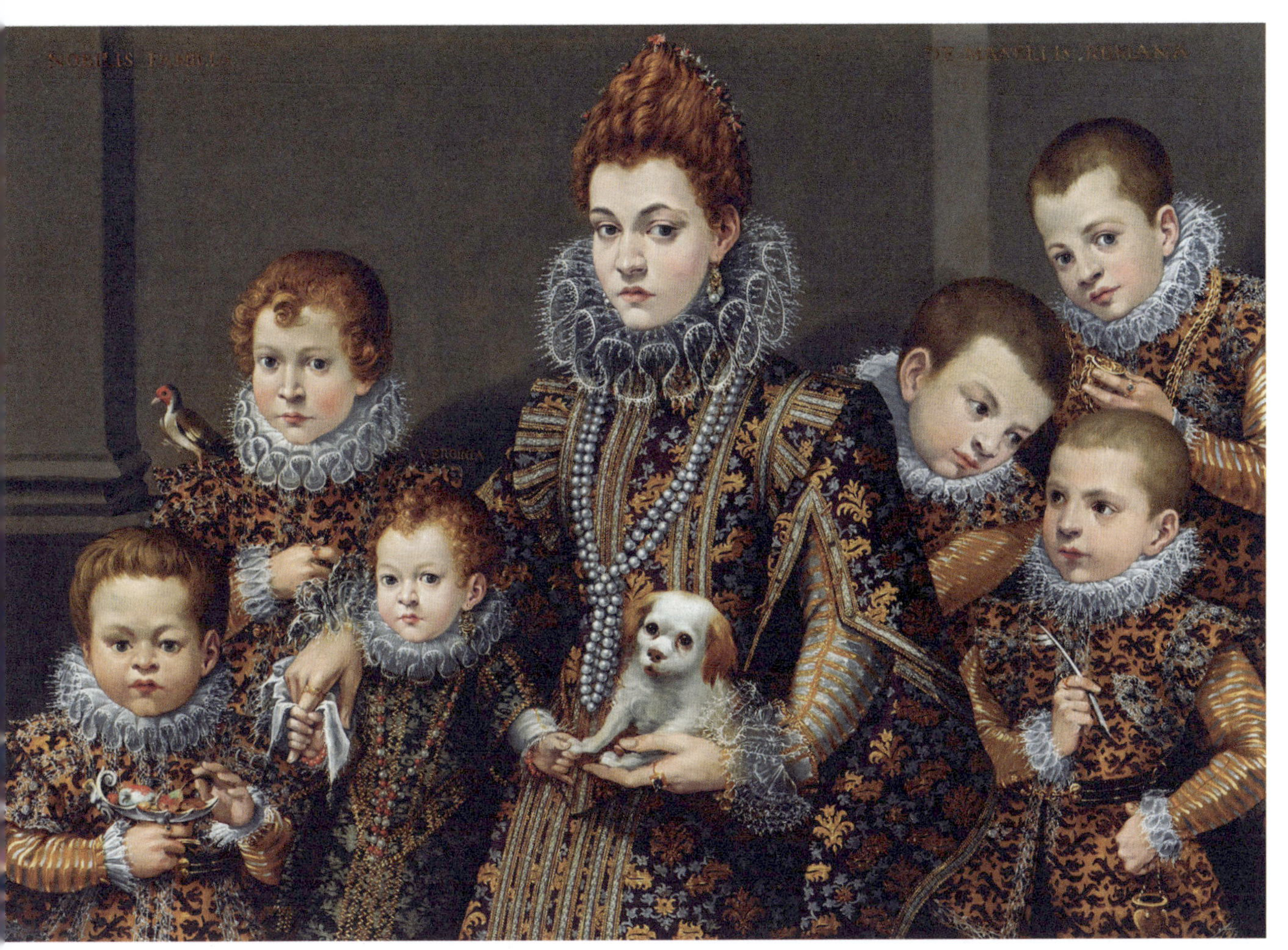

A stricken artist

Lavinia Fontana's career was so prestigious that in 1611, the sculptor Felice Antonio Casone produced an honorary medal stamped with the painter's profile. On the reverse, he depicted an allegory of inspiration, sitting in front of an easel, her hair electrified by creativity.

Meanwhile in India

Miskin shows off his most beautiful feathers

In the 16th century, India was dominated by the rulers of the Mughal dynasty. Between the Muslim and Hindu religions, a refined art of miniature painting appeared, promoted by Emperor Akbar, who founded a productive artistic studio.

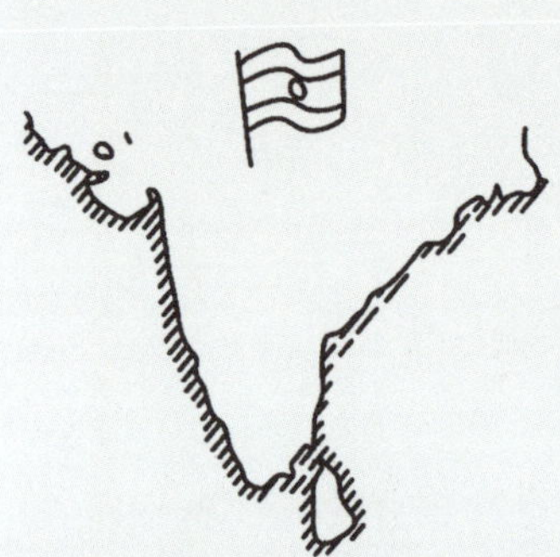

Setting the scene

Indian painting on paper first appeared in the 14th century, when northern India was occupied by the Mughal Empire, founded by Badur. The golden age of Mughal art really began somewhat later, under the reign of Badur's grandson, Emperor Akbar, who came to power in 1556.

Akbar practised an open and enlightened Islam. His studios were home to both Muslim painters from Persia and Hindu painters. These artists were also exposed to European art, which was spread in the illustrated books brought by the Jesuits.

The masterpiece

- This scene is inspired by the Shâhnâmeh, the Persian Book of Kings, which glorifies the ancient kings of Iran in the form of a long mythological poem, narrated by the poet Firdousi, in the 11th century.
- In this episode, the magician Zal is attempting to save his son Rustam, who is fighting a losing battle against Isfendiar. He summons a fabulous bird, the Simurgh, to make his wish come true. To call the bird to him, he climbs to the top of the mountain, accompanied by three men. They are carrying flaming cassolettes. In one of them, he burns a piece from a feather.
- This sumptuous page was likely produced for Emperor Akbar. The decor is inspired by Persian art. Through the great diversity and vividness of the colours, the painter rendered the wondrous appearance of the bird and the beauty of nature. The artist has meticulously painted the variety of shades of the rocks, and the river is teeming with fish and ducks.

WHO IS MISKIN?

Miskin was active between 1580 and 1604. He was the son of the painter Mahesh, from whom he certainly received his training. Both father and son were cited, in their time, as being among the greatest painters to the court of Emperor Akbar.

Miskin's art elegantly combined Persian influences and European conventions in the rendering of volumes. He cut his teeth in the 1580s, first working as a colourist, a position entrusted to young artists. He thus contributed to creating works commissioned by the emperor, notably the *Razmnāna*, a Persian translation of the famous *Mahābhārata*.

He then took on greater responsibilities, to the point where he overshadowed his father's work. He notably illustrated the *Rāmāyana* and the *Akhbarnāma*, which recounts the story of Akbar. His compositions are sophisticated, and he excelled in the representation of animals and human expressions.

WHAT ARE THE *RĀMĀYANA* AND THE *MAHĀBHĀRATA*?

While the Mughal Empire that ruled India was Muslim, the daily lives of the people of South India were influenced by the Hindu religion – in particular by great epics such as the *Rāmāyana* and the *Mahābhārata*, which tell the tale of the god Vishnu's incarnations on Earth. These works have inspired artists throughout the ages, resulting in illustrated books in the 16th century and film adaptations in the present day.

THE FIRST RECRUITS TO AKBAR'S STUDIO

After founding the studio, Emperor Akbar entrusted two artists who had previously worked for his father, Huamayun, at the court of Shah Tahmasp I in Persia, where he lived in exile.

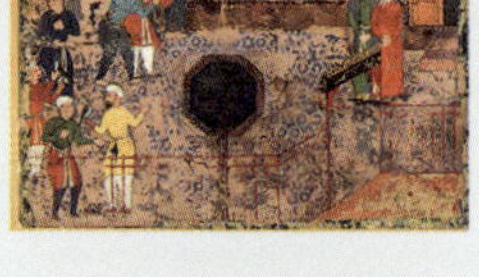

Mir Sayyid Ali
Emissaries bring news from the provinces of Khaybar and Chin to Anoshirvan,
page from the album *Hamzanama*,
16th century
Museum of Applied Arts, Vienna

Abd al-Samad
Hunters in a Forest,
page from the album *Golšan*,
mid-16th century-
early 17th century,
LACMA, Los Angeles

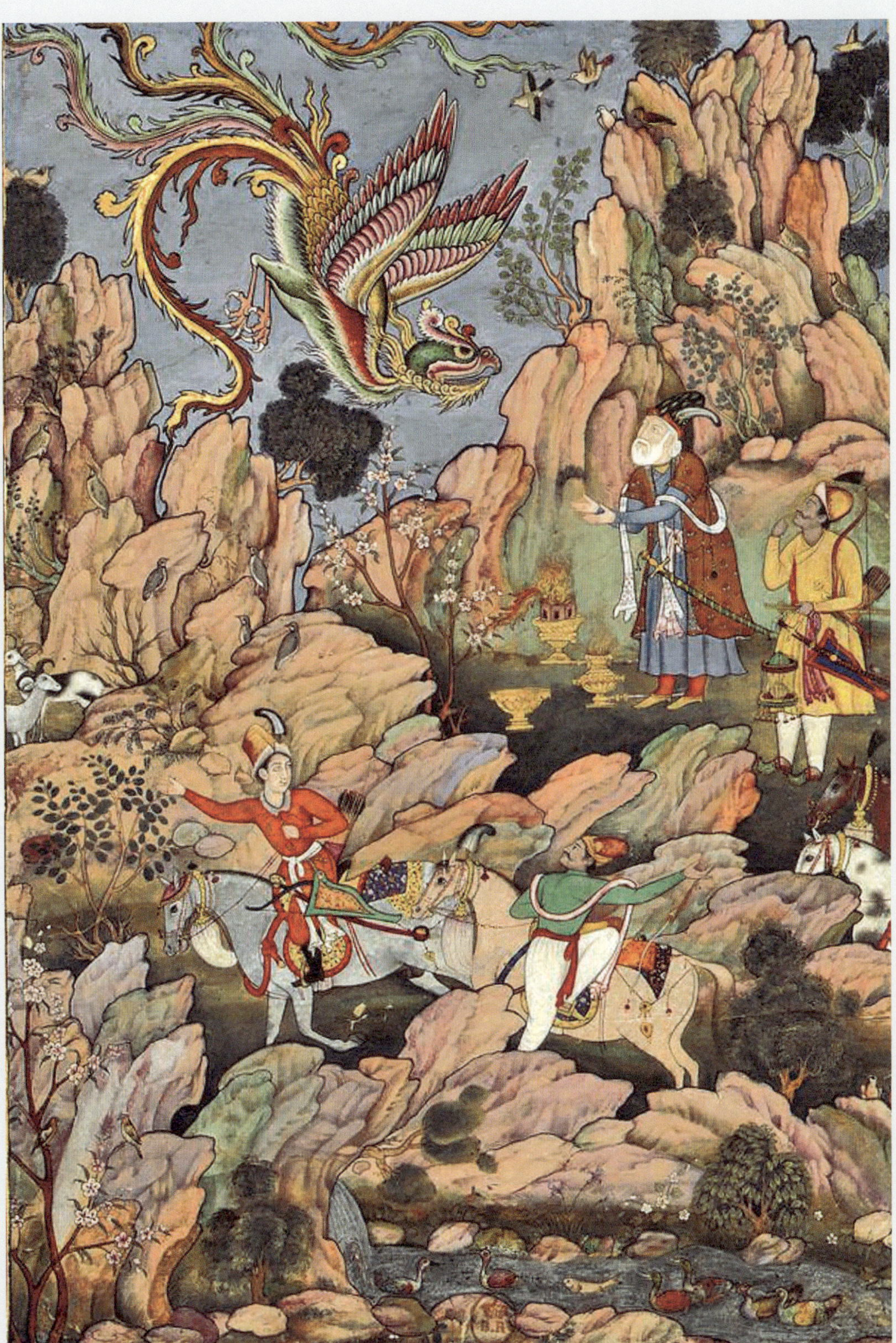

Attributed to Miskin
ZAL PLEADS WITH THE SIMURGH TO SAVE HIS SON RUSTAM
Folio 30 / Mughal School
Circa 1595–1605
Gouache and gold on paper
40.3 × 27.3 cm
Bibliothèque nationale de France, Paris

All forms of Baroque

16TH–18TH CENTURY

A spectacular style of painting that aims to convey emotion, featuring bold colours and lines of force

In Italy

Caravaggio
p. 78

Annibale Carracci
p. 82

Guido Reni
p. 86

Artemisia Gentileschi
p. 88

Economic and commercial vitality in a region that benefited artists

In the Netherlands

Peter Paul Rubens
p. 98

Anthony Van Dyck
p. 114

In Spain

Diego Velázquez
p. 112

GOLDEN AGE DUTCH

17TH CENTURY

Judith Leyster
p. 104

Johannes Vermeer
p. 106

Rachel Ruysch
p. 108

Rembrandt Van Rijn
p. 118

In France

Georges de La Tour
p. 94

Simon Vouet
p. 122

For the glory of the kingdom, an authentic French school, between Baroque and Classicism, is promoted by the Académie Royale de Peinture et de Sculpture (p. 132).

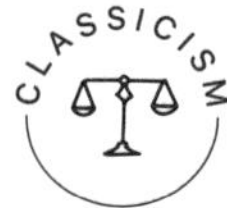

17TH CENTURY

Nicolas Poussin
p. 124

Charles Le Brun
p. 130

PART

2

From Caravaggio to Charles Le Brun

Triumphant painting

The influence of power, from Rome to Versailles

The Protestant Reformation incited the Catholic Church to react and to reassess its foundations. This period marked the advent of grandiose and theatrical art, aiming to move people. From Baroque to Classicism, painting became a communication tool for both religious and political powers.

Caravaggio
An artist who left a mark

Michelangelo Merisi da Caravaggio, a brilliant and restless Baroque painter, left his mark on the history of art. The author of simple and effective compositions, he constructed dramatic settings, while his penchant for chiaroscuro made him famous.

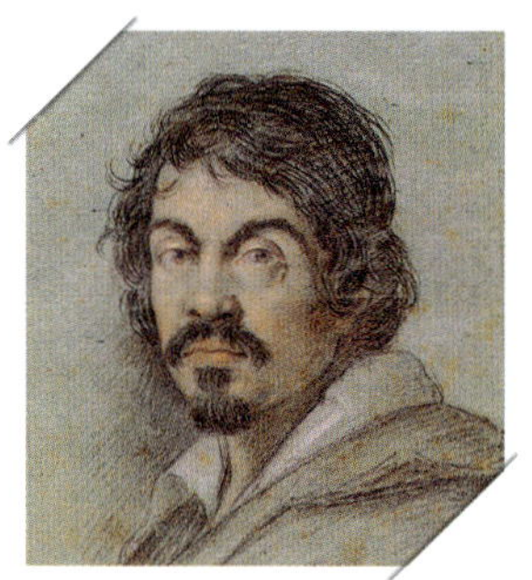

A taste for realism

The realism of Caravaggio's style is what made it unique. Virgins and saints have wrinkled faces and dirty feet; Greek gods have black fingernails. The artist anchors religious painting in everyday life.

Not entirely Catholic

The painter is also the author of a remarkable secular production, highly realistic in style. He painted genre scenes that illustrated the vices of human nature. Often framed at mid-body level, his works featured drunken faces, games, cheating and fortune-telling.

A bad boy

Caravaggio was not "your local friendly artist". He was a tavern brawler, and was guilty of murder. Having been jailed several times, he also spent part of his life in exile. He died on the way back to Rome, in circumstances that remain shrouded in mystery to this day.

TREND SETTER

Even when Caravaggio was alive, his style was emulated by many, and gradually spread throughout Europe. The movement would be called "Caravaggisti".

Lavinia Fontana
Page 72

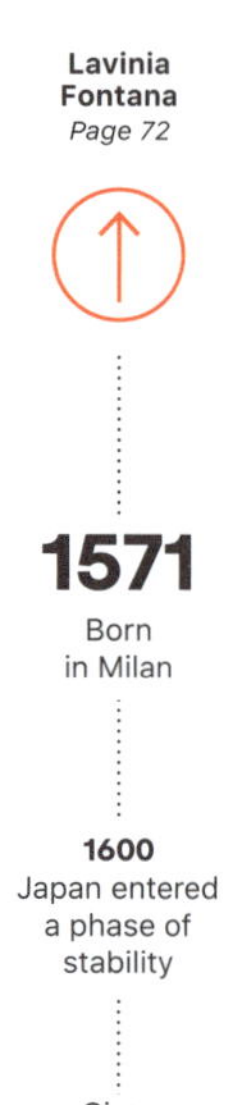

1571
Born in Milan

1600
Japan entered a phase of stability

Circa
1600 to **1604**
Painted *The Entombment*

1609
Galileo, from Italy, created the first astronomical telescope

1610
Died in Porto Ercole, in Tuscany

Annibale Carracci
Page 82

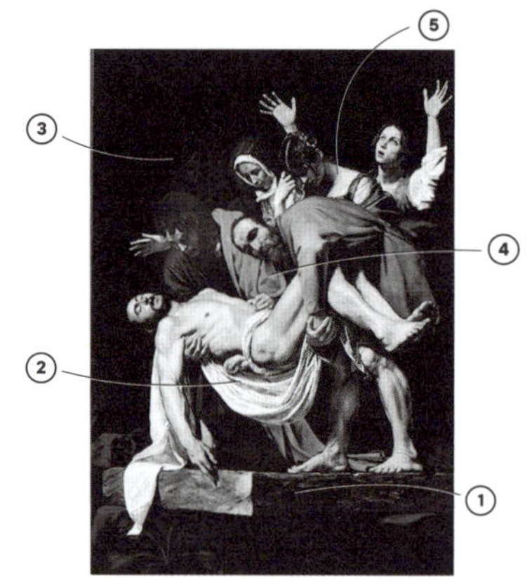

THE ENTOMBMENT

Circa 1600–1604
Oil on canvas
300 × 203 cm
Vatican Museums, Rome

WHAT ARE WE LOOKING AT?

The entombment depicts the moment when the defunct Christ is laid in his tomb. Here, he is carried above the stone that will close off his tomb. This is one of Caravaggio's greatest masterpieces.

① A level composition

The tombstone at the bottom of the painting is at eye level, as this painting is an altarpiece. It was therefore intended to be displayed in a church, on high.

② Michelangelo *vs* Michelangelo

The artist drew inspiration from sculptures to depict this group of characters. In particular, the position of Christ is reminiscent of Michelangelo's *Pietà* (p. 54). In fact, the altar for which this painting was commissioned was in fact dedicated to the *Pietà*. Light strikes and highlights Christ's body, contrasting starkly with the dark background.

③ Virtual reality

This composition features hardly any depth: while the horizon is hidden by the figures, Caravaggio has cleverly pivoted the tombstone towards the viewers, producing an impression of three-dimensionality. It feels like the tombstone is entering our space, and that one could almost touch the body of Christ.

④ A faithful rendition

According to the Gospel of John, Nicodemus helps lower the body into the tomb. Here, he stands on the right, recognisable by his beard. On the left is John, helping him. He can be recognised by his youthful appearance and his red coat.

⑤ A set of three

The women standing just behind are all named Mary: on the left stands the other of Jesus; her wrinkled face goes against the grain of idealised representations. Mary Magdalene, at the centre, is weeping, while Mary of Clopas' attitude intensifies the scene's drama.

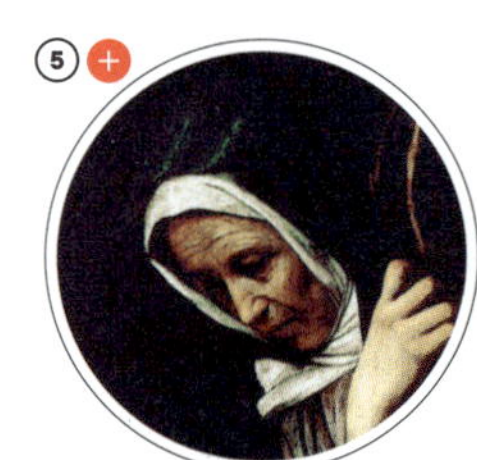

THE CARAVAGGISTI IN A NUTSHELL

- Pronounced realism.
- A dark palette and dramatic lighting.
- Simple compositions.
- Framing at mid-body level.
- Trivial scenes depicting life inside a tavern.
- Religious episodes with secular overtones.

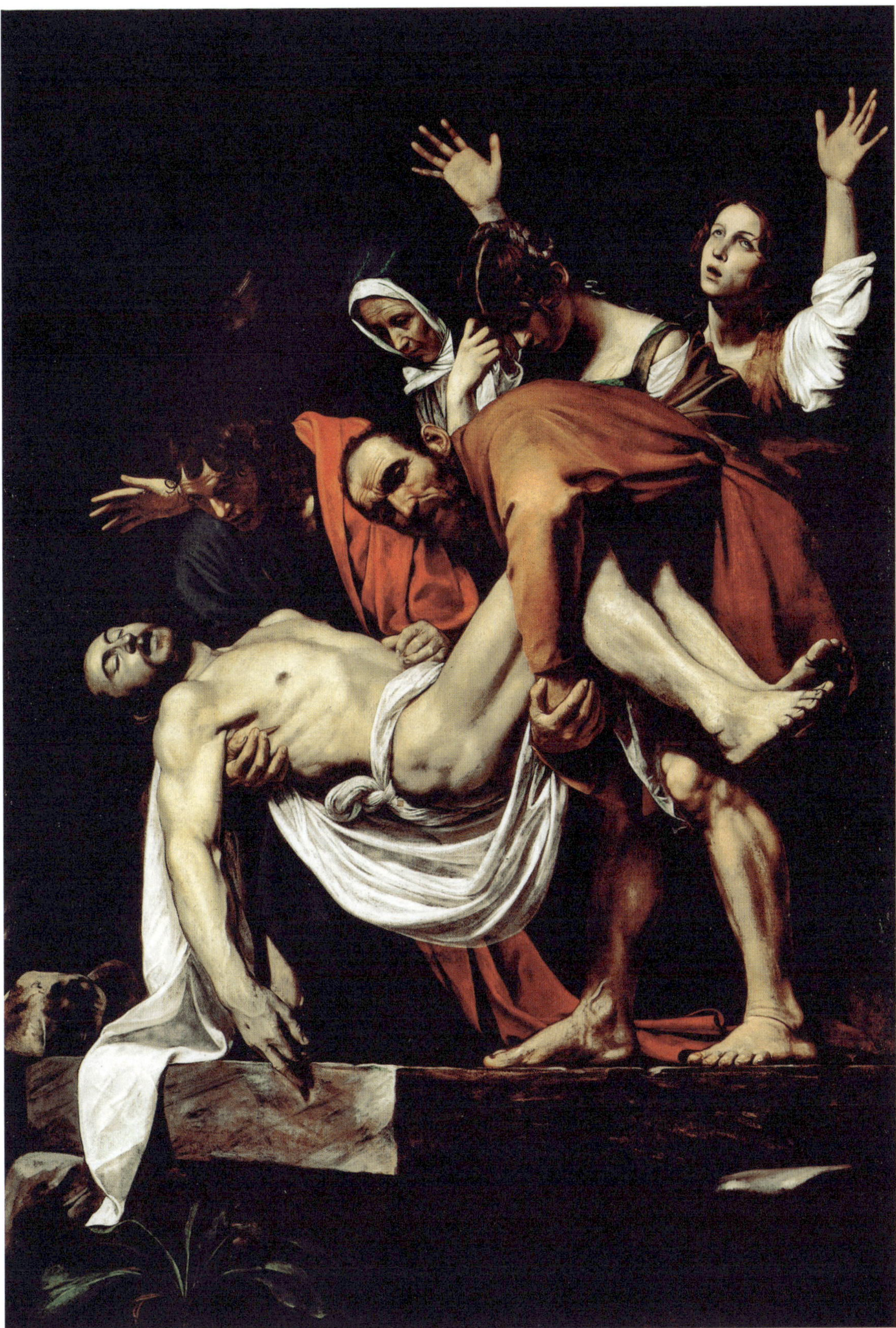

Completely Baroque

The Council of Trent set the record straight

At the end of 1517, the Protestant Reformation swept across Europe, under the impetus of Luther. The Catholic Church sought to reassert its influence, and art became a means to convey its message.

Saint Sebastian, before and after the Reformation

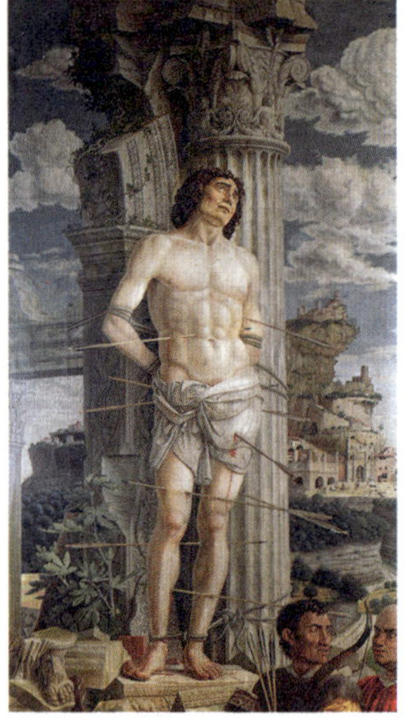

RENAISSANCE

The colour scheme is luminous, and the painting harks back to antiquity, featuring magnificent sculpted ruins. The body is modelled according to the rules of antique art. The trompe-l'œil technique and the landscape testify to the period's interest for perspective and proportion.

Andrea Mantegna

Circa 1480,
Louvre Museum,
Paris

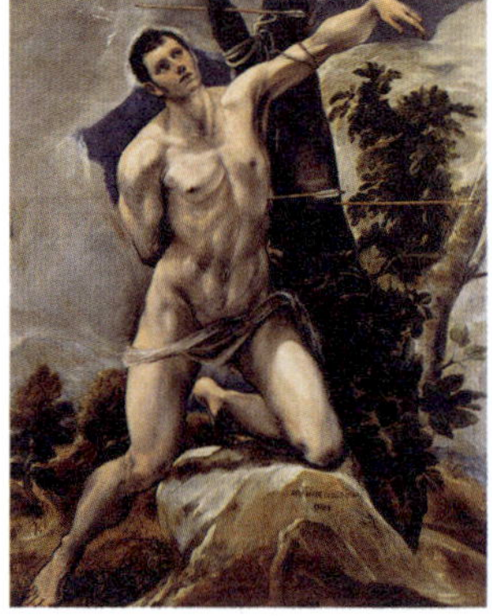

MANNERISM

The body is contorted into a strange, unstable position. The figure's head is too small in relation to its body. Mannerism extrapolates the art of the Renaissance to the point of bizarreness, allow painting to become more expressive.

El Greco

Circa 1577
Catedral de San Antolín,
Palencia

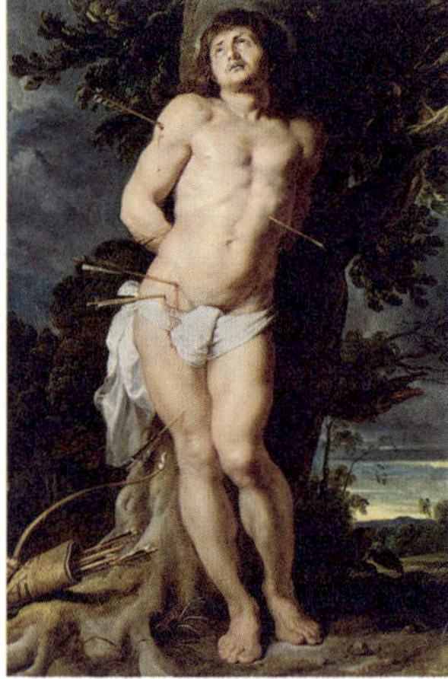

BAROQUE

The emphasis is placed on the scene's dramatic character. The setting is plunged into darkness, while a source of light illuminates the body of the saint from the side. The painting aims to move the faithful, to better spread the message of the Church.

Peter Paul Rubens

1614
Gemäldegalerie,
Berlin

WITH OR WITHOUT IMAGES

In reaction to the Reformation, the Church of Rome gathered at the Council of Trent. While Protestants rejected the worship of images, the Council reaffirmed their power, claiming that they participated in the adoration of Christ, the Virgin Mary and the saints. The art of the Counter-Reformation became an instrument of propaganda and recapture for the Catholic Church.

WHAT'S BRED IN THE BONE ...

Alongside powerful religious images, other secular scenes were produced, appealing to the viewers' senses. They represented popular pastimes, such gambling, taverns, music, some even including depictions of violence and triviality.

The components of the Baroque style

① **Contrasting light**
The lighting accentuates the message's dramatic flair.

② **The palette**
Bold colours are emphasised, taking precedence over drawing.

③ **Selective lighting**
Martyrs, ecstatic saints and spectacular biblical episodes are presented within a scene. Works aim to convey a sense of exaltation in believers.

④ **Compositions**
They are structured around great lines of force or swirling movements.

⑤ **Emotions**
They are visible, accentuated: the artist seeks to appeal to the viewer's empathy, in an attempt to engage them.

⑥ **Triviality**
The figures' nails are black, their feet are dirty, their faces red and wrinkled. The painting's movement brings out a naturalism that anchors the scenes in reality.

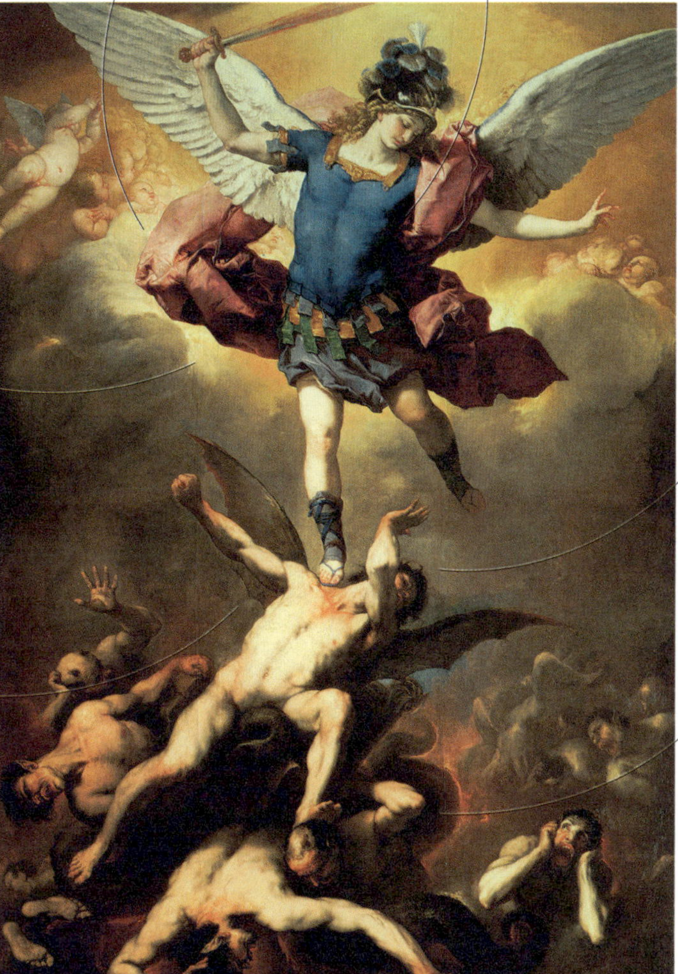

LUCA GIORDANO
The Fall of the Rebel Angels
1660–1665
Kunsthistorisches Museum,
Vienna

Annibale Carracci

Painting with a Bolognese twist

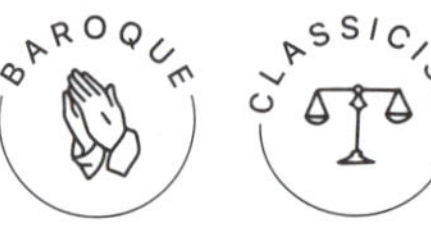

After the eccentricities of Mannerism, Carracci's art advocated the observation of nature. He was a leader of the Bolognese school, and his style is sometimes difficult to distinguish from that of his brother Agostino and his cousin Ludovico, both also painters.

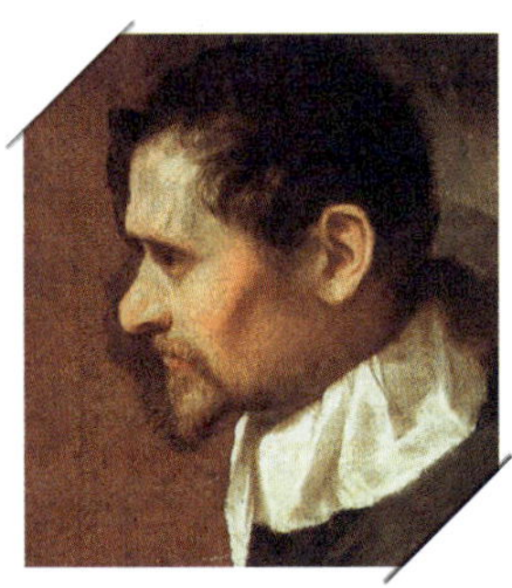

All gifts are in nature

Nature was Carracci's first school, and early on, he showed talent as a draughtsman. Viewers were awed by his sculptural and illusionist style. This inventive artist embodies the combination of Baroque and Classicism.

Family spirit

The Carracci were a dynasty. Together with his brother Agostino and his cousin Ludovico, Annibale founded the Accademia degli Incamminati in Bologna, where they taught their painting skills. Renowned artists such as Domenichino, Guido Reni (p. 86) and Francesco Albani would study with them.

Jack-of-all-trades

Carracci was at the forefront of trends. Beyond traditional religious and historical paintings, minor genres earned well-earned prestige through his works. He excelled in the art of landscape painting, and his genre scenes are highly empathetic, maybe because of his humble origins.

FORMATIVE TRAVELS

Invited to Rome, Carracci immersed himself in the works of antiquity, Michelangelo and Raphael – an influence that is visible in the sumptuous decor of the Farnese Gallery.

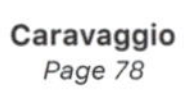

Caravaggio
Page 78

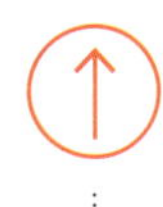

1560
Born in Bologna

1595 to **1596**
Painted *The Choice of Hercules*

1609
Died in Rome

1611
Birth of Charles de Batz de Castelmore d'Artagnan, whose "Mémoires" inspired Alexandre Dumas

1618
The Thirty Years' War broke out

Guido Reni
Page 86

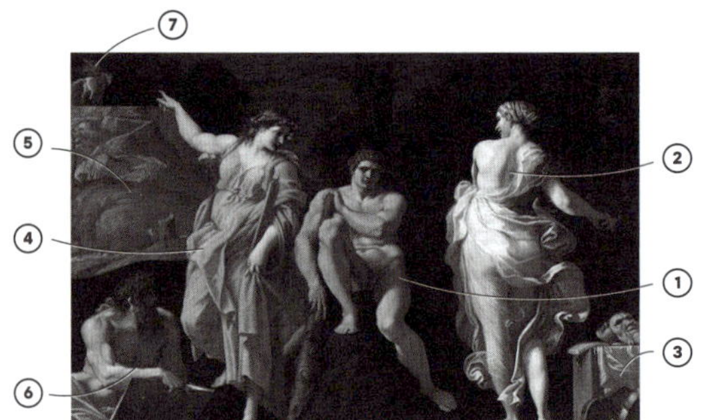

THE CHOICE OF HERCULES

1595–1596
Oil on canvas
167 × 223 cm
National Museum of Capodimonte, Naples

WHAT ARE WE LOOKING AT?

This painting was inspired by the *Apology*, an ancient text attributed to Prodicus, a Greek philosopher. It depicts the hero Hercules hesitating between vice and virtue, represented here by allegories.

① Between a rock and a hard place

Hercules, son of Jupiter (p. 156), is recognisable by his club. His monumentality is reminiscent of Michelangelo's figures on the ceiling of the Sistine Chapel (p. 54). The hero's central position in the image sets the scene for his hesitation between vice and virtue.

② Appearances are deceiving

From the flowers at her feet to her hairstyle and the transparent drape she is wearing, the allegory of vice is deliberately attractive. She is pointing out a lush forest to the hero.

③ Seductive arguments

Music, theatre and games could distract the hero from his destiny. The masks also offer a warning against the futility of appearances.

④ Another kind

Virtue is more chastely dressed. In her hand, she holds a *parazonium*, a dagger carried by Roman officers.

⑤ A lesser temptation

The landscape that virtue is pointing to is also less compelling. The mountain is barren; a broken tree trunk can be seen. The hero's path will be arduous.

⑥ It will be known

The poet has been summoned to reward the hero's efforts. He stands ready to write the story of Hercules and to spread his fame.

⑦ A source of motivation

The winged horse is Pegasus, an attribute of the Farnese family, by whom this work was commissioned. The mountain is therefore the Helicon, home to Pegasus and the Muses. This painting, which is stimulating for inspiration, likely adorned a study.

⑦ +

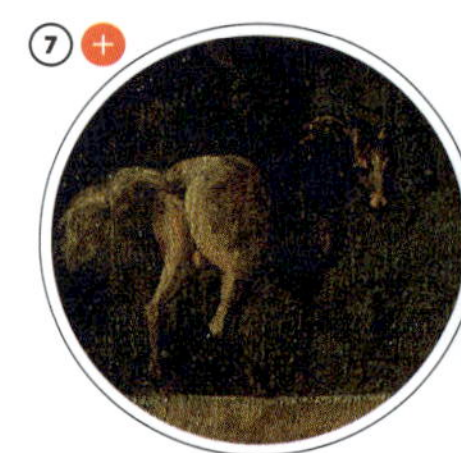

A MEETING THAT NEVER TOOK PLACE

Pegasus is a winged horse. According to Apollodorus of Athens in *Library*, he is the son of Poseidon and the Gorgon Medusa, who was killed by the hero Perseus. In the ancient myths, his path never actually crossed that of the demigod Hercules. His presence here is purely symbolic.

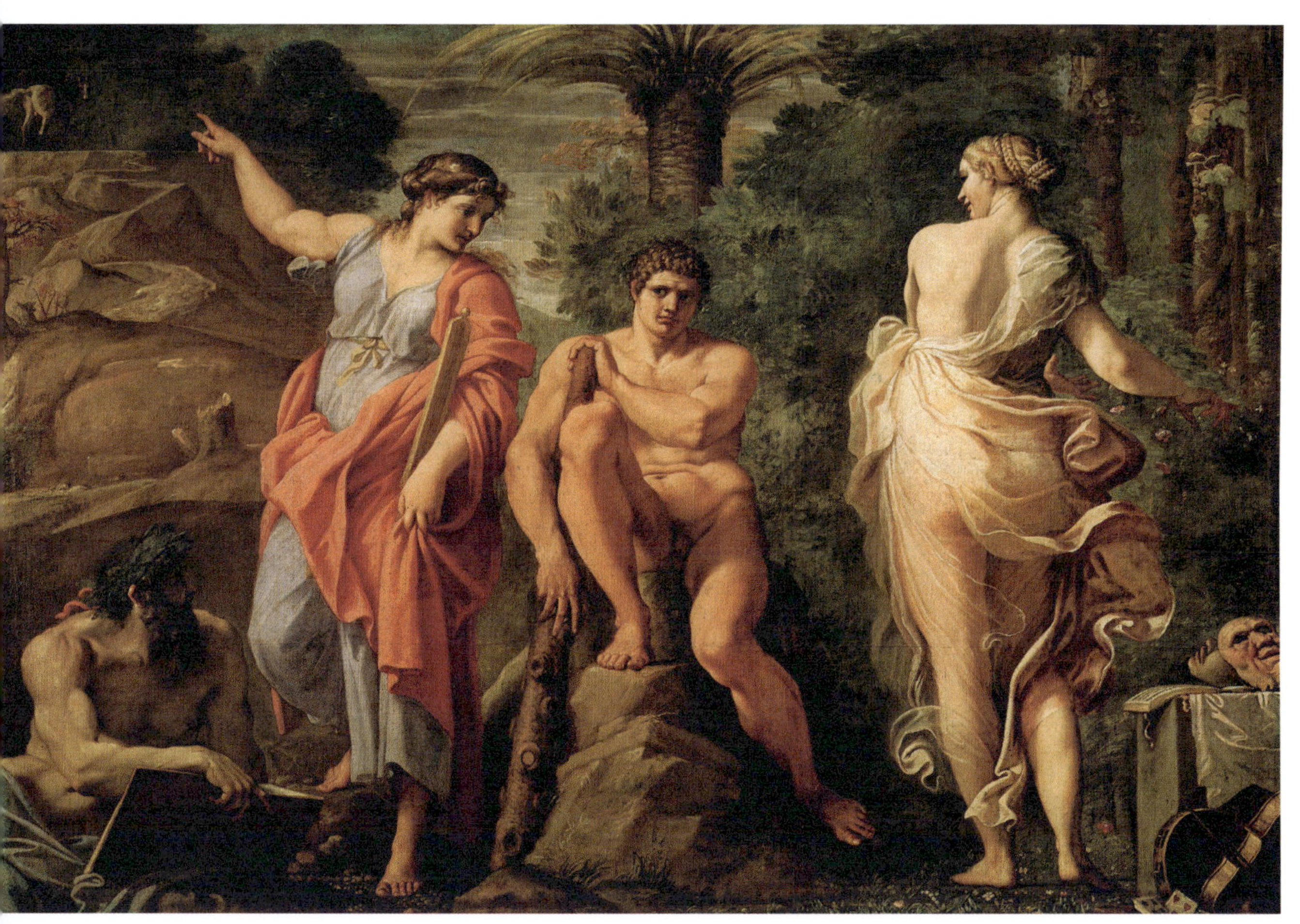

Why are they always naked?

Greek heroes are not exhibitionists. Under the brushes of artists, they were depicted as "heroic nudes", allowing the author to present an idealised human body, whose beauty reflected virtue. For reasons of propriety, women were exempt from this rule, save for goddesses and allegories, as they are imaginary characters.

Carracci and Cézanne

Farmers are kings

Both painters focused on the peasant condition. Their monumental figures are graced with a noble, imposing presence. Carracci used a genre scene as a pretext to paint this motif, while Cézanne entirely freed himself from the constraints of any subject.

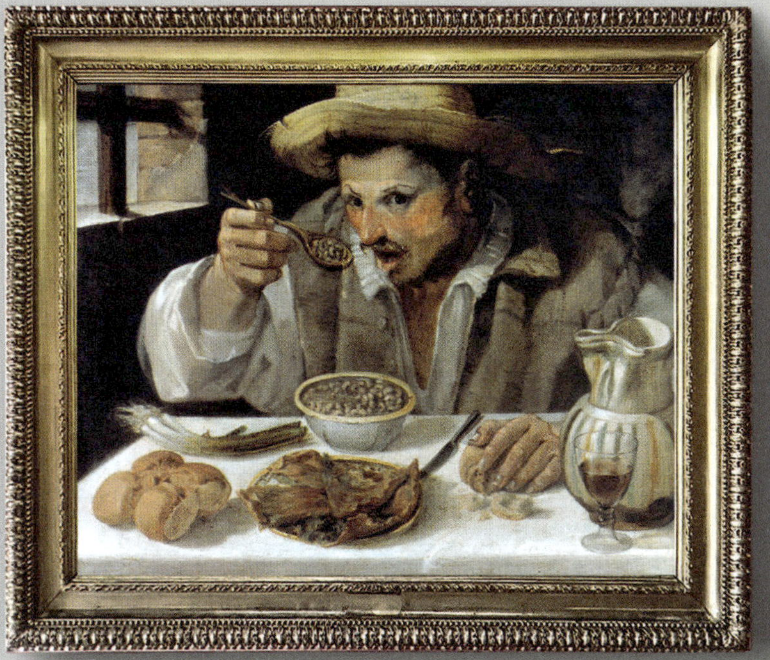

***THE BEAN EATER* BY ANNIBALE CARRACCI**
1584–1585

The scene is particularly striking. The peasant is eating greedily, clutching a piece of bread. The location is dark, the subject's hat is worn and the bars on the window are reminiscent of a prison. Despite this, the meal looks appetising, and the table depicted in the front of the painting invites viewers to sit down.

Oil on canvas, 57 × 68 cm
Colonna Palace, Rome

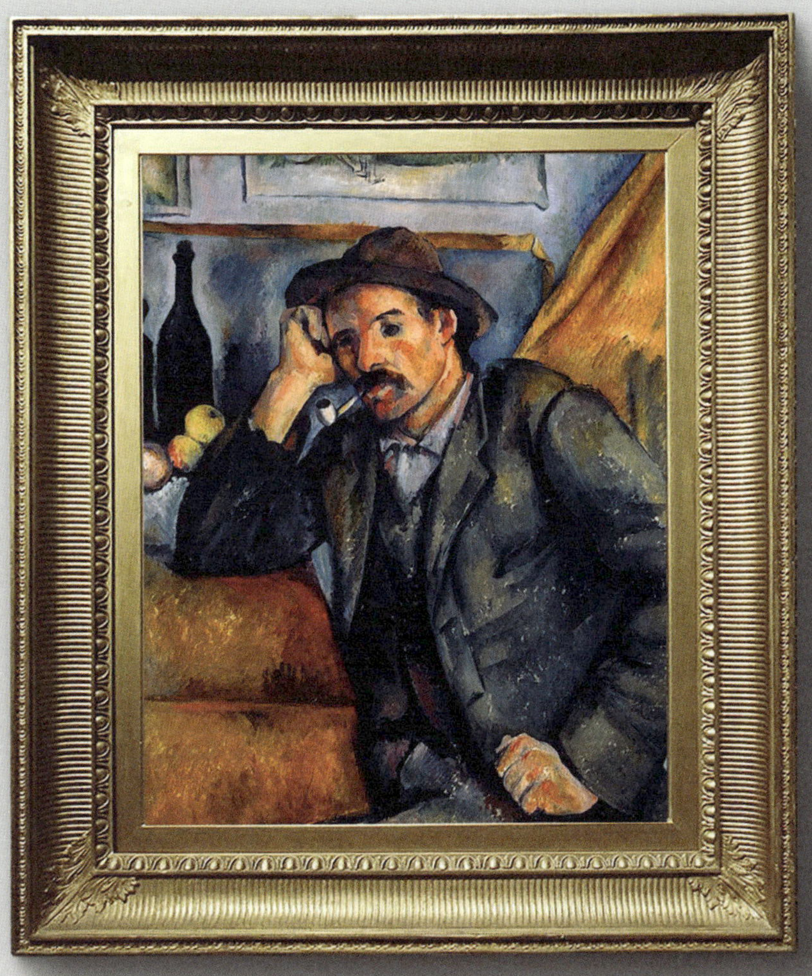

***MAN WITH A PIPE* BY PAUL CÉZANNE**
1890–1892

This man is peaceful, lost in an unending reverie. The unstable lines and contrasting perspective reinforce the model's solidly seated position, as he "stands firm" against this imbalance. The greys and mauves play with tawny tones evocative of the South of France.

Oil on canvas, 82.5 × 73.5 cm
State Hermitage Museum, Saint Petersburg

Guido Reni
Sehnsucht

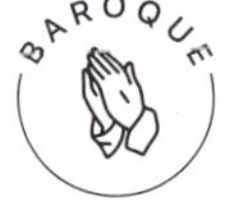

A major artist of his time, Guido Reni was influenced by the art of Carracci and Caravaggio; however, he was in search of an ideal of beauty and purity. Between Bologna and Rome, he carved a unique path, inspired by Raphael.

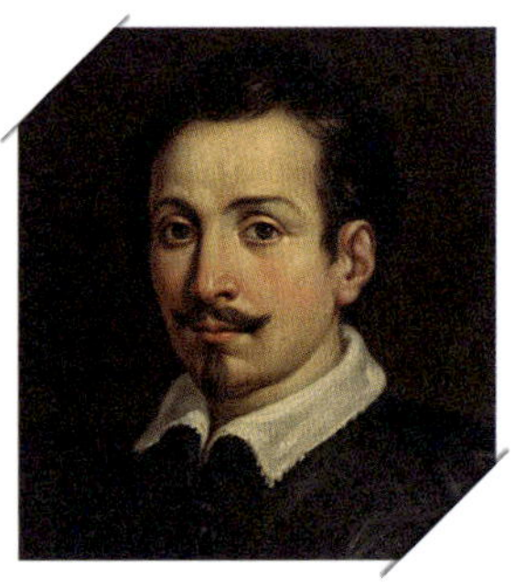

The pupil surpassed the teacher

Reni was trained by Calvaert, a painter from Antwerp. He then joined the academy founded by the Carracci (p. 82). In spite of his abilities, he parted ways with the establishment because of a rivalry with Ludovico, against whom he won a commission.

A nest of vipers

He was invited to Rome by Giuseppe Cesari, who aspired to compete with Caravaggio (p. 78) by bringing in new talent. Agostino Carracci, who also resided in Rome, favoured the careers of other painters to limit Reni's growing popularity. Reni's gifts, however, would allow him to make the most of his situation.

Unconditional groupie

Reni admired the effectiveness of Caravaggio's compositions, but rejected his realism. In search of an ideal of divine beauty that would serve the messages of the Church, he revered Raphael (p. 46).

FRONT ROW WITNESSES

The tale of Reni's life has reached us thanks to Carlo Cesare Malvasia, who recounts the lives of the painters of Emilia-Romagna in the 17th century in his book *Felsina Pittrice*.

Annibale Carracci
Page 82

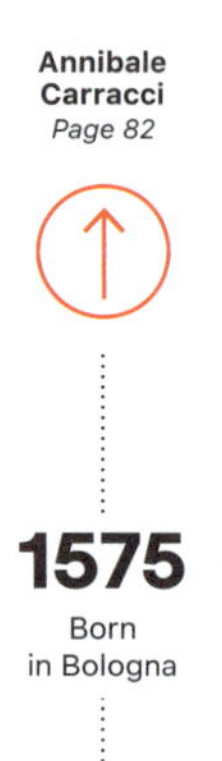

1575
Born in Bologna

Circa
1611
Reni painted *Massacre of the Innocents*

1631
The foundation stone of the Taj Mahal was laid. The construction would require many years

1642
Died in Bologna

1642
Blaise Pascal invents the Arithmetic Machine

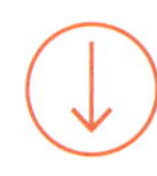

Artemisia Gentileschi
Page 88

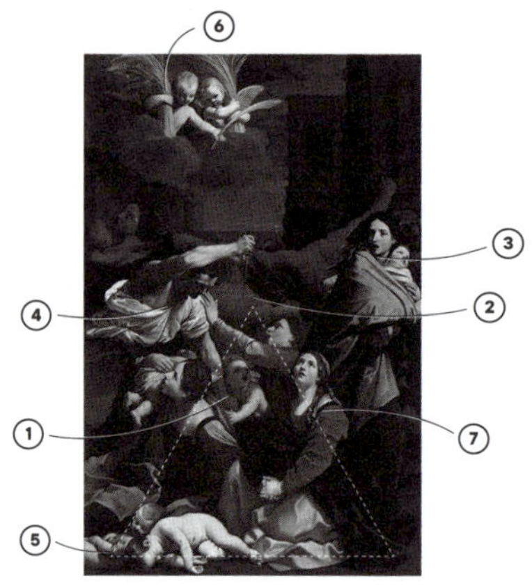

MASSACRE OF THE INNOCENTS

Circa 1611
Oil on canvas,
268 × 170 cm
National Art Gallery of Bologna, Italy

WHAT ARE WE LOOKING AT?

In the Gospel according to Matthew, King Herod received an omen: the king of the Jews (Jesus Christ) would be born in Bethlehem. He ordered that all the children in the town be killed to eliminate this future rival.

① Movements that flow together

This painting is the perfect synthesis of the classical ideal inspired by Raphael and the dynamism of Italian painting in the 17th century. The foreground's pyramidal construction forms part of a tragic movement.

② A meaningful void

The top of the pyramid remains empty. This void, in the centre of the image, emphasises the characters' dramatic momentum and highlights the dagger held by one of the executioners.

③ No escape

The tall framing creates the impression of a narrow space, like a trap closing in on the women who are attempting to escape on either side of the scene.

④ Before and after

Characters are arranged in several close-up shots, presenting various actions: the attempted escape, the tragedy that has occurred, and the one that is about to. However, the painter does not display the crime itself.

⑤ Eternal rest

In the foreground on the left, two small victims can be seen, as if asleep. Their chubby bodies contrast with the absence of life.

⑥ A break in the clouds

Above them, up high, two *putti* reflect the victims, offering them palm branches, the symbol of martyrdom.

⑦ She has eyes only for God

Their resigned mother is already seeking consolation in Heaven. Sublimated by the drama, she is the embodiment of the graceful ideal sought by Reni.

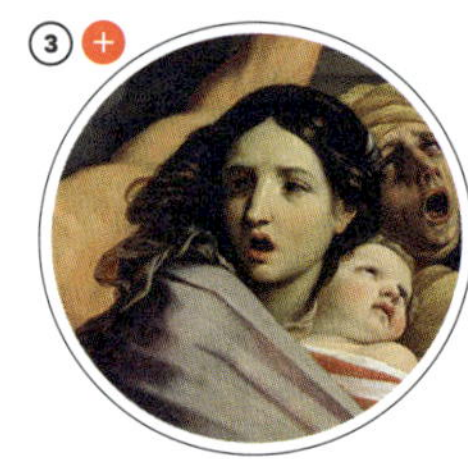

ONE PUTTO, TWO PUTTI

Also known as amoretti, the *putti* are chubby babies with wings. They often have a mischievous attitude, and are amusing figures. While they do not necessarily have an identity or function of their own, they are the best known walk-on actors in Western painting.

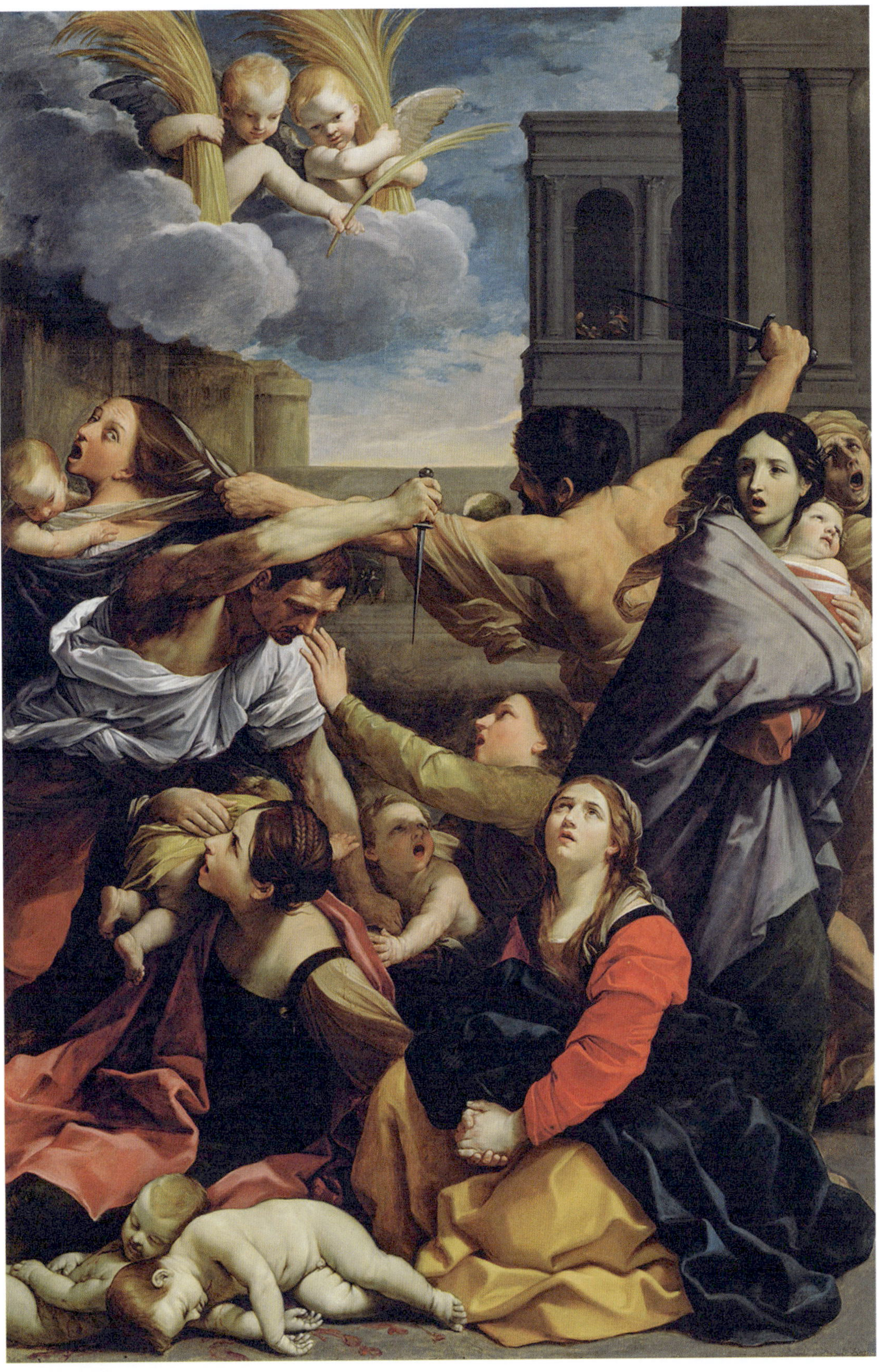

Artemisia Gentileschi

Fierce talent and a character to match

Artemisia Gentileschi learned the art of painting in her father's studio, influenced by the art of Caravaggio. Her talent and boldness made her one of the greatest names in Baroque painting. During her lifetime, she was internationally renowned.

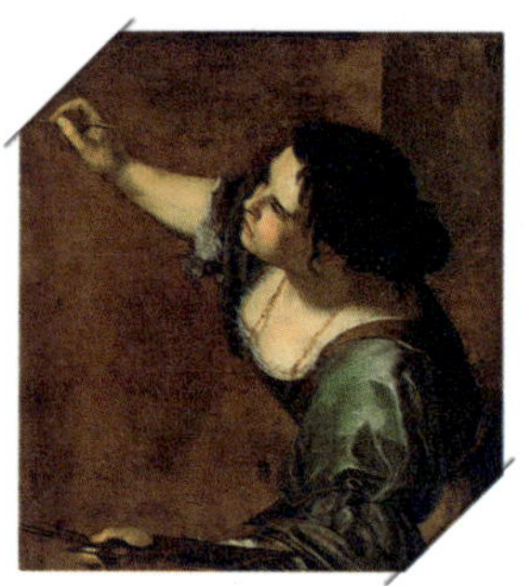

A liberated woman

Under the influence of a brutal father, and raped by one of his associates, Gentileschi emancipated herself through painting. She tried her hand at all genres, even those reserved for men, such as history painting. Her works are filled with courageous and tragic heroines.

Social pressure

After a humiliating and resounding trial, Artemisia had no choice but to marry to regain her respectability. With her spouse, she moved to Florence, where she was asked by the Grand Duke of Tuscany to join the Academy of Art – a first, for a woman.

A solid network

Freed from her husband, she pursued her career, surrounding herself with renowned artists: Simon Vouet (p. 122), Anthony Van Dyck (p. 114) and Guercino. She travelled to Italy, London and France, where she was invited to the Royal Court. She settled in Naples, where she was assigned commissions from prestigious patrons.

IT WAS SAID OF HER

"She has no peers, having created such works of art that perhaps even the most important masters of this profession cannot achieve." Orazio Gentileschi, Artemisia's father.

Guido Reni
Page 86

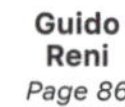

1593
Born in Rome

1606
European eyes contemplated Australian shores for the first time

1625 to **1626**
Painted *Penitent Magdalene*

1635
Foundation of the Académie Française by Cardinal Richelieu

1654
Died in Naples

Georges de La Tour
Page 94

PENITENT MAGDALENE

1625–1626
Oil on canvas
122 × 97 cm
Seville Cathedral

WHAT ARE WE LOOKING AT?

This is a typical representation of Saint Mary Magdalene doing penance. In the Catholic religion, she is the symbol of repentance.

Association

The history of art associates Mary Magdalene, a disciple of Jesus, with the image of the repentant sinner and Mary of Bethany. One or the other, according to the Gospels, washed Christ's feet with her hair and anointed them with perfume. Here, Marie-Magdalene can be identified by the perfume bottle that glows in the darkness, and by her long, beautiful hair.

Pure Baroque

The viewer is presented with a legible image, featuring an immediately identifiable saint, set in a clear composition. The red drapery, meticulously painted by Artemisia Gentileschi, creates a theatrical atmosphere that is reinforced by the chiaroscuro recalling the art of Caravaggio. An off-camera light source on the left brightly illuminates the saint's face, drawing pronounced shadows on her flesh.

Changing her mind

Magdalene's attitude is melancholic. Her eyes are half closed, and a tear is beading on her face. She is slumped in her chair, and her uncomfortable position evokes deep inner suffering. However, Gentileschi painted other signs stating that she is not yet repentant.

Vestiges of love

She is still wearing her jewellery, symbols of her dissolute life, and her hand is sensually playing with her hair. Similarly, the low-cut neckline of her garment reveals her bare shoulder and the top of her breasts, both manifestations of the ambiguous limbo in which Magdalene is suspended. In another version of the work kept in the Seville Cathedral, the linen veil covering her throat was widened by another artist.

THREE HEROINES BY ARTEMISIA

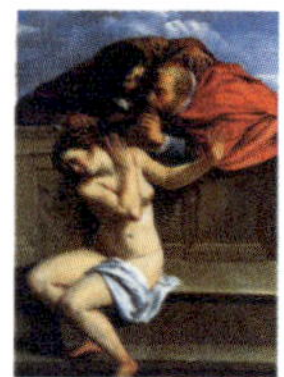

Susanna and the Elders
Circa 1610
Schloss Weißenstein, Pommersfelden

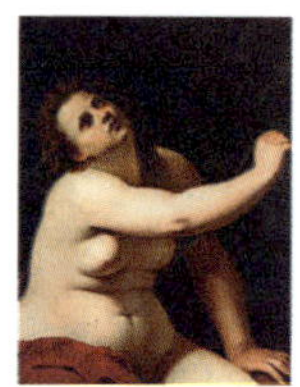

Cleopatra
1630
Private collection

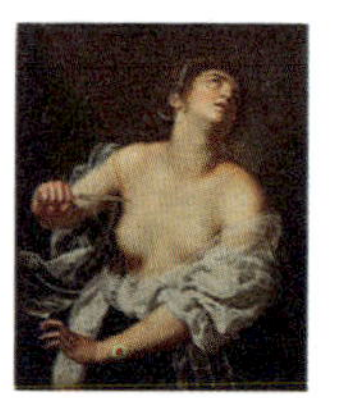

Lucretia
1630–1635
Private collection

LATE RECOGNITION

After centuries spent in oblivion, the historian Roberto Longhi invited the public to rediscover Gentileschi in 1916, with the essay *Orazio and Artemisia Gentileschi: Father and Daughter*. In the 1960s, she was considered "lustful and precocious". The feminist research that ensued is contributing to a more accurate representation.

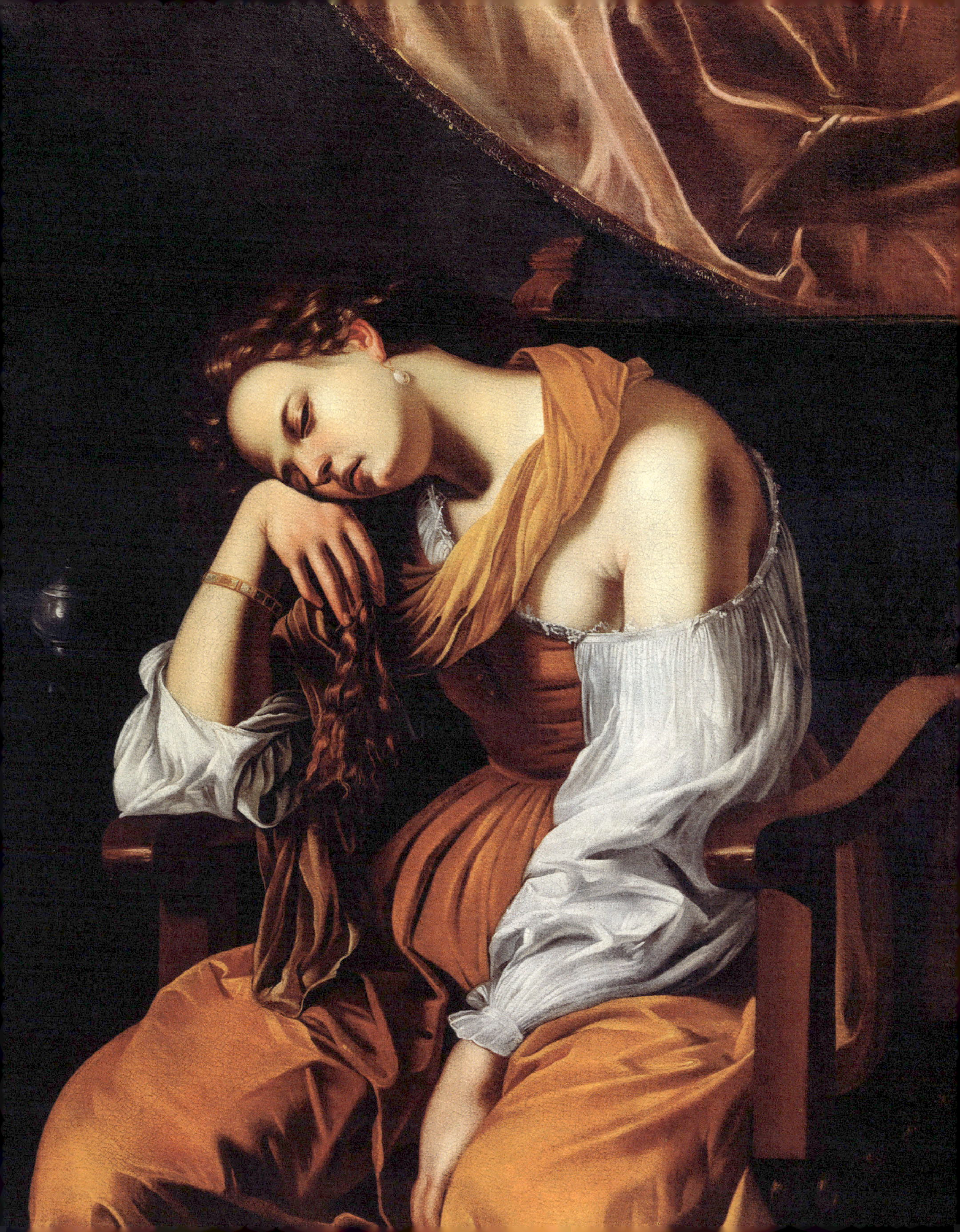

Caravaggio and Gentileschi

Sore throats

The Old Testament tells of the siege of Bethulia by the troops of General Holofernes. As the villagers were preparing to surrender, Judith travelled to the enemy camp to murder the villagers' oppressor.

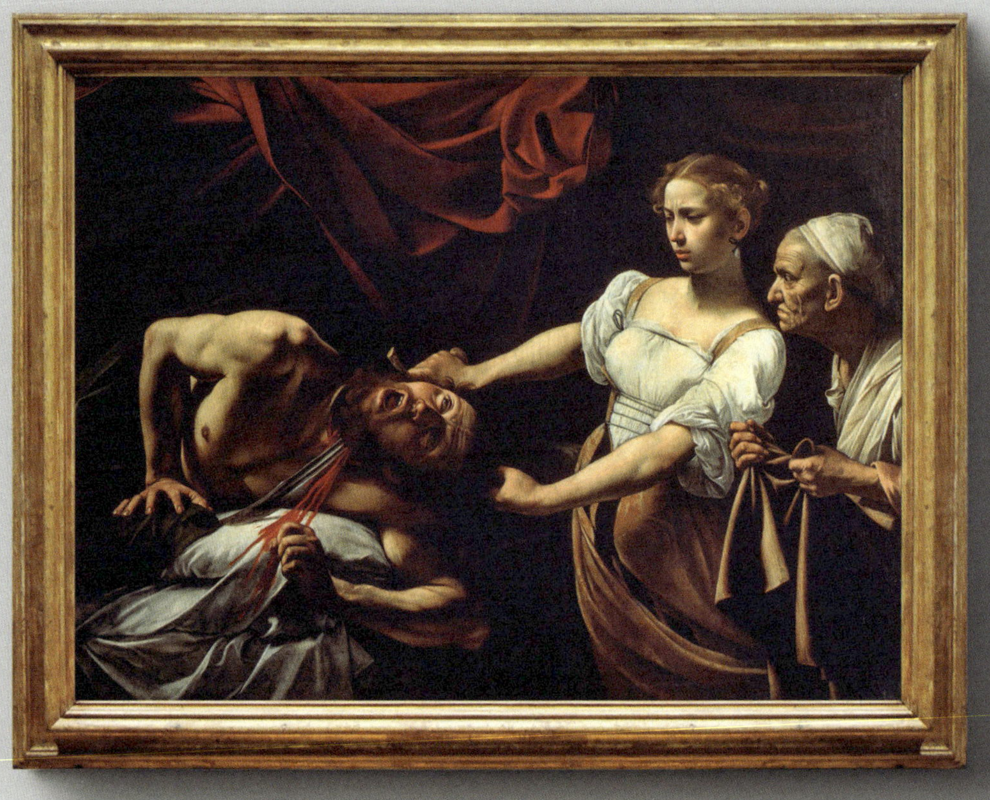

***JUDITH AND HOLOFERNES* BY CARAVAGGIO**
Circa 1598

Caravaggio's Judith seems repulsed by her task and evokes empathy, while the servant woman embodies unhealthy curiosity. The painting should be read horizontally, inviting viewers to observe the protagonists' expressions. It produces a highly dramatic atmosphere, reinforced by the red curtain.

Oil on canvas, 145 × 195 cm
National Gallery of Ancient Art, Rome

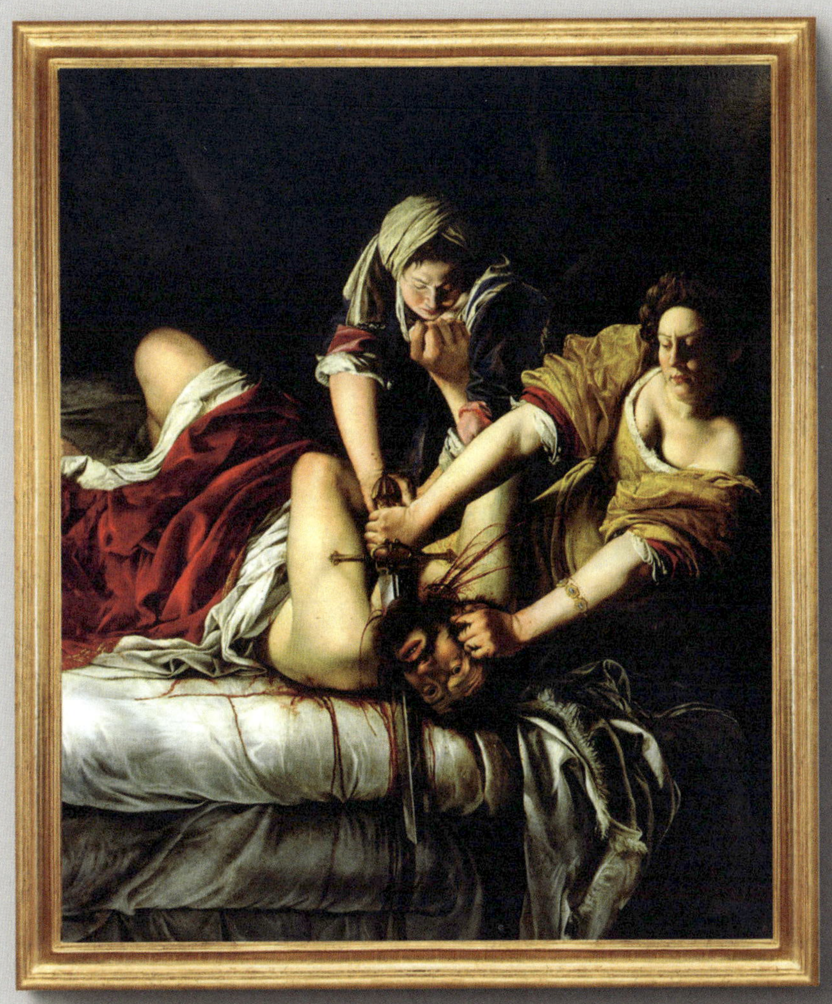

***JUDITH BEHEADING HOLOFERNES* BY ARTEMISIA GENTILESCHI**
Circa 1614–1620

Gentileschi's Judith leaves no room for doubt. The characters faces are concentrated; they are focused on their task. The painter proposes a more vertical composition, which enhances the women's confidence and emphasises the brutality and implacability of their act.

Oil on canvas, 199 × 162.5 cm
Uffizi Gallery, Florence

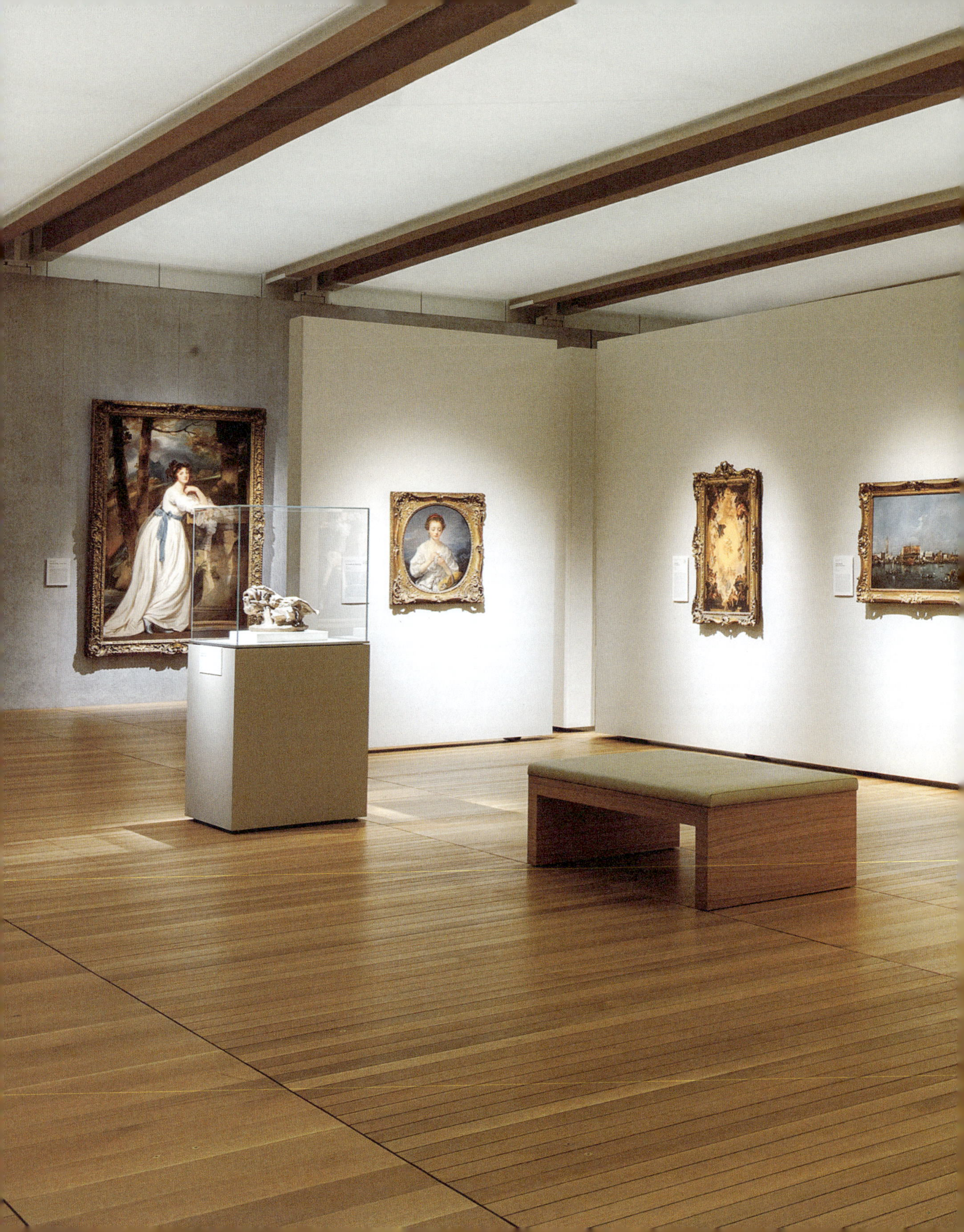

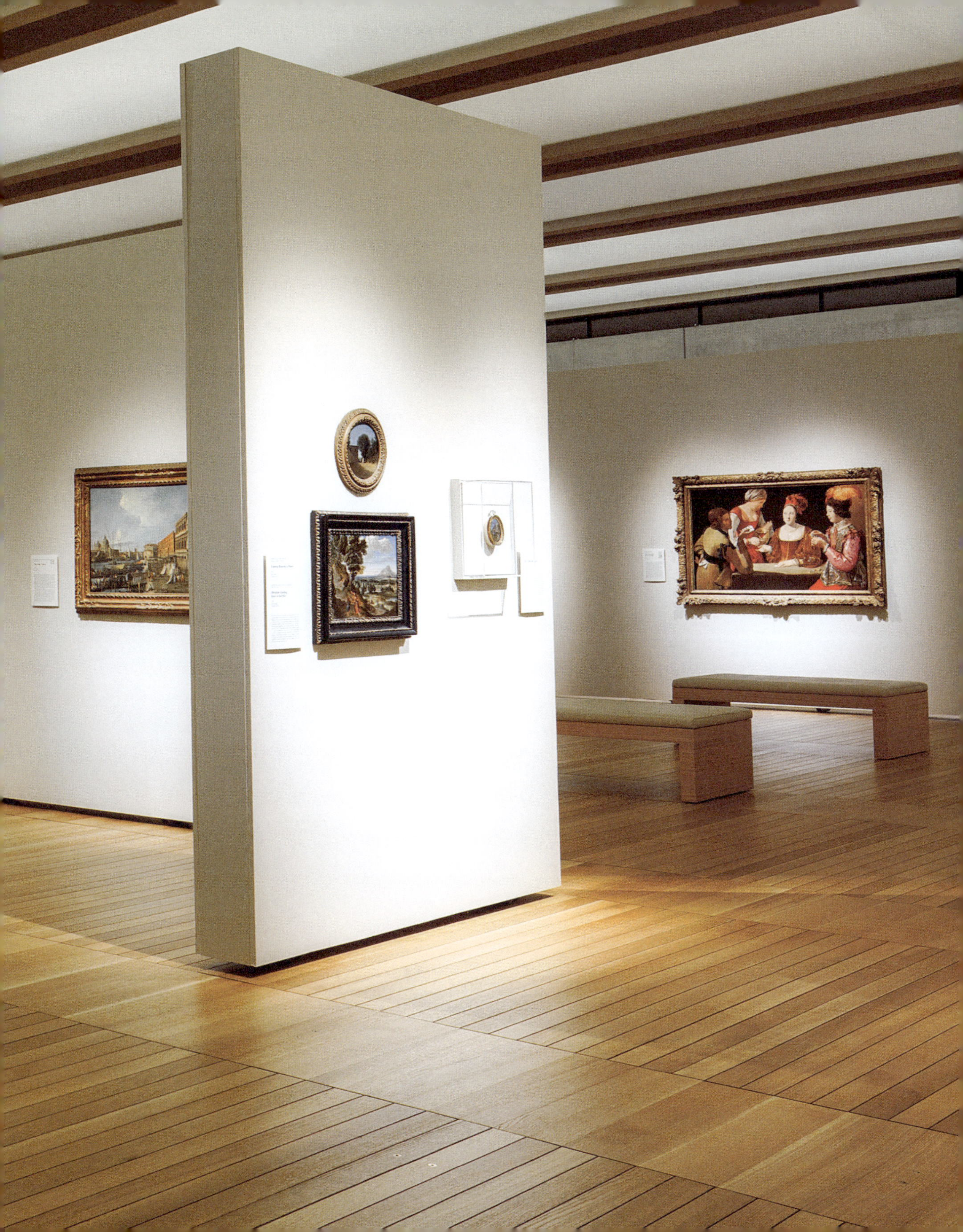

Georges de La Tour

Nocturnes that light a flame

Forgotten after his death, to the point that in the 19th century, none of his works even featured his name in French museums, La Tour is one of France's greatest painters. He owes his reputation to his prodigious candlelight nocturnes.

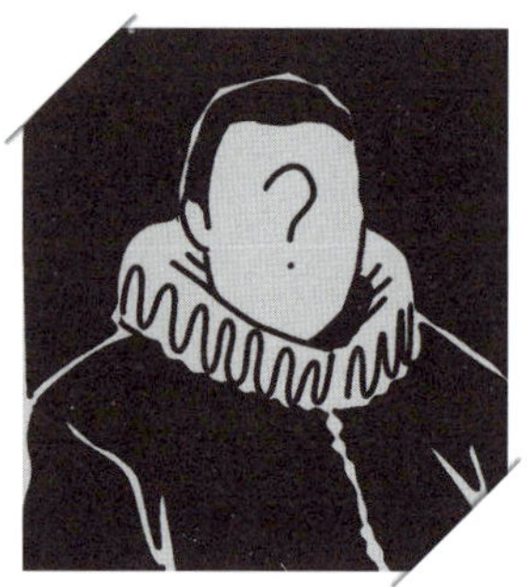

Extra and ordinary

La Tour was born in Lorraine, which was independent from France at the time. He travelled to Paris, where he became the "ordinary painter" to King Louis XIII. Among his clients were the most important names in the capital, including Cardinal Richelieu.

Day and night

The painter's character was the opposite of his art: his works are as humanistic as he was passionate. His work also features contrasting daytime and nighttime paintings. The latter are generally associated with his mature period; however, he painted nocturnes earlier in his career.

What a show-off!

La Tour's realism and chiaroscuro evoke the art of Caravaggio, but his famous "nocturnes" were an opportunity for him to fully express his creative fibre. Through studies of lighting, he evolved towards a certain innovative geometrisation of forms.

THE KING'S CHOICE

It is said that Louis XIII appreciated the artist's *Saint Sebastian Tended by Saint Irene* so much that he had his bedroom cleared of all other paintings, and kept only this one.

Artemisia Artemisia Gentileschi
Page 88

1582
The Gregorian calendar was established, including leap years

1593
Born in Vic-sur-Seille, Moselle

Circa
1636
to
1640
Painted *The Card Sharp with the Ace of Diamonds*

1652
Died in Lunéville

1668
La Fontaine published *Fables*, with great success

Peter Paul Rubens
Page 98

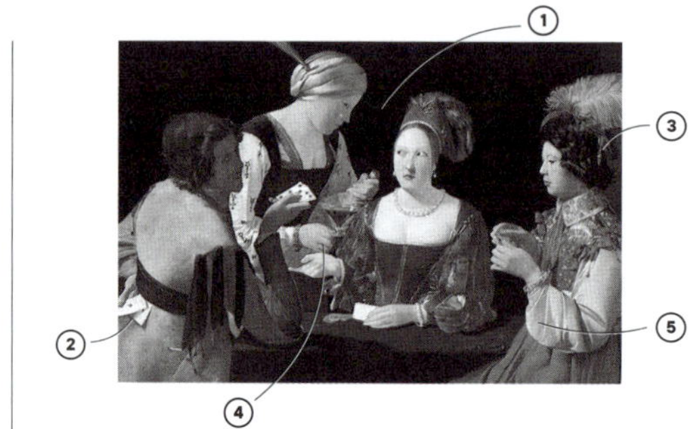

THE CARD SHARP WITH THE ACE OF DIAMONDS

Circa 1636–1640
Oil on canvas
106 × 146 cm
Louvre Museum, Paris

WHAT ARE WE LOOKING AT?

This painting is a genre scene, describing a card game where three accomplices have planned a ruse to cheat the fourth player.

① Look them in the eyes

The courtesan is making a discreet gesture with her hand; she and her servant are exchanging intriguing glances, telling us of their intention to commit an evil deed.

② Straight flush

The man on the left is about to grab an ace of diamonds hidden behind his back to complete his set of the same suit, which is facing us. The viewer is an accomplice of the deception. A second version of this painting exists, featuring an ace of clubs.

③ The butt of the joke

Isolated in the foreground, this young man, dressed in his Sunday best, is about to get fleeced; the feather on his hat refers to the French expression for this, "se faire plumer". Concentrating on his game, he sees nothing of this organised attempt at cheating. This character might echo the biblical episode of the prodigal son, who squandered his father's possessions and returned home penniless.

④ Kinky

Deep necklines, wine glasses and money – all vices are featured at this table. The untied aiguillettes on the cheater's shoulder are also a symbol of moral laxity. The painter is denouncing them, but he also seems to laugh at the future victim's foolishness.

⑤ Too well dressed

While our contemporary eyes see nothing but antique clothing from the painter's time, there is nothing ordinary about these outfits. These are most likely theatre costumes.

① +

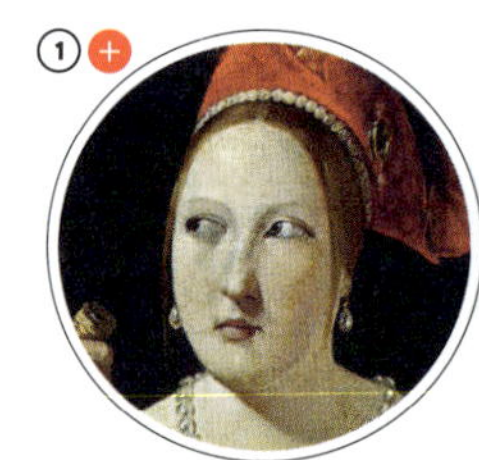

A RARE ARTIST

Today, only 48 paintings throughout the world are attributed to Georges de La Tour. This low number explains the success met by the painter's work in auction houses. In 2020, *A Girl Blowing on a Brazier* was auctioned off for 4.34 million euros.

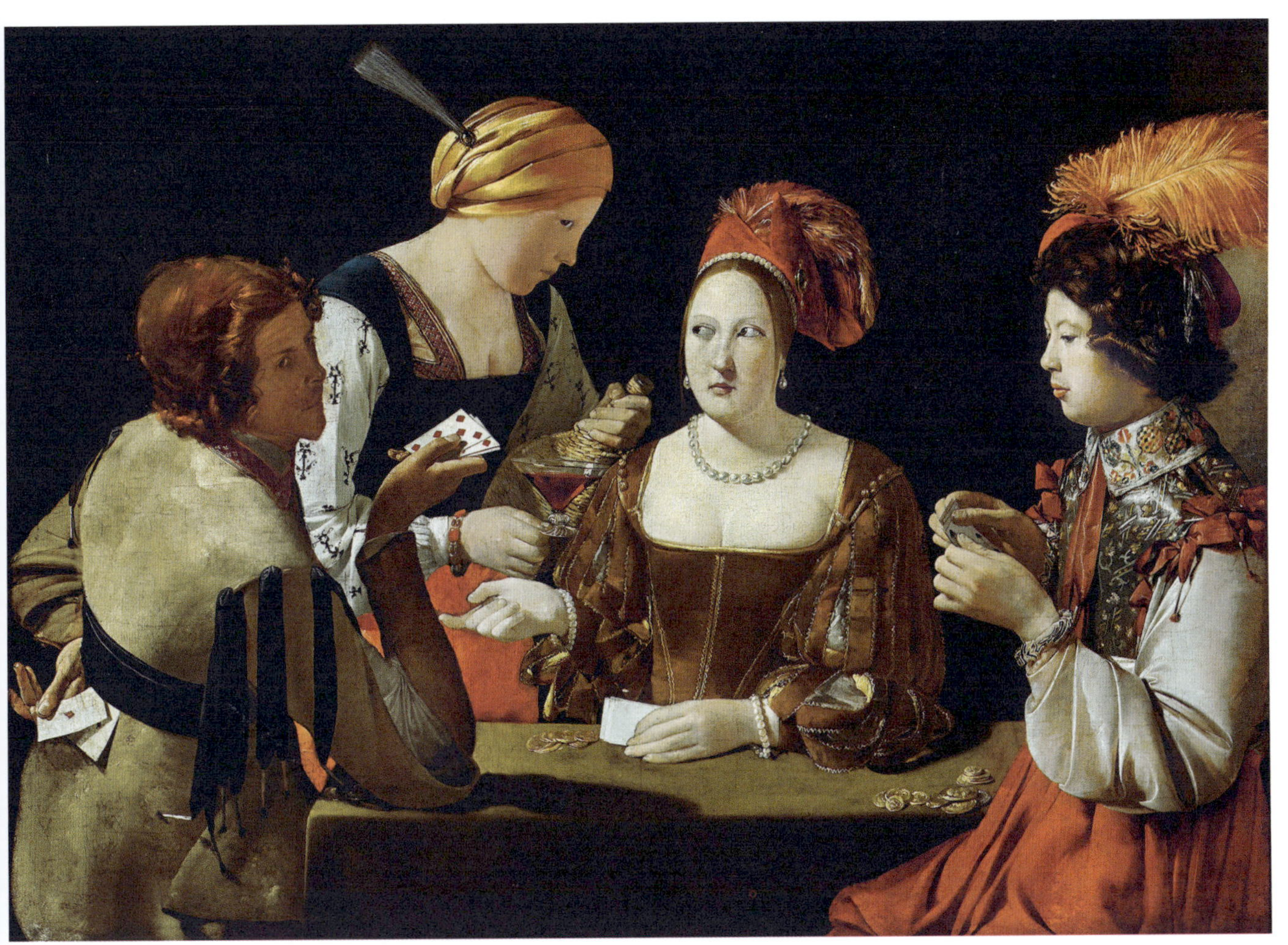

The cheater's ace

A second version of this painting exists in the United States where the ace, hidden by the cheater on the left, is an ace of clubs, not of diamonds. In the course of their existence, both versions were enlarged by a strip located on the upper part. However, only the painting in the Louvre still retains this strip, where the feather of the maid's headdress was extended.

Learn to decipher attributions like a professional

A highly nuanced lingo

**Captions specify the names of the painters.
Sometimes, however, some indications can seem rather difficult to understand.
Here is an overview of the attributions lingo, featuring a practical case study: Rubens.**

The artist at the helm

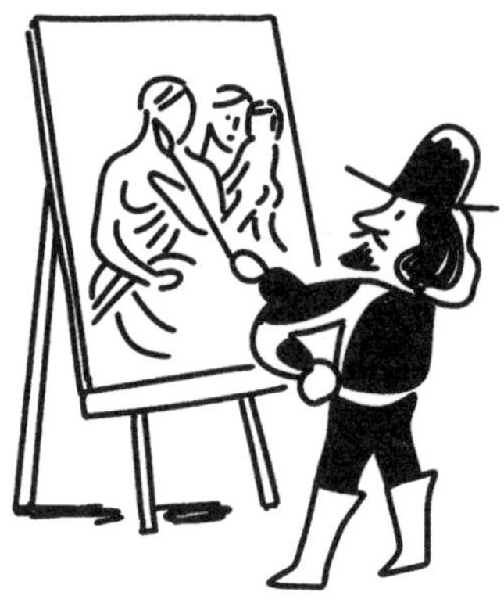

By Rubens

When the title of a work is associated with the artist's name, with no other indication, or when a work is indicated as "by" the artist, the painting was indeed produced by the prince of Flemish baroque.

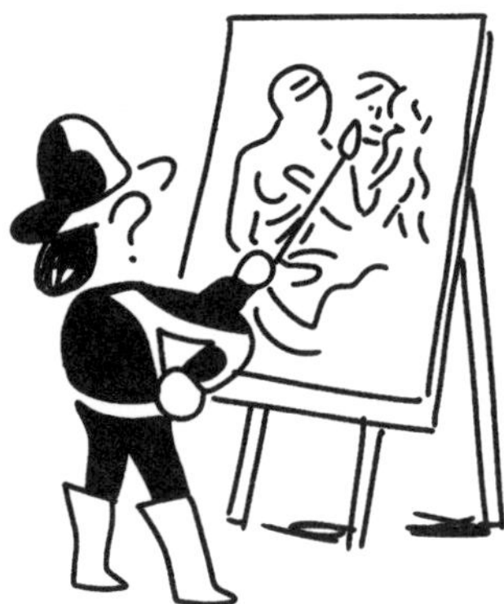

Attributed to Rubens

This indication means that there is a solid chance that this painting was indeed produced "by the hand of", but some doubts remain. When viewing a painting "attributed to", you may indeed be looking at a painting by the master.

EXPERTS AND EXPERTISES

In the absence of the artist's signature or of any document referring to the work, expert eyes are able to identify a master's "touch" and determine whether the artist has intervened in the painting, in whole or in part. However, extensive scientific analyses may also be conducted to assist with authentication (p. 326).

WITH NO LEGAL GUARANTEE

In the absence of identification, the expression **"in the taste of Rubens"** provides some context. This expression refers to a painting that is similar to the style of the master, however, without offering any guarantee that it was painted in the same period or in the same region.

As followers take over

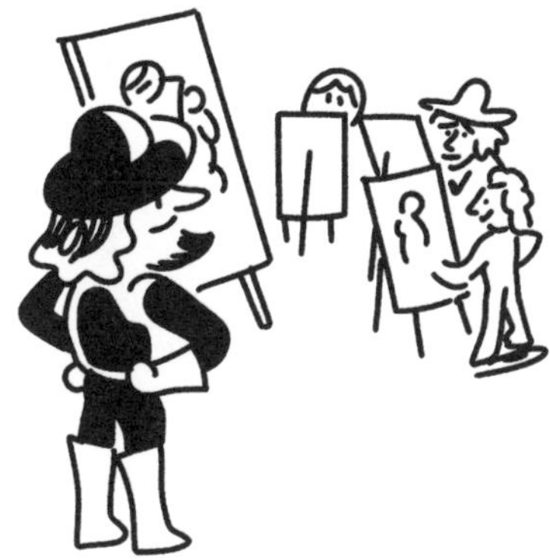

Rubens's studio

Many painters relied on their studio to help them. A painting "from the studio of" means that the work was produced in the artist's studio or under their supervision.

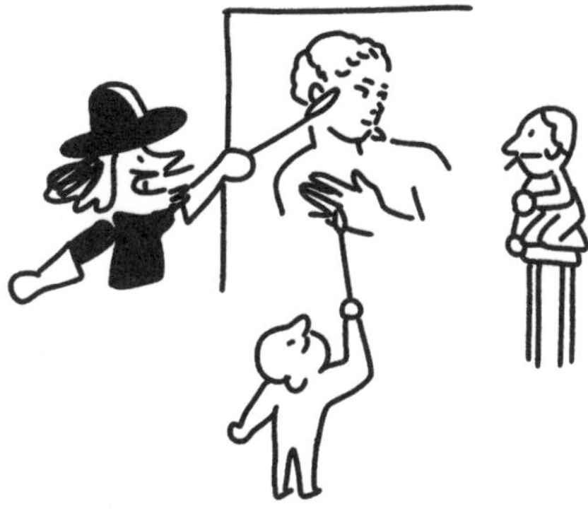

Rubens and studio

This nuance means that the master painted certain parts of the picture (the faces, for example), and entrusted the rest to his studio.

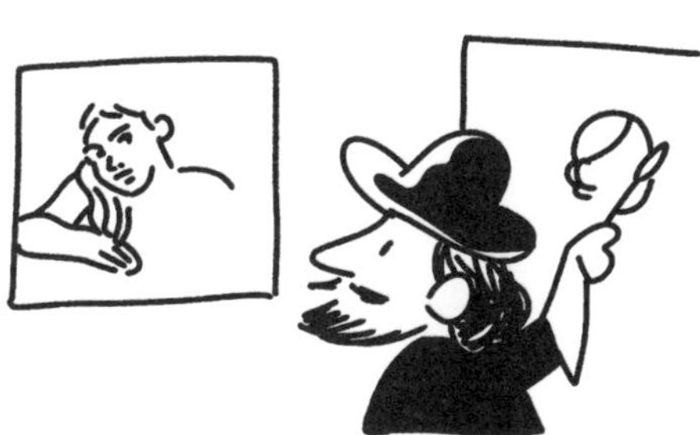

Rubens, after Titian

Artists often learned by copying their elders. A painting by "Rubens, after Titian" is a work of art produced by Rubens, using a painting by Titian as a model.

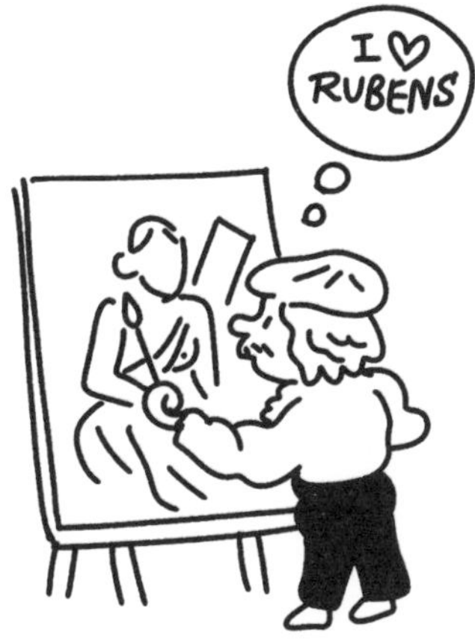

School of Rubens

A portrait from the school of Rubens indicates that the painter benefited from the master's teachings, influence or technique.

The indication "School of Rubens" is valid if the work was produced during Rubens's lifetime or within 50 years of his death, at the most.

Peter Paul Rubens

European before it became a thing

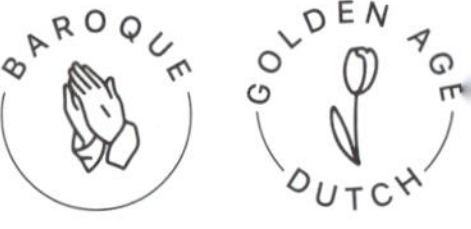

Rubens's paintings are brimming with sensuality. He painted life with tumult, passion and violence; under his brush, flesh became voluptuous, pearly and shaded with blue reflections.

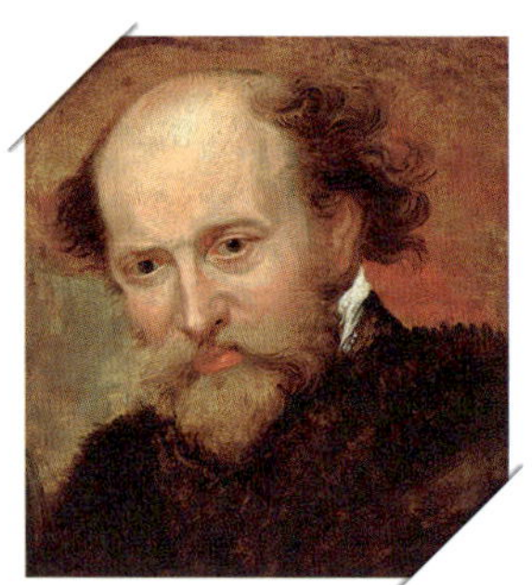

Soft power

Popular with sovereigns, Rubens used his talents for diplomatic purposes. He accompanied official delegations, and used his brush as a lobbying instrument. He travelled all over Europe, settled for a while in Italy, and contributed to peace between the Netherlands, Spain and England.

A business manager

Rubens was highly ambitious and ran a successful studio in Antwerp, which he described as a genuine factory. He surrounded himself with multiple collaborators and apprentices, which he organised to their individual specialities: landscapes, animals, still lifes and others. Many hands contributed to his works.

The artist's muse

Widowed, Rubens remarried at the age of 53 to the young Hélène Fourment. The couple was intimate, and the painter was in love. Hélène became his muse; she would appear in all his paintings, in the guise of a nymph, a goddess or a saint.

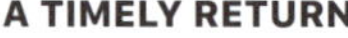

A TIMELY RETURN

After spending eight years in Italy, Rubens moved to Antwerp in 1609. The Twelve Years' Truce and the Counter-Reformation fostered creation. At this time, he founded his prestigious studio.

Georges de La Tour
Page 94

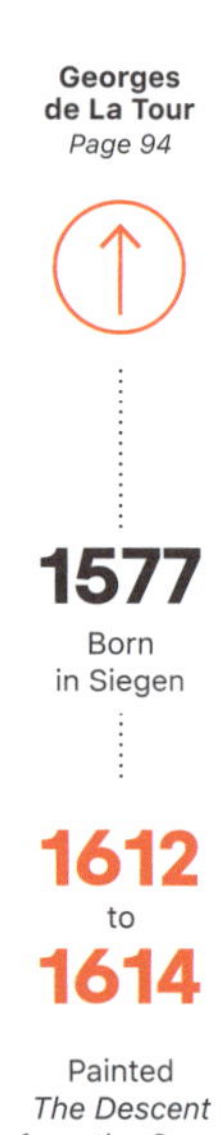

1577
Born in Siegen

1612 to **1614**
Painted *The Descent from the Cross*

1640
Died in Antwerp

1651
The treatise *Le Cuisinier François* marked the history of French gastronomy

1678
Madame de La Fayette published *La Princesse de Clèves*

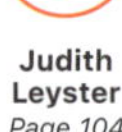

Judith Leyster
Page 104

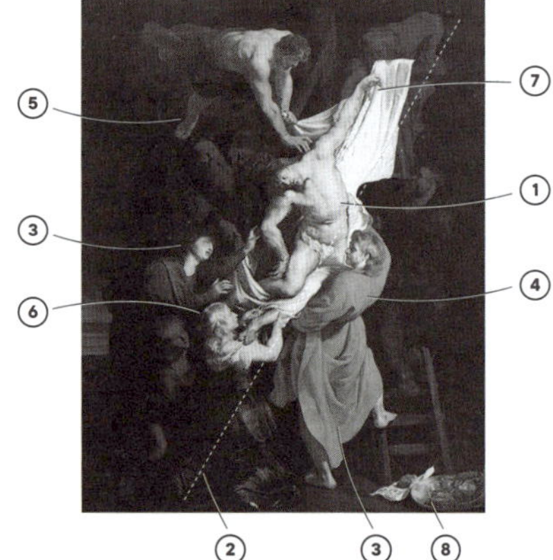

THE DESCENT FROM THE CROSS

1612–1614
Oil on canvas
420 × 310 cm
Cathedral of Our Lady, Antwerp

WHAT ARE WE LOOKING AT?

The Descent from the Cross **represents the moment when the disciples took the lifeless body of Christ down from the cross. It is one of Rubens's most famous paintings, and is an expression of Flemish baroque in all its splendour.**

① A light in the darkness

The pallor of Christ's figure in his shroud contrasts with the work's twilight atmosphere: Rubens sought to remind viewers that Christ is the "light of the world".

② Baroque through and through

A diagonal line produces a dynamic composition, reinforcing the scene's dramatic atmosphere.

③ Holy empathy

The Virgin Mary's face is depicted in the cadaverous hue of her son's body, demonstrating that she shares his pain.

④ That's flashy

The apostle John is depicted with a red coat and a young face. The colour of his outfit contrasts with the monotonous tones of the chiaroscuro, reinforcing the impression of physical proximity to the viewer.

⑤ Background work

In contrast, the disciple's foot, suspended in the void, in the upper left-hand section of the background, provides depth to the composition.

⑥ A memorable foot

Christ's foot rests on Mary Magdalene's shoulder, evoking the passage in the Gospels where she washed Christ's feet and wiped them dry with her hair.

⑦ It looks like it's real

The humanity of the attitudes, the realism of the tears and the bloody wounds invite believers to feel compassion.

⑧ Guilty objects

On the ground, one can see the crown of thorns and the three nails of the torment of Christ; next to them, the parchment that was nailed to the cross, according to Pilate's will, states: "Jesus of Nazareth, King of the Jews."

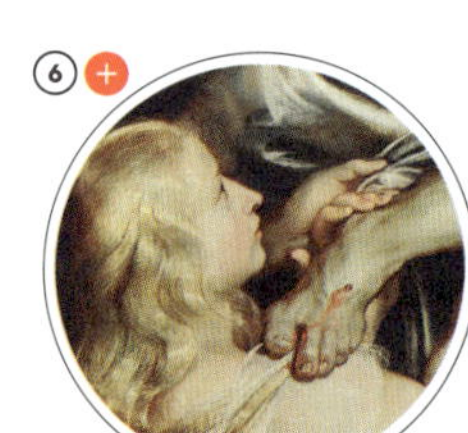

THE DUTCH GOLDEN AGE

The 17th century was a prosperous economic period in the Netherlands. The presence of wealthy patrons coincided with the emergence of exceptional skilled artists, whose fame extended beyond the country's borders. This period was known as the "Dutch Golden Age".

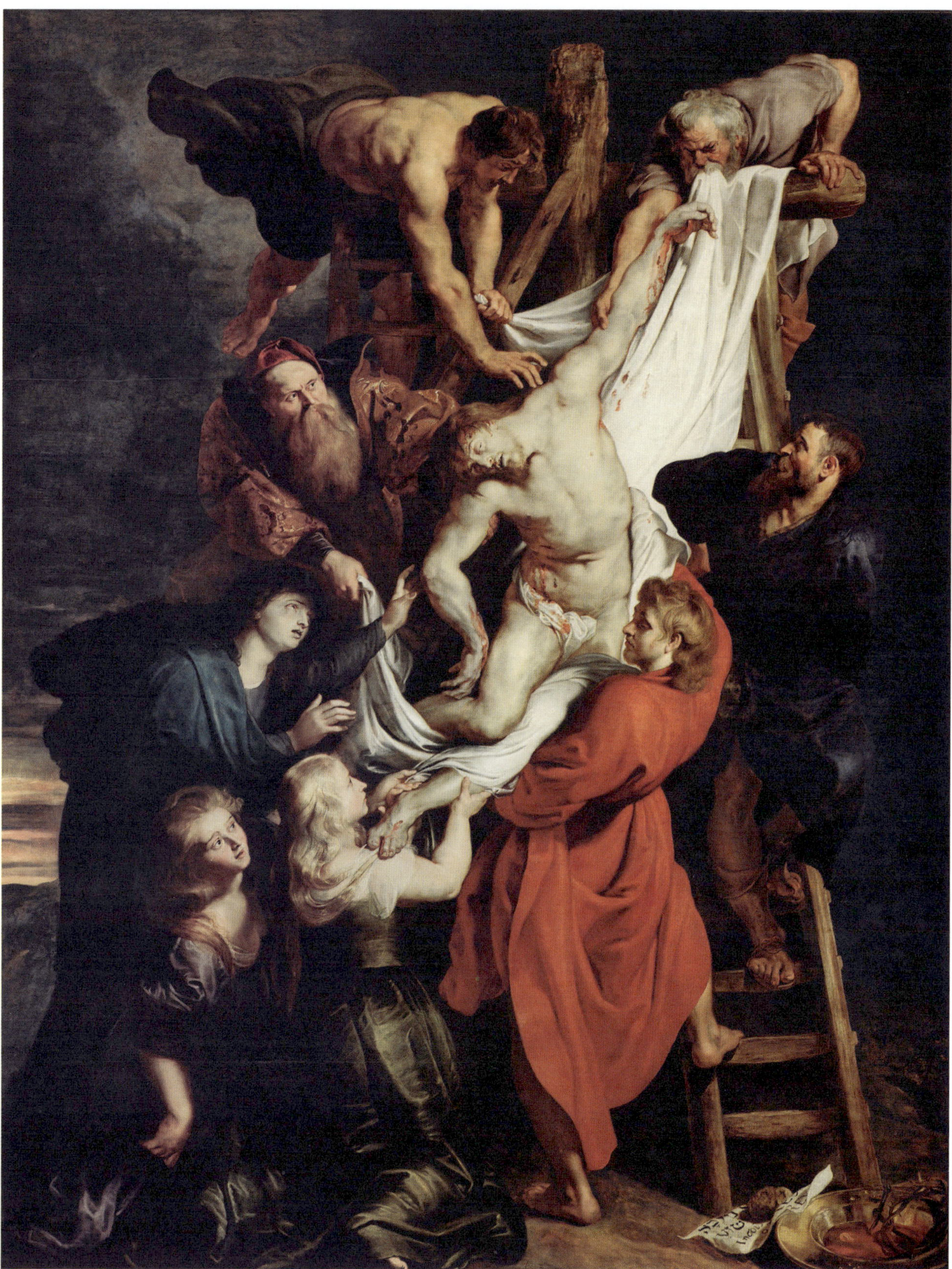

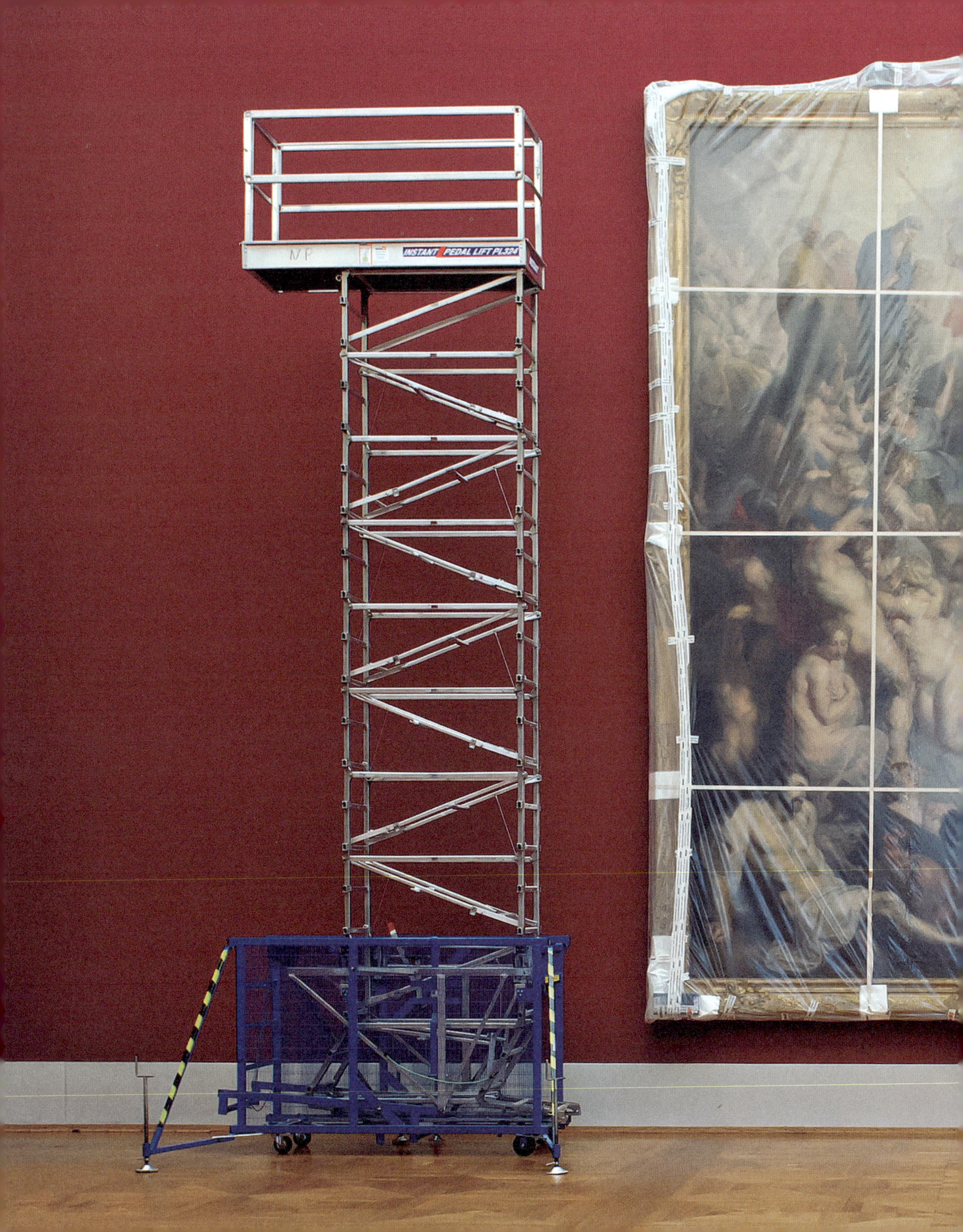
INSTANT PEDAL LIFT PL324

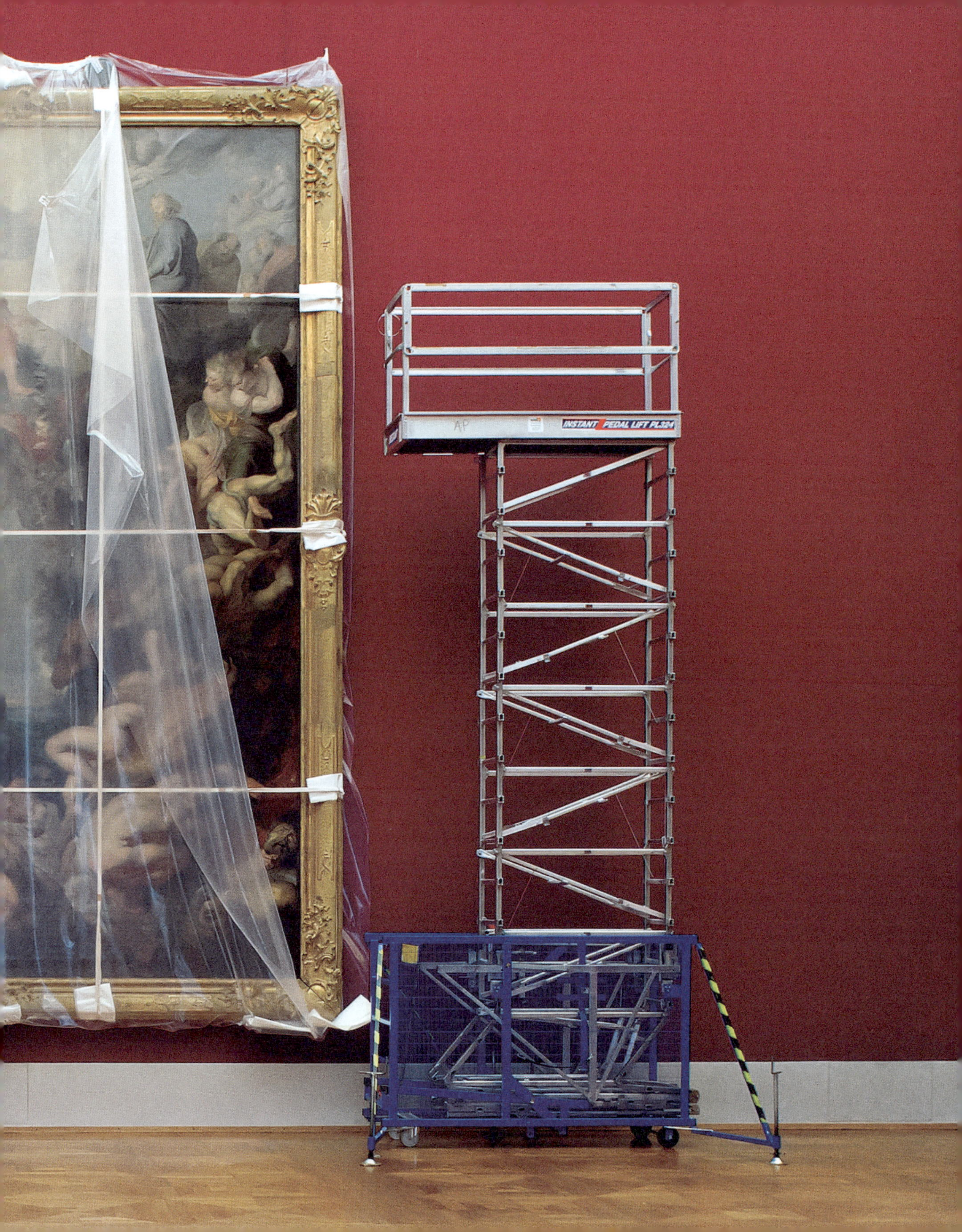
AP
INSTANT PEDAL LIFT PL324

Brueghel, Rubens and Rousseau

Paradises truer than life

Lush, bountiful vegetation, teeming with animals – this is the cliché of Paradise inherited from the Old Testament. While the Flemish painters closely followed the biblical text, Rousseau composed a profane Eden that he invented entirely.

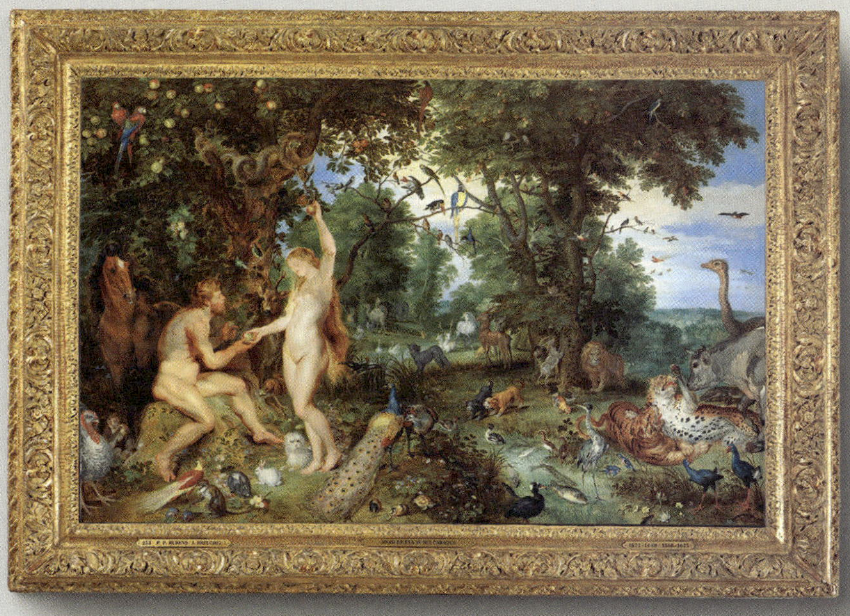

***THE GARDEN OF EDEN* BY JAN BRUEGHEL THE ELDER AND PETER PAUL RUBENS**
1615

This idealised vision of a pastoral scene set in the forest was likely influenced by the natural scenery observed by both painters; however, its peace would be short-lived: Eve is already sharing with Adam the fruit that she picked from the tree of knowledge, under the serpent's malevolent gaze.

Oil on wood, 74.3 × 114.7 cm
Mauritshuis, The Hague

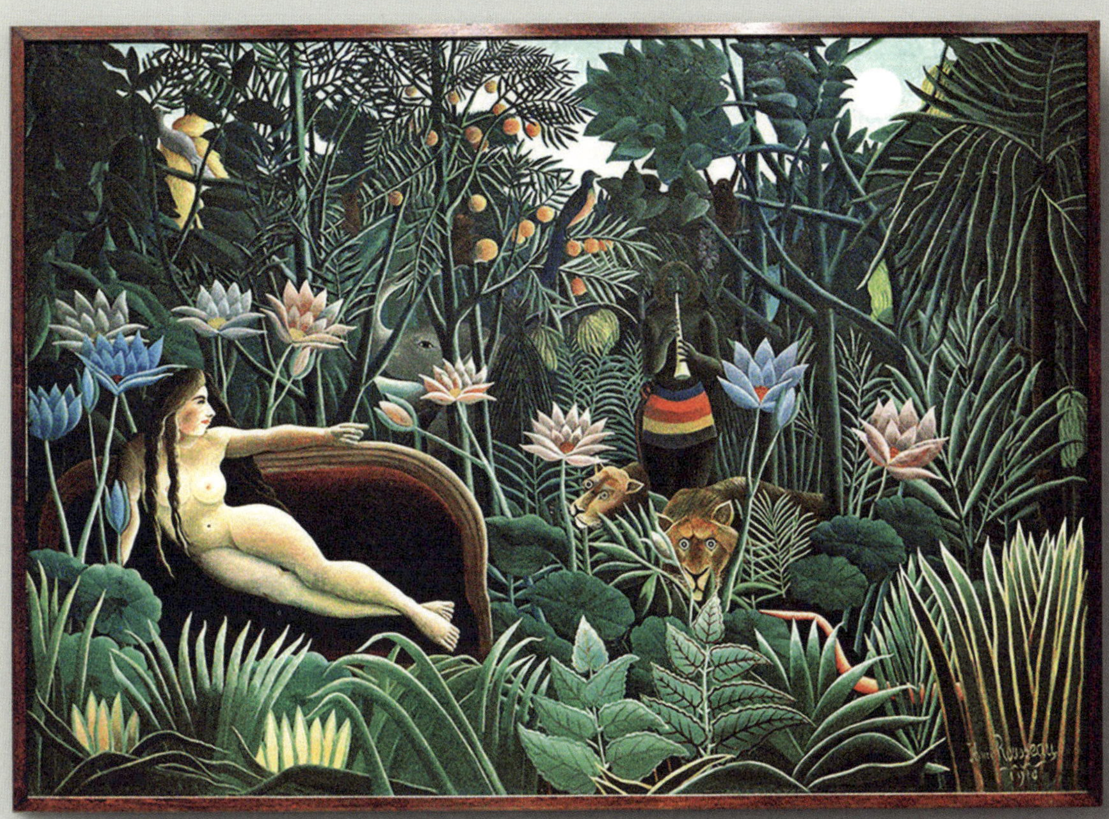

***THE DREAM* BY HENRI ROUSSEAU**
1910

Rousseau never travelled outside France. The jungles that he painted were influenced by magazines and his visits to the Jardin des Plantes, in Paris. The sofa, an incongruous item, proves that this scene is a dream. Its owner has probably fallen asleep in it, and has been transported to this wonderful world.

Oil on canvas, 204.5 × 298.5 cm
MoMA, New York

Judith Leyster
A brush with flair

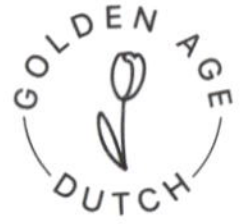

Leyster was one of the greatest female artists of the Dutch Golden Age. Her intelligence, her business acumen and her painting skills enabled her to distinguish herself in a profession saturated by men.

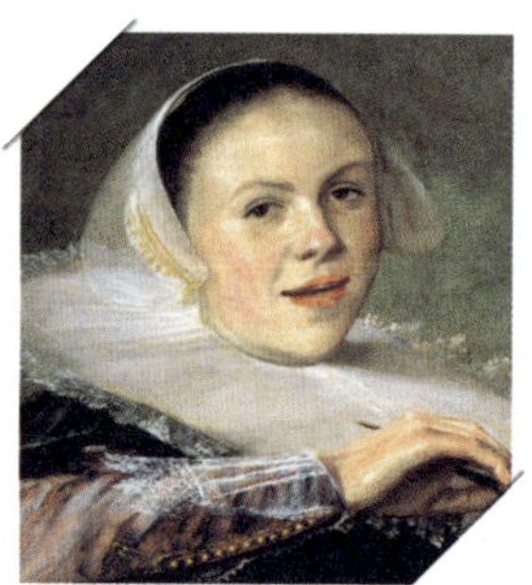

The exception to the rule

A rare occurrence for a painter in Haarlem, Judith Leyster was not born into a family of artists. This did not prevent her from asserting herself in a predominantly male environment, however. She joined the painters' guild, where she was the only woman to own a studio.

The businesswoman

Leyster had a solid market perception. She did not seek to invent a style, but rather to produce fashionable images that would sell well. By producing paintings in modest formats, she appealed to the middle class, who purchased artworks at reasonable prices.

A real star

She developed her reputation by signing her works with an "L", followed by a star (*Leyster* can be translated as "leading star"). When she married, however, her name disappeared in favour of her husbands, also a painter. She would nonetheless continue to paint, while also playing an active role in his business.

TRADE UNION MEMBERS

The guilds or academies of Saint Luke, the patron saint of painters, are local guilds that enable artists to defend their interests collectively.

Peter Paul Rubens
Page 98

1609
Born in Haarlem

Circa
1629
Painted *The Last Drop*

1660
Died in Heemstede

1673
Molière died after the performance of *Le Malade Imaginaire.*

1687
The English mathematician Newton theorised universal gravitation

Johannes Vermeer
Page 106

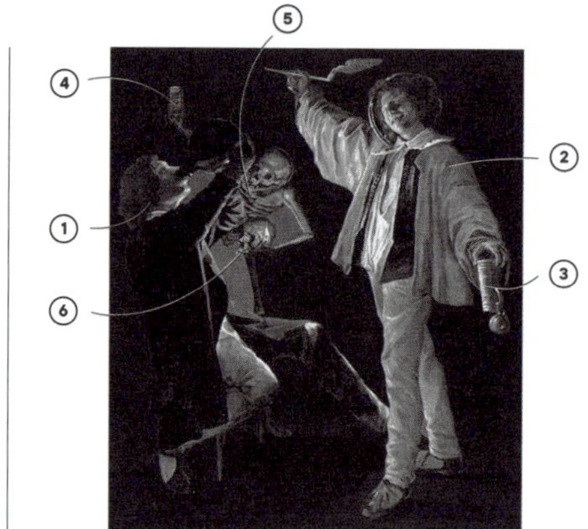

THE LAST DROP
(OR THE GAY CAVALIER)

Circa 1629
Oil on canvas
89.1 × 73.5 cm
Philadelphia Museum of Art, Philadelphia

WHAT ARE WE LOOKING AT?

These two men, who are partying, appear to be unaware of the sinister skeleton in their company. Its presence turns this genre scene into a vanitas (p. 110).

① To the dregs

The drinker is tipping his jug, drinking it to the last drop. Visibly inebriated, he is attempting to steady himself by awkwardly spreading his legs.

② Drunk as a skunk

His companion's silly expression is amusing, and leaves little doubt that he too is drunk. His undone clothes convey his decadence.

③ Things in hand

The smoker is brandishing items that are typically associated with the vice of drinking. In his left hand, he is holding an overturned tankard; it is empty, meaning that he has drunk his fill. In his other hand, he is holding a lit pipe, a symbol of an existence that is going up in smoke.

④ Time flies ...

The skeleton is a representation of death. It is looking closely at the drinkers, and appears to gleefully contemplate the man who is greedily emptying the jug. It is holding a candle and an hourglass, symbols of the transience of life. This scene is a vanitas.

⑤ Seeing double

In the Middle Ages and the Renaissance, death was represented by a skeleton, then reduced to its most basic embodiment: a skull. By depicting both, Leyster is emphasising the message she wants to convey to the viewer.

⑥ The last one before a long time

The lit candle places this scene at night. The undone suit worn by the figure on the right tells us that the two men may be celebrating Shrove Tuesday before fasting for Lent.

⑤ +

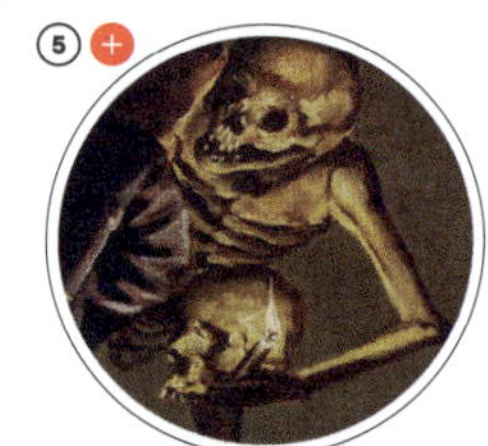

DOUBLE-EDGED

Leyster's works were influenced by the painter Frans Hals. The latter's popularity helped ensure Leyster's return from oblivion in the 20th century; however, her works were often attributed to her colleague, before being rightfully returned to her.

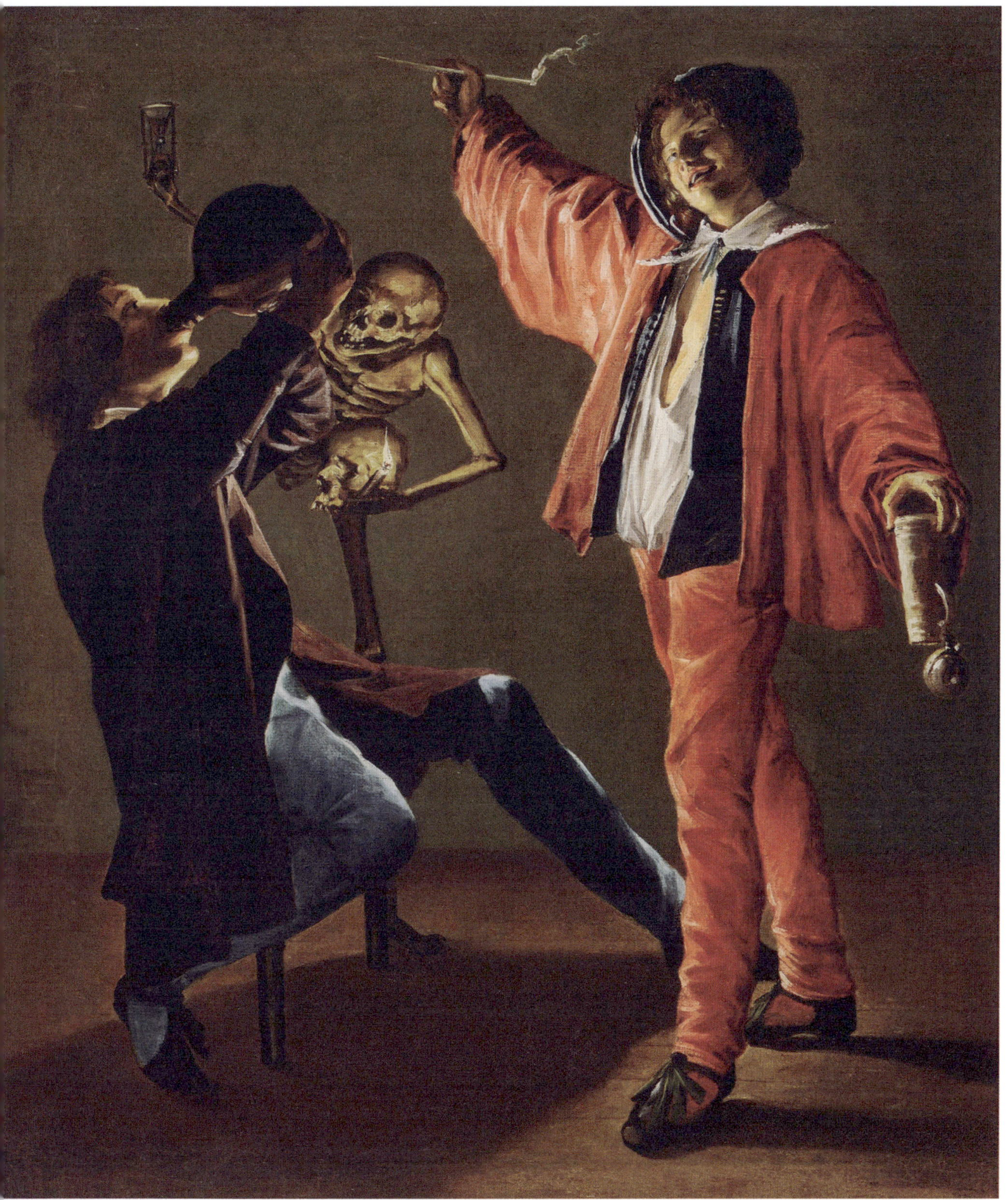

Johannes Vermeer

And the ordinary becomes extraordinary

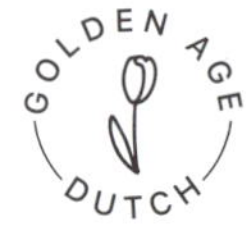

Despite the limited number of works attributed to him and a life that remains somewhat shrouded in mystery, Vermeer was celebrated throughout the world. While his genre scenes earned the admiration of wealthy patrons, this would not be enough to save him from difficult times towards the end of his life.

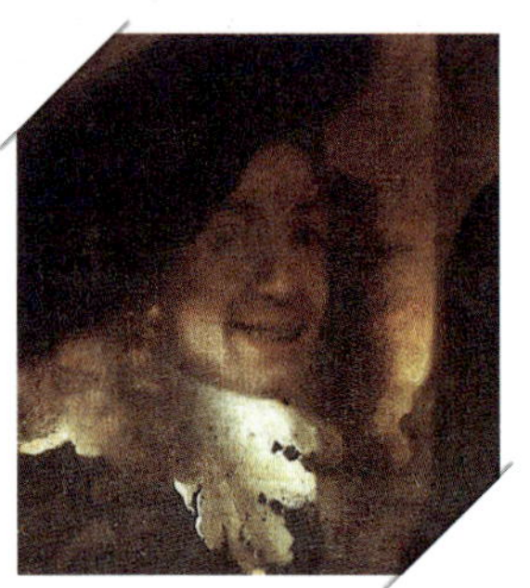

An enigmatic beginning

There is very little written information on Vermeer's life. No preparatory drawings or sketches were found after his death, and only about thirty identified works of his exist today. This mystery has earned him the nickname of the "Sphinx of Delft".

A high-end clientele

Vermeer likely belonged to the Delft elite. His clients were wealthy patrons, including Van Ruijven, who possessed a large collection of his works. However, the war between Holland and France left the painter with meagre resources to feed his eleven children.

A silence worth its weight in gold

Vermeer was celebrated for his genre scenes (p. 166). He painted well-arranged, hushed interiors, in which mostly middle-class women are engaged in music or writing alone, in gallant company or accompanied by a female servant.

DISSATISFIED?

Dazzled by Vermeer's *View of Delft*, Bergotte, the protagonist created by Marcel Proust, compared his writing to this painting: "My last books are too dry, I ought to have gone over them with a few layers of colour, made my language precious in itself, like this little patch of yellow wall."

Judith Leyster
Page 104

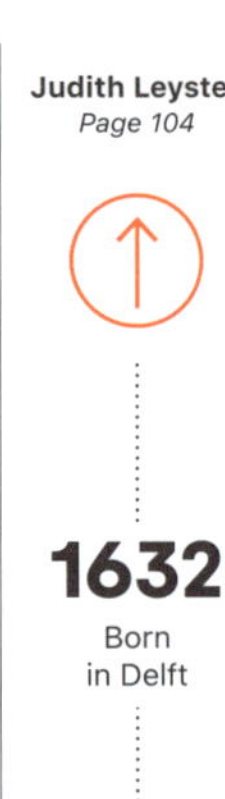

1632
Born in Delft

1636
First performance of *Le Cid* by Corneille

Circa
1660
Painted *The Milkmaid*

1670
Madame de Montespan officially became the mistress of Louis XIV

1675
Died in Delft

Rachel Ruysch
Page 108

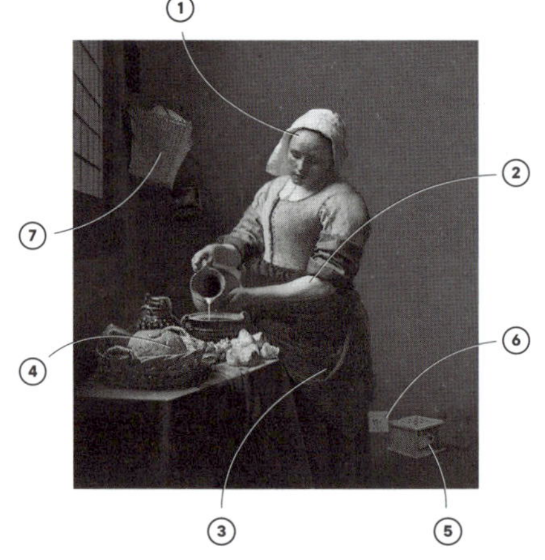

THE MILKMAID

Circa 1660
Oil on canvas
45.5 × 41 cm
Rijksmuseum, Amsterdam

WHAT ARE WE LOOKING AT?

In this genre scene, Vermeer has depicted a servant, rather than a bourgeois woman. She is pouring milk into a bowl, with conscientious dedication.

① Do not disturb

The milkmaid's face stands out against the fabrics that she is dressed with. The impasto of the brushstrokes on her forehead highlight her presence, emphasising her beautiful concentration.

② Work that takes a toll

She is wearing work sleeves that reveal her skin. The whiteness of her arms contrasts with the complexion of her hands, reddened by domestic chores.

③ An overpriced apron

This deep blue hue is obtained from lapis lazuli, a very expensive pigment that may have been purchased for the painter by his patron Van Ruijven.

④ Let's eat!

The transparent, irregularly flowing milk and the loaves of bread in the foreground form an appetising still life for the viewer. This appeal to the senses echoes the servant's corseted sensuality.

⑤ A warm underside

The small stove is both a testimony to everyday domestic life and a sexual allusion: women would place their feet on it, so that the heat would rise up under their petticoats.

⑥ Ambiguous love

One of the tiles in the plinth features a Cupid, recognisable by his bow. This symbol reinforces the sensual interpretation of the scene. However, painted tiles were common at the time, so its presence may be entirely coincidental.

⑦ Hanging hamper

With the suspended objects, the painter seized the opportunity to display his talent in the rendering of textures. The juxtaposition of matt wicker and shiny copper creates a nice contrast.

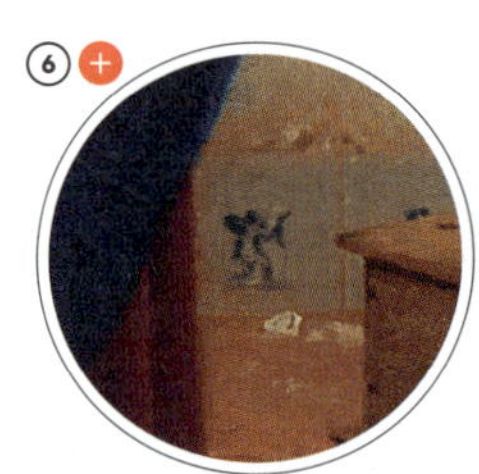

LEADING FIGURES OF THE DUTCH GOLDEN AGE

- Johannes Vermeer
- Peter Paul Rubens (p. 98)
- Jacob Jordaens (1593–1678)
- Judith Leyster (p. 104)
- Anthony Van Dyck (p. 114)
- Frans Hals (1582–1666)
- Rembrandt (p. 118)
- Rachel Ruysch (p. 108)

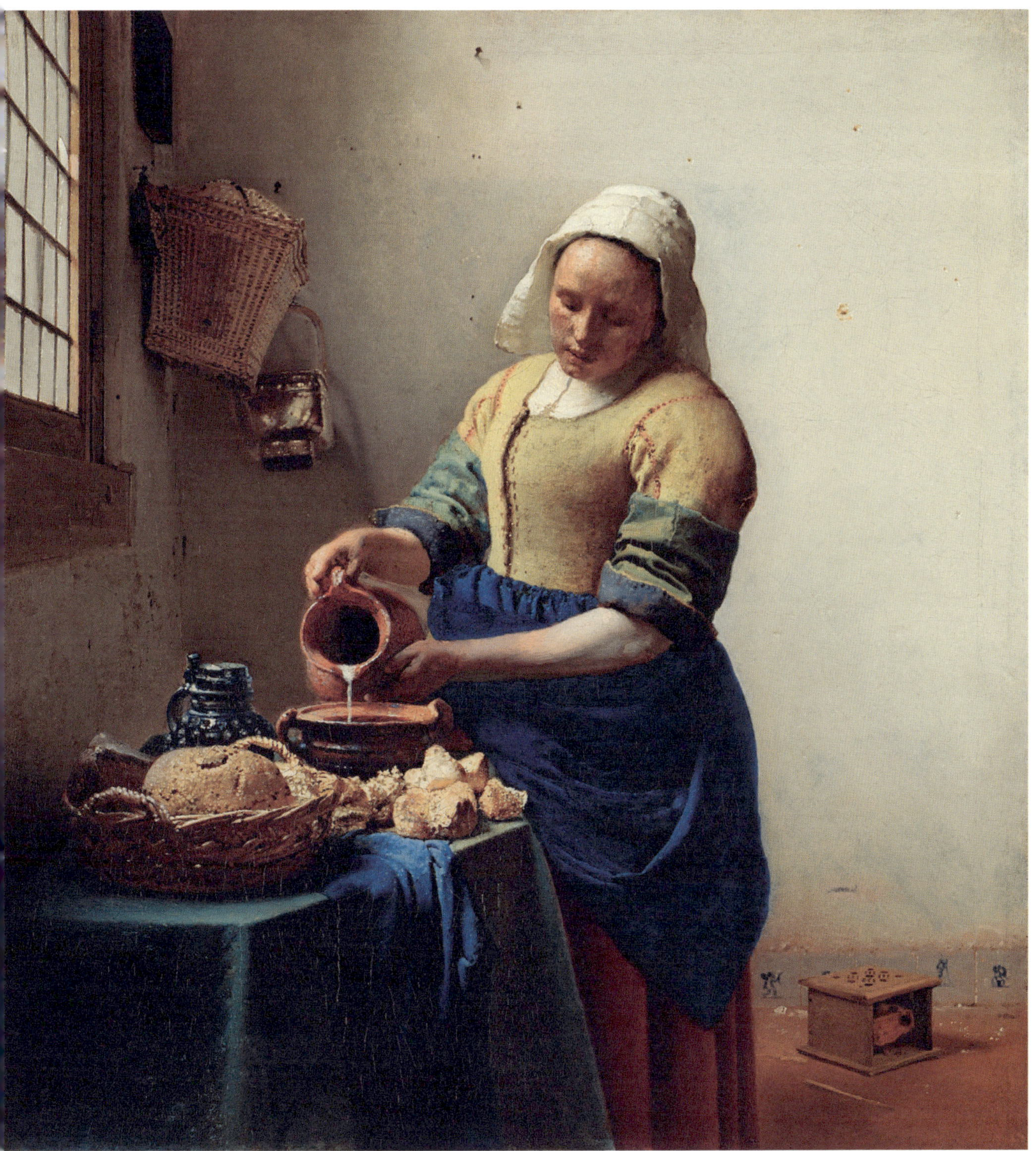

Rachel Ruysch

The fine flower of Dutch painting

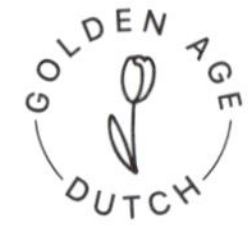

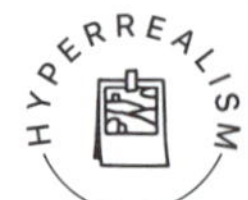

**Ruysch was the best still life painter in Amsterdam. Her talent, inspired by her father's botanical activities, earned her a renown beyond her country's borders.
She sold her works at very high prices to the European nobility.**

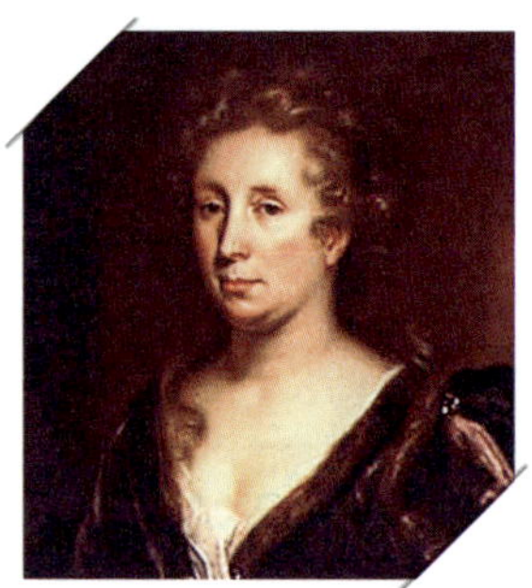

A debut at home

From childhood, Ruysch closely observed, then copied the flowers and plants collected by her father, a professor of anatomy and botany. At the age of 15, showing remarkable abilities, she was admitted into the studio of Willem Van Aelst.

A flourishing career

Her depictions of elegant bouquets in vases resting on marble borders were met with success. The painter continued to work until the end of her life, even after giving birth to ten children – a rare occurrence among female artists of her time.

A good turn from a patron

Wealthy collectors and aristocrats couldn't get enough of Ruysch's works, which she sold for high prices. So remarkable was her talent that she was granted a pension by the German Prince John William of Neuburg-Wittelsbach; he didn't even require that she live in Germany, provided that she sent him one painting every year.

EVERY WINNER TRIED THEIR LUCK

At the age of 59, Ruysch and her husband won 75,000 guilders in a lottery. Money would never be an issue for her.

Johannes Vermeer
Page 106

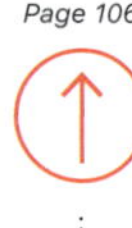

1664
Born in The Hague

1711
Painted *Still-Life with Fruit, Flowers, and Insects*

1721
Montesquieu published *Persian Letters*

1750
Died in Amsterdam

1775
The United States entered the War of Independence.

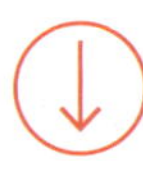

Diego Velázquez
Page 112

STILL-LIFE WITH FRUIT, FLOWERS, AND INSECTS ↗

1711
Oil on canvas
87 × 69.5 cm
Private collection

WHAT ARE WE LOOKING AT?

This magnificent still life, featuring sun-drenched fruit, conceals a religious message. It is, in fact, a vanitas (p. 110).

Luxury at low prices

In the 17th century Netherlands, flowers were a mark of opulence. Still lifes cost less than natural flowers, and allowed their owners to enjoy unlikely bouquets comprising extraordinary varieties throughout the year, regardless of the season.

A reliable recipe

For this composition, Ruysch was inspired by Otto Marseus Van Schrieck, who popularised still lifes representing undergrowth teeming with insects and creepy crawlies ready to devour one another. Here, Ruysch combined them with sun-drenched, sweet fruits that whet the viewer's appetite.

Fruits of passion

The choice and juxtaposition of the fruits leave no doubt as to the religious interpretation of this painting. The ears of wheat evoke bread, and thus the body of Christ, while the grapes are the symbol of his blood. Next to the grapes, the red colour of the pomegranate seeds reminds us of the passion of Christ and the resurrection.

A halftone image

The perishable fruits and ephemeral insects also symbolise the transience of existence. The ray of sunlight illuminating this still life contrasts with the ominous black background and, in the foreground, the shadow that threatens to spread as the radiant star sets. All things must come to an end.

TULIP MANIA IN THE 17TH CENTURY

To denounce the exorbitant price of tulips, in 1636, a pamphlet circulated, describing everything that could be purchased for 2,500 guilders.

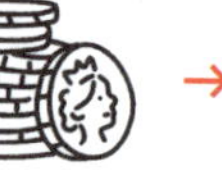

→

Several tons of wheat and rye
4 fat oxen
8 pigs, 12 sheep
casks of wine and beer
2 tonnes of butter
3 tonnes of cheese
1 bed with sheets
1 wardrobe
1 silver vase

→

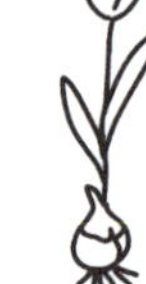

By comparison, at the time, a rare Semper Augustus *tulip bulb could fetch up to 13,000 guilders!*

PAINTERS FAMOUS FOR THEIR STILL LIFES

- Pieter Claesz (circa 1597–1661)
- Louise Moillon (1609/10–1696)
- Jean Siméon Chardin (p. 144)
- Henri Fantin-Latour (1836–1904)
- Paul Cézanne (p. 242)
- Henri Matisse (p. 262)

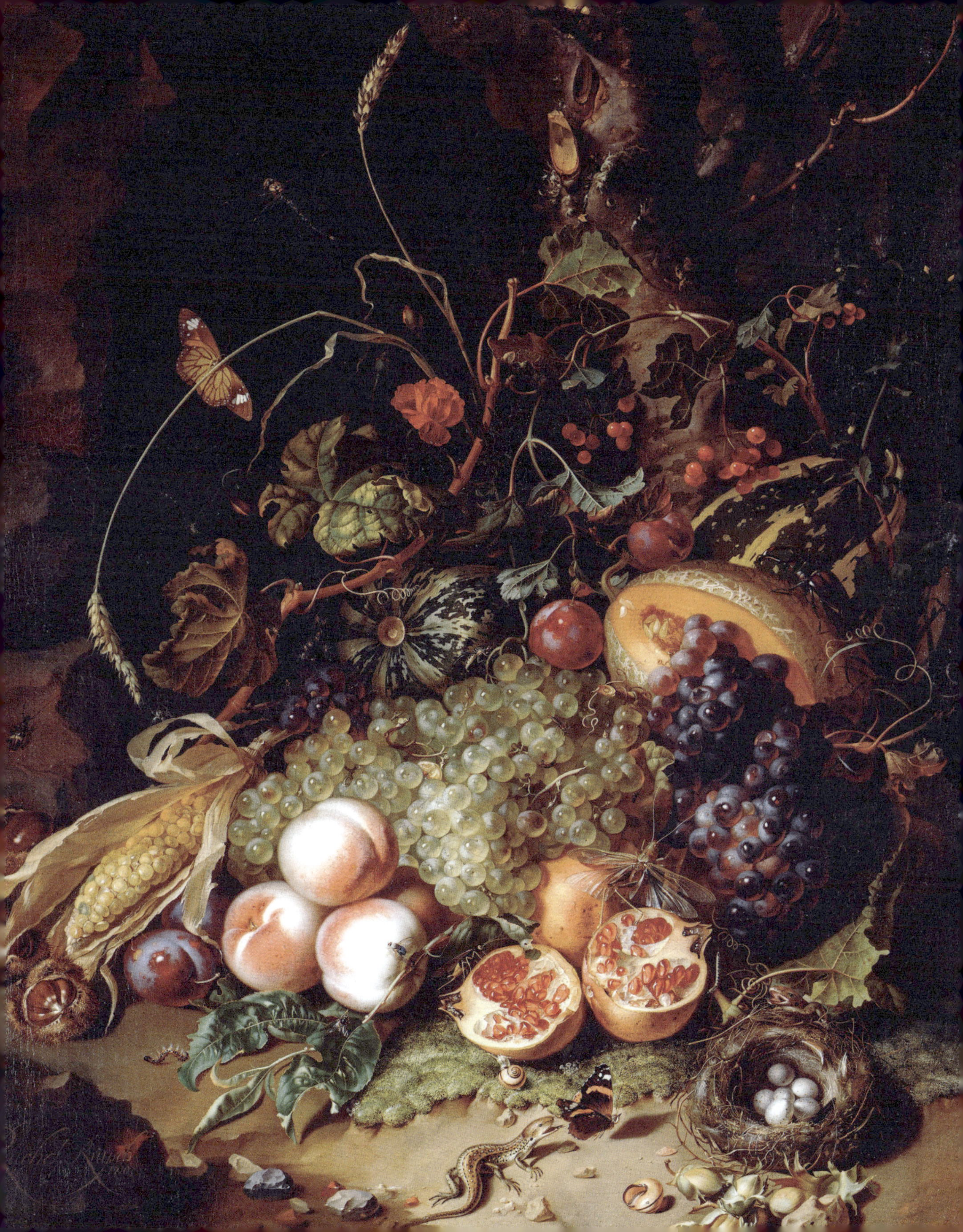

When vanities tame death

Skulls and paintings

The representation of death has always been a feature of the history of painting. From the 17th century onward, death was often represented in a "vanitas", a tradition born in northern Europe, which conveyed a religious and moral message.

Representing death

Originating in the Protestant countries of northern Europe in the 17th century, a vanitas traditionally featured a still life with a skull. The skull motif is derived from the representation of death in the Middle Ages. This representation first appeared in Dances of Death (or "Danses Macabres"), which featured skeletons dragging the living to their deaths.

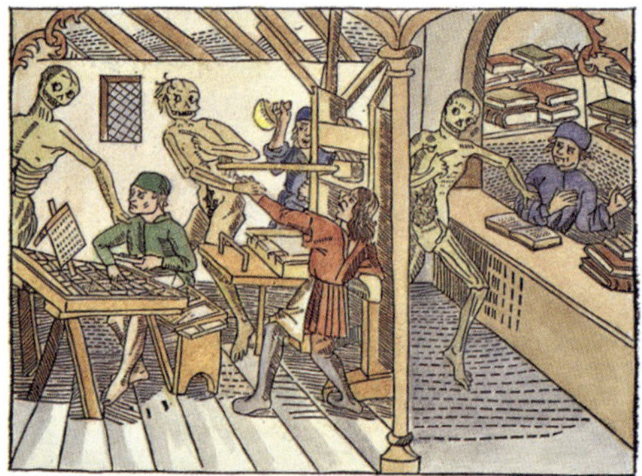

SKULLS AND SKELETONS

The skeleton itself became an allegory of Death. The dancing attitudes in which it is often depicted may be confusing, but they testify to how familiar the living were with death, in the past. Indeed, death was an integral part of their daily lives, due to wars, epidemics and infant mortality.

Mathias Huss

Death Taking the Printers and a Bookseller,
coloured engraving, 1499,
private collection

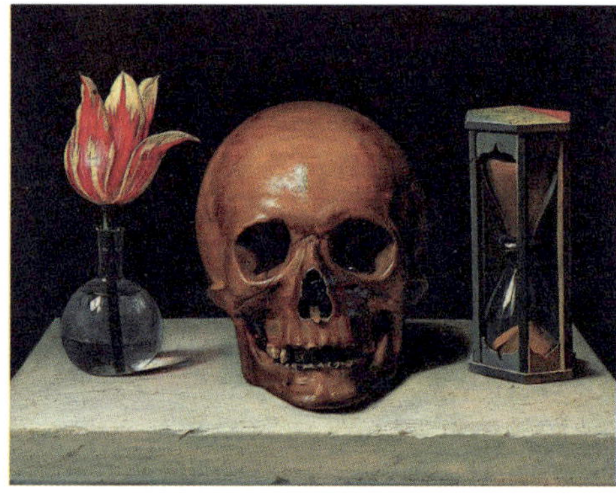

A LESSON IN LIFE

A vanitas is not only an evocation of death, but also a lesson in life. By reminding us of its transience, a vanitas encourages the viewer to lead an exemplary life, and to use the time available to them here on Earth for essential actions. A vanitas is also, by contrast, a means of denouncing the vices and futility of human nature.

Philippe de Champaigne

Still-Life with a Skull
17th century vanitas,
Musée de Tessé, Le Mans

VANITAS AND *MEMENTO MORI*, TWO SIDES OF A SAME COIN

The name "vanitas" may seem strange, so far removed is it from the meaning that we give the word "vanity" today. It originates in "Vanity of vanities; all is vanity", the words that introduce the book of Ecclesiastes (Old Testament), a text that invites the faithful to enjoy life with wisdom. It is also the meaning of *memento mori*, a Latin locution, which conveys the same message. These words mean "Remember that you will die", a synonym for "vanity".

Symbols to be decoded

The notion of death is also reflected in other symbols evoking the transience of life. It can also be featured in religious paintings and depictions of genre scenes. Its explicit representation may be abstracted when the painter wishes to emphasise the necessary morality of human existence.

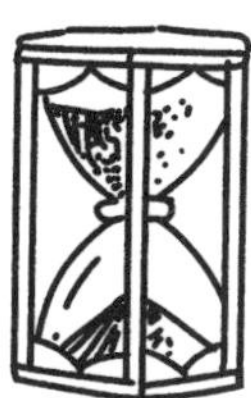

Hourglass

The hourglass is a classic motif: it evokes the brevity of the time that is available to us on Earth, and the necessity to find meaning in one's life.

Candle

With its melting wax, the candle reminds us of the passing of time and the burning of life. Does one not say, "burning the candle at both ends"?

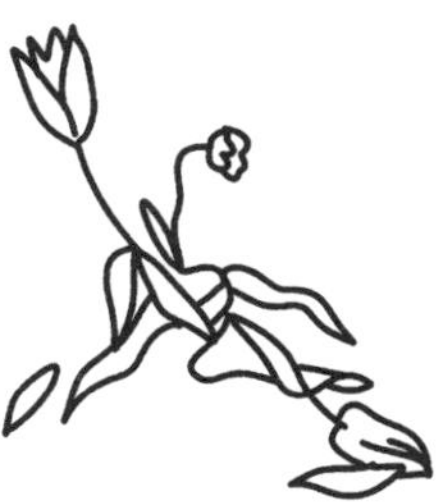

Flowers

They are often depicted for their ephemeral beauty. They reflect attraction for futile earthly pleasures, of which nothing remains after death.

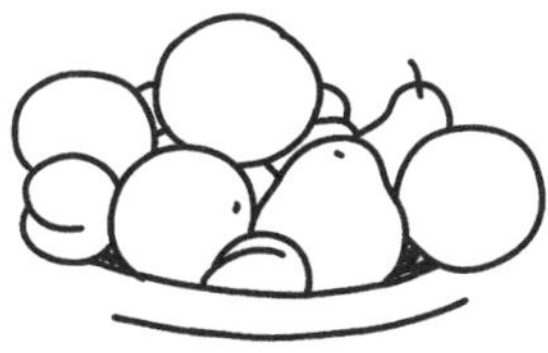

Fruit

Fruit evokes immediate pleasures that spoil over time. It is sometimes associated with insects, symbolising the decay of flesh.

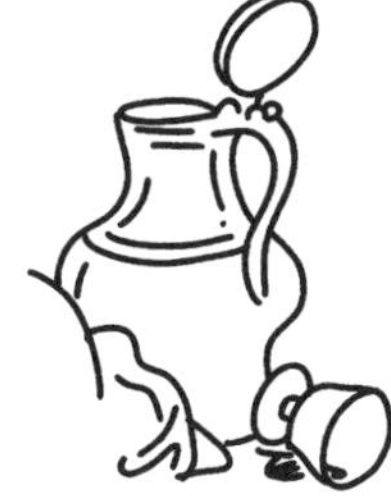

Alcohol

It evokes vice. Depicted as opened or empty bottles, its presence denounces unreasonable consumption. It sometimes associated with gambling and lust.

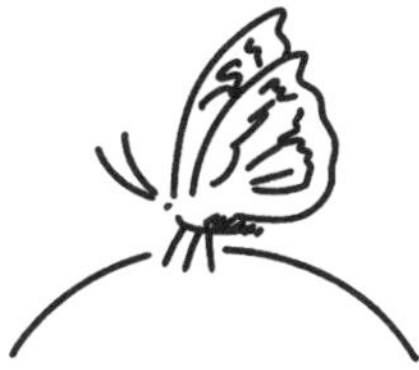

Butterfly

This insect carries an ambiguous message. It is, par excellence, the symbol of the ephemeral nature of life, but it may also evoke the resurrection – the journey of man into another world.

Books

According to their nature and position, open or closed, they convey different messages: the manifestation of a pious life spent in meditation or the pride of man's knowledge, as he attempts to surpass God.

Diego Velázquez

In his majesty's service

Velázquez was the greatest painter of the Spanish Golden Age. His portraits were based on colour and light. This precocious talent would earn him the admiration of the king of Spain and of many painters after him, such as Manet and Picasso.

In the big league

From the very beginning, Velázquez surpassed the painters of Seville, who would copy his works out of envy or admiration. He was then introduced to the King of Spain, and soon became his portraitist.

Inclusive diversity

Aristocrats, philosophers, dwarfs or jesters – Velázquez confronted his science of portraiture with numerous models. He rendered the physiognomy of people without any judgement of value, and attempted to capture, with his brush, the depth of human nature.

In good form

In Italy, he would extensively copy Raphael (p. 46) and Michelangelo (p. 54). He was impressed by Caravaggio's modernity (p. 78); however, it was Titian (p. 62) whom he admired the most. Velázquez was a talented colourist: he created tones and textures using all the possibilities offered by pigments, and treated light and black tones with great sensitivity.

INCOGNITO

Velázquez would only rarely sign or date his paintings, which greatly complicated the study of his works.

Rachel Ruysch
Page 108

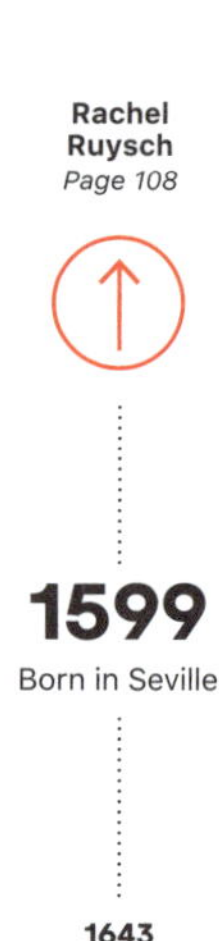

1599
Born in Seville

1643
Evangelista Torricelli invented the barometer

1656
Painted *Las Meninas*

1659
The Treaty of the Pyrenees brought a 27-year war between France and Spain to an end

1660
Died in Madrid

Anthony Van Dyck
Page 114

LAS MENINAS

1656
Oil on canvas
320.5 × 281.5 cm
Prado Museum, Madrid

WHAT ARE WE LOOKING AT?

This dynastic portrait was commissioned by the king to show off the infanta Margarita, heir to the crown, but Velázquez was required to modify the painting when a male heir was born.

① Harsh competition

At the time of the commission, the five-year-old infanta Margarita was presented as the heir to royal power. However, the birth of her younger brother would change the situation. Here, the infanta is surrounded by her attendants, the Meninas, to whom this painting owes its name.

② *Photobombing*

The painter has layered sources of light to create a sense of depth in the picture, all the way up to the door at the back, through which the queen's chamberlain can be seen.

③ One ring to rule them all

Dwarfs were present in European courts. Here, the dwarf Maribarbola is making a strange gesture: in her hand, she was holding a ring representing the power held by the infanta, but Velázquez erased it.

④ Product placement

The painter boldly represented himself in the painting. In his place stood a page, who was presenting a baton of command to the infanta. As he was required to remove this item, Velázquez took the opportunity to produce a new version of the painting, in which he appears to be looking at the viewer, as if they were posing as a model.

⑤ A well thought-out trick

Velázquez is in fact looking at the queen and the king: they can be seen in the mirror at the back. This artifice, featured in the painting since its creation, served to bring the infanta closer to her parents; with this skilful transformation of his work, however, Velázquez reversed the scene: he appears to be painting the portrait of the couple while the infanta visits them.

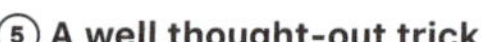

③ +

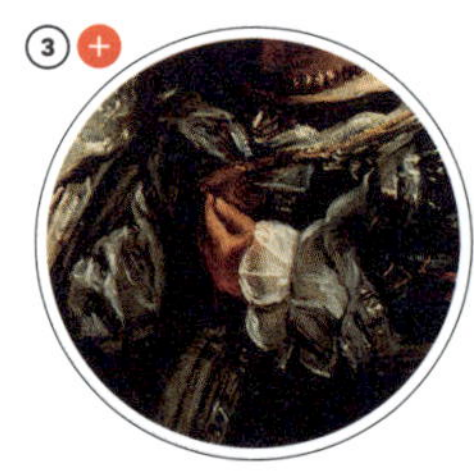

THE SPANISH GOLDEN AGE

In the 17th century, Spain became a wealthy and conquering nation, and experienced a Golden Age. Buzzing with life, the nation birthed great authors, such as Cervantes, and great artists, such as Velázquez, Zurbarán, Murillo and El Greco. The emulation between these artists radiated throughout Europe.

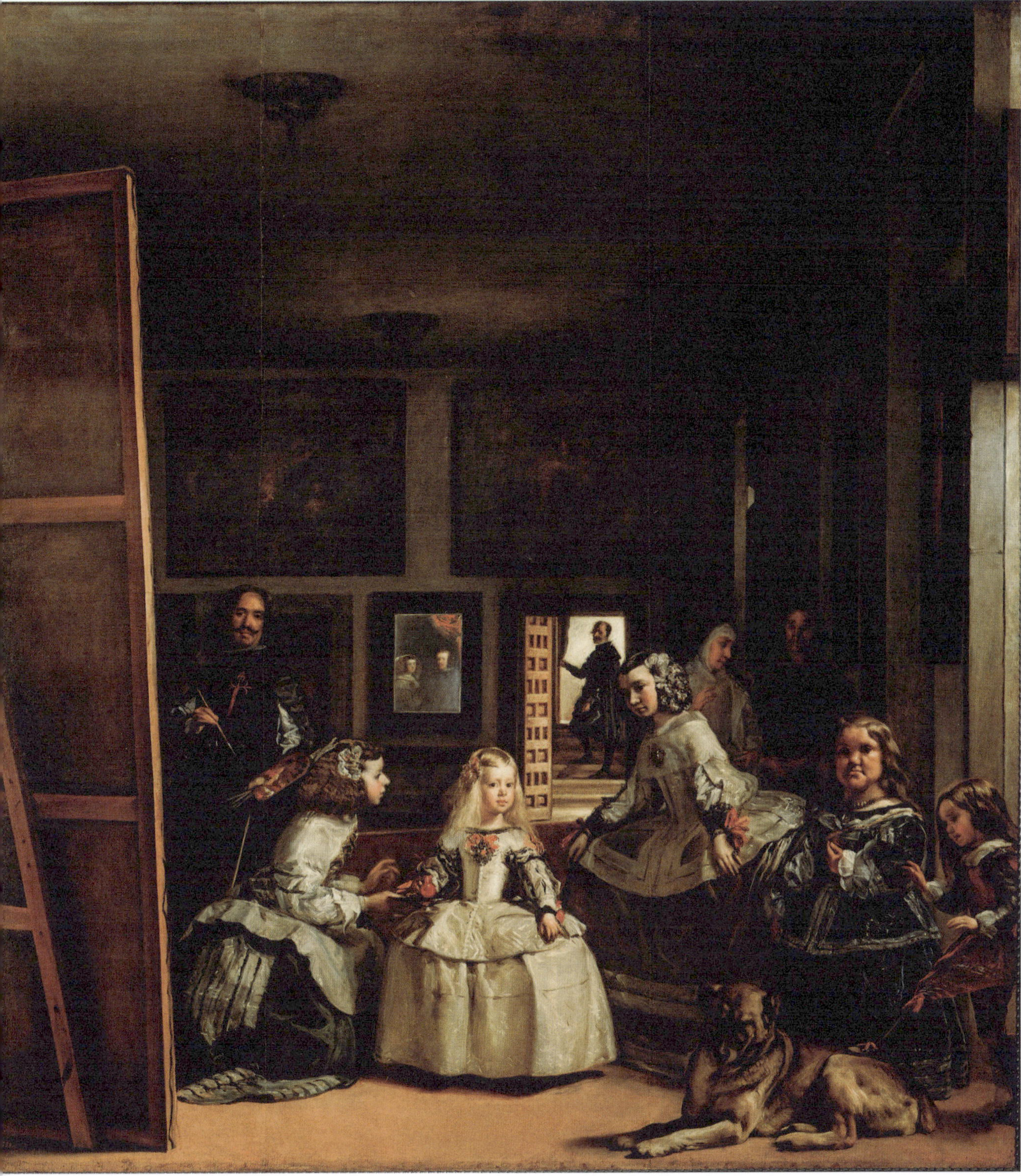

Anthony Van Dyck

The pupil who was his teacher's equal

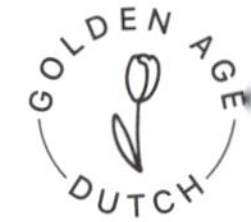

Together with Rubens, Van Dyck is one of the greatest painters ever born in Antwerp. He possessed a dazzling talent for portraiture, and graced his models with a nonchalant elegance that was prized by the European aristocracy.

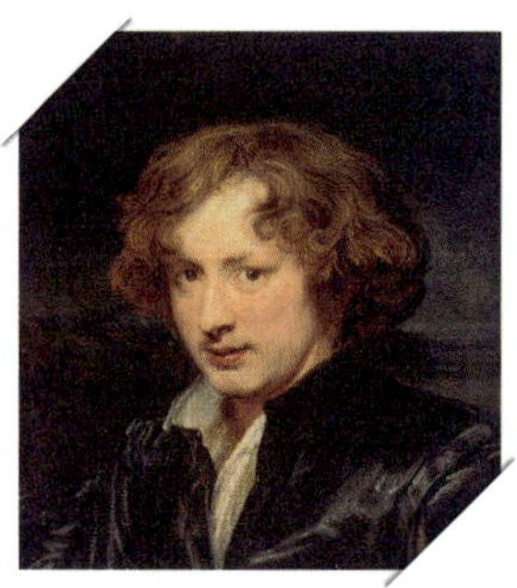

A cumbersome mentor

Van Dyck learned painting from Rubens (p. 98). This was a godsend, since the two men worked together for ten years; however, it would also prove to be a burden for the young painter, who struggled to free himself from the shadow of his master, who likely became jealous of him.

Venetian escape

Van Dyck broke away from Rubens's influence by studying Titian. In Italy, he admired and copied the Venetian, collecting his works so assiduously that his cabinet of masterpieces impressed Marie de' Medici, queen of France.

King-size painting

A brilliant and precocious artist, Van Dyck produced exceptional portraits at the age of 14. Sovereigns from all over Europe were eager to secure his services, in particular King Charles I of England, for whom Van Dyck produced numerous effigies that marked the history of English painting.

IT WAS SAID OF HIM

"You triumph, Van Dyck, prince of mild gestures, in each of these splendid creatures soon to die."
Marcel Proust, in "Portrait de peintre", *Le Gaulois*, 1895.

Diego Velázquez
Page 112

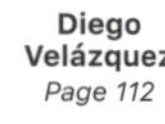
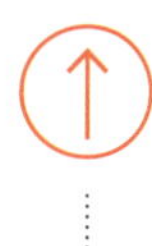

1599
Born in Antwerp

1606
In the famous port of Amsterdam, tea arrived from China

1636
Painted *Charles I at the Hunt*

1640
The portrait of Louis XIII began circulating in France, in the form of the Louis d'Or

1641
Died in Blackfriars

Rembrandt Van Rijn
Page 118

CHARLES I AT THE HUNT ↗

1636
Oil on canvas
266 × 207 cm
Louvre Museum, Paris

WHAT ARE WE LOOKING AT?

Van Dyck graces Charles I of England with a romantic flair, portraying him hunting, in keeping with the characteristics expected of a 17th-century gentleman.

Private turf

Van Dyck portrayed King Charles I in many ways, as a monarch by divine right or in a double portrait, with his wife Henrietta Maria of France, sister of Louis XIII. Here, he depicted a romantic vision of the monarch at the hunt, a favourite pastime of his.

Coolness before it was a thing

Charles I adopts the distinguished casualness that is characteristic of Van Dyck's portraits. He is standing in a majestic pose, and while the staff on which he is leaning is a stark reminder of his power, the king also displays a casualness that reflects the poise of the well-born.

Class at the palace

Van Dyck depicts the king as the leading gentleman of the kingdom, according to the period codes described in *The Book of the Courtier* (1528) by Balthazar Castiglione and *The Compleat Gentleman* (1622) by Henry Peacham. Both writings evoke the natural poise of superior people. Castiglione described this poise as *"sprezzatura"*, which, in modern terms, can be translated as "class".

Ruthless attention to detail

To create a sense of relief and depth on the king's arm, whilst painting this limb in a frontal perspective, the painter played with effects of light on the sovereign's clothing. The silky texture contrasts with the matt finish of the red short trousers. The horse with its head down, conveying a notion of deference, is borrowed from Titian's work *Adoration of the Magi*.

3D BEFORE ITS TIME

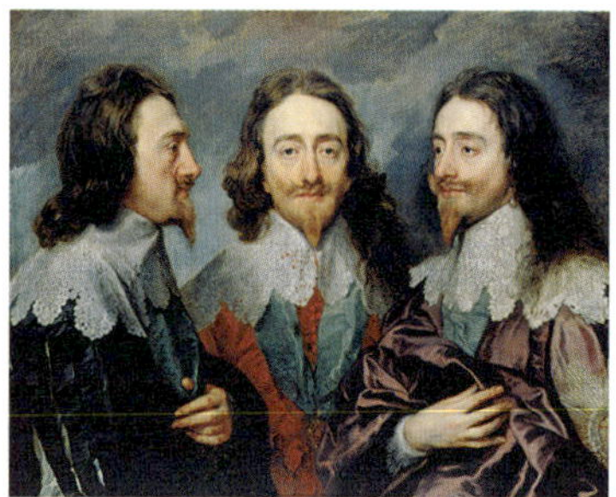

Charles I in Three Positions, 1635–1636
Windsor Castle

In 1635, Antony Van Dyck painted a famous portrait of King Charles I from three different angles. It was intended for the sculptor Bernini, who was commissioned to create a marble bust of the monarch. The bust was destroyed in a fire in 1698.

VAN DYCK'S ART IN A NUTSHELL

- Portraits displaying natural attitudes, between conformism and expressiveness.
- Characters posing with nonchalant elegance.
- A sensual touch, inherited from Venetian painting.
- A palette that grew richer and warmer over the years.

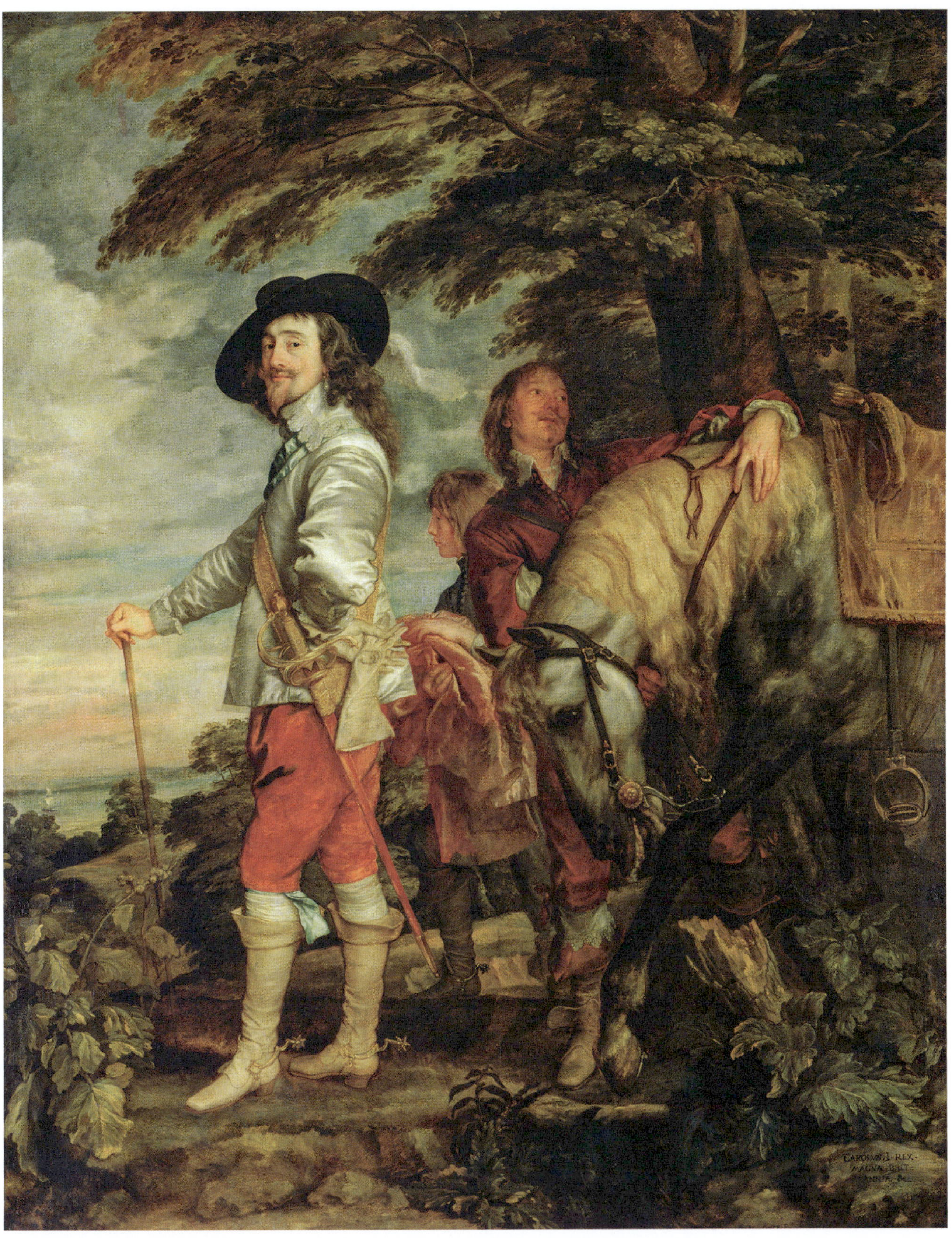
CAROLVS · I · REX ·
MAGNÆ · BRIT ·

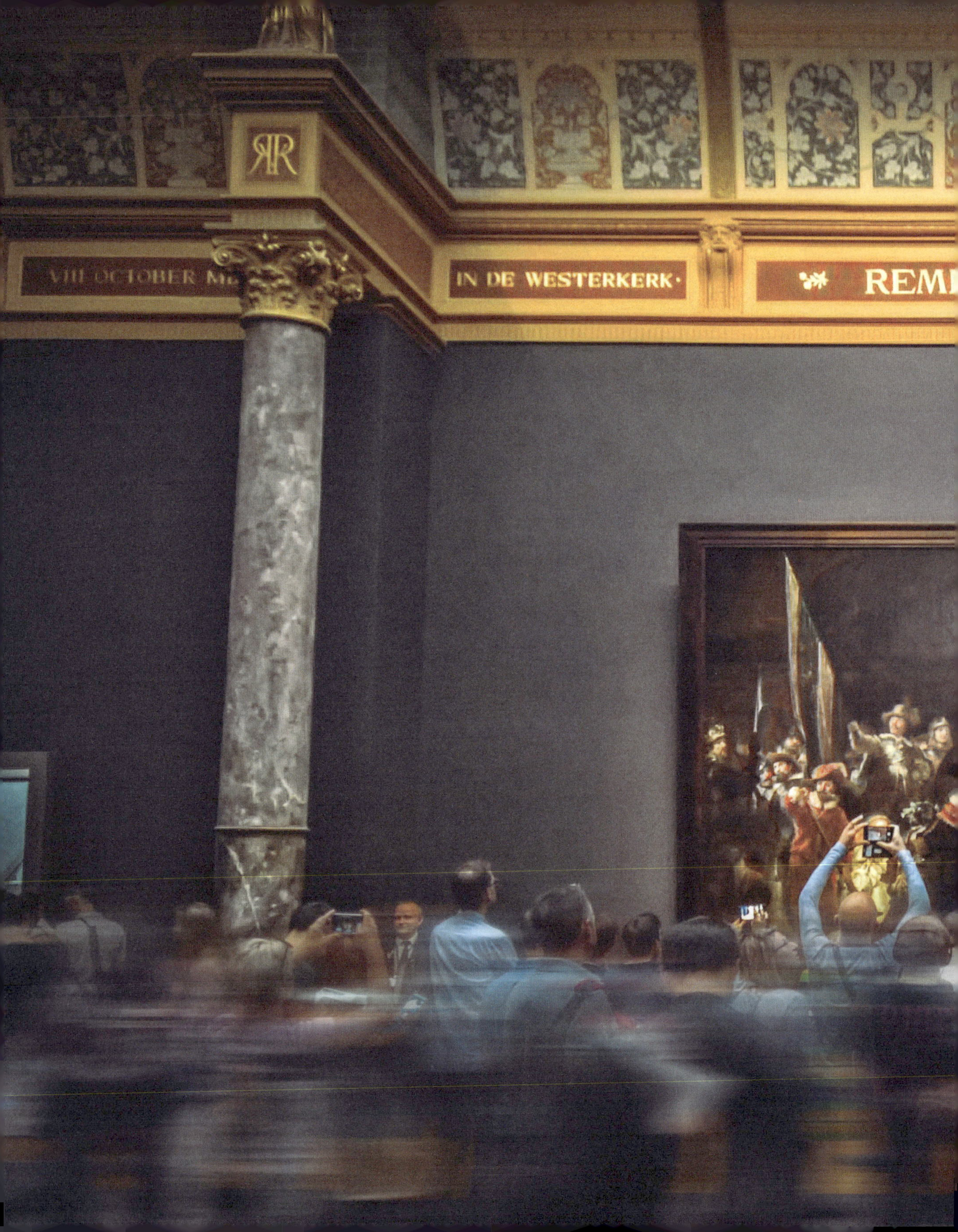
IN DE WESTERKERK·

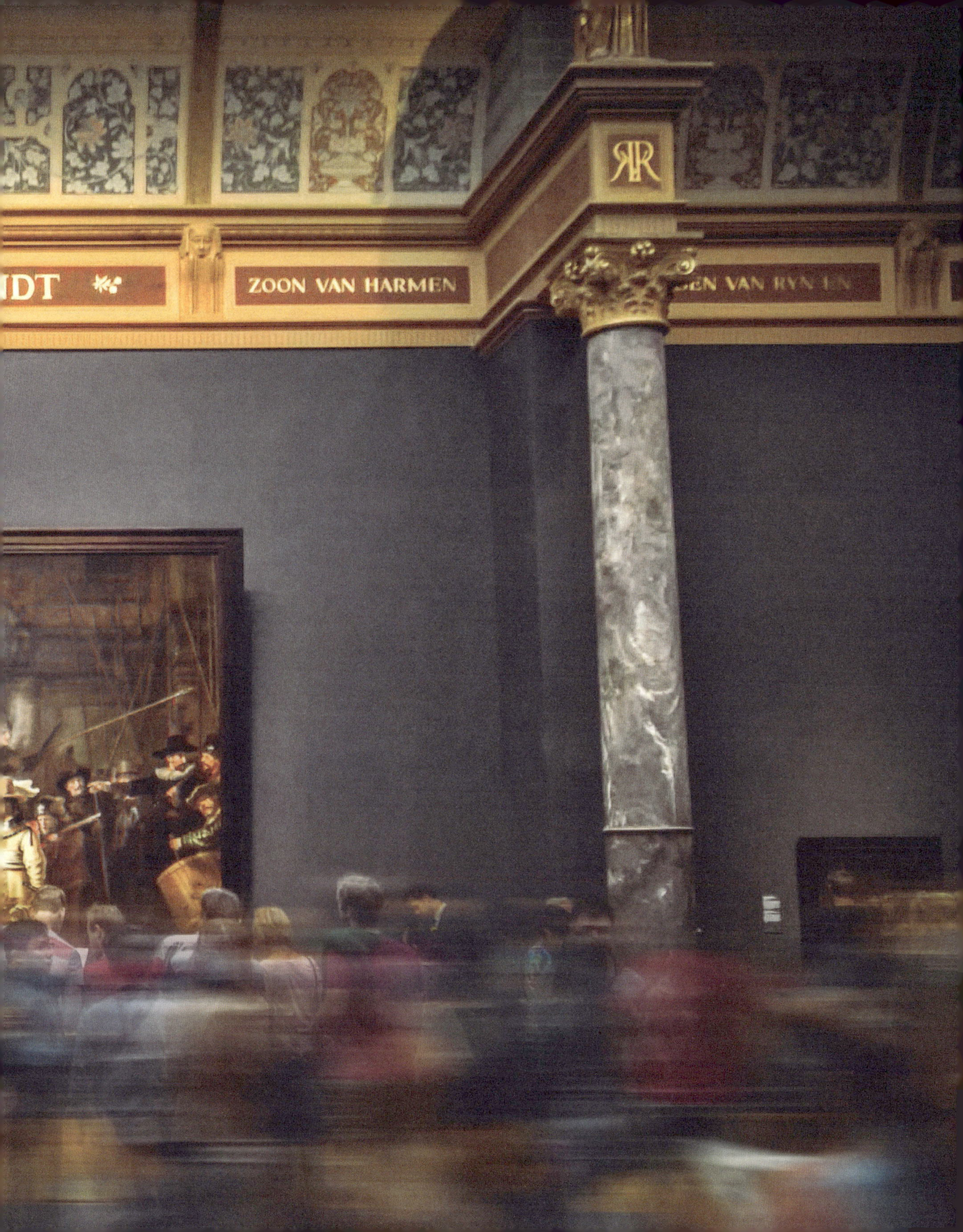
ZOON VAN HARMEN

Rembrandt Van Rijn

He was his own model

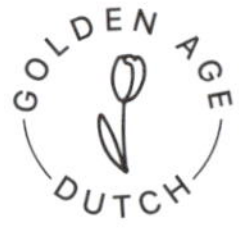

Rembrandt, a brilliant illustrator and engraver, was recognised during his lifetime as a star of painting. He was the heir of both Flemish realism and Caravaggio's chiaroscuro, inspired by the art of Italian and other artists.

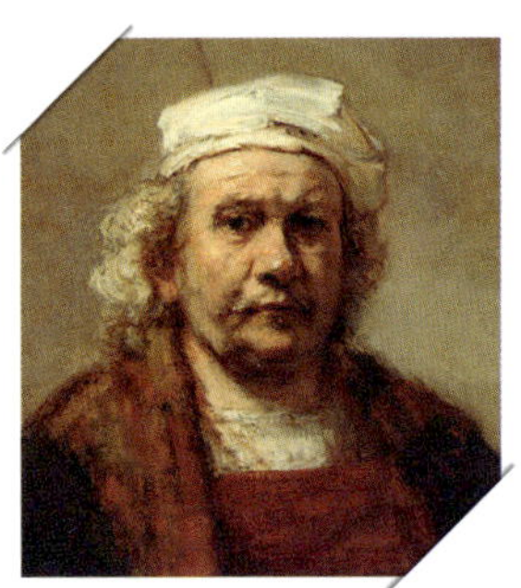

Narcissistic?

At the age of 25, Rembrandt settled in the flourishing city of Amsterdam; there was no shortage of wealthy patrons, and they would support his rise to fame by asking him to paint individual portraits or group portraits. His favourite model, however, was himself. He painted over 80 self-portraits at all ages of his life.

Exotic influences

The painter was passionately interested in the Orient, whose influences are apparent in the costumes and accessories of his portraits. It was suspected that he owned a collection of costumes; in reality, however, he was inspired by engravings.

Ah! Love...

Rembrandt was very much in love with his wife Saskia. He painted on many occasions, in the guise of various characters. Her death would cause the artist great distress, which would be perceptible even in his paintings.

COMPULSIVE BUYER

Despite his fame, the painter's finances were chaotic; he collected numerous works of art – engravings, objects and drawings – from the East and West.

Anthony Van Dyck
Page 114

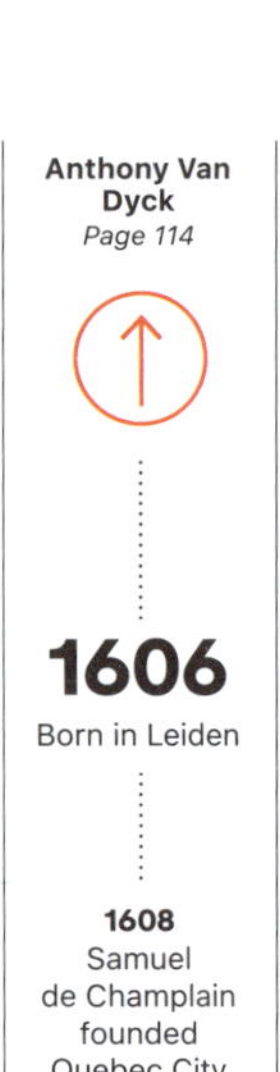

1606
Born in Leiden

1608
Samuel de Champlain founded Quebec City

1642
Painted *The Night Watch*

1665
Bernini sculpted the bust of Louis XIV

1669
Died in Amsterdam

Simon Vouet
Page 122

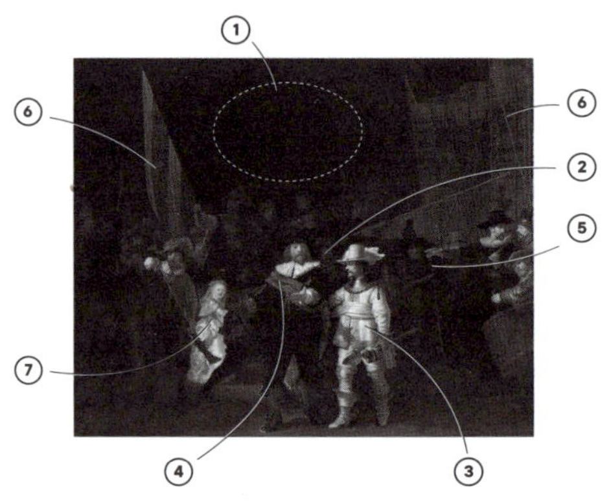

THE NIGHT WATCH

OR THE SHOOTING COMPANY OF FRANS BANNING COCQ AND WILLEM VAN RUYTENBURCH

1642
Oil on canvas
379.5 × 453.5 cm
Rijksmuseum, Amsterdam

WHAT ARE WE LOOKING AT?

This painting, which appears like a historical fresco, is in fact a group portrait. The painter resorted to various tricks and techniques to make the composition more dynamic and dramatic.

① False impression

In the 19th century, this work was renamed *The Night Watch*, because the background was thought to indicate a nocturnal atmosphere. It is not the case, however – Rembrandt simply liked to play with chiaroscuro.

② *Who's who?*

This company is led by Captain Frans Banning Cocq, in the left foreground, and Lieutenant Willem Van Ruytenburch, on the right.

③ Clothes woven from light

The painter captivates the spectator's gaze with touches of light. The young girl's light-coloured garment matches that of the lieutenant in the foreground.

④ In red and black

The touches of red on the captain's scarf and on the clothes of the soldiers to his left and right also add rhythm to the painting.

⑤ Speaking with their hands

The figures' gestures grace this portrait with a dynamic and narrative impetus, reminiscent of history paintings. They also encourage the viewer's gaze to skip from one character to another.

⑥ To-and-fro

The spears shafts echo the flagpole and the barrels of the rifles. The painter has created a network of lines streaking across the composition's space, making the portrait seem dynamic.

⑦ The White Lady

In the midst of all these men, the young girl resembles a supernatural apparition. Some believe that she is Saskia, the painter's wife. On her belt, chicken feet (*klauw*) refer to the name of the soldiers, *Klaweniers*, i.e. arquebusiers.

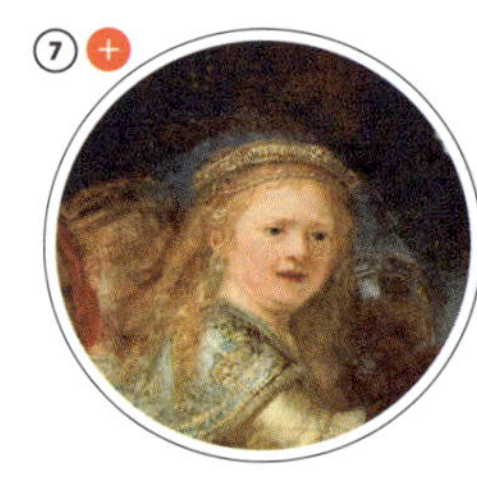

REMBRANDTS GALORE

Up to 1,000 works have been associated with the painter's name; in reality, however, his production is estimated at 500 paintings, of which 200 are said to have been "lost" – that is to say that they were mentioned in the artist's time, but are yet to be identified today. Today, some 300 identified paintings are said to exist.

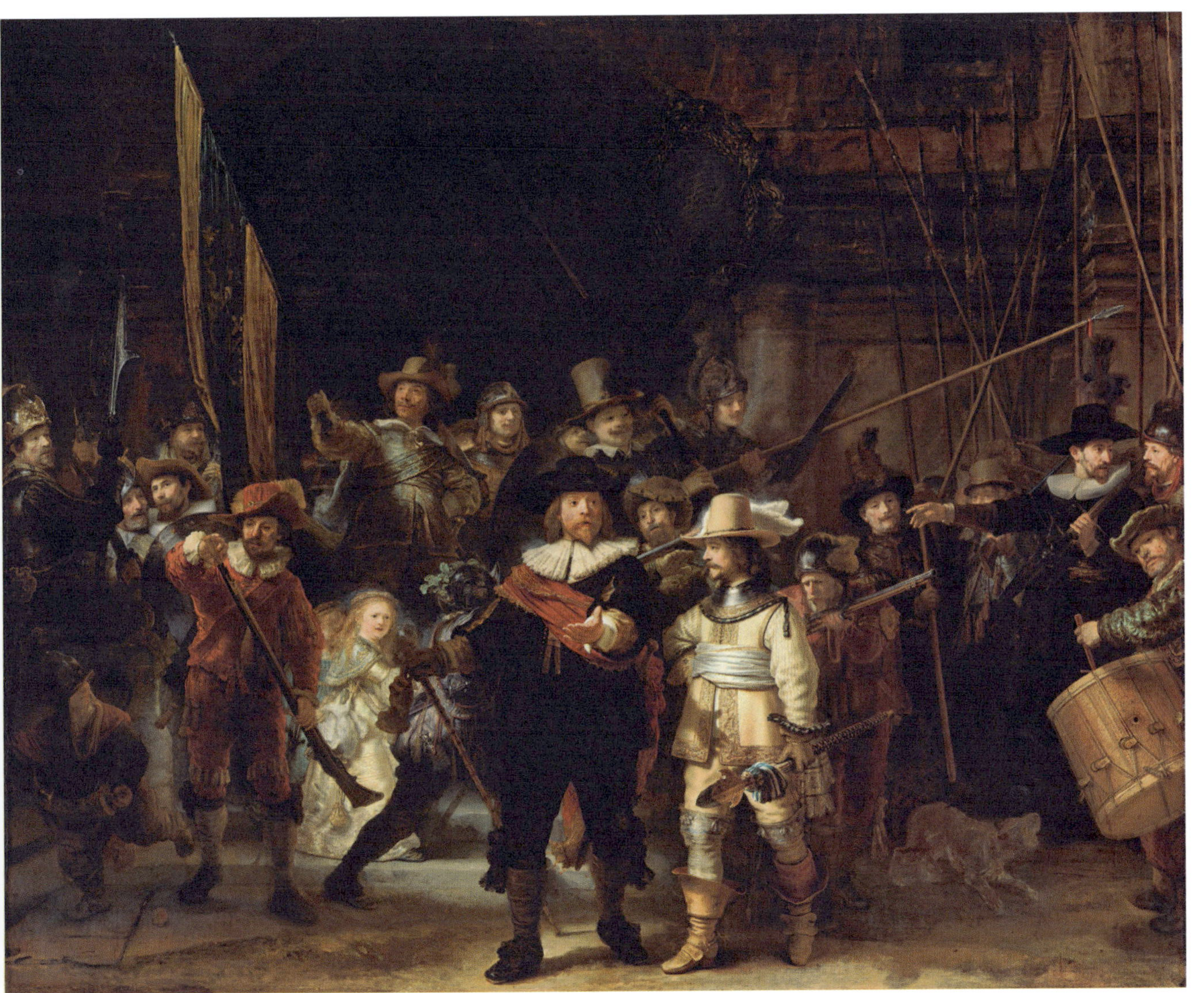

Sure of himself (and his brushstroke)

Between 2019 and 2022, *The Night Watch* underwent a spectacular restoration, which was performed in the museum, before the very eyes of the visitors. Examinations carried out on this occasion revealed that, under the paint, the preparatory drawing is very similar to the final result: Rembrandt was satisfied with his composition.

Rembrandt and Velázquez
In darkened tones

Rembrandt and Velázquez were contemporaries, but never had the opportunity to admire their respective works. Yet, they displayed the same taste for chiaroscuro and the same palette, giving pride of place to brown and black tones.

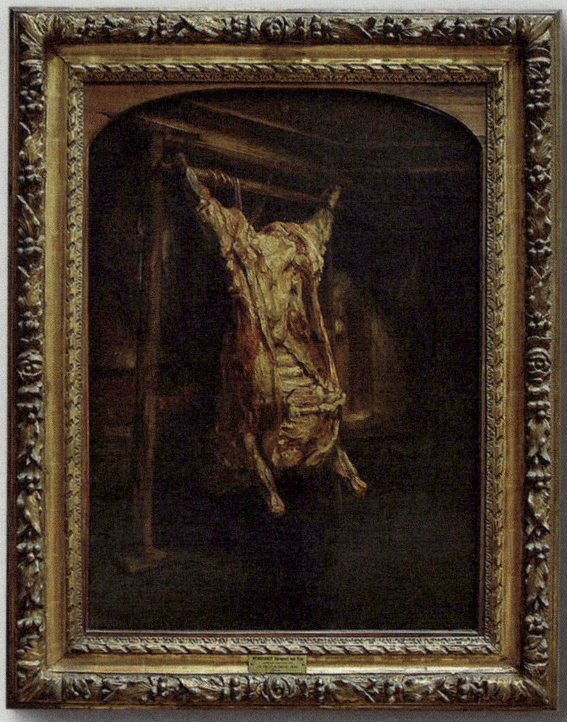

***SLAUGHTERED OX* BY REMBRANDT VAN RIJN**
1655

Rembrandt explored the possibilities of matter, which appears to writhe before the viewer's eyes. Never has dead flesh looked so alive. However, this ox suspended in the crucified position may be a vanitas (p. 110), a religious message reminding us that death is inevitable.

Oil on wood, 94 × 69 cm
Louvre Museum, Paris

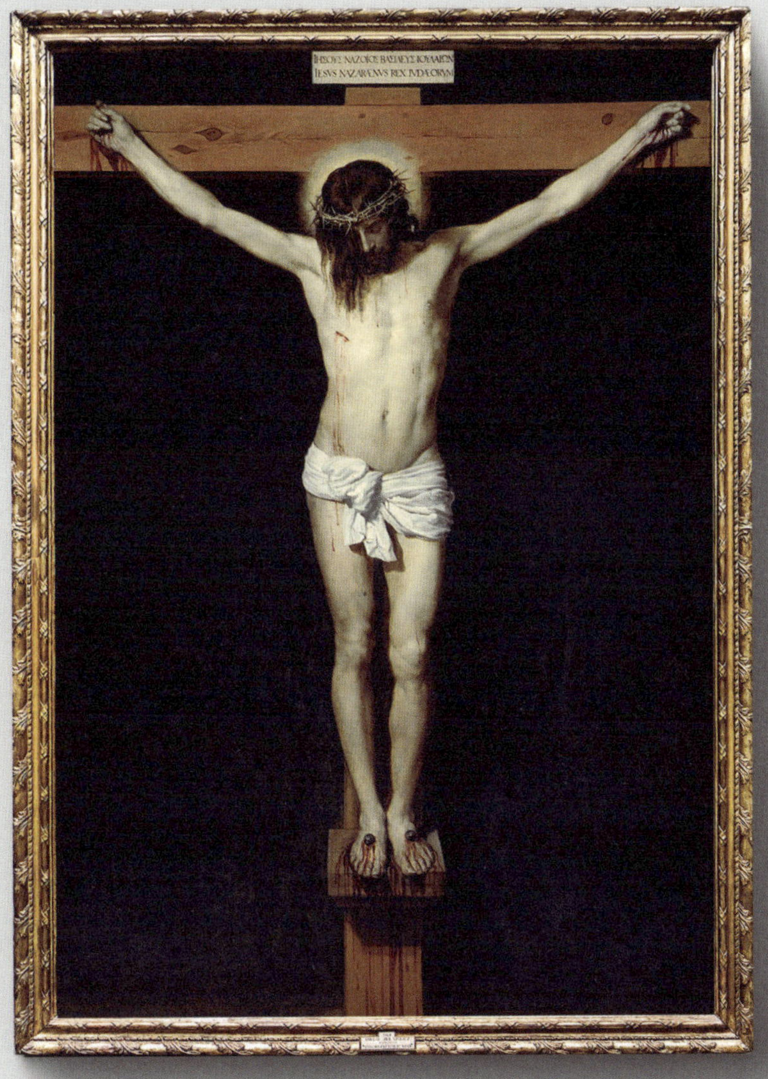

***CHRIST CRUCIFIED* BY DIEGO VELÁZQUEZ**
Circa 1632

Here, Christ is represented in the flesh. The modelling of the delicately rendered body is evocative of the most beautiful marble figures of Apollo, which the painter likely admired in Italy. In torment, expressed in the blood flowing from his wounds, Christ remains perfectly divine.

Oil on canvas, 248 × 169 cm
Prado Museum, Madrid

Simon Vouet

An unsung hero

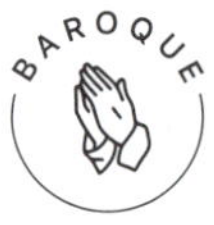

With his outstanding drawings and his fresh palette, Vouet was one of the greatest French painters. Sadly, the French Revolution did not take kindly to his imposing religious altarpieces, and he was forgotten by history, to the point that his works were still very much set aside in the 20th century.

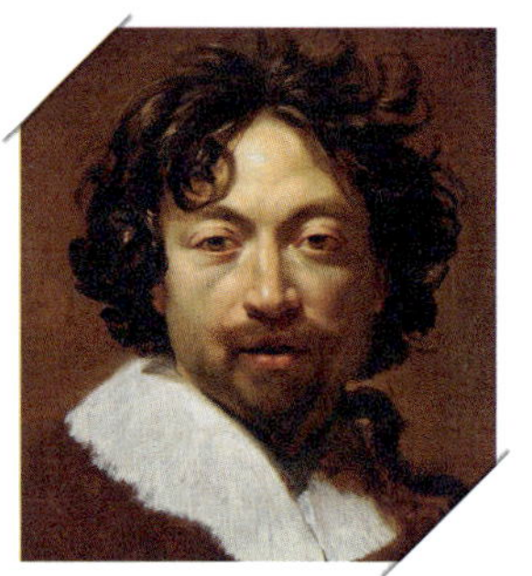

A traveller at heart

As a young man, Vouet travelled from London to Constantinople. At the age of 22, he moved to Rome, where he found love, and his works were met with success. Fifteen years later, he returned to France, at the height of his career. Louis XIII welcomed him enthusiastically, and he soon became the greatest painter of France.

The big picture

In Italy, he immersed himself in the works of the Mannerists and Caravaggio (p. 78). His painting was humanistic; faces were individualised, and bodies were depicted with a consistent approach. His art struck a balance between colour and drawing, baroque and academic technique. His favourite supports were large altarpieces and vast sets.

A good teacher

Vouet, who also managed a renowned studio, was apparently also a highly talented teacher. He trained many apprentices, who went on to become recognised artists, such as the painters Eustache Le Sueur and Charles Le Brun, and the architect André Le Nôtre.

ROYAL JEST

"Vouet has been caught out!" – this sentence was famously uttered by Louis XIII, amused by the return to France of Vouet's rival, Nicolas Poussin (p. 124).

Rembrandt Van Rijn
Page 118

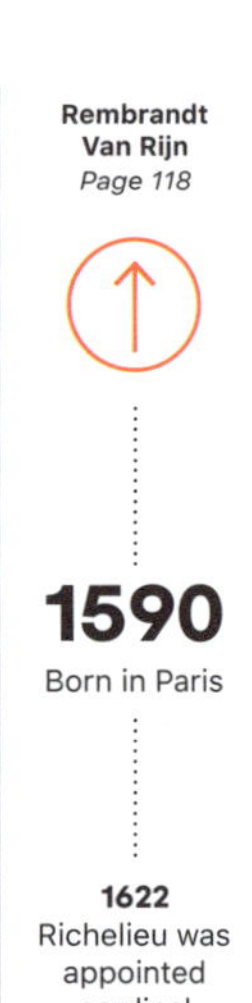

1590
Born in Paris

1622
Richelieu was appointed cardinal

1638 to **1640**
Painted *Allegory of Faith and Contempt of Wealth*

1643
Louis XIV acceded to the throne

1649
Died in Paris

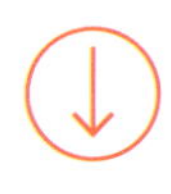

Nicolas Poussin
Page 124

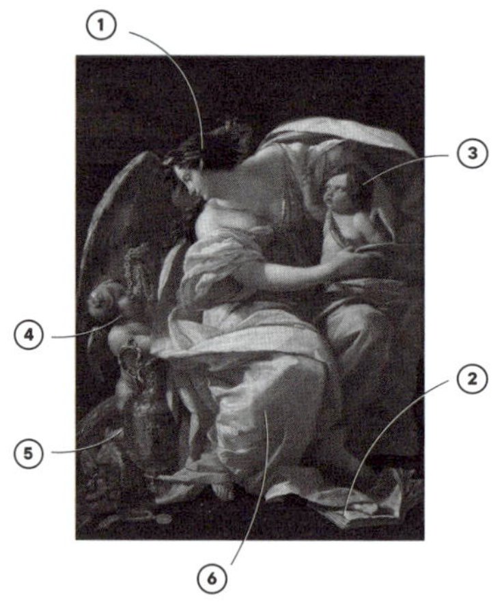

ALLEGORY OF FAITH AND CONTEMPT FOR WEALTH

1638–1640
Oil on canvas
170 × 124 cm
Louvre Museum, Paris

WHAT ARE WE LOOKING AT?

This is an allegorical representation, i.e. a concept embodied by a figure. The monumentality of the figure, its crown of laurels and its wings affirm its supernatural and hieratic character.

① The stage is set

In the 19th century, this work was catalogued under the title *Allegory of Wealth*, but it is in fact an allegory of Christian faith.

② How obvious was it?

Faith can be identified by the attributes placed at her feet, on the right: a cornerstone and a book.

③ Cloudless love

In her arms, she is holding a *putto*, or amoretto, who is pointing towards the sky. This is a metaphor for celestial love, as opposed to the other *putto*, who represents earthly love.

④ An attempt at corruption

Earthly love is attempting to interest faith by offering her riches, but faith is turning away from it and remains faithful to heavenly love. The painter has arranged the composition in such a way that faith is looking down on him, as a sign of contempt.

⑤ A lesson cast in silver

The beautiful metal vase features a relief depicting the myth of Apollo (p. 156) and Daphne, in which the Greek god pursued the nymph, who prayed to be turned into a laurel tree to escape his advances. Earthly pleasures are but mere vanity.

⑥ An in-between without compromise

With great accuracy, Vouet draws from baroque and classic influences: the sinuous and sensual drapery covering faith is balanced by the clarity of the composition. The palette's luminosity, and the yellow drapery in particular, already heralds the penchant of the 18th century.

⑤ +

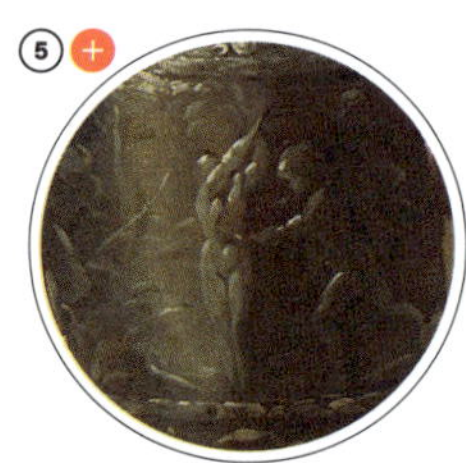

A LITTLE CHAUVINISTIC...

In the 17th century, French painting attained a high level of refinement. It was in this context that the Académie Royale de Peinture et de Sculpture was founded (p. 132). It would allow artists to raise the French school to the level of the great European schools and extend its renown beyond the kingdom.

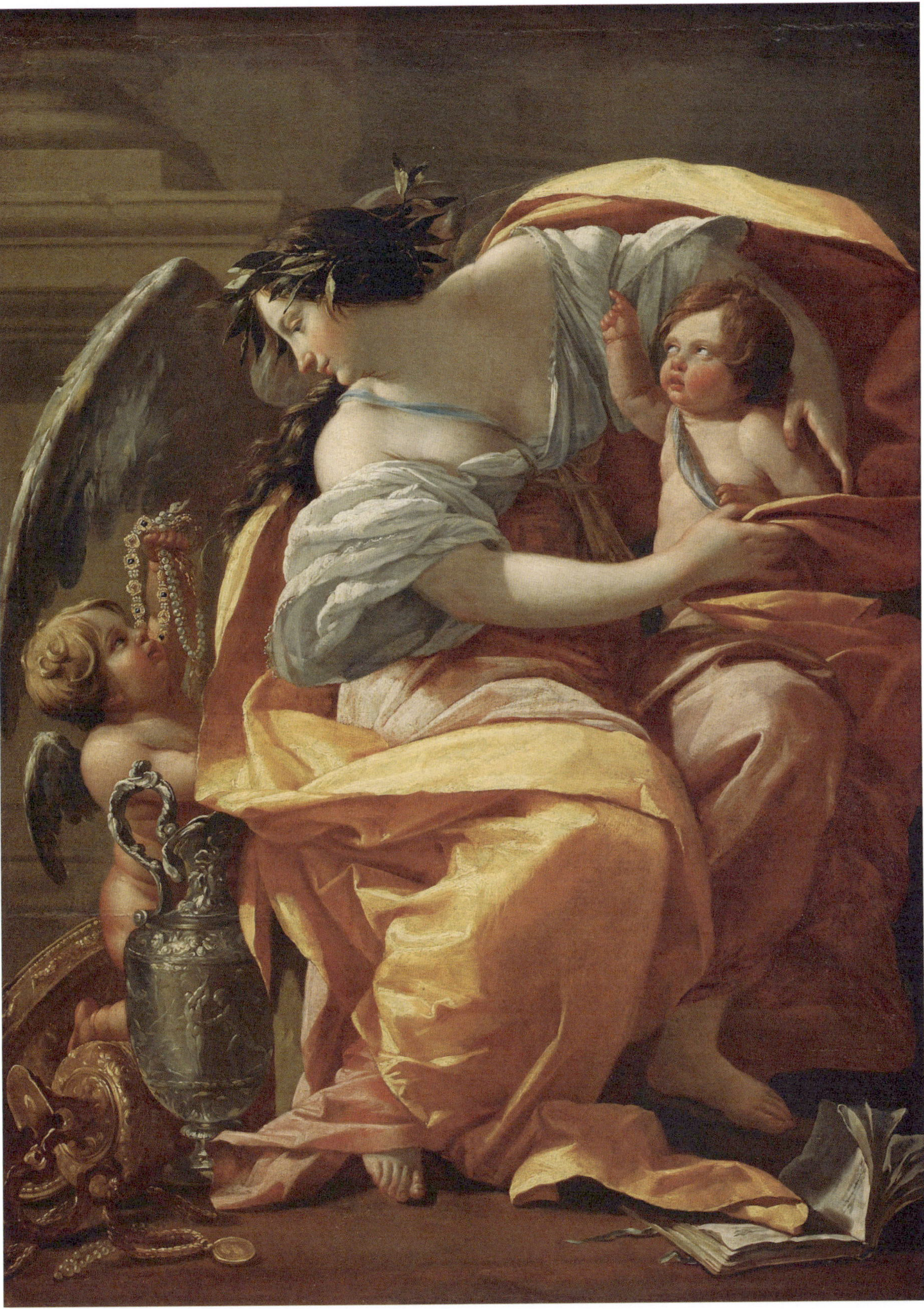

Nicolas Poussin

The nerd of the bunch

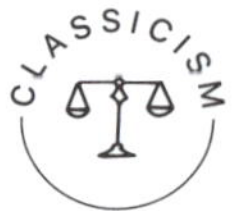

Considered by some as the greatest French painter, Poussin was an intellectual artist. His works, sometimes mysterious, were the subject of much discussion.

Stirring the brains

Poussin was a cultured, sometimes inaccessible painter. His paintings are sometimes difficult to understand, because within them, he hid double meanings or referred to complex biblical or mythological episodes.

Not so classical

His rigorous compositions often highlighted him as the poster boy of classicism; however, there is another, more sensual dimension to Poussin's work. To his impeccable drawings, he knew how to add the luminous colours of the Venetian school.

Camembert or burrata?

Born in Normandy, Poussin spent most of his life in Rome, which made him the most Italian of French painters. Summoned by Louis XIII in 1640, he would stay in France for only two years, being rather adverse to court intrigues.

ALL ONE'S EGGS IN ONE BASKET

Forty – this is the number of Poussin's paintings kept in the Louvre, which thus holds the largest collection in the world.

Simon Vouet
Page 122

1594
Born in Les Andelys

1636
Foundation of Harvard University

Circa
1638
Painted *Et in Arcadia Ego*

1665
Died in Rome

1693—1694
A great famine caused 1.3 million deaths in the kingdom of France

Charles Le Brun
Page 130

ET IN ARCADIA EGO

Circa 1638
Oil on canvas
85 × 121 cm
Louvre Museum, Paris

WHAT ARE WE LOOKING AT?

This work has been often commented on, because it still remains mysterious. Here, Poussin evokes the topic of death and its omnipresence.

Inspired by a mentor

When Poussin painted this work, the subject depicted was practically unheard of. Before him, it was proposed by a great Italian artist whom he admired, Giovanni Francesco Barbieri, known as Guercino.

Promising land

The title sets the scene in Arcadia, a mountainous region of Greece, considered an idyllic land and the scene of many myths. In the centre, three shepherds are dressed in ancient fashion. They are accompanied by an unidentified woman, who could embody an allegory.

An enigmatic sentence

The men are resting against a tomb, which bears the Latin inscription: *"Et in Arcadia ego"* – "And I too am in Arcadia". Also present in Guercino's version, this sentence is not an excerpt from any known text.

Memento mori

It could be a message from Death, speaking directly to viewers to warn them that it is present everywhere, even in the most paradisiacal places, and that all things must come to an end.

One last message for the road

It may also be an inscription left by the deceased on their tomb to warn the living, as was done in ancient times. This would be an invitation to celebrate life, to enjoy it while there is still time, as life is fleeting.

THE UNFILTERED VERSION

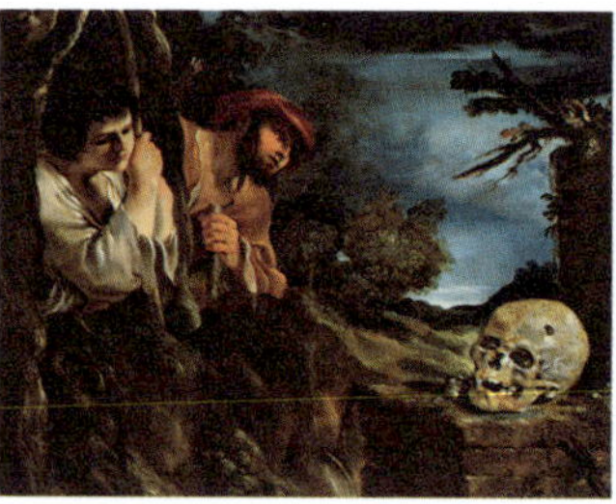

Giovanni Francesco Barbieri, known as Guercino, *Et in Arcadia Ego*, circa 1618
National Gallery of Ancient Art, Rome

In Guercino's version of *Et in Arcadia Ego*, death is explicitly present: the artist painted a vanitas in the foreground (p. 110), represented by a skull. The terror caused by this skull is intensified by the rodent attempting to enter its jaw and the insect on its forehead; the shepherds, meanwhile, are deep in thought, ignoring each other.

CLASSICISM IN A NUTSHELL

- The search for general harmony between forms and colours, but drawing is most important.
- Stable and balanced compositions, often in the form of a triangle or a frieze.
- Moral subjects inspired by antiquity or the Bible.

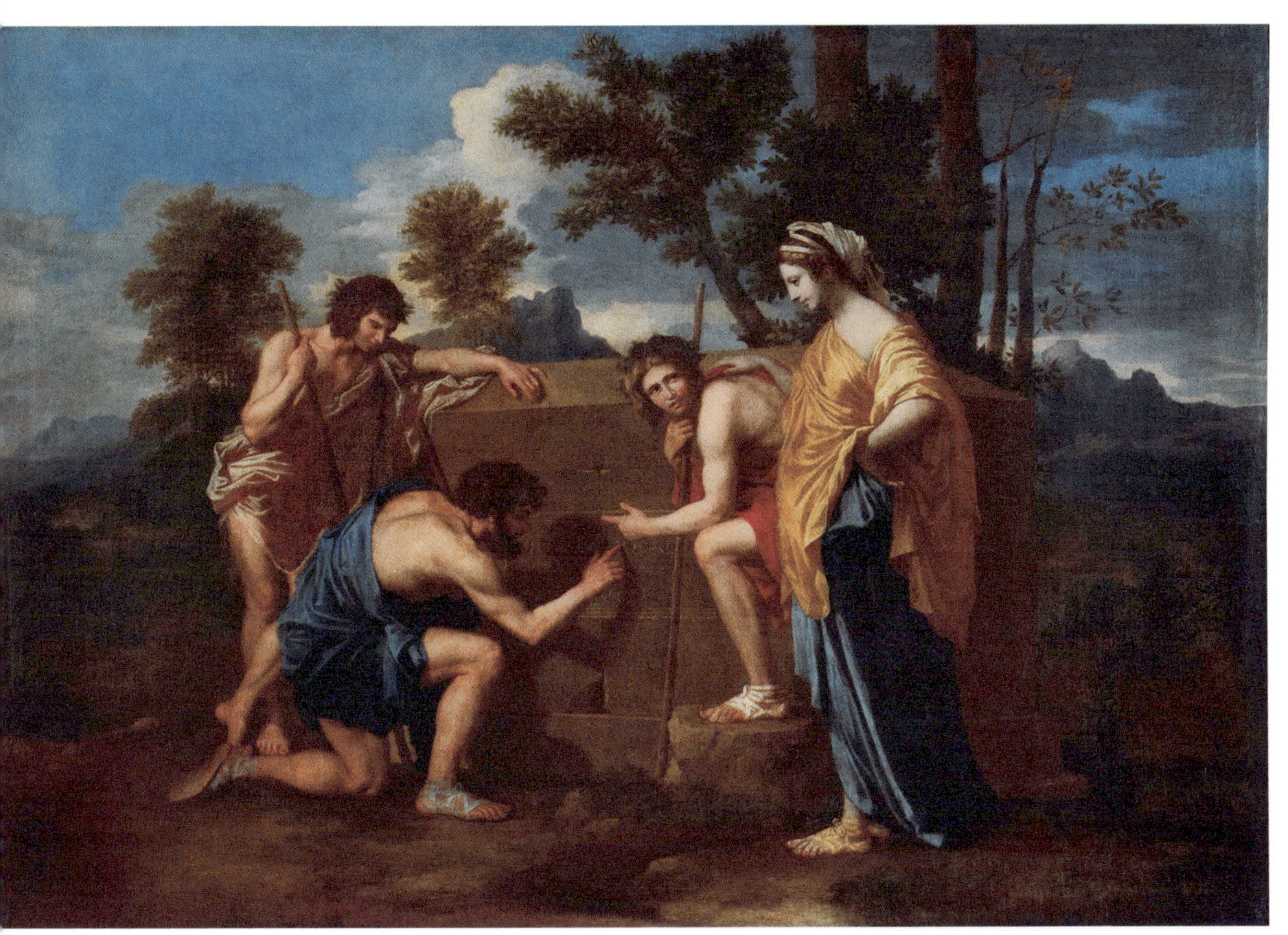

From Russia with love

One of the greatest experts on Nicolas Poussin was Anthony Blunt. Curator of the Royal Collection, he was also a Soviet spy. The discovery of his betrayal was kept quiet until Margaret Thatcher entered Downing Street and revealed the truth in 1979.

Poussin and Twombly

Flowers that endure the seasons

Both foreigners living in Italy, Poussin and Twombly share a passion for the myths of antiquity. Three centuries apart, both succeeded, in their own way, in depicting the sensuality and the poetic impulse of *The Empire of Flora*.

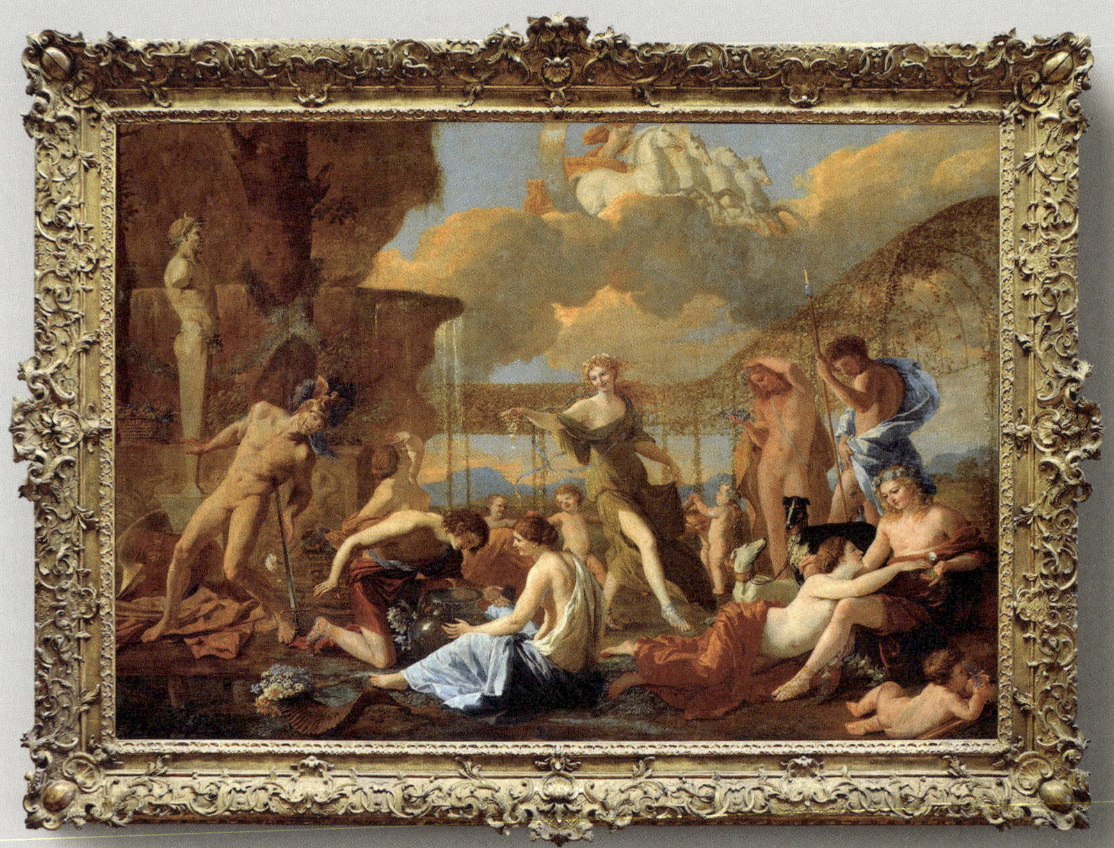

***THE EMPIRE OF FLORA* BY NICOLAS POUSSIN**
1631

In this painting, Poussin has gathered several myths from Ovid's *Metamorphoses*, depicting heroes transformed into flowers. Dominated by the sun, they bask in a sensual languor that contrasts with the geometric decor, as flowers appear on their bodies.

Oil on canvas, 132 × 181.4 cm
Gemäldegalerie, Dresden

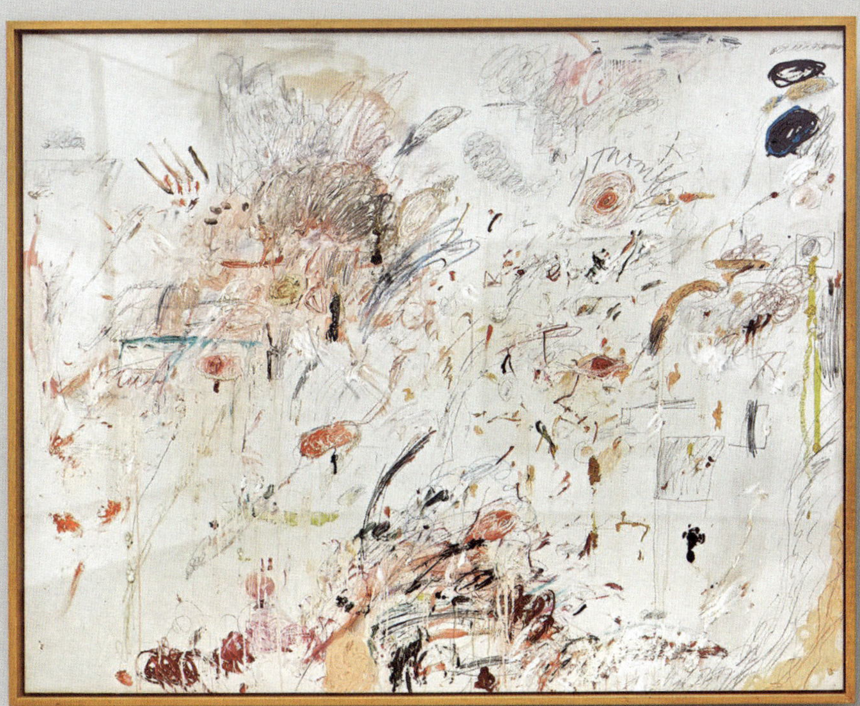

EMPIRE OF FLORA BY CY TWOMBLY
1961

One should not seek to identify a literal transposition of Poussin's work. The viewer's gaze catches on to elements that it seems to recognise, but foremost, the artist has aspired to amplify the scene's sensuality and spirituality. The image disappears, allowing us to better capture its essence.

Mixed media, 101.2 × 148 cm
Cy Twombly Foundation

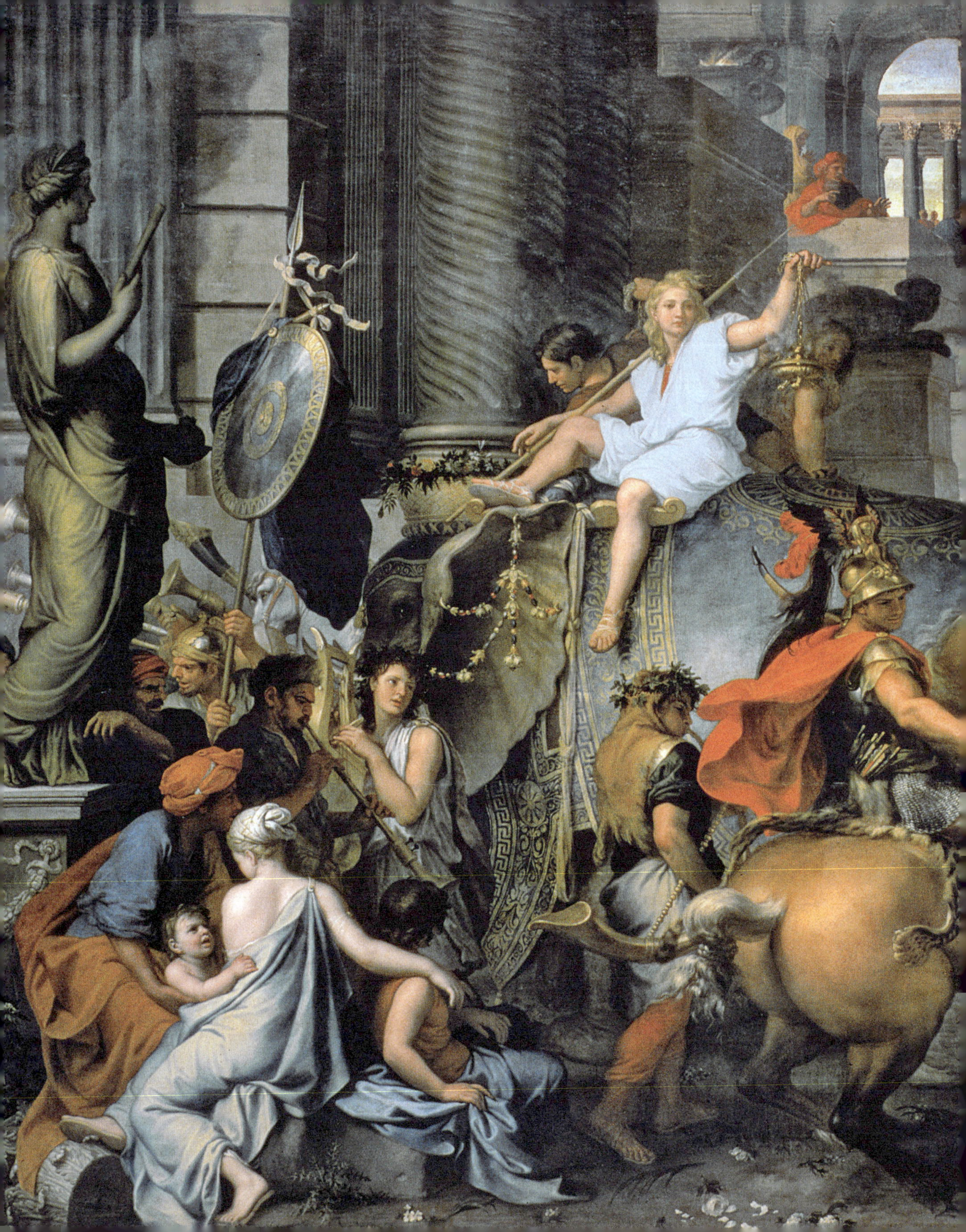

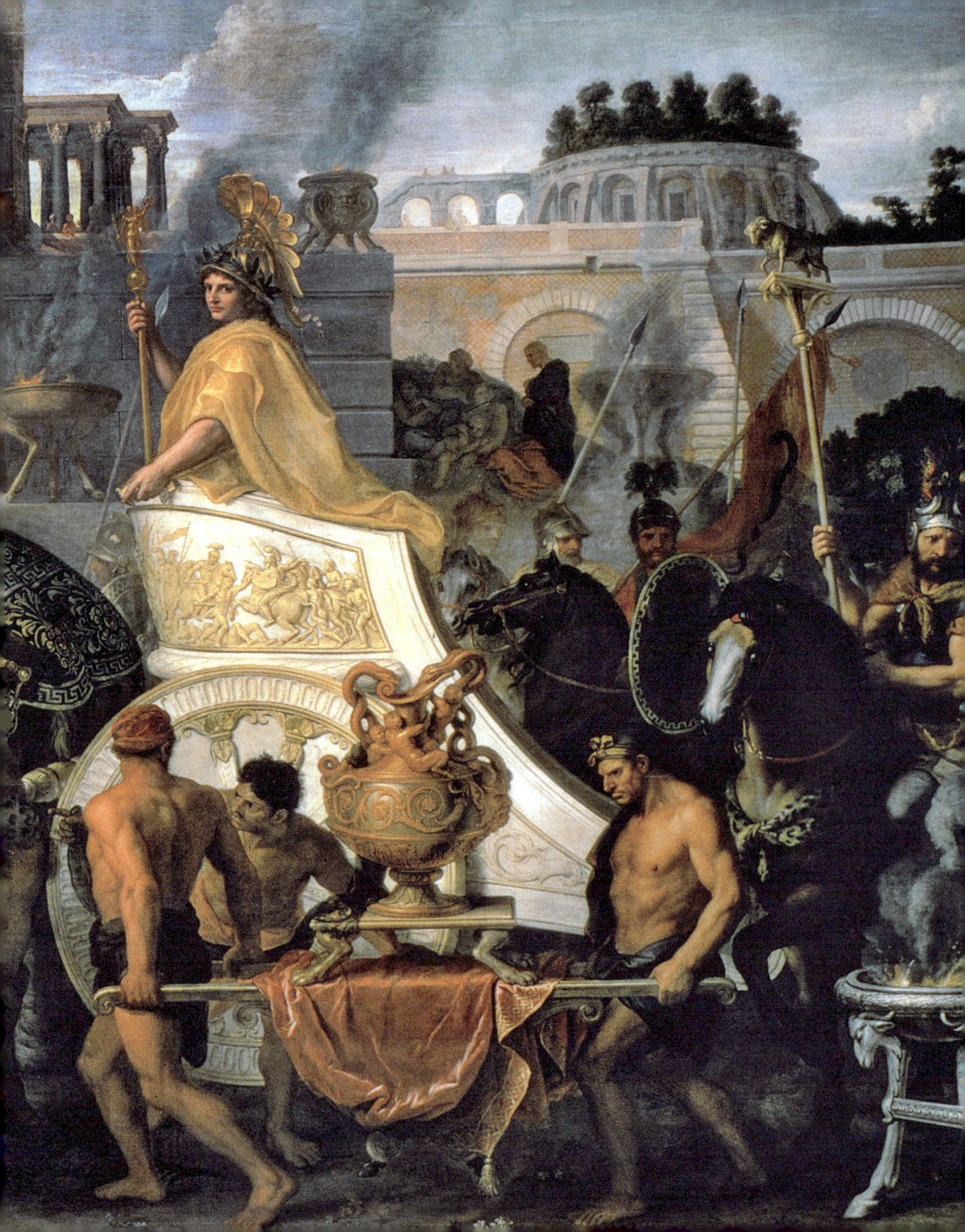

Charles Le Brun

He made the Sun King shine

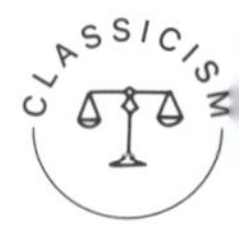

First painter to King Louis XIV, Le Brun was known for his radiant decorations of Versailles; however, he also worked on ephemeral decorations and church altarpieces, and became famous for his animal paintings.

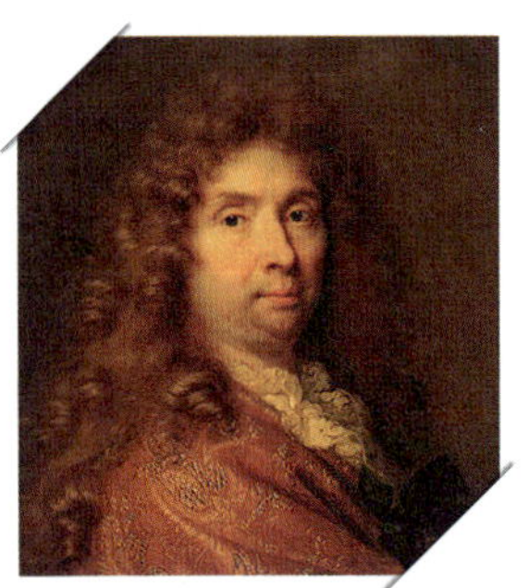

An impressive boss

Although Le Brun served the Church with his art throughout his life, he was best known for his work as a painter to Louis XIV, in particular for the imposing ceiling of the Hall of Mirrors at Versailles. His name is associated with the Sun King and the Palace of Versailles.

The customer is king

For the monarch, he painted monumental works that required him to surpass himself in the mastery of composition. He elaborated his paintings as pictures that involve the viewer, rather than as decors. He also produced sumptuous ephemeral ornaments for parties and ceremonies.

An instant classic

Educated and curious about his time, he directed the Académie Royale de Peinture et de Sculpture (p. 166), where he defended the rigour of drawing against the excessiveness of colour. However, his inventive and eloquent painting set the codes of the "Louis XIV" genre, and inspired following generations.

MULTIPLE MANDATES

In 1662, Colbert founded the Gobelins Manufactory, which would mark the history of tapestry in France. Le Brun became its first director.

Nicolas Poussin
Page 124

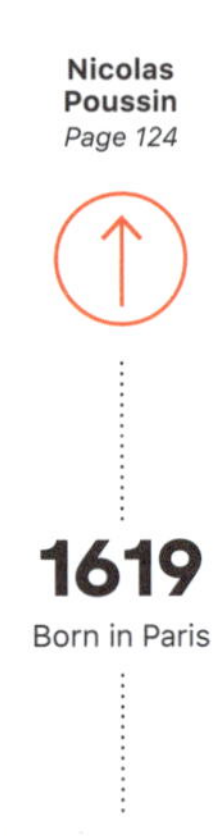

1619
Born in Paris

1642
The Dalai Lama was proclaimed ruler of Tibet

1664 to **1665**
Painted *Entry of Alexander into Babylon*

1685
Birth of the composer Johann Sebastian Bach

1690
Died in Paris

Antoine Watteau
Page 138

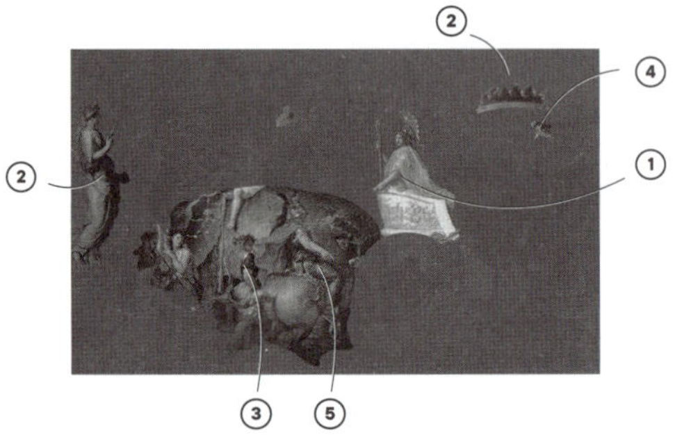

ENTRY OF ALEXANDER INTO BABYLON

Circa 1664–1665
Oil on canvas
450 × 707 cm
Louvre Museum, Paris

WHAT ARE WE LOOKING AT?

King of Macedonia and limitless conqueror, Alexander the Great, enters Babylon, which has fallen under his rule. Reclaimed for political reasons, the conqueror's legend would serve the image of Louis XIV.

(1) Royal mascot

Adorned in gold, wearing a prodigious helmet girded with laurels, Alexander appears in a solar glory that is associated with Louis XIV. Here, the warrior interacts with the viewer, looking him straight in the eye. The richly decorated elephants pulling his chariot were taken from Darius, the defeated king of Persia. They are the symbol of the warrior's dominance.

(2) We know where we are

Le Brun took care to situate the scene. On the left is a statue of the legendary queen Semiramis, and on the right, in the background, rise the famous Hanging Gardens, described as one of the Seven Wonders of the World.

(3) Well studied

The Persians welcome the conqueror with music. The curved trumpet is a *lituus*, which originated from the Etruscan civilisation that thrived in the Mediterranean region before the Greeks.

(4) God willing...

Rams are the attributes of the Greco-Egyptian god Zeus Ammon. When Alexander visited the deity's sanctuary of at Siwa, the priest who welcomed him told him that he was the son of the god. The mention of this affiliation of a god with a sovereign resonates with the policy of divine right conducted by Louis XIV.

(5) Local colours

The rider could be the Persian governor welcoming the victor, or Ephesus, Alexander's general and friend. The Greek-style harnessing of the horse favours the second option.

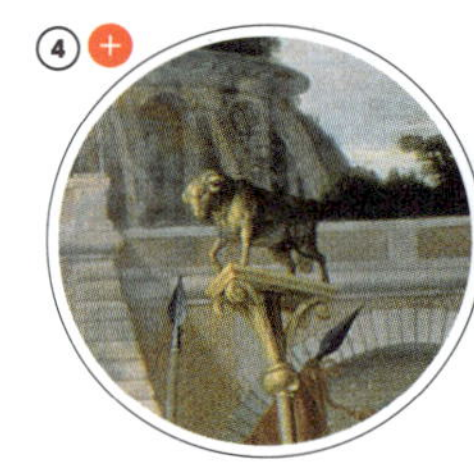

LE BRUN'S ART IN A NUTSHELL

- Political art that served the glory of the king.
- A sense of composition.
- A commitment to the viewer.
- A classical approach, favouring drawing over colour.

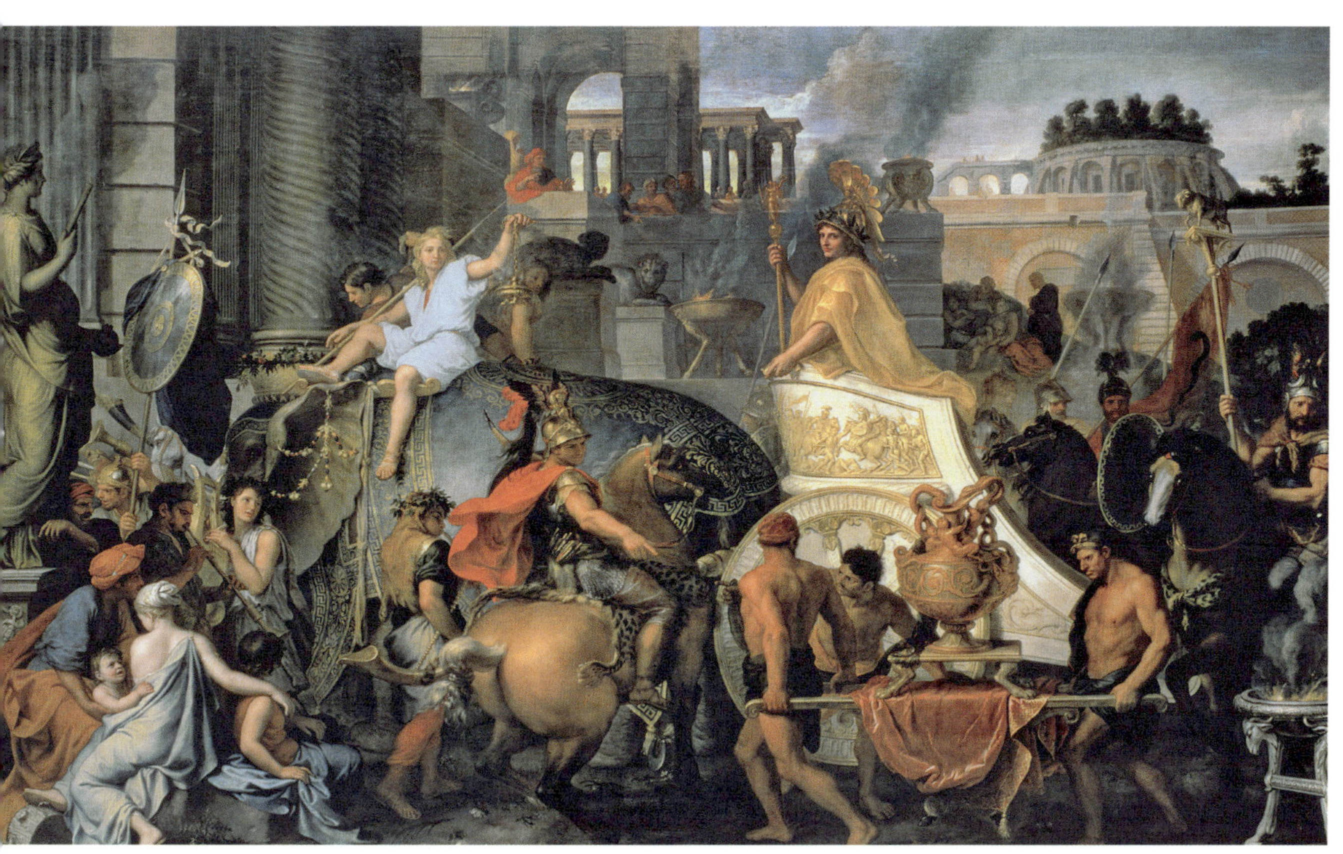

Wonders from another time

While they no longer exist, the Hanging Gardens of Babylon are described by authors from the antiquity. Some viewed this extraordinary green construction as one of the Seven Wonders of the World, of which only the Great Pyramid of Giza remains today.

Becoming a painter for the Palace of Versailles

The ideal curriculum vitae in the 17th century

Under the reign of Louis XIV, the arts were institutionalised with the creation of new establishments, among which the Académie Royale de Peinture et de Sculpture. Such institutions protected painters and traced a path of excellence, enabling them to access the most prestigious commissions.

Guidance sheet

Studios run by painters who were members of the Académie Royale ensured that pupils benefited from their support and their network.

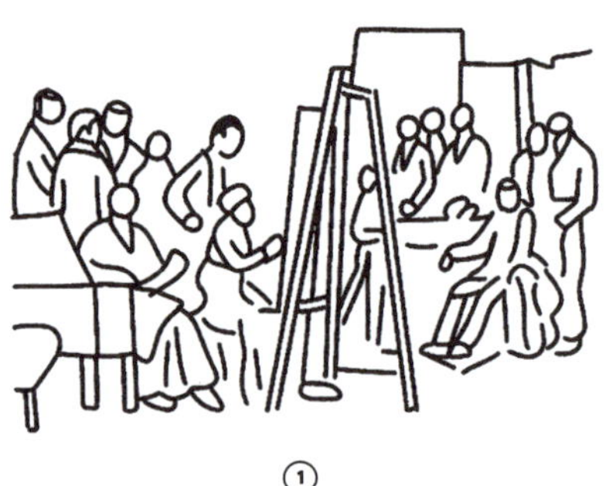

①

TRAINING

Training took place in a painter's studio. Pupils were introduced to the preparation of pigments and canvas, the use of brushes and the fundamentals of the discipline.

Women were not allowed in the institution, where male models posed nude.

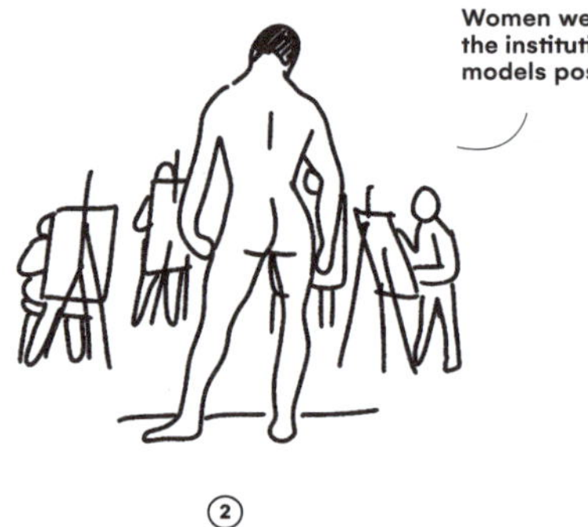

②

SCHOOL

At the Académie Royale de Peinture et de Sculpture, artists attended courses in drawing live male models. Pupils were taught by the Academicians themselves, who also corrected their drawings.

The competitive entry examination was only opened to women in 1903!

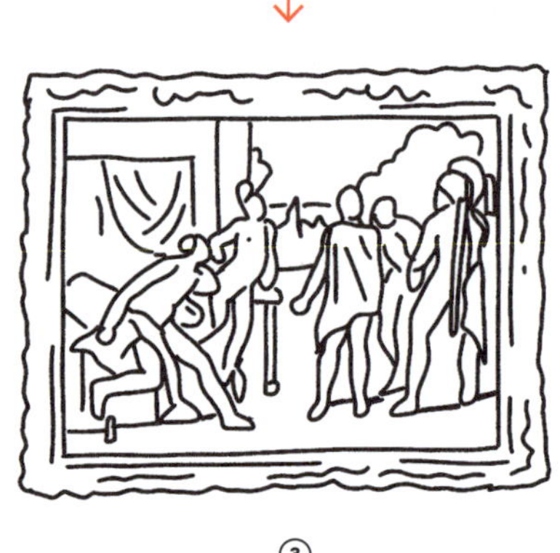

③

COMPETITION

The competition for the Prix de Rome marked the end of the apprenticeship. Candidates were required to present a painting on a given historical theme. Awarded to Hyacinthe Rigaud, François Boucher (p. 154) or Jacques-Louis David (p. 170), this was the most prestigious award; however, most of its winners are unknown today.

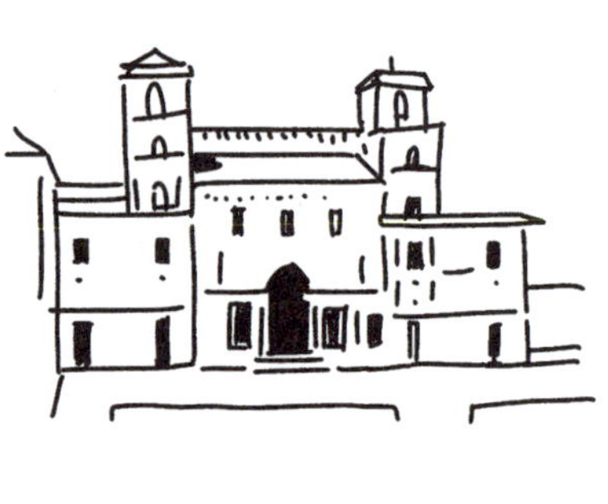

④

INTERNSHIP ABROAD

The Académie de France in Rome welcomed the winners of the Prix de Rome for a three-year period. Initially housed in the Palazzo Mancini, the Académie de France relocated to the Villa Medici, which continues to welcome artists and researchers today, despite the abolition of the prize by André Malraux in 1968.

Becoming an Academician

①

APPROVAL

The artist presented a work on the basis of which Academicians would assess his talent. If he passed this first test, he earned the right to exhibit at the Salon (p. 220).

②

PROJECT VALIDATION

The artist was required to propose a draft, consisting of a sketch based on a subject imposed by the Académie Royale de Peinture et de Sculpture.

③

RECEPTION

After the project was approved, the artist created and finalised the work; this reception piece was then donated to the Académie Royale.

A selection of iconic reception pieces

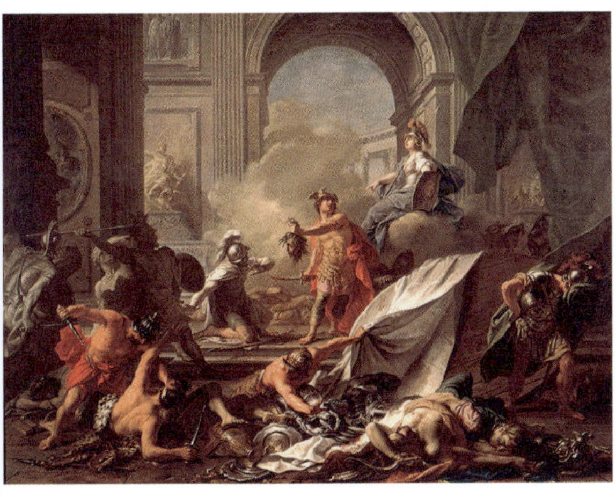

Jean-Marc Nattier
Perseus Petrifies Phineas and his Companions with the Head of Medusa
1718
Musée des Beaux-Arts, Tours

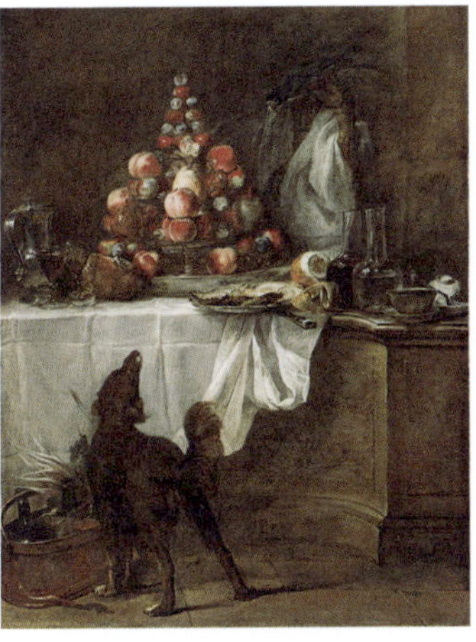

Jean Siméon Chardin
The Buffet
1728
Louvre Museum, Paris

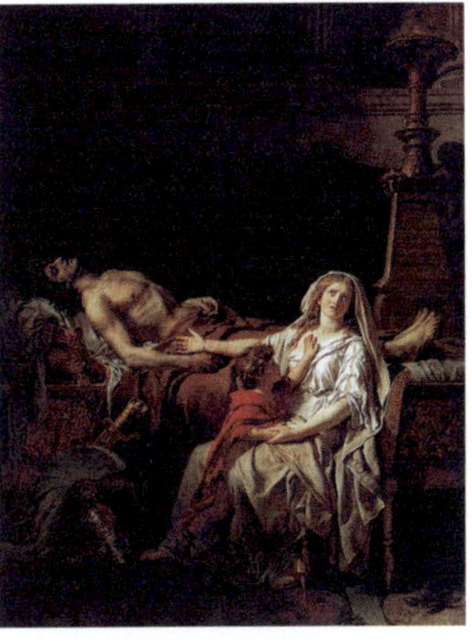

Jacques-Louis David
Andromache Mourning Hector
1783
Louvre Museum, Paris

Not as rigid as it seemed

Despite its conservative image, the Académie Royale de Peinture et de Sculpture, founded in 1648, was a place for the confrontation of ideas, and many of the great debates that shook the history of art were held there.

This royal institution governed the arts in France for 150 years. From the French Revolution onward, it evolved in various forms. Today, it is known as the Académie des Beaux-Arts, a part of the Institut de France.

BEING AN ACADEMICIAN MEANT...

- Benefiting from exclusive royal commissions.
- Meeting and discussing the arts.
- Teaching pupils of the Académie Royale de Peinture et de Scultpure.

THE SECOND SEX

Women were rarely admitted to the Académie Royale. However, as early as 1663, Catherine Duchemin would become the first female artist to join the ranks of the Académie Royale, as a "flower painter".

Meanwhile in China

Shitao cultivated the art of nature

While China was shaken by political upheavals, Shitao chose to live on the fringes of society and returned to nature. His art was captivating, both for its authenticity and its audacity.

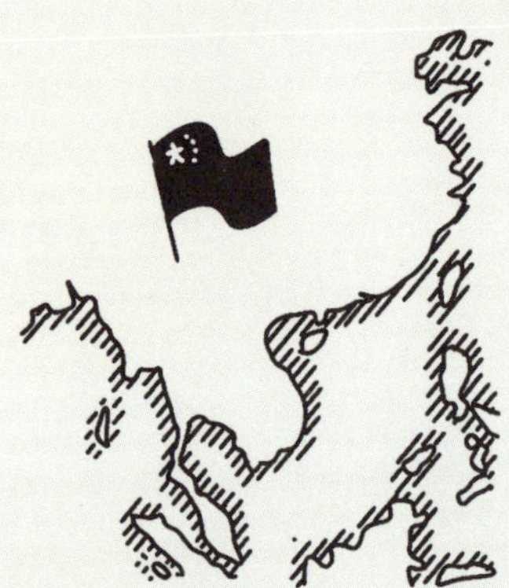

Setting the scene

In China, in the 17th century, the Ming dynasty came to an end and the Manchus rose to power. Artists withdrew to Xuancheng, sheltered from court intrigues and removed from the political life of the country.

Enjoying the natural paradise that they inhabited, amidst forests and rivers, they strayed from the academic orientation of Chinese painting and returned to using nature as a model. Among them, Shitao forged his personality as an artist, far from the Manchu oppression that sealed the fate of his family.

The masterpiece of the moment

- His painting displayed an innovative trait, featuring the codes of the past while also offering a renewed approach to art. This work is the synthesis of his work. Shitao has created a charming landscape that unfolds according to the traditional Chinese perspective, using the verticality of the scroll to tier the planes and connect them in an audacious manner.
- The first plane, at the bottom, takes up almost half of the image. It depicts a calm river flowing near a hermit's hut. In the second plane, a wilder forest appears, dotted with rocks between which the river's water cascades.
- At the top, the mountain appears unreachable, draped in cottony clouds. The viewer's gaze meanders through the three planes, descending from the high–altitude mist to the river as it forms different forks, before becoming the quiet stream that weaves a winding path towards the foreground. The painter conveys the feeling of peace and harmony that inhabits him.

SHOCK QUARTET

In the 17th century, the Beijing "orthodox school" of painting was dominated by the "Four Wangs": Wang Shimin, Wang Jian, Wang Hui and Wuang Yuanji.

WHO WAS SHITAO?

A painter, a poet and a philosopher, Shitao advocated personal expression, the perfection of the gesture and nature as an inspiration.

Born in 1642, he was a descendant of the Ming dynasty. His family was murdered by the Manchus, but he was saved by a servant who entrusted him to the care of monks. He travelled from monastery to monastery until he eventually settled in Xuancheng.

When Kangxi, the new monarch, appeared to be more lenient towards artists, Shitao came out of retirement. From Nanjing to Beijing, he travelled and socialised with poets and painters. He would find himself competing with the "Four Wangs".

Shitao then returned to solitude, building a modest cottage in Yangzhou, where he would appear to embody the hermit depicted in his paintings. He passed on his thoughts in a treatise that marked the history of Chinese art.

SOME ANCIENT MASTERS OF CHINESE PAINTING

Unlike in the West, where the preferred media were wood, then canvas, traditional Chinese painting was commonly produced on rolls of silk or paper. Wooden rods attached to the end of the rolls were used to manipulate them.

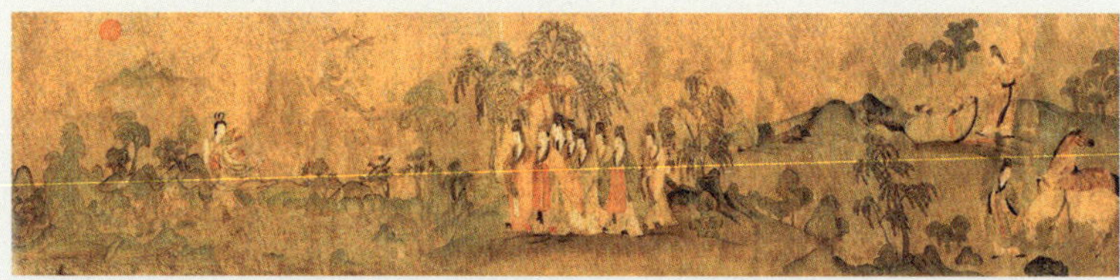

Gu Kaizhi
Nymph of the Luo River
Circa 344–406
The Palace Museum, Beijing

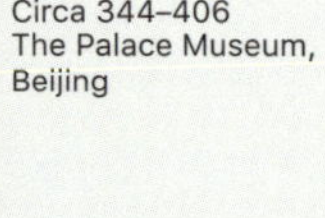

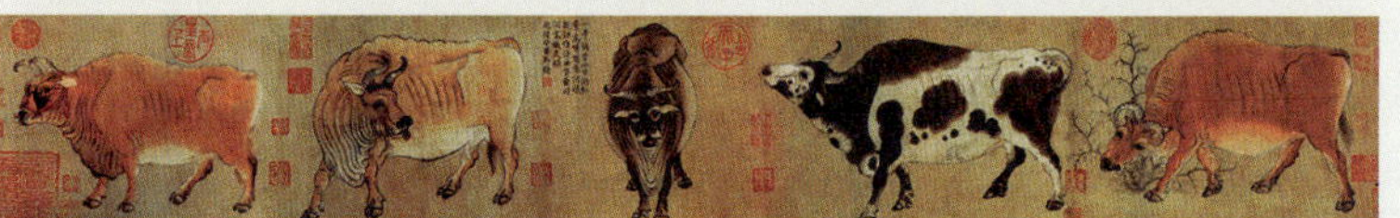

Han Huang
Five bulls
723–787
The Palace Museum, Beijing

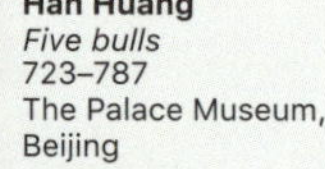

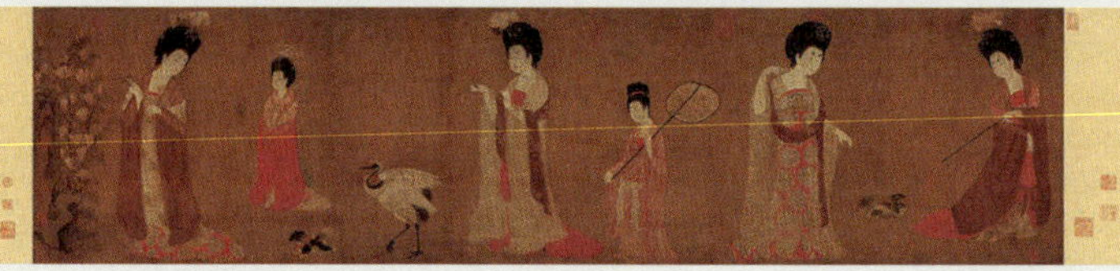

Zhou Fang
Court Ladies Adorning Their Hair with Flowers
Circa 730–800
Provincial Museum, Liaoning

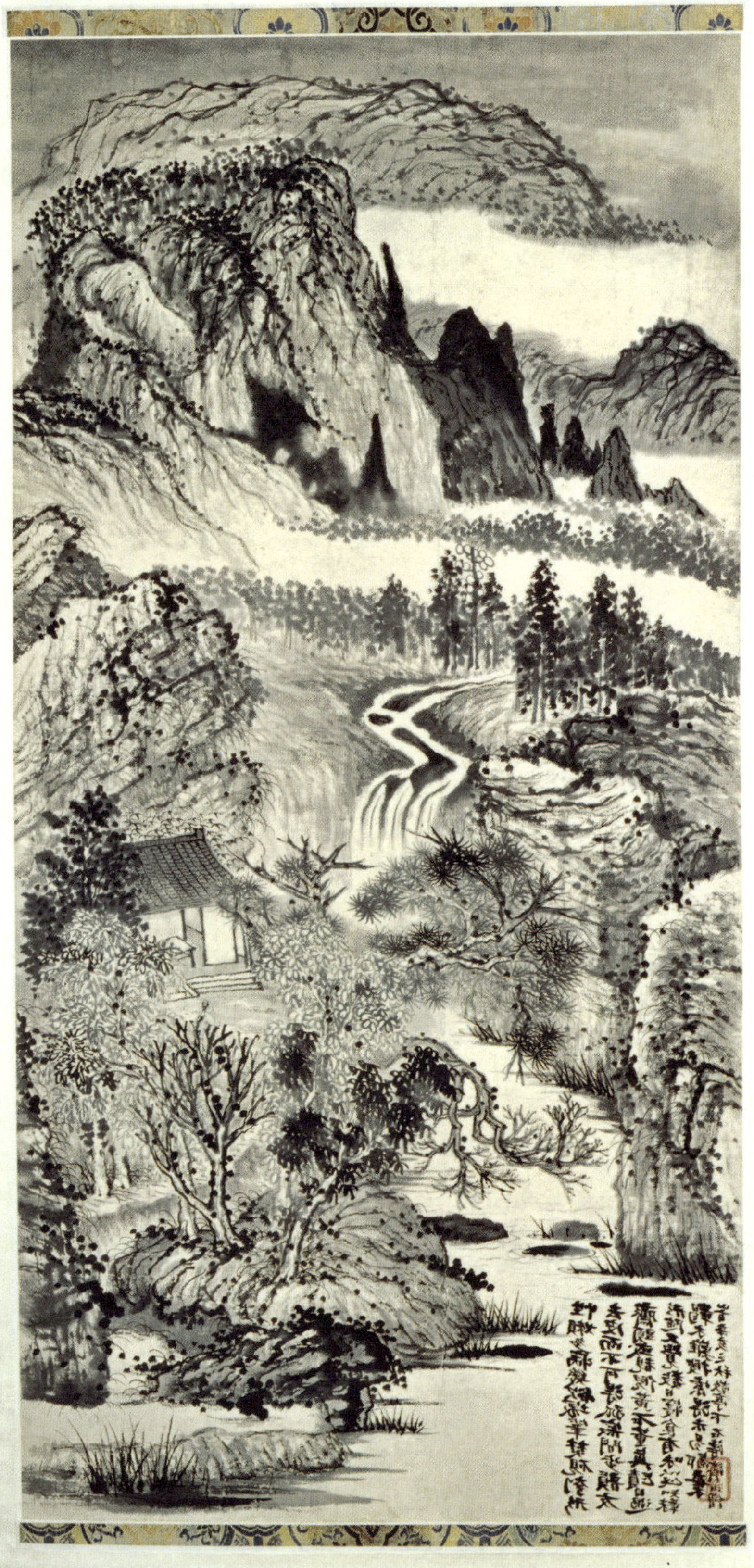

Shitao
JINGTING MOUNTAINS IN AUTUMN
1671
Ink on paper,
86 × 41.7 cm
Musée Guimet, Paris

The leading painters of the Enlightenment

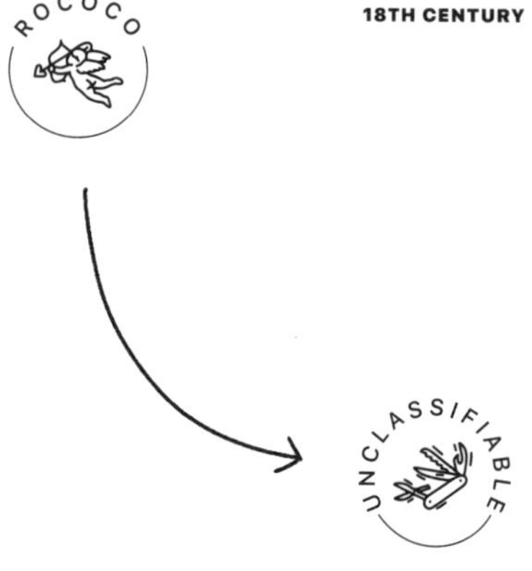

18TH CENTURY

A lighter and more libertine, and also more intellectual approach to painting. A light palette...

Antoine Watteau
p. 138

François Boucher
p. 154

Jean-Honoré Fragonard
p. 158

Giambattista Tiepolo
p. 150

...that also captivated artists whose work evades any classification

Jean Siméon Chardin
p. 144

William Hogarth
p. 148

The great masters of neoclassicism

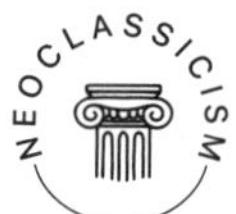

18TH-19TH CENTURY

A return to the moral and aesthetic rigour, in line with the advent of the Empire

Adélaïde Labille-Guiard
p. 164

Élisabeth Vigée Le Brun
p. 168

Jacques-Louis David
p. 170

Marie-Guillemine Benoist
p. 172

Jean-Auguste-Dominique Ingres
p. 180

The great romantic painters

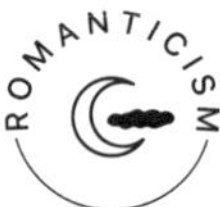

19TH CENTURY

An exalted approach to art, narrating great events and contemporary phenomena in painting

Francisco de Goya
p. 174

Caspar David Friedrich
p. 176

Joseph Mallord William Turner
p. 178

Théodore Géricault
p. 184

Eugène Delacroix
p. 191

PART

3

From Antoine Watteau to Eugène Delacroix

Sensitive painting

From libertinism to contemporary dramas

Art was transforming with society, within which the bourgeois classes were asserting themselves. Alongside official painting, a new, more intimate and sensitive approach to painting emerged. This trend would become the source of the pictorial revolutions for the following century.

Antoine Watteau

An aptly handled transition between two centuries

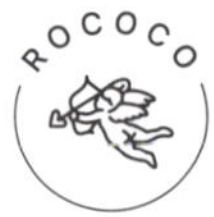

Forming a link between the 17th and 18th centuries, Watteau was neither a classical nor a rococo painter. His unclassifiable "fêtes galantes" symbolised the need for renewal at the end of the reign of Louis XIV.

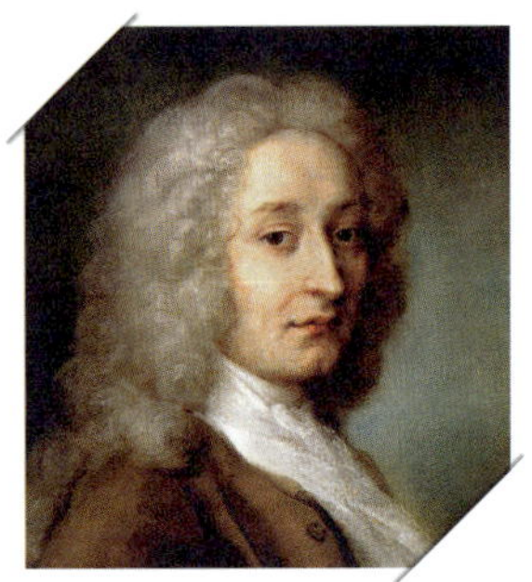

Free from Parisian ties

Born in Valenciennes six years after the city was attached to France, Watteau was as Flemish as he was French. His origins shone through in his paintings: he observed Rubens's art of colouring (p. 98). In Versailles, he was inspired by the Venetians invited by the Regent.

A genre all his own

Drawn to the music and characters of the Commedia dell'arte, he invented the genre called the "fêtes galantes". His silky-coloured paintings weave a path between realism and poetry. This remarkable artist knew how to pause movements with accuracy and fluidity.

A phenomenal career

His painting was soon met with public and critical success, which would be reinforced by his admission to Académie Royale. However, a solitary character, the artist was distressed by the unwelcome admirers who crowded to his home. A shooting star in the world of painting, Antoine Watteau died at the age of only 37.

MUSICAL BRUSHWORK

In a third of his works, Watteau depicted musicians playing.

Charles Le Brun
Page 130

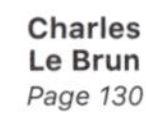

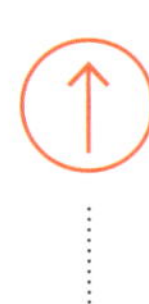

1684
Born in Valenciennes

1689
The Bill of Rights – the foundation of the British parliamentary monarchy

1717
Painted *Pilgrimage to Cythera*

1720
A plague epidemic struck Marseille

1721
Died in Nogent-sur-Marne

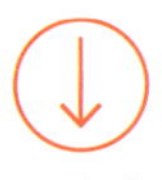

Jean Siméon Chardin
Page 144

PILGRIMAGE TO CYTHERA ↗

1717
Oil on canvas
129 × 194 cm
Louvre Museum, Paris

WHAT ARE WE LOOKING AT?

In this "fête galante" (a courtship party), Watteau depicted pilgrims in love on their way to Cythera, or returning from the island. The painting's atmosphere is both mysterious and sensual.

Situating Cythera

This island is mentioned as one of the possible birthplaces of the goddess Venus (p. 156), represented, on the right, as a statue on a pillar covered with flowers. A pilgrimage to Cythera is a pilgrimage dedicated to love and carnality. But are these characters embarking to travel to the island or returning from it?

A pas de deux

The three couples on the right are telling the same story, in a choreographic arrangement. Sitting down, they are flirting, oblivious to the world, then getting up before heading for the boat. The standing woman, looking back, appears to evoke regret, which supports the idea that she is departing from the island where her love flourished.

In the footsteps of giants

Rubens's influence is apparent in the treatment of the figures, but also in the way nature is depicted to express feelings.
The autumnal greenery contributes to a melancholic and poetic emotion. The distant blue horizon, where sky and sea merge, evokes the background of Leonardo da Vinci's *Saint Anne* (p. 44).

A timeless scene

The mystery thickens, as one cannot place this scene in time. The pilgrims are wearing contemporary clothes, but the statue of Venus, the little amoretti suspended in the air, the half-naked mariners hark back to antiquity.

A SENSITIVE MATTER

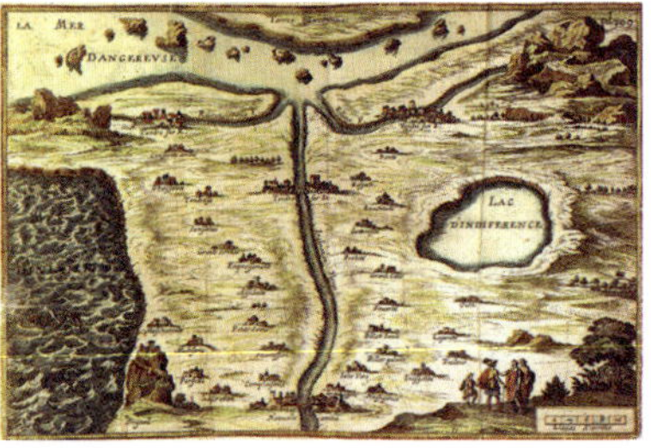

The Map of Tendre, 1856,
Bibliothèque Nationale de France, Paris

In the 17th century, the idea of a land of love emerged, materialised by *The Map of Tendre*, a geographical representation of feelings inspired by the novel *Clélie* by Madeleine de Scudéry.

A PROCRASTINA-TOR

Approved by the Académie Royale de Peinture et de Sculpture (p. 166) in 1712, Watteau was required to present his reception piece. After several reminders and a firm injunction, he finally delivered this painting in 1717. With this unclassifiable work, Watteau was accepted by the Académie Royale as a painter of "fêtes galantes".

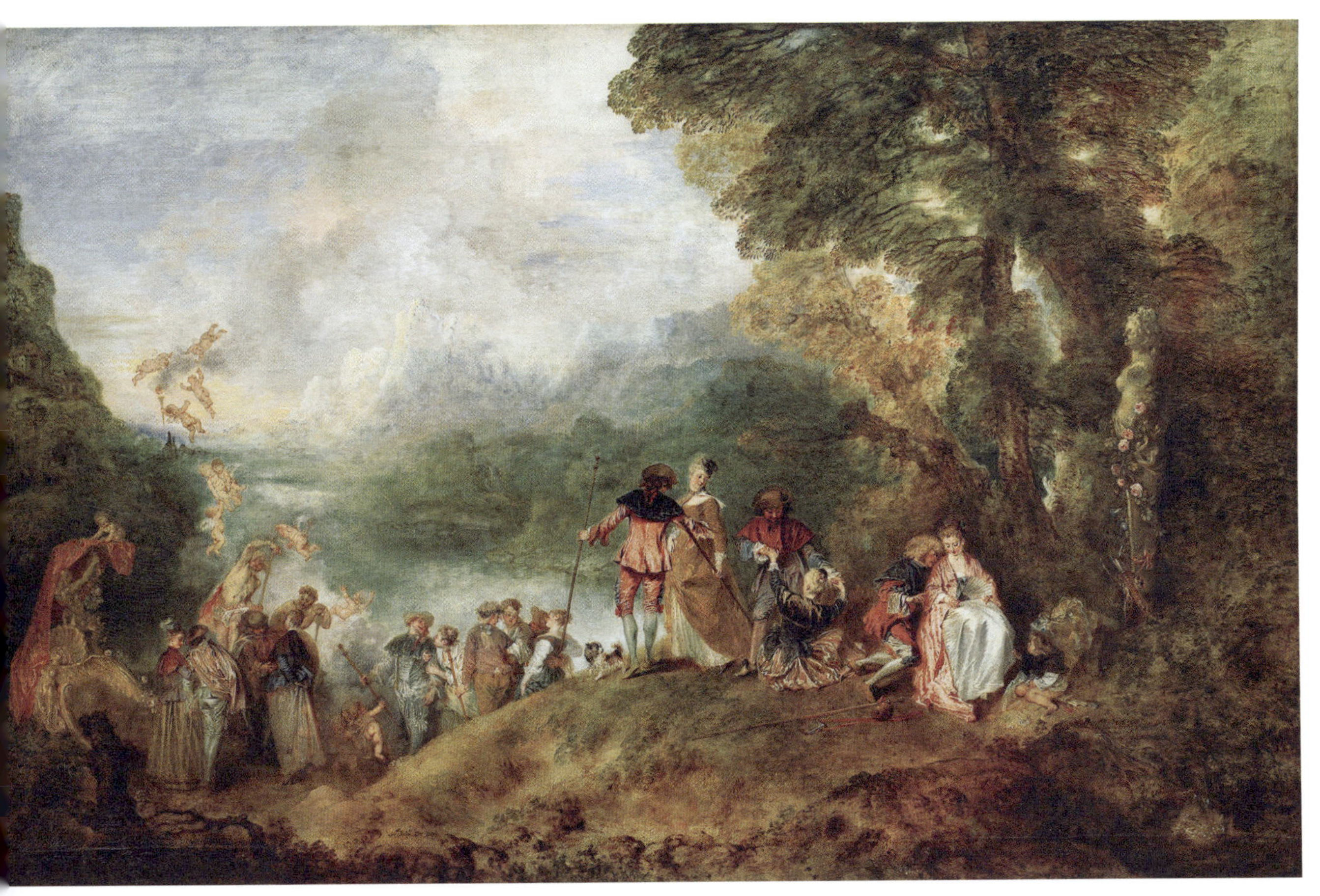

His mother was the sea

According to the Greek poet Hesiod, Aphrodite, known as Venus to the Romans, was born off the island of Cythera, hence the name that Hesiod gave her: Venus of Cythera. In *Theogony*, the story of the birth of the gods, he presented her as the daughter of the sea, impregnated by the titan Ouranos, who would be emasculated by his son Cronos during the fight that opposed them.

The most beautiful views

Seeing the world in paint

GIORGIONE
The Tempest

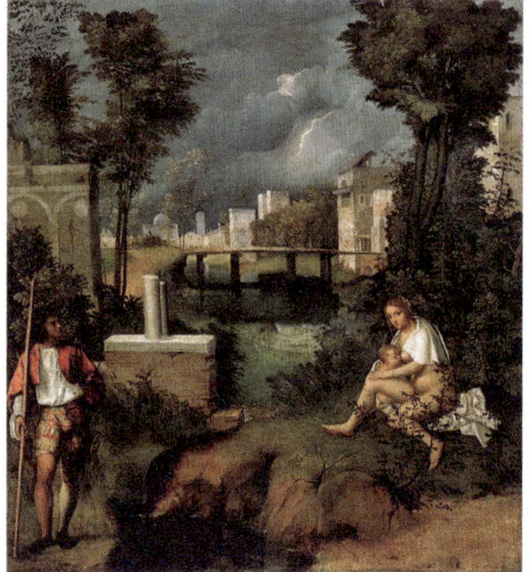

EL GRECO
View of Toledo

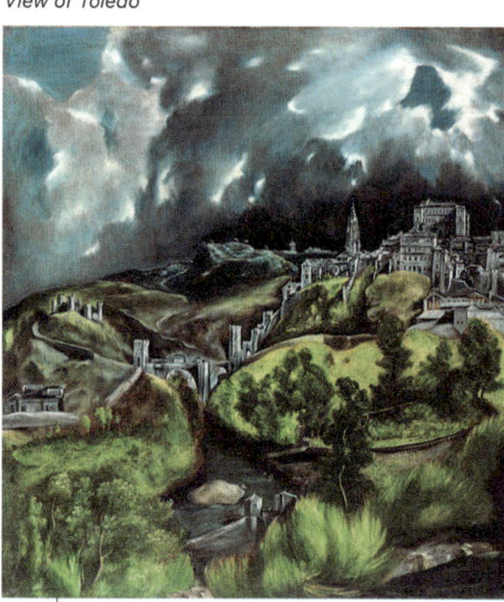

CANALETTO
The Entrance to the Grand Canal, Venice

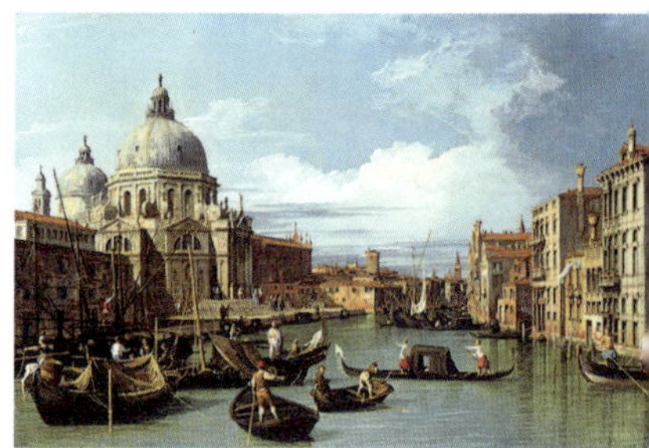

1506 **1596** **1730**

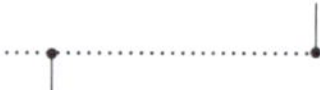

1529 **1648** **177**

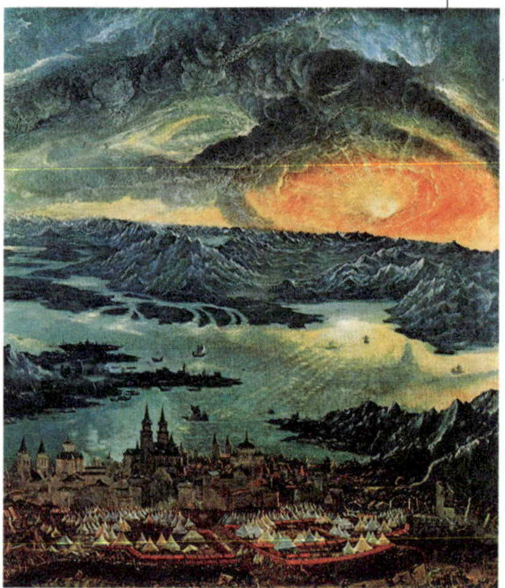

ALBRECHT ALTDORFER
The Battle of Alexander at Issus

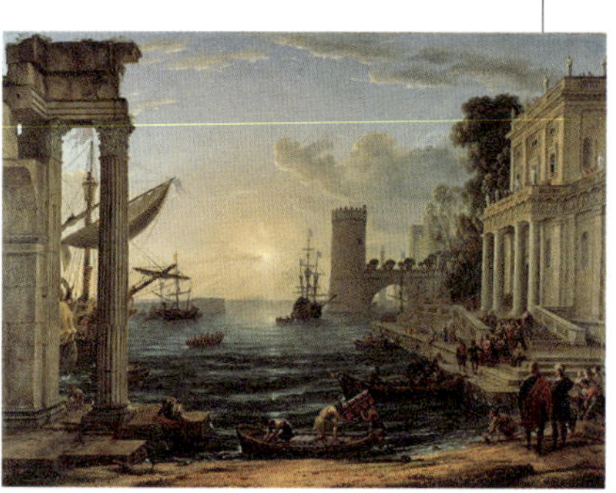

CLAUDE GELLÉE
The Embarkation of the Queen of Sheba

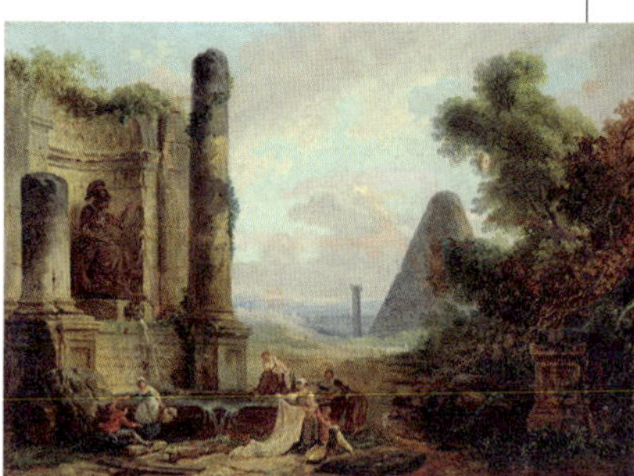

HUBERT ROBERT
Fountain of Minerva

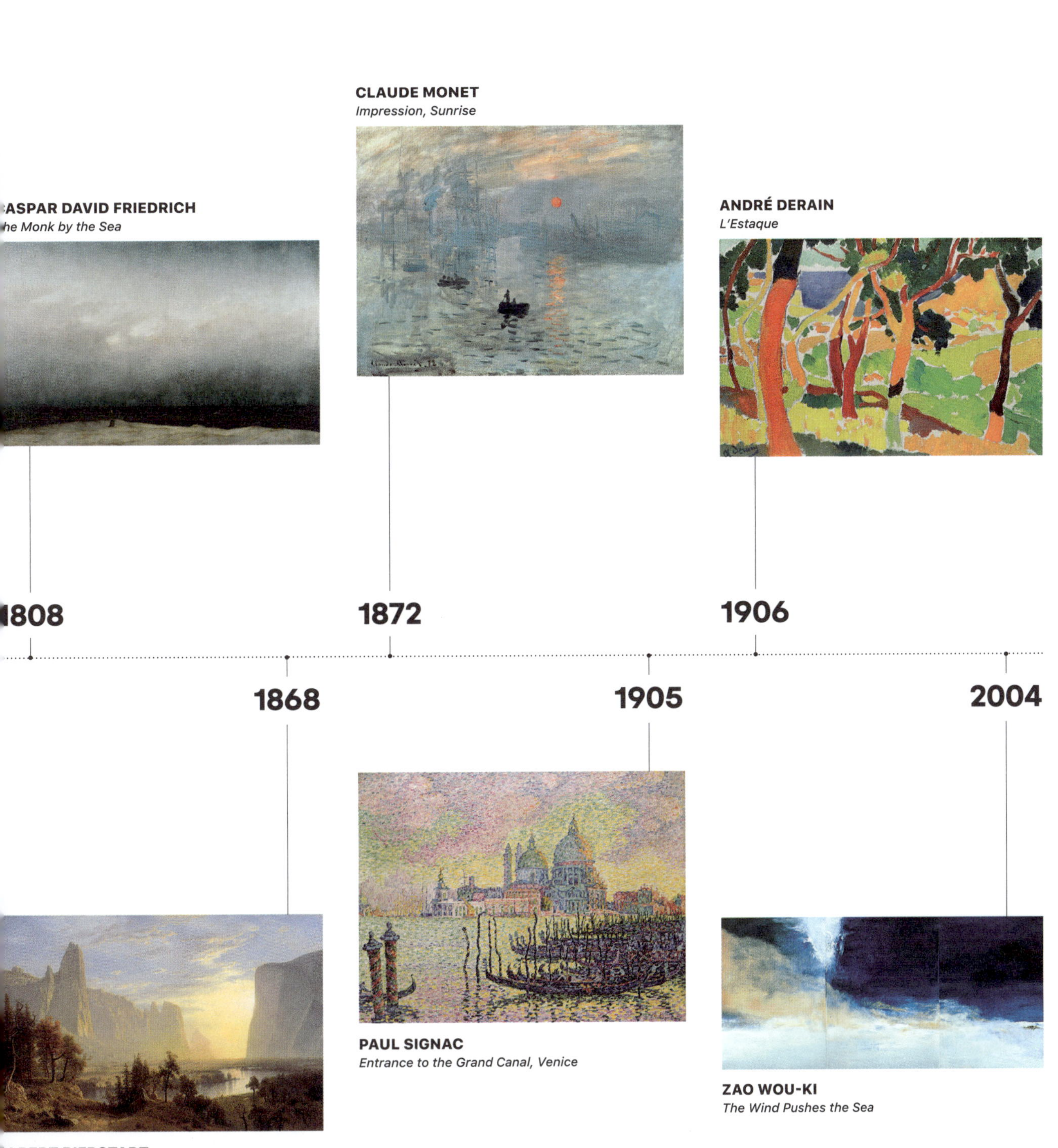

ASPAR DAVID FRIEDRICH
he Monk by the Sea
808
CLAUDE MONET
Impression, Sunrise
1872
ANDRÉ DERAIN
L'Estaque
1906
1868
LBERT BIERSTADT
osemite Valley, Yellowstone Park
1905
PAUL SIGNAC
Entrance to the Grand Canal, Venice
2004
ZAO WOU-KI
The Wind Pushes the Sea

CHARDIN
Le panier de fraises des bois

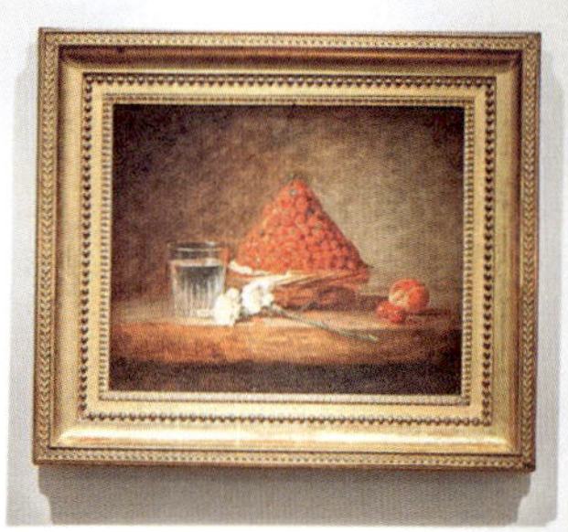

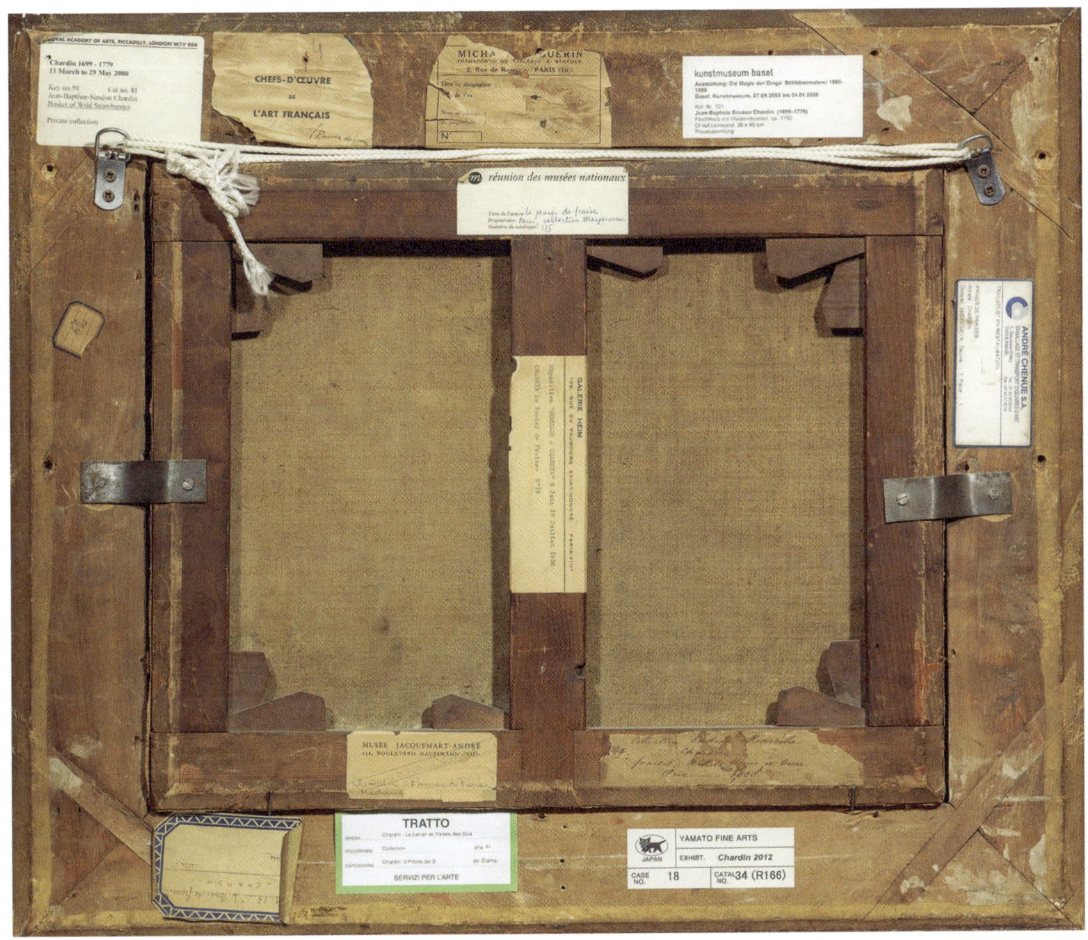

Front and back

Opposite, *Basket with Wild Strawberries* by Chardin, presented for sale by Artcurial on 23 March 2022. Above, the back of the work, featuring labels that testify to its presentation in various institutions: Musée Jacquemart-André (Paris, 1961), Royal Academy of Arts (London, 2000), Kunstmuseum (Basel, 2008) and others.

Jean Siméon Chardin

Still life truly comes to life!

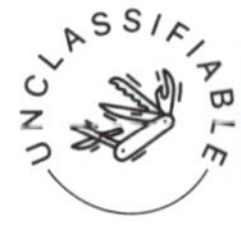

Chardin's work defies classification. His works stood out amidst the enthusiastic and light-hearted production of the Enlightenment. Painting was a difficult exercise for him, but his hard work would earn him the admiration of many painters after his time.

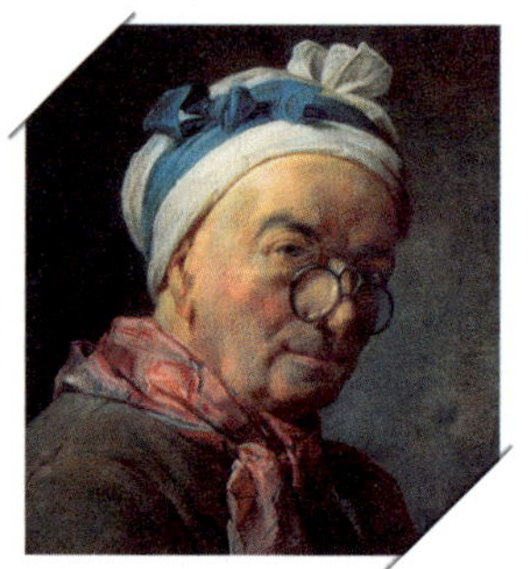

Reaping the fruits of his labour

Chardin was admitted to the Académie Royale de Peinture et de Sculpture as a painter "in the talent of animals and fruits". He was also fond of genre scenes where time seems to stand still. Towards the end of his life, pigments would make him ill, causing him to swap oil painting for pastel.

It's not an easy ride for everyone

He received a modest education, which gave him a complex; however, Denis Diderot would describe him as a brilliant conversationalist. He was a hard worker, who devoted long hours to his art in the secrecy of his studio.

He bewitched the gaze

Jean Siméon Chardin did not care for painting perfect illusions, but he rendered the truth. In his compositions, he arranged objects that he had chosen for their formal aspect, rather than for their utility. Their presence radiates a kind of magic that continues to confuse the most expert observers.

IT WAS SAID OF HIM

"This magic cannot be explained. [...] Come closer, and everything blurs, flattens and disappears; move away, and everything is recreated and reproduced." Denis Diderot, Salon of 1763.

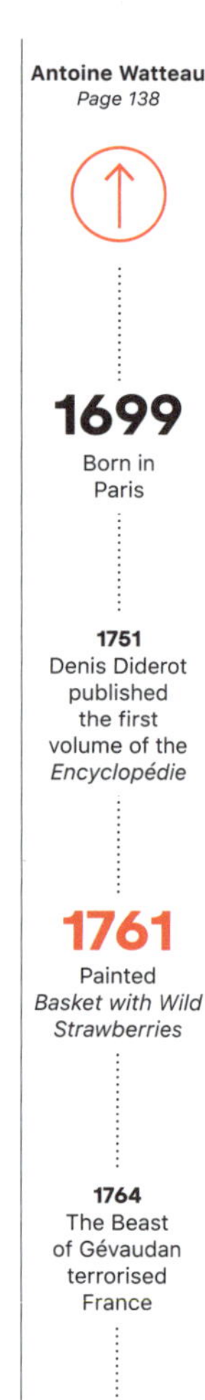

BASKET WITH WILD STRAWBERRIES

1761
Oil on canvas
38 × 46 cm
Currently being acquired by the Louvre Museum

WHAT ARE WE LOOKING AT?

Chardin painted this masterpiece of the still life genre at a time when strawberries were in fashion. Two years earlier, Louis XV had a greenhouse built, which housed the most beautiful collection of strawberry plants in Europe.

Playing on textures

The artist had entered his mature period. The composition of this work is simple, and the fruits are summarily detailed. Nonetheless, the painter succeeds in producing materiality; his quest is that of truth. The light renders the texture of each fruit. It bounces off the smooth skin of cherries, but is absent from the matte, fluffy skin of peaches, while the shards of light on the strawberries reflect their graininess.

Vivid hues of red

The colour palette is limited; white and red stand out beautifully against the brown background, contrasting beautifully with each other. Splashes of red dot the canvas: cherries colour the wood of the table, a crushed piece of strawberry appears just in front of the carnations, and the strawberries themselves are reflected in different parts of the glass.

A lesson from Cézanne

With the glass, the strawberries arranged in the form of a pyramid and the fruit on the right of the painting, Chardin produced an image that would later inspire a rule stated by Cézanne, laying the foundations of avant-garde painting: "Treat nature by the cylinder, the sphere, the cone."

Something is happening

The flower is unbalanced and is threatening to fall off the table at any moment. The painter expertly used effects to captivate the viewer with his images and breathe life into his still lifes.

IN CHARDIN'S PAINTINGS, ONE CAN SEE ...

Still lifes | **Genre scenes in a kitchen** | **Children learning or having fun**

AN EXPENSIVE TREAT

In 2022, *Basket with Wild Strawberries* was auctioned and sold by Artcurial to an American gallery owner for 24.3 million euros. However, the Louvre Museum requested that it be classified as a "national treasure" by the French State, which gave the institution 30 months to raise the funds required to acquire the work for its collections.

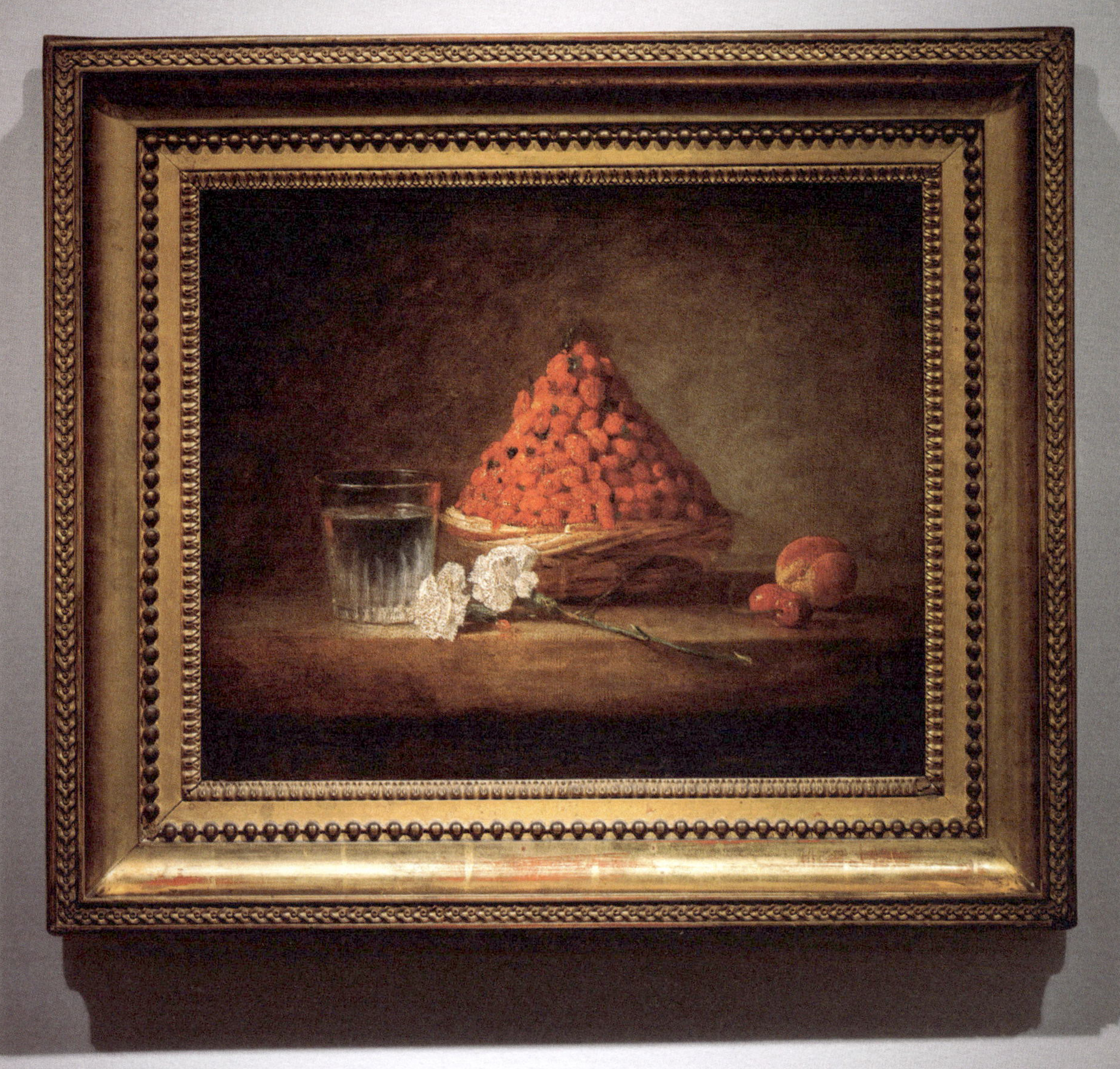

Ducreux and Chardin

He who laughs last, laughs hardest!

Jean Siméon Chardin and Joseph Ducreux were contemporaries, but the former's silence and paused time seem opposed to the latter's outrageous and fluid attitudes. Yet, each in their own way, they succeeded in engaging the viewer.

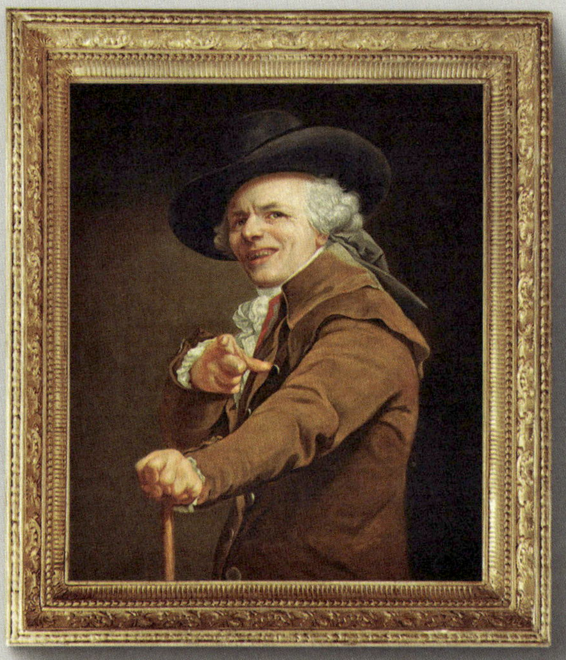

SELF-PORTRAIT IN THE GUISE OF A MOCKINGBIRD **BY JOSEPH DUCREUX**
1783

The artist has established explicit frontal contact with the viewer, an approach that was as destabilising at the time as it remains now. Despite earning the freedom to exhibit his works at the time of the French Revolution, the painter remained heavily criticised. His "lackey humour" stood in defiance of social codes.

Oil on canvas, 55.4 × 46.3 cm
Musée National des Châteaux de Versailles et de Trianon

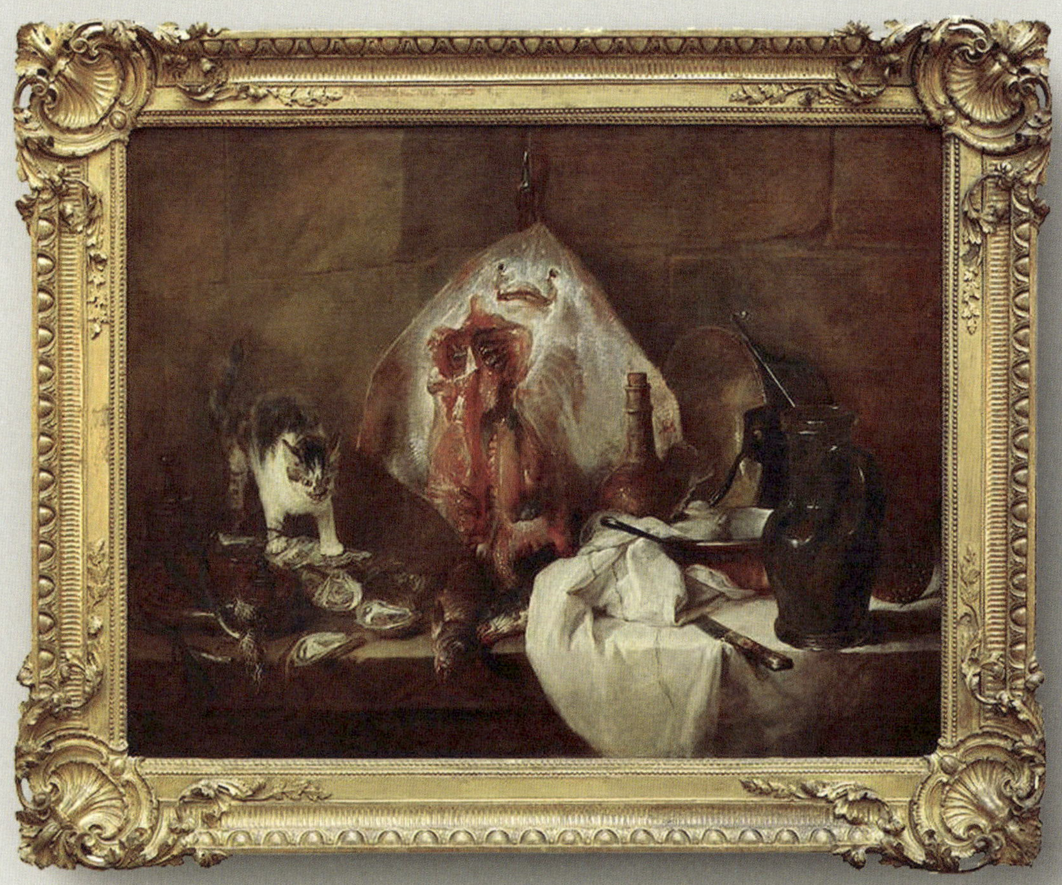

***THE RAY* BY JEAN SIMÉON CHARDIN**
1728

The gaze is drawn to the suspended ray, to which this work owes its name. One cannot help but distinguish a face – a strange and sad clown, engaging in a face-to-face encounter with the viewer. This anthropomorphic allusion and the fish's exposed entrails may also evoke a martyr.

Oil on canvas, 114 × 146 cm
Louvre Museum, Paris

William Hogarth

The Human Comedy through the lens of English humour

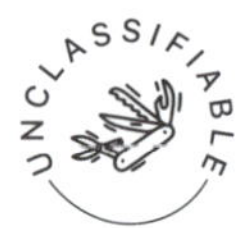

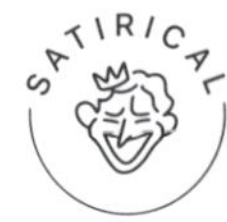

Hogarth was a remarkable engraver and an innovative painter. He was also a committed man, no doubt marked by his troubled childhood, known for his satirical wit that appealed to the public.

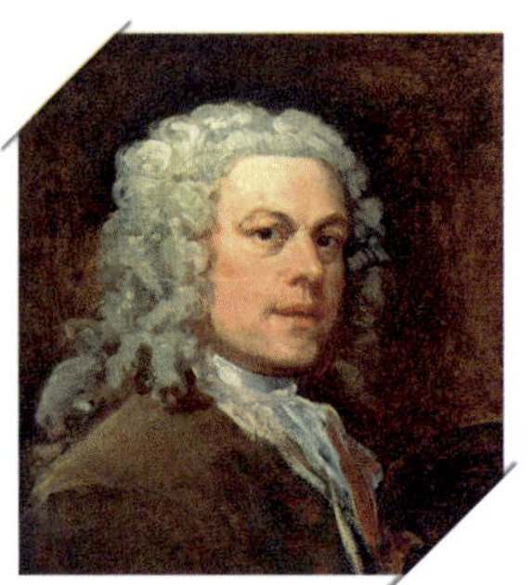

A committed man

When Hogarth was a child, his father was jailed for debt. This event awakened, in the artist, a tenacity that would mark his career. He was also involved in institutions to reflect on the role of art, and contributed to the Foundling Hospital of London.

Piracy is killing engraving

Hogarth was foremost a renowned engraver. In his studio, among other works, he produced successful social satires that were copied and distributed without his permission. He lobbied the British parliament for the creation of the Engraver's Copyright Act (known as "Hogarth's Act"), which protected engravers.

Quality humour

Hogarth's involvement in painting came late in his life. He tried his hand at historical painting, portraits and "conversation pieces", genre scenes depicting English society. He was renowned as a "comic history painter" for his satirical talents.

WILLIAM HOGARTH SAID

"I know no such thing as genius – genius is nothing but labour and diligence."

Jean Siméon Chardin
Page 144

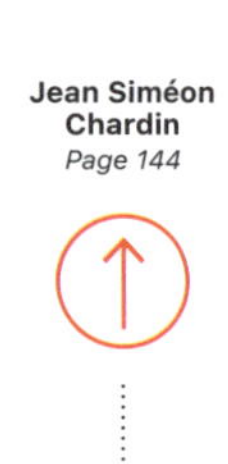

1697
Born in London

1742
Anders Celsius invented the thermometer scale that bears his name

1743 to **1745**
Painted *Marriage à-la-Mode: The Tête à Tête*

1764
Died in London

1776
On 4 July, the United States signed the Declaration of Independence

Giambattista Tiepolo
Page 150

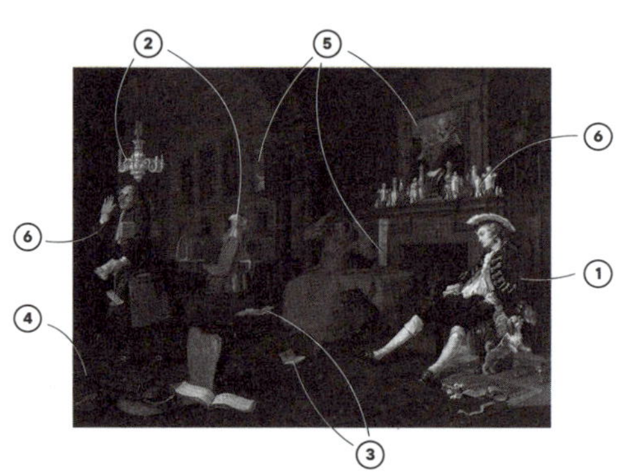

MARRIAGE À-LA-MODE: THE TÊTE À TÊTE

1743–1745
Oil on canvas
69.9 × 90.8 cm
National Gallery, London

WHAT ARE WE LOOKING AT?

In a series of six paintings, Hogarth recounts the consequences of an arranged marriage. Here, the bride and groom are reunited after spending a dissolute night, each on their own.

① Dangerous liaisons

The husband looks weary. The black spot on his neck suggests that he has contracted syphilis, while his broken sword on the ground evokes impotence; the dog is sniffing a woman's cap sticking out of his pocket.

② Burning the candle at both ends

His wife has stayed up all night, as indicated by the tired look on her servant's face and the burned-out candles. These are also a vanitas (p. 110).

③ A bluff

The cards indicate that she has been playing. At her feet lies a whist rule book; whist was a fashionable game created by Hoyle, known for his books on card games.

④ False note

The two violin cases placed on top of each other symbolise the lovemaking that she has engaged in, while the overturned seat indicates the presence of a lover, who has left suddenly. From the look of satisfaction on her face, she quite enjoyed herself.

⑤ An idea in the back of the artist's head

The decor confirms the licentious atmosphere. The sculpted profile behind the wife evokes her lover, and behind the columns, the green curtain hiding an erotic nude whose foot can be seen echoes the amoretto above the fireplace.

⑥ Misplaced priorities

The accumulation of trinkets on the mantelpiece is a testament to the couple's poor taste and their penchant for frivolous spending; meanwhile, a servant is fleeing the room, holding unpaid bills in his hand.

⑥ +

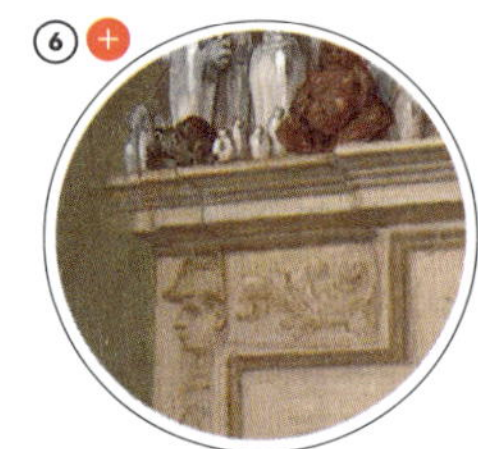

COMPLETE SERIES

Hogarth's series *Marriage à-la-Mode* is composed of six scenes:

- *The Marriage Settlement (name on the frame: The marriage contract)*
- *The Tête à Tête (name on the frame: Shortly after the marriage)*
- *The Inspection (name on the frame: The visit to the quack doctor)*
- *The Toilette (name on the frame: The countess's morning levee)*
- *The Bagnio (name on the frame: The killing of the earl)*
- *The Lady's Death (name on the frame: The suicide of the countess)*

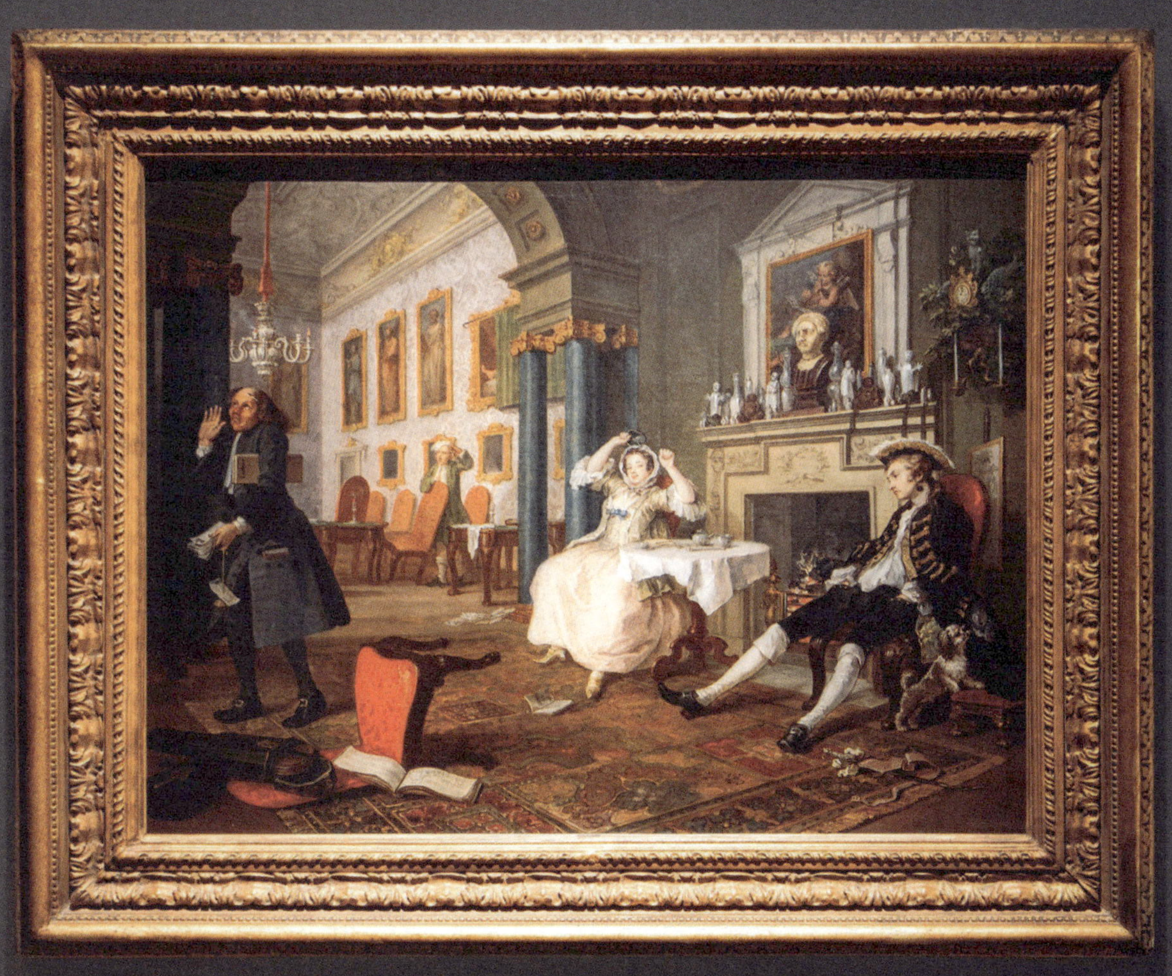

Giambattista Tiepolo

Formidable decors

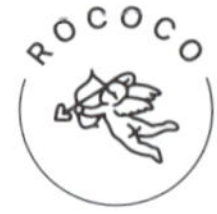

In the vibrant 17th-century Venice, Tiepolo became a leading artist, influenced by the great masters who preceded him. His bright palette and ethereal compositions would seduce the courts of Europe.

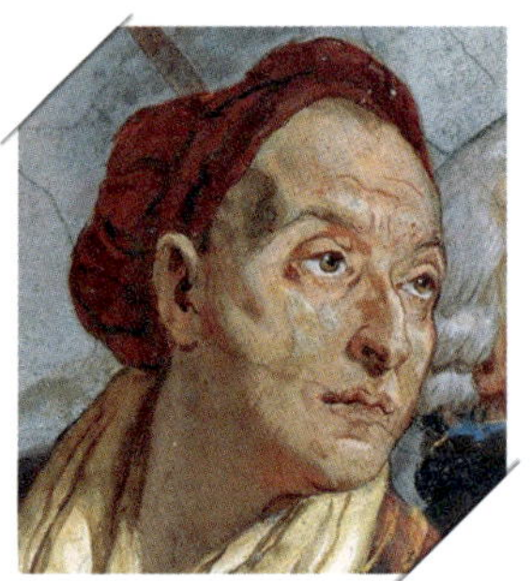

Learning can happen at any age

Tiepolo was taught in the studio of the Venetian painter Gregorio Lazzarini. He copied the works of his master and other painters, and learned to structure his compositions, acquiring a solid visual culture that he would enrich throughout his life.

Clear thinking

Tiepolo's palette is luminous. In his maturity, he favoured brilliant tones and coloured shadows in the manner of Veronese (p. 68). The painter was known for his speed of execution, which proved useful when producing fresco decorations, for which he was highly demanded.

Tiepolo, father and son

The artist's two sons, Giandomenico and Lorenzo, would accompany him on his building sites, from Germany to Spain. Aged 66, he placed himself at the service of the prestigious Spanish monarchy, while Venice was won over by neoclassical taste, which he didn't care for.

SIMPLY SHAMEFUL!

Tiepolo also used his skills as a forger. With the help of a friend, he "embellished" a sketch, in order to sell it under the Veronese's name.

William Hogarth
Page 148

1696
Born in Venice

1718
Foundation of New Orleans in the Gulf of Mexico

1743 to **1744**
Painted *The Banquet of Cleopatra*

1762
Catherine the Great became Empress of Russia

1770
Died in Madrid

François Boucher
Page 154

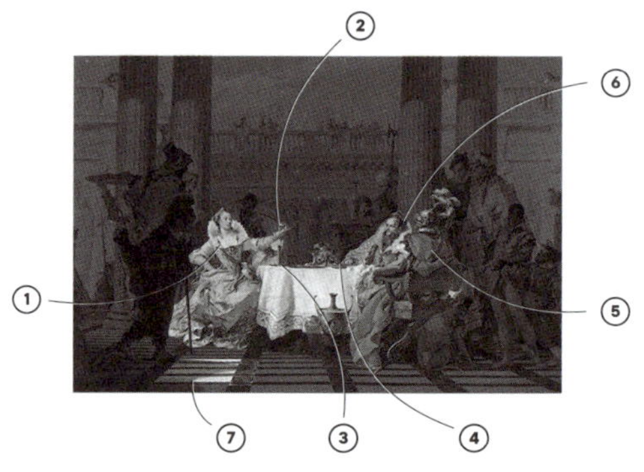

THE BANQUET OF CLEOPATRA

1743–1744
Oil on canvas
250.3 × 357 cm
National Gallery of Victoria, Melbourne

WHAT ARE WE LOOKING AT?

In *Natural History*, the Latin author Pliny the Elder recounts how Queen Cleopatra served her lover, the Roman consul Mark Antony, the most expensive meal in the world.

① *Makeover*

Described as a nefarious seductress, Cleopatra is depicted dressed in European fashion, in majesty, and surrounded by busy servants.

② Dissolved solution

Promising her lover a sumptuous meal, Cleopatra has kept her word: she has seized the sumptuous pearl hanging from her earring and is dissolving it in vinegar to drink it. The other pearl is still hanging from her ear.

③ Tested, but not approved

It is likely that Pliny the Elder invented this fable, as however corrosive vinegar may be, it would not be able to completely dissolve Cleopatra's pearl – and, moreover, in such a short time.

④ No dessert for Mark Antony

On the table, the meal is frugal. All its luxury lies in the pearl drunk by Cleopatra. The fruit bowl is decorated with representations of Isis, an Egyptian goddess associated with love and fertility.

⑤ Secondary role

Mark Antony's features are largely hidden by his richly decorated warrior's helmet. He is recognisable by the ample red Roman general's cloak that he is wearing.

⑥ No extra time

Lucius Plancus was the judge of this bet between the two lovers. He declared Cleopatra the winner before she could dissolve the second pearl.

⑦ Entering through the front door

The balanced architectural decor is reminiscent of Veronese's compositions. The tiled foreground welcomes the viewer to enter the scene – a feeling reinforced by the painting's dimensions.

② +

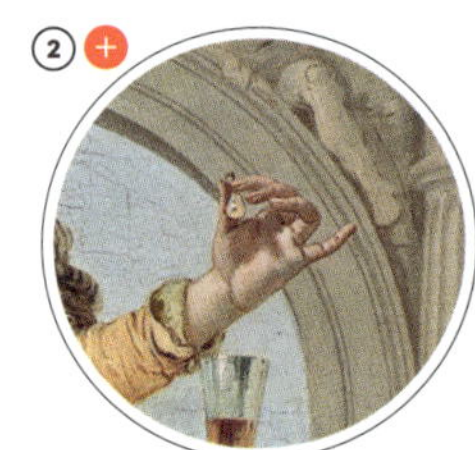

TIEPOLO'S ART IN A NUTSHELL

- A bright palette.
- Coloured shadows.
- Ethereal and dynamic compositions.
- Illusionary decors.
- Frescoes and oil paintings.

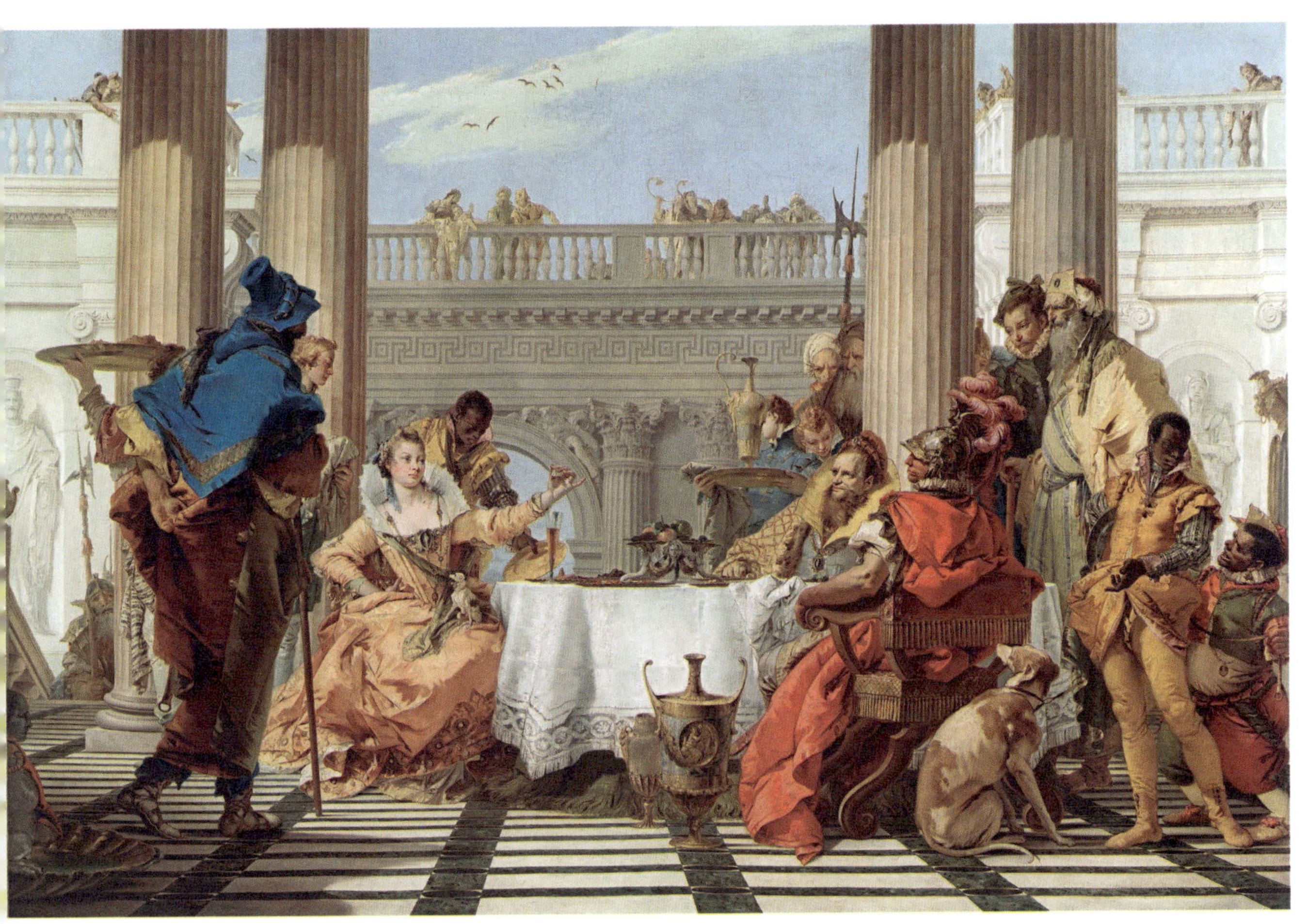

Pliny's words

"She took one earring off, and dropped the pearl in the vinegar, and when it was melted, swallowed it. Lucius Plancus, who was umpiring the wager, placed his hand on the other pearl when she was preparing to destroy it also in a similar way, and declared that Antony had lost the battle [...]. With this goes the story that [...] the second of this pair of pearls was cut in two pieces, so that half a helping of the jewel might be in each of the ears of Venus in the Pantheon at Rome."

Natural History, Book IX.

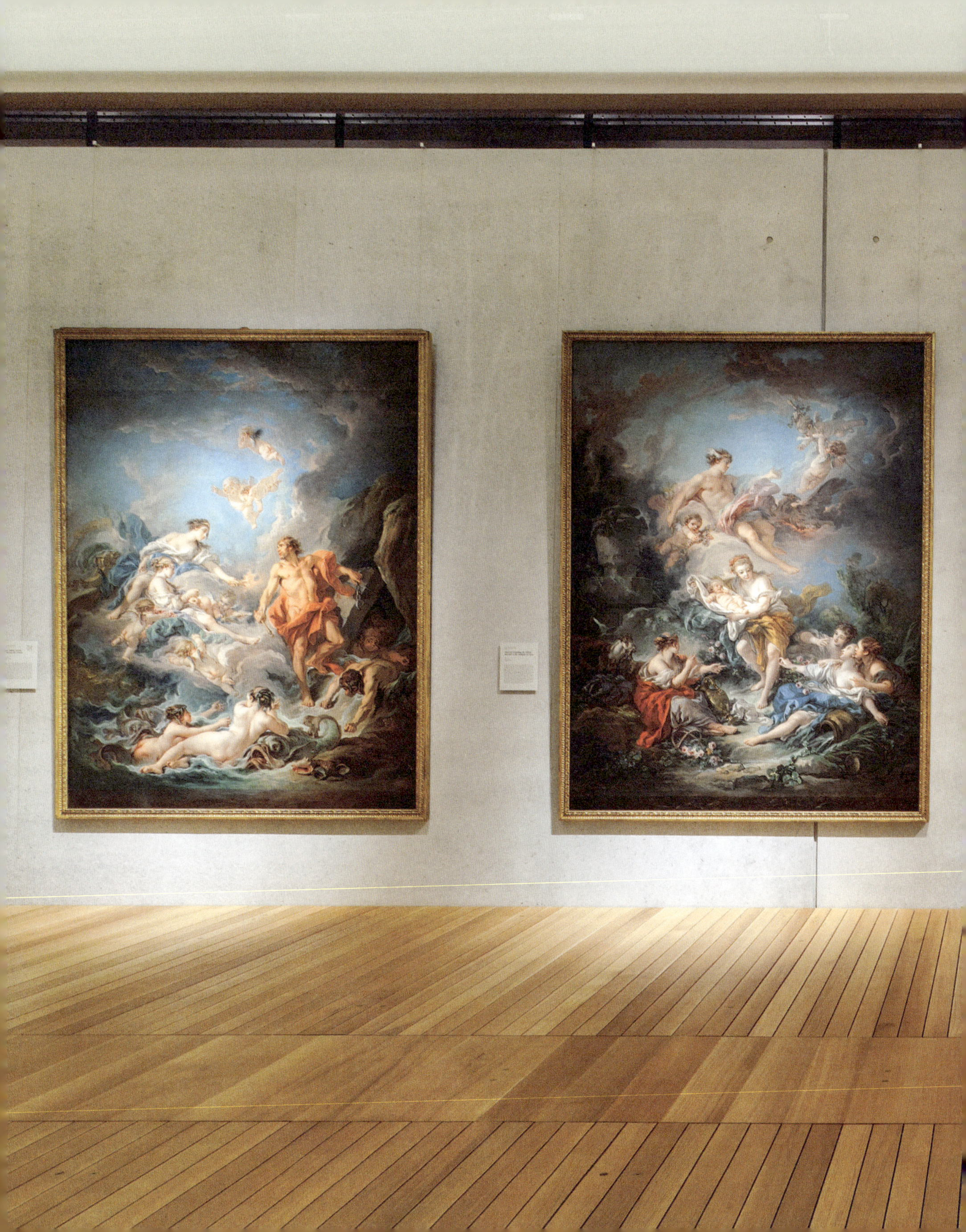

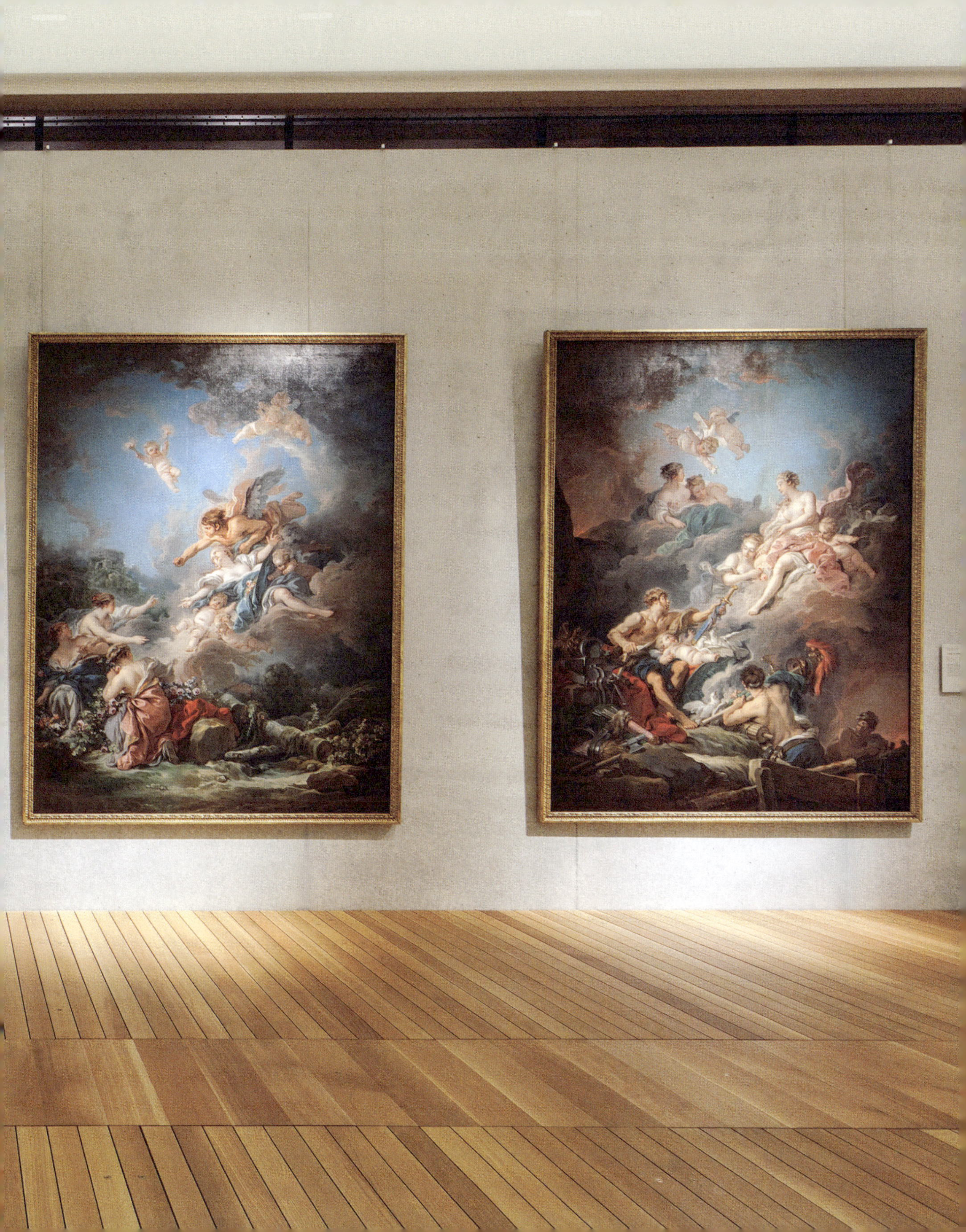

François Boucher

A cutting-edge painter

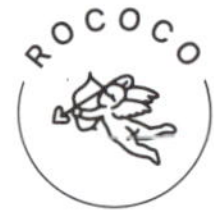

Boucher was a born painter. He was immensely talented, tried his hand at all subjects and was awarded with great prestige. His highly decorative painting set trends for the aristocracy in France and Europe.

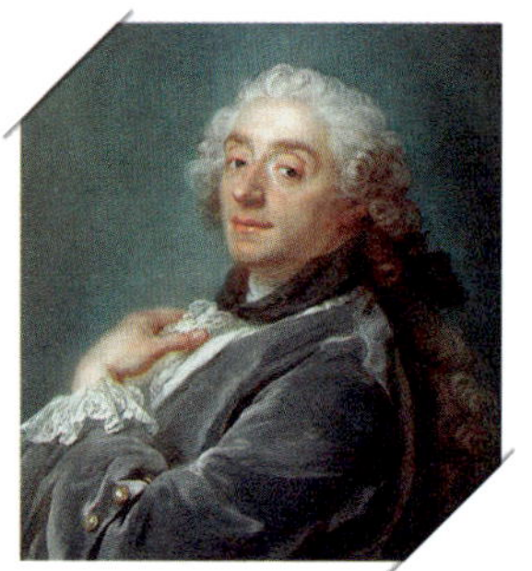

False start

The son of a relatively unknown illustrator, Boucher briefly visited François Lemoyne's studio. Despite winning the Prix de Rome (p. 132), he was refused a stay in Italy. He turned to engraving to finance his trip. During his journey, he would become sensitive to the art of Sebastiano Ricci.

Well-balanced curves

He was greatly talented and used his skills to try his hand at all subjects, from history painting to libertine nudes. His highly decorative art, which features a vivid palette combined with sensual and mellow curved lines, is emblematic of the Rocaille spirit.

A trendy artist

First painter to Louis XV and favourite of Madame de Pompadour, he was renowned from Denmark all the way to Russia. His paintings would decorate fashionable interiors, but from the 1760s onward, the graceful fantasy depicted in his works found its detractors, including the philosopher Denis Diderot.

A GRATEFUL PUPIL

"Not everyone can be a Boucher." With these words, Jacques-Louis David (p. 170), a prestigious pupil of François Boucher, expressed his admiration for his master's genius.

Giambattista Tiepolo
Page 150

1703
Born in Paris

1741
Voltaire wrote *Candide*

1769
Painted *Venus at Vulcan's Forge*

1770
Died in Paris

1789
"Nothing", Louis XVI wrote in his diary on 14 July

Jean Honoré Fragonard
Page 158

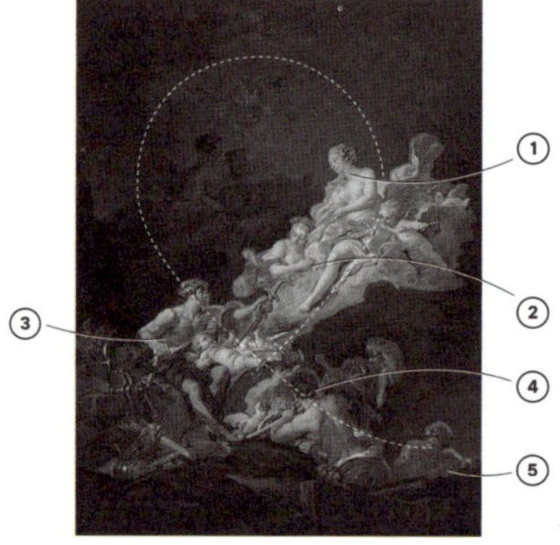

VENUS AT VULCAN'S FORGE

1769
Oil on canvas
273.5 × 204.7 cm
Kimbell Art Museum, Fort Worth

WHAT ARE WE LOOKING AT?

In this painting, Boucher recounts an episode from the *Aeneid*, a Latin epic by Virgil. It depicts the goddess Venus coming to persuade the god Vulcan to help her.

① Convincing arguments

As a war looms in the region of Rome, Venus worries about her son Aeneas, who is mortal. She visits her husband, Vulcan, using her charms to convince him to forge weapons that will protect Aeneas.

② First-class travel

The goddess is represented amidst an avalanche of feathers, clouds, drapery and flesh, featuring very sensual accents. She is also recognisable by the flowers, doves and *putti* (p. 86) accompanying her.

③ Under her spell

The god Vulcan is captivated by the goddess's aura. Venus's sway on the god is symbolised by the *putto* and the doves descending on his lap. He is already handing her a sword that can be interpreted as a sexual hint.

④ Follow the movement

The image's structure is based on a vast dynamic curve. It begins at the lower left, rises diagonally, following the back of the figure turning away from the viewer, then continues towards the peak of the rock at the top left; it then follows the pattern of the clouds, before leading us back to Venus and down to Vulcan.

⑤ A painter with a trained eye

This composition allows for clear delimitation of each god's universe: clear, celestial and ethereal for Venus, and dark, volcanic and rocky for Vulcan, who is assisted by the Cyclops, recognisable by the third eye present on the forehead of the one facing the viewer.

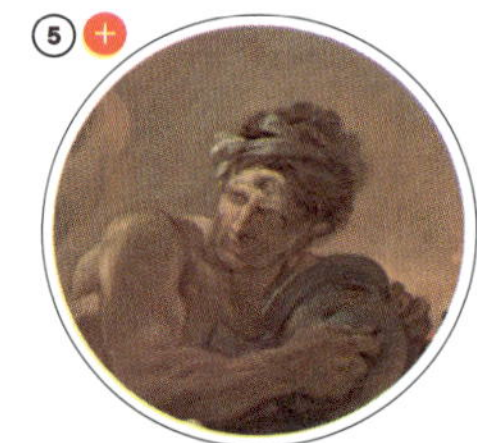

THE ROCAILLE OR ROCOCO MOVEMENT IN A NUTSHELL

- A luminous and vivid palette, that was, however, gentler and more nuanced than in the previous century.
- Dynamic curves and counter-curves.
- Sensual and soft textures.
- A gallant and pastoral world.

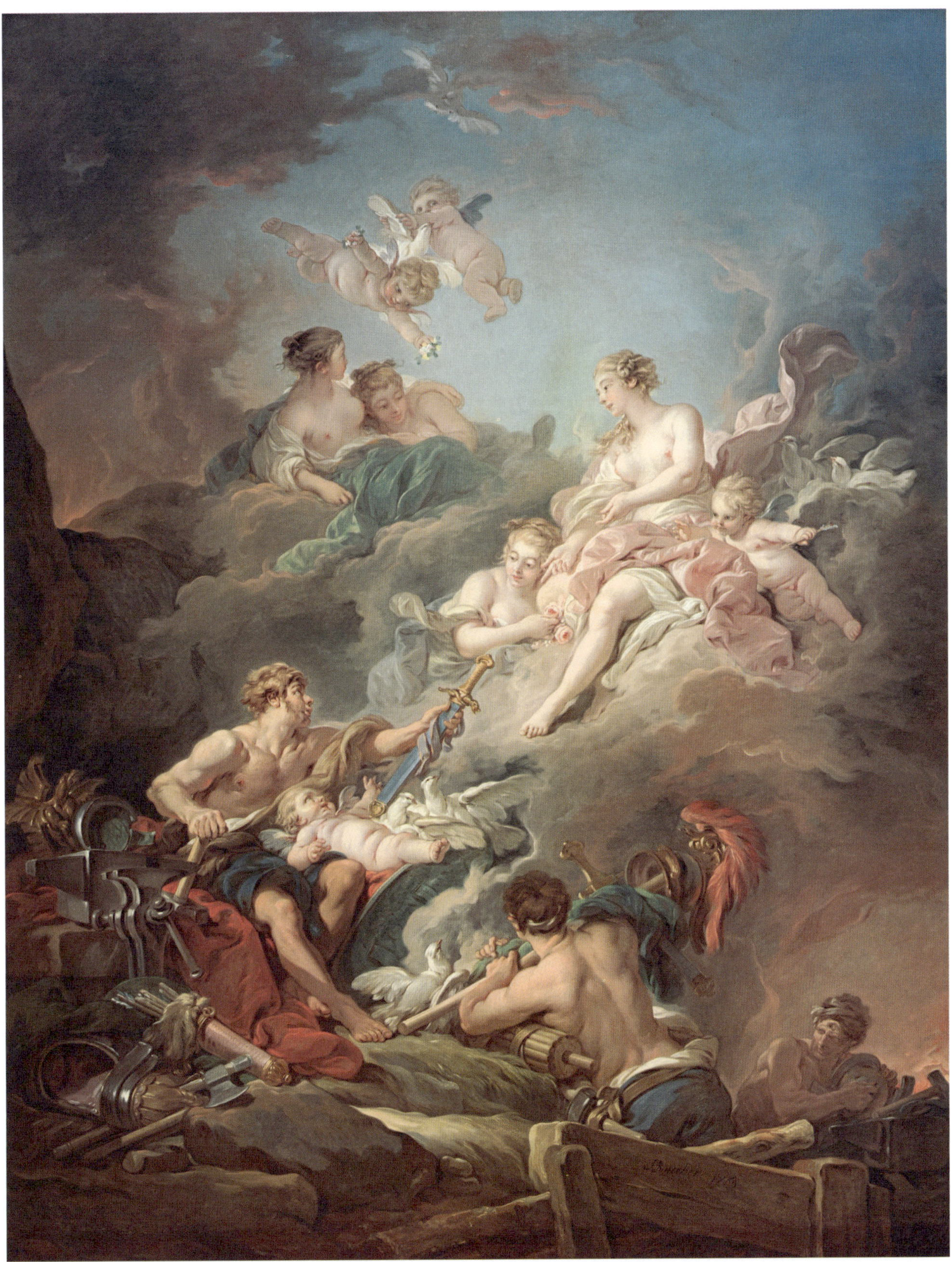

A meeting at the summit of Mount Olympus
Mythical decipherments

Agitators of myths, grandiose and angry, accomplices of both the vilest and the worthiest, the Greek-Roman gods and goddesses have been a staple of Western painting for centuries. But how can one recognise them? Please join us on a guided tour of the most exclusive location of all antiquity: Mount Olympus.

First generation — The children of Cronos and Rhea

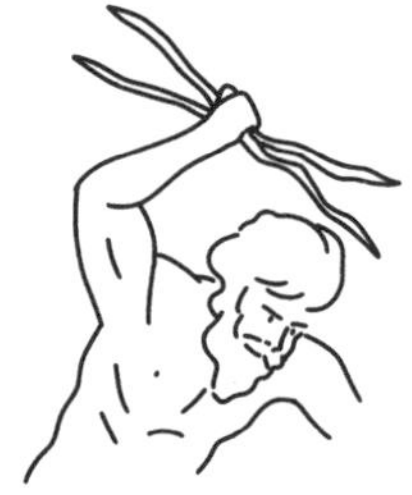

Zeus

Roman name: Jupiter
Attributes: Lightning, eagle, beard

The god of gods, he was the most powerful and the most revered of all; however, he was also unfaithful and lustful. Zeus had no qualms about misleading any young women and men who crossed his path.

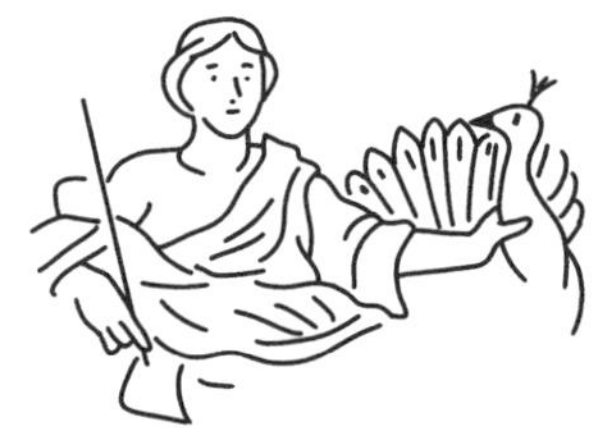

Hera

Roman name: Juno
Attributes: Diadem, sceptre, veil, peacock

The wife of Zeus, she was associated with marriage. Renowned for her temper and her jealousy, she would castigate any female rivals who diverted her husband's gaze from her. The couple's spats were largely responsible for adverse weather.

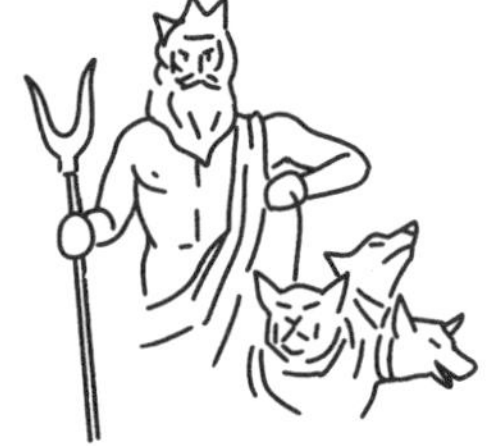

Hades

Roman name: Pluto
Attributes: Crown, two-pronged sceptre

He was the god of the Underworld – which, by metonymy, was also named "Hades". He was a terrifying god, and few temples and altars were consecrated to him.

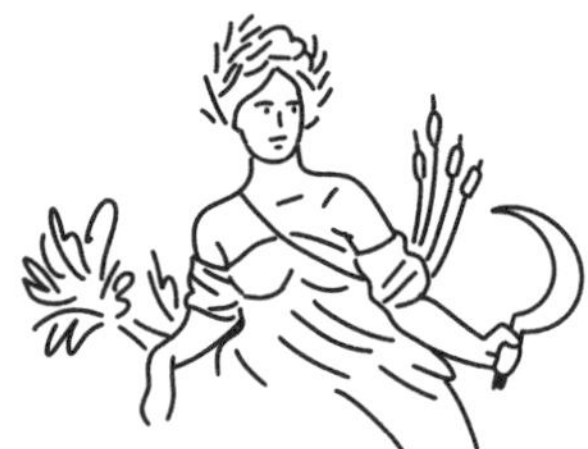

Demeter

Roman name: Ceres
Attributes: Wheat, sickle, flowers, in a crown or held in the hand

She was the goddess of harvests and of agriculture. Together with her daughter Persephone, the wife of Hades, she would return to the Underworld in autumn and winter; she was therefore associated with the cycle of the seasons.

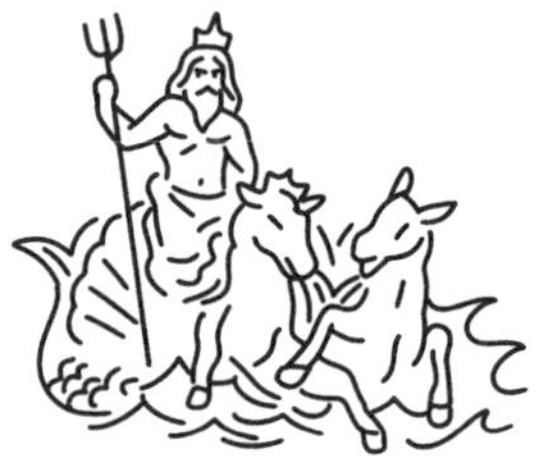

Poseidon

Roman name: Neptune
Attributes: Dolphin, horse, crown, trident

While Zeus ruled the earthly world and Hades ruled the underworld, Poseidon was the king of the oceans and waters. Being also the creator of the horse, he was depicted riding a chariot.

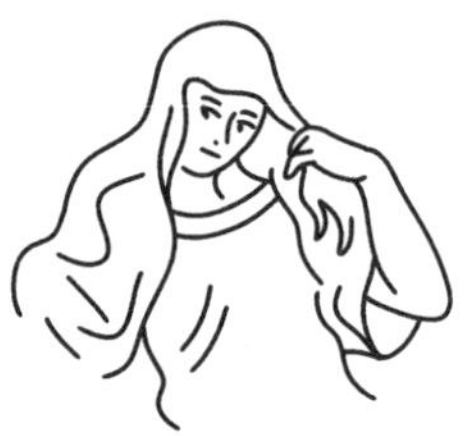

Hestia

Roman name: Vesta
Attributes: Fire, horn of plenty, often depicted wearing a veil

Goddess of the hearth, home and family, she was rarely represented in paintings. Coveted by the gods, she took refuge with her brother Zeus and decided to remain a virgin forever.

Second generation, a few of Zeus's children

WHAT IS MOUNT OLYMPUS?

Mount Olympus was the home of the gods. At its peak, the Greek deities observed the world and interfered in the lives of humans, while feeding on nectar and Ambrosia, the food reserved for them. Mount Olympus is also a massif in the Greek landscape. Culminating at 2,917 metres, it is the country's highest mountain.

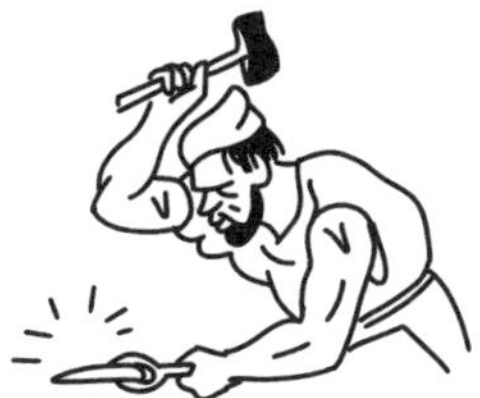

Hephaestus

Roman name: Vulcan
Mother: Hera
Attributes: Anvil, fire, hammer, pincers, tunic and cap

Unsightly and lame, he was rejected by Hera. In exile, he learned to master fire, and became the official blacksmith to the gods. His wife was Aphrodite.

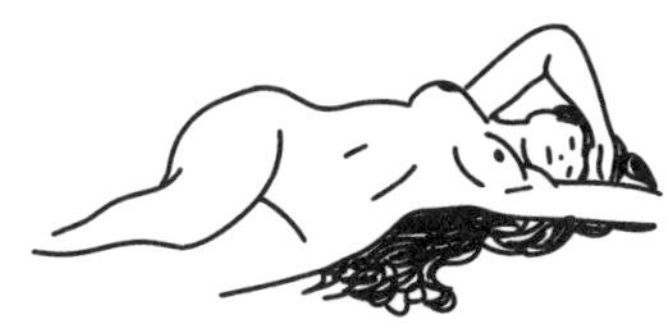

Aphrodite

Roman name: Venus
Mother: The foam of the sea
Attributes: Dove, swan, shell, apple (golden), pomegranate

She was the goddess of love. Depicted in voluptuous poses, she was easily recognisable by her beauty and sensuality. While she was Hephaestus's wife, she had many lovers.

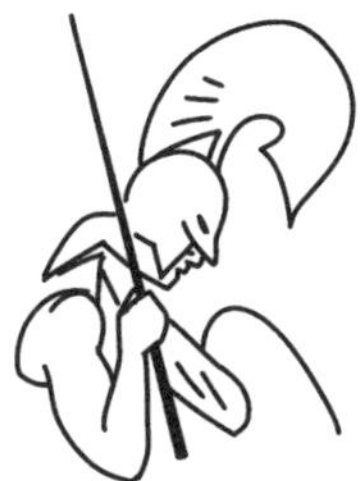

Ares

Roman name: Mars
Mother: Hera
Attributes: Helmet, shield, sword

He was a violent and bloodthirsty god, associated with war. He was shunned by the denizens of Mount Olympus, especially by his father Zeus. On the battlefield, he was accompanied by Discord, Fear, Terror and War. He was one of Aphrodite's lovers.

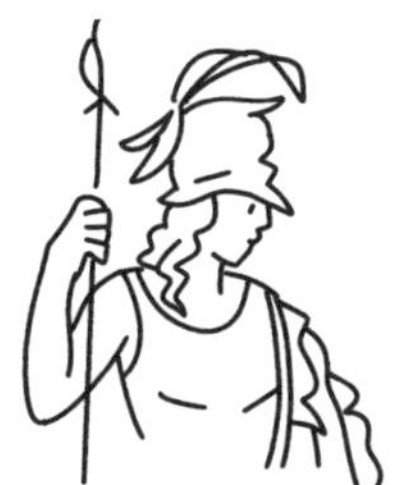

Athena

Roman name: Minerva
Mother: Metis (Wisdom)
Attributes: Helmet, spear, shield adorned with the head of a Gorgon, owl

Athena was the goddess of war and of wisdom. She was one of the most beloved among the Greek pantheon. When Metis became pregnant, Zeus swallowed her. Suffering from a headache, he asked Hephaestus to crack his skull open: from this wound, Athena was born.

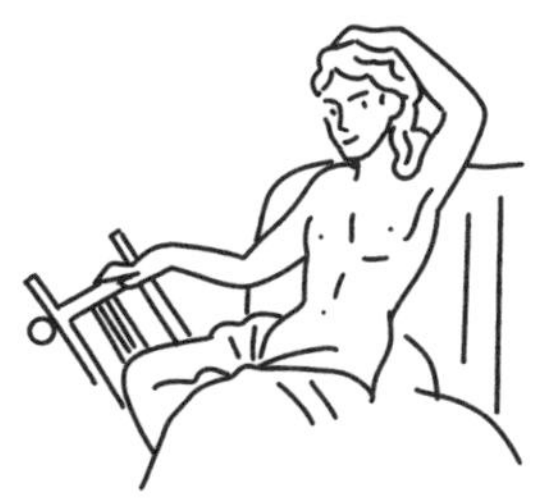

Apollo

Roman name: Apollo (the same!)
Mother: Leto
Attributes: Sun, lyre, bow, chariot

The god of beauty, arts and light, Apollo embodied ideal and perfection. His lovers were innumerable, and he led the Chorus of the Muses. He was a gifted healer, and his oracles were both sought after and feared. He was Artemis's twin brother.

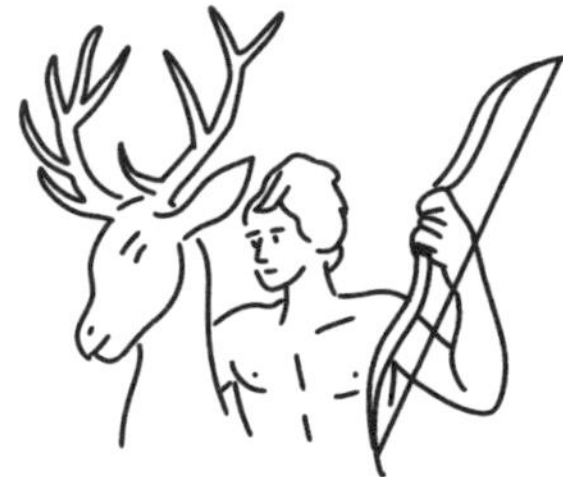

Artemis

Roman name: Diana
Mother: Leto
Attributes: Crescent moon, bow and arrow, doe, dogs

Apollo's sister, Artemis was the goddess of the hunt and the forests, which she roamed with the Nymphs. A chaste goddess, she would make any men pay dearly for their curiosity if they attempted to spy on her bathing.

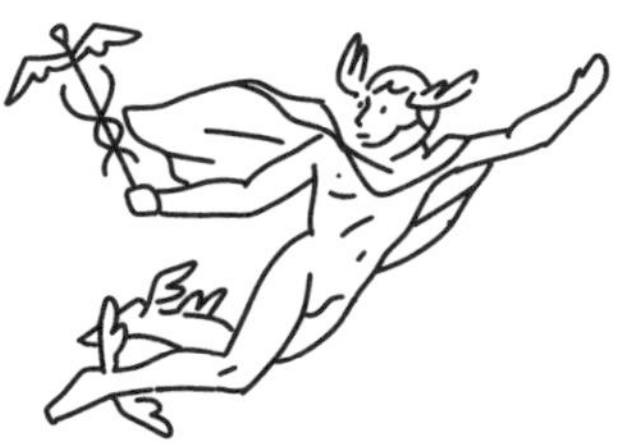

Hermes

Roman name: Mercury
Mother: Maia
Attributes: Winged sandals or helmet, caduceus, purse

Hermes was the messenger of the gods; his winged attributes allowed him to bear news quickly. He watched over travellers, merchants and thieves. He was a clever, cunning and ambiguous god.

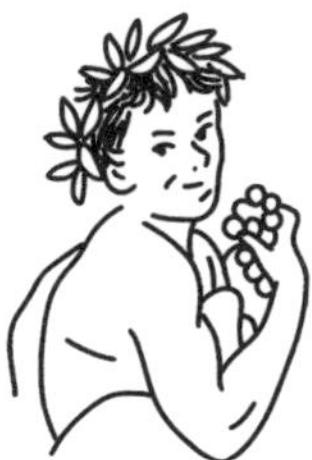

Dionysus

Roman name: Bacchus
Mother: Semele
Attributes: Vine leaves, bunches of grapes, wine, ivy, panther skin

When Semele died, pregnant with Bacchus, Zeus concealed the foetus in his thigh, from which the god of wine would emerge. Bacchus embodied the passions that dominate reason.

Jean Honoré Fragonard

The enlightened art of the Enlightenment

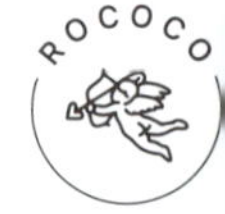

A libertine and enlightened painter, Fragonard was a perfect reflection of his time. Winner of the Prix de Rome in 1756, he turned his back to the official path and to history painting, favouring private commissions from rich clients, which would make his fortune.

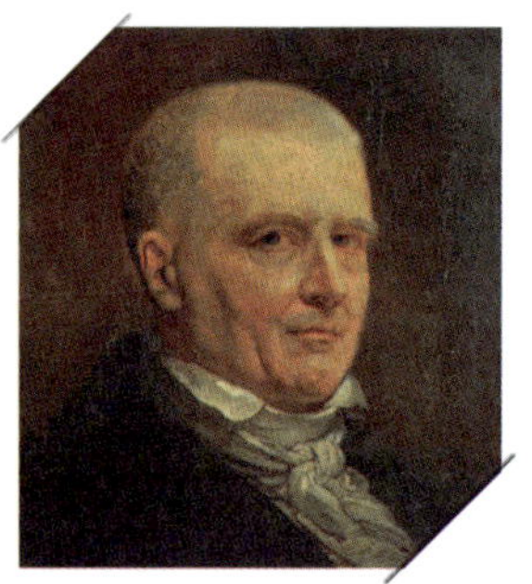

A way with words

Fragonard, nicknamed "Frago", was known for his fashionable libertine paintings. Far from being merely frivolous, however, these works – and in particular, the bucolic exteriors that they depicted – reflected his taste for the works of the 17th-century Dutch painters. They conveyed an artistic freedom that the painter would one day express by declaring: "I would paint with my ass."

An illustrious illustrator

He was also renowned for his great drawing talent, which he used to immortalise the surroundings of the Villa d'Este in Tivoli, or to illustrate 57 plates of La Fontaine's *Fables*.

Family comes first

The painter collaborated with his sister-in-law, Marguerite Gérard, whom he had trained in his art. They got along well, and would often produce "four-handed works", to the extent that it was sometimes difficult for historians to distinguish their respective creations.

A CHOICE CASTING

François Boucher, Jean Siméon Chardin, Charles-André Van Loo and Charles-Joseph Natoire were the four great masters who played an important role in Fragonard's training.

François Boucher
Page 154

1732
Born in Grasse

1748
First archaeological excavations in Pompeii

1767 to **1768**
Painted *The Happy Accidents of the Swing*

1782
Pierre Choderlos de Laclos published *Les Liaisons dangereuses*

1806
Died in Paris

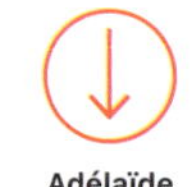

Adélaïde Labille-Guiard
Page 164

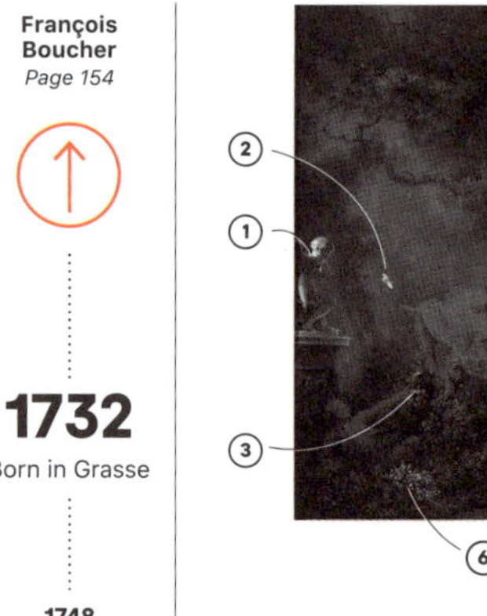

THE HAPPY ACCIDENTS OF THE SWING

Circa 1767–1768
Oil on canvas
81.8 × 64.8 cm
Wallace Collection, London

WHAT ARE WE LOOKING AT?

The subject of this libertine scene, typical of the 17th century, can be read in the eyes of the enthralled man on the left. His gaze guides us under the skirts of the young woman (his mistress, no doubt), while in the background, a husband left in the shadows suspects nothing.

① One work may hide another

This statue represents Étienne Maurice Falconet's *Seated Cupid (L'Amour menaçant)*. Ready to draw an arrow, this figure demands secrecy, while also evoking the perils of passion.

② It's a gift

Carried away by the momentum, the young woman is throwing her shoe to her lover – both a sensual and mischievous offering and a testimony of abandon.

③ Hats off

The hat is a sexual allusion. When removed, it is the sign of capitulation to overwhelming desire. It appears to be gathering rosebuds, a metaphor for the female sex.

④ Truer than life

Adding mischief to his work, Fragonard gave the illusion that the cherubs, though statuesque, are fascinated by the scene being played out.

⑤ Canine senses tingling

Often represented as a symbol of loyalty, the dog is barking; is this a warning of what is to come, or does it reflect impatient desire instead?

⑥ A fine figure set amidst beautiful plants

The lush vegetation highlights the work's erotic charge. While the husband is standing next to a trunk displaying dry, bare roots, the lover is sprawling on a bed of greenery dotted with blooming flowers.

② +

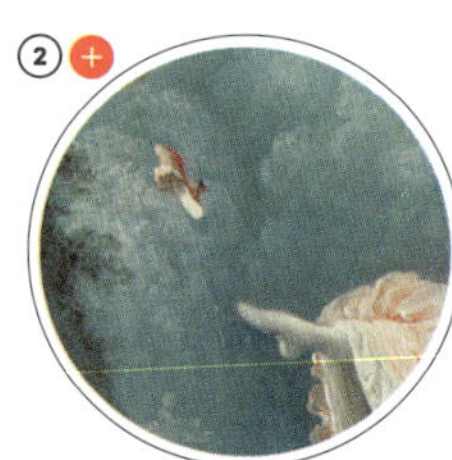

A SPECIFIC ORDER

This painting was commissioned by Baron de Saint-Julien: "I should like Madame on a swing that a bishop would set going. You will place me in such a way that I would be able to see the legs of the lovely girl..." Fragonard, overcome with scruples, would replace the bishop with a cuckold.

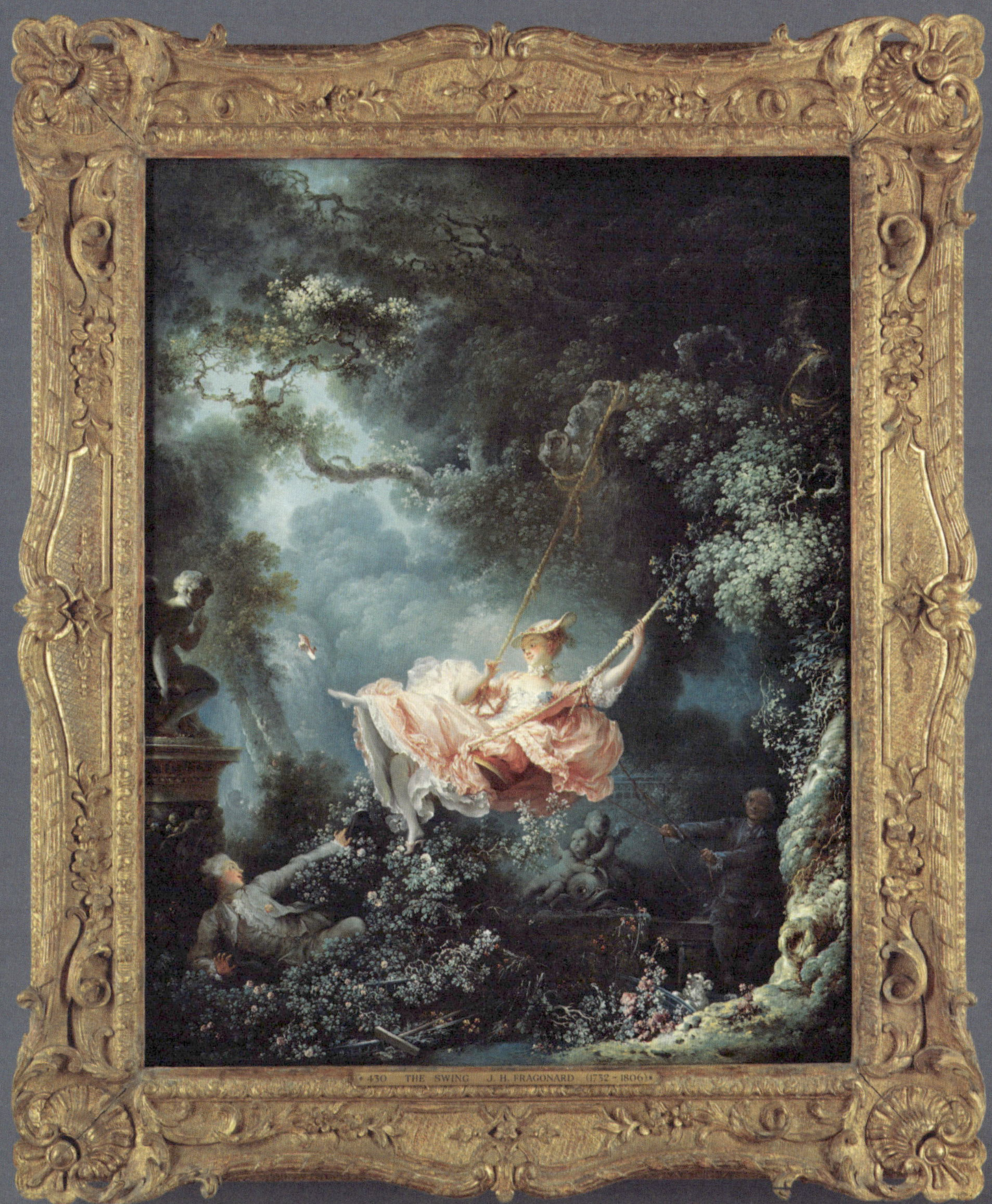
430 THE SWING J. H. FRAGONARD (1732 - 1806)

Ter Borch, Gérard and Fragonard

A fashion show

Alongside the great academic paintings, a taste for genre scenes developed in the 18th century. Using small, intimate formats, French painters distinctly paid tribute to the Dutch masters of the previous century.

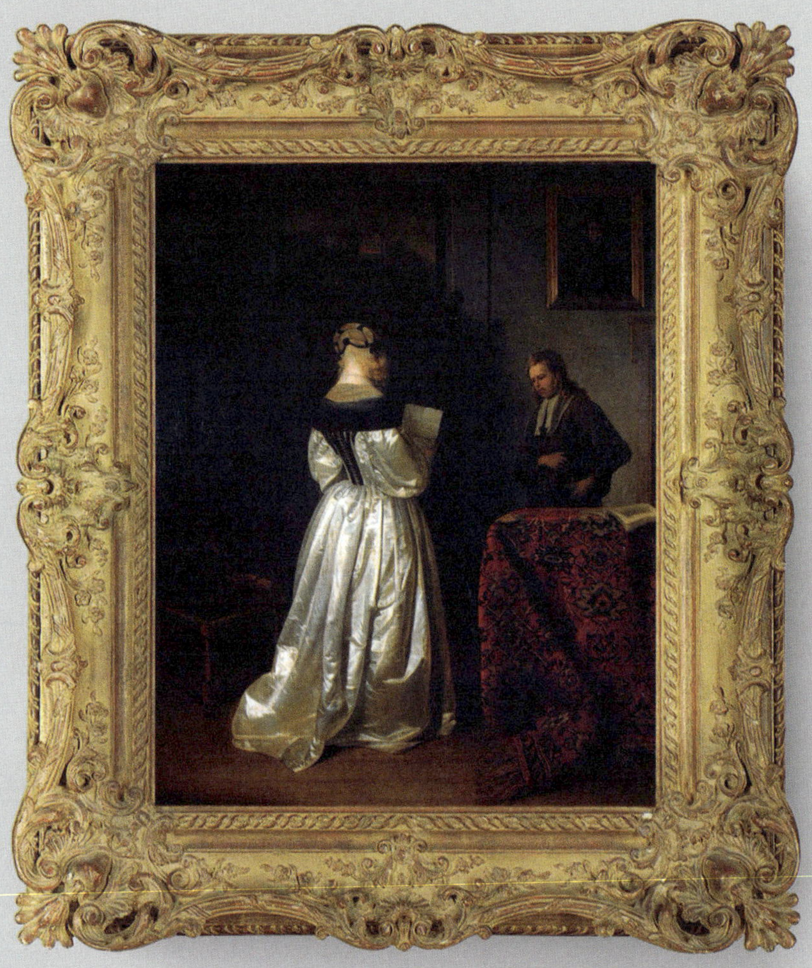

***THE MESSENGER ("THE UNWELCOME NEWS")* FROM THE STUDIO OF GÉRARD TER BORCH**
1650–1660

Borch was a *fijnschilder*, meaning that he was an artist who painted with a fine style. His technique is skilfully applied to depict the satin and sensual appearance of the dress. He was adept at painting figures from the back, and his paintings reveal a great psychological finesse.

Oil on canvas, 70 × 54 cm
Hermitage Museum, Saint Petersburg

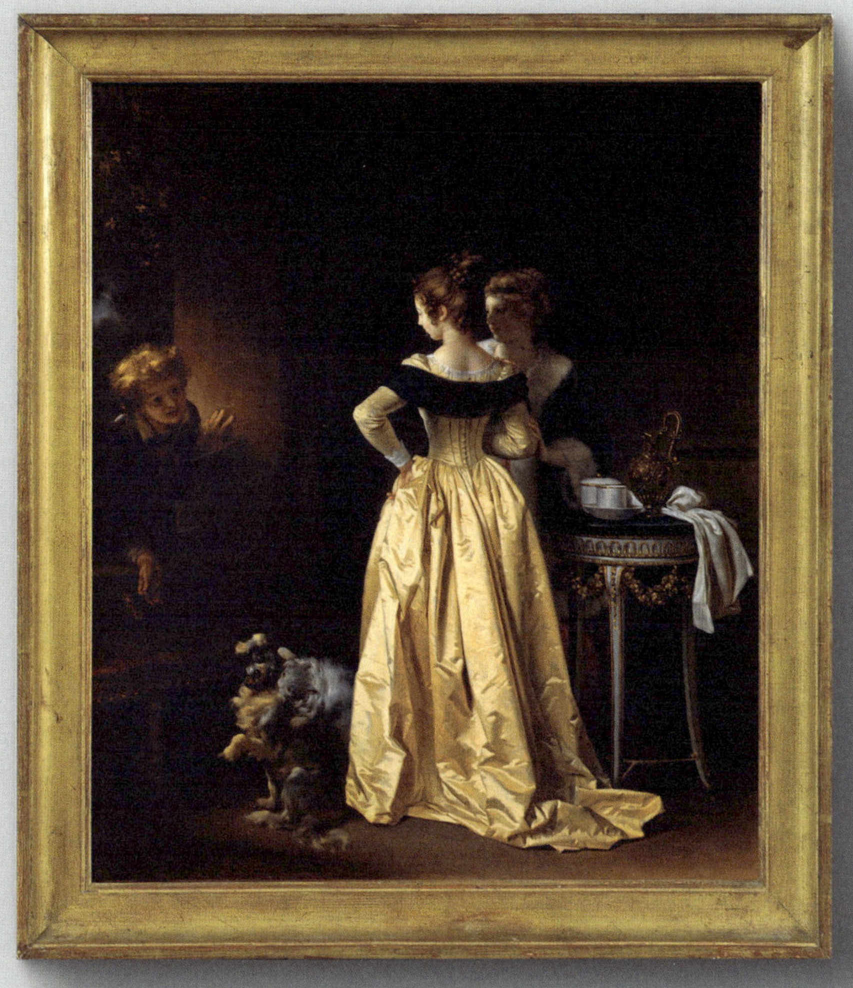

***LE BOUQUET* BY MARGUERITE GÉRARD AND JEAN HONORÉ FRAGONARD**
1783–1784

Marguerite Gérard discovered Gérard Ter Borch's work through the collection of engravings of Jean Honoré Fragonard, her brother-in-law. The duo of painters clarifies the ambiguity introduced by the Dutch artist: the visitor is holding a rose, a sexual allusion, while his lustful intentions are illustrated by the two animals.

Oil on canvas, dimensions unknown
Private collection

Meanwhile in Turkey…

Şahkulu produced his most beautiful works

In the 16th century, the Ottoman Empire experienced a golden age under the reign of Suleiman the Magnificent. His prolific workshops would contribute to the expansion of the empire's cultural influence. In these, the painter Şahkulu rose to fame by becoming the master of the "Saz" style.

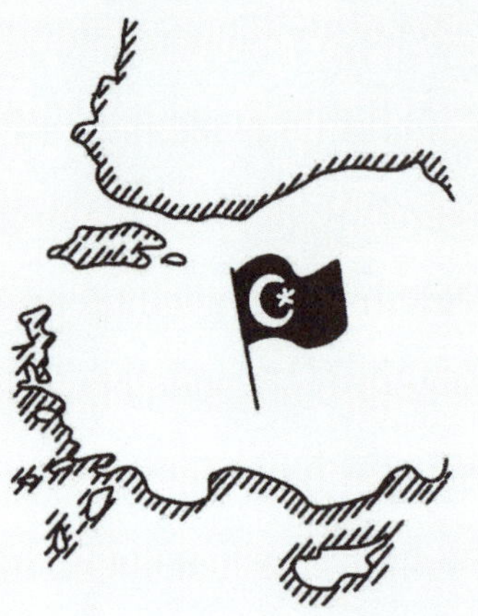

Setting the scene

In the 16th century, the Ottoman Empire reached its pinnacle under the reign of Suleiman I, who would become known as Suleiman the Magnificent in the western world. He was both a powerful conqueror and a discerning collector, particularly of Chinese porcelain, which influenced the artists at his court.

Topkapı Sarayı, the Sultan's palace, housed numerous workshops that bore witness to the empire's cultural wealth; among these were goldsmiths' and booksmiths' workshops, where a refined art of bookbinding and illumination thrived. The Turkish 16th century was also the golden age of Iznik ceramics, as well as textiles in Istanbul and Bursa.

The masterpiece of the moment

- Drawing allowed Ottoman artists to express their creativity freely, outside of the illustration of books, by inventing their own motifs. Here, Şahkulu illustrated a dragon on a bed of spiralling twisted leaves, in the Saz style that was popular at the time.
- The dragon's silhouette is structured by the thick black line that runs along its back. The dynamic undulation produces an impression of movement, reinforced by the rhythmic arrangement of the legs, which seem to move. The end of the animal's tail lies beyond the frame, while its mouth is about to extend beyond it too. Everything here is designed to produce the illusion of life and movement.
- Near the dragon's head, an inscription states that the work is a study by Şahkulu. The inscription was added after the drawing was completed, but the artist's style can be recognised in the precise rendering of the dragon's mottled skin and the veins of the leaves.

THE SAZ STYLE IN A NUTSHELL

Inspired by the arts of China and Iran, this style developed in Turkey in the 16th century. It featured jagged and stylised foliage, often associated with creatures from Chinese mythology.

WHO WAS ŞAHKULU?

Şahkulu is considered the instigator of the Saz style, which he founded in the decade of 1530 in the workshops of Suleiman the Magnificent, when he became the head of the Nakkaşhane, the royal workshop dedicated to bookmaking.

He trained in Tabriz, Persia (which would later become Iran) with the master of miniature painting Aqa Mirak. Exiled, he travelled to Anatolia, then joined the Sultan's workshops in Istanbul, around December 1520 or January 1521. His productions were appreciated by Suleiman who, according to the writings, granted him a workshop where he enjoyed watching him work.

The artist was renowned for his refined touch, the quality of his drawing and his sense of movement. Many followers continued the Saz style, influencing not only the book arts, but also ceramics, textiles and carpets, which constituted the bulk of artistic creation under the reign of Suleiman the Magnificent.

SOME GREAT ARTISTS OF THE ROYAL BOOK WORKSHOP

These artists worked during the reign of Suleiman and his successors, Sultans Selim II and Murad III.

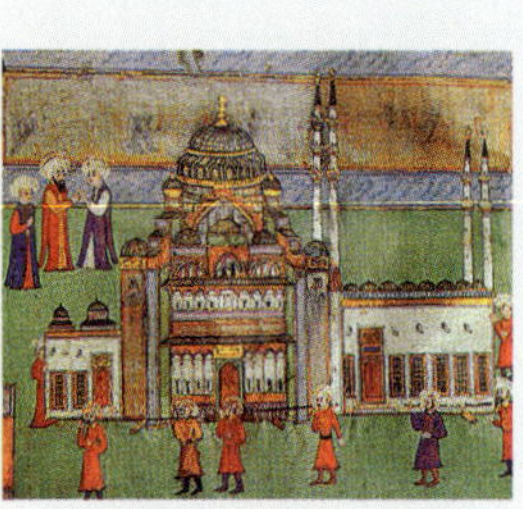

Nakkach Osman, painter
The Carrying-in of a Model of Süleymaniye Mosque (detail from *Surname-i Hümayun*)
1582–1588
Topkapı Palace, Istanbul

Like Şahkulu, he had his own workshop.

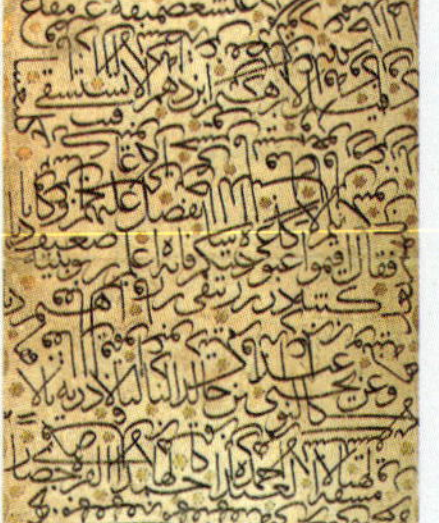

Ahmed Karahisari, calligrapher
Calligraphy Exercise
16TH CENTURY
Sakıp Sabancı Museum, Istanbul

He passed on his art and his position to his pupil Hasan Çelebi.

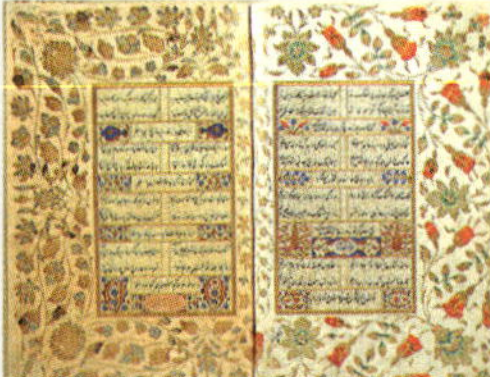

Kara Memi, painter
Divan-i Muhibbi
1566
Istanbul University library

Memi would become Şahkulu's successor.

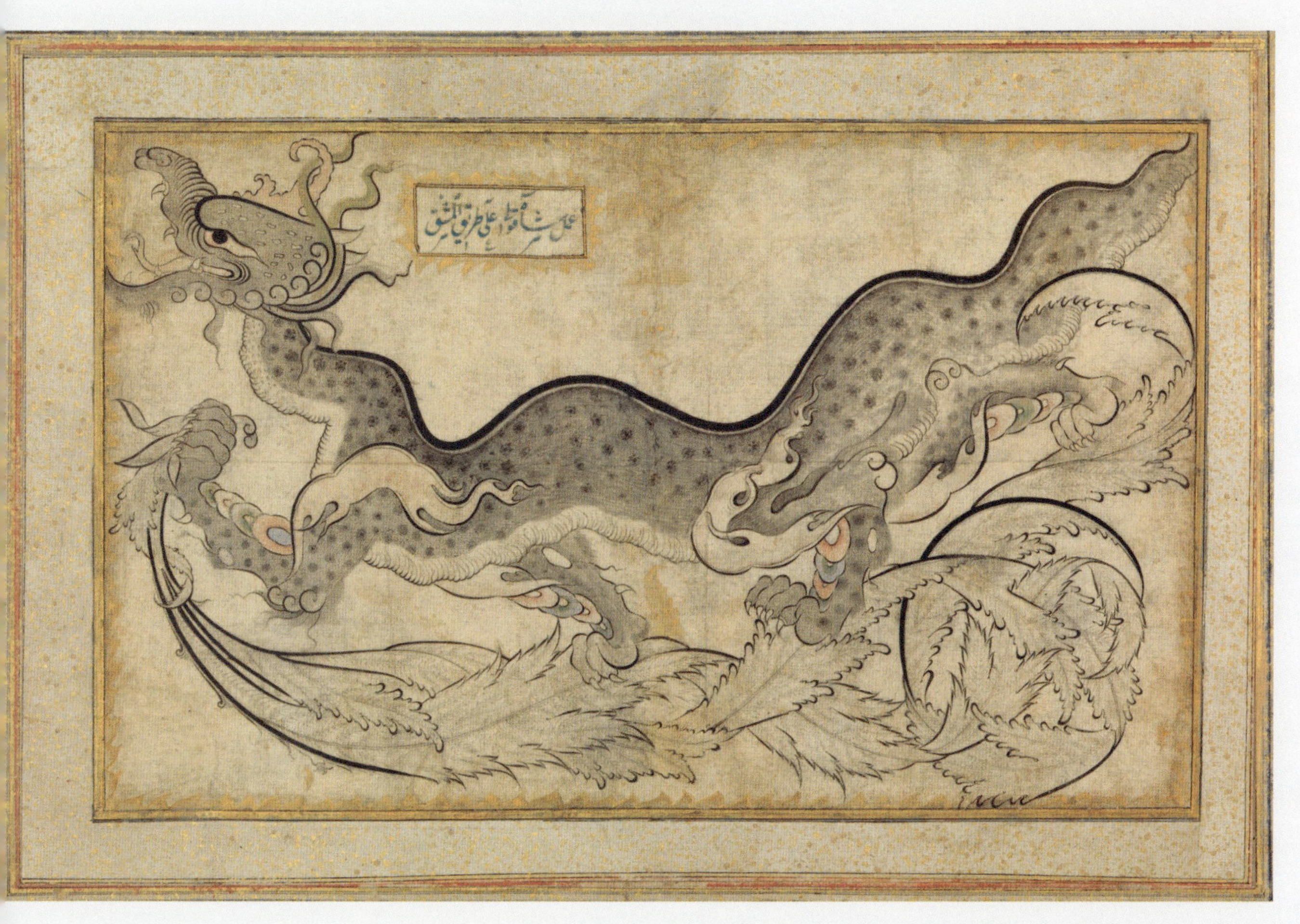

Şahkulu
"SAZ"-STYLE DRAWING OF A DRAGON AMID FOLIAGE
1540–1550
Ink, watercolor and gold on paper, 27.2 × 40.6 cm, 1789, New York,
The Metropolitan Museum of Art

Adélaïde Labille-Guiard

A liberated woman's life ain't an easy one

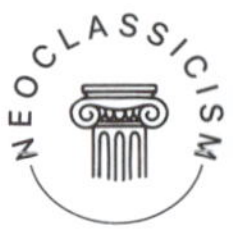

Adélaïde Labille-Guiard was a miniaturist and pastellist. Her portraits were lauded by the critics, who admired their realism. An ambitious artist, she enriched her talents with the technique of oil painting in order to join the Académie Royale de Peinture et de Sculpture.

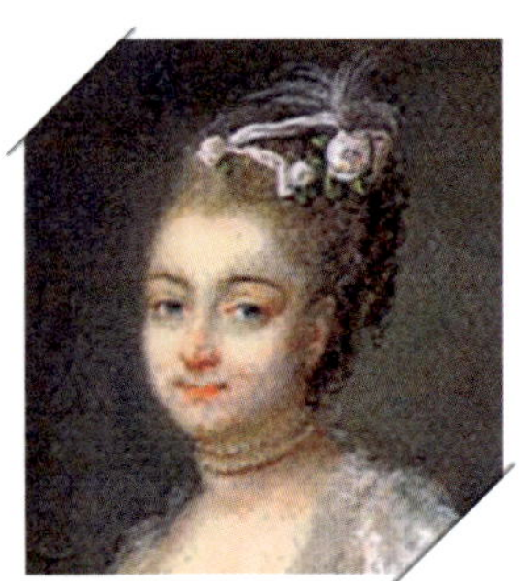

Breaking the Académie Royale's mould

The Académie Royale considered Élisabeth Vigée Le Brun's (p. 168) and Adélaïde Labille-Guiard's candidacies with misogyny. The institution required them to find patrons amidst high-ranking representatives of the state to signal the exceptional nature of their admission. Labille-Guiard refused, and was admitted solely on the basis of the quality of her works.

The royal way

Teaching painting to women, she was unable to secure a studio in Louvre Palace, where her young pupils would have frequented a male audience. As a measure of compensation, Louis XVI granted her a government pension. The artist would also be named the official painter of the "Mesdames of France", the king's aunts.

Changing sides

Abandoned by her royal patrons during the French Revolution, she rebuilt a clientele from proponents of the parliamentary monarchy and deputies. She escaped the most dire fate; however, "citizen Guiard" was obliged to surrender her royal portraits, which were burned.

A QUESTION OF PARITY

The presence of women in the Académie Royale was limited to four members. Carried by the wind of freedom during the French Revolution, Adélaïde Labille-Guiard demanded that this rule be lifted. Her proposal would be voted on, but never implemented.

Jean Honoré Fragonard
Page 158

1749
Born in Paris

1783
First manned balloon flight from Versailles

Circa
1785
Painted *Self-portrait with Two Pupils*

1792
Rouget de Lisle composed *La Marseillaise*

1803
Died in Paris

Élisabeth Vigée Le Brun
Page 168

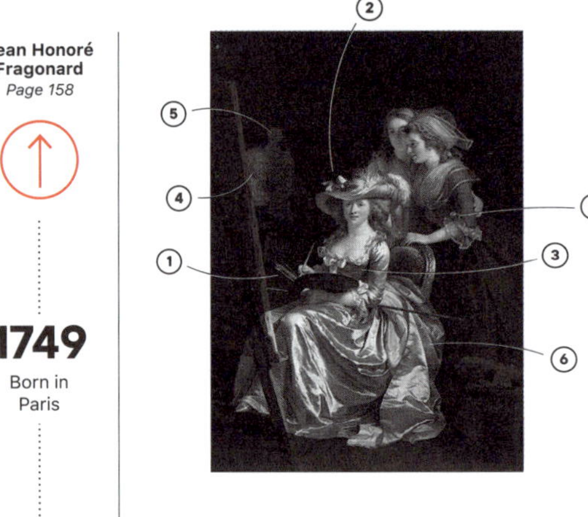

SELF-PORTRAIT WITH TWO PUPILS

Circa 1785
Oil on canvas
210.8 × 151.1 cm
Metropolitan Museum of Art, New York

WHAT ARE WE LOOKING AT?

Two years after her complicated admission into the Académie Royale, Adélaïde Labille-Guiard painted a self-portrait as a response. In this work, she asserted herself as an independent and confident painter, and as a teacher passing on her knowledge to two pupils, potential future candidates to the Académie Royale.

① Taking her future in her own hands

With her palette in hand, Adélaïde Labille-Guiard sends a clear message: she is a painter and an independent woman, and asserts herself as such.

② An impressive presence

The painter boldly returns the viewer's gaze, challenging and questioning them at the same time.

③ Freedom of body and spirit

The deep neckline is yet another sign of emancipation for the painter, who hereby asserts her femininity and her freedom of conduct.

④ Worthy heiress

The daughter of a man of status and a respectable woman, she places herself under the protection of her father, represented by this head.

⑤ Not prude, but cautious nonetheless

The statue of a vestal, a virgin Roman priestess, compensates for the audacity of her cleavage and protects her honour.

⑥ The makings of a heroine

She likely acquired her ability to render fabrics and textures from her childhood spent in her father's fashion shop.

⑦ Sorority

As a further message to the Academicians, Adélaïde Labille-Guiard's pupils are standing close, together with her, linked to their teacher by the placement of their hands.

⑥ +

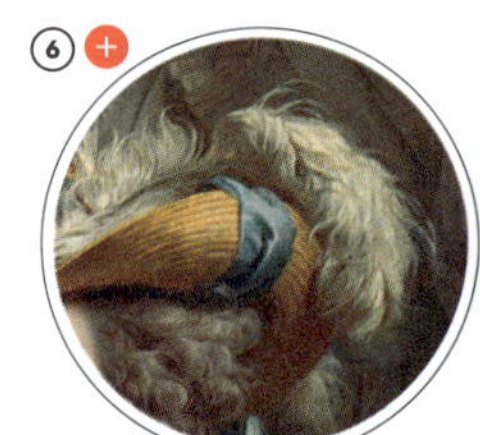

PAINTERS FAMOUS FOR THEIR SELF-PORTRAITS

- Albrecht Dürer (p. 58)
- Sofonisba Anguissola (1532–1625)
- Rembrandt Van Rijn (p. 118)
- Gustave Courbet (p. 198)
- Vincent Van Gogh (p. 246)
- Frida Kahlo (p. 306)

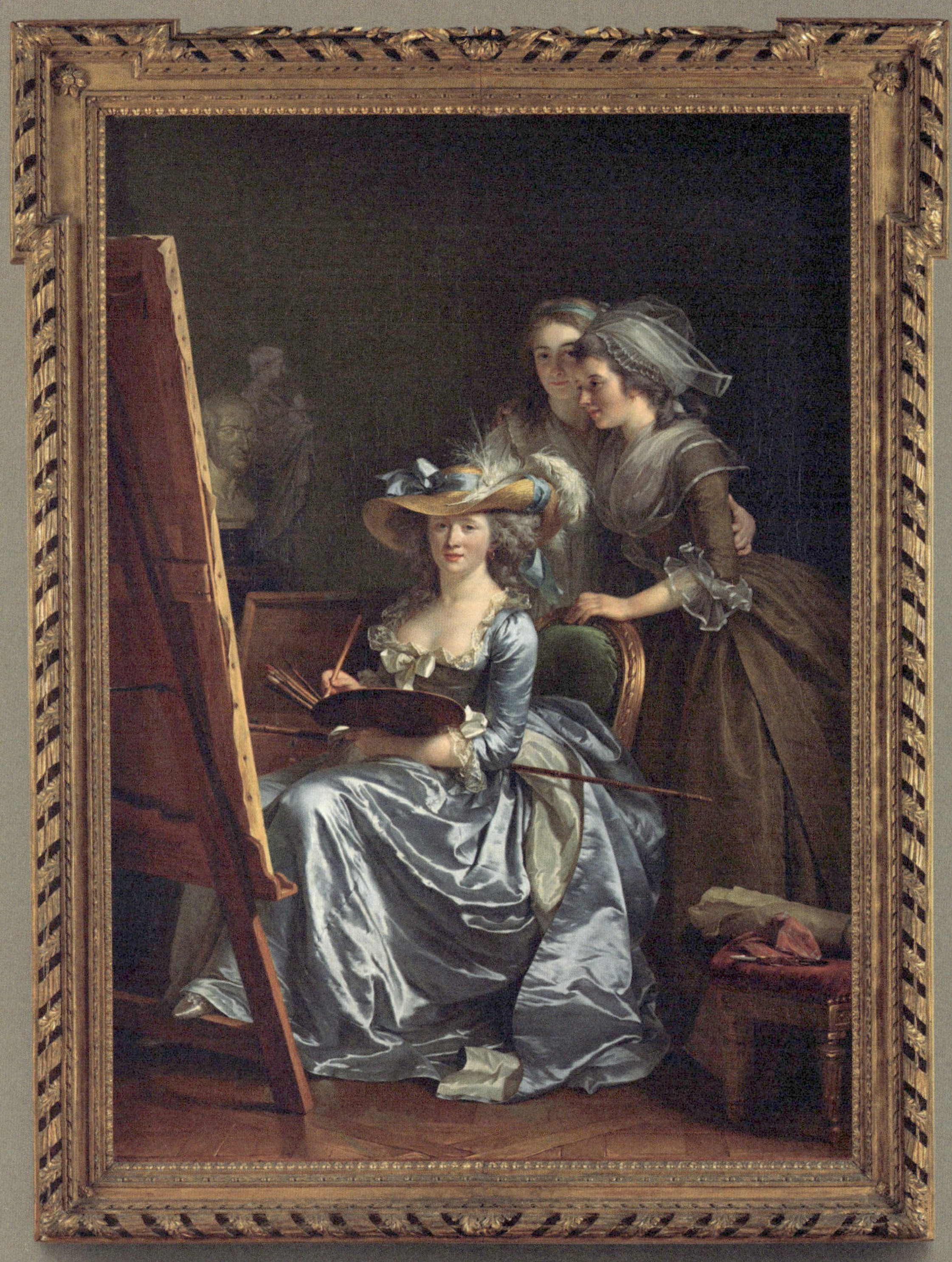

All genres are found in painting

To the test of a rigorous hierarchy

**As early as the 15th century, historians and theorists questioned the idea of classifying paintings by genre, according to the nobility of the subject and the inherent difficulty of its representation.
With the foundation of the Académie Royale de Peinture et de Sculpture in 1648, a strict hierarchy was established within the French school.**

The art of classification

In 1668, in a preface to the *Conférences de l'Académie Royale de Peinture et de Sculpture*, André Félibien established a classification of genres, from the least noble to the noblest. This architect and historiographer (that is, a writer of history) established his classification in a way that conferred greater value to the capacity for imagination, which he considered to be a more complex undertaking than the capacity for imitation. He viewed ideation as a principle higher than realisation.

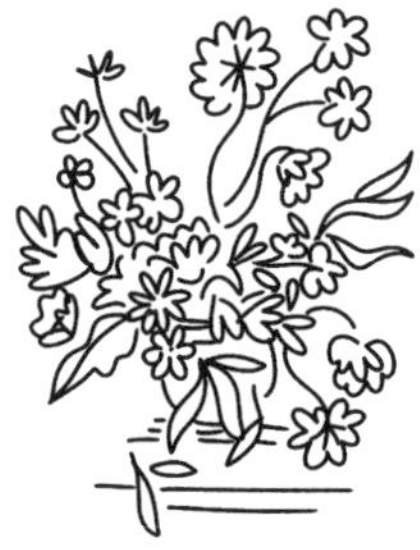

Still life

This genre concerned everything that is inanimate, and therefore easy to reproduce: objects, plants, food, dead animals, etc.

6

Rachel Ruysch *(p. 108)*
Jean Siméon Chardin *(p. 144)*

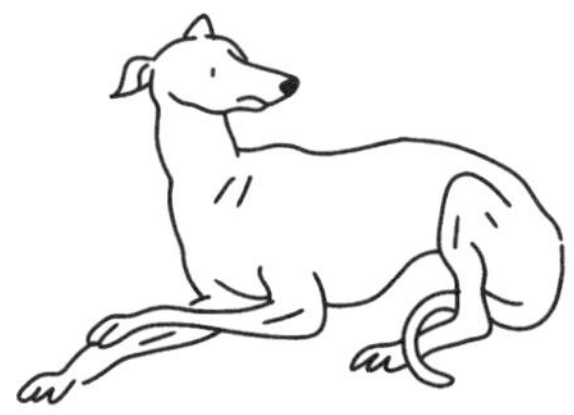

Animal painting

Compared to still life, the depiction of animals represented an additional difficulty, as it required the artist to render the impression of life that animates the models.

5

Frans Snyders
Jean Siméon Chardin *(p. 144)*

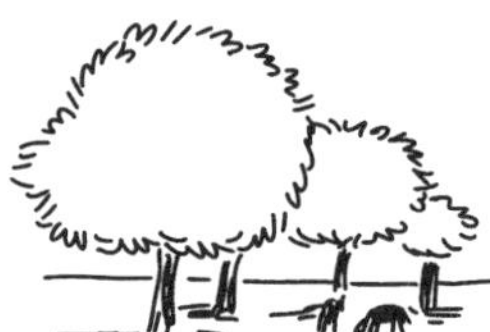

Landscape

Landscape painting, while simple in appearance, earned prestige with painters such as Nicolas Poussin and Annibale Carracci, who depicted historical scenes in sublime natural settings.

4

Claude Gellée, Claude Lorrain
John Constable
Camille Corot

A TOUCH OF FLEXIBILITY

Despite the apparent rigidity of this hierarchy, the Académie Royale also took into account the specificities of the painters that it welcomed: Antoine Watteau was accepted for a "courtship subject", Jean Siméon Chardin's report states that he was a painter "in the talent of animals and fruits", while the Le Nain brothers were admitted as "painters of bambocciades" – genre scenes depicting popular or peasant life.

A NUDE MODEL OR NOTHING

History painting required the representation of heroic nudes. This prerequisite became an argument of oppression, as women artists were not granted access to live models.

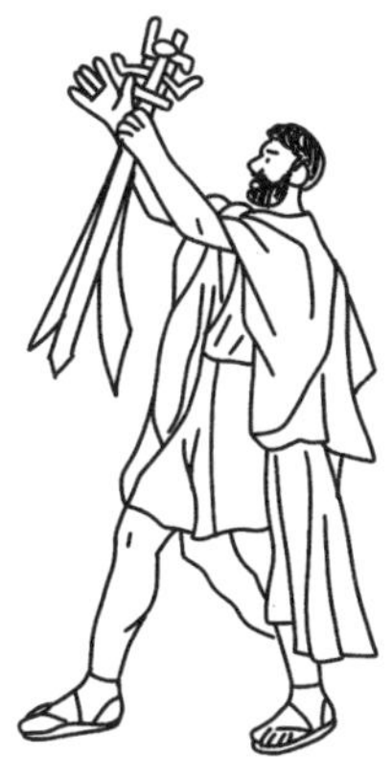

History

Félibien spoke of history, for secular historical scenes and religious painting, and of "fables", for mythological subjects. Above them all, he placed the allegory, a genre featuring extraordinary and divine characters performing noble deeds. It required a creative effort on the artist's part, as he could not imitate something that he had witnessed; it was inherently an invention of the mind.

1

Artemisia Gentileschi *(p. 88)*
Nicolas Poussin *(p. 124)*
Jacques-Louis David *(p. 170)*

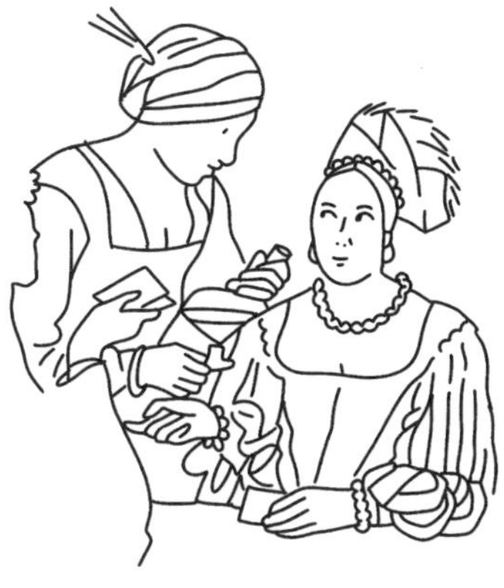

Genre scene

In the 18th century, the Académie Royale added this genre to its list. It depicted the daily life of ordinary and anonymous people, and could also evoke peasant scenes, as well as the life of the bourgeois or aristocratic classes.

2

Georges de La Tour *(p. 94)*
Judith Leyster *(p. 104)*
Jean Honoré Fragonard *(p. 158)*

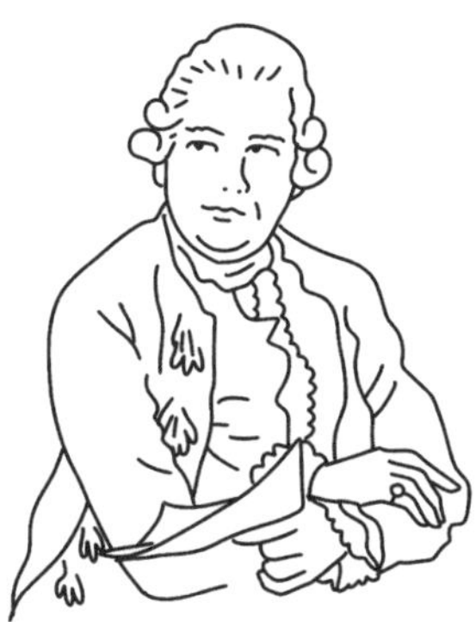

Portrait

The portrait surpassed the landscape because it needed to breathe life and movement into an image to make it feel lifelike. Some portraitists, using allegorical portraiture, were successfully admitted as history painters to the Académie Royale.

3

Antoine Van Dyck *(p. 114)*,
Élisabeth Vigée Le Brun *(p. 168)*
Thomas Gainsborough

Élisabeth Vigée Le Brun

The artist of a waning regime

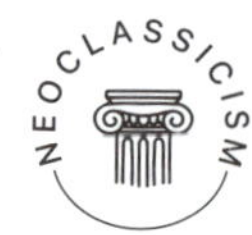

Élisabeth Vigée Le Brun was appreciated for her use of colour and her creativity, but she was best known for embellishing her models. Her self-portraits depicting herself as an accomplished artist and woman were the best form of advertisement for her talent.

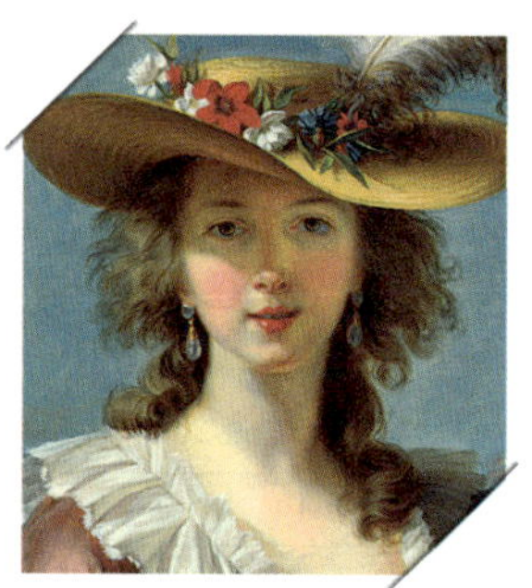

A successful career

Everybody who was anybody in Parisian circles flocked to her salon and, at the age of only 23, her services were requested by Marie-Antoinette. Her first portrait of the Queen of France would become her first success: she became an official painter, and many other commissions followed.

A fierce admission process

The artist sought glory and applied to the Académie Royale, but her acceptance required the intervention of the king; only then would the Academicians "execute with profound respect the orders of their Sovereign". This indication in the minutes clearly highlights the Academicians' reluctance to comply with this obligation.

On tour

Her proximity to the Court became unacceptable during the French Revolution. The artist left France and began a long journey, which would contribute to her reputation. Everywhere she stayed, her talent would be in great demand.

AN ARTIST ON THE MOVE

Between 1789 and 1808, Elisabeth Vigée Le Brun successively travelled through Italy, Austria, Bohemia, Germany, Russia, England, Holland, Belgium and Switzerland.

Adélaïde Labille-Guiard
Page 164

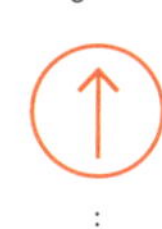

1755
Born in Paris

1782
Posthumous publication of the first volume of Rousseau's *Confessions*

1787
Painted *Marie-Antoinette and Her children*

1815
Birth of the mathematician Ada Lovelace

1842
Died in Paris

Jacques-Louis David
Page 170

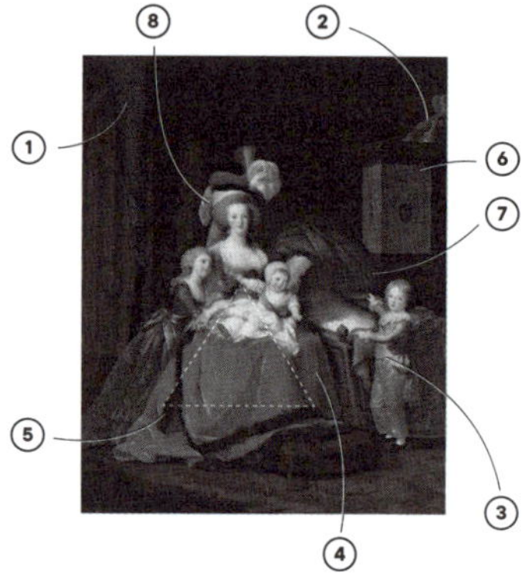

MARIE-ANTOINETTE AND HER CHILDREN

1787
Oil on canvas
275 × 215 cm
Musée National des Châteaux de Versailles et de Trianon

WHAT ARE WE LOOKING AT?

In 1785, Marie-Antoinette was caught up in the affair of the diamond necklace; this scandal contributed to her reputation as a spendthrift queen, who was bringing ruin to France. She called on Élisabeth Vigée Le Brun in an attempt to restore her image. Behind the family portrait lay a political campaign.

① The stage is set

Palace, colonnade, drapery... The splendour reminds us that we are in Versailles, but the scene is plunged into shadow. It is a time for sobriety.

② Job description

The crown on the cushion bearing a Fleur-de-Lys is a reminder of the figures' prestige and the queen's mission: to give birth to descendants.

③ Just like Dad

The first Dauphin is recognisable by the blue ribbon of the Order of the Holy Spirit, the insignia worn by kings in official portraits.

④ *Dress code*

The Queen follows in the footsteps of the pious Marie Leszczynska, wearing a red velvet dress similar to that of Louis XV's wife.

⑤ Strong value

The triangular composition is inspired by the Holy Family of the Italian Renaissance, and adds to the models' prestige.

⑥ Stored away

In response to criticism, the Queen's jewel case depicted is darkened by shadows. Apart from discreet earrings, Marie-Antoinette is wearing no ornaments.

⑦ Gone too soon

The cradle covered with a black shroud should have been that of Princess Sophie, who died at only 11 months. The artist aimed to create empathy.

⑧ A razor-sharp brush

Public opinion would not be impressed by this portrait of a placid-looking queen, especially since Vigée Le Brun tended to make her look younger and more beautiful.

② +

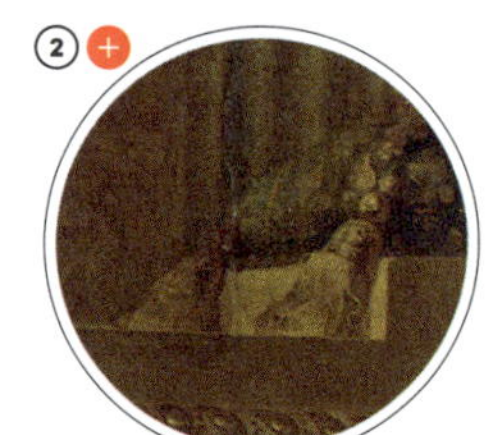

OTHER WELL-KNOWN FRENCH WOMAN PAINTERS OF THE 18TH CENTURY

- Adélaïde Labille-Guiard (p. 164)
- Marguerite Gérard (1761–1837) (p. 160)
- Angelica Kauffmann (1741–1807)
- Marie-Thérèse Reboul (1728–1805)
- Anne Vallayer-Coster (1744–1818)

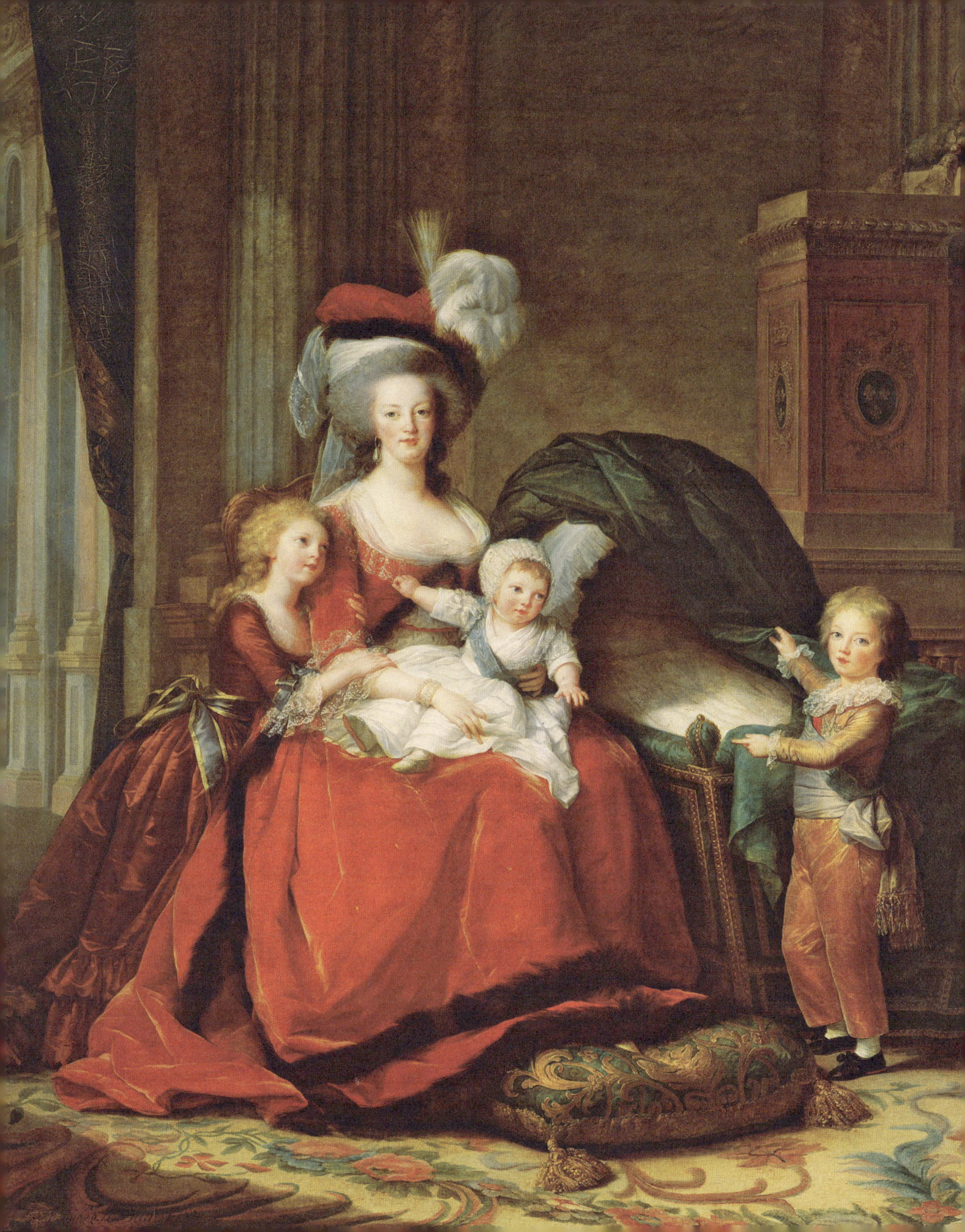

Jacques-Louis David

The French Empire's greatest ambassador

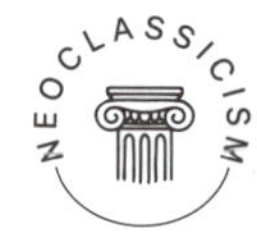

An ambitious painter in search of honours, Jacques-Louis David led a career that was close to government circles and to Napoleon I. He was a leading figure of the neoclassical movement, which marked a return to moral rigour.

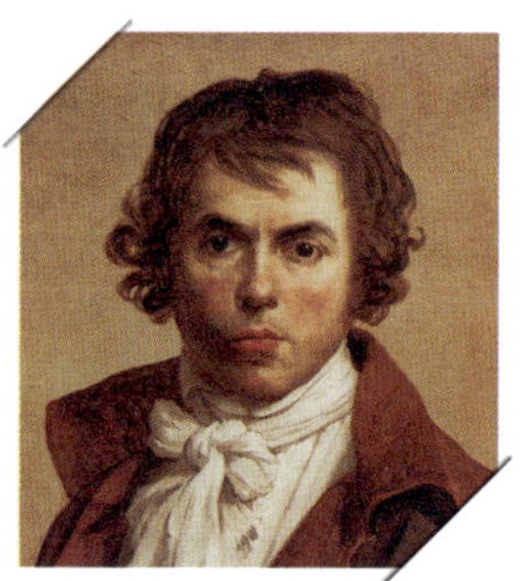

A slow start

After training with Joseph-Marie Vien, Jacques-Louis David unsuccessfully entered the competition for the Prix de Rome three times, thereafter attempting suicide. He was successful on his fourth attempt, and spent several years in Italy, where he immersed himself in antique art and the works of Caravaggio.

A conventional rebel

While the rigour and moral values of his art led him to become the most celebrated representative of neoclassicism, David was also an independent artist, and would defy the established institutions and the Académie Royale, even organising paid exhibitions in his studio on the fringes of official salons.

The wrong horse

Involved in politics, he voted for the execution of Louis XVI and became the official painter to Napoleon I, whom he immortalised as a conqueror, a warrior or a sacred emperor in monumental formats. Following the Restoration, he was exiled to Brussels, where his career would end.

OUT OF SIGHT, OUT OF MIND

After his death, the French government refused to repatriate his remains to France. Only his heart remains preserved in the Père-Lachaise cemetery, next to his wife.

Élisabeth Vigée Le Brun
Page 168

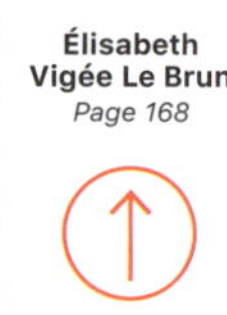

1748
Born in Paris

1781
Foundation of the City of Los Angeles

1784
Painted *Oath of the Horatii*

1813
Jane Austen's Pride and Prejudice became a best-selling book

1825
Died in Brussels

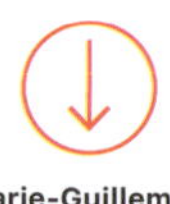

Marie-Guillemine Benoist
Page 172

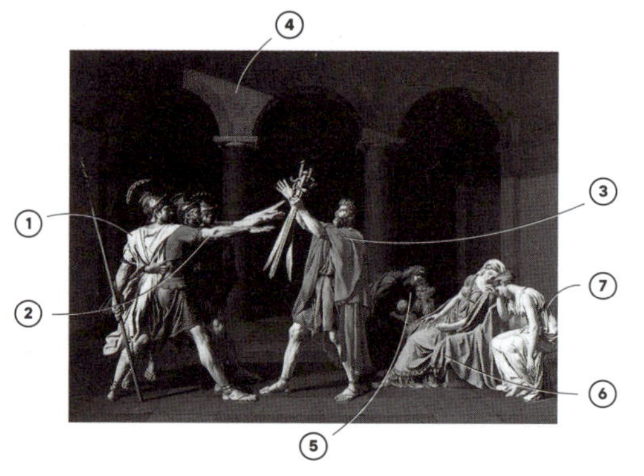

OATH OF THE HORATII

1784
Oil on canvas
330 × 425 cm
Louvre Museum, Paris

WHAT ARE WE LOOKING AT?

In Titus Livius's *History of Rome*, the three Horatii of Rome fight the three Curatii of Alba to decide the fate of the two cities at war. Here, the Horatii take an oath of victory or death.

① Three brothers

The Horatii are taking an oath to their father. Under Jacques-Louis David's brush, the story takes on a moral and political tinge, as it represents the sacrifice of the individual for the collective.

② Synchronicity

The three heroes' coordination testifies to their determination and solidarity; in the foreground, one of them is encircling his brother's waist with his hand.

③ No choice

The father is looking up to the sky with imploring eyes, but resignedly handing the weapons of battle to his sons; this work depicts the triumph of morality over passions.

④ A well-set stage

Rigorous ancient architecture provides stability to the scene, divided into three groups: the Horatii, the father, the women. The balanced composition makes this work a neoclassical model.

⑤ *Mater Dolorosa*

The dramatic atmosphere is amplified by the female figures. The mother is embracing her two remaining children, protecting those who can still be saved from harm.

⑥ Theatrical pain

Dressed in yellow and blue, Sabine is the wife of the eldest of the Horatii, but she is Albanian, and the Curiatii's sister. Whatever the outcome, she is a victim of cruel fate. Her character was inspired by *Horace*, a play written by the French tragedian Pierre Corneille.

⑦ No silver linings

At her side, the lamenting Camilla, sister of the Horatii, promised to a Curiatius. According to Titus Livius, she would be killed by her brother when she overwhelmed him with reproaches, after he defeated her betrothed.

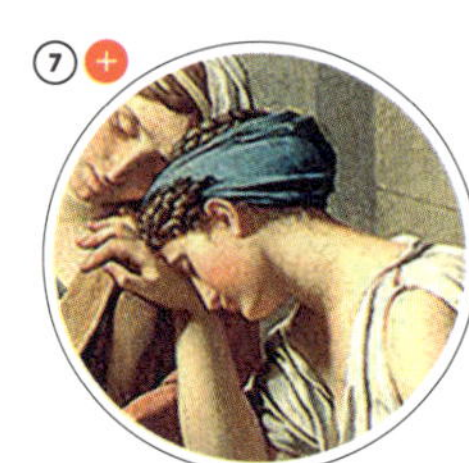

NEOCLASSICISM IN A NUTSHELL

- Subjects featuring a high moral value.
- A movement inspired by classical painting and antique art.
- Rigorous and balanced compositions.
- The search for a Raphaelian ideal of beauty.

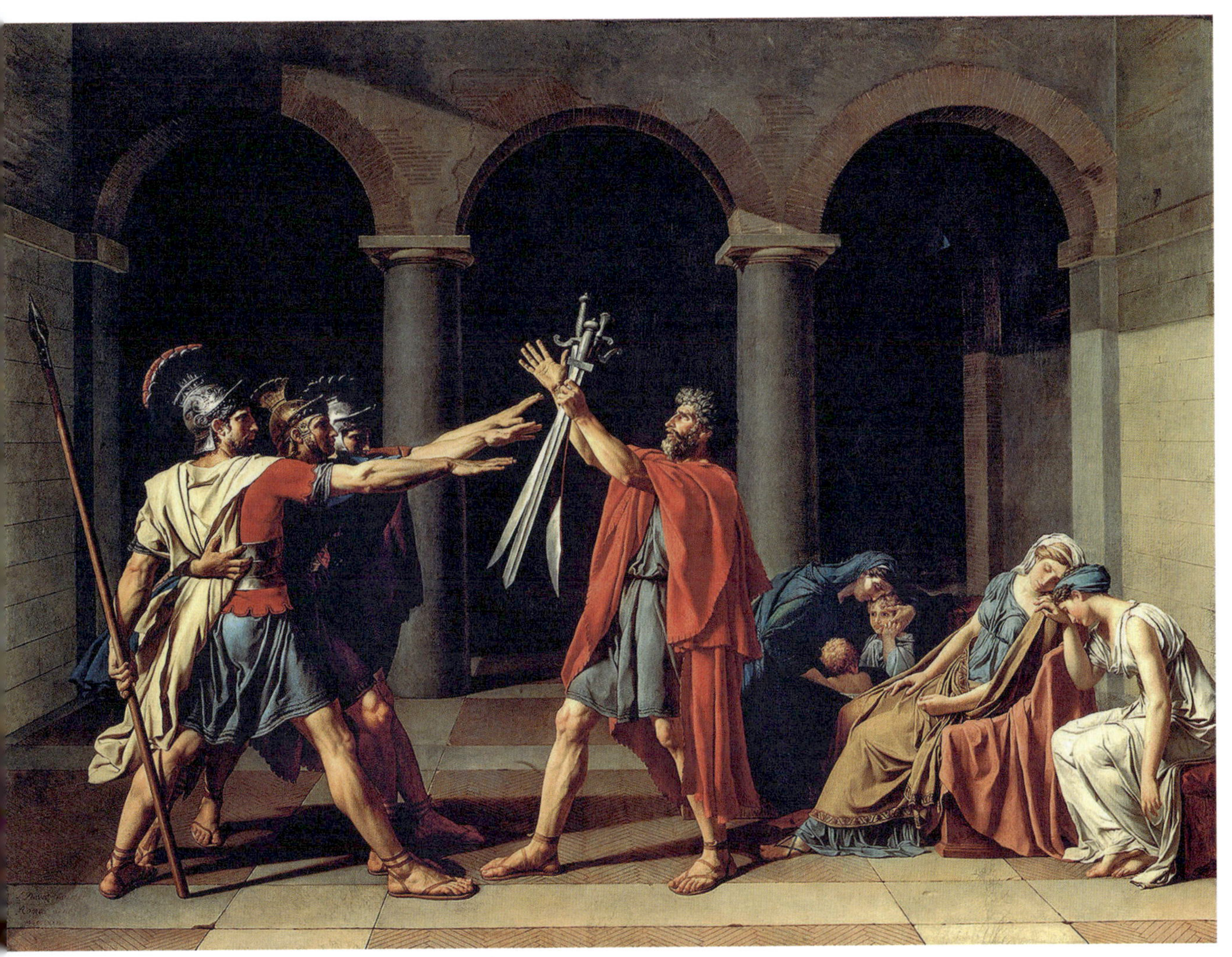

Your money or your life

Following the episode narrated by Titus Livius, Horatius was sentenced to death by the Roman Senate and people for killing his sister. His father intervened to defend him, arguing that he was the saviour of Rome and the last of its children. Horatius's sentence was commuted to a fine.

Marie-Guillemine Benoist

Caught between history and stories

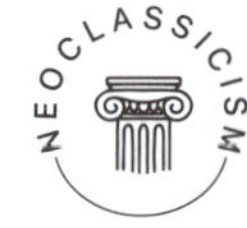

A brilliant portraitist in the service of Napoleon I, Marie-Guillemine Benoist was a pupil of Jacques-Louis David. She was recognised for the "vigour of her talent", which she would even confront with history painting. Sadly, her career would be short-lived.

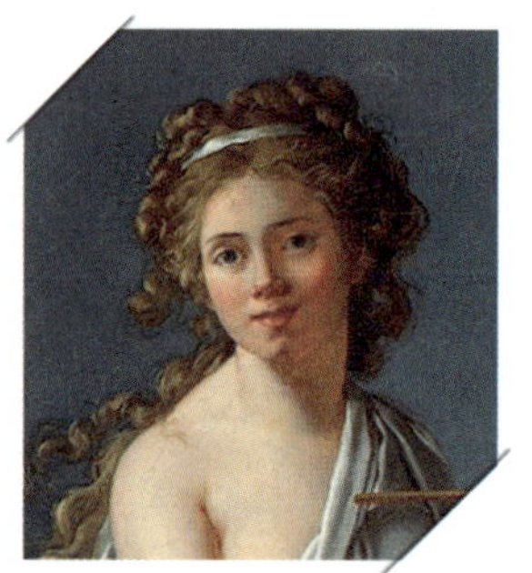

The cream of the crop

Driven towards an artistic career by her family, Benoist learned painting with Vigée Le Brun (p. 168), and then with Jacques-Louis David (p. 170), whom she admired. From his teachings, she retained a taste for vivid and sharp colours.

A painting with stories

A skilful portraitist, whose talents were recognised by critics, she also tried her hand at history painting, embracing this genre even in her self-portrait in antique dress. Akin to other successful women painters of her time, she was subjected to criticism and slander.

Stopped in her tracks

She had a fantastic career, and painted several portraits of Napoleon I and members of his family; however, she was pressured to end her career by her husband, who considered her work incompatible with his own political ambitions.

IT WAS SAID OF HER

"With pastel, she painted heads that already heralded the talent that she justly became famous for." Élisabeth Vigée Le Brun, *Souvenirs*, 1869.

Jacques-Louis David
Page 170

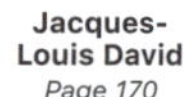

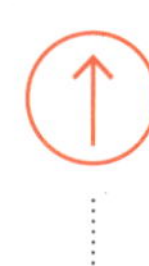

1768
Born in Bordeaux

1791
In Haiti, slaves led their first revolt

1800
Painted *Portrait of Madeleine*

1804
General Bonaparte became Napoleon I

1826
Died in Thomery

Francisco de Goya
Page 174

PORTRAIT OF MADELEINE ↗

1800
Oil on canvas
81 × 107 cm
Louvre Museum, Paris

WHAT ARE WE LOOKING AT?

This is an ambiguous portrait: is Marie-Guillemine Benoist painting a plea against slavery, or is she rather reproducing the stereotypes of her time?

A difficult story

The young woman would be one Madeleine, who was probably conscripted as a slave in Guadeloupe before serving in the house of Benoist's brother-in-law. There is no document to prove her citizenship, but she entered France as a domestic servant.

Stereotypes die hard

Madeleine's nudity, her earring and the kerchief that she wears on her head leave not doubt about her condition, close to slavery. The artist may have aspired to represent the spirit of "exoticism", which was fashionable at the time.

A domestic socialite

However, her perception of Madeleine seems respectful. The painting emphasises her individuality, reinforcing the impression of a portrait depicting a high society woman, like Jacques-Louis David's Portrait of Madame Récamier (p. 170). Her bare breast could also evoke La Fornarina, the Portrait of a Young Woman by Raphael (p. 46).

Measures still fragile

The colours blue, white and red are reminiscent of the French Revolution, tipping the scales towards the representation of an egalitarian ideal, at a time where the application of the first measures aiming to abolish slavery proved difficult.

Beautiful skin

Beyond the political message, this portrait is a masterpiece. The painter depicted Madeleine's expression with sensitivity. She perfectly mastered the rendering of Madeleine's black complexion, which was still rarely practised in studios.

A WOMAN OF INFLUENCE

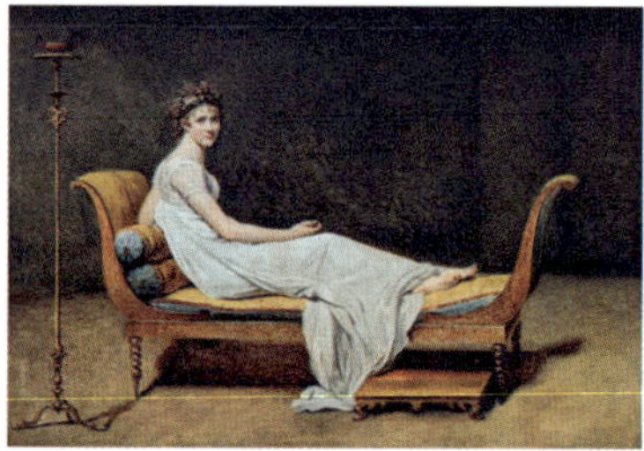

Jacques-Louis David,
Portrait of Madame Récamier
1800, Louvre Museum, Paris

The *Portrait of Madeleine* draws inspiration from the Portrait of Madame Récamier, by Jacques-Louis David. At the turn of the 19th century, Juliette Récamier was renowned for her wit and beauty. Her salon was frequented by many artists.

A TITLE THAT SAYS IT ALL…

Formerly titled *Portrait of a Negress*, this work was renamed *Portrait of a Black Woman*, to erase the racism conveyed by the original title. In 2019, it was exhibited at the Musée d'Orsay as *Portrait of Madeleine*, a new title designed to acknowledge the model's individuality.

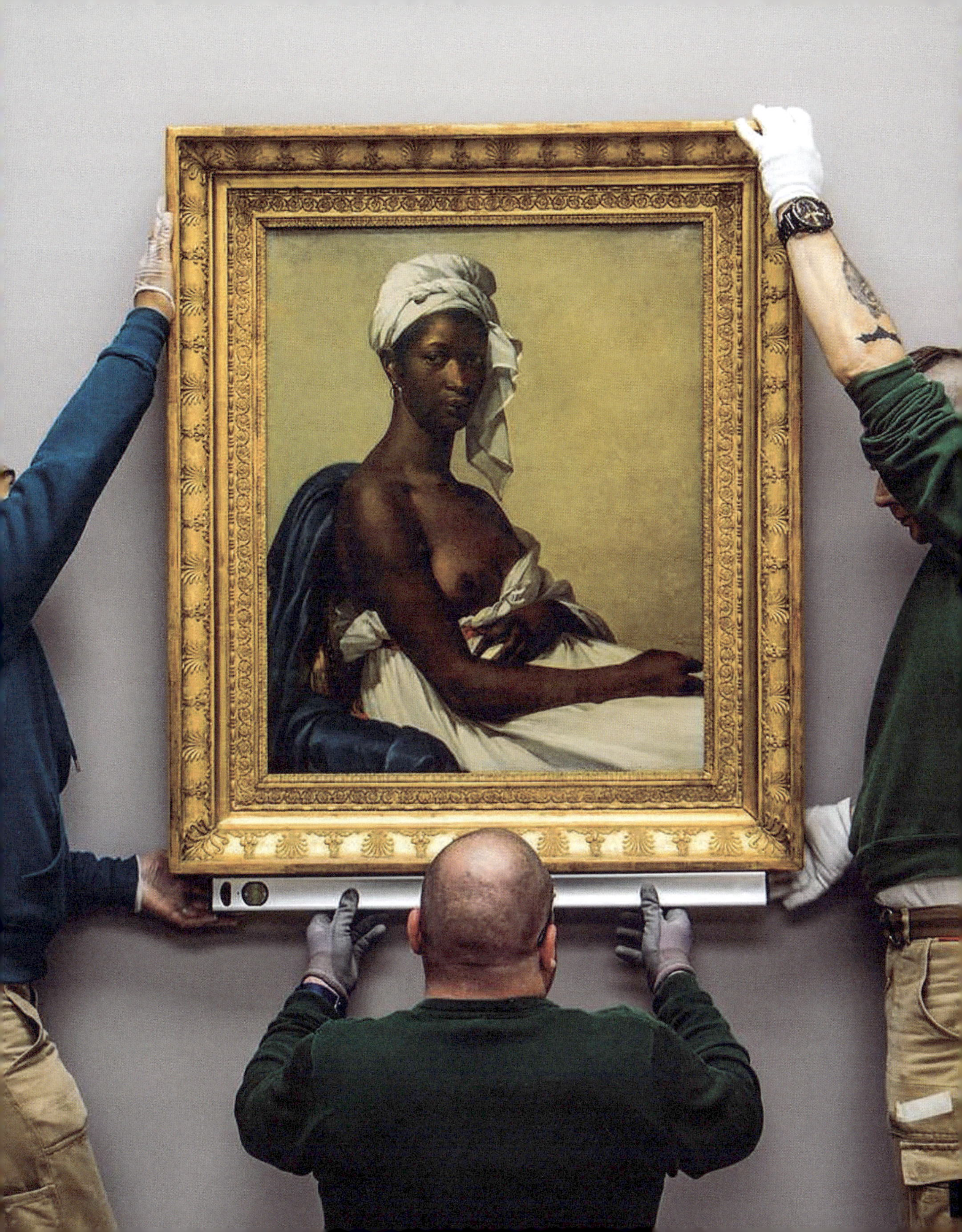

Francisco de Goya

Vitriolic paintings

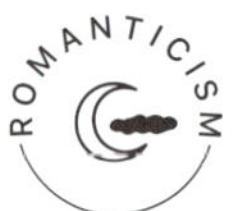

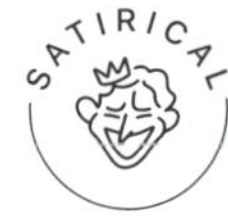

At the age of only 30, he received his first official commission and moved to Madrid. He impressed the Court with his speed of execution and his talent. His career had begun, and he would become the great portraitist of the Spanish nobility.

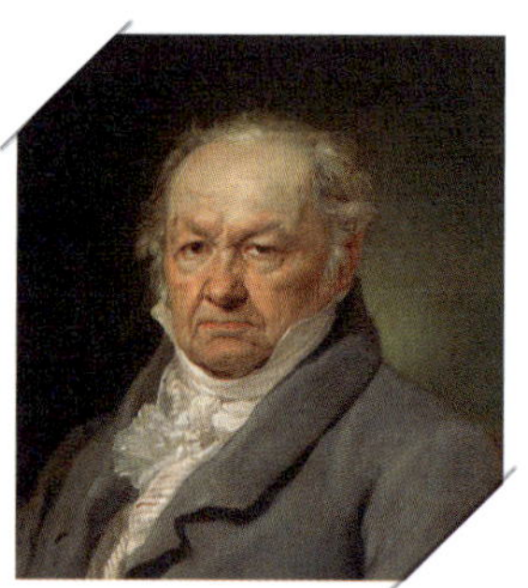

A caricaturist before his time

Goya lived in turbulent times: Spain was at war, and the spirit of the Enlightenment spread across Europe, upsetting the powerful. Far from being under the government's thumb, the painter was an independent spirit, and did not hesitate to denounce the failings of his time with images that were, in turn, amusing and cruel.

A permanently engraved consequence

Goya was an exceptional engraver. Struck deaf in 1792, he aspired to "give free rein to invention, fantasy, and caprice", and began work on the series titled *Los Caprichos* (The Caprices") – more personal works, tinged with black humour, which would guide the rest of his work.

Interior decorator

This acerbic irony would be expressed in the last period of his career, with his series of "Black Paintings". These frescoes would adorn the *Quinta del Sordo*, the "House of the Deaf", located in the Madrid countryside, where Goya retired for a time.

IT WAS SAID OF HIM

"No one, more than him, has dared in the sense of the possible absurd."
Charles Baudelaire, *Curiosités esthétiques*, 1868.

Marie-Guillemine Benoist
Page 172

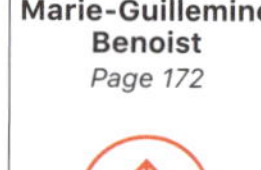
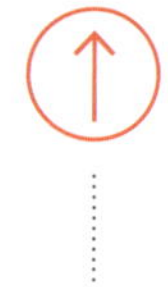

1746
Birth in Fuendetodos (near Zaragoza)

1814
The French monarchy attempted to restore itself to health

Circa
1813 – 1820
Painted *The Letter*

1824
Beethoven, despite being deaf, gave the first performance of the *Ninth Symphony*

1828
Died in Bordeaux

Caspar David Friedrich
Page 176

THE LETTER
OR THE YOUNG

Circa 1813–1820
Oil on wood
181 × 125 cm
Palais des Beaux-Arts, Lille

WHAT ARE WE LOOKING AT?

This genre scene depicts two young women of good character. They are wearing the traditional Spanish dress: they are *Majas*. However, in the guise of innocuous appearances, Goya may be issuing a sharp social critique.

Visible affluence

Many clues are revealing of the young woman's status. She is flanked by a female companion, who is holding an umbrella to protect her from the sun, and is accompanied by a small dog, the indispensable pet of the wealthy young women of her time. Also, she knows how to read – a skill prevalent only in the wealthier tiers of society.

At the centre of her concerns…

In the centre of the canvas is a letter. Held close to the young woman's heart, its white colour echoes her bodice. Could this be a love note? Often perceived as a symbol of loyalty, the dog may be consistent with this theory; however, its eager attitude may suggest a lighter connotation.

Class contempt?

The whiteness of the young woman's bodice is a sign of moral purity, which also reflects affluence. This *Maja* has enough money to hire a laundress. In the background, washerwomen are indeed, working diligently, while the protagonist turns her back to them. The young bourgeois woman therefore ignores those who enable her to present such an image.

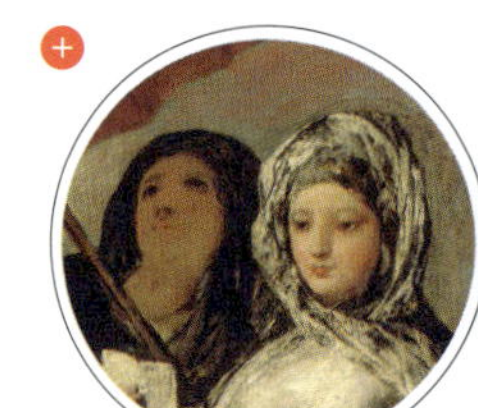

FAKE TWINS

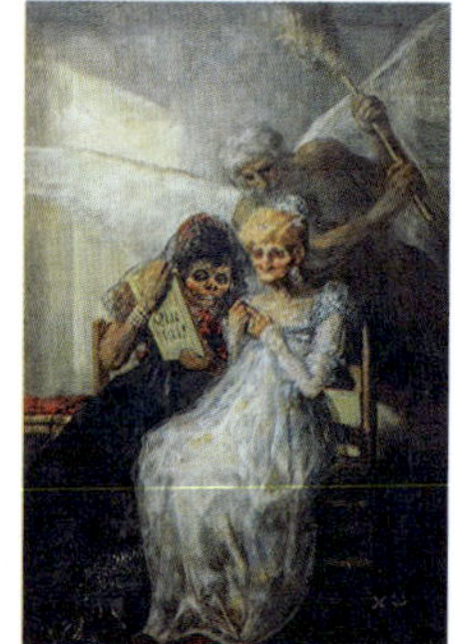

The Letter was nicknamed "The Young", in reference to *Time*, another painting by Goya renamed "The Old Women". Linked by their titles and their identical format, these two works are thought to be counterparts; however, this is not the case: Goya painted them at two different times, and they were not initially of the same size. *Time* was enlarged to match the format of *The Letter*. This was likely requested by the art dealer Durlacher, who acquired the works at the sale of King Louis-Philippe's collection in 1853.

The Old Women or *Time*, 1808–1812
Palais des Beaux-Arts, Lille

HEADLESS

Where is Goya's skull? After his burial, for reasons unknown, Goya's body was decapitated. His skull was last seen in Bordeaux in 1955. It has been missing ever since.

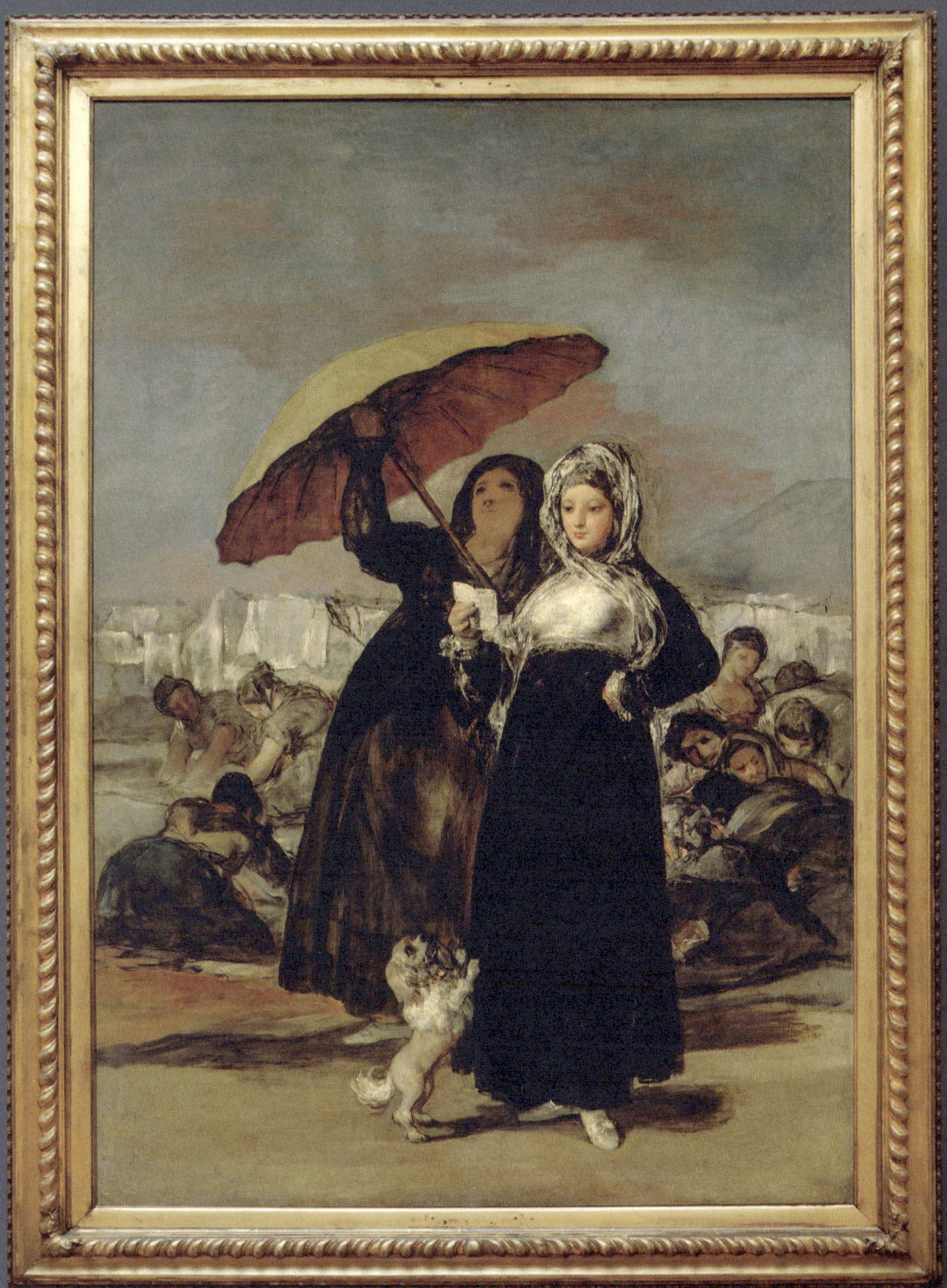

Caspar David Friedrich

Nature pervades religion

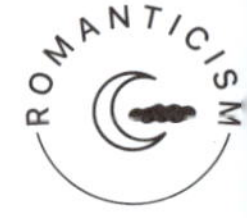

Star of the German Romantics, Friedrich is undoubtedly one of the best known and most appreciated German painters in the world. His melancholic landscapes are haloed with light, bearing a spiritual message.

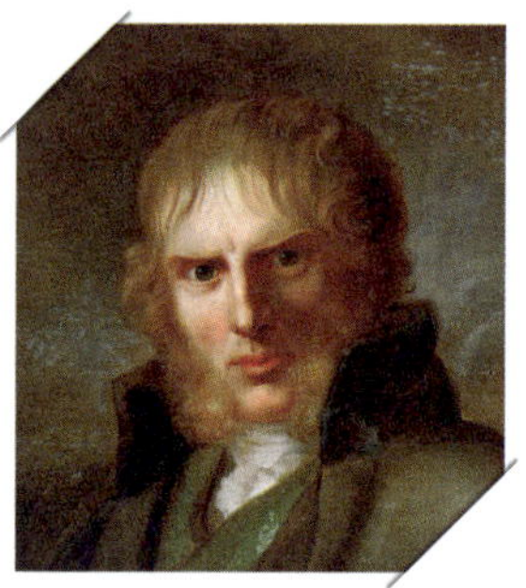

Off the beaten track

In his youth, Friedrich was a writer before becoming a painter. He likely embraced painting because he felt the need to illustrate his ideas. He avoided the classic Italian journey, and instead, trained at the Copenhagen Academy. He settled in Dresden, maybe seduced by the beauty of the area's landscapes.

Mountains of piety

Imbued with Pietism, he painted landscapes with great spirituality. His paintings depicted an exalted and grandiose nature, carrying within itself the ambivalence of eternity and finitude, in the vein of German Romanticism.

A reputation set in stone

Friedrich was an academician in Dresden and Berlin. He was supported by the great German romantic writer Goethe, and by the King of Prussia. In France, the sculptor David d'Angers cele-brated his painting as the "tragedy of the landscape".

CASPAR DAVID FRIEDRICH SAID

"The artist should paint not only what he has in front of him, but what he sees inside himself."

Francisco de Goya
Page 174

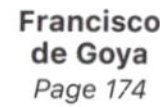

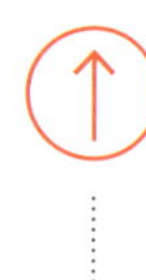

1774
Born in Greifswald

1800
Alessandro Volta created the first electric battery

Circa
1818
Painted *Wanderer above the Sea of Fog*

1830
Chopin composed his first *Nocturnes*

1840
Died in Dresden

J.M.W. Turner
Page 178

WANDERER ABOVE THE SEA OF FOG ↗

Circa 1818
Oil on canvas
94.8 × 74.8 cm
Kunsthalle, Hamburg

WHAT ARE WE LOOKING AT?

This famous traveller, renowned throughout the world, is both an ode to the grandeur of nature and the bearer of a spiritual message.

Subject to interpretation

With his back turned to the viewer, the wanderer leaves it to us to interpret his state of mind. Maybe he is at a loss when faced with the vastness of the world and the grandeur of the nature that dominates him, or maybe he is captivated by the immensity and the sense of escape that it inspires.

A force of nature

His three-quarter position indicates that he is looking precisely at the Rosenberg Glacier, which rises at the bottom of the valley. And while the mountain is far away, it still dominates him, even though he is perched on a vantage point.

With his head in the clouds

His contemplation may be meditative. The cul-de-sac formed by the promontory that he stands on seems to indicate that he has reached the end of a path; however, his journey is spiritual and religious, above all. Feeling inspired, he beholds the work of the Creator. He has risen above the fog, the uncertainties of his existence, and reached a clairvoyance that allows him to apprehend the world rightly.

Symbiosis

The wanderer also displays his profound communion with the landscape that he is contemplating. The shape of his shoulders echoes that of the Rosenberg, and one can observe a form mimicry between the folds of his frock coat and the rock formations protruding from the clouds.

THE GRAND RETURN OF THE GOTHIC STYLE

Friedrich's painting is part of a revival of the Gothic style in Europe. This resurgence was expressed in various disciplines: in painting, with the British pre-Raphaelites (p. 214) and the Troubadour style in France; in architecture, with important theorists such as John Ruskin or Viollet-le-Duc; and in literature.

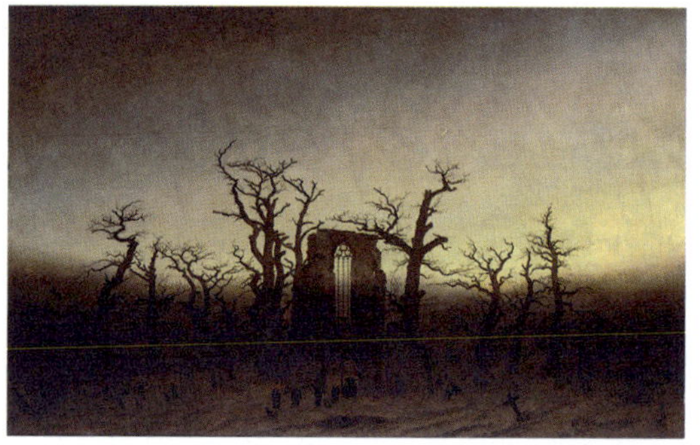

The Abbey in the Oakwood, 1809–1810, Alte Nationalgalerie, Berlin

GERMAN ROMANTICISM IN A NUTSHELL

- The expression of feelings overriding reason.
- Reconnecting with nature.
- Exalted landscapes conveying emotions.
- A reaction of national preference against the Enlightenment and Napoleon.

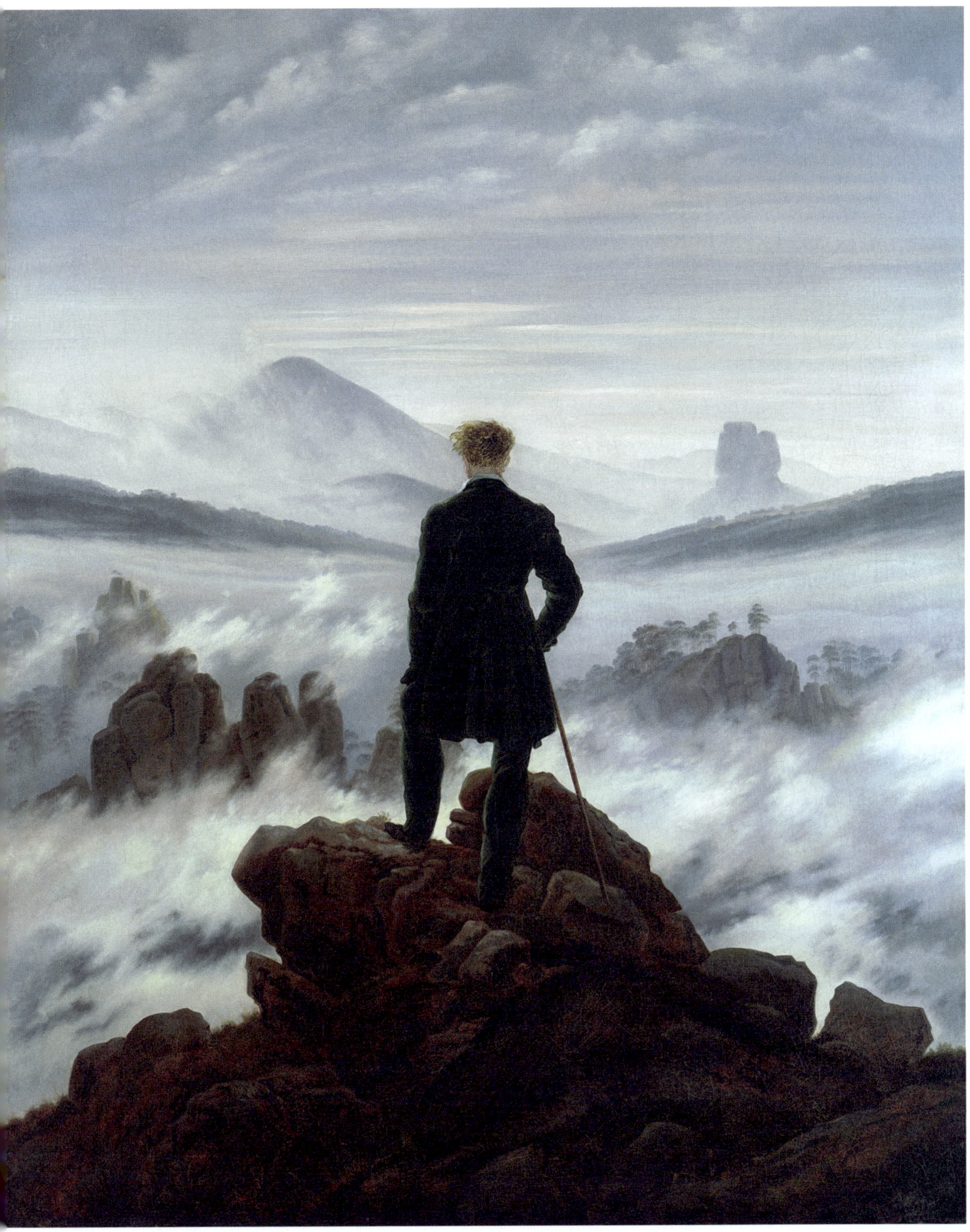

Joseph Mallord William Turner

An unconventional artist

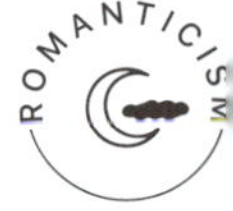

Turner was one of the greatest British painters. He distinguished himself as a landscape artist, where his bold use of colour overturned convention. He was also a celebrated watercolourist.

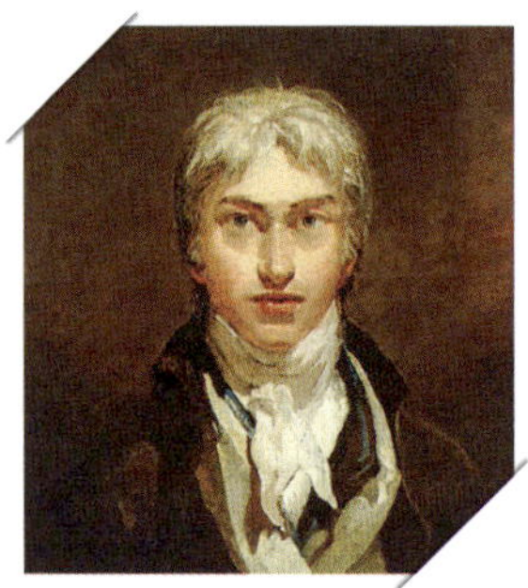

Unbelievable but true

The son of a barber and wigmaker, Turner began his career with an architect, drawing city views. At 26, he became the youngest academician at the Royal Academy of Arts, where his manners shocked his contemporaries. He did not hesitate to retouch his works during exhibitions, in front of an astonished audience.

Following the flow

Imbued with Romanticism, he used historical subjects to raise landscape painting to its most noble status. His golden lights, influenced by the French landscape painter Claude Gellée (also known as Claude Lorrain) graced his works with symbolist accents (p. 212), drawing them towards abstraction.

Dipping his brushes and feet in water

Turner was a tireless traveller. He travelled the UK and Europe, from Brittany to the Loire and Venice. He frequently transcribed landscapes in watercolour, a discipline in which he excelled.

IT WAS SAID OF HIM

"I was a good deal entertained with Turner. I always expected to find him what I did. He is uncouth but has a wonderful range of mind." Letter from John Constable to Maria Bicknell, 30 June 1813.

Caspar David Friedrich
Page 176

1775
Born in London

1793
Marie-Antoinette walked up the steps to the guillotine

1844
Painted *Rain, Steam and Speed*

1849
The first French stamp was released

1851
Died in London

Jean-Auguste-Dominique Ingres
Page 180

RAIN, STEAM AND SPEED

1844
Oil on canvas
91 × 121.8 cm
National Gallery, London

WHAT ARE WE LOOKING AT?

In a cloud of fog haloed by light, a train is heading towards us, on a bridge whose perspective is reinforced by brown tones. Does Turner embrace modernity, or does he resent it?

Catching a running train

The train, appearing from the background of the painting, is piercing the fog and will soon reach the viewers' level. This movement in space could also symbolise a shift in time: the background is the past and the viewer's perspective is the future, which the train has not yet reached. In any case, progress is depicted as inevitable.

La Fontaine revisited

The accentuated perspective conveys the idea of speed, which the painter also evokes in other ways. In the middle of the tracks, one can see the footprints of a hare, which have almost been erased. On the left, a small boat and, on the right, barely visible, horses and a man evoke slower means of locomotion. These small figures, integrated into the landscape, are reminiscent of the art of Claude Gellée and Nicolas Poussin (p. 124).

A cult work

Turner did not seek to precisely transcribe reality; rather, he aspired to render a feeling, of a luminous atmosphere blurred by fumes and bad weather. Impressionists would become fervent admirers of the practice of capturing such "snapshots".

Experiencing a downpour

The art critic John Ruskin told the tale of a female traveller who once saw a man stick his head out of the train window for nearly ten minutes, in the midst of a storm. On seeing the painting, she reportedly stated that this man must have been Turner.

TURNER'S WORK IN FIGURES

Turner bequeathed his works to the National Gallery in London, to ensure his posterity. This collection is now housed in Tate Britain.

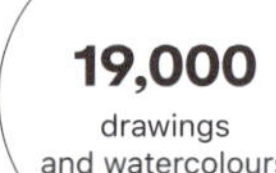

19,000
drawings and watercolours

100
completed paintings

182
works drafted

MADE IN ENGLAND

Watercolour was a British speciality. In 1766, William Reeves perfected the preparation of dry colours, a technical advance that contributed to the democratisation of watercolour, which became increasingly practised as a hobby.

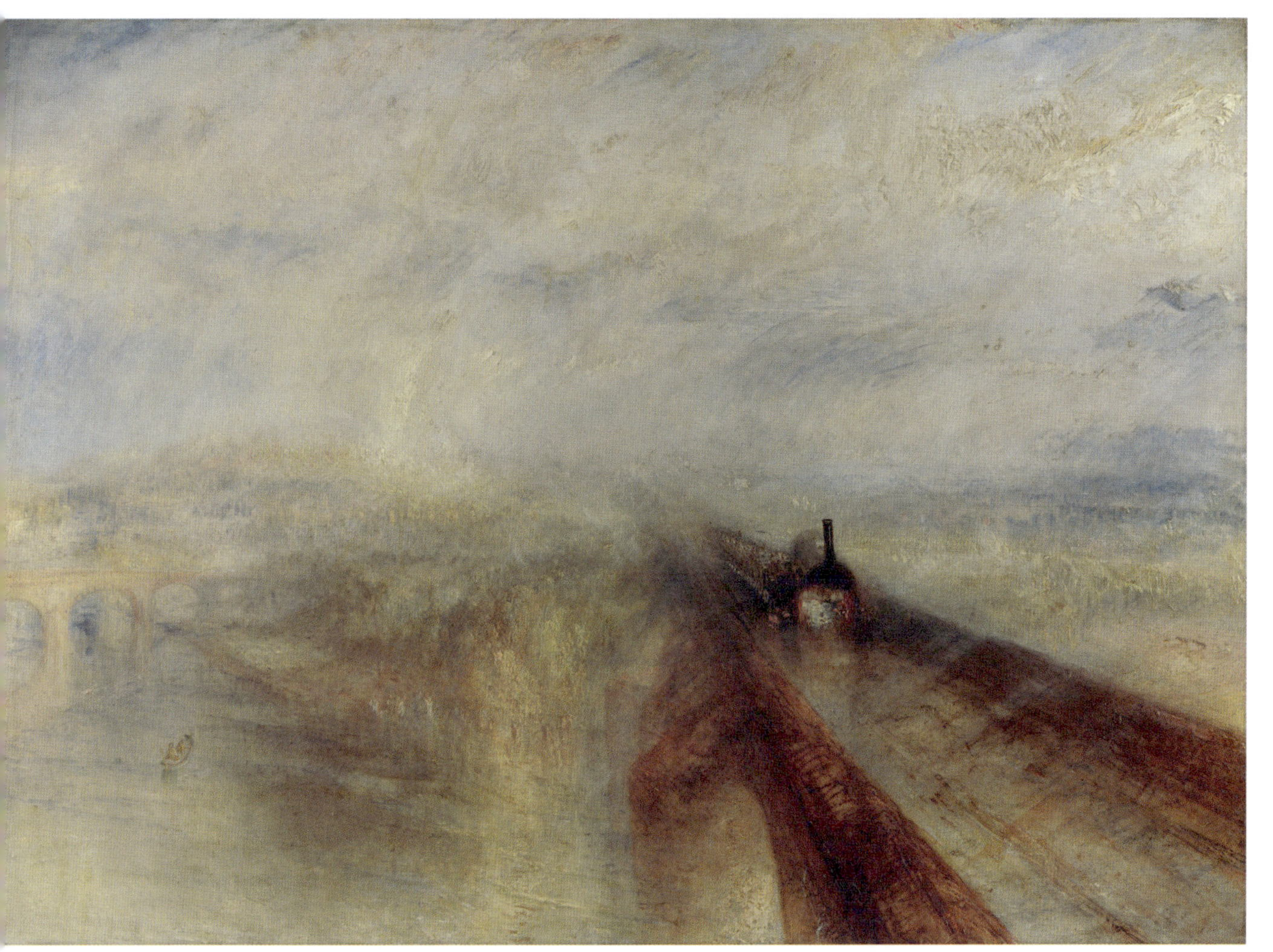

Railways and a golden age

The democratisation of railways in Great Britain occurred in the context of the Victorian era, during the reign of Queen Victoria, from 1837 to 1901. An industrial, colonial and diplomatic power, Great Britain experienced unprecedented growth, despite the great precariousness of the more modest working classes.

Jean-Auguste-Dominique Ingres

A passion for the flesh

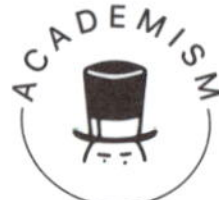

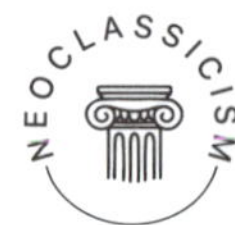

Known for his anatomical eccentricities, Ingres adhered to a classicism that he inherited from his master Jacques-Louis David and his admiration for Raphael. The artist's relationship with critics was somewhat fractious, but his talent was highly sought after.

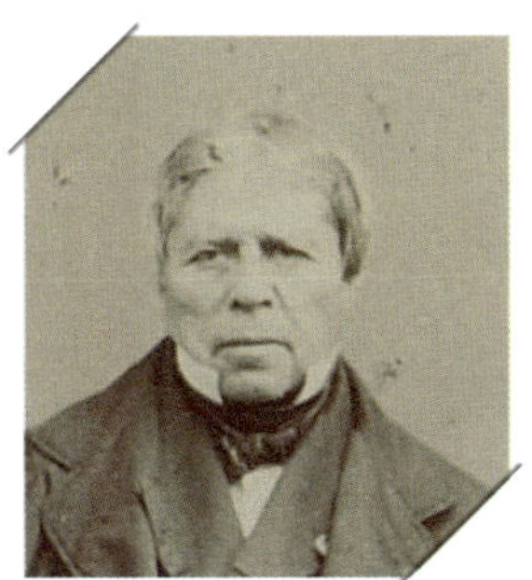

"Ingrou" for those who knew him well

The son of an artist, the young "Ingrou", as his parents called him, first learned to paint in Montauban, then moved to Toulouse. He copied the old masters, which he reworked to his liking, then joined Jacques-Louis David's studio in Paris (p. 170), before leaving for Rome.

A fetishist

In Italy, Ingres unconditionally worshiped Raphael, religiously preserving a piece of bone and a drawing by the master – that were, in fact, false relics. A brilliant draughtsman and colourist, he rejected romanticism and defended classicism, within the realms of which he nevertheless allowed himself some eccentricities.

Dragging his feet

His early portrait of Napoleon I was criticised, but the artist's talents were sought after by the polite society, including the restored monarchy. However, he was reluctant to produce these commissions, which were too time-consuming to his liking.

AN ARTIST WITH MORE THAN ONE STRING TO HIS BOW

An experienced violinist, the painter left his name to the French expression "violon d'Ingres", which describes a hobby at which one excels.

J. M. W. Turner
Page 178

1780
Born in Montauban

1841
Palaeontologist Richard Owen invented the word "dinosaur"

1845
Painted *Louise de Broglie, Countess d'Haussonville*

1847
The Brontë sisters published *Jane Eyre*, *Wuthering Heights* and *Agnes Grey* under pseudonyms.

1867
Died in Paris

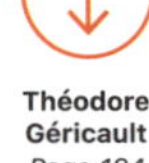

Théodore Géricault
Page 184

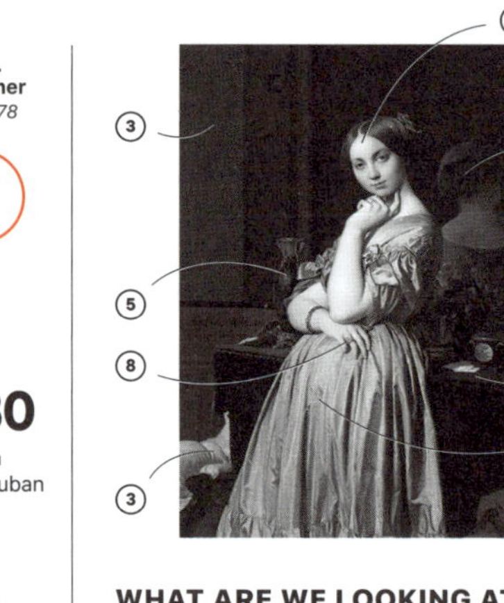

LOUISE DE BROGLIE, COUNTESS D'HAUSSONVILLE

1845
Oil on canvas
131.8 × 92.1 cm
The Frick Collection, New York

WHAT ARE WE LOOKING AT?

This is one of the portraits that Ingres produced during his golden age. When the painter returned from Rome, showered with praise, he painted the Countess d'Haussonville, whom he had met in Italy.

① An air of mystery

The young woman seems both deep in thought and amused to leave the viewer in a state of uncertainty. Her pose is inspired by the statue of Hannah, sculpted by Lorenzo Ghiberti during the Renaissance.

② Bottomless depth

With the mirror, Ingres gave volume to his model; in the absence of other elements appearing in the reflection, this object also creates an air of mystery.

③ Great comfort

The interior is discreetly luxurious and comfortable, featuring silk-lined walls and the two soft, white armchairs, to either side of the fireplace.

④ Go blue!

Ingres painted a harmonious range of blues. This cameo is enhanced with touches of red, with the flowers and the ribbon, which are cleverly repeated in the mirror.

⑤ *Comeback*

This vase may be Japanese or French, of Oriental inspiration. It is mounted on a bronze base. Rococo fashion regained popularity in the middle of the 19th century.

⑥ The curtain falls

The countess has placed opera glasses on the edge of the mantelpiece, and has hung a lace-up bag just above them. On the armchair, next to it, is her shawl. She may have just returned from the show.

⑦ A trendy woman

These cards were left in her hallway by visitors in her absence. They are a testimony to her active social life.

⑧ There is a catch

She is wearing a so-called "Cleopatra ring" on her finger. It may reflect her interest for history and morbidity, which are reflected in her writings.

⑦ +

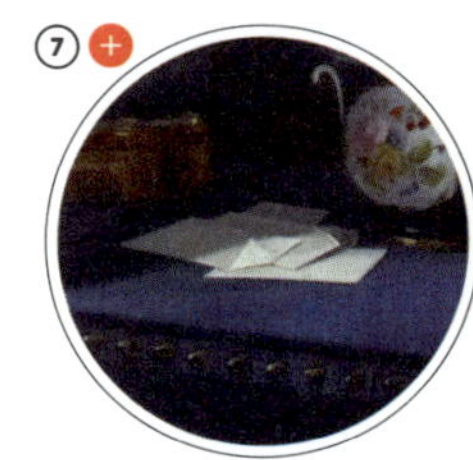

INGRES'S ART IN A NUTSHELL

- A taste for classical art, inspired by David and Raphael.
- Nudes with sometimes questionable, strange anatomy.
- Erotic depictions of women's bodies and harems, painted in an Orientalist taste.
- Refined portraits featuring sublimely rendered materials.

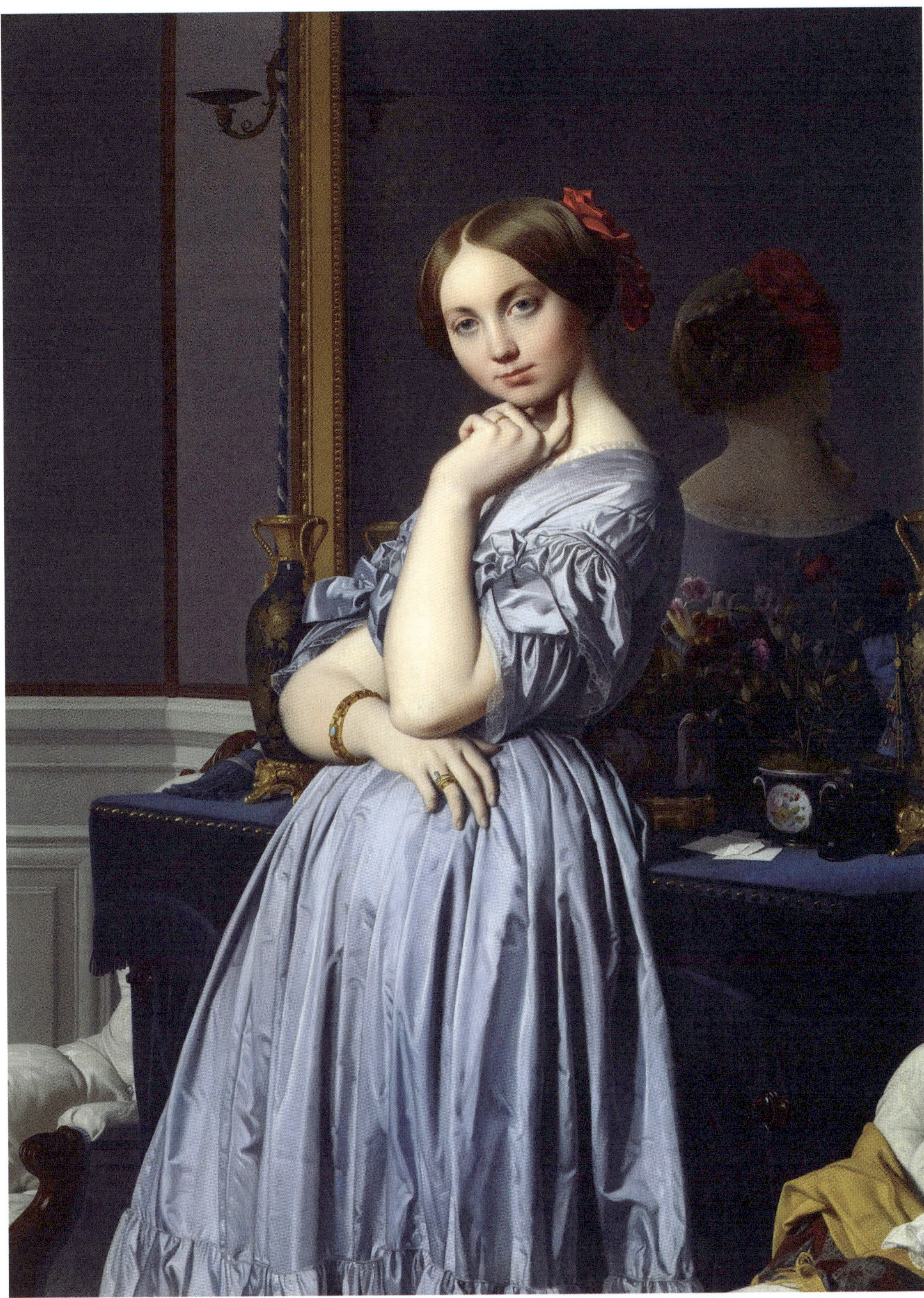

Ingres and Valadon

Contradicting visions of the female body

The odalisques are a variant of the reclining nude, introduced by the Renaissance figure of Venus. In the midst of the Orientalist wave, Ingres invented this tradition, a pretext for eroticising the female body. This motif would be emulated by others, from Eugène Delacroix to Henri Matisse.

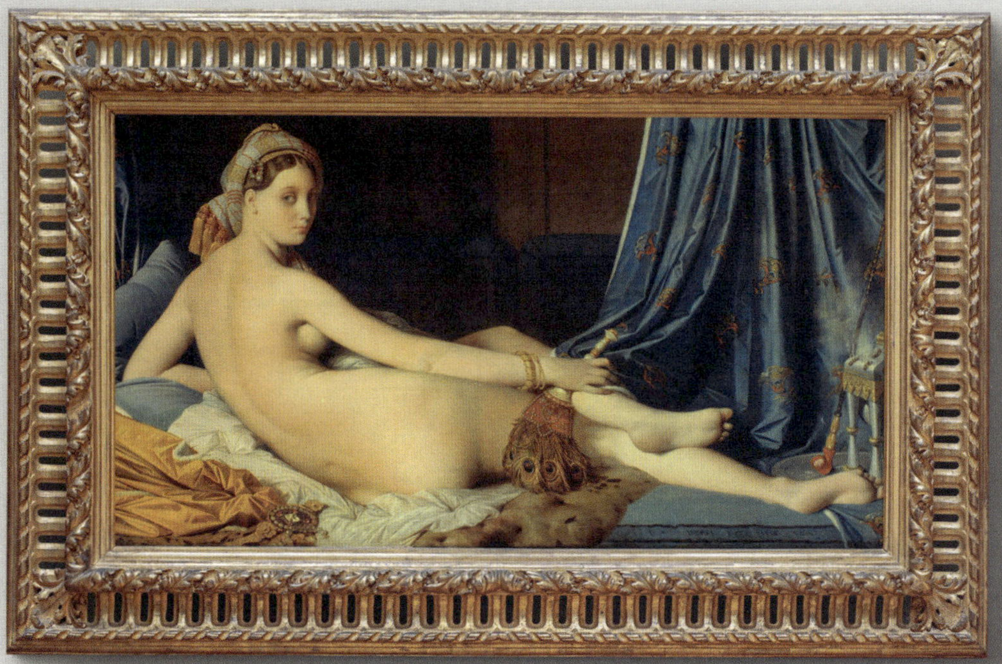

LA GRANDE ODALISQUE **BY JEAN-AUGUSTE-DOMINIQUE INGRES**
1814

This odalisque, with her elongated back, conveys a strange and mysterious sensuality. She represents the fantasised vision of Orient in the 19th century. Far-flung countries, and the bodies of the women who inhabited them were then perceived as territories offered to conquest by men.

Oil on canvas, 91 × 162 cm
Louvre Museum, Paris

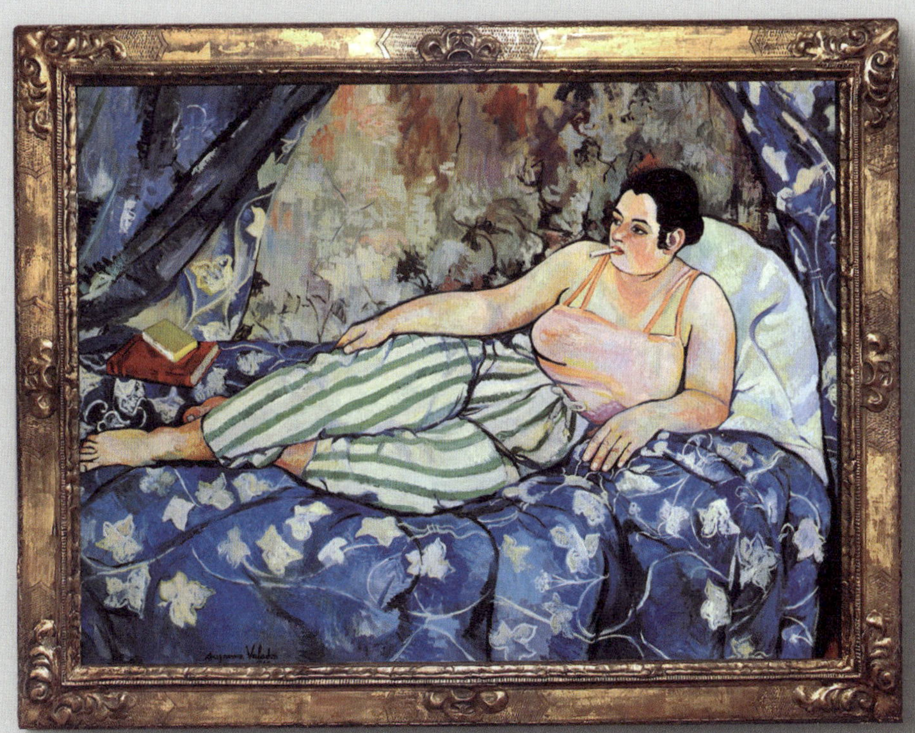

***THE BLUE ROOM* BY SUZANNE VALADON**
1923

While Valadon adhered to the codes of the reclining nude, she broke with the sensuality perceived by the male gaze. Her odalisque is more realistic, wearing pyjamas that evoke the everyday life of Parisian bohemians. The cigarette is a symbol of emancipation.

Oil on canvas, 90 × 116 cm
Musée des Beaux-Arts, Limoges
(on deposit at the Musée National d'Art Moderne, Paris)

Théodore Géricault

Drifting against the flow

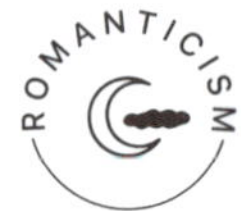

Géricault, who died at the age of 33, led an excessive and unreasonable life, and had a brilliant artistic career. Known for his paintings of horses, he was, with Eugène Delacroix, the other great figure of French Romanticism.

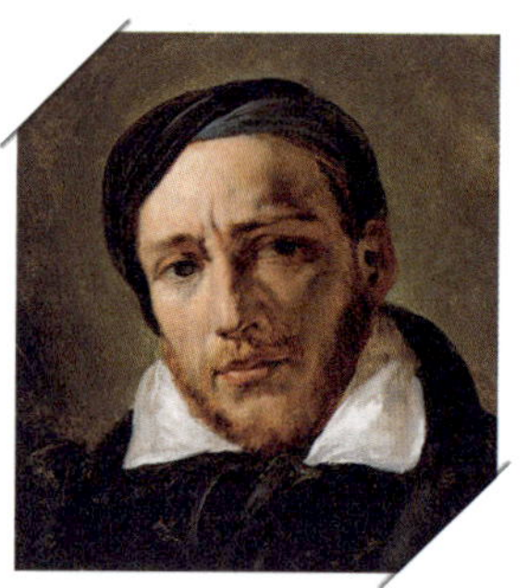

Counting and writing

Born into a bourgeois family, Géricault attended high school. He won prizes for spelling and Latin. His uncle hired him as an apprentice accountant; as a teenager, however, Géricault already secretly frequented Claude-Joseph Vernet's studio, before officially joining Pierre-Narcisse Guérin's.

Life in the fast lane

The painter lived a life of excess and drama. Expelled twice from the Louvre in his youth, he was both a royalist musketeer and a rebel at heart. He had a history of problems, among which paranoia, horse-riding accidents, bankruptcy and illness.

Passion bears fruit

Géricault's work was ambivalent, brilliant and tortured. As a painter, he was impressed by his master's classicism and Michelangelo's *terribilità*. He painted morbidity and madness, stormy battle scenes, portraits with pervaded by an eerie presence and horses on the qui-vive.

A WORD FROM THE KING

"Monsieur Géricault, the shipwreck that you have painted is certainly no disaster." This is the compliment that Louis XVIII is said to have addressed to the painter on discovering *The Raft of the Medusa*.

Ingres
Page 180

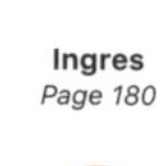

1791
Born in Rouen

1815
Napoleon went into exile on Saint Helena

1818 to **1819**
Painted *The Raft of the Medusa*

1821
The Greek War of Independence broke out

1824
Died in Paris

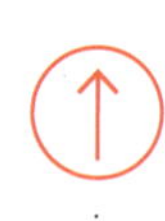

Eugène Delacroix
Page 190

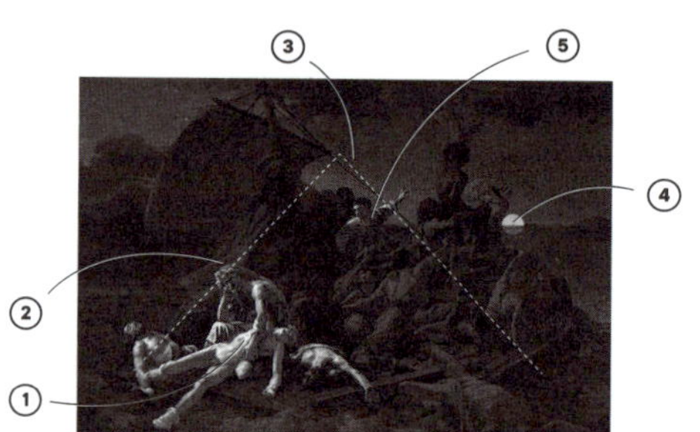

THE RAFT OF THE MEDUSA ↗

1818–1819
Oil on canvas
491 × 716 cm
Louvre Museum, Paris

WHAT ARE WE LOOKING AT?

Géricault piled up the corpses to describe the horror experienced by the shipwrecked crew of *The Medusa*, creating a spirited composition that laid the foundations for great Romantic paintings.

A little context information

In 1816, the French frigate *Méduse* was shipwrecked. The captain abandoned 150 men on a makeshift raft, without oars, driving survivors to the worst extremes of human nature, as they were required to drink their own urine, eat their dead and cast the wounded to the waves to save food.

① The propriety of the nude

Corpses are piled up, about to collapse into the sea. The artist transgresses codes by representing death with brutality, but Géricault's academic depiction of nude corpses is evocative of his admiration for the paintings of Pierre-Narcisse Guérin and Jacques-Louis David.

② Gazing into the waves

Facing us, this castaway is the embodiment of humanity in tragedy. With his gaze filled with emptiness by despair or madness, he refuses to surrender his son's corpse to the sea.

③ The bleakest of storms...

The pyramidal construction confirms the painter's classical training, but the highly dynamic composition, highlighted by the stormy sea and the twilight sky, reflect the romantic ideal.

④ ...And a glimmer of hope

The gazes of the remaining lucid shipwrecked sailors are converging towards the horizon, in a single movement. In the distance, one can see the French brig *Argus*, coming to save them. Barely visible in this painting, it represents a fragment of hope.

⑤ Identified witnesses

The painter portrayed engineer Alexandre Corréard pointing towards the horizon, drawing the attention of Doctor Henri Savigny. Both survivors would sign the account of this shipwreck, which terrified France.

② +

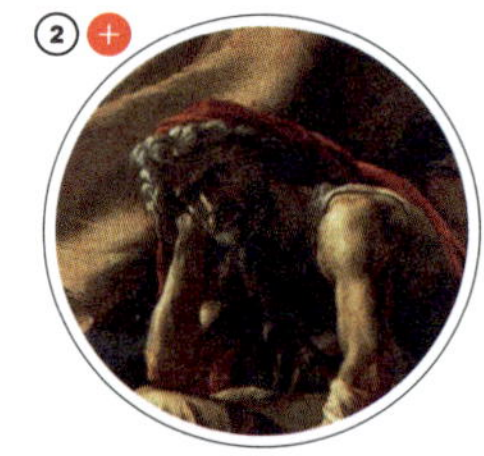

ROMANTICISM IN A NUTSHELL

- A movement that spread throughout Europe in the first half of the 19th century.
- An exalted approach of painting that stood against the mastery promoted by classicism.
- Medieval, Oriental and Gothic sources of inspiration.
- An interest in current affairs and contemporary history.

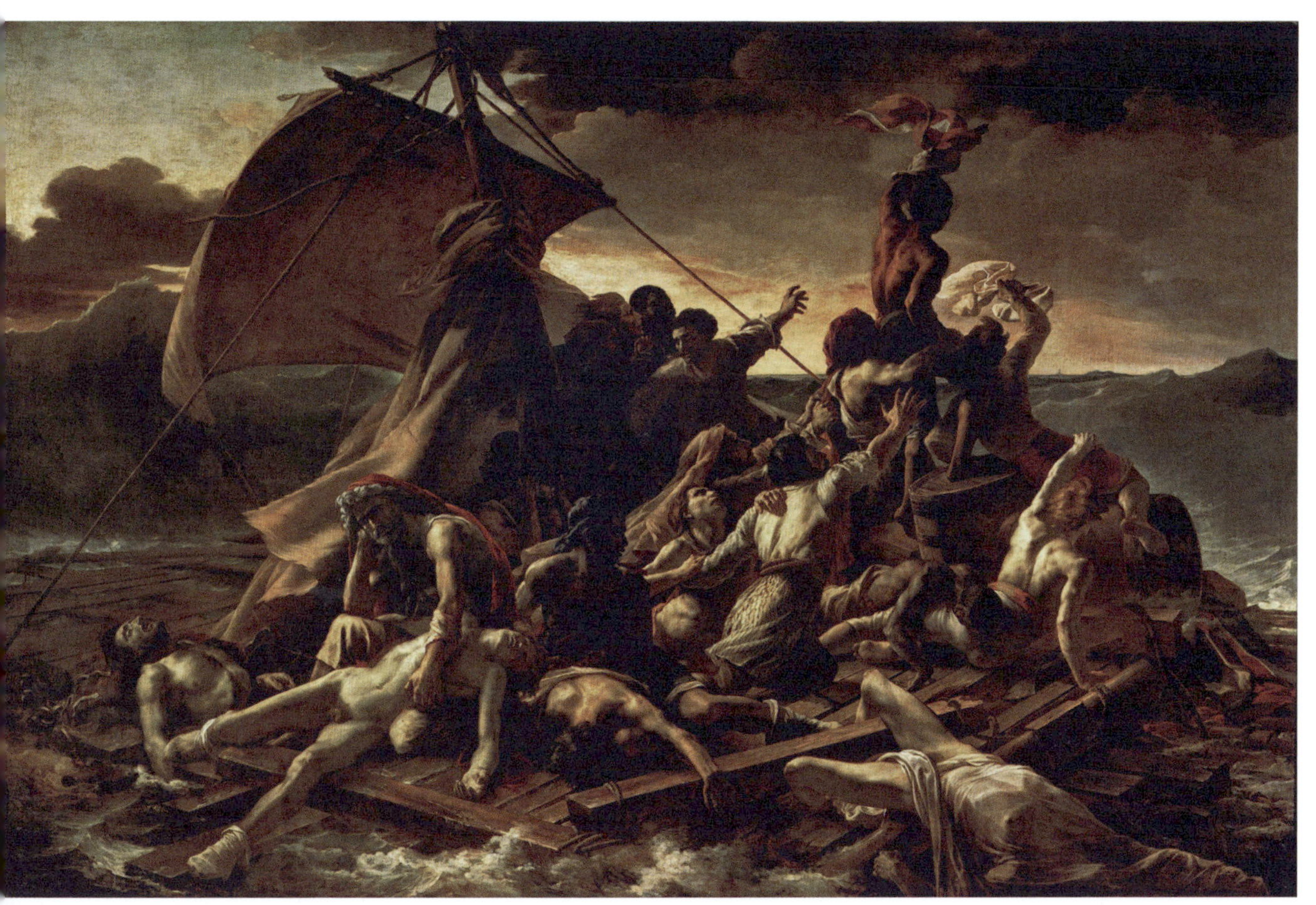

Unbearable

"Those whom death had spared in the disastrous night which we have just described, fell upon the dead bodies with which the raft was covered, and cut off pieces, which some instantly devoured." Excerpt from *An Account of the Shipwreck of the Medusa*, by Alexandre Corréard and Henry Savigny.

The cornerstones of art

The greatest paintings are carved in ancient marble

The study of sculpture, in particular antique sculpture, was essential to artists. It enabled them to comprehend volumes and light. It is therefore not uncommon, in paintings, to find compositions or characters inspired by sculpture.

Winged Victory of Samothrace

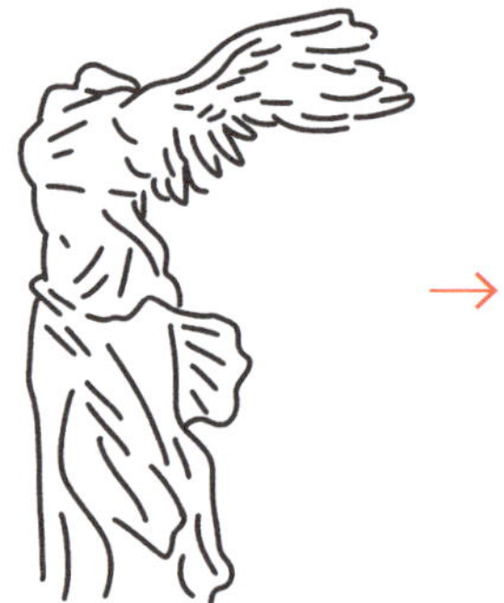

Winged Victory of Samothrace, *circa 220–185 BC, Louvre Museum, Paris.*

→

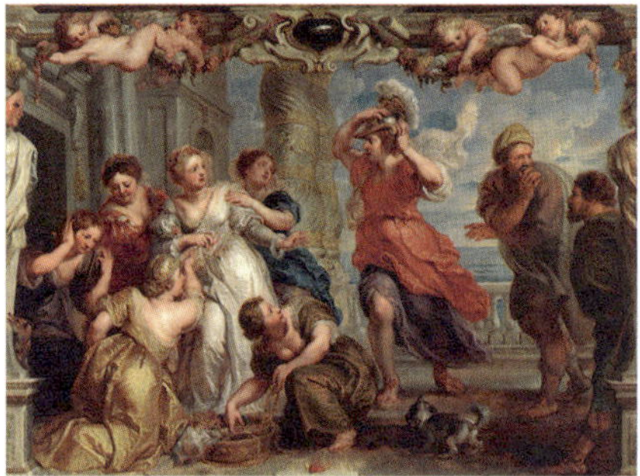

Rubens
Achilles Discovered by Ulysses Among the Daughters of Lycomedes, *1630–1635, Prado Museum, Madrid.*

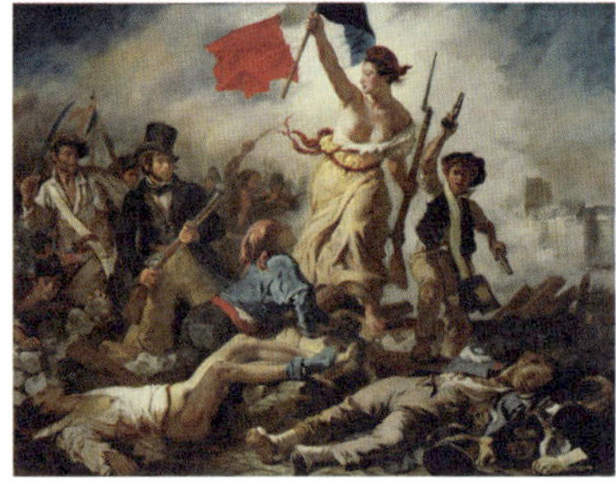

Delacroix
Liberty Leading the People, *1830, Louvre Museum, Paris.*

Capitoline Venus

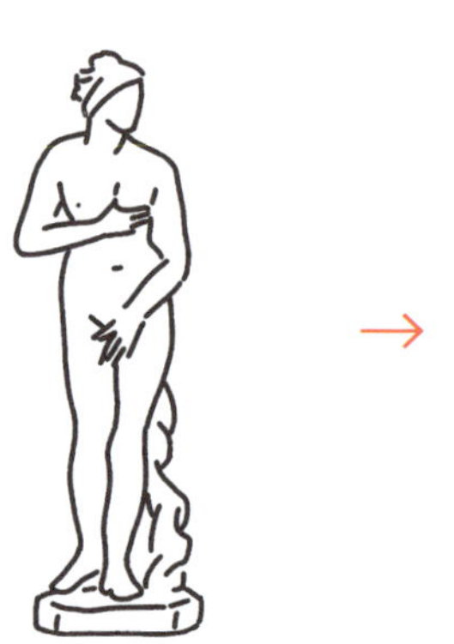

Venus de' Medici, *50 BC, Uffizi Gallery, Florence.*

→

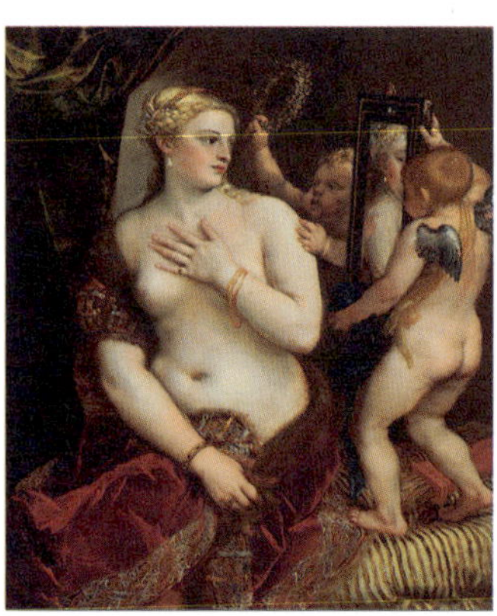

Titian
Venus with a Mirror, *circa 1555, National Gallery of Art, Washington.*

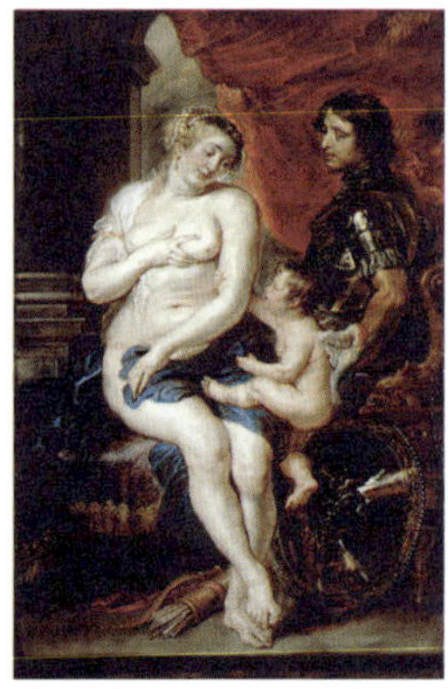

Rubens
Venus, Mars and Cupid, *circa 1635, Dulwich Picture Gallery.*

PROTECTED DESIGNATION OF ORIGIN

To produce their most sumptuous masterpieces, sculptors would search for the most beautiful marble. The Carrara quarries, in Italy, are particularly famous for the whiteness of their marble. In his book *The Lives of the Most Excellent Painters, Sculptors, and Architects*, Giorgio Vasari recounted that Michelangelo himself used to travel to Carrara to extract blocks for his works with his pupils.

Apollo Belvedere

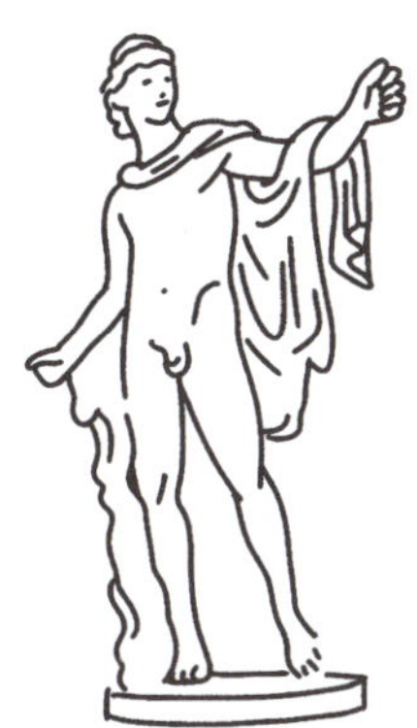

Apollo Belvedere, *second half of the 4th century BC, Vatican Museums.*

→

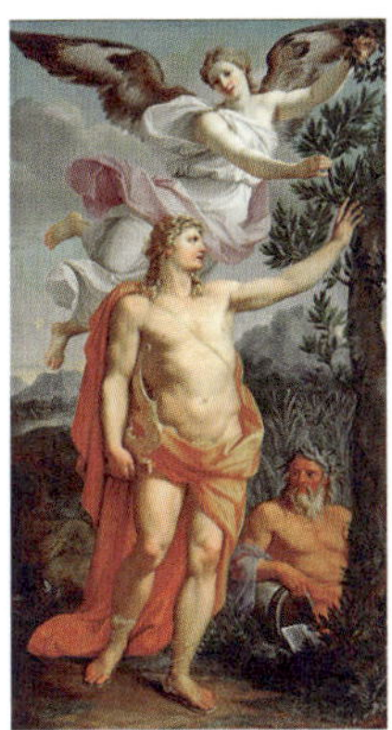

Coypel
Apollo crowned by Minerva, *1667–1668, Louvre Museum, Paris.*

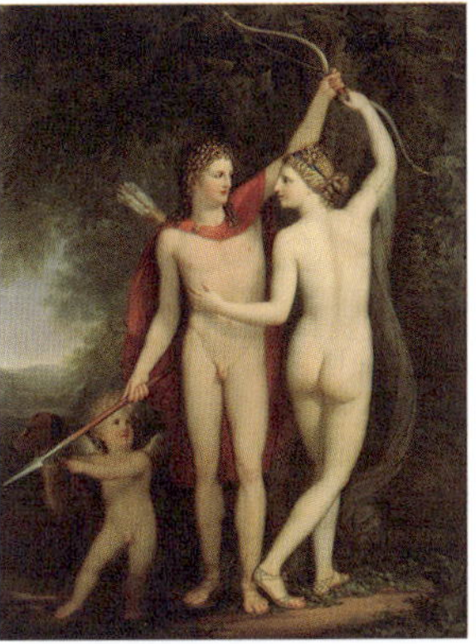

Åkerström
Venus, Adonis and Cupid, *18th century, Nationalmuseum, Stockholm.*

The Three Graces

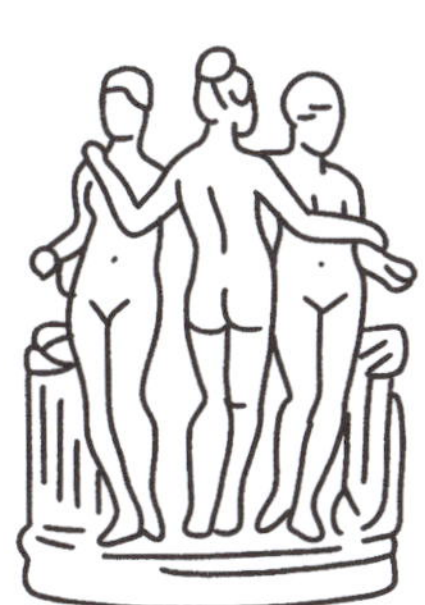

The Three Graces, *2nd century, Louvre Museum, Paris.*

→

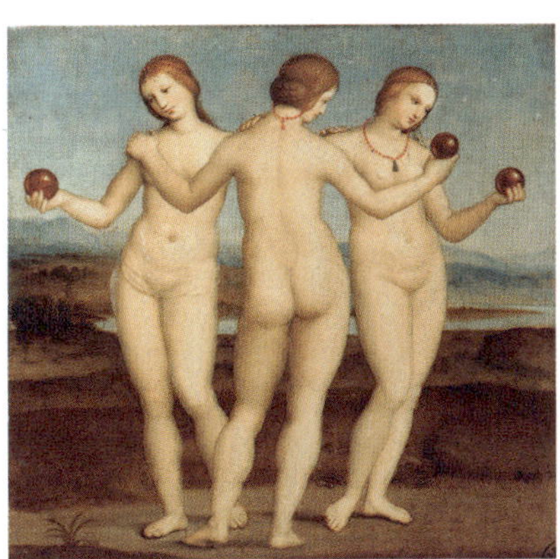

Raphael
The Three Graces, *1503–1505, Château de Chantilly.*

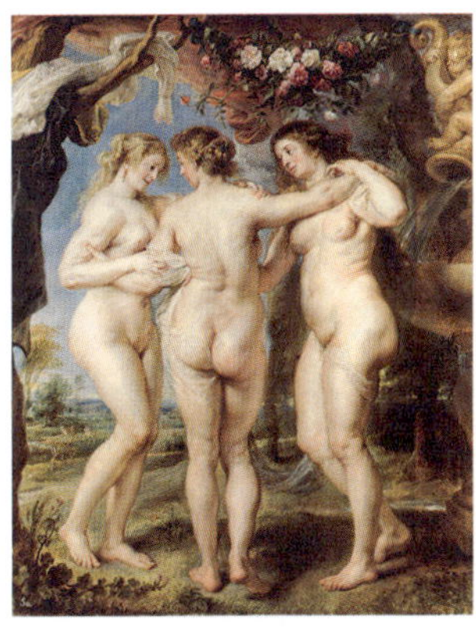

Rubens
The Three Graces, *1630–1635, Prado Museum, Madrid.*

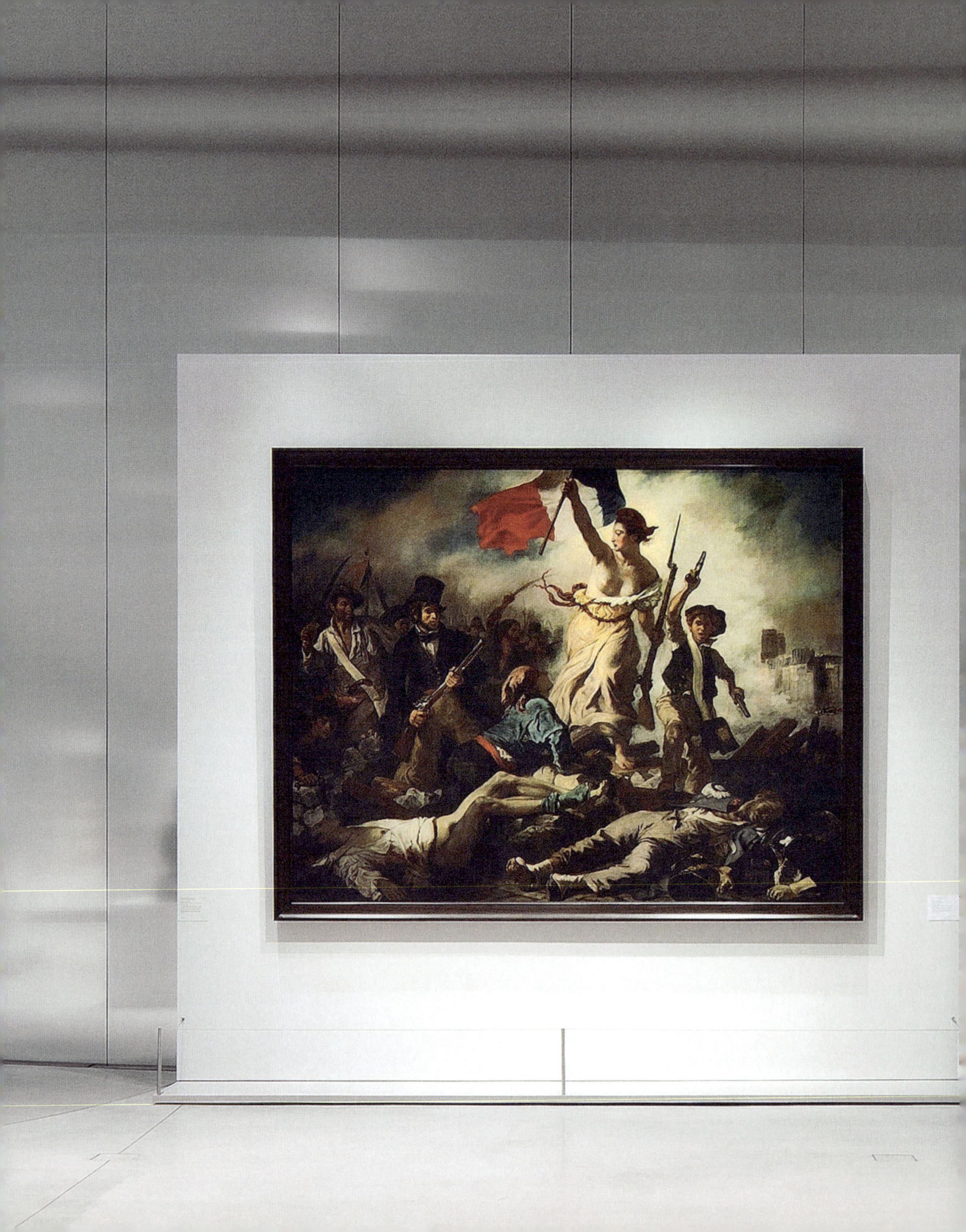

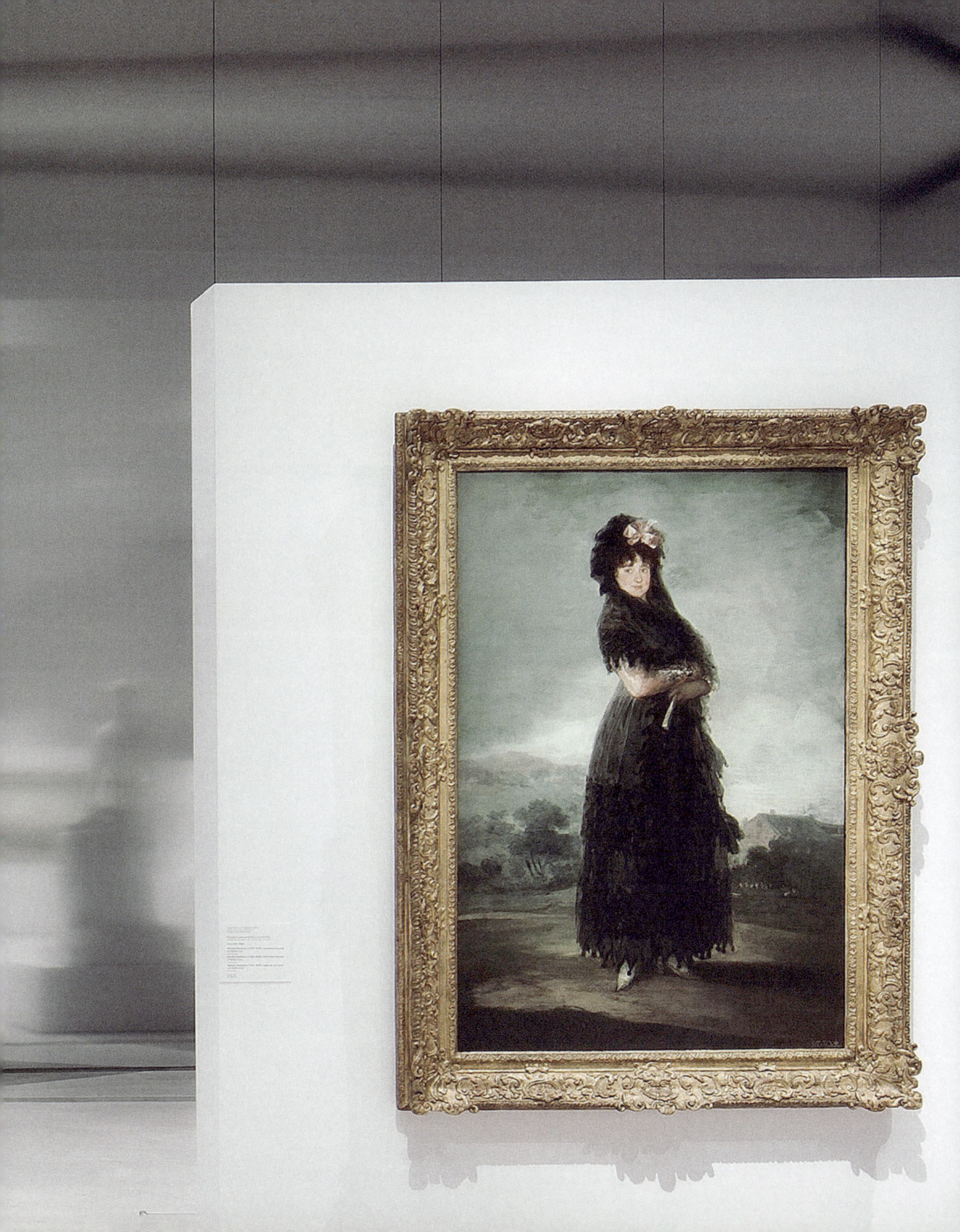

Eugène Delacroix

A chronicler of his time

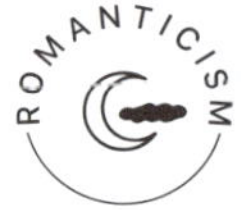

Along with Géricault, Delacroix was the other leading figure of French Romanticism. However, isolated from the movement, Delacroix refused this categorisation. Indeed, even today, this term fails to fully encompass the variety of his work, influenced by classicism, but also breaking with tradition.

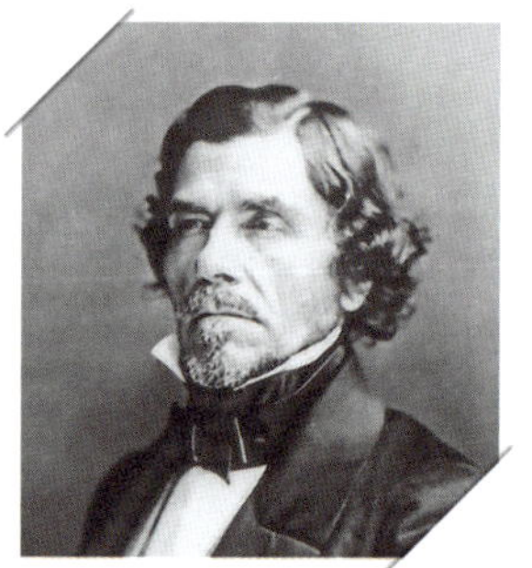

The brush *vs* the pen

Ranging from portraits to animal paintings and vast decors, Delacroix's works are extremely varied. He was also close to literary circles, and numerous writings remained after his death, including a very extensive diary.

New horizons

Delacroix was impressed by Orientalism – a taste, among French society, for distant lands marked by colonialism. In 1832, he travelled to Morocco, and was amazed by the local culture, the colours and the light.

Setting the tones

The painter was also a fantastic colourist. He used saturated tones that critics did not always approve of, and rendered shadows using colour. He followed in the footsteps of great painters, from Veronese to Rubens, and became an inspiration for the avant-garde painters, years later.

EUGÈNE DELACROIX SAID

"A painting creates a mysterious bridge between the souls of the characters and that of the spectator."

Théodore Géricault
Page 184

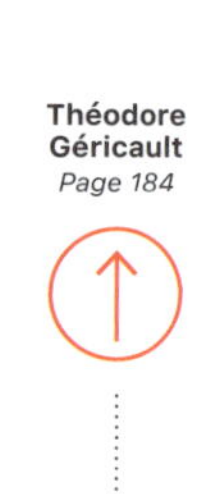

1798
Born in Charenton-Saint-Maurice

1799
Discovery of the Rosetta Stone

1816
In Africa, Shaka began the foundation of the Zulu Kingdom

1830
Painted *Liberty Leading the People*

1863
Died in Paris

Gustave Courbet
Page 198

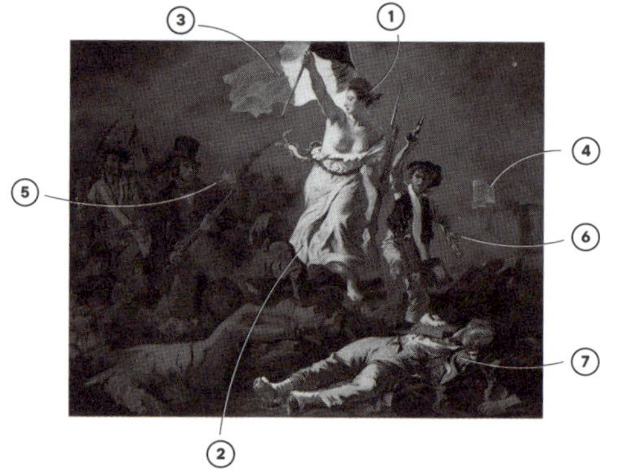

LIBERTY LEADING THE PEOPLE

1830
Oil on wood
260 × 325 cm
Louvre Museum, Paris

WHAT ARE WE LOOKING AT?

This painting depicts the July Revolution of 1830, in France. The people revolted against Charles X, who censored the press and constrained voting rights.

① A mythical image

This woman is an allegory, the representation of an idea – in this case, Liberty.

② Shocking details

Her dress is soiled, and her armpit is unkempt. The homage paid here is ambiguous: Delacroix was both a dandy who worked for the king and a chronicler who was fascinated by the inception of democracy.

③ Always with a raised fist

This allegory of Liberty is perfectly suited to the iconography of revolts; her raised fist remains a symbol used today by activists and militants.

④ This is Paris

The French flag, a symbol raised in open support of the king in the aftermath of the July Revolution, can be seen everywhere, from the clothes to the clouds. It is difficult to identify the location of the event, but the towers of Notre-Dame appear in the distance.

⑤ Headgear for wise heads

The bicorn hat is the uniform of Polytechnique. The school's students were keen actors of the July Revolution.

⑥ It's the other way around

This isn't Gavroche, as has often been said, as the painting predates *Les Misérables*. However, Victor Hugo may have been inspired by this work when he created his character.

⑦ Security breach

The Swiss Guards were the regiment dedicated to ensuring the safety of the king. The corpse of one of these soldiers, in the foreground, symbolises the downfall of Charles X.

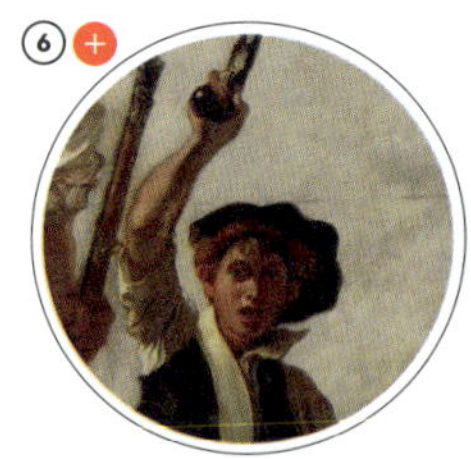

LEGWORK

To represent his allegory, Delacroix was inspired by antique statuary, in particular by the Winged Victory of Samothrace. Beneath the drapery of the dress, the movement of Liberty's legs is identical, pressing the fabric of her dress against her skin (p. 186).

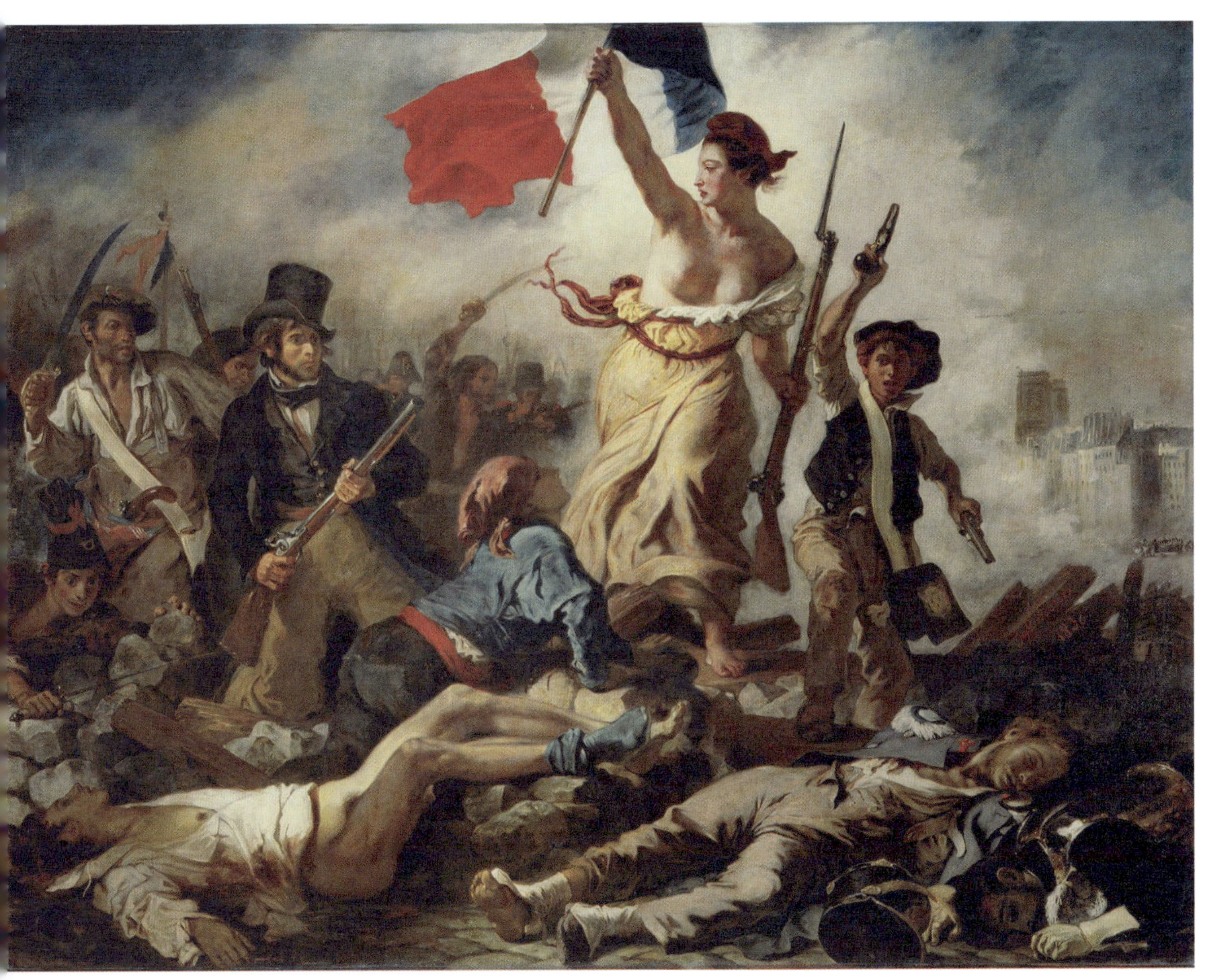

Three days that made history

The July Revolution is named the "Trois Glorieuses", as it took place over the course three days: on 26, 27 and 28 July 1830. It drove King Charles X to abdicate. Louis-Philippe, the last monarch to rule France, took his place and acted as "King of the French people".

Delacroix and Rubens

In league with colour

In the 17th century, the "colour dispute" broke out within the Académie Royale de Peinture et de Sculpture (p. 166). It opposed the Rubenists, proponents of colour, and the Poussinists, supporters of drawing. Delacroix, in the tradition of the Flemish artist, was one of the leading colourist painters.

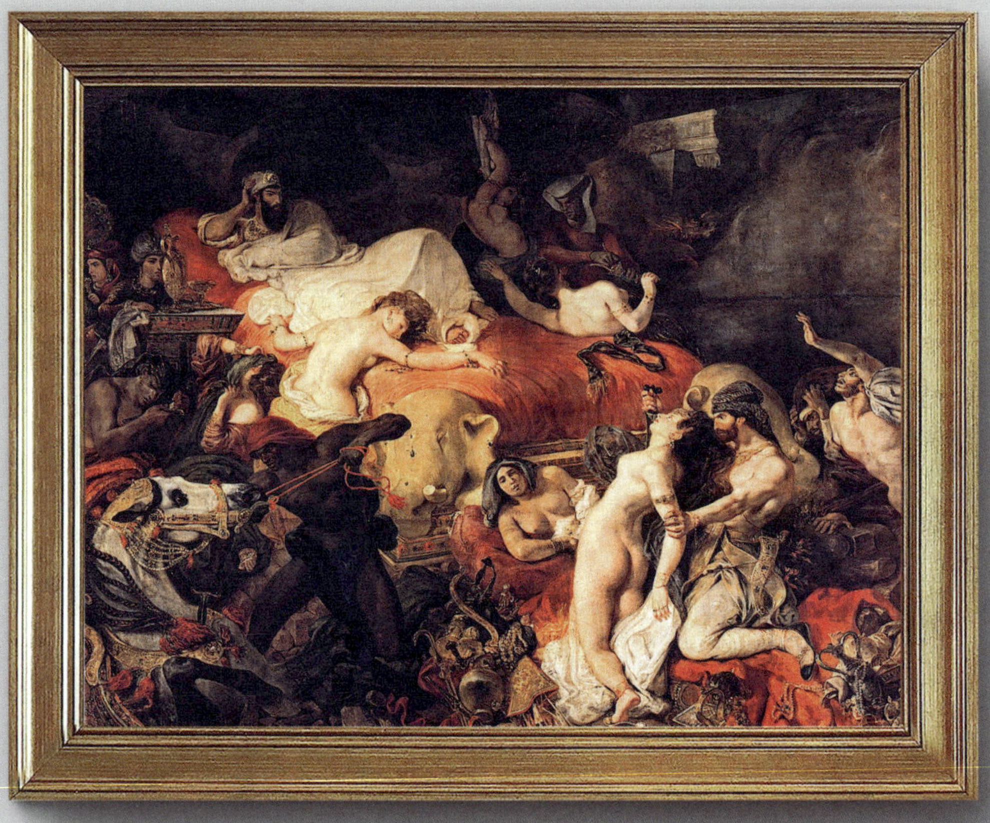

***THE DEATH OF SARDANAPALUS* BY EUGÈNE DELACROIX**
1827

Delacroix staged the myth of King Sardanapalus who, besieged by his enemies, sacrificed women, animals and treasures so that nothing would survive him. The painter played on the red tones of the draperies and the whiteness of the skin to create a striking contrast that conveys the horror of the moment.

Oil on canvas, 392 × 496 cm
Louvre Museum, Paris

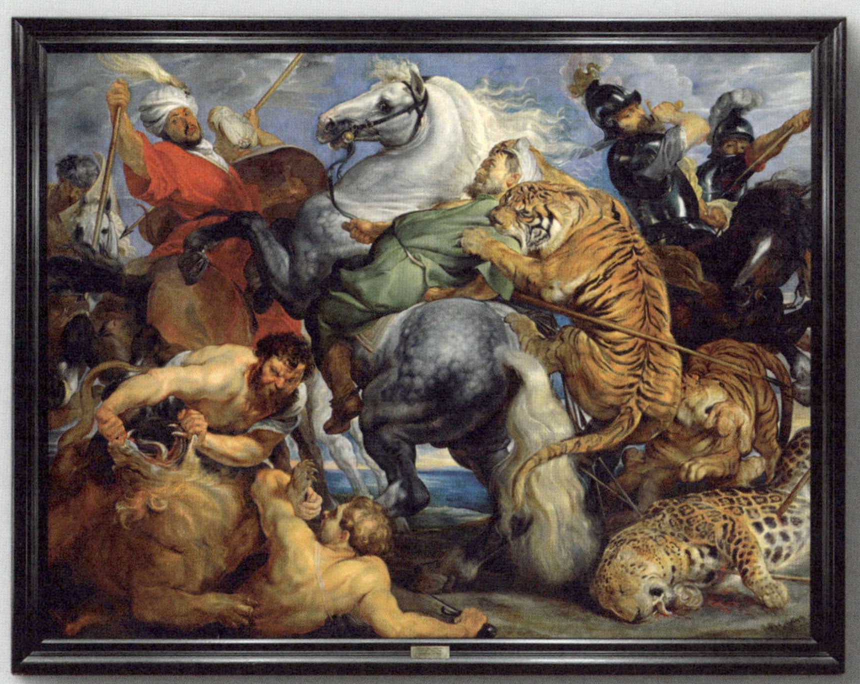

THE TIGER HUNT BY PETER PAUL RUBENS
1615–1617

Rubens combined shapes and colours to perfection, creating a powerful centrifugal effect that draws the viewer's gaze in. This eventful composition brilliantly conveys the tumult and violence of the struggle between men and wild beasts.

Oil on canvas, 248.2 × 318.3 cm
Musée des Beaux-Arts, Rennes

Meanwhile in Japan...

Katsushika Hokusai's tidal wave caused a landslide

Just as the art of printmaking named *ukiyo-e* threatened to run out of steam, Hokusai gave it a new lease of life with the series titled *Thirty-Six Views of Mount Fuji. The Great Wave off Kanagawa* would be the first, and also the most famous of these prints.

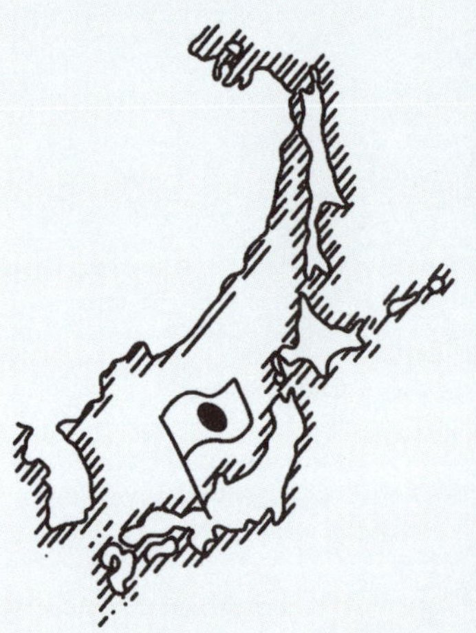

Setting the scene

In the early 19th century, *ukiyo-e* was at its peak; however, it threatened to decline, as the government circulated edicts aiming to moralise these sometimes sensual, and even erotic images.

Hokusai gave this art form a new lease of life, renewing the genre by imagining the landscape print. This inspiration took the form of *Thirty-Six Views of Mount Fuji*, featuring the volcano, a sacred mountain to the Japanese people.

This aesthetic upheaval was all the more welcome, as it invited spectators to reconnect with nature and the principles of Shintoism, the country's ancestral religion, which preceded Buddhism.

The masterpiece

- In *The Great Wave off Kanagawa*, Mount Fuji, visible in the background, is used as a pretext to depict the mighty forces of nature. The towering wave, standing out against the sky, evokes yin and yang, a reminder of the spiritual character borne by the print.
- It is about to engulf a fishermen's boat; the fishermen's figures are insignificant, compared to the immensity of the ocean. The foam takes on the shape of claws, preparing to tear the fragile boats apart. This series of prints was an opportunity for Hokusai to try his hand at rendering atmospheres, lights and weather phenomena.

He also experimented with Western innovations that had reached Japan by means of maritime trade, in particular the use of linear perspective (p. 34) and Prussian blue, a pigment that produced a blue of unequalled depth and added to the virtuosity of his art.

WHO WAS HOKUSAI?

Born in 1760, Hokusai was a great artist of the Edo period (1600–1868). This period marked a time of Japanese retrenchment, combined with strong economic growth.

Known for renewing the art of *ukiyo-e* with landscape prints, the artist, throughout the 70 years of his career, was given many nicknames – the most outstanding being *Gakyōjin*, which means "the Old Drawing Fool".

He was also known for his *Manga*, a repertoire of motifs from everyday life, which he propagated and would influence the image of Japan. Even though his art is very far removed from it, Hokusai was also an originator of the Japanese manga.

He passed away in 1849, at the dawn of modernity in European painting. Soon afterwards, he became an inspiration for many artists such as Vincent Van Gogh (p. 246), Claude Monet (p. 224) and Auguste Renoir (p. 232), as Japan opened up to the world again and took part in the World's Fairs. His work would then give rise to a fashion known as "Japonism".

WHAT IS *UKIYO-E*?

Ukiyo-e, which can literally be translated as "images of a floating world", was an art of printmaking. It depicted scenes of everyday urban life, which became fashionable with the rise of the big cities. Often connected to the world of entertainment, it featured actors and courtesans.

VARIATIONS ON THE SAME THEME

The series of Thirty-Six Views of Mount Fuji *was, for Hokusai, a pretext to represent the beauty of the Japanese landscapes and the mountain in all weathers.*

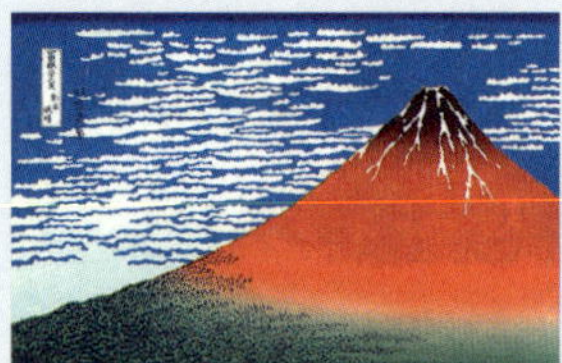

Mount Fuji on a Clear Day, view no. 2.

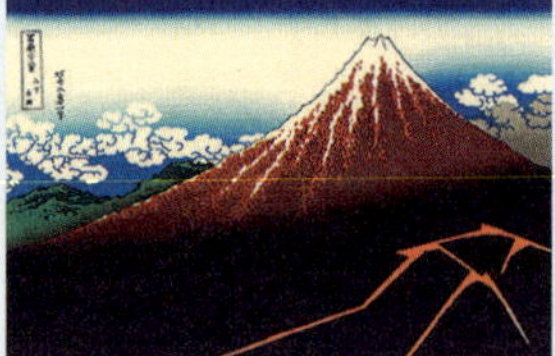

Thunderstorm Beneath the Summit, view no. 3.

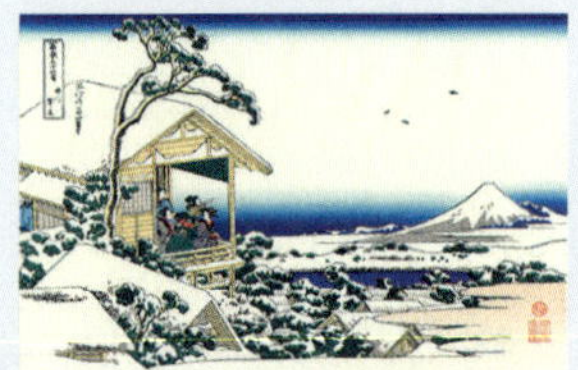

Morning after a Snowfall at Koishikawa, view no. 24.

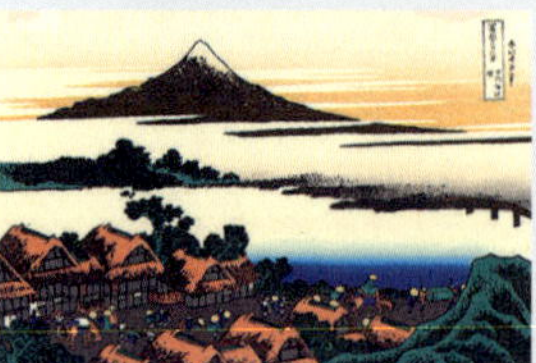

Dawn at Isawa in Kai Province, view no. 41.

Katsushika Hokusai
THE GREAT WAVE OFF KANAGAWA
1831
Thirty-Six Views of Mount Fuji, view no. 1
Print
Bibliothèque Nationale de France, Paris

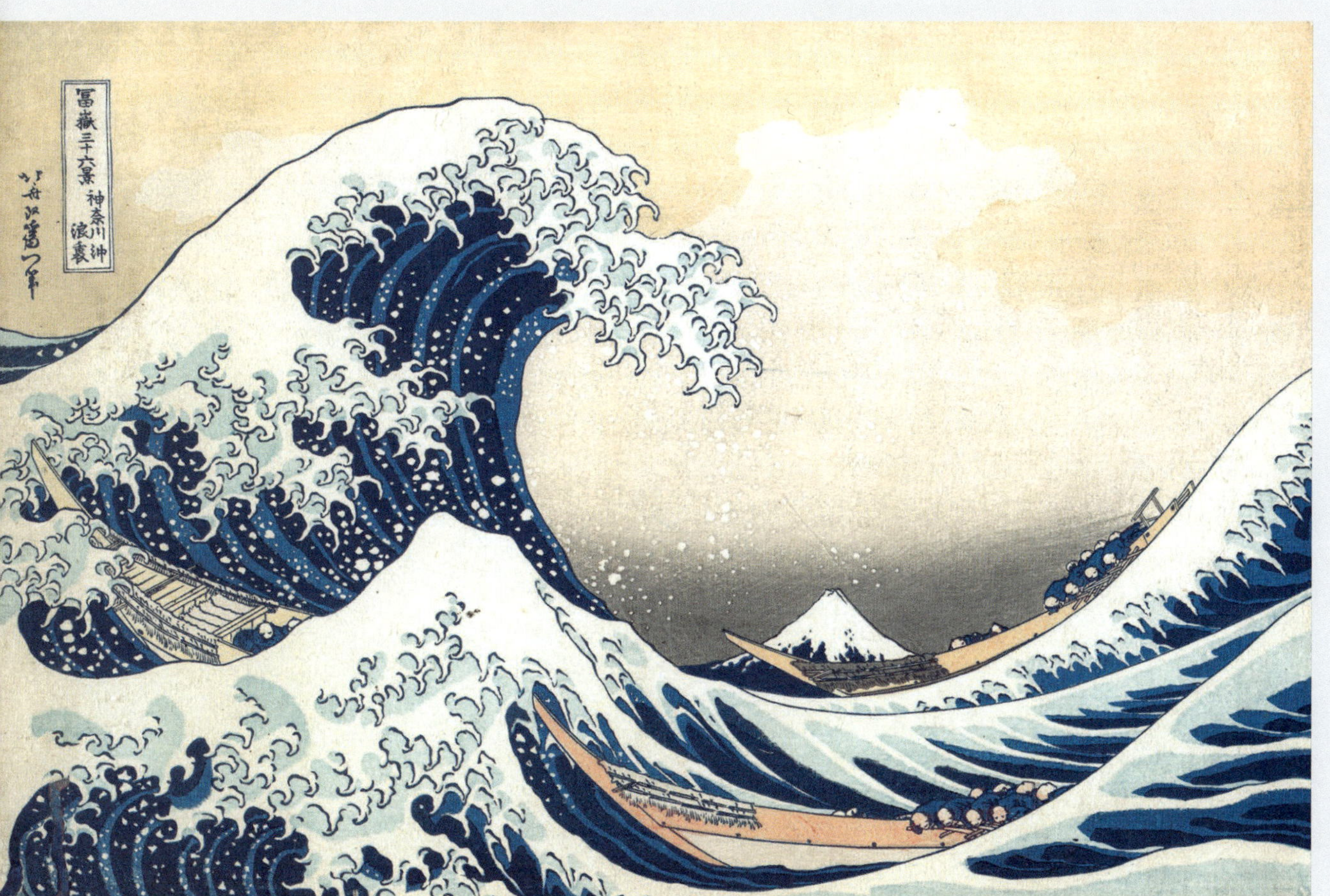

Riding the wave

Following the success of this first series, Hokusai produced *One Hundred Views of Mount Fuji*, which were published between 1834 and 1840. For this occasion, the artist created an inverted version of *The Great Wave off Kanagawa*, devoid of any human activity, but ever as poetic, with the wave's foam merging to depict a bird's flight.

The realist break

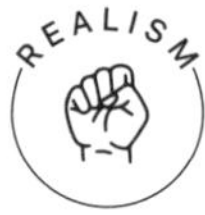

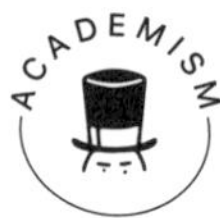

The style of a new world

An abundant new creativity

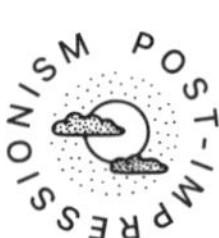

The last dreamers

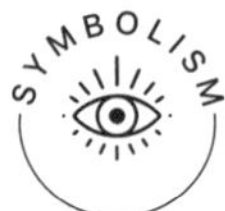

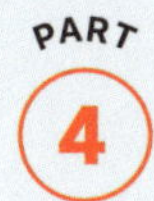

From Gustave Courbet to Gustav Klimt

Rebellious painting

The lights and colours of a changing world

From railways to the birth of photography, society was undergoing a profound transformation. Artists rejected academicism and invented a style of painting inspired by modernity, the great outdoors and light, driving them to increasingly audacious formal experiments.

Gustave Courbet

Boldness in spades

A master of realism, Courbet announced modernity through the sheer audacity of his works. He would stand by them, even if it meant shocking spectators, which did not hinder his success. Due to his political positions, as a proponent of the Paris Commune insurrection, he would be forced into a tragic exile that would ruin the end of his career.

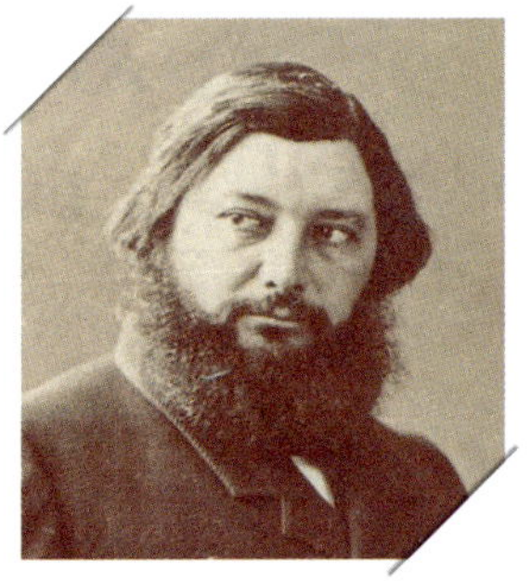

An inhospitable Salon

After arriving in Paris at the age of 20, Courbet embraced the lifestyle of a solitary painter. As he frequented salons and museums, his technique progress swiftly, but he was rejected several times before being admitted to the Salon (p. 220). Within a few years, he would become a recognised master.

An agitator

His rural realism and his nerve shocked spectators and peers. He advertised these traits, organised tours of his works, encouraging his own marginalisation. In parallel with the 1855 World's Fair, he created a counter-exhibition that would be remembered as a manifesto of realism.

Inhabited by nature

Courbet painted many landscapes that contributed to his commercial success, yet he was not considered a landscape painter. He painted an intimate and sensitive vision of nature, as we humans perceive it, composed of darkness, rocks and water.

GUSTAVE COURBET SAID

"I have been painting for ten years; newspapers have already honoured me by mentioning my work."

Eugène Delacroix
Page 190

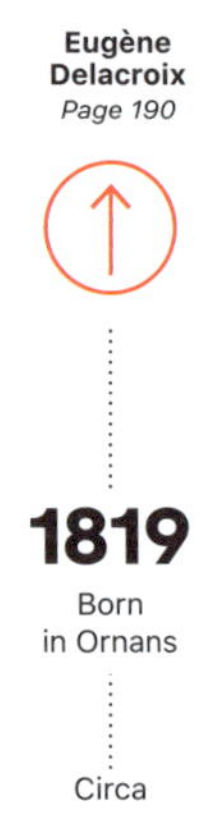

1819
Born in Ornans

Circa
1844 to **1845**
Painted *The Desperate Man*

1862
Victor Hugo published *Les Misérables*

1870
Rome became the capital of Italy, unified as a kingdom

1877
Died in La Tour-de-Peilz

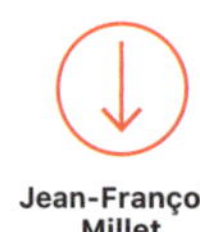

Jean-François Millet
Page 202

THE DESPERATE MAN

Circa 1844–1845
Oil on canvas
45 × 54 cm
Private collection

WHAT ARE WE LOOKING AT?

Throughout his career, Courbet produced self-portraits which, considered as a whole, formed a kind of autobiography. Here, he represented himself with the features of a desperate man.

Drama king

The closeness of the viewer to the artist, the frontality and the dramatic expression, accentuated by the movement of the arms and the intense gaze, made this work famous. It remains fascinating, even today. Painted in the artist's youth, this work enabled him to tap into his romantic vein.

Comedy or tragedy?

The question arises: does this a self-portrait truly capture his state of mind at that time? Or is it a "tête d'expression", an expressive head – in other words, an academic exercise consisting of a simple study of a face expressing an emotion, for which the painter would have taken himself as a model?

Soft toy or lucky charm

This work is significant, because it would remain with Courbet until the end of his life: he kept it in his room in Switzerland, according to the testimony of the doctor who was at his side during his final moments. In fact, Courbet did not exhibit this painting – only twice, and long after it was completed, in 1873 and 1876.

Tough times: an allegory

The painter was known for his jovial nature, which could tip the balance in favour of the expressive head, but he also had moments of despondency. This self-portrait was likely painted around 1844, when Courbet was setting up his life as an artist, but consistently seeing his works refused at the Salon (p.220).

FINAL SUCCESSES

Credited with over a thousand paintings, Courbet is a regular fixture in auction houses, delighting collectors. Here is a review of his best trades… post mortem.

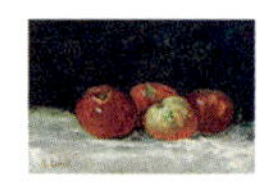

Still life
Red Apples, 1872.

Sold in 2011 for 409,250 pounds.

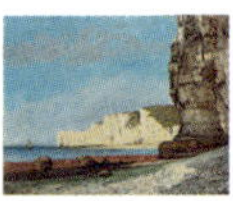

Landscape
The Cliffs at Étretat, ca. 1870.

Sold in 2013 for 2.8 million dollars.

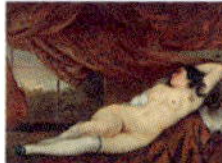

Nude
Reclining Nude, 1862–1863.

Sold in 2015 for 15.28 million dollars.

Genre scene
Poor Woman of the Village, 1866.

Sold in 2022 for 1.73 million dollars.

REALISM IN A NUTSHELL

- A preoccupation with social issues, far from the heroism of history painting.
- The end of the idealisation of bodies and faces.
- The emergence of modern themes such as everyday life, work or modern life.
- A visible and assertive touch.

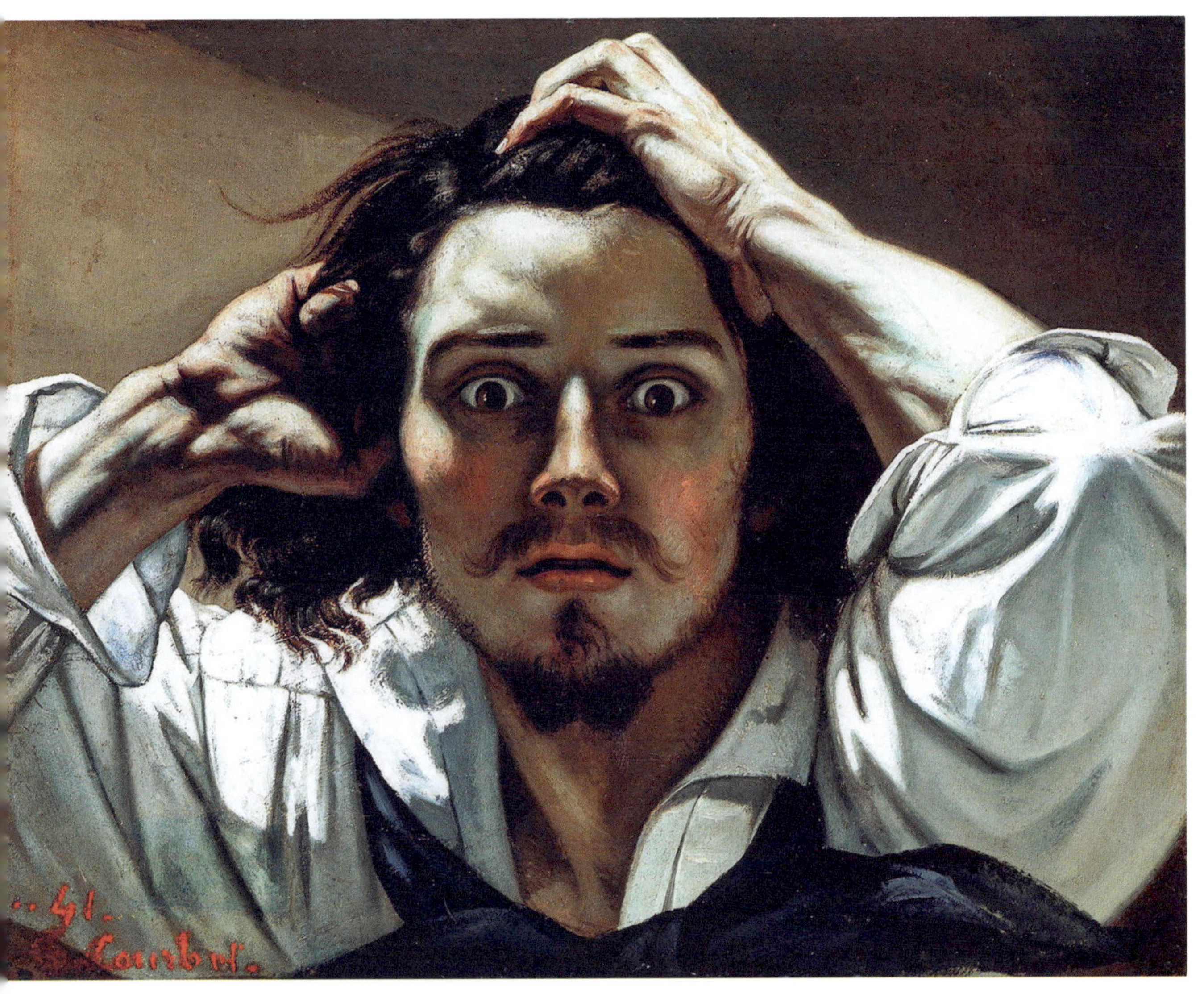

His heart sways

While Courbet is considered one of the greatest names in realism, this youthful self-portrait, with its particularly dramatic expressiveness, rather bears the hallmark of the romantic influences of his early works.

Courbet and ORLAN

Opposing sexes

Is it pornography to paint or photograph an offered sex with such realism? Gustave Courbet, through the refinement of his execution, and Orlan, through the political statement that she defended, enabled their creations to rise above triviality.

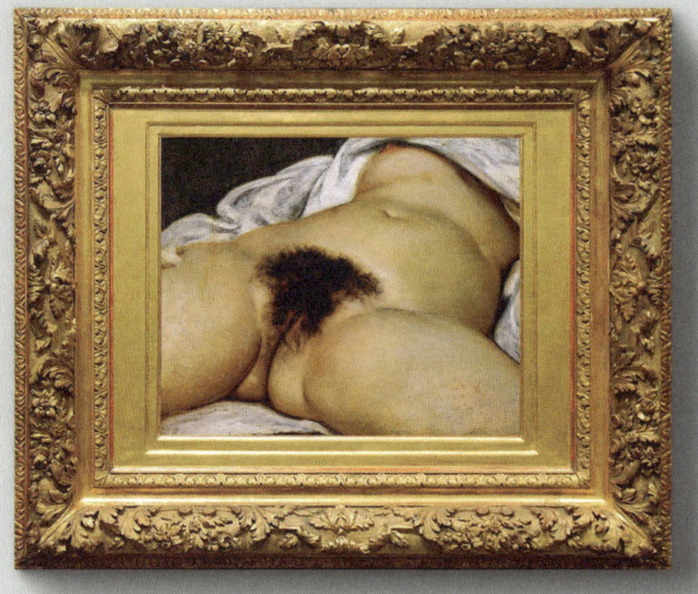

***THE ORIGIN OF THE WORLD* BY GUSTAVE COURBET**
1866

Courbet produced a brilliant and provocative work, commissioned by the Turkish-Egyptian diplomat Khalil Sherif Pasha. Hidden behind a curtain or an innocent landscape painting, this work was only revealed in private. One hundred and fifty years after its creation, it continues to fascinate or disturb.

Oil on canvas, 46.3 × 55.4 cm
Musée d'Orsay, Paris

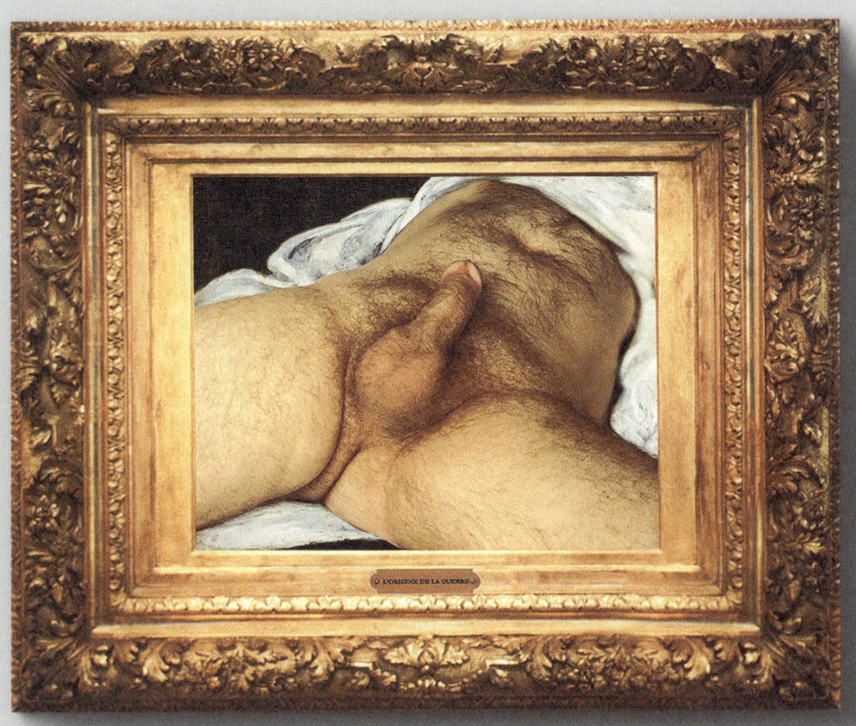

***THE ORIGIN OF WAR* BY ORLAN**
2011

This feminist version is a denunciation of the harmful effects of toxic masculinity in a world normed by patriarchy. The phallus is also a symbol of desire for the French psychoanalyst Jacques Lacan, who owned Courbet's painting. Thus, the circle is complete!

Cibachrome pasted on aluminium, 88 × 105 cm
Artist's collection

Jean-François Millet

Earning a living from the countryside

Born into a family of farmers, Millet would find success with his paintings that celebrated and ennobled agricultural work. After his career came to a hesitant start, he moved to Barbizon (in Seine-et-Marne), where many painters practised outdoor painting.

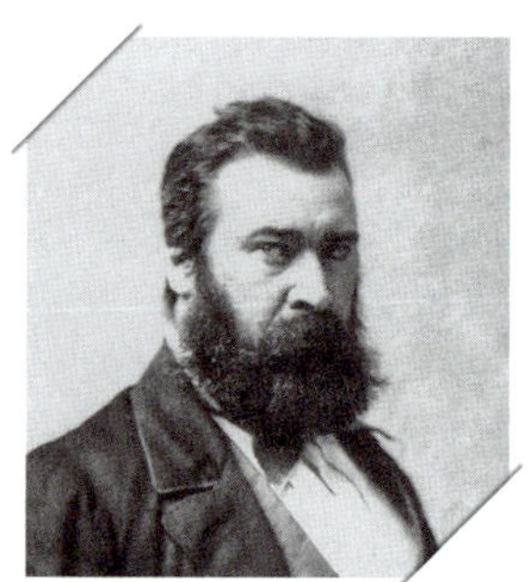

A slow start

Millet took his first drawing lessons at the age of 19. He trained between Normandy and Paris, where he attended the Louvre. He experienced both successes and failures at the Salon (p. 220), and lived meagrely from his portraits and small nudes.

Success in the great outdoors

From 1848 onward, he received his first commissions from the French state. He hoped to make a name for himself in history painting; however, due to social and political developments in France, he found himself drawn to agricultural themes, which would make him successful.

The era of the countryside

In 1849, cholera swept through Paris. Millet fled to Barbizon with his family. There, he painted numerous scenes of rural life, depicting peasant work, presented in peaceful interiors or under twilight skies.

JEAN-FRANÇOIS MILLET SAID

"I will confess, at the risk of sounding even more of a socialist than I am, that it is the human, the frankly human side that moves me most in art."

Gustave Courbet
Page 198

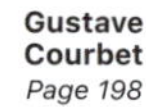

1814
Born in Gréville-Hague

1830
Stendhal published *The Red and the Black*

1857 to **1859**
Painted *The Angelus*

1870
France declared war on Prussia

1875
Died in Barbizon

Rosa Bonheur
Page 206

THE ANGELUS

1857–1859
Oil on canvas
55.5 × 66 cm
Musée d'Orsay, Paris

WHAT ARE WE LOOKING AT?

Subverted many times by the arts and marketing, *The Angelus* is Millet's great masterpiece. It depicts simple and dignified peasants interrupting their work to pray.

Prayer time

The setting sun indicates that the scene takes place at the end of the day. The title allows us to determine the exact time, as the Angelus is a prayer that took place three times a day, including once in the evening, at 6 p.m. Behind the woman, the church can be seen, its bells ringing to invite worshippers to reverence.

Rooted in earth

The woman is clasping her hands together, while the man is holding his hat in his hands; both have put down their pitchforks and potatoes to pray. One can only be struck by their humble and dignified attitude. The high skyline anchors them deeply in the land that they are cultivating.

Like at grandma's house

In this intimate and universal work, the church bells ring out the hours and the stages of life. However, this mystical reading falls far from the painter's intention, who was recounting his childhood. He remembered his grandmother interrupting the family when the bells chimed. As if in a distant memory, the protagonists' faces are blurred.

A celebrated arrival

Millet painted a rural scene in line with his previous successes. This painting's destiny, however, would be different: it would be passed from hand to hand, from Belgium to the United States, before finally reaching the Louvre Museum in 1909. Its arrival was celebrated as an event, and it became a masterpiece for the moral and religious example that it set in a French nation wounded by a turbulent 19th century.

AN INFLUENCED INFLUENCER

Influences		Influenced
Diego Velázquez (p. 114)	→ MILLET →	**Vincent Van Gogh** (p. 246)
Jean-Baptiste Greuze (1725–1805)		**Salvador Dalí** (p. 296)
Thomas Couture (1815–1879)		**Edward Hopper** (p. 302)
Narcisse Diaz de la Peña (1807–1876)		**Terrence Malick** (born in 1943)

THE BARBIZON SCHOOL

From the 1830s to the 1860s, artists in search of landscapes to paint at the location gathered in Barbizon, on the edge of the Fontainebleau Forest. They were attentive to atmosphere and nature, and are often presented as the precursors of Impressionism.

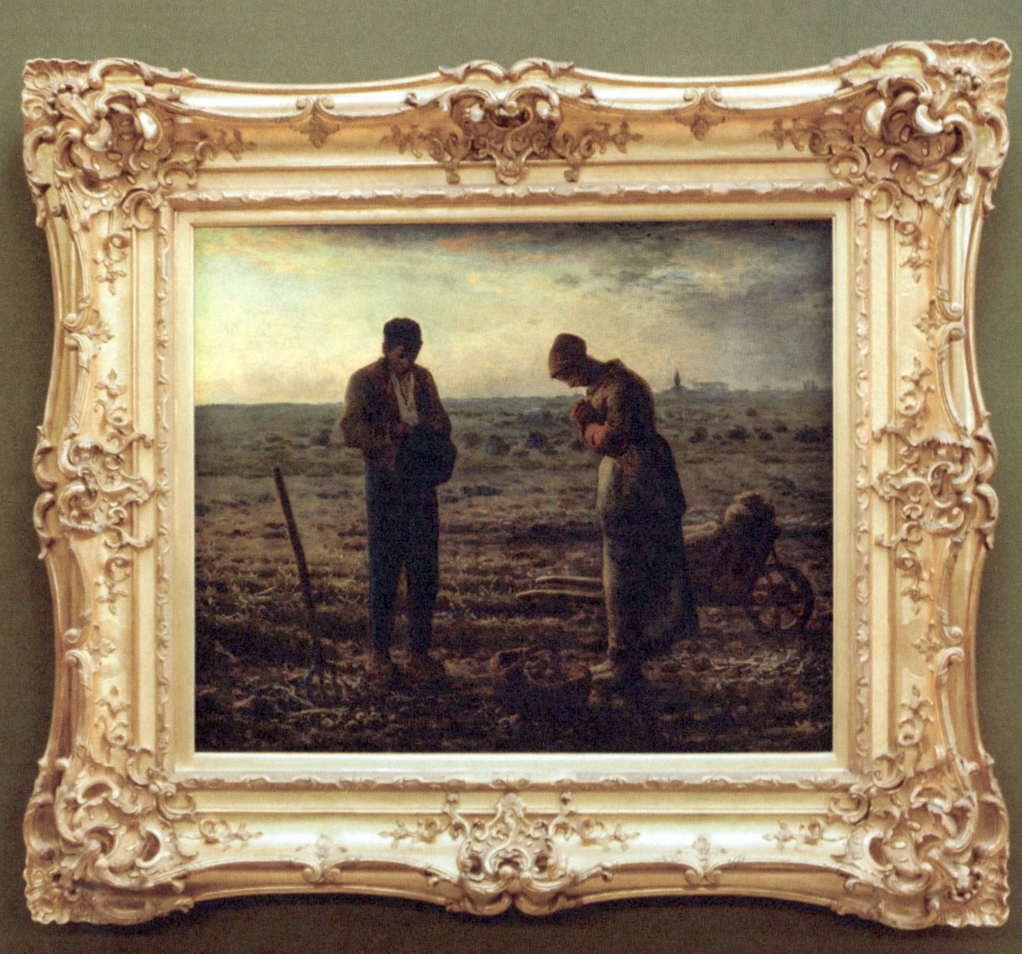

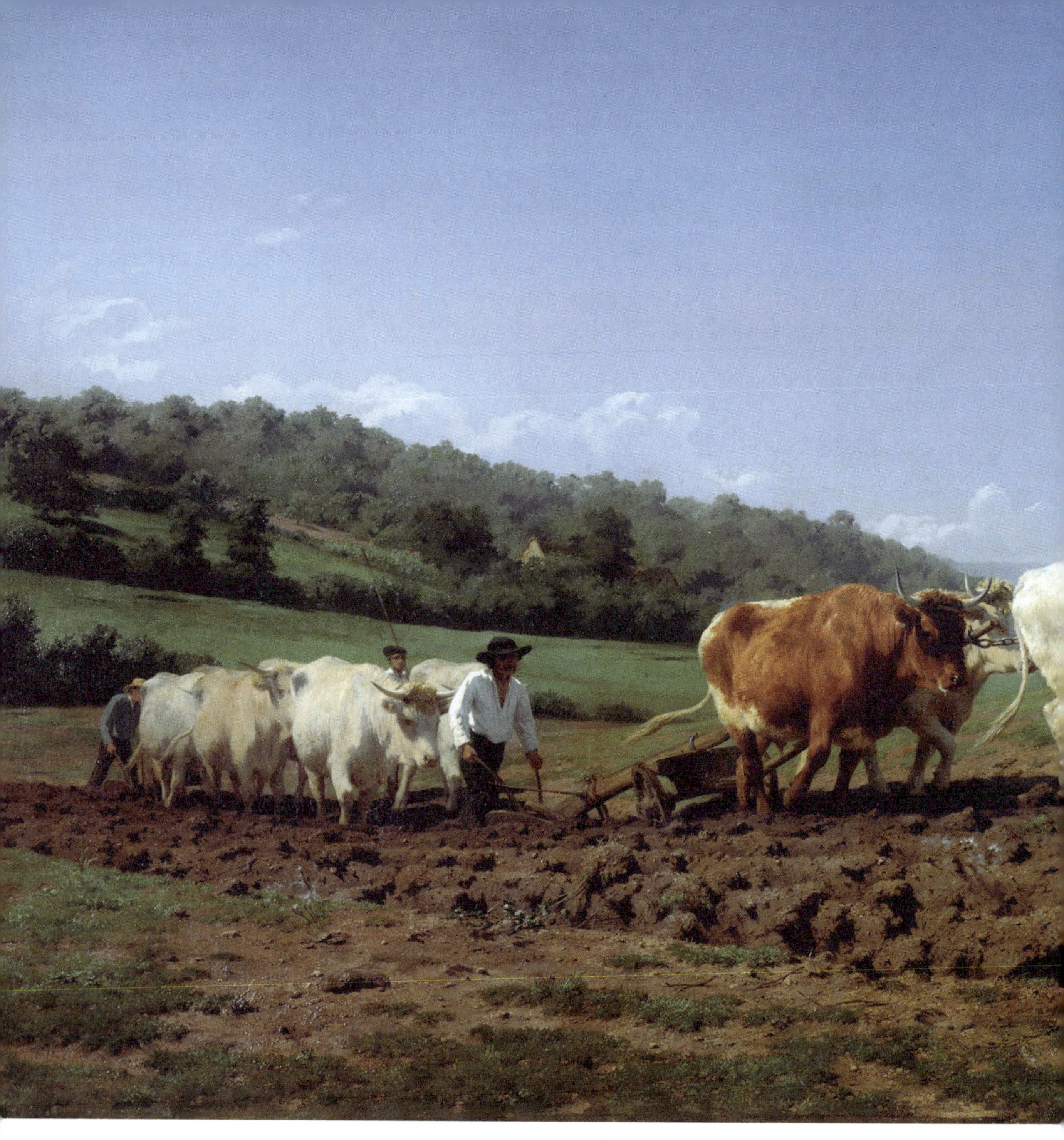

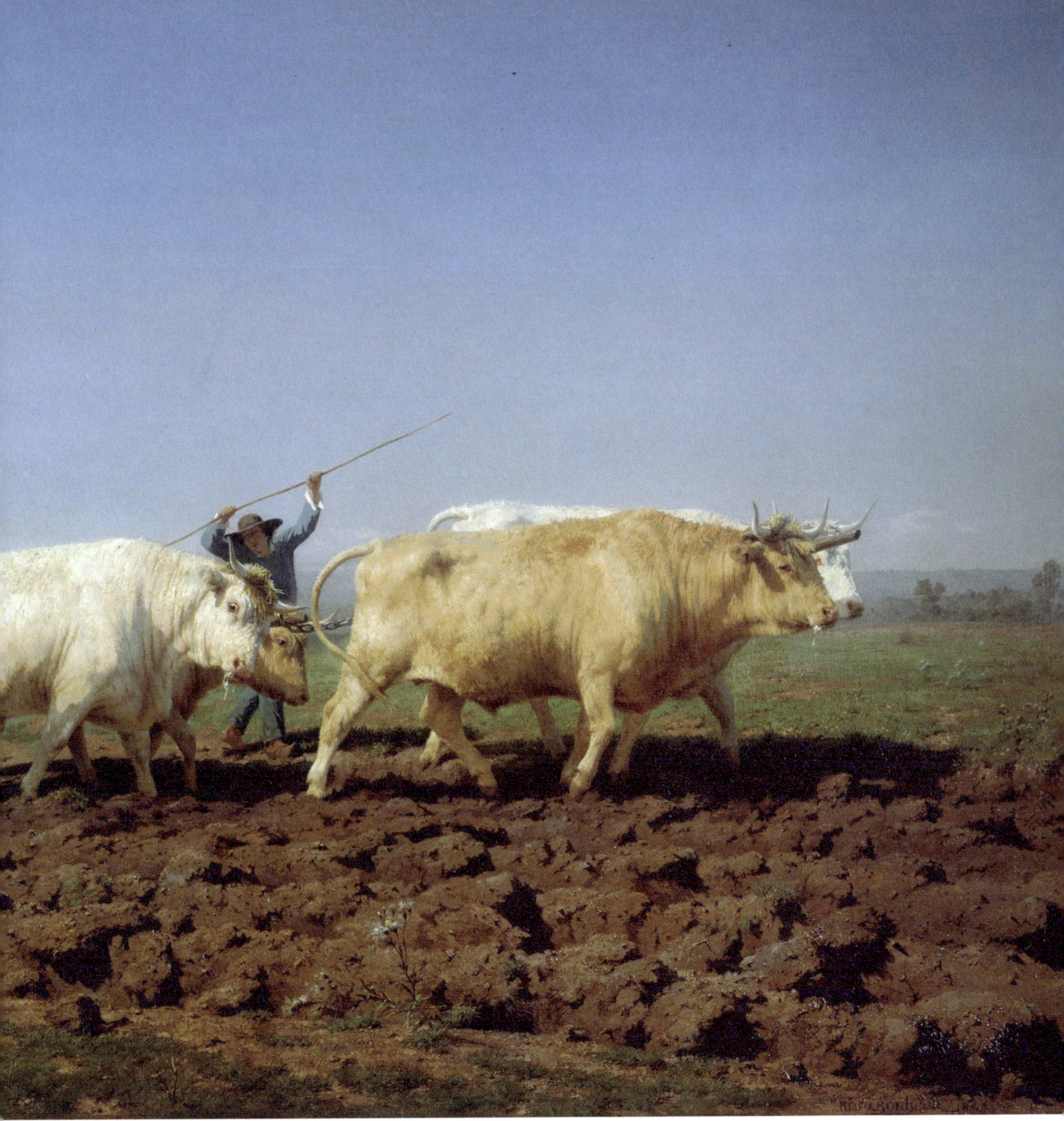

Happiness isn't always in the field

Raymond Bonheur, the artist's father (p. 206), was proud of his daughter's success; however, he would not be able to attend the consecration of this masterpiece, as he passed away a few weeks before the opening of the 1849 Salon. Sadly, the 3,000 francs received by the painter for this commission would be used to pay for her father's funeral.

Rosa Bonheur

Always found in the field

Bonheur dominated the genre of animal painting. Famous during her lifetime for her agricultural paintings, she also depicted wildlife, from African felines to majestic deer, as well as the great American wilderness, inspired by Buffalo Bill.

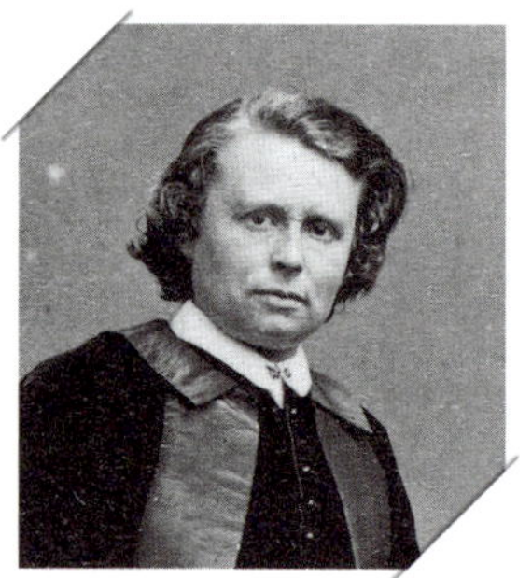

Rooted in tradition

Rosa Bonheur was born into a family of painters, and received an academic education in art. Between realism and naturalism, she studied anatomy and drawing, which enabled her to faithfully reproduce the muscles and the texture of the fur of the animals that she painted.

Smart animals

However wild her subjects may be, she managed to convey their intelligence in her paintings. Her studies evoke portraits. Breaking free from anthropocentrism, which places mankind at the centre of everything, she placed men on an equal footing with animals. She faithfully painted their behaviour, and sometimes their distress in the face of their exploitation.

The ruthless world of the salons

While animal painting was rather dominated by male artists, Rosa Bonheur imposed herself by her sheer talent and her monumental formats. Assertive and daring, she obtained a cross-dressing permit, which enabled her to paint more comfortably and free herself from the male gaze.

ROSA BONHEUR SAID

"I was only happy when I was in the midst of these beasts; I studied them with passion in their ways."

Jean-François Millet
Page 202

1822
Born in Bordeaux

1825
Photography came into the world with Nicéphore Niépce

1832
Aurore Dupin made a name for herself: George Sand

1849
Painted *Ploughing in the Nivernais*

1899
Died in Thomery

William Bouguereau
Page 210

PLOUGHING IN THE NIVERNAIS ↗

1849
Oil on canvas
133 × 260 cm
Musée d'Orsay, Paris

WHAT ARE WE LOOKING AT?

With this traditional rural scene, the painter is offering an idealised celebration of peasantry, in which 19th century spectators could already perceive the underlying question of animal welfare.

An outdoor view for the indoors

In 1848, Rosa Bonheur was crowned with all honours during the official Salon. This consecration would be confirmed by the French State: the Ministry of the Interior commissioned her to paint a picture of animals in a pasture. While staying in the Nièvre region for her studies, at the home of some friends of her father's, she decided on the subject of the commission.

Break out the popcorn

Ploughing in the Nivernais is a painting presented in a monumental and panoramic format, which graces the scene with cinematic dynamism, recreating the appearance of a history painting. The pronounced perspective allowed the artist to demonstrate the full extent of her talent. With this work, Bonheur upset the hierarchy of genres, dividing critics between praise and annoyance.

Hard, hard work

While the men are painted quickly, their faces presenting summarily sketched features, the real heroes are the cattle. They are detailed with great precision, to the extent that animal experts have been able to identify two breeds of ox that are now extinct. The white ox, in the centre of the image, is exhibiting signs of stress, with a widened eye and drool pouring from its snout.

Problematic quality

The painter also took great care in painting the upturned earth. This realism displeased some critics, who considered it to be "excessively well painted". Here, Bonheur offers an idealised landscape and vision of rural life, perhaps inspired by the romantic literature of George Sand.

NEITHER HUSBAND NOR CHILD

Outside the conventions of her time, Rosa Bonheur settled far from urban life, sharing her home with women who would contribute to her works and her posterity.

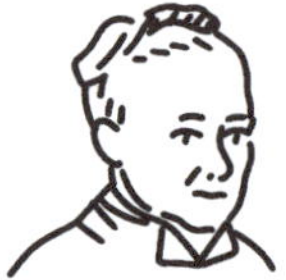

Nathalie Micas
Micas worked as an assistant to the painter. She prepared canvases and transferred reproductions. Her death would leave the painter in despair.

Anna Klumpke
The artist's last companion, the American painter was also her legatee. After her death, she inventoried and photographed her works.

NATURALISM IN A NUTSHELL

- A movement that emerged in the 1870s.
- A name borrowed from the natural sciences: living things studied with scientific exactness.
- An extension of realism, with a darker, more social approach.
- Topical issues, whether urban or rural.
- A genre embodied by Émile Zola in literature.

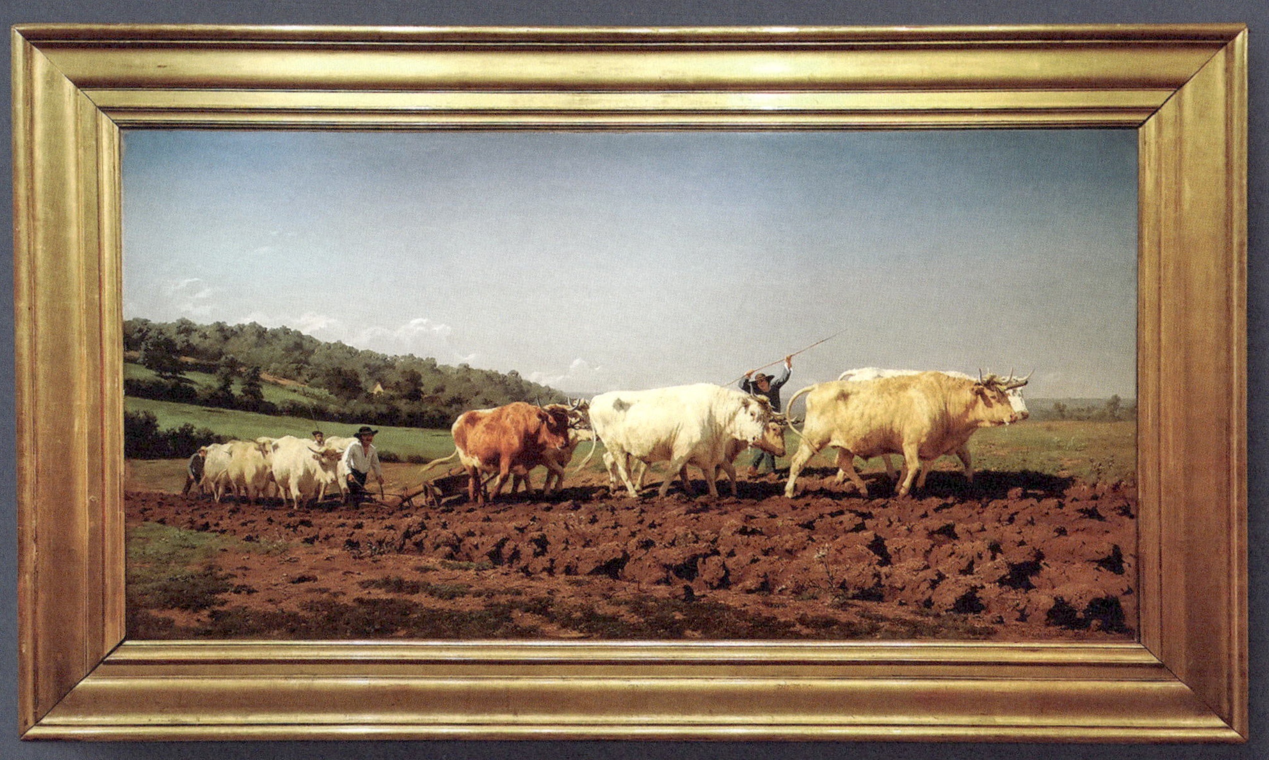

Horned beasts

The artists' cash cow

JACOB CORNELISZ VAN OOSTZANEN
Portrait of an Ox Won in a Parrot Shooting Contest

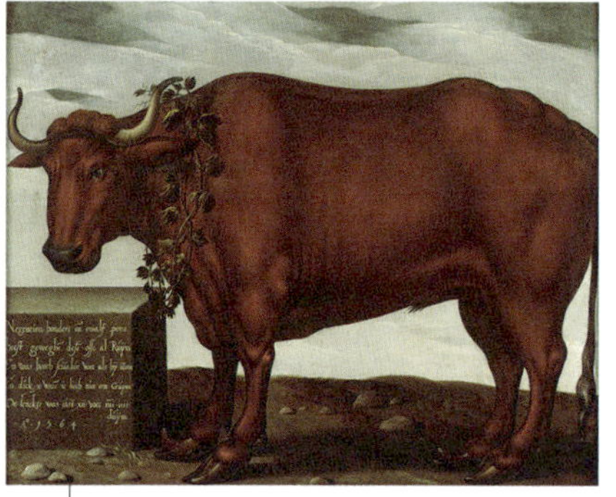

1564

1634–1652

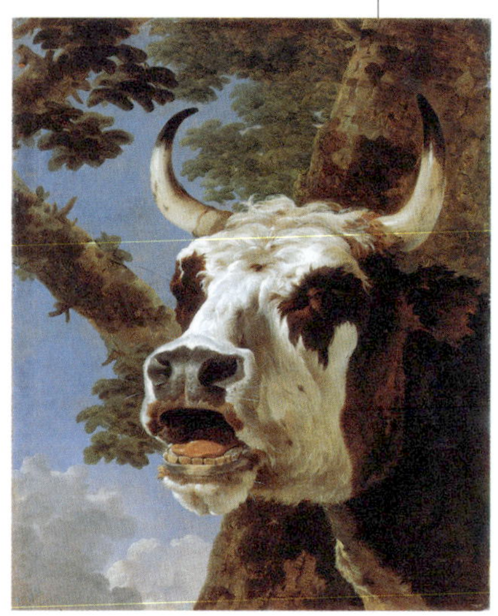

JAN ASSELIJN
Head of a Lowing Ox

PAULUS POTTER
The Young Bull

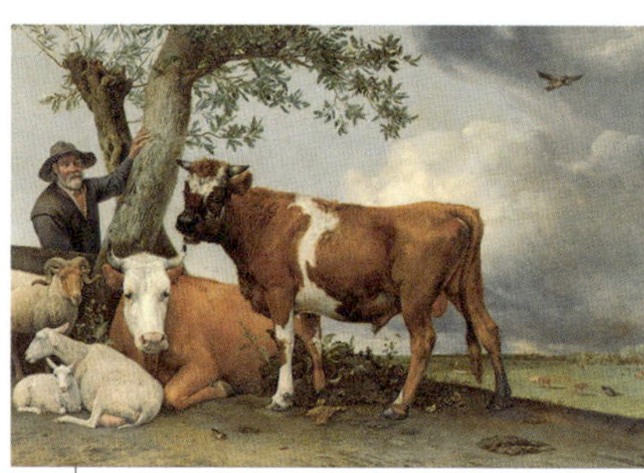

1647

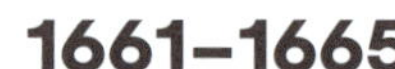

1661–1665

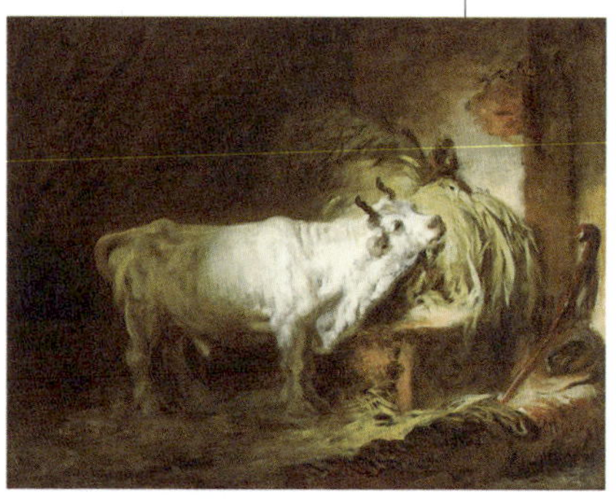

JEAN HONORÉ FRAGONARD
The White Bull in the Stable

WILLIAM MERRITT CHASE
The Family Cow (Calf's Head)

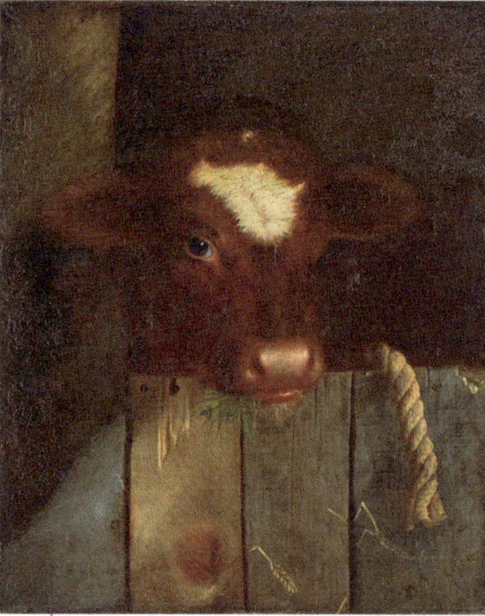

1869

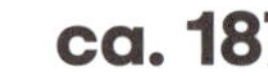

ca. 187

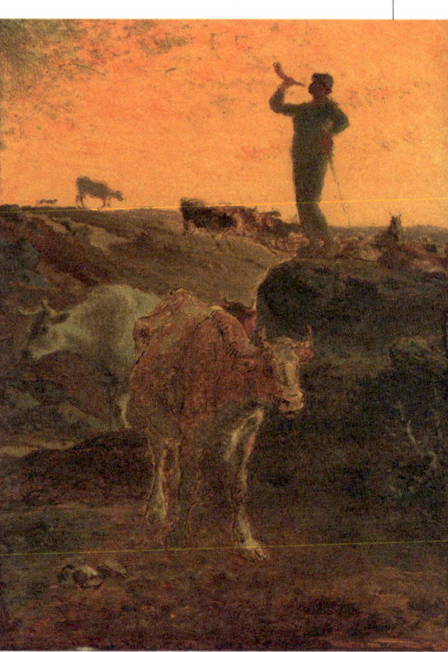

JEAN-FRANÇOIS MILLET
Calling the Cows Home

VINCENT VAN GOGH
The Cows

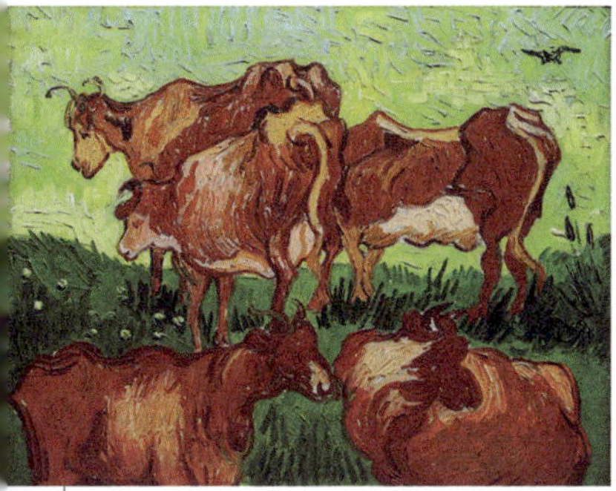

1890

1891

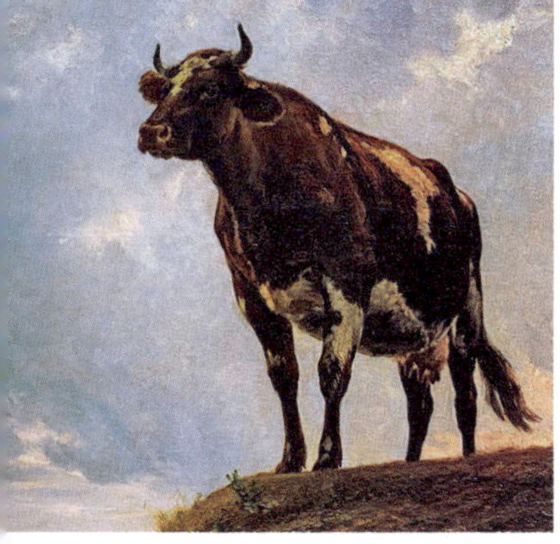

LÉON BARILLOT
La Vache brune (The Brown Cow)

PAUL SÉRUSIER
White Cow

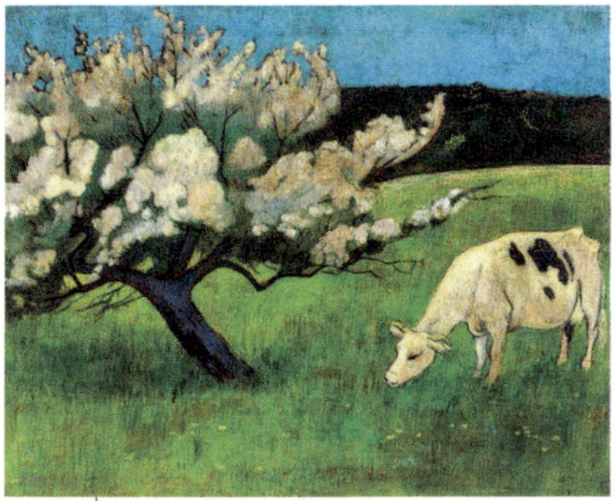

ca. 1895

1911

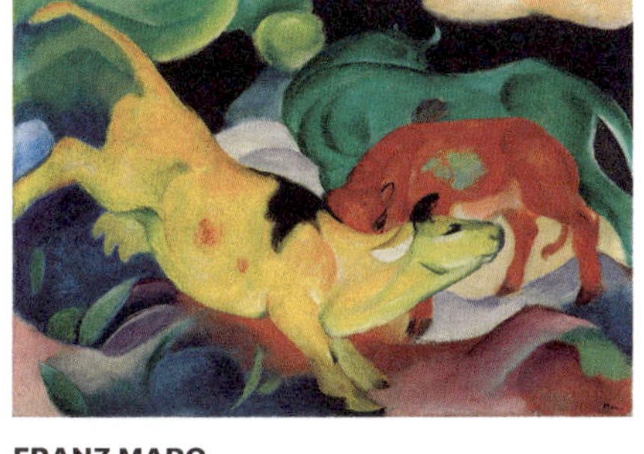

FRANZ MARC
Cows, Red, Green, Yellow

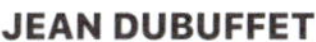

JEAN DUBUFFET
Cow

1966

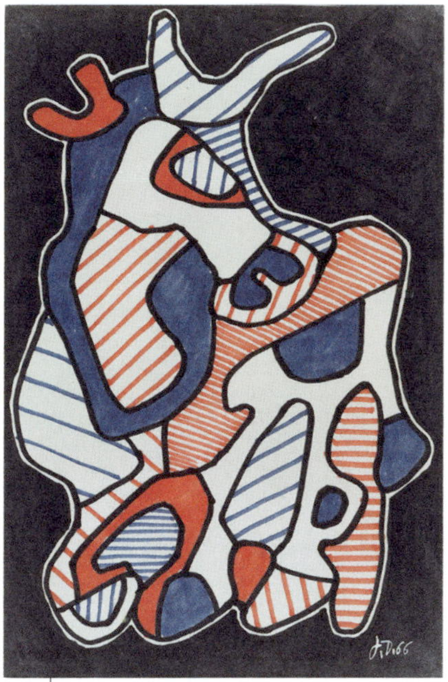

ca. 1970

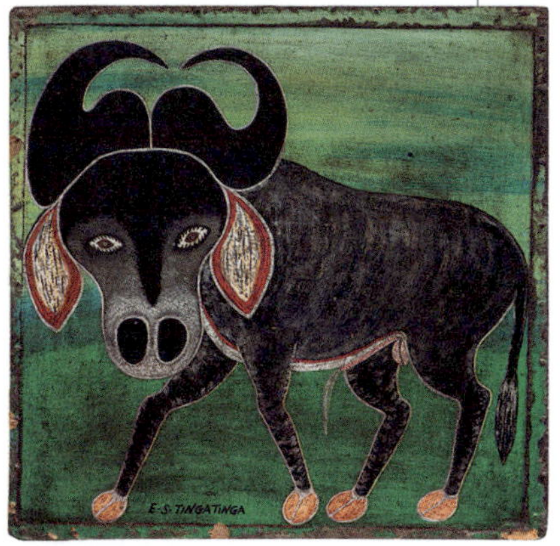

EDWARD SAIDI TINGATINGA
The Buffalo

William Bougeureau

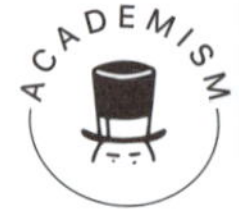

A firefighter under fire

During the 19th century, a period marked by political upheavals and modernity, Bouguereau continued the tradition of classical painting with dazzling technical mastery. However, his academic approach irritated the Modernists.

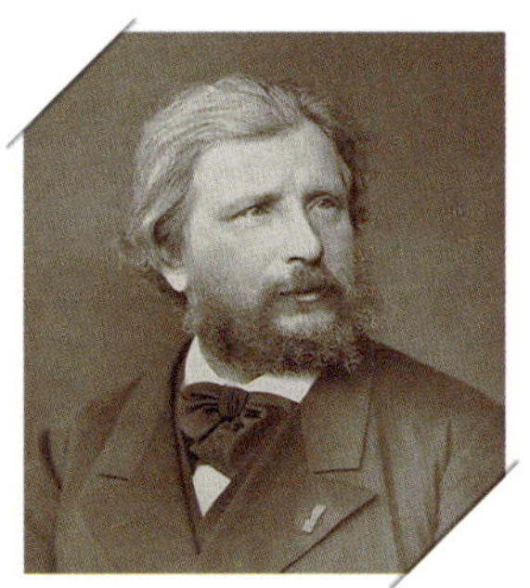

Success story

The son of a provincial bourgeois merchant, Bouguereau climbed the ladder of his artistic career one step at a time. Famous in France and as far away as the United States, he received every possible honour. A prolific artist, he left over 800 completed works.

Countering photography with art

His productivity allowed him to try his hand at all genres, ranging from charming peasant scenes to highly sensual mythological paintings. His talent for rendering physiognomies is unsettling, and the smoothness of his works produces results similar to those of photography, which was then in full development.

A hot topic

The academic approach that characterised Bouguereau's and his colleagues' works was ironically given the nickname of "Art Pompier" (fireman's art), a pejorative term derived implying that it was "Pompeian" and "pompous". The painter alienated the modern Impressionists who, to use Cézanne's words, would go so far as to tell him to "piss off". Neither his merits nor his fame would survive the Avant-Garde.

IT WAS SAID OF HIM

"Those who reproach him for [...] perfecting his painting too much cannot suspect that they are paying him the most wonderful compliment." Jean de La Rouvière, art critic.

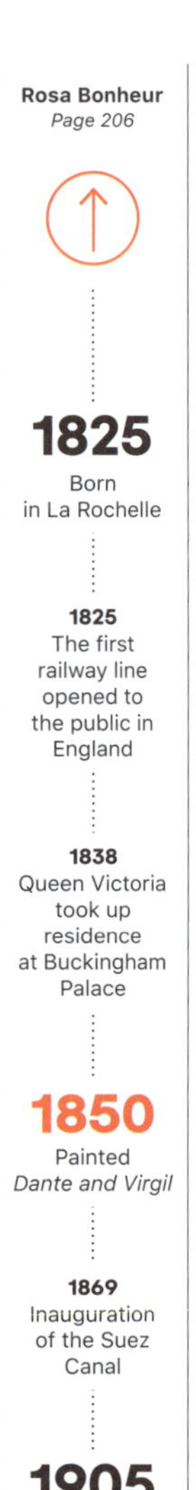

Rosa Bonheur
Page 206

1825
Born in La Rochelle

1825
The first railway line opened to the public in England

1838
Queen Victoria took up residence at Buckingham Palace

1850
Painted *Dante and Virgil*

1869
Inauguration of the Suez Canal

1905
Died in La Rochelle

Gustave Moreau
Page 212

DANTE AND VIRGIL

1850
Oil on canvas
280.5 × 225.3 cm
Musée d'Orsay, Paris

WHAT ARE WE LOOKING AT?

Bouguereau was inspired by a scene from Dante's *The Divine Comedy*, which he used to demonstrate his prodigious talents in a violent and sensual duel, testing the limits of humanity.

Spirit of revenge

After having failed twice to win the Prix de Rome, Bouguereau would finally come second in the competition. This raging enthusiasm stands as a testament to the young man's state of mind, after his lacklustre victory.

An unambiguous depiction

The scene is inspired from Canto XXX of *The Divine Comedy*, which describes the eighth circle of Hell, populated by deceivers. In this place, the deceitful Gianni Schicchi attacks the heretical forger Capocchio. Dante's work indeed mentions that Schicchi assaulted Capocchio, biting him on the neck.

Business first

Here, the painter created a prodigious aesthetic of horror, in which he exaggerated the torsion of the bodies. Protruding veins and tendons and contracted muscles reflect the scene's violence. After this work, Bouguereau would return to more conventional, more easily marketable subjects.

Well placed

As privileged spectators, Dante and Virgil are depicted standing, on the left. Virgil is recognisable by his antique garment and his laurel crown; he is holding his hand to his mouth, in revulsion. Dante, wearing his usual red headgear, is attempting to appease him with a hand gesture.

Devilish smile

The background glows red, amidst in sulphurous fumes through which a demon is flying with a chilling, cynical grin. An avalanche of bodies, both dead and living, is being cast into a molten abyss.

OTHER LEADING FIGURES OF ACADEMISM

Large formats, moral subjects and a smooth style – the Academicians are the heirs of the great historical painting, rooted in tradition. Their productions are also referred to as "official art".

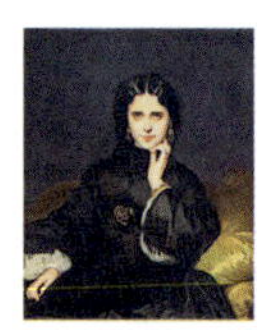

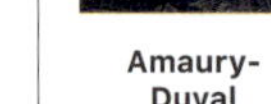

Amaury-Duval (1808–1885)

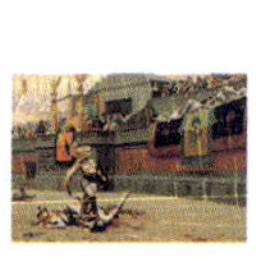

Jean Léon Gérôme (1824–1904)

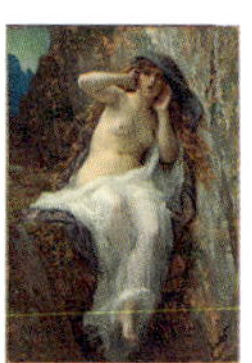

Alexandre Cabanel (1823–1889)

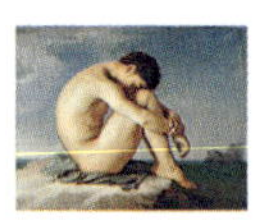

Hippolyte Flandrin (1809–1864)

ACADEMISM IN A NUTSHELL

- A taste for classical, antique and literary subjects, among others.
- Idealised, excessively sensual depictions of bodies, especially those of women.
- An invisible touch producing smooth, polished paintings.
- Meticulously detailed paintings, with an emphasis on drawing.

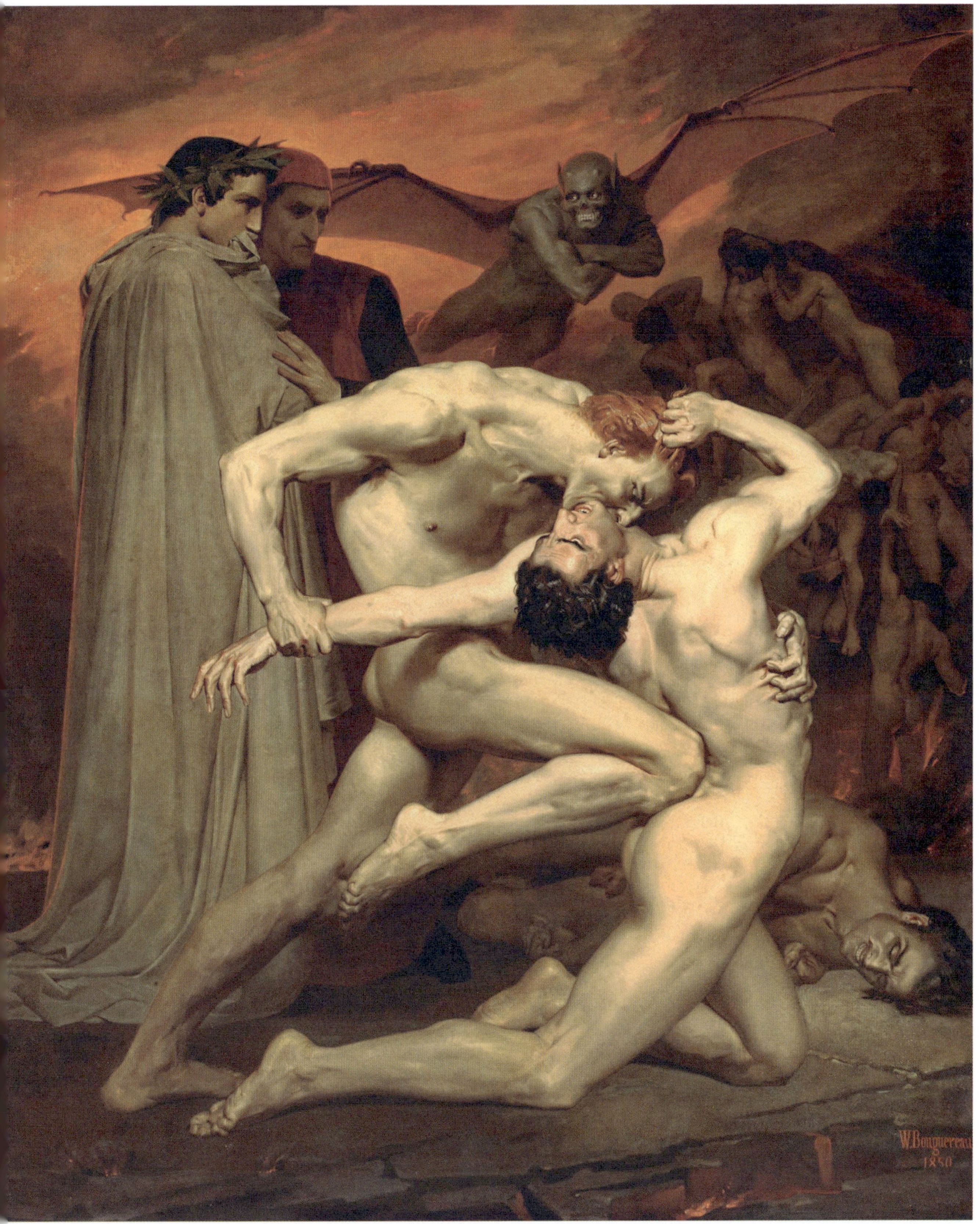
W.Bouguereau
1850

Gustave Moreau

Strange and penetrating dreams

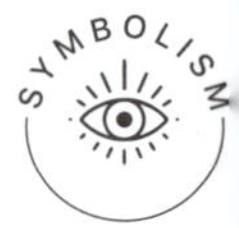

Inspired by Poussin and the Renaissance masters that he saw in the Louvre and in Italy, Moreau was a purveyor of "enigmatic reveries", as Zola wrote. Moreau's uncommon paintings made him the leading figure of symbolism.

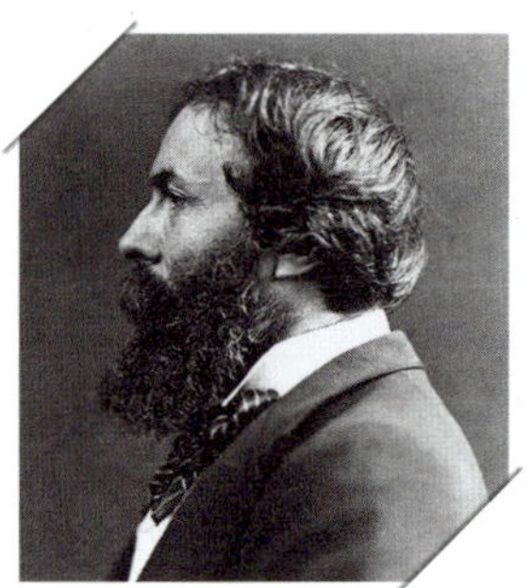

School comes first!

Moreau had been drawing since childhood, but he was only allowed to attend drawing classes in the evening, after school. After he obtained his baccalauréat, his father finally gave him permission to fully devote himself to art.

A style of his own

This unclassifiable painter experienced late, but certain success. His mythological and religious paintings are overflowing with details, and are shrouded in golden light. Moreau would be the only artist to adorn his works with ornaments in ink, inspired by oriental dreams influenced by Pharaonic Egypt and Indian miniatures.

A poisoned gift?

At the end of his life, Moreau bequeathed his house and works to the state, so that his home could be turned into a museum. The administration was reluctant, given the number of drafts and unfinished works, but finally accepted the bequest with conditions. The museum opened in 1903, and remains open to the public today.

GUSTAVE MOREAU SAID

"I love my art so much that I will only be happy when I do it for myself alone."

William Bouguereau
Page 210

1826
Born in Paris

1857
Gustave Flaubert published *Madame Bovary*

Circa
1876
Painted *The Apparition*

1896
Sigmund Freud invented psychoanalysis

1898
Died in Paris

Edward Burne-Jones
Page 214

THE APPARITION ↗

Circa 1876
Oil on canvas
142 × 103 cm
Musée Gustave Moreau, Paris

WHAT ARE WE LOOKING AT?

Here, the painter creates a fable from an episode from the New Testament, featuring Salome, who was known for having demanded and obtained John the Baptist's head.

A sad story

Moreau was deeply misogynistic, and while this belief was his own, it was also prevalent at his time. He saw women as dangerous seductresses who corrupt men, and was fascinated by damned heroines such as Cleopatra or, here, Salome.

A head to die for

In the Gospels of Mark and Matthew, Salome danced at King Herod's birthday banquet. As a reward, he promised to give her whatever she wanted. She then demanded the head of John the Baptist, on her mother's advice. This harmful maternal influence would make Salome a symbol of perdition for men, and would lastingly inspire the history of art.

A breach of the Bible

The scene painted here was entirely invented by the painter; it depicts the saint's head returning to haunt Salome, who is pointing at it with a terrified look. Here, the painter reflected upon the possibility of remorse and repentance felt by the young woman, manipulated by her mother.

Like in fairy tales

Moreau did not place the scene in time or space; Salome still appears to be dancing for the king, though John the Baptist is already dead. The rich ornamentation is reminiscent of medieval art and the Orient. It is rumoured to have been added a posteriori by the painter, at the end of his career, when he had embraced the depiction of these decorative interlaces.

SERIAL APPEARANCES

For some twenty years, Moreau never tired of representing Salome in paintings, drawings and engravings.

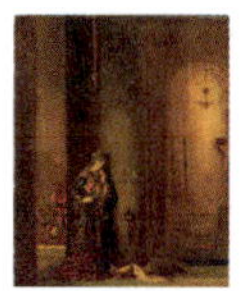

Salome at the prison
1873–1876
National Museum of Western Art, Tokyo

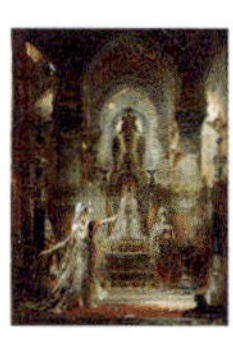

Salome Dancing before Herod
1876
Hammer Museum, Los Angeles

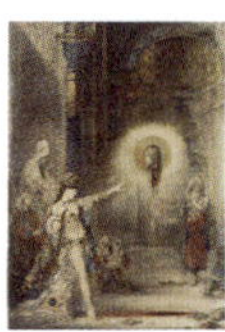

The Apparition (watercolour)
1876
Musée d'Orsay, Paris

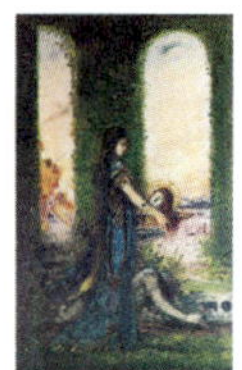

Salome in the Garden
1878
Private collection

WHAT IS SYMBOLISM?

- Strictly speaking, Symbolism is a late 19th-century movement that distanced itself from the rational thinking of an evolving world.
- In the broadest sense, it applies to all periods: it represents the propensity of artists to imitate, in their paintings, a part of an invisible, spiritual world.

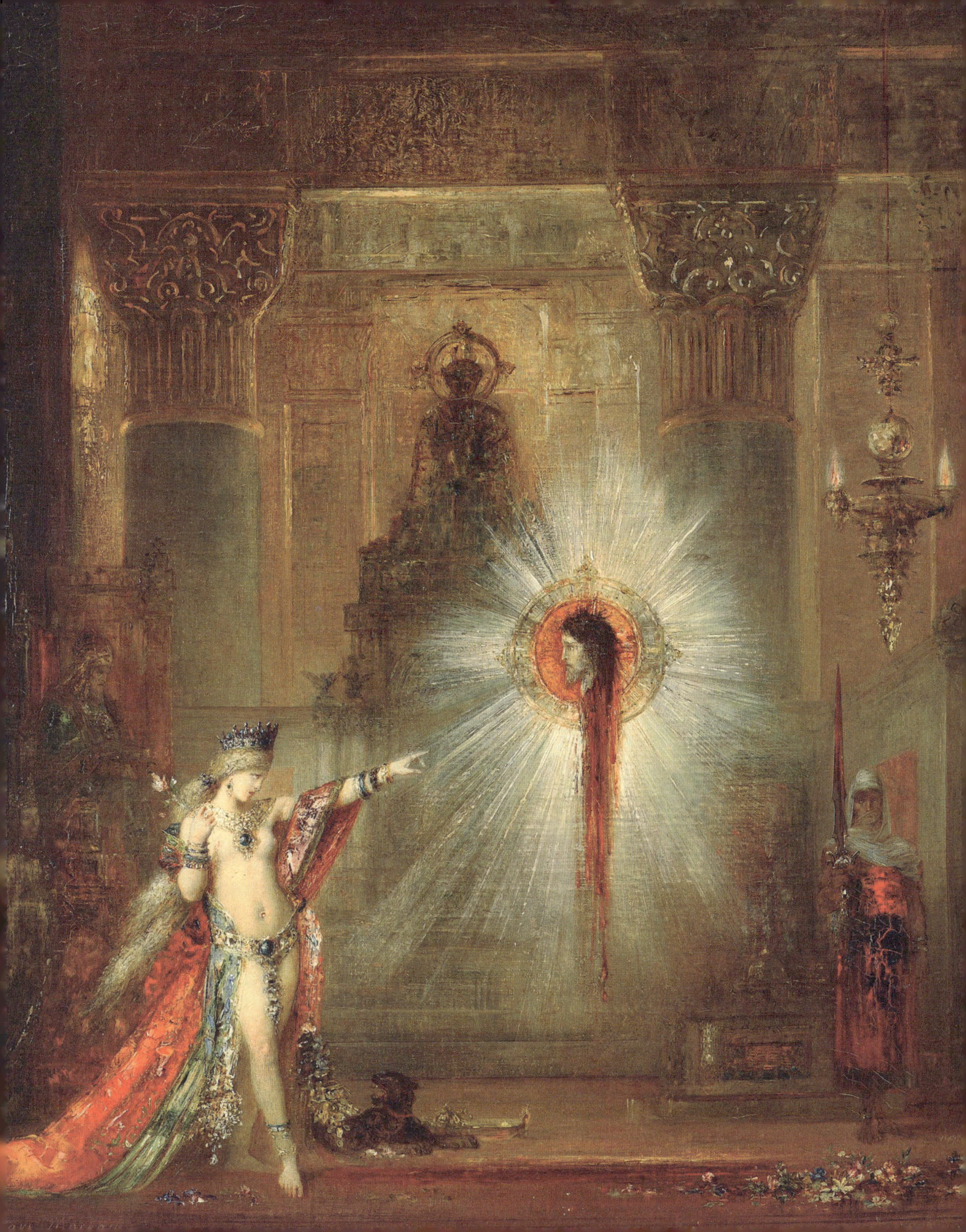

Edward Burne-Jones

The Middle Ages return to favour

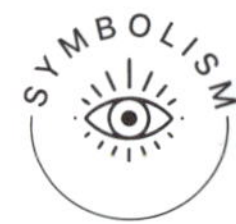

Along with Rossetti, Burne-Jones is one of the best-known figures of Pre-Raphaelitism. His erudition and taste for drawing enabled him to perfect a free form of art that promotes beauty for all.

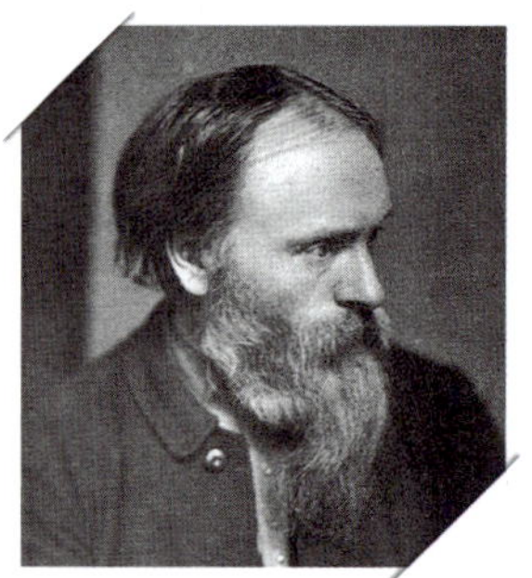

A crisis of faith

Burne-Jones came from a relatively poor background, and studied with the aim of pursuing a career in the Church. At Oxford, he met William Morris; they would both embrace art when they discovered the Pre-Raphaelite Brotherhood.

Aesthetic desertion

Burne-Jones developed an instinct for beauty. Trained by Dante Gabriel Rossetti, he cultivated a taste for the Middle Ages; however, his penchant for drawing also led him to admire the artists of the Renaissance, which his mentor, however, rejected. His approach to painting is decorative and perfected.

Quality public service

The artist held public art in high esteem, considering that it should be seen and appreciated by all. To this end, he worked for the Church, produced numerous stained glass windows for William Morris, and promoted a comprehensive approach to art, ranging from ceramics to tapestry and jewellery.

EDWARD BURNE-JONES SAID

"I have learned to recognise beauty when I see it, and that is what matters most to me."

Gustave Moreau
Page 212

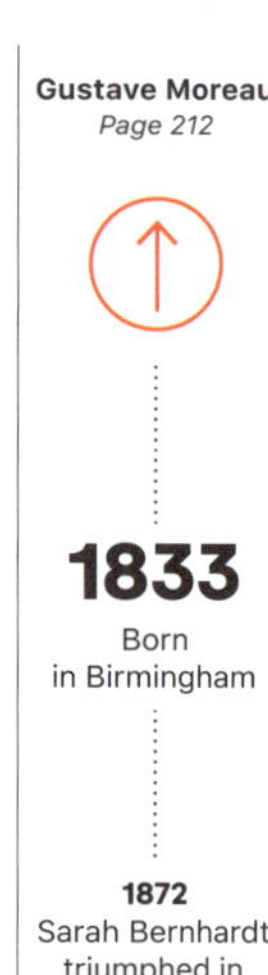

1833
Born in Birmingham

1872
Sarah Bernhardt triumphed in *Ruy Blas*

1875 to **1883**
Painted *The Wheel of Fortune*

1886
Inauguration of the Statue of Liberty in New York

1898
Died in London

Édouard Manet
Page 216

THE WHEEL OF FORTUNE ↗

Between 1875 and 1883
Oil on canvas
200 × 100 cm
Musée d'Orsay, Paris

WHAT ARE WE LOOKING AT?

Inspired by a medieval ballad, Burne-Jones painted an allegory of Fortune spinning her wheel. The work may also convey a political message.

Poetic inspiration

The source of this painting is a ballad by the poet Alfred Tennyson, from *Idylls of the King*, which recounts love affairs inspired by Arthurian legend.

Fortuna, fortunae

The woman on the left is an allegory of Fortune, in the Latin sense of the word, i.e. fate, destiny. Her gigantism is amplified by the surrounding architecture, which seems tiny by comparison. The palette of browns and greys accentuates the oppressive atmosphere.

Italian origins

The drapery of Fortune's dress is reminiscent of the works of Botticelli and Mantegna. She is turning a wheel – a symbol of destiny which, at any given moment, can define the existence of humans. Three men are tied up on this wheel, their sensual and tortured bodies evoking the art of Michelangelo (p. 54).

A reversal of fortune

The men can be identified by their attributes.
At the bottom, the head covered with laurels is that of a poet. The man in the middle, with a sceptre in his hand and a crown on his head, is a king. Above him is a slave, who can be recognised by the chain hanging down his leg.

Class struggle

The different statuses of the characters, successively being crushed by fate, and the slave's foot pressing down on the king's head, make this work a possible political allegory; it was met with great enthusiasm when it was presented in France.

CLICHÉS GONE OUT OF FASHION

Often featured in paintings, the Pre-Raphaelite feminine ideal is frequently ambiguous and associated with a misogynistic image of women. They are depicted as sensual, by turns idle, desperate or venomous. Their melancholic gaze is lost in the distance.

Lady Lilith

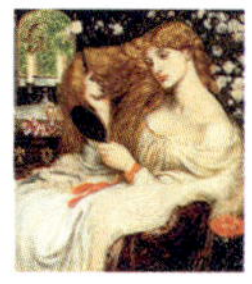

Dante Gabriel Rossetti, 1866–1873, Delaware Art Museum

Mariana

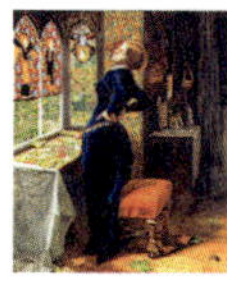

John Everett Millais, 1851, Tate Britain, London

Flaming June

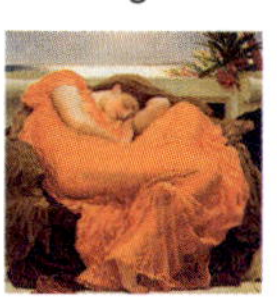

Frederic Leighton, circa 1895, Museo de Arte de Ponce, Puerto Rico

THE PRE-RAPHAELITE MOVEMENT IN A NUTSHELL

- A brotherhood of painters that reacted to British Academism.
- Inspired by Gothic art and the early Renaissance, "before Raphael".
- A very polished form of art, attentive to details, founded on drawing.
- Melancholic and nostalgic atmospheres.

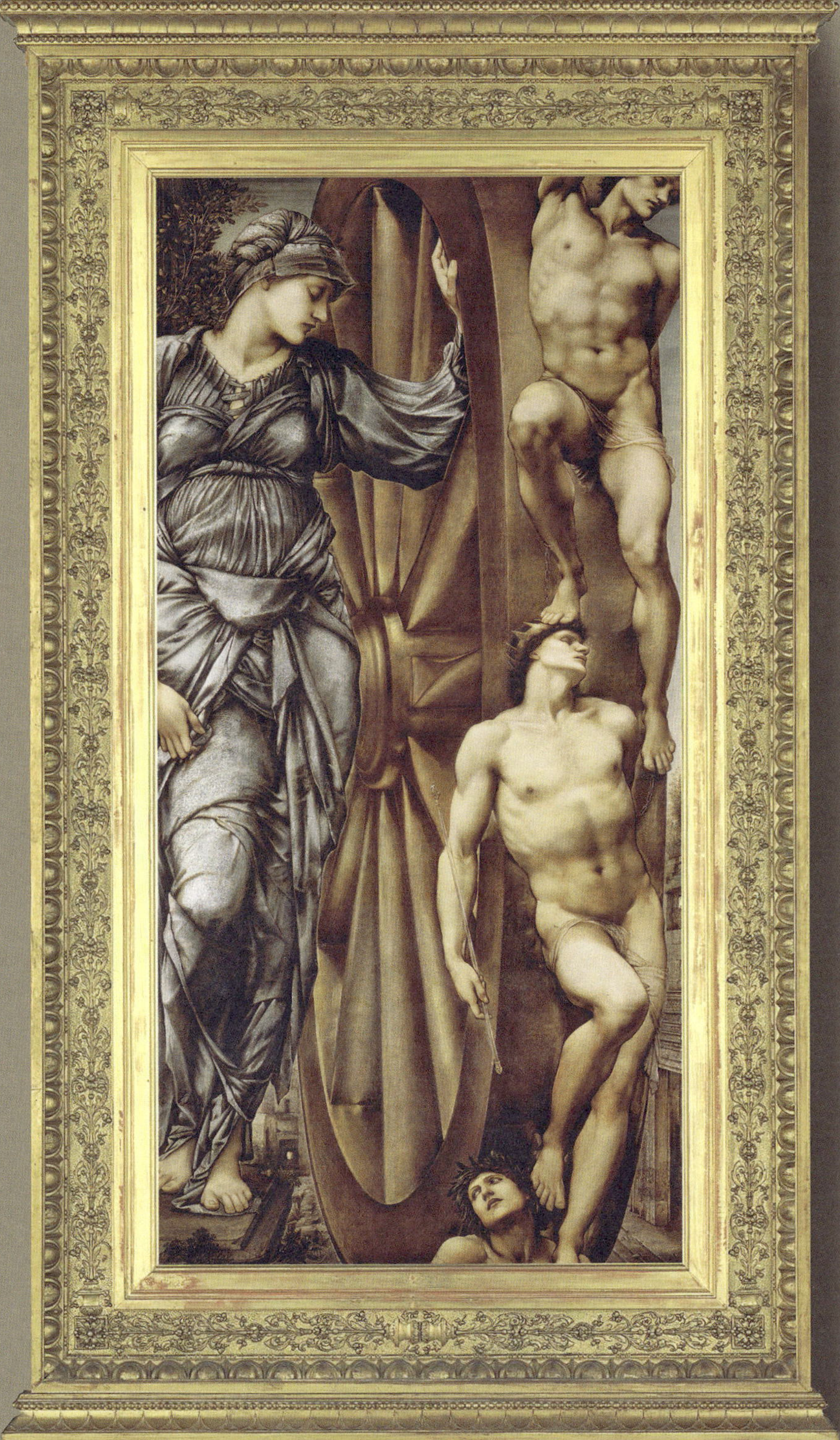

Édouard Manet

A lunch scene that whet the critics' appetite

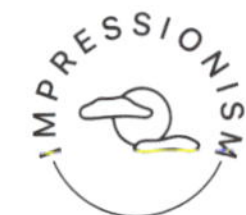

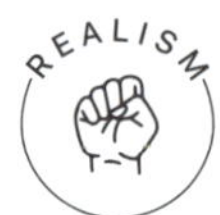

Despite the controversial nature of his works, Manet was inspired by the great masters, and was keen to exhibit at the Salon. He shook up a system that he admitted to wanting to be part of. The audacity of his works was his way of demonstrating modernity.

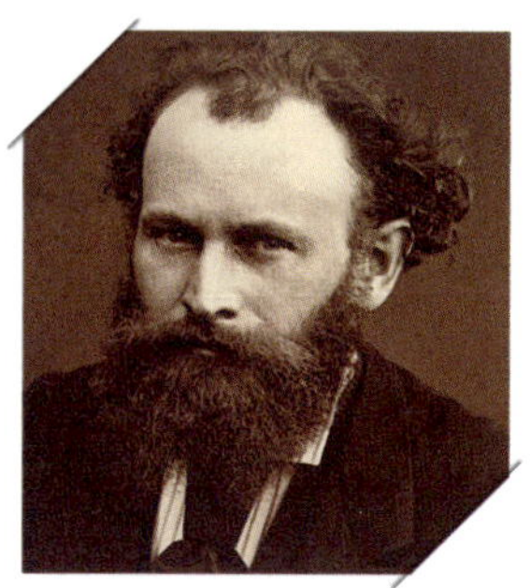

A slight struggle

After two unsuccessful attempts at the competitive examination for the French Naval School, Manet entered the studio of Thomas Couture. He observed Watteau (p. 138) and the Le Nain brothers at work, and trained during his travels in Europe. He experienced an aesthetic shock when discovering the works of Velázquez (p. 112) in Madrid.

A fusion of classes

A modern painter, Manet did not deny tradition, but transformed it to the point of transgression. Criticised for the raw realism of his works, his approach disrupted the hierarchy of genres, abolishing both narrative and drama. His contemporaries alleged he deprived his subjects of their moralvalue.

Valuable friendships

Throughout his life, the artist experienced scandals and rejections at theSalon. A fervent Republican, he was experienced political censorship. Hisfriends included Berthe Morisot (p. 234), Henri Fantin-Latour, along withauthors Charles Baudelaire, Stéphane Mallarmé and Émile Zola, who took uptheir pens to defend him.

PETTY-MINDEDNESS

"Gaining a few years on Monsieur Manet: what a sad policy!"
The French poet Stéphane Mallarmé denounced the rejection of modernity, nonetheless inescapable, when two of Manet's works were refused at the 1874 Salon.

Edward Burne-Jones
Page 214

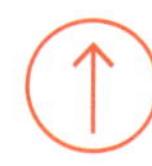

1832
Born in Paris

1840
Railway Mania

1863
Painted *The Luncheon on the Grass*

1871
Rimbaud wrote the poem *Le Bateau ivre*

1883
Died in Paris

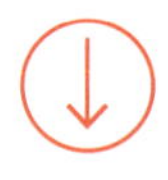

Claude Monet
Page 224

THE LUNCHEON ON THE GRASS ↗

1863
Oil on canvas
207 × 265 cm (214 × 270 cm before two size reductions)
Musée d'Orsay, Paris

WHAT ARE WE LOOKING AT?

Manet painted much more than an incongruous picnic that caused a scandal: what he produced is indeed a manifesto of modern painting.

It's a remix!

In this work, Manet twisted tradition. He was inspired by Italian art: the young woman's pose is an excerpt from a lost work by Raphael, the *Judgement of Paris*, known from an engraving. The painting also refers to *The Pastoral Concert* by Titian, where two musicians are surrounded by idealised naked women.

The naked truth

In this painting by Manet, the naked woman's figure has no justification, as this work depicts neither a mythological nor a historical scene; it is made all the more shocking by the woman's gaze, which engages viewers.

But what are we doing here?

Around her, the men are acting nonchalantly; the one facing us seems absent. Viewers don't really know what is going on in this scene, which features no real subject.
This is another affront to Academism.

Driving the nail in

Far from being stingy in his provocations, Manet also opted for a very large format for this genre scene, normally reserved for history painting (p. 166), which was considered the noblest genre. There is no question that he definitely did not shy from thumbing his nose at propriety.

Curveless shapes

Manet was also criticised for his approach to painting; he was accused of creating flat, boneless bodies, with thick, imprecise contours. Here, the scene appears to lack depth, as if the characters had been pasted onto a landscape. The artist experimented with formal effects, challenging habits.

A LANDMARK LUNCHEON

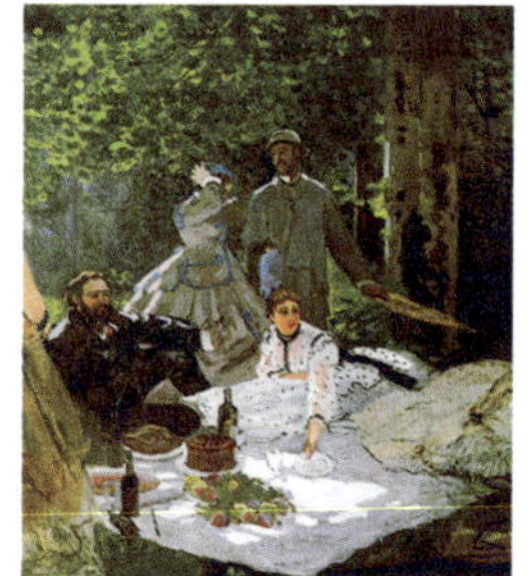

Claude Monet
Luncheon on the Grass
1865–1866, Musée d'Orsay, Paris.

- **Claude Monet** (p. 224) painted his own *Luncheon on the Grass* between 1865 and 1866.
- **Paul Cézanne** (p. 242) sought to compete with Manet with *The Eternal Feminine* in 1877.
- **Paul Gauguin** (p. 248) depicted the same nude motif in *Where Do We Come From? What Are We? Where Are We Going?* between 1897 and 1898.
- **Pablo Picasso** (p. 264) produced variations of the theme in the 1960s.
- **Alain Jacquet** presented his own screen-printed version in 1964.

AN AIR OF DÉJÀ VU ...

The young woman is Victorine Meurent, a professional model who regularly posed for Manet. He would also immortalise her in his work *Olympia* (p. 219).

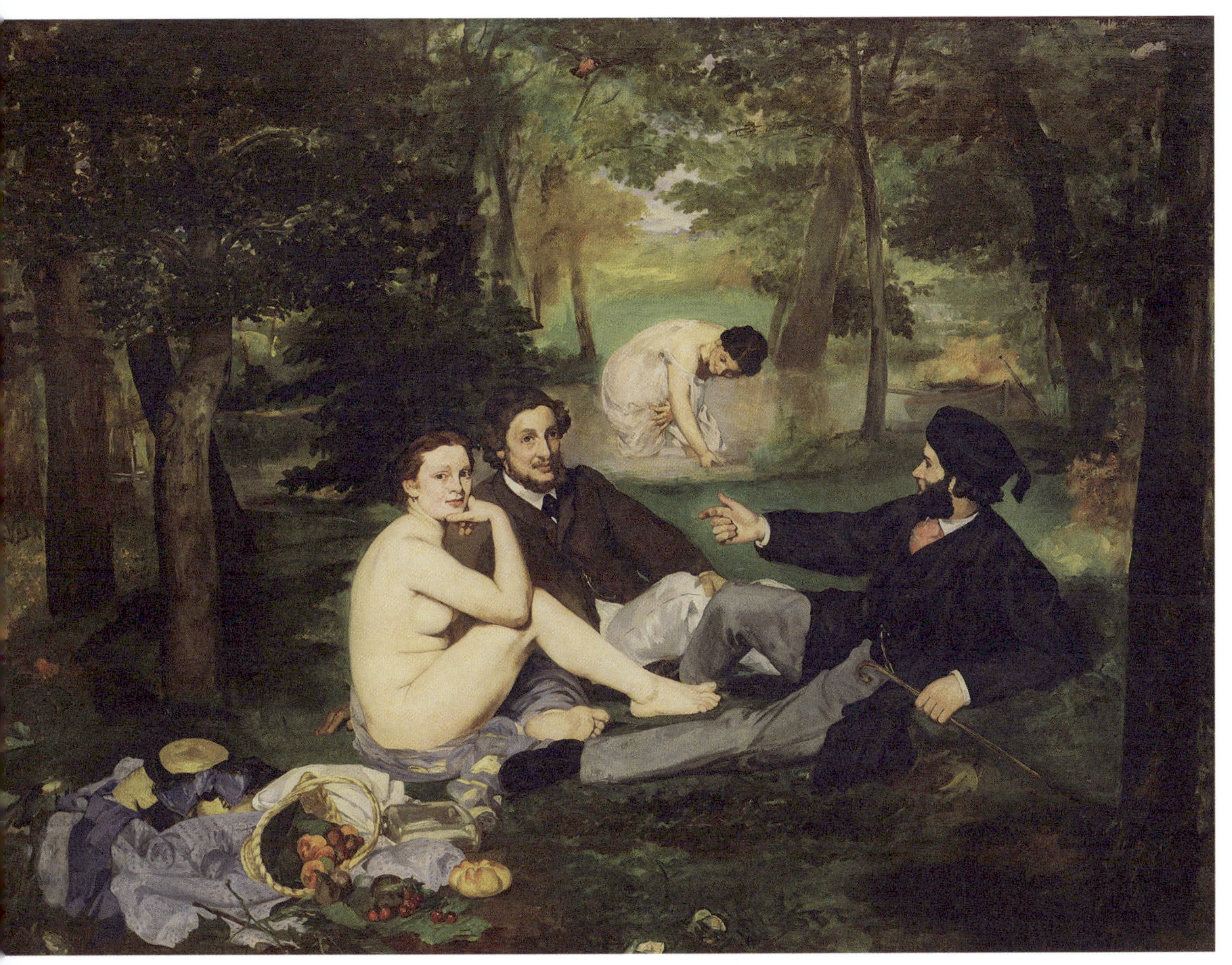

The work in *The Masterpiece*

Zola was not content with defending Manet. In his novel *The Masterpiece*, he described a painting of monumental dimensions that strongly resembled *The Luncheon on the Grass* by Manet: "On the grass, amidst the summer vegetation, a nude woman was stretched. [...] This gentleman had his back turned. One saw nothing of him but his left hand, with which he was supporting himself on the grass."

Manet and Cabanel

Settling scores

In 1863, the official Salon and the Salon des Refusés jousted with each other over nudes. Goddesses and prostitutes were the heroines of a new quarrel between the Ancients, championed by Alexandre Cabanel, and the Moderns, championed by Édouard Manet.

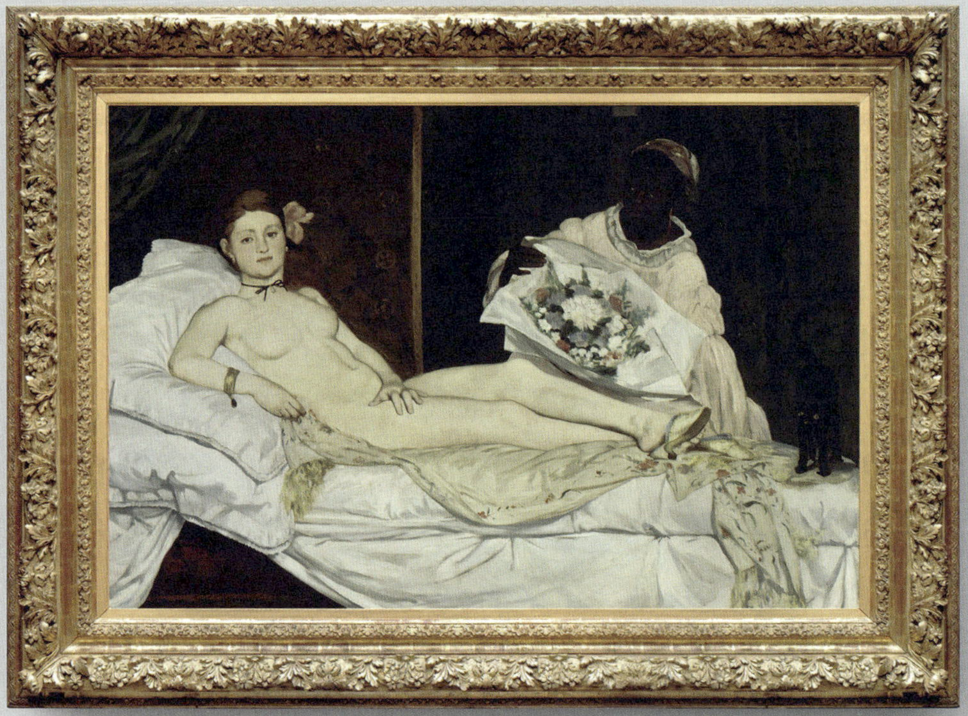

***OLYMPIA* BY ÉDOUARD MANET**
1863

Manet accepted no compromise, reinterpreting Titian's *Venus of Urbino* as a prostitute. The model's air of disinterest, the absence of voluptuousness and the realistic treatment underpin a commercial and well-controlled relationship to sex.

Oil on canvas, 130.5 × 191 cm
Musée d'Orsay, Paris

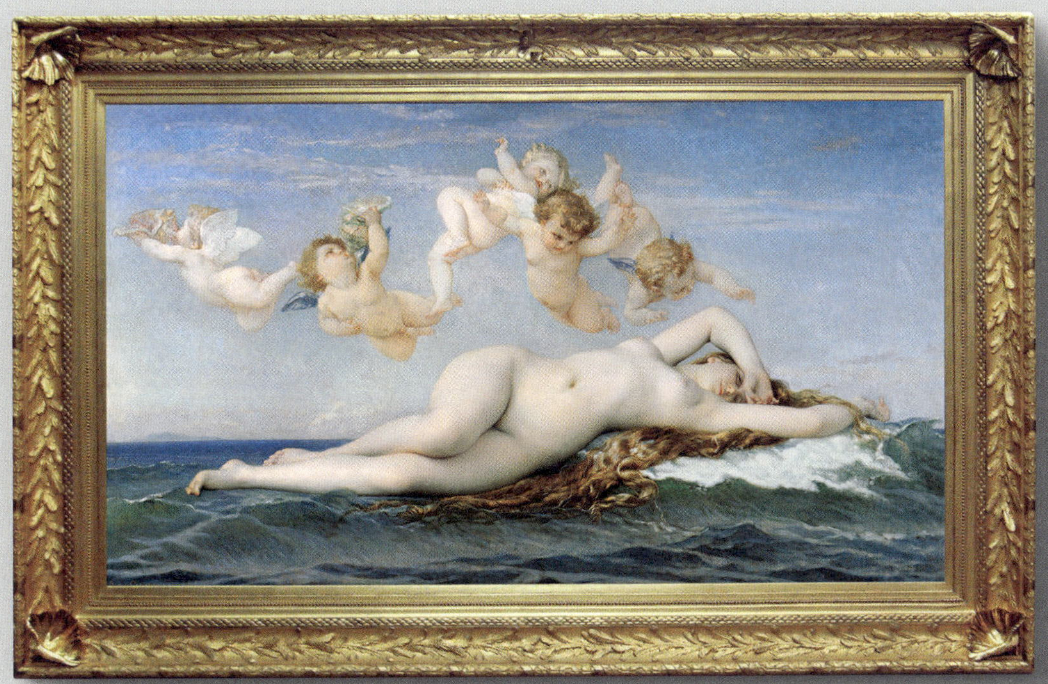

***THE BIRTH OF VENUS* BY ALEXANDRE CABANEL**
1863

Cabanel offers a languid nude subject to the viewer's gaze. However, the mythological pretext made its eroticism tolerable, and the work was met with success. Some critics nonetheless denounced the compromise between academic seriousness and the popular features with which the goddess is represented.

Oil on canvas, 130 × 225 cm
Musée d'Orsay, Paris

The official Salon and the Salon des Refusés

Two Salons, two atmospheres

From the 17th century to the beginning of the 20th century, French artistic life was largely influenced by the "Salon".
It commanded good taste, sealed the fate of artists and saw the birth of the discipline of art criticism.
However, this academic posture was overturned in the 19th century.

The *in*

"The Salon is a vast theatre, where neither rank nor favour nor wealth can reserve seats for bad taste," wrote the artist Louis Carrogis de Carmontelle in 1785.

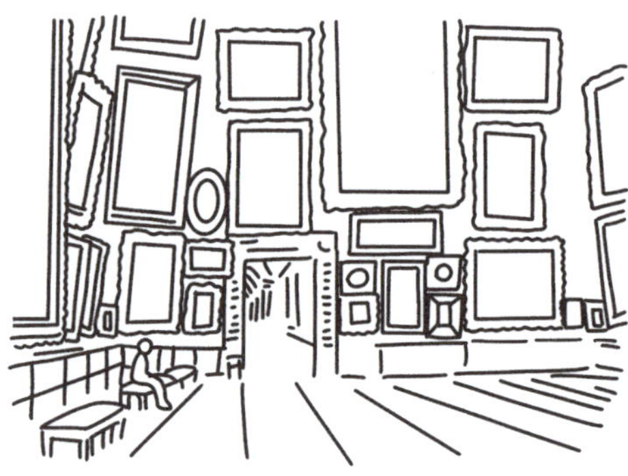

A very strict Salon

As early as 1667, the Académie Royale de Peinture et de Sculpture (p. 132) began exhibiting its members' works. For the artists, this annual presentation became the means to make themselves known and obtain commissions. These exhibitions were named "Salon", in reference to the square-shaped Salon Carré of the Louvre, where they were held from 1725 to 1748.

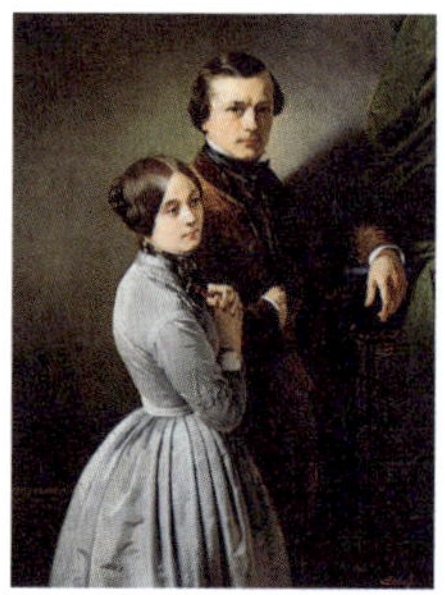

↑
ACCEPTED

Claude-Marie Dubufe
Édouard and Juliette Dubufe
1846
Château de Compiègne

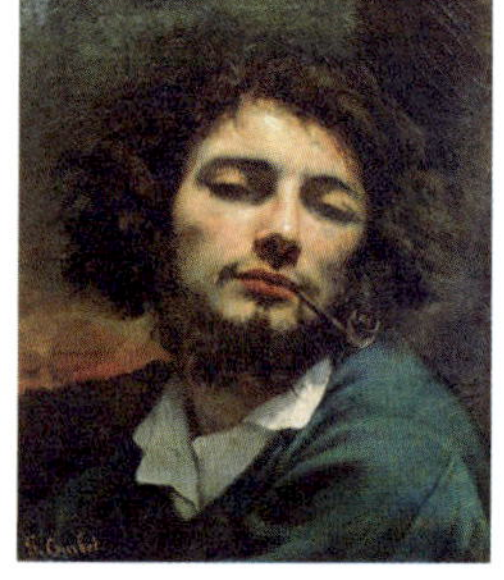

↑
REFUSED

Gustave Courbet
Self-Portrait (The Man with a Pipe)
1846
Musée Fabre, Montpellier

A poorly accepted refusal

After the Revolution, works were submitted for approval to a jury that defended an academic style, refusing to take into account the appearance of new movements that challenged this influence.
In 1846, the writer Charles Baudelaire took offence at the rejection of the very talented Gustave Courbet (p. 198).

THE BIRTH OF A NEW DISCIPLINE

- A spiritual period par excellence, the 18th century encouraged debate and reflection, and also witnessed the affirmation of an intellectual discipline, closely linked to art, which remains in force today: criticism.
- In the 19th century, as this literary genre became more popular, a number of writers tried their hand at the genre; not least Baudelaire, Balzac, Zola and Hugo would in turn comment on the art of their time.

The off

A rebellious Salon

In 1863, the jury of the official Salon was more demanding than ever: out of 5,000 works submitted, 2,000 were refused. The "Salon des Refusés" was born out of this severity. Édouard Manet's *The Luncheon on the Grass* (p. 216) would appear among the rejected works. While this exhibition had a rebellious flair, it was created on the initiative of Napoleon III, who wished to "let the public judge the legitimacy of these claims".

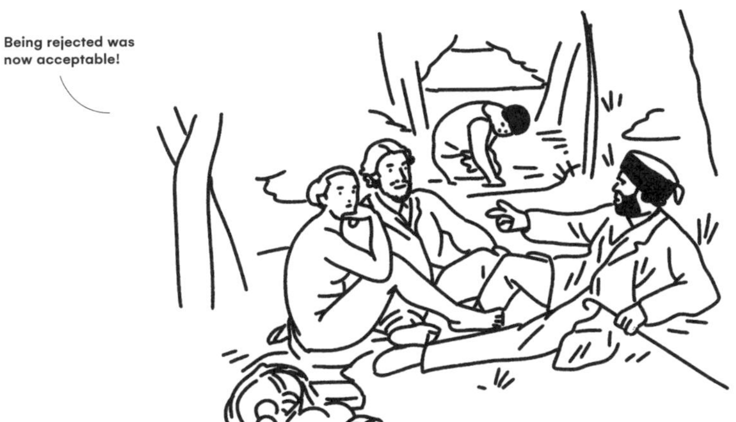

NOTORIOUS "REFUSÉS"

- Henri Fantin-Latour (1836–1904)
- Johan Barthold Jongkind (1819–1891)
- Édouard Manet (p. 216)
- Camille Pissarro (1830–1903)
- Henri Fantin-Latour (1844–1910)
- James Abbott McNeill Whistler (1834–1903)

Independent Salons

Out of the frustration of many rejections, an exhibition that took place in 1874, organised by the "Société Anonyme des Artistes Peintres, Sculpteurs et Graveurs", would forever mark the history of art... Today, it is better known as the "Première Exposition des Peintres Impressionnistes".

It occurred from 15 April to 15 May 1874, in one of the photographer Félix Nadar's studios, located at 35 Boulevard des Capucines in Paris. The term "Impressionism" is derived from Monet's painting *Impression, Sunrise* (p. 141) that was exhibited on this occasion.

THE "PREMIÈRE EXPOSITION DES PEINTRES IMPRESSIONNISTES" IN NUMBERS

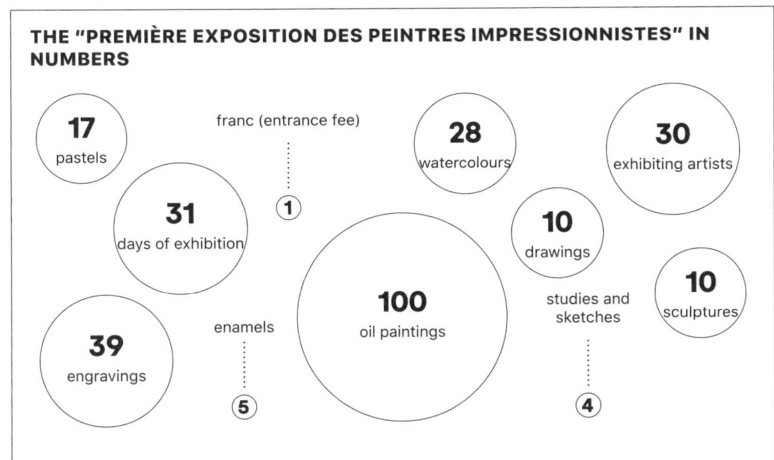

TRADITION COMPROMISED

In the second half of the 19th century, the Salon experienced continuous upheavals, to the point that the French State withdrew from it in 1881, leaving the artists to organise it through the Salon des Artistes Français. This event led the creation of other events, such as the Salon des Indépendants or the Salon d'Automne.

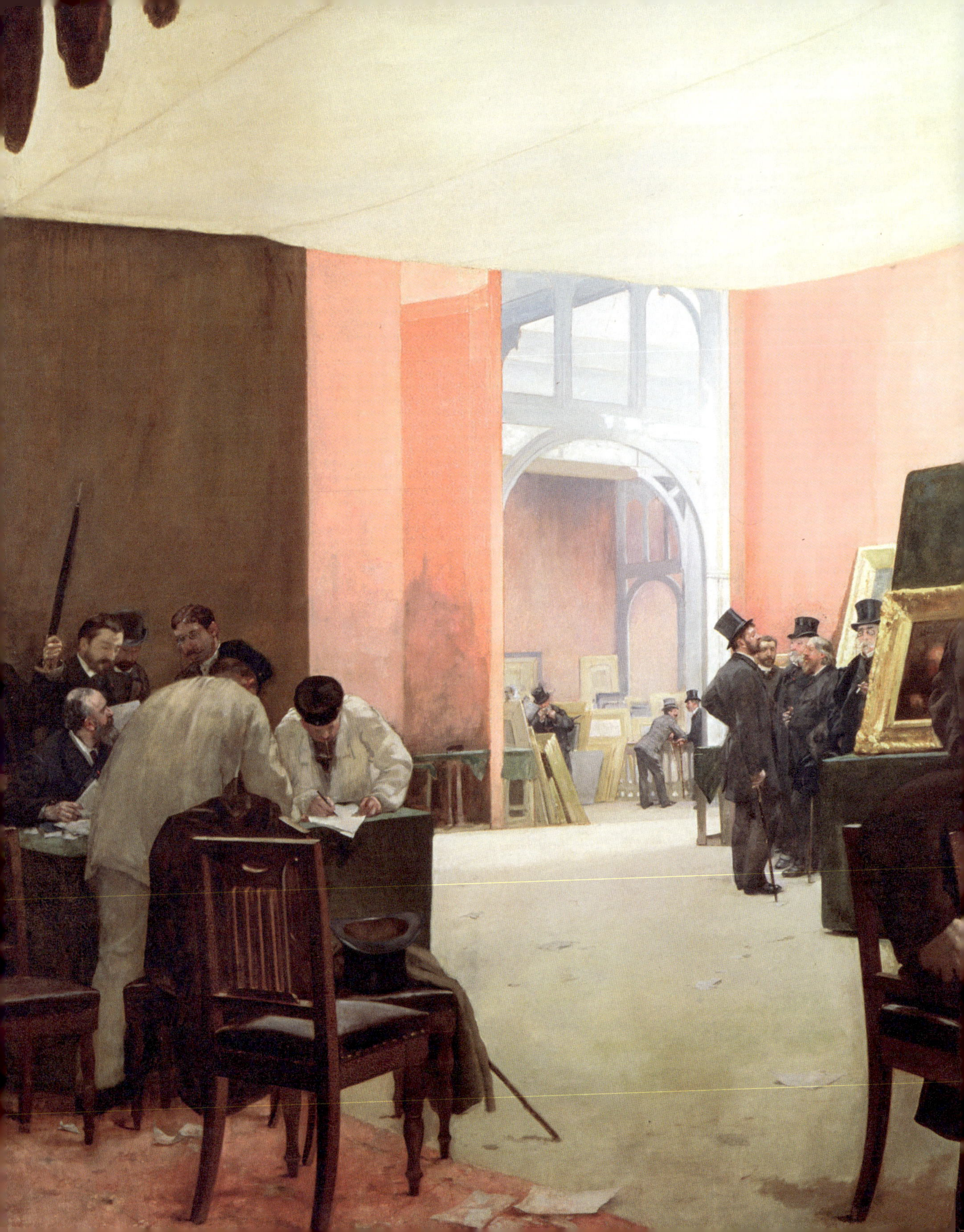

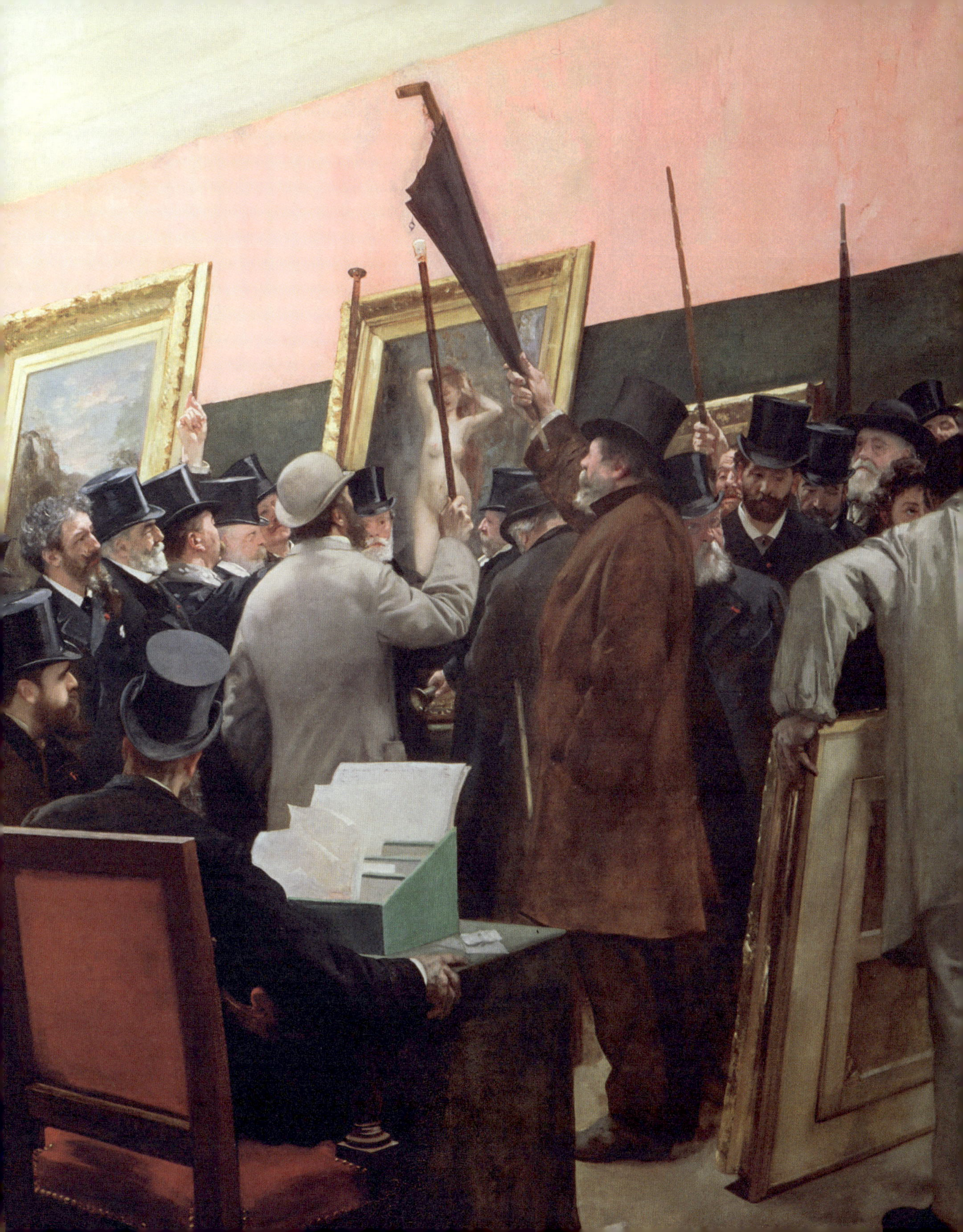

Claude Monet

Outdoor enthusiast

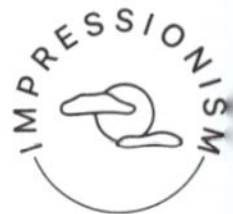

An avid painter who painted outdoors and constantly observed the effects of light, Monet is probably the most famous of the Impressionists. Indeed, one of his paintings would give the movement its name in 1874.

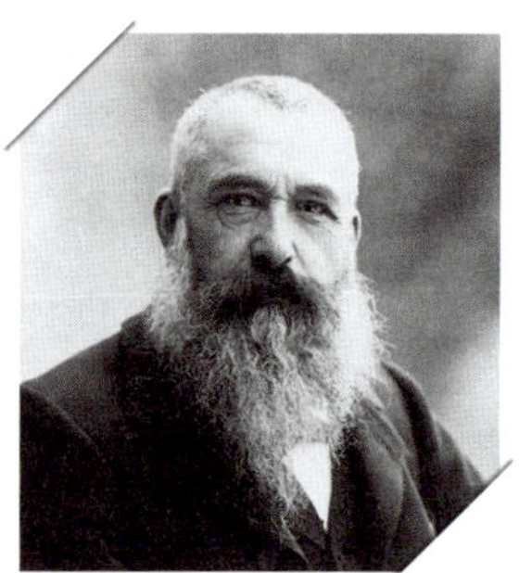

Talent produced in Normandy

Born in Paris, the son of a prosperous merchant from Le Havre, Monet first established a reputation as a caricaturist. His drawings caught the eye of the artist Eugène Boudin, who trained him in painting, including outdoors. He was also influenced by the painter Johan Barthold Jongkind, who stayed in Normandy.

The exhibition that changed everything

In 1874, he participated in the "Première Exposition des Peintres Impressionnistes", held in the studio of the photographer Félix Nadar, where he presented his painting *Impression, Sunrise*. From this, an ironic art critic derived the neologism "Impressionist", which gave its name to the movement.

Nature is the future

In 1890, Monet finally managed to make a living from his work. He acquired a house in Giverny, and had its garden landscaped. Nature would inspire him to paint his *Water Lilies*, his last series, in which the beginnings of abstract painting are already apparent.

A LESSON FOR LIFE

"Three brushstrokes from nature are worth more than two days of work at the easel," was the lesson Boudin passed on to Monet.

Édouard Manet
Page 216

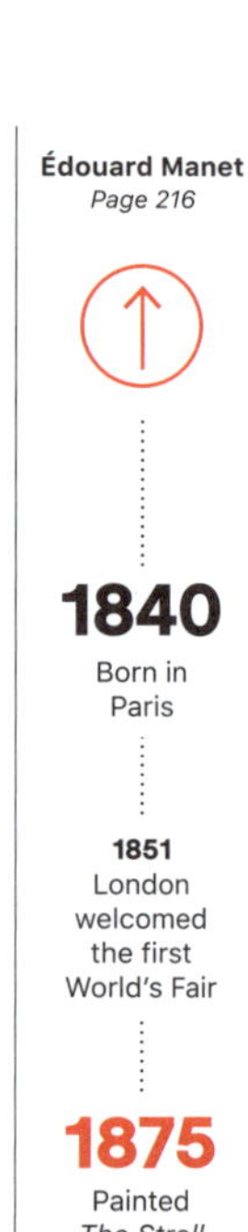

1840
Born in Paris

1851
London welcomed the first World's Fair

1875
Painted *The Stroll*

1876
Alexander Graham Bell invented the telephone

1881
The Little Dancer of Fourteen Years by Degas caused a scandal

1926
Died in Giverny

Edgar Degas
Page 230

THE STROLL

1875
100 × 81 cm
Oil on canvas
National Gallery of Art, Washington, DC

WHAT ARE WE LOOKING AT?

In 1871, Monet and his family moved to the suburbs of Argenteuil, where they enjoyed walks in the countryside and long painting sessions outdoors. Here, the painter immortalised his wife, Camille, and their son Jean.

Spontaneity studied

Although the session probably lasted several hours, Monet aspired to give the impression that he was capturing the moment. The models' pose seems to indicate that they are interrupting their walk to turn towards the viewer. The painter frees himself from academic conventions, introducing viewers to his family.

Variable skies

The free and flowing brushstrokes also grace this work with a feeling of spontaneity and dynamism. In places, Monet plays with the incompleteness and the preparatory layer of the canvas, which remains apparent as a means of shading the sky.

Airy and breezy

Blue and white tones are used to depict both the sky and Camille's dress. Using this technique, Monet appears to materialise the atmosphere; he gives the viewer the impression that he has succeeded in painting the wind.

The colours of light

The light is expressed with highlights of white on his wife's dress, and with warmer yellow touches on his son's shoulders. In the grass, the painter played with shades of green to render shadows and recreate the density of the vegetation.

IN MONET'S PAINTINGS, ONE CAN SEE ...

Throughout his career, Monet repeated the same motifs. This was an excellent way for him to study the light according to the season or the time of day.

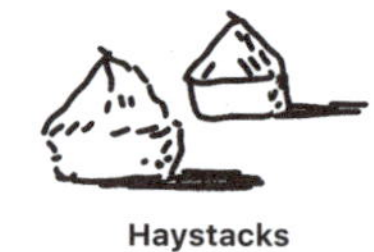

Haystacks

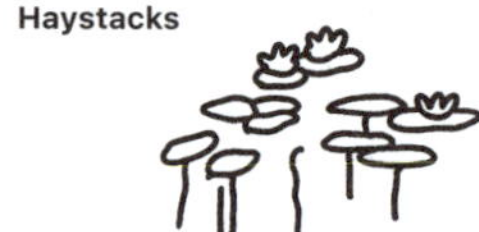

Water lilies

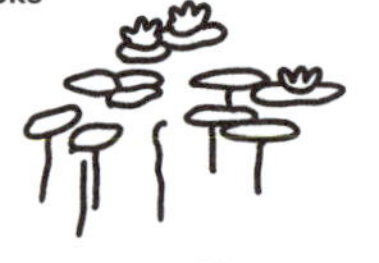

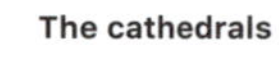

The cathedrals of Rouen

IMPRESSIONISM IN A NUTSHELL

- The representation of light and the transience of the moment.
- A swift, visible, easily distinguishable touch.
- Colours are applied side by side; the viewer's gaze blends them together.
- Landscapes and scenes of modern life, painted at the location.

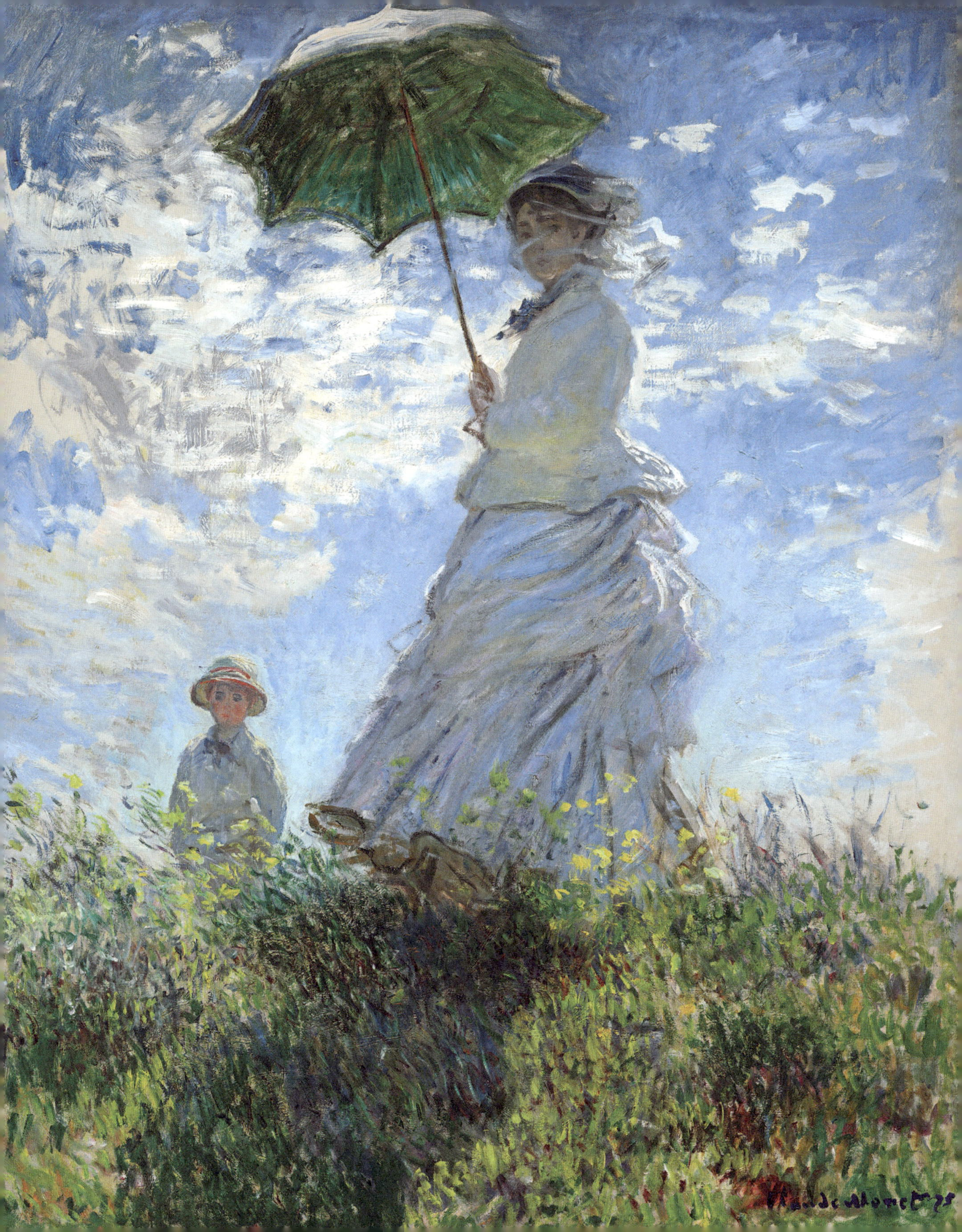

Monet and Mitchell

When painting goes green

From Monet to Mitchell, there is only one step ... or a few yards. Joan Mitchell settled in Vétheuil, where the Impressionist lived before moving to Giverny. While Monet, a Norman by adoption, looked for motifs at the water's edge, the American artist recreated her perception of them in her studio.

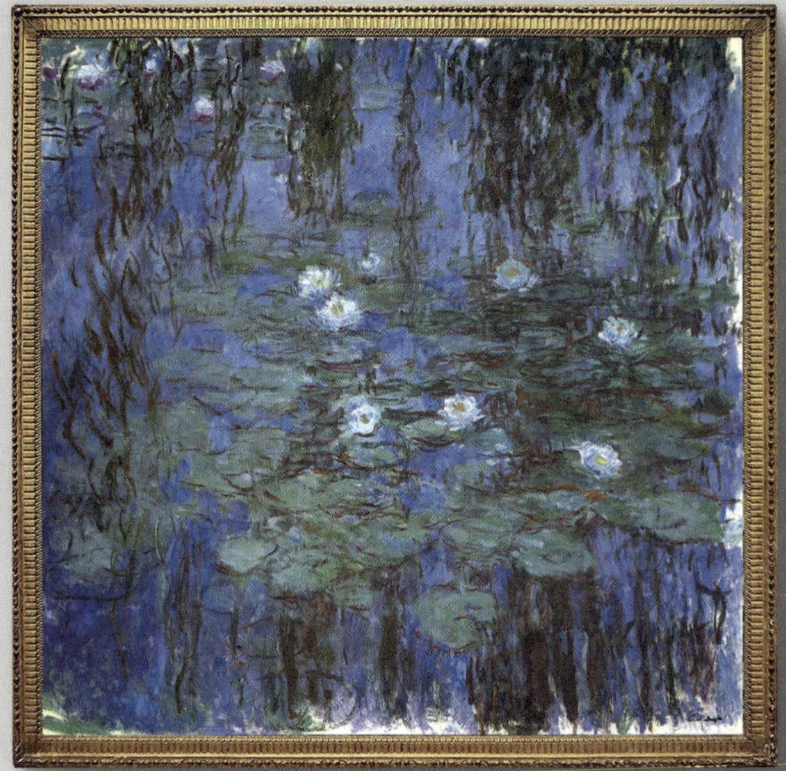

***BLUE WATER LILIES* BY CLAUDE MONET**
1916–1919

In 1893, Monet moved to Giverny, where he had a garden landscaped, which he considered a work of art. The vegetation inspired him to create the *Water Lilies* series, which spanned the entirety of the end of his career. The painter's motifs capture the elusive variations of time, tending towards abstract art.

Oil on canvas, 204 × 200 cm
Musée d'Orsay, Paris

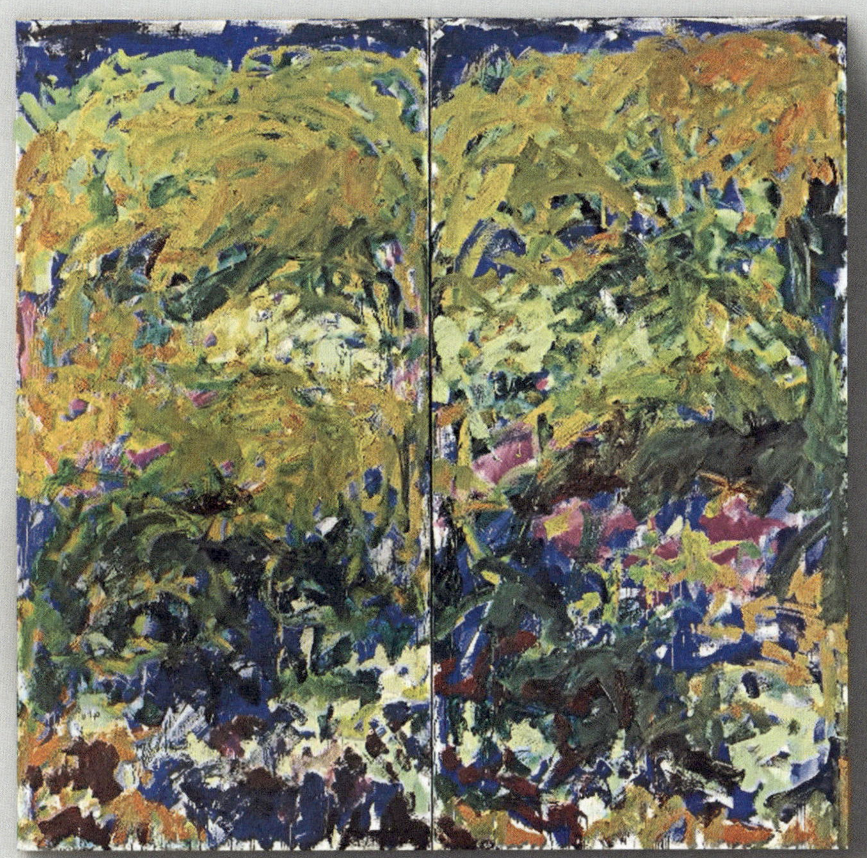

***LA GRANDE VALLÉE IX* BY JOAN MITCHELL**
1983–1984

In 1968, Mitchell moved to Vétheuil. Under her brushes, nature embraced abstraction and adopted the codes of American abstract expressionism: large formats, ample gestures and pure colours that rendered the artist's inner sensitivity, as she distanced herself from the motif.

Oil on canvas, 260 × 260 cm
Collection FRAC Normandie, Rouen

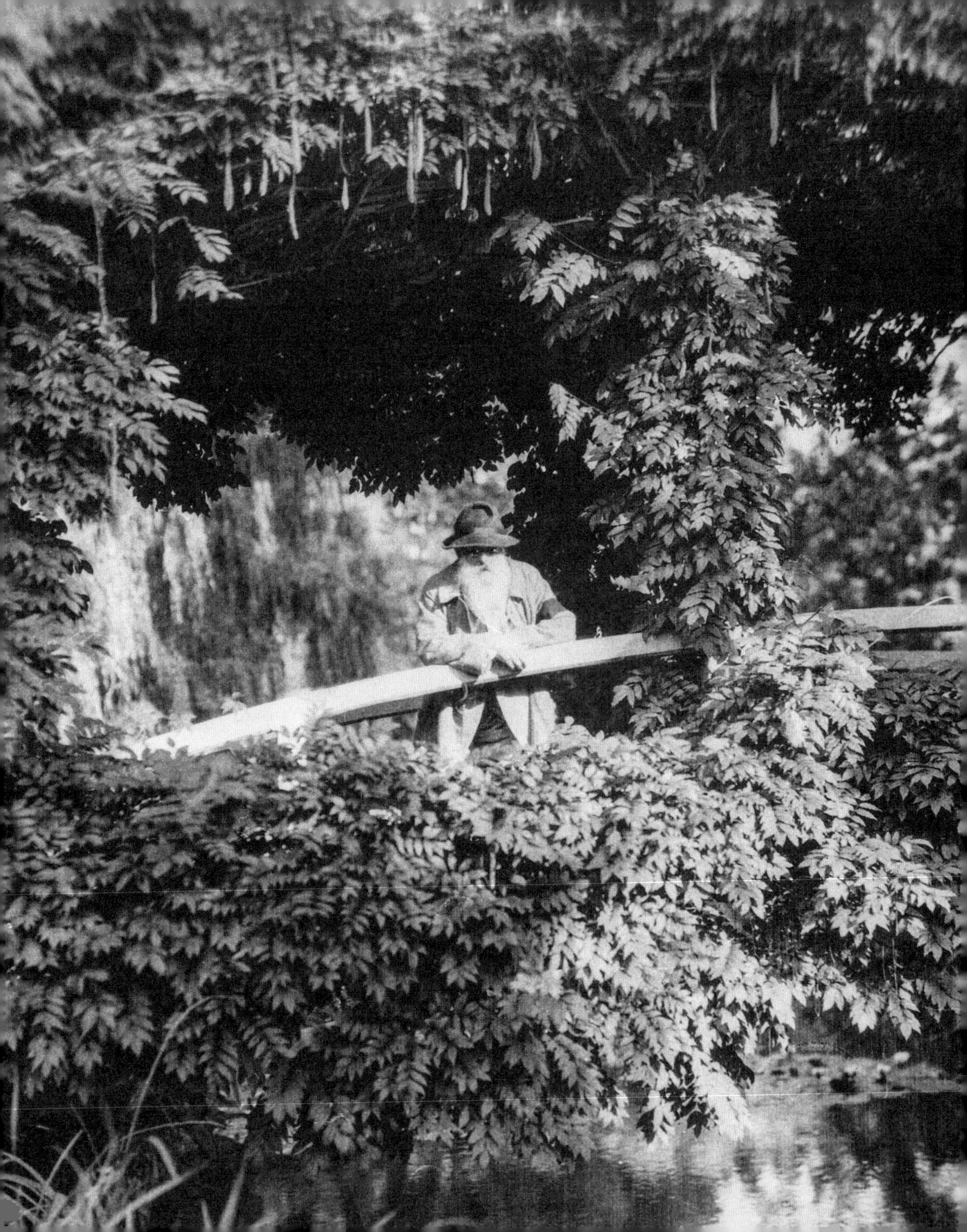

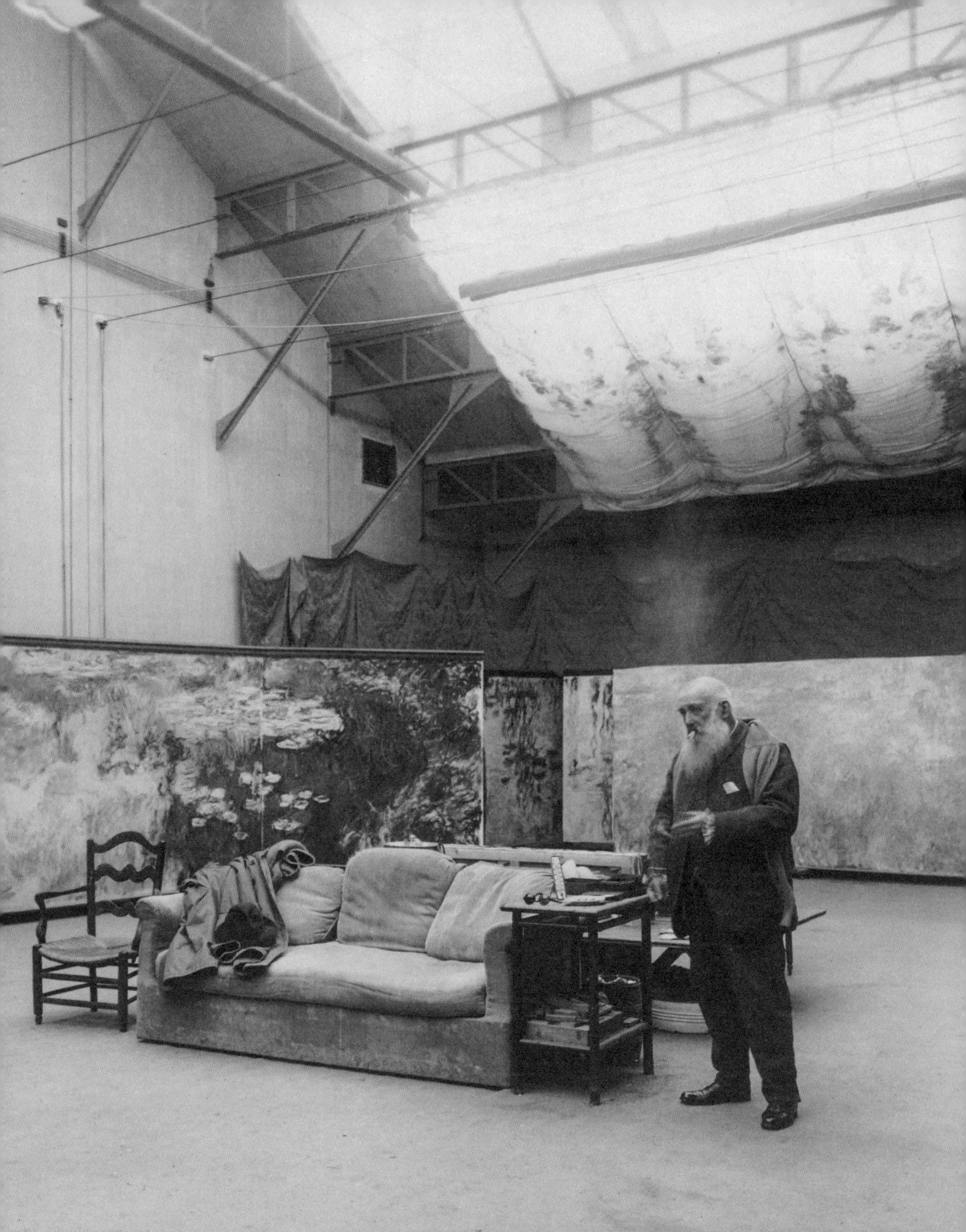

Edgar Degas

Gracing the body with the right touch

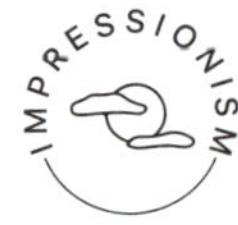

Edgar de Gas, known as Degas, was a cultured painter who strayed from the official ways. He is known today for his dancers, whose attitudes he captured in oil paintings, and with pastels and pencils, seeking to render an expression of truth in his art.

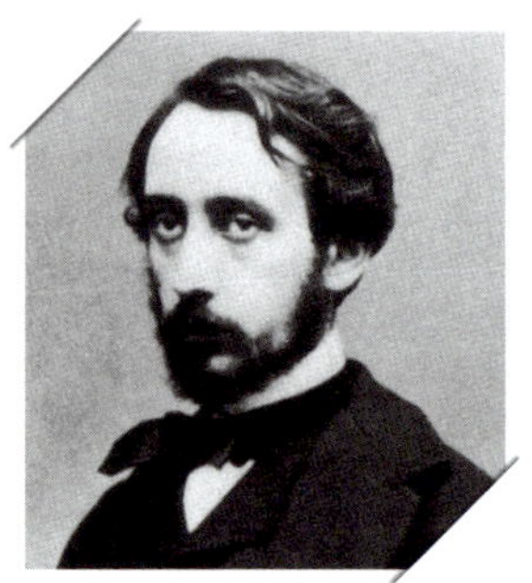

A course of action

After passing a baccalauréat in literature, Degas copied the works of the Louvre and enrolled in the classes of Louis Lamothe, heir to Ingres. Degas admired Jean-Auguste-Dominique Ingres for his penchant for line work. The painter also spent several years in Italy, where he rubbed shoulders with Gustave Moreau (p. 212).

In tune with the times

As a painter of modern life, Degas depicted both everyday life in the Parisian bourgeoisie and scenes of work. He sought the path of independence by participating in impressionist exhibitions; however, his realism and the subjects that he chose brought him closer to Manet, with whom he had a stormy friendship.

Sidesteps

Fascinated by women's bodies, milliners' workshops and movement, which he also tried to capture using photography, Degas chose the opera as his favourite venue. He became famous for his dancers, whom he liked to paint in the privacy of the backstage and during lessons.

COLOURFUL PASTELS

Suffering from a condition that would gradually leave him blind, towards the end of his life, Degas traded oil painting for pastel, with which he would never cease to innovate.

Claude Monet
Page 224

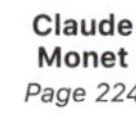

1834
Born in Paris

1855
Gérard de Nerval committed suicide in Paris

Between
1875
and
1876
Painted *In a Café*

1913
The Rite of Spring caused a scandal at its performance

1917
Died in Paris

Pierre-Auguste Renoir
Page 232

IN A CAFÉ

ALSO KNOWN AS L'ABSINTHE

Between 1875 and 1876
Oil on canvas
92 × 68.5 cm
Musée d'Orsay, Paris

WHAT ARE WE LOOKING AT?

With this work, which caused a scandal in its time, Degas illustrates the harm caused by alcohol on Parisian bohemians and the life of cafés in modern Paris.

From Greece to Japan

The scene takes place at the Café de la Nouvelle Athènes, which was frequented by the artists of Pigalle. However, the juxtaposition of the tables, creating a geometrical and serpentine line, and the work's format, stretched in height, draw their inspiration from elsewhere: they recall the art of Japanese prints, which were in vogue at the time.

The little sister

This construction also allowed the artist to create an imbalance accentuated by the absence of legs under the marble table tops. This instability echoes the advanced state of inebriation of both protagonists. Their gazes are empty, but their glasses are full; this is probably not their first round.

Wallflowers

This painting is a genuine public service advertisement against the evils of alcoholism. The two characters are sitting side by side, but they are ignoring each other, lost to apathy. They are but a shadow of their former selves, which can be seen on the wall… The carafe echoes the woman's silhouette and her emptiness.

Likely, but untrue!

Despite the moral message, the work caused a scandal: akin to Manet, Degas illustrated a vulgar, low-class subject that was not suitable for painting. The work is so realistic that Degas had to deny the alcoholism of his models, the actress Ellen Andrée and the artist Marcellin Desboutin. This would not prevent Zola from drawing inspiration from his painting for some pages of the novel *L'Assommoir*.

MONTMARTRE'S PROMINENT CAFÉS IN THE NINETEENTH CENTURY

1. **Le Guerbois**, Avenue de Clichy.
2. **La Nouvelle Athènes**, Place Pigalle.
3. **La Rochefoucauld**, at the corner of Rue La Fontaine and Rue La Rochefoucauld.
4. **Le Rat mort**, Place Pigalle.
5. **Le Chat noir**, 84, Boulevard de Rochechouart and Rue Laval *(now Rue Victor-Massé)*.

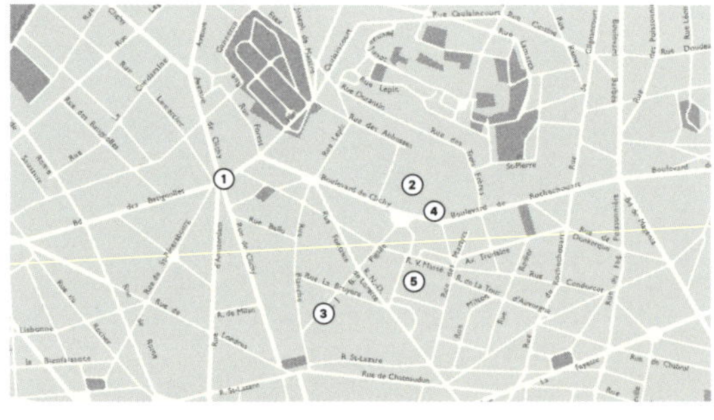

WHO WERE THE FIRST IMPRESSIONISTS?

The "Première Exposition des Peintres Impressionnistes" (p. 221) brought together thirty artists, including:

- Edgar Degas
- Eugène Boudin (1824–1898)
- Marie Bracquemond (1840–1916)
- Paul Cézanne (p. 242)
- Claude Monet (p. 224)
- Berthe Morisot (p. 234)
- Camille Pissarro (1830–1903)

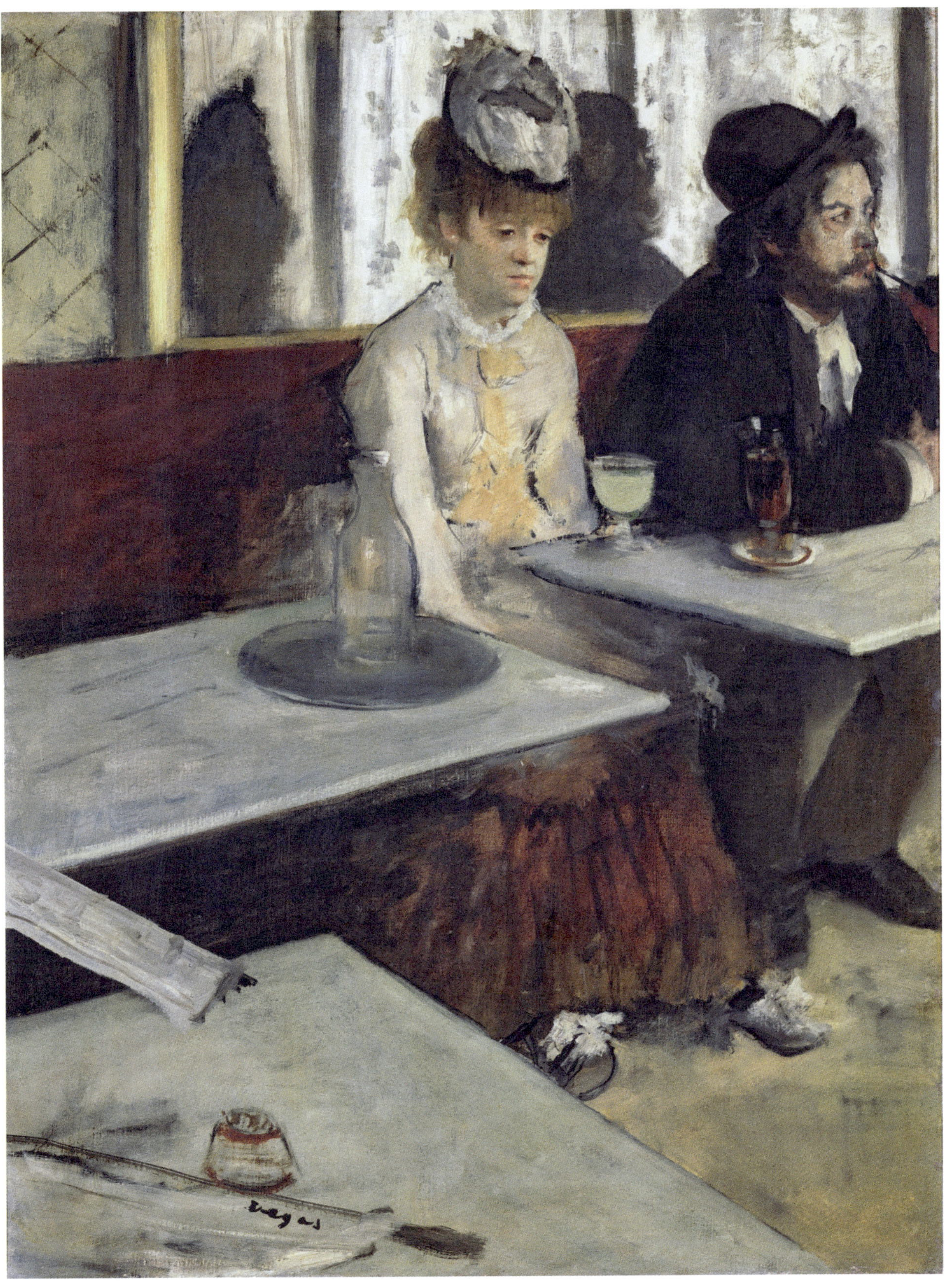
Degas

Pierre-Auguste Renoir

A joyful existence

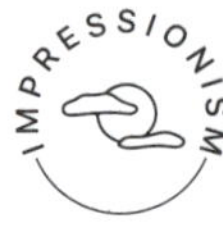

A leading figure an Impressionism that exudes joie de vivre, Renoir built up a vast network of friends and connections. The artist left behind no less than 4,000 works, which bear witness to the evolutions of his style.

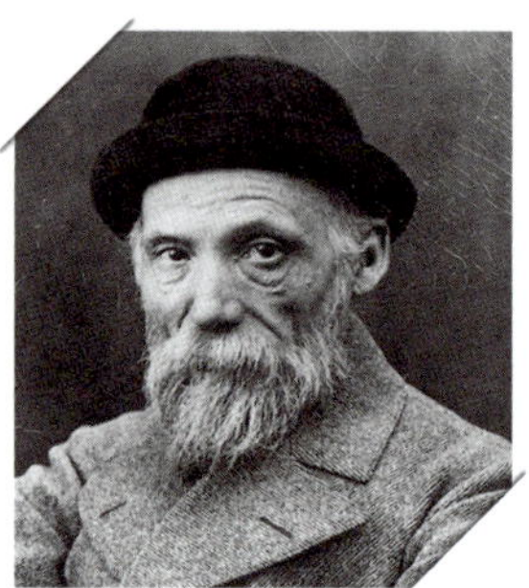

Job cuts

Born in Limoges, Renoir began by painting on porcelain, but the industrialisation of this discipline left him with no choice but to embrace another path. He then attended the Beaux-Arts and the studio of the painter Charles Gleyre.

Outings with friends

At Gleyre's studio, he met Claude Monet (p. 224), Alfred Sisley and Frédéric Bazille. Together, they settled down to paint in Barbizon, where Renoir was influenced by Camille Corot, but also by Jean-Auguste-Dominique Ingres (p. 180), Eugène Delacroix (p. 190) and the Realists. He had many connections among art dealers, such as Paul Durand-Ruel.

A part-time rebel

At the Salon, he in turn experienced success and rejection, and occasionally participated in Impressionist exhibitions. His painting was sensual and joyful. His style would evolve through a "sour" period, featuring acidic colours, and a "pearly" period, rife with pink and white tones.

PIERRE-AUGUSTE RENOIR SAID

"Painting is not daydreaming. It is, first of all, a manual task, and you have to perform it as a good worker would."

Edgar Degas
Page 230

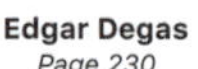

1841
Born in Limoges

1863
The Salon des Refusés marked the end of Academism

1876
Painted *Bal du Moulin de la Galette*

1883
Zola published the novel *Au Bonheur des Dames*

1919
Died in Cagnes-sur-Mer

Berthe Morisot
Page 234

BAL DU MOULIN DE LA GALETTE

1876
Oil on canvas
131.5 × 176.5 cm
Musée d'Orsay, Paris

WHAT ARE WE LOOKING AT?

This work is one of the masterpieces of Impressionism. In a large format, Renoir depicts a modern ball scene, expressing his optimistic vision of life.

A well-framed party

Renoir recreates a general impression of good humour and bustle, true to the atmosphere of the "Guinguette" that Parisians would flock to on Sundays, at the Moulin de la Galette, in Montmartre. Despite the profusion of details, the artist has produced a harmonious palette of blues and greens, creating a coherent whole.

It takes what it takes

To capture this atmosphere so accurately, Renoir would remove the canvas from his studio, Rue Cortot, to the "Guinguette", where he was able to capture the vibrant atmosphere at the location, forever rendering this fleeting moment in oil painting.

An enlightened look

Under this natural and artificial lighting, the painter conscientiously rendered the light, which takes the form of furtive spots that perfectly capture the rays of sun filtering through the trees. This constellation is reflected by the white globes of the chandeliers hanging over the stage.

In Spain

The impression of effervescence is carefully balanced by a well-structured composition. The figures in the foreground on the right form a first space, which the painter separates from the background occupied by dancers, by means of the diagonally placed bench. The standing couple depicted in full length appears to be looking at the viewer, inviting them to the dance.

SILENCE ... AND ACTION!

The painter's descendants would become particularly well known in the film industry.

Pierre-Auguste Renoir
(1841–1919)

Pierre Renoir *(1885–1952)*	Jean Renoir *(1894–1979)*	Claude Renoir *(1901–1969)*
As an actor, he played the roles of Commissaire Maigret and Charles Bovary.	A great Oscar-winning filmmaker based in Hollywood, he directed *The Grand Illusion*, *The Human Beast* and *The Rules of the Game*.	Nicknamed "Coco", he was a ceramic artist, and worked on several films in the 1930s and 1940s.

RENOIR'S ART IN A NUTSHELL

- An art that expresses the painter's joie de vivre.
- Women placed in the spotlight, from portraits of Renoir's relatives to opulent, naked bathing women.
- A style that evolved over the years, with contours becoming more uncertain or more defined, according to periods.

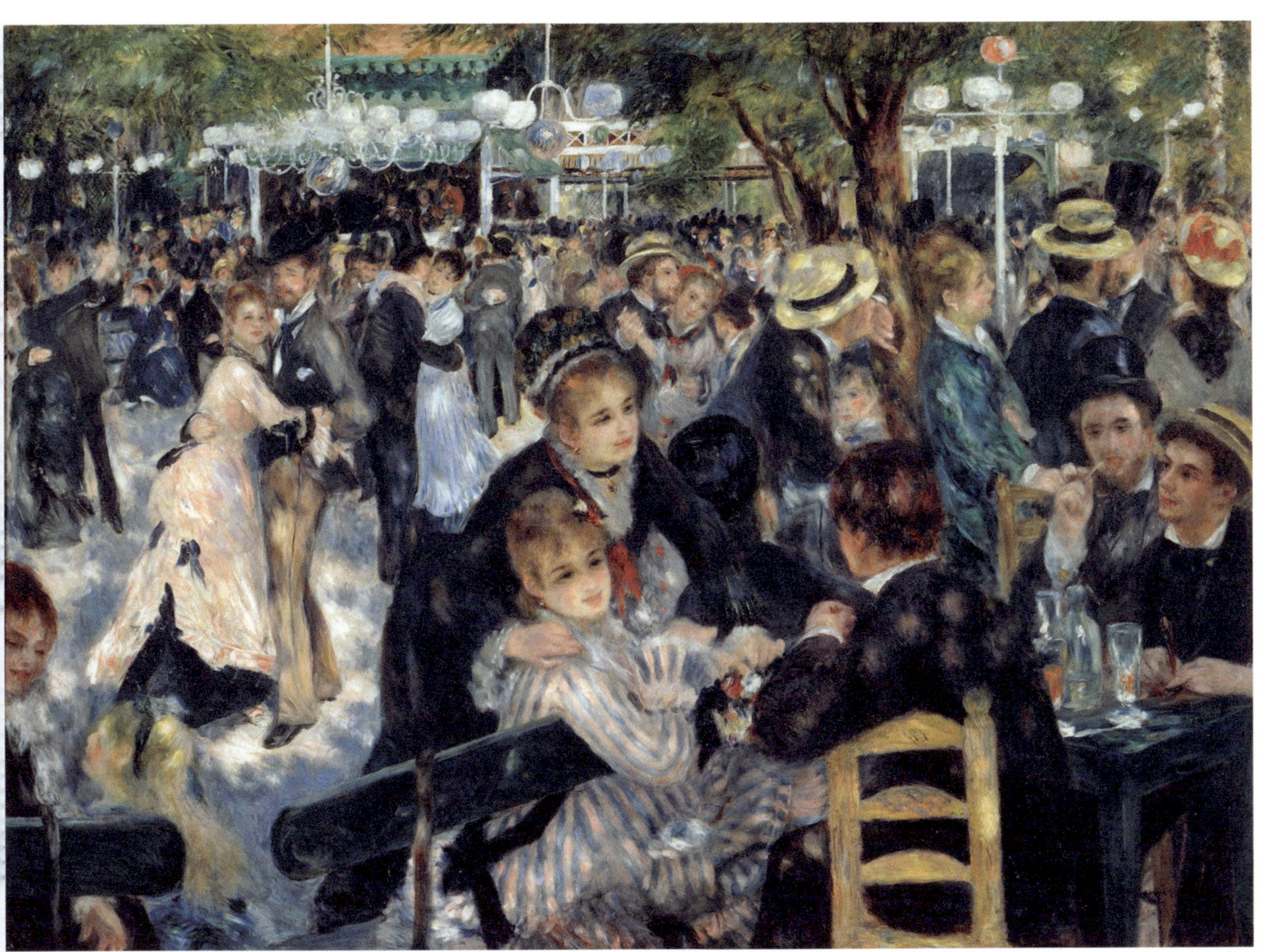

The café near the windmills

The Moulin de la Galette took its name from the two neighbouring windmills that once surrounded the location where the "Guinguette" took place, Le Radet and Le Blute-Fin, respectively. Both windmills still exist, and are the last two remains of windmills on the Montmartre Hill. While Le Blute-Fin has retained its original location, Le Radet has been relocated, and now overlooks a restaurant.

Berthe Morisot

The accomplishment of the unfinished

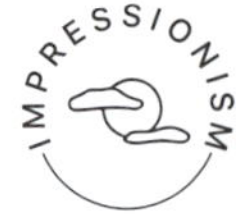

Morisot was one of the most daring artists of her time.
She exhibited assiduously at the official Salon, then, from the first year, with the Impressionists.
She painted with speed and ease, mainly depicting female figures.

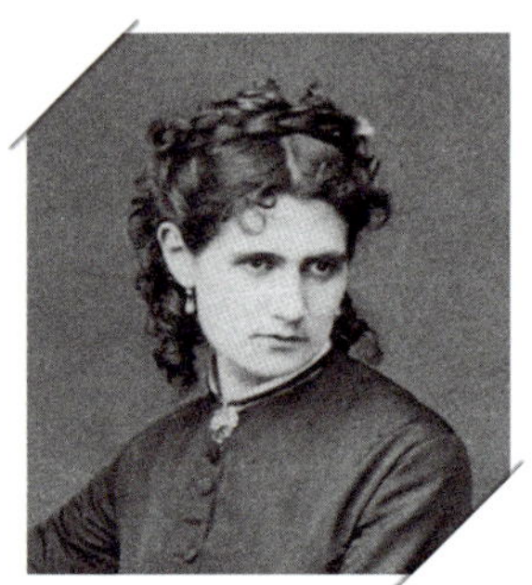

Man is a wolf to his fellow woman

Trained by Camille Corot, Morisot was supported by a cultured bourgeois family. Despite the audacity of her style, the artist navigated between affirmation and doubt. She struggled to attain recognition as a professional artist.

No time to wait

As a painter of the human figure, she told the tale of modernity in urban exteriors and bourgeois interiors. As time went by, her brushwork became increasingly spontaneous. She painted without waiting for layers to dry, scraping the material from her brush handle to create textured effects.

In between

Her art cultivated ambiguity, playing on the unfinished, the *"non finito"*. She depicted young women with absent or absorbed gazes. Her paintings bridged the gap between inside and outside, between intimacy and the public sphere.

A LUCID WOMAN

"I don't think there ever was a man who treated a woman as an equal, and that is all that I would have asked for, because I know that I am worth as much as they are," Berthe Morisot wrote in her diary in 1890.

Pierre-Auguste Renoir
Page 232

1841
Born in Bourges

1861
The construction of the Opéra Garnier began

1872
Painted *The Cradle*

1874
Première Exposition des Peintres Impressionnistes

1895
Died in Paris

Gustave Caillebotte
Page 236

THE CRADLE ↗

1872
Oil on canvas
56 × 46.5 cm
Musée d'Orsay, Paris

WHAT ARE WE LOOKING AT?

Morisot portrayed her sister, leaning on her child's cradle. The young woman's attitude is ambiguous, between contemplation and melancholy.

Lifting the veil on intimacy

The artist reveals a private moment, painting her sister Edma Pontillon contemplating her child. The moment seems peaceful; the mother, with a protective gesture, holds the veil in her hand, creating a filter between the child and the viewer.

Postpartum depression?

Celebrated as an exaltation of motherhood, this image nonetheless causes doubt. Edma's attitude is melancholic; her chin rests on her hand and her gaze is lost in emptiness.

Life choices

The scene is all the more ambiguous when one knows that both sisters followed opposite paths: while they were both artists, Edma gave up painting after marrying, while Morisot remained single for a long time and never stopped painting.

In the starting blocks

Painted in 1872, two years before the first Impressionist Exhibition, this work already bears the hallmark of the aesthetic revolution to come. However, Morisot's touch still remains too orthodox. She failed to adopt the free-form and unfinished manner that characterised her later works.

Transparency by transparency

The work is very well finished, and the artist's delicate touch allows her to reflect the gentleness and the comfort of the moment. The painter has wonderfully worked the glaze, enabling her to render the transparency of the curtain and shades of white tinged with pink, yellow and blue.

MORISOT'S WORK IN FIGURES

The artist was distinguished in all fields, and while she produced some fine landscape paintings, figures largely dominate her work.

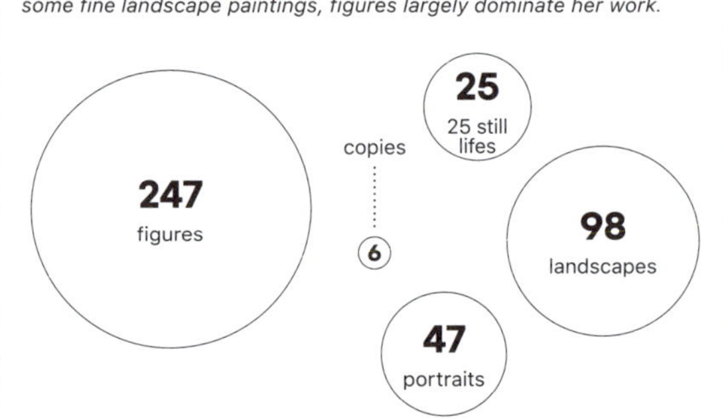

OTHER RENOWNED IMPRESSIONIST PAINTERS

- Éva Gonzalès (1849–1883). A pupil of Manet, she painted the bourgeois society.
- Mary Cassatt (1844–1926) produced touching portraits of mothers and children.
- Marie Bracquemond (1840–1916). A pupil of Ingres, she also worked in ceramics.

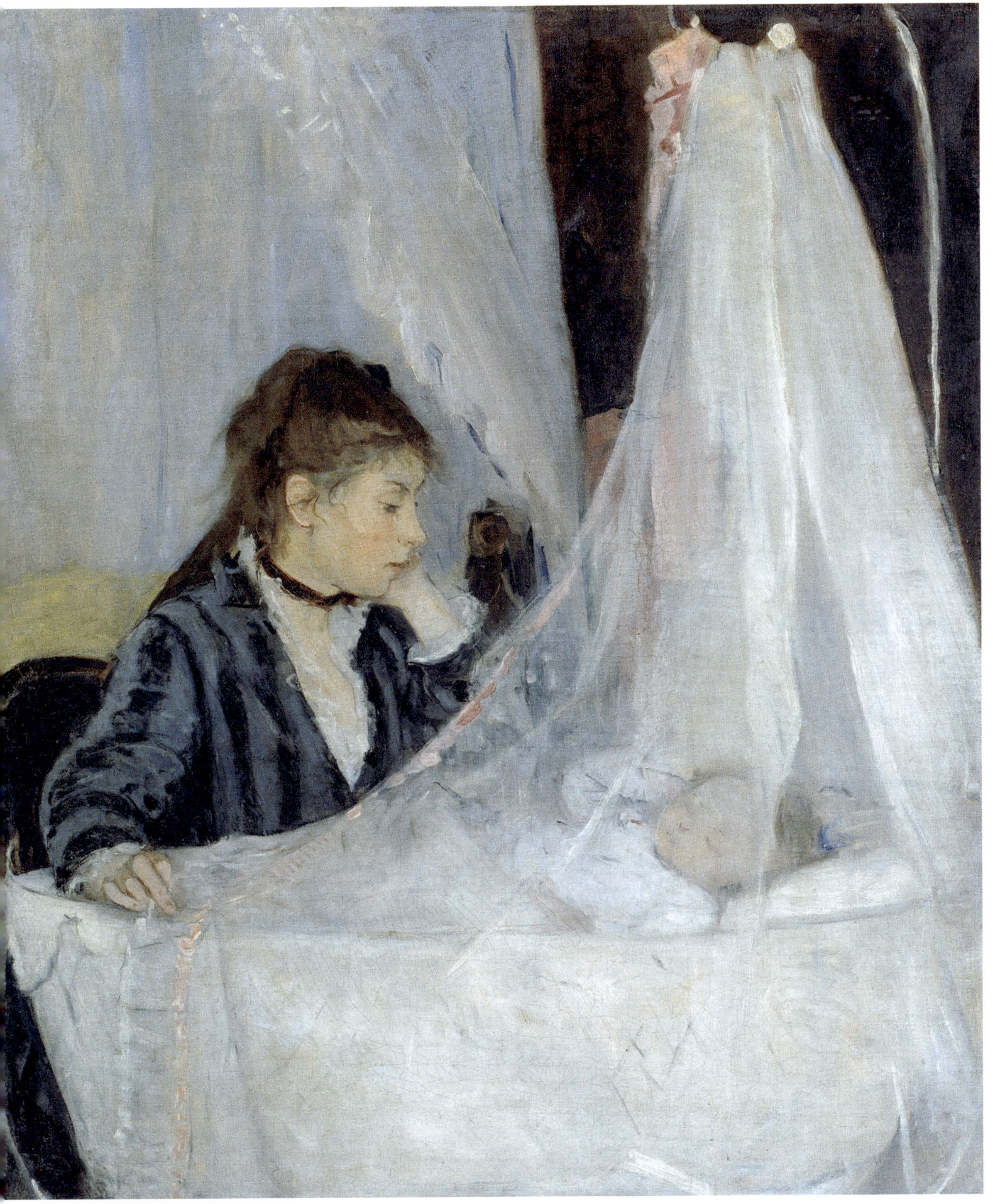

Gustave Caillebotte

The gentleman artist

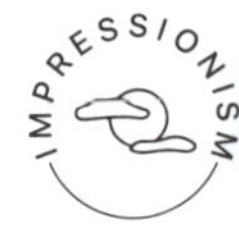

Caillebotte was primarily known as a patron of the arts; yet he exhibited alongside the Impressionists. His works accurately render the atmosphere of the Parisian streets. He was very close to his brother Martial, a photographer.

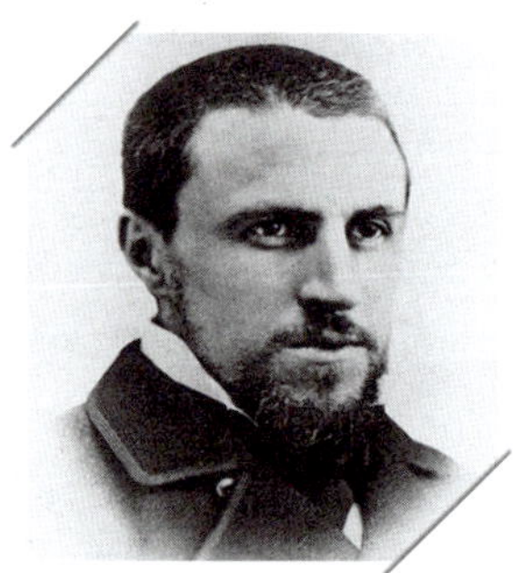

Curious by nature

Caillebotte was born into an affluent family; he received a solid education and enjoyed many hobbies, such as boating and gardening. His interest in art was reflected in his own paintings, but also in his collection and his activities, as a patron of the arts.

Crossroads

He attended Léon Bonnat's studio and the Beaux-Arts, but preferred the company of the Impressionists, who invited him to participate in their second exhibition. His work received positive attention.

Art in the street

Like his friends, Caillebotte painted modern life – particularly street scenes, as viewed from balconies or from the pavement, to better capture the attitudes of passers-by. His views and perspectives are remarkable. His passions for horticulture and canoeing are reflected in his paintings.

JACQUES CAILLEBOTTE SAID

"So, four Impressionists set themselves the task of reproducing Paris. Monsieur Caillebotte chose the street; Monsieur Renoir, the ball; Monsieur Degas, the theatre and the café concert; and Madame Berthe Morizot [*sic*], the boudoir," summarised the critic Jacques Caillebotte in 1877.

Berthe Morisot
Page 234

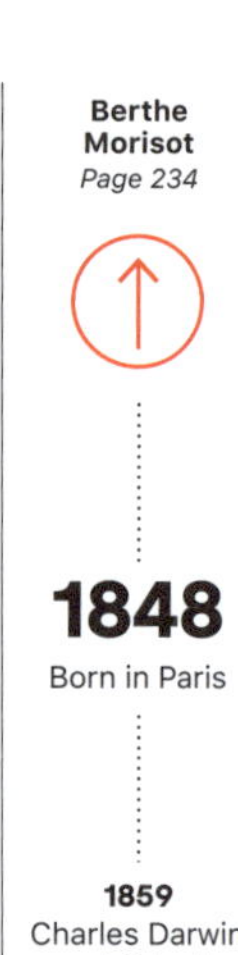

1848
Born in Paris

1859
Charles Darwin published his theory of evolution

1877
Painted *Paris Street; Rainy Day*

1894
Died in Gennevilliers

1896
First edition of the modern Olympic Games in Athens

Georges Seurat
Page 238

PARIS STREET; RAINY DAY

1877
Oil on canvas
212.2 × 276.2 cm
Art Institute, Chicago

WHAT ARE WE LOOKING AT?

This view of Paris, where the rain produced reflections on the pavement, is one of the painter's masterpieces, demonstrating the originality of his approach of the city and its modernity.

The best of both worlds

The rigorous construction and detailed drawing defy classification. Caillebotte embraced the very fine style of academic painting, but borrowed the novelty of the subject from Impressionism.

Careful, works in progress

The painter depicted the modernity of Paris after its transformation by Baron Haussmann. The regular rhythm of the architecture, the cobblestones lining the ground and the anonymous figures under their umbrellas denote a certain monotony that the prefect's detractors would complain about.

Zoom in

The image is divided in two by the streetlight. On one side, the wide image reveals perspectives that grow narrower as the viewer's gaze moves towards the horizon. On the other side, the close-up scene produces a magnifying glass effect. The left-hand section of the painting is relatively empty, while the other side is crowded.

A nice district

Only the figures in the right foreground are showing their faces. Visibly belonging to a well-to-do class, they set the social tone for this street, which is part of a new district elected by the bourgeoisie.

Look ahead!

Some small details disturb the scene's tranquillity. On the right, the passer-by is tilting his umbrella to avoid the collision that the viewer will soon witness, as the couple's attention is focused on an event taking place beyond the frame. Behind him, the man staring at the ground is about to bump into the lamppost, while the legs sticking out from under his umbrella produce an amusing effect.

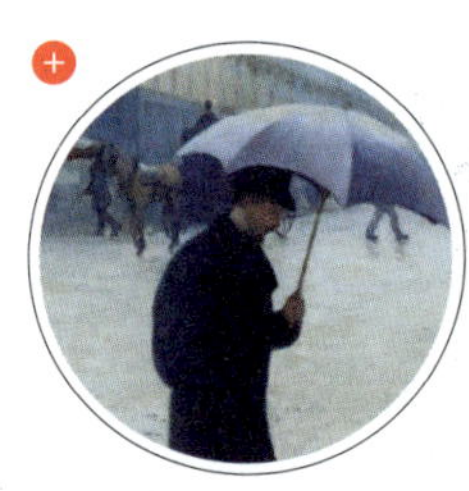

A HARSH SELECTION PROCESS

Caillebotte bequeathed his collection to France after his death, with the obligation to exhibit it. Faced with this requirement, the French State, in agreement with Renoir, his executor, selected 40 paintings, including masterpieces by Claude Monet, Paul Cézanne and Camille Pissarro. These paintings are now exhibited at the Musée d'Orsay.

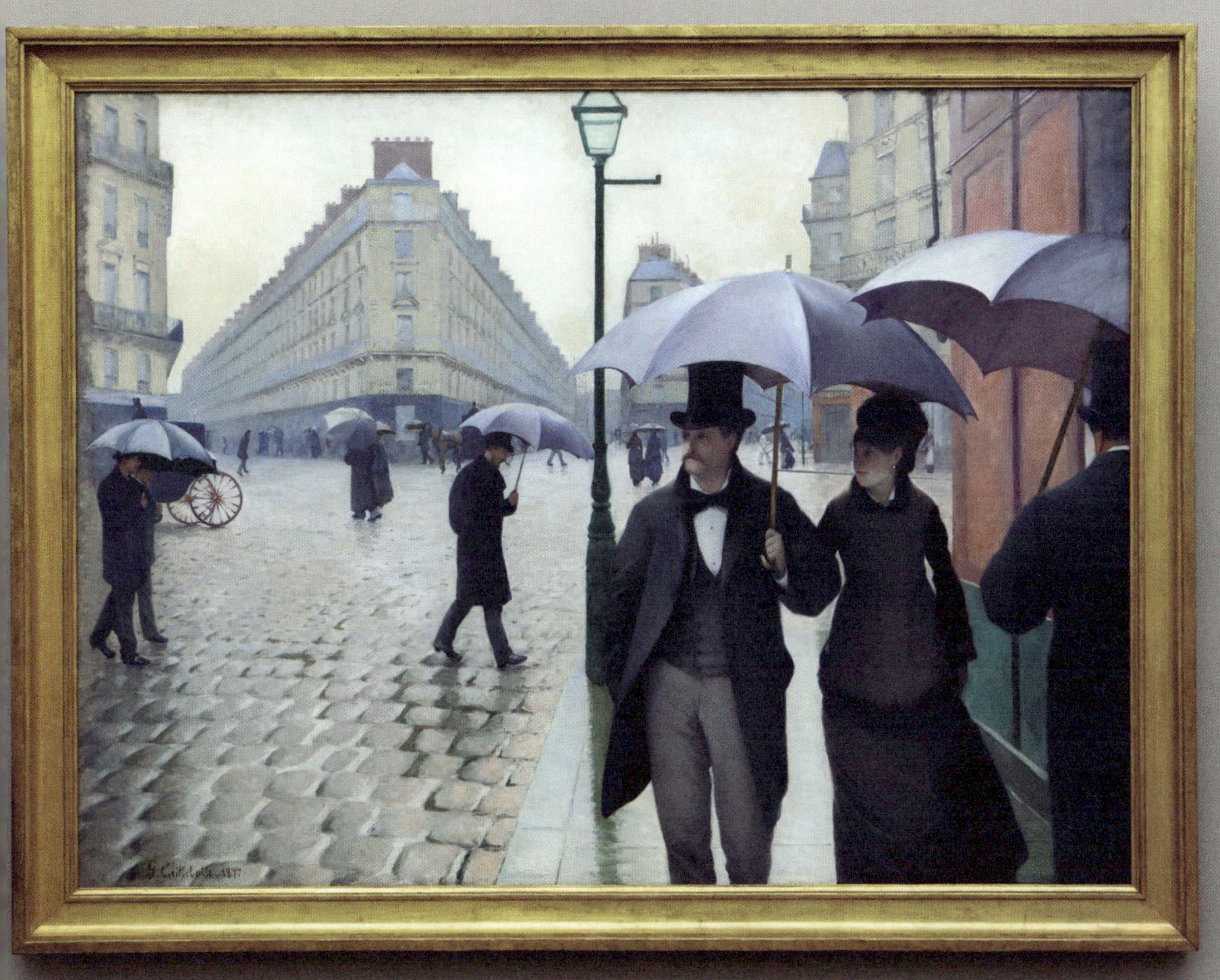

Georges Seurat

Punctilious and efficient

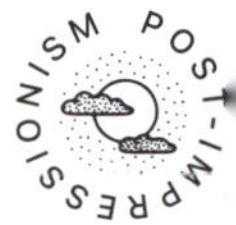

Seurat had a very short career, during which he demonstrated his great drawing skills. He devised the principle of colour division, which gave rise to the Neo-Impressionist movement.

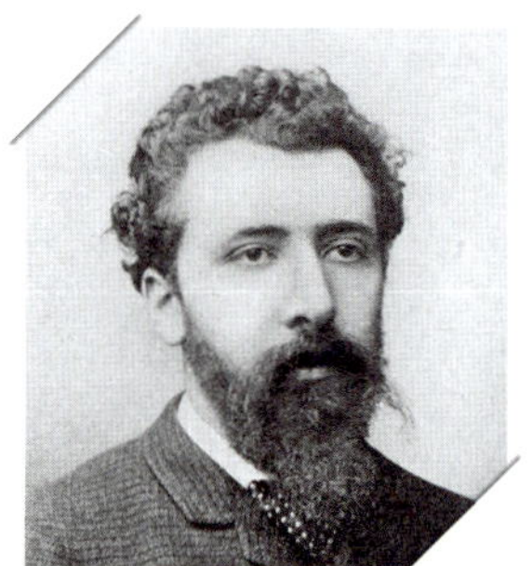

Solid drawing technique

Seurat was one of the greatest illustrators of the 19th century. He learned the rudiments of drawing at the municipal school, copied the old masters and confirmed this talent at the Beaux-Arts, in Henri Lehmann's studio, where he swiftly honed his skills.

Selected references

He embraced modernity and colour. The artist painted genre scenes and landscapes, like the Barbizon artists, but also riverbanks in the Parisian suburbs, like the Impressionists. Rejected at the Salon (p. 220), he joined the Société des Artistes Indépendants, where he met his friend Paul Signac.

A whole science

Studying treatises on colour, he approached painting from a scientific perspective that was sometimes caricatured. Although he adopted a disciplined and systematic method, this pointillist approach was also the expression of a highly personal creativity.

BRIEF, BUT INTENSE

Seurat died at the age of 31, and did not have time to convince detractors of his art.
In the ten years of his career, however, he produced over 240 paintings and hundreds of drawings.

Gustave Caillebotte
Page 236

1859
Born in Paris

1882
Alphonse Bertillon founded the first police laboratory dedicated to criminal identification

1890
Painted *The Channel at Gravelines, Evening*

1891
Died in Paris

Paul Cézanne
Page 242

THE CHANNEL AT GRAVELINES, EVENING

1890
Oil on canvas
65.4 × 81.9 cm
MoMA, New York

WHAT ARE WE LOOKING AT?

This stylised landscape, devoid of depth, allows the painter to carry out a plastic experiment. However, it also conveys a certain melancholy, fed by the paleness of the colours.

A trendy destination

From 1886 onwards, Seurat spent his summers by the sea, in Normandy. This would be an opportunity for him to paint seascapes, following a long pictorial tradition, from Vernet to the Impressionists. Like the latter, throughout these months spent painting at the location, he sought to capture the effects of light.

A change of course

During his stay in Gravelines, Seurat produced four paintings representing different moments of the day. Unlike the Impressionists, however, he did not seek to render nature through the prism of emotions; instead, he focused on a plastic experimentation based on shapes and colours.

Flattening

The composition is arranged in horizontal bands. The lamppost and the anchors, as vertical elements, form the junction between these different planes, reinforcing the absence of depth, reminiscent of Japanese prints. The pastel and lavender tones are reminiscent of the nocturnes by Whistler, a painter who also focused on formal research, and whom Seurat admired.

Is anyone there?

Despite the importance given to form, a certain melancholy still pervades this work. It is reinforced by the pale colours and the spread of long horizontal stripes, but also by the absence of any figures, while the street lamp, the boats and the anchors all evoke human activity. Seurat produced a calm and serene composition that is conducive to meditation.

A recomposed moment

True to his classical training, the painter has rendered the landscape authentically, but he has based this composition on drawings made at different times. Indeed, the buildings and the lamppost are part of the original setting, while the anchors and the boats belong to other studies.

OTHER LEADING FIGURES OF NEO-IMPRESSIONISM

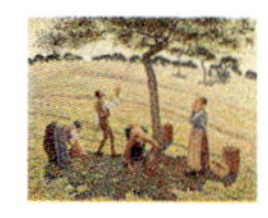

Camille Pissarro
Apple Picking at Éragny-sur-Epte, 1888
Dallas Museum of Art

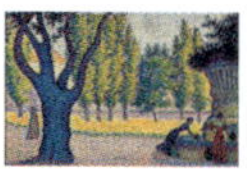

Paul Signac
Saint-Tropez, Fontaine des Lices, 1895
Guggenheim Museum, Bilbao

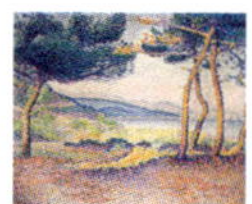

Henri Edmond Cross
Pines on the Coastline, 1896
Private collection

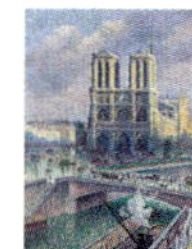

Maximilien Luce
Notre-Dame de Paris, 1900
Private collection

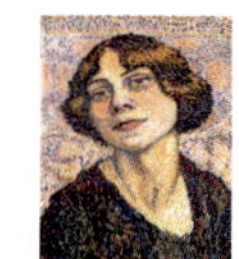

Lucie Cousturier
Self-portrait, 1905–1910
Indianapolis Museum of Art

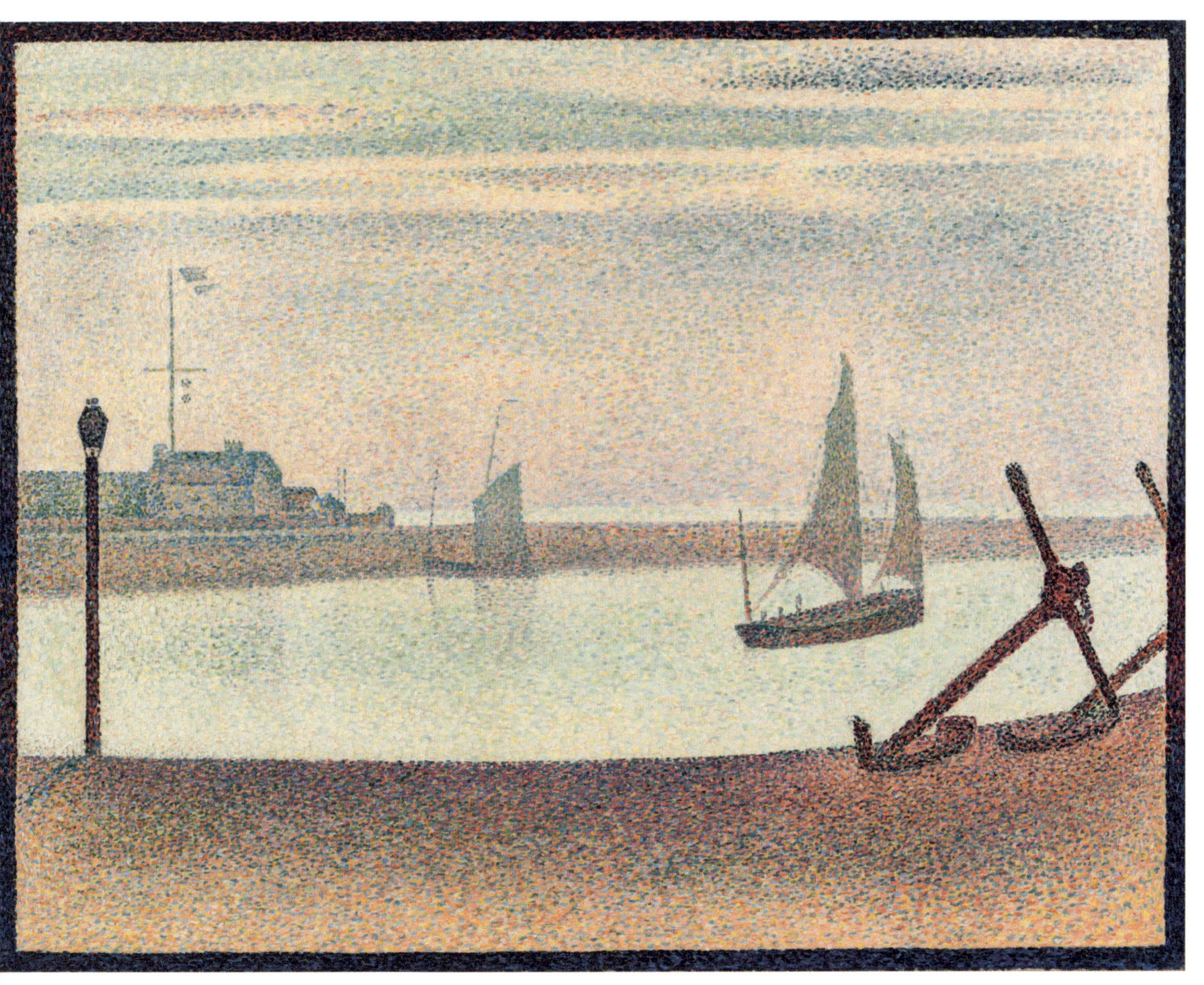

Neo-Impressionism

Also known as "pointillism", this movement was born in the mid-1880s, and consists in the application of pure colours in small strokes. The viewer's eye combines them into new shades, following the principle of optical mixing.

Anatomy of a painting

The chic underbelly of painting

Only the surface of the painting is visible to the viewer; other layers are present behind the paint layer, however. Although they are undetectable to the untrained eye, from the material of the support to the state of the varnish and the preparatory layer, these elements can influence the work's final appearance.

Three common supports

Most paintings in museums are painted on canvas. However, the oldest works are often painted on wood, a medium that has been used less frequently over the course of centuries. Some works in small formats are also painted on copper.

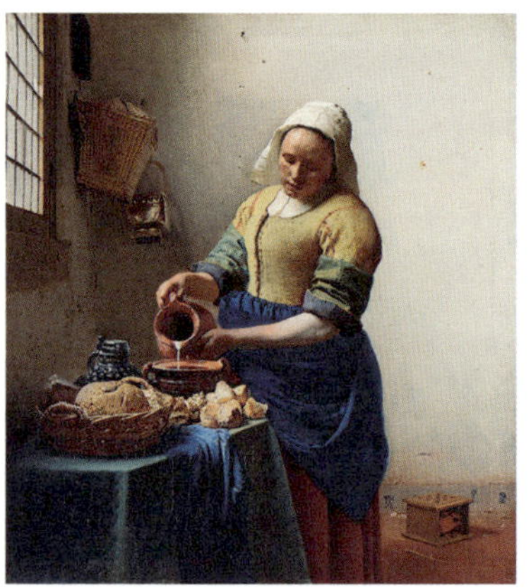

↑ **PAINTED ON CANVAS**

Johannes Vermeer
The Milkmaid,
1660, Rijksmuseum,
Amsterdam

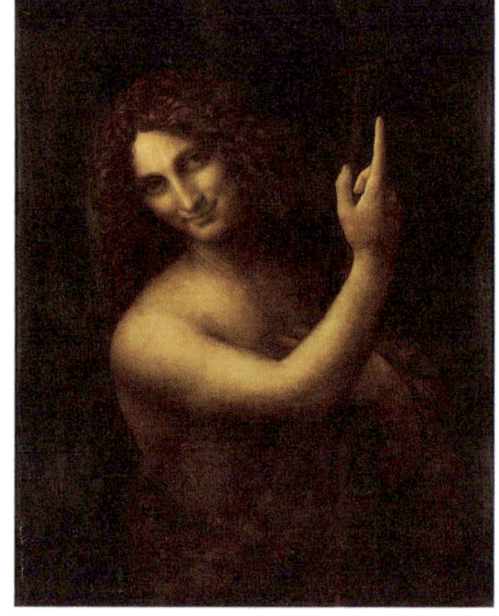

↑ **PAINTED ON WOOD**

Leonardo da Vinci
Saint John the Baptist,
1508–1519,
Louvre Museum, Paris

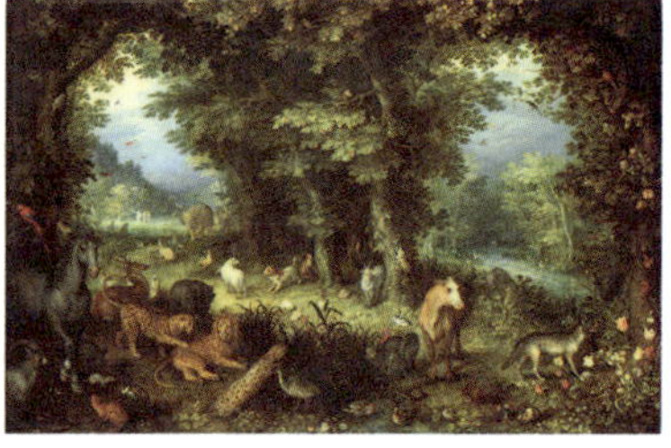

↑ **PAINTED ON COPPER**

Jan Brueghel the Elder
Earth or The Earthly Paradise,
1607–1608,
Louvre Museum, Paris

LEAVING THE BEATEN TRACK

Modern artists sometimes leave the undercoat or canvas visible. This was, for instance, a common practice for Berthe Morisot (p. 234). Paul Gauguin (p. 248), for lack of money, sometimes painted on jute canvas, the roughness of which is apparent under the paint.

LAST RESORT

Should the original support become too fragile, the paint layer can be transferred to a new support. This operation is referred to as a "transposition".

Well-ordered layers

①

The chassis

When the support used is canvas, it is usually fixed on a frame. The canvas's tension can be adjusted using "keys". These are small, bevelled pieces of wood that can be inserted to slightly spread the frame's uprights.

②

The support

Wood, canvas, copper, cardboard, ivory, glass and more: many supports are available. The most popular, however, remain wood and canvas. Wood was one of the first movable supports. Used since antiquity, it spread widely from the Italian Primitives (p. 20), who initiated the trend of easel painting. Canvas dominated from the 17th century onwards, but was already used as early as the 15th century.

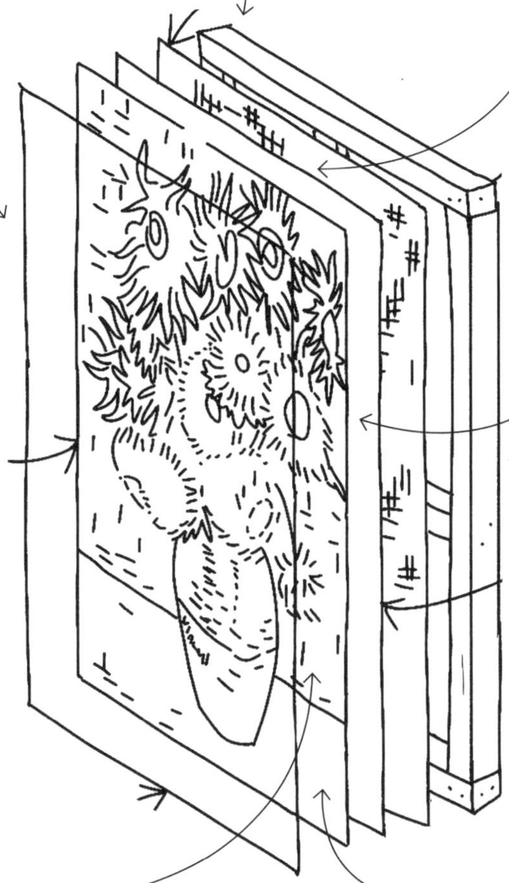

⑤

The varnish

Paintings can be varnished to protect them; however, this can be counterproductive. Indeed, applying additional coats of varnish to a work of art can make it turn yellow. Sometimes, mould can appear: these alterations of the varnish or the pictorial layer create an opacity, making the painting less visible. The work can then be restored (p. 299) in order to enhance its visibility, by thinning the coats of varnish.

③

The preparation layer

The artist does not paint directly on the canvas; they apply an undercoat, whose colour can influence the final result of the painting: Georgia O'Keeffe (p. 304) painted on a white undercoat to enhance the luminosity of her works. In contrast, Gustave Courbet (p. 198) prepared his canvases in black.

④

The brushwork

This is the trace left by the brush. It can be smooth or thickly textured ("impasto"), and can help to attribute an unsigned work to an artist. Raphael (p. 46) and David (p. 170) are known for their smooth, finished touch. On the contrary, Van Gogh (p. 246) is known for his use of impasto, which enhances his works with a three-dimensional appearance.

④

The paint layer

It is called "material" or "paint layer". The manner in which paint is applied to the canvas changes throughout the course of history, according to fashions, movements or painters. Most often, paint is applied using a brush or a knife.

Paul Cézanne

The antechamber of the Avant-Garde

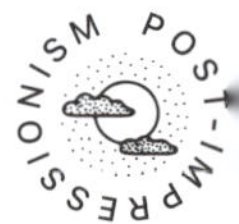

Born in Provence, where he was Émile Zola's classmate, Cézanne moved to the capital, where he met Auguste Renoir, Claude Monet and Camille Pissarro. Despite the criticism that he received and the rejection that he experienced, he left his mark on the history of art by paving the way for the 20th century modern artists.

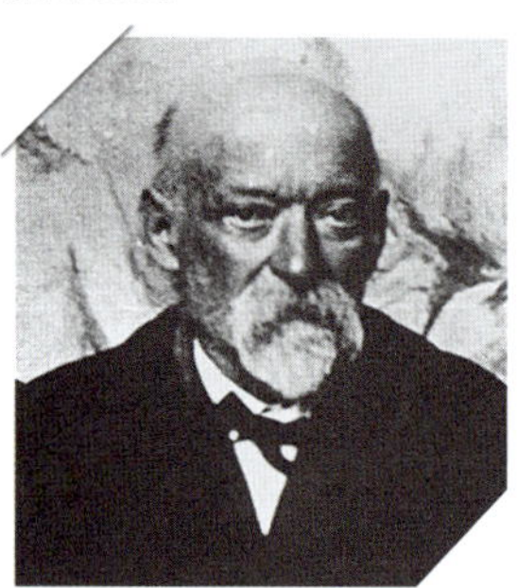

Classic, but not too classic

In his early years, Cézanne employed what he described as a "manière couillarde" (from the French word "couilles", meaning testicles), meaning a crude style. The brushstrokes are thick and dark, inspired by classical painting, particularly the Spanish masters. While he admired the great masters in the Louvre, he refused to accept Academism and associated himself with modern artists.

Directing good shots

From Impressionism, Cézanne retained a taste for light. In his homeland, he adopted a new way of painting, featuring rigorous constructions. He would describe his art as doing "Poussin all over from nature". He broke down landscapes into geometric colour planes, prefiguring cubism.

Volume equals colour

His still lifes were an opportunity for elaborate research, using colour, rather than light, to render volumes. His unstable compositions, featuring impossible perspectives, are one of his major inventions – lessons that the 20th century Modern artists would not forget.

PAUL CÉZANNE SAID

"With an apple, I will astonish Paris."

Georges Seurat
Page 238

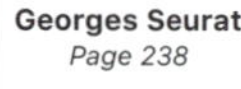

1839
Born in Aix-en-Provence

1848
Victor Schœlcher signed the abolition of slavery

Between **1888** and **1890**
Painted *Kitchen Table*

1889
Inauguration of the Eiffel Tower

1895
The screening of the first film took place: *Workers Leaving The Lumière Factory in Lyon*

1906
Died in Aix-en-Provence

Vincent Van Gogh
Page 246

KITCHEN TABLE ↗
(OR STILL LIFE WITH BASKET)

Between 1888 and 1890
65 × 81.5 cm
Oil on canvas
Musée d'Orsay, Paris

WHAT ARE WE LOOKING AT?

An admirer of Chardin, Cézanne joins a long pictorial tradition with this still life; however, this work's composition, with its imperfect geometry, makes it a precursor of modernity.

Geometry lesson

Cézanne said: "Treat nature by the cylinder, the sphere, the cone."
This is exactly the principle that he applied here. The pears have no tails, and are now shaped like cones; their volumes are rendered by colour. In the foreground, a yellow fruit has been transformed into an almost perfect sphere.

White on white

The white draperies grace this composition with a traditional allure, while also allowing Cézanne to play with shades by placing porcelain dishes on top of them. The shades of white overlap, but never merge. In the basket, on the contrary, the drapery enhances the blazing colours of the fruit.

On the move

While the subject may seem static, in this painting, it is not. The distorted perspective creates dynamism, and forces the viewer's gaze to move around the composition. The fruit in the foreground appears to be ready to roll to the ground, while the porcelain lids almost seem to be sliding off the pots. Further up, the viewer's gaze lingers on another round pot,

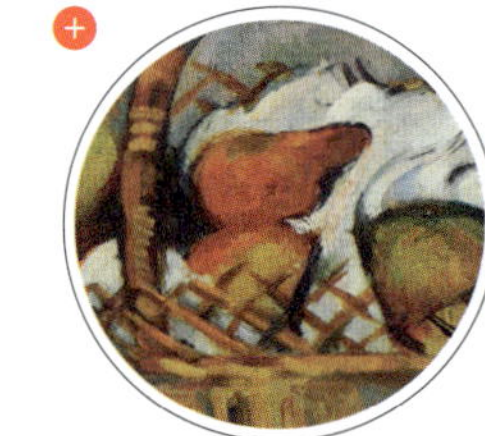

whose opening is excessively visible. The angle is too steep, while the basket next to it appears to have been observed from a lower point. In the background, a chair leg appears to be bending under an invisible weight.

IN CÉZANNE'S PAINTINGS, ONE CAN SEE ...

Like many artists, Cézanne produced series of motifs. Here are the most emblematic of his art.

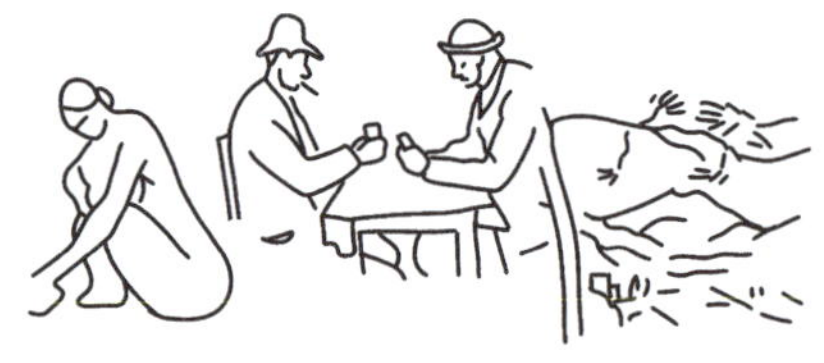

Bathers, male and female **Card players** **Representations of Montagne Sainte-Victoire**

POST-IMPRESSIONISM IN A NUTSHELL

- This term refers to artists who took part in an artistic explosion at the end of the 19th century.
- It defines a tendency, embraced by artists, to capitalise on the advances of Impressionism to conduct various formal experiments.

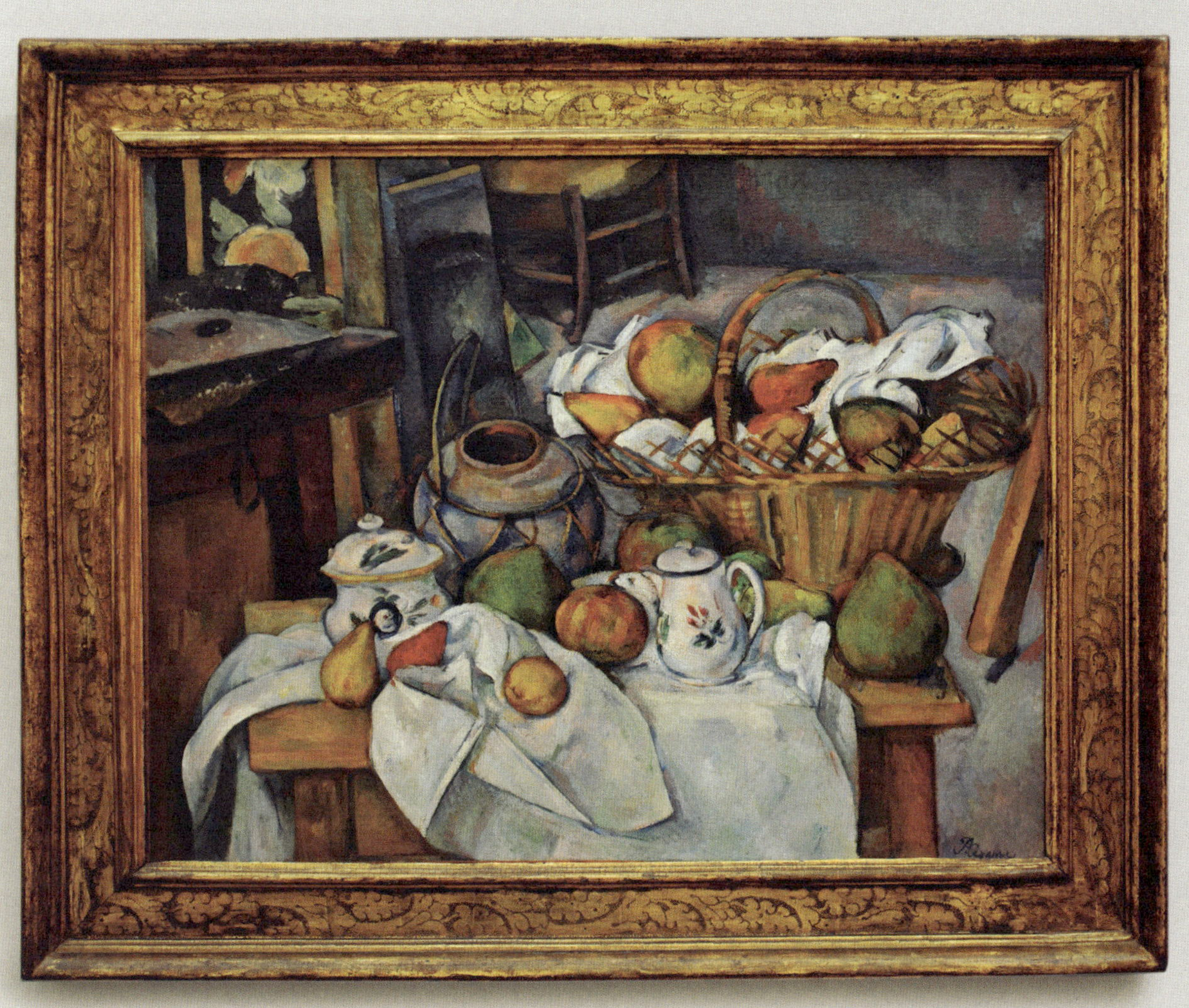

No quarters

Apples served with all manners of oils

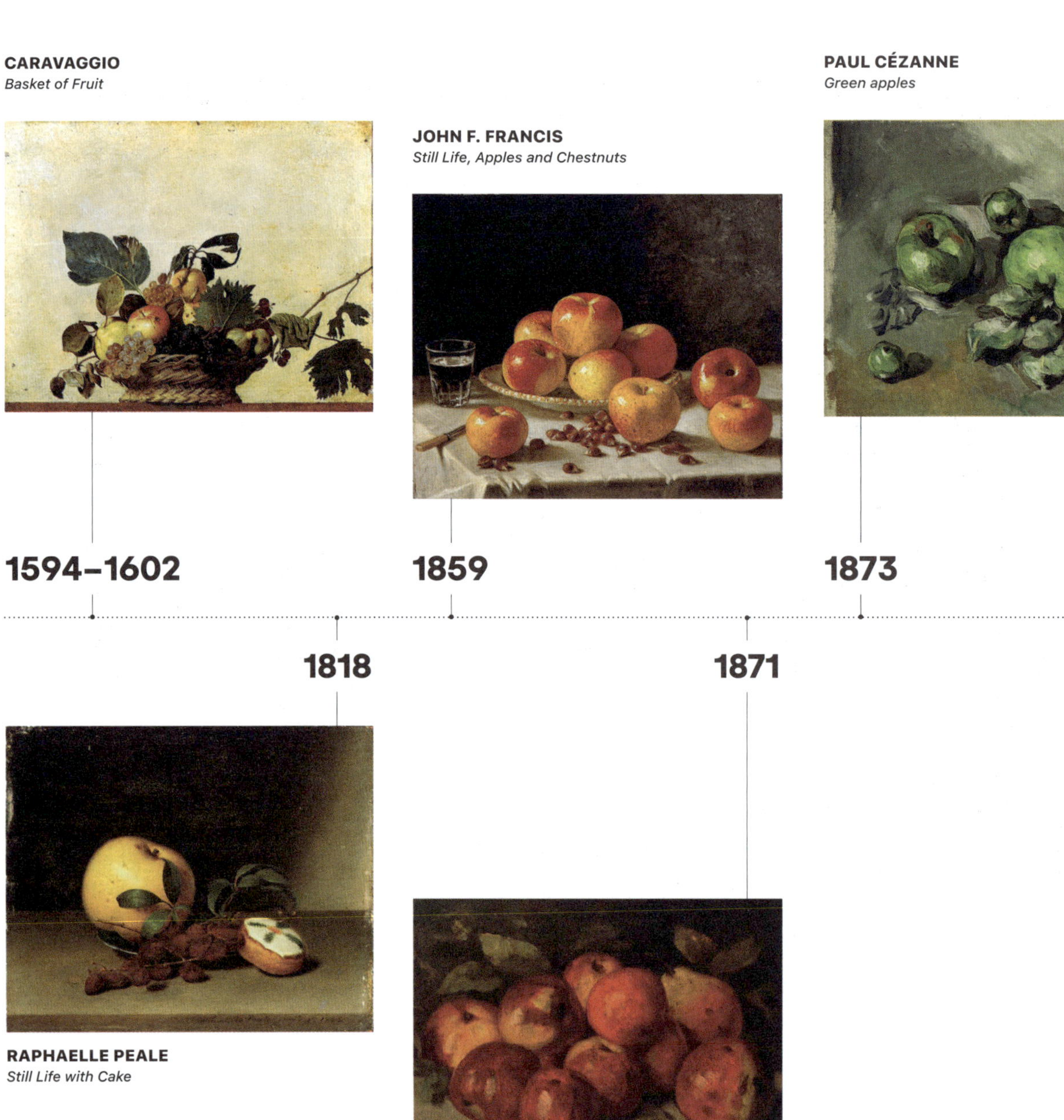

CARAVAGGIO
Basket of Fruit

1594–1602

1818

RAPHAELLE PEALE
Still Life with Cake

JOHN F. FRANCIS
Still Life, Apples and Chestnuts

1859

1871

GUTAVE COURBET
Still Life with Apples and a Pear

PAUL CÉZANNE
Green apples

1873

VINCENT VAN GOGH
Still Life with Apples

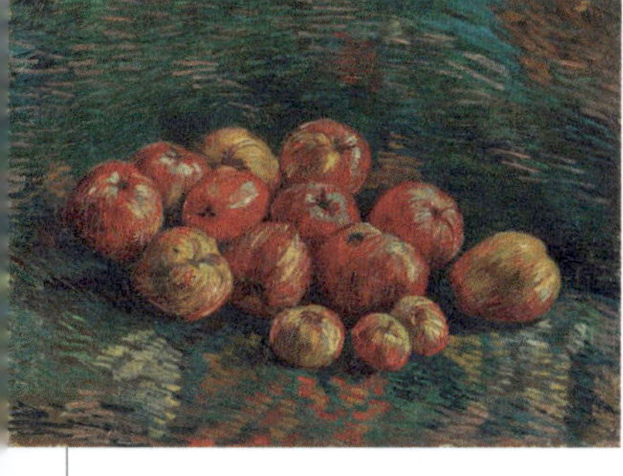

1887

1889

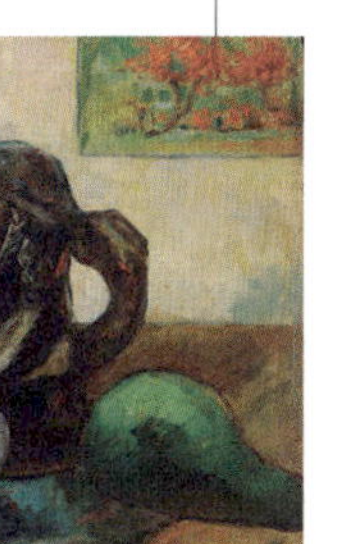

PAUL GAUGUIN
Still Life with Apples, a Pear, and a Ceramic Portrait Jug

ZINAIDA SEREBRIAKOVA
Apples on the Branches

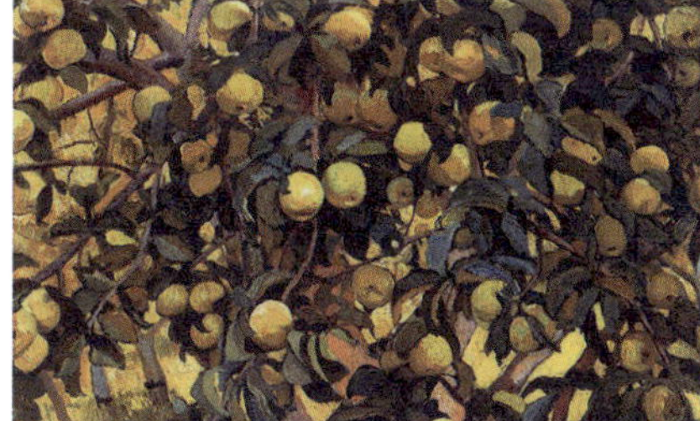

1910s

1910

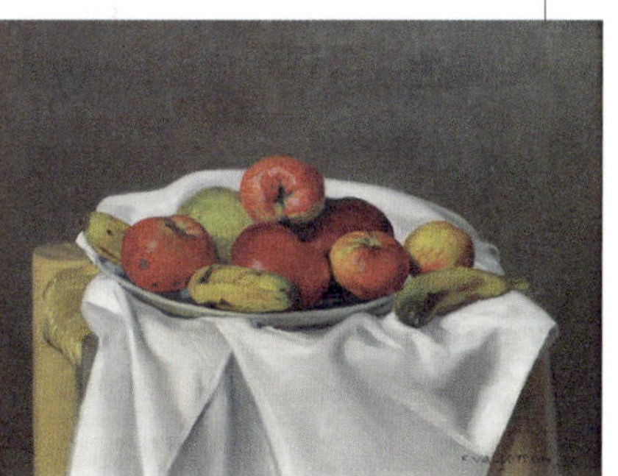

FÉLIX VALLOTTON
Still Life with Apples

JUAN GRIS
Apples

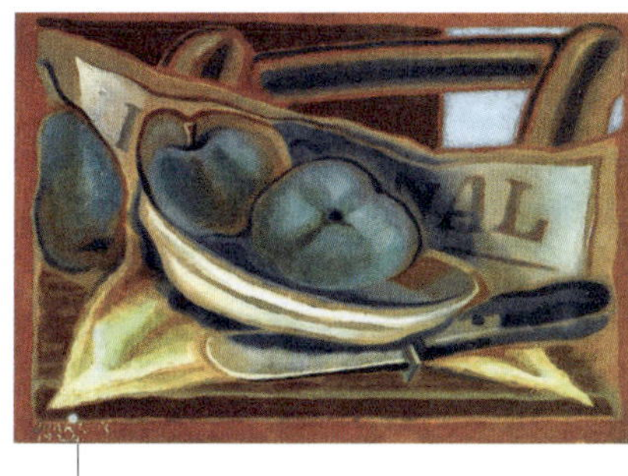

1924

Vincent Van Gogh

Thickening brushwork

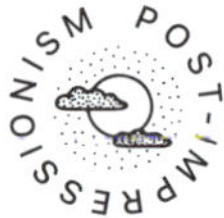

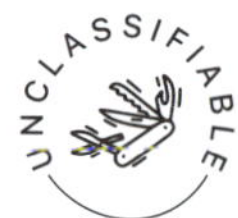

Van Gogh was one of the greatest artists of the Post-Impressionist movement. He learned from the Impressionists' achievements, cultivating a singular form of art in which he broke away from realism. Between his late calling and his premature death, Van Gogh's career was short-lived.

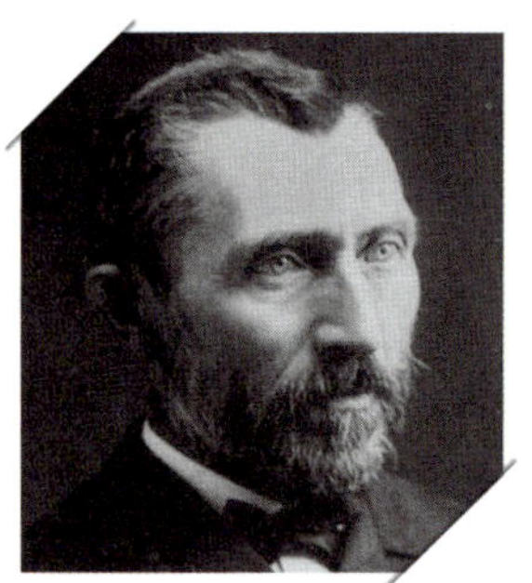

Late in life

Van Gogh decided to become an artist at the age of 27. After a disappointing experience at the Beaux-Arts, he learned watercolour and oil painting with Anton Mauve. He was particularly fond of drawing from live models.

His greatest fan

Throughout his life, the artist would be supported, morally and materially, by his brother Theo. Vincent joined Theo in Paris, where he discovered Impressionism and its developments, such as pointillism (p. 239). He remained in France until the end of his life, between Arles and Auvers-sur-Oise.

Generously applied

The artist detached himself from the necessity to transcribe reality. His brushwork became thicker as he used impasto, producing an almost three-dimensional effect on the canvas. His technique gave rhythm to his landscapes, composed of moving forms, while his colours were vivid, featuring deep blues, with strident or warm yellow and green hues.

DUE DATE

Psychologically unstable, Van Gogh died prematurely in circumstances that remain unclear today, joining the list of great painters that passed at the age of 37, like Raphael, Caravaggio, Antoine Watteau and Henri de Toulouse-Lautrec.

Paul Cézanne
Page 242

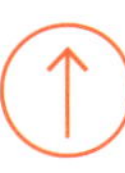

1853
Born in Groot-Zundert

1857
Flaubert was taken to court following the publication of *Madame Bovary*

1889
Painted *The Starry Night*

1890
Died in Auvers-sur-Oise

1898
Émile Zola's article "J'accuse" was published on the front page of *L'Aurore*

Paul Gauguin
Page 248

THE STARRY NIGHT ↗

1889
Oil on canvas
73.7 × 92.1 cm
MoMA, New York

WHAT ARE WE LOOKING AT?

This is one of Van Gogh's greatest masterpieces. However, if we are to believe the letters written to his brother Theo, this was a simple sketch, inspired by the view from his room.

Convalescence with a view

Van Gogh painted this work in Saint-Rémy-de-Provence, where he was interned to treat his mental illness. He was inspired by the view from his room, which he reinterpreted, as the village was not visible from his window.

A long story

In his correspondence, Van Gogh evoked his fascination for the night, which he inherited from the masters who preceded him, and whom he admired: the Dutch landscape painters of the 17th century or the Barbizon artists, such as Camille Corot and Jean-François Millet (p. 202).

A little closer to the stars

The painter has freed himself from realism. Although the sky is full of celestial waves, one can see Venus, just to the right of the cypress tree, and the moon, in the corner of the canvas. Van Gogh haloes the celestial bodies with an artificial glow, which contributes to the enchanting appearance of the night.

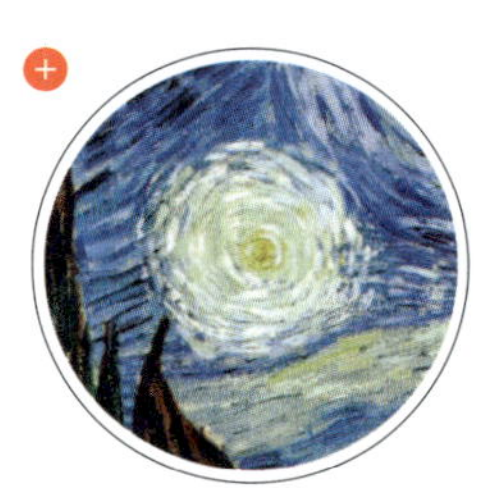

Saved as a draft

This work is now one of the artist's best-known paintings; an unexpected turn of events, as in his letters, he mentioned a "study of the night" to his brother Theo. It was probably made without any preparatory drawings, and the painter even left the canvas visible in places.

VAN GOGH'S LETTERS IN NUMBERS

Van Gogh wrote many letters to his family, most of which are now kept in the Van Gogh Museum in Amsterdam.

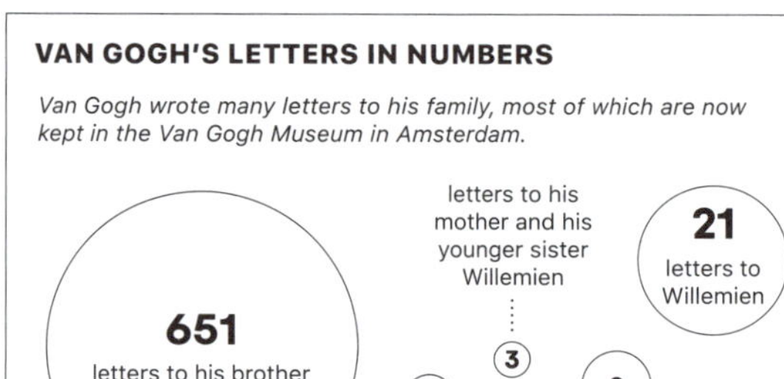

HOUSE-SHARING GONE WRONG

In 1888, Paul Gauguin joined Van Gogh in Arles, but the relationship between the two artists turned sour. During a violent argument, Vincent had a fit of dementia and cut off part of his ear, which he offered to a prostitute. Following this event, he decided to be hospitalised.

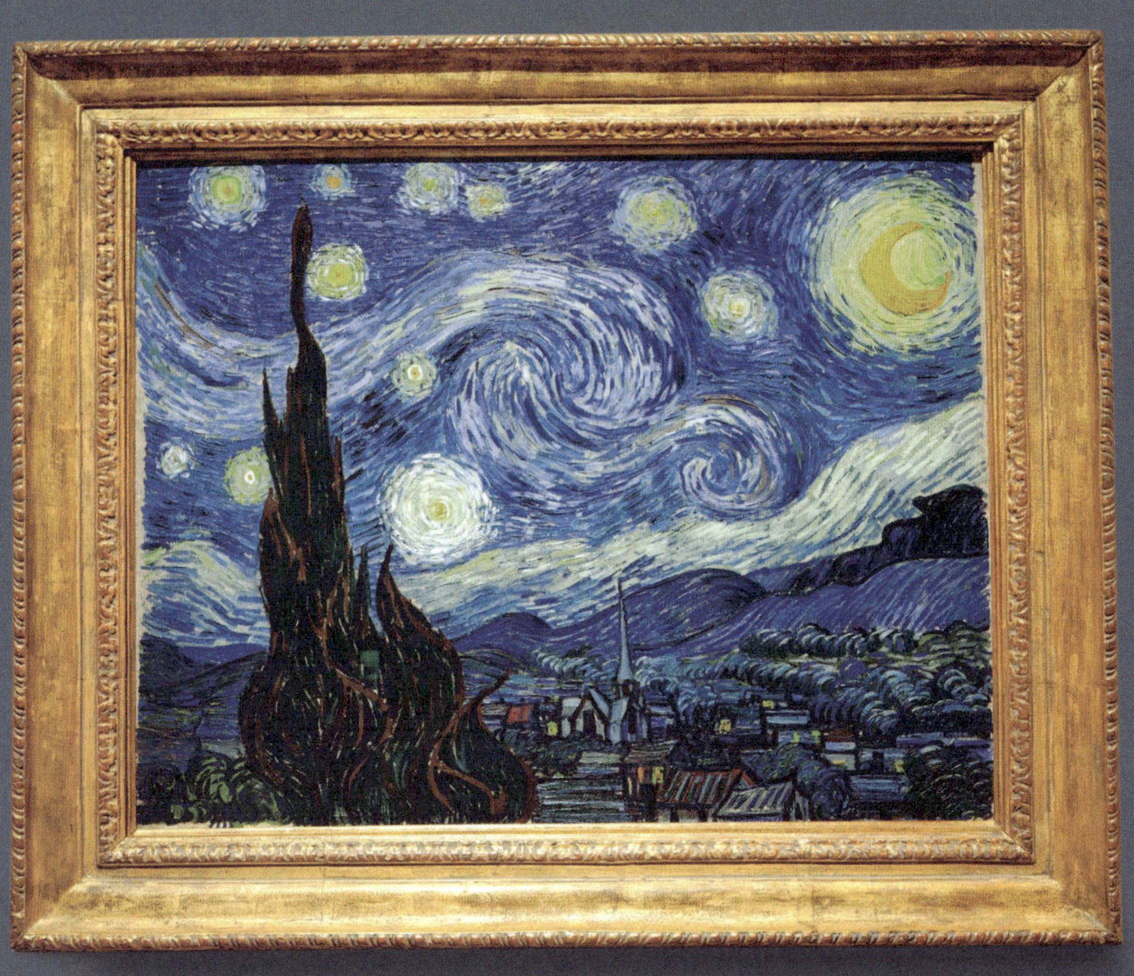

Paul Gauguin

Wanderlust

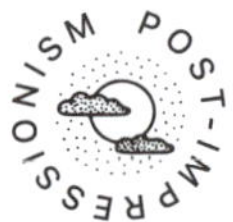

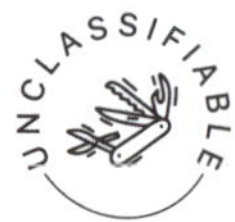

A tortured painter who fled to Polynesia to escape Western civilisation, Gauguin was artistically nourished by his travels. His works are filled with mysticism and the promise of unknown landscapes. With Gauguin, painting truly became a territory for experimentation.

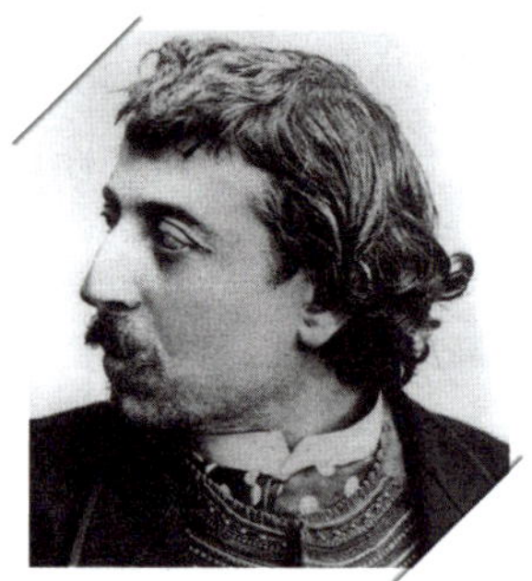

Weekend painter

Gauguin first practised painting as a hobby. He also learned modelling. He met Camille Pissarro, who likely influenced his artistic aspirations, and then Paul Cézanne. He collected works by the Impressionists, alongside whom he exhibited.

An invitation to travel

Gauguin grew up in Peru, and joined the Merchant Navy. He was an insatiable traveller, who roamed the world from Copenhagen to Panamá. His travels forged his visual culture. He was inspired by antiquity and by classical painting, as well as by his non-Western discoveries.

Calculated risks

He created a form of art based on borrowing, experimentation and accidental discoveries, between hesitations and brilliant intuitions. He liked to paint on rough surfaces, which gave his works a distinctive appearance. His daring use of colour left its mark on painting, and paved the way for the Avant-Garde.

PAUL GAUGUIN SAID

"Nothing so resembles a daub as a masterpiece."

Vincent Van Gogh
Page 246

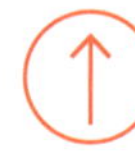

1848
Born in Paris

1879
Thomas Edison invented the first electric light bulb

1891
Painted *Tahitian Women on the Beach*

1903
Died in Hiva Oa, Marquesas Islands

1906
Proust began writing *In Search of Lost Time*

Félix Vallotton
Page 250

TAHITIAN WOMEN ON THE BEACH ↗

1891
Oil on canvas
69 × 91.5 cm
Musée d'Orsay, Paris

WHAT ARE WE LOOKING AT?

**Very recently arrived on the island, with this painting, Gauguin displayed all the enthusiasm and fascination that he felt for the Tahitians.
He was intrigued by the calm and mystery that surround them.**

Zen retreat

In 1891, Gauguin landed in Tahiti. He sought to escape Western civilisation and to return to the sources of creation, far from the official art that was fashionable in Paris. There, he mingled with the inhabitants, and was fascinated by their serenity. This work was given to a ship's captain, who commissioned the painter to paint a portrait of his wife, which Gauguin never delivered.

Genuine goddesses

The young women's peaceful demeanour is also tinged with a certain enigmatic melancholy, which testifies to the artist's still unsatisfied curiosity for the people that he was discovering. Through the tight framing, the two figures, who are not communicating with each other, become monumental and sacred, isolated from the outside world.

Mismatched pareos

The sadness that could pervade this scene is countered by the vivid palette. The women are sitting on a terrace, probably made of wood; the direction of the slats is depicted discreetly in the background. The yellow tones contrast with the dark blue, producing an audacious harmony with the young women's pink and red clothes.

Shirtless

The very chaste pink dress is a reminder of the presence of Protestant missionaries on the island; in *Parau Api*, a second version of this work, the painter replaced it with a black and yellow pareo.
He also transposed this motif into a larger composition, entitled *Te Fare Hymenee*.

THE PONT-AVEN SCHOOL

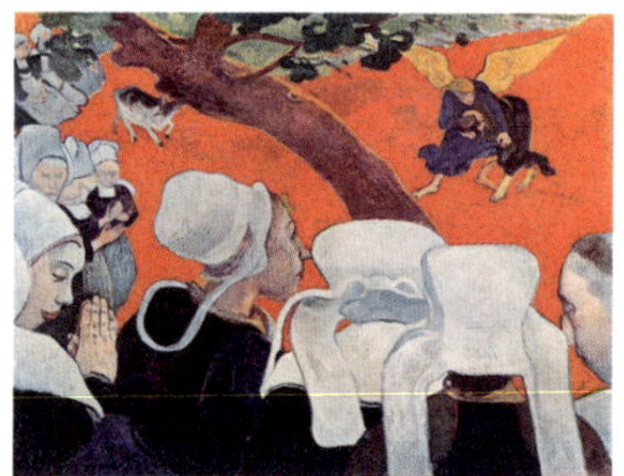

Vision after the Sermon, 1888
National Gallery of Scotland, Edinburgh

Gauguin's career briefly led him to Brittany, where he joined the colony of local artists who formed the Pont-Aven School. They were influenced by the spiritual and religious atmosphere of rural Brittany, which remained, at the time, relatively untouched by technical progress.

AWARENESS

How should one exhibit Gauguin in the 21st century? Between the colonialist vision and the sexualisation of young girls, the artist's work raises questions at a time when consciences are awakening. An increasing number of cultural institutions throughout the world are taking up these issues, in order to provide context to his work.

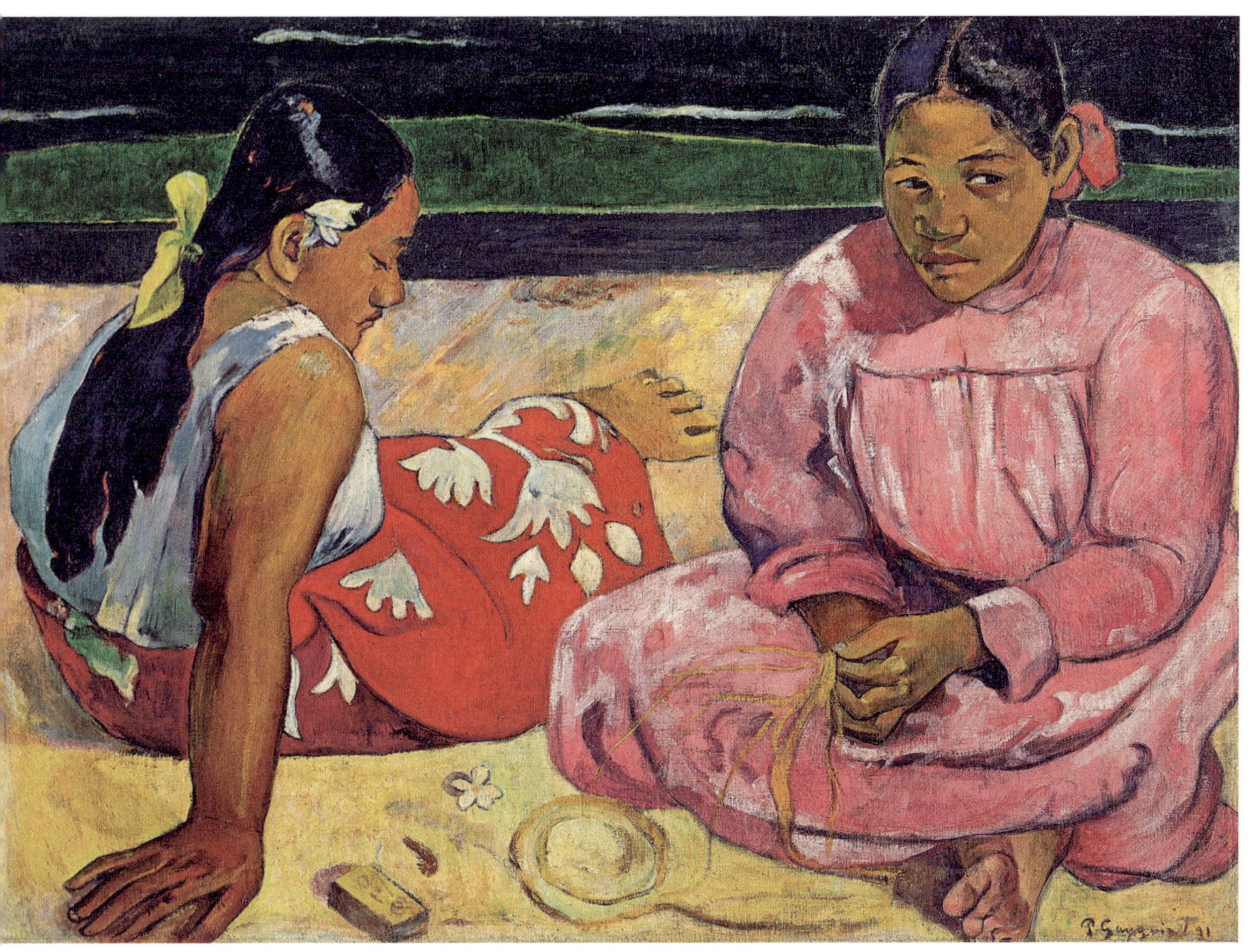

Paradises forever lost

Despite his travels and his constant thirst for change, Gauguin was tormented by depression. In Tahiti, instead of the idyllic land he had hoped for, he experienced new disappointments, and found himself in conflict with the local authorities. Ill and alcoholic, he passed away at the age of 55.

Félix Vallotton

Silences that speak volumes

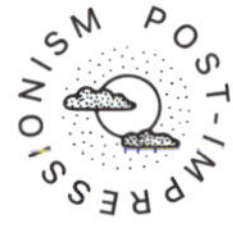

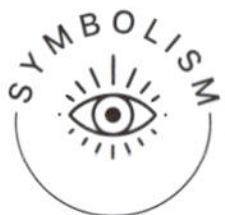

Vallotton, a Swiss native who became a French citizen, was a talented engraver and a multifaceted painter. He marked his time with his unclassifiable works, in which a silent battle of the sexes, tinged with misogyny, played out in cold atmospheres.

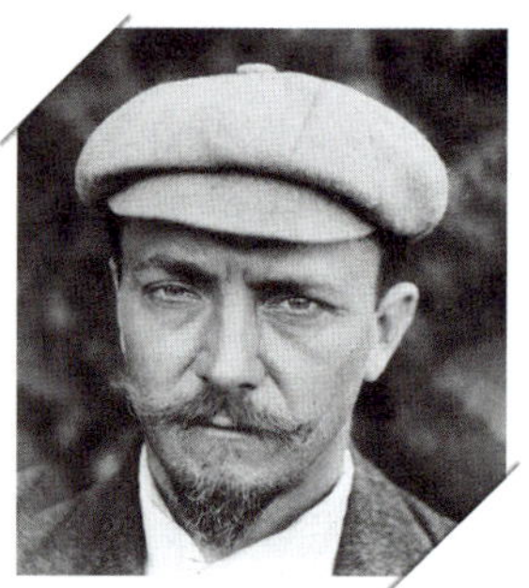

In the capital

Vallotton produced his first paintings as a teenager. At the age of 17, he moved to Paris to train at the Académie Julian. He first earned a modest living taking commissions, while also exhibiting in the salons. His works were noticed by the Nabis group, which he joined.

Digging his own furrow

A writer, an art critic and a press illustrator, the artist had many strings to his bow; above all, however, his works as a wood engraver would earn him great recognition. He practised this discipline all his life, with great talent.

Bourgeois dramas

Vallotton combined precise drawing with a choice of subtle colours, producing works infused with great plasticity, in which perspectives clashed with flat coloured tints. The artist painted strange and muffled atmospheres, where complex relationships between men and women were formed.

THE AWARENESS OF BEING AN ARTIST

At his first exhibition in 1885, Vallotton began his "Livre de raison", a catalogue raisonné of his works, in which he carefully described each one.

Paul Gauguin
Page 248

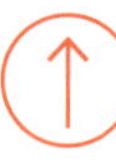

1865
Born in Lausanne

1871
The Commune of Paris

1909
Painted *Box Seats at the Theatre, the Gentleman and the Lady*

1909
Robert Peary became the first man to reach the North Pole

1925
Died in Paris

Edvard Munch
Page 252

BOX SEATS AT THE THEATRE, THE GENTLEMAN AND THE LADY

1909
Oil on canvas
46 × 38 cm
Private collection

WHAT ARE WE LOOKING AT?

Between the mystery of the scene being played out and the combination of coloured flat tints, this work bears witness to Vallotton's qualities as a painter, both for his intellectual approach and his plastic rendering.

A crowded balcony

Although there is little information available, the edge of the wall on which the woman's hand is resting and the dark background indicate that the couple, who are barely visible, are sitting in a theatre box.

Zoom in

Félix Vallotton cleverly places the viewer in a low-angle position, suggesting an exchange of glances that takes place between boxes. However, the viewer appears to be too close to the box's edge, as if they were observing the scene through binoculars. With this close framing, Vallotton was able to emphasise the coloured flat tints, positioning himself as a precursor of conceptual painters such as Rothko (p. 308).

In a velvet case

This low-angle view also preserves the mystery of the scene unfolding before the spectator's eyes. True to his habits, the painter has recreated a hushed atmosphere, in which a silent, tension-filled relationship seems to be playing out, highlighted by the acidity of the yellow tint.

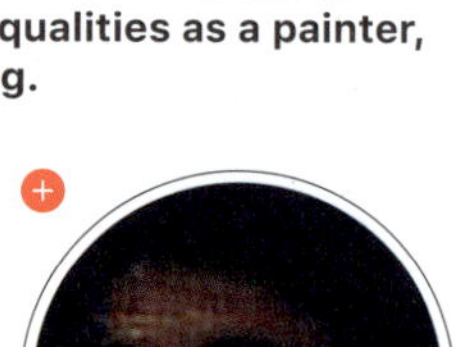

A black look

The man's face, cut off, deprives him of a mouth that would complete his expression and perhaps lift the mystery. Here, only his eyes, which are left in shadow, are discernible, framed by hair that is almost as black as the background.

A shadow of a doubt

The woman's head is fully visible, but barely sketched, and overshadowed by her large hat. Her expression is every bit as enigmatic: is it a shadow, or is a tear flowing down her face? Is she moved by the show playing out before her eyes, or rather by the exchange taking place inside the theatre box?

WHO WERE THE NABIS?

- *Nabis*, in Hebrew, means "prophets".
- These young artists advocated art for the sake of art, beauty in things mundane.
- They abolished the boundaries between the so-called noble disciplines and the decorative arts.
- They gave each other nicknames; Vallotton was the "Foreign Nabi".

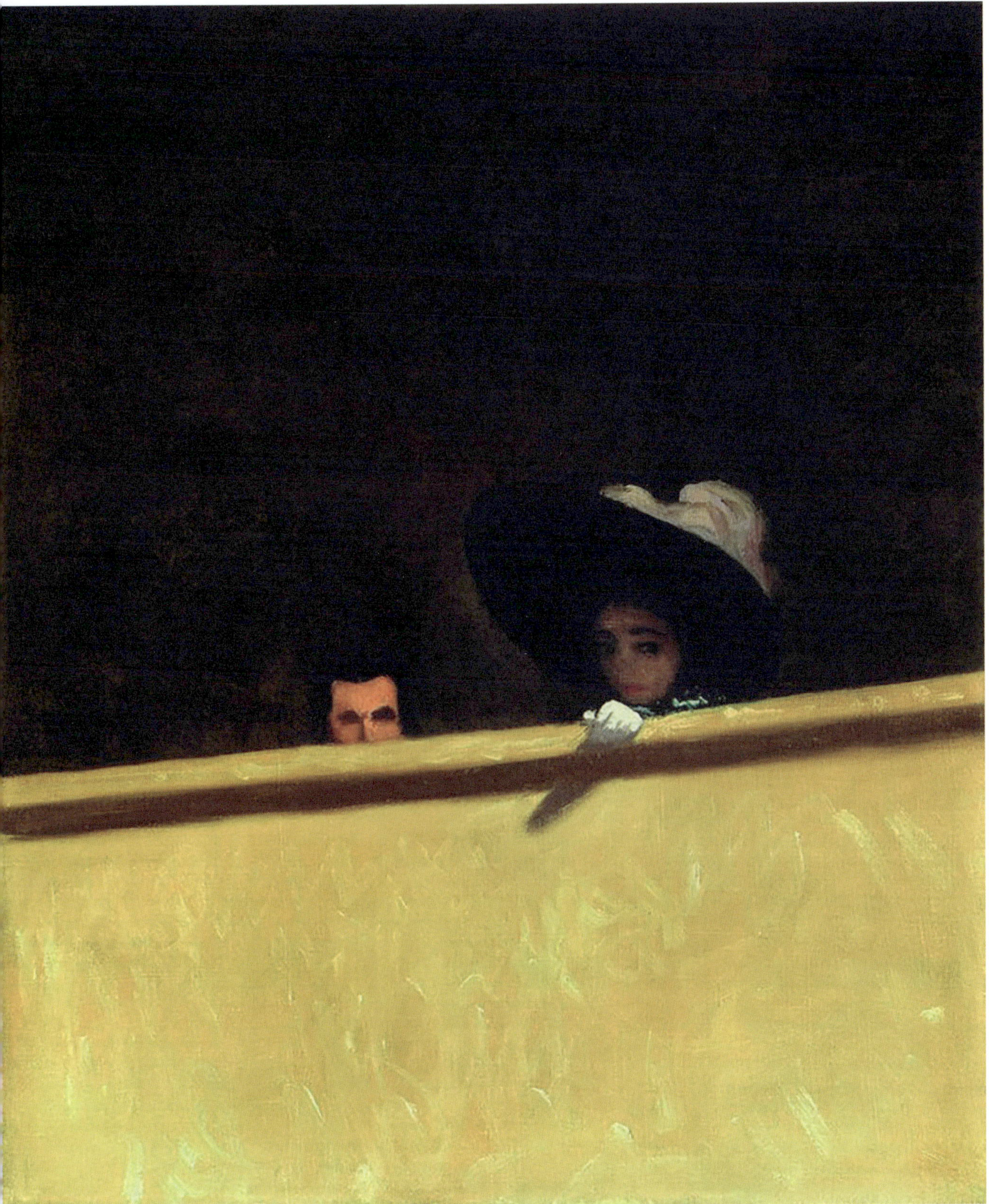

Edvard Munch

When depression leads to expression

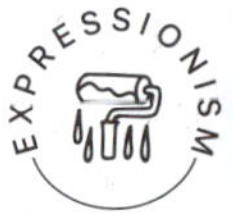

A pioneer of Expressionism, Munch painted a disturbing work, influenced by his grief and his anguished personality. Repeating the same motifs, he may have found, in this process, a way to exorcise his pain or return to the source of his emotions.

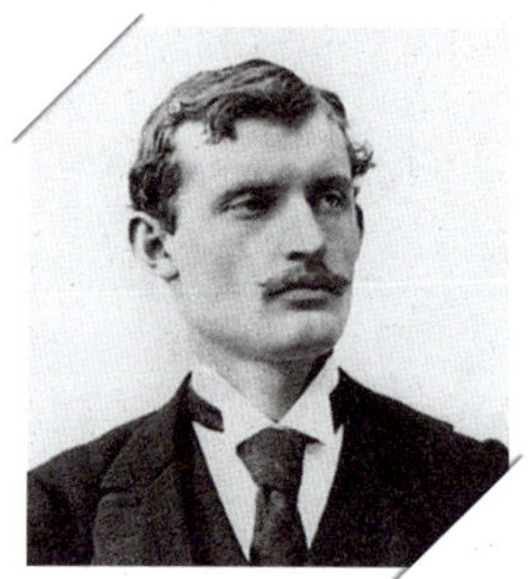

A difficult start

In his youth, the painter experienced a number of difficulties. Bereft by the disappearance of members of his family, he underwent the rigorous education of his father, a military doctor. Often ill, he learned to draw to keep himself busy, which is how his vocation was born.

Art therapy

Munch travelled to France, where he was inspired by Impressionism. In Berlin, he met other Scandinavian artists, with whom he exhibited and caused a scandal. Strange and anguished, his works caused confusion; they reflected his psychological state, making him one of the precursors of Expressionism.

A happy ending

Anxious and alcoholic, he was interned for several months in 1908. After he became sober, his paintings were filled with a newfound energy. Having become a well-known artist over the years, he moved to a house in the suburbs of Oslo, where he continued creating.

EDVARD MUNCH SAID

"I don't paint what I see, but what I saw."

Félix Vallotton
Page 250

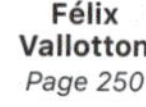

1863
Born in Ådalsbruk (Løten), Norway

1897
First performance of *Cyrano de Bergerac*

1910
Painted *The Scream*

1911
The Mona Lisa was stolen; Camille Picasso and Guillaume Apollinaire were suspected

1912
Sinking of the Titanic

1944
Died in Oslo

Gustav Klimt
Page 254

THE SCREAM

1910
Tempera and oil
83.5 × 66 cm
On cardboard
Munch Museet, Oslo

WHAT ARE WE LOOKING AT?

***The Scream* is a moral self-portrait of the painter, seized by profound anguish, which materialises in the form of a shifting, tormented landscape that reflects Munch's feelings.**

He who screams isn't he who is!

The character is holding his hands to his ears: he is terrorised when he hears a piercing scream splitting the air.

Dear Diary

Before it became an image, *The Scream* was a note written by Munch in his diary, in which he described the hallucination embodied by this landscape, turning red and black and overwhelming him.

Inner anguish

While Munch's anguish is visible throughout the landscape, he is the only one to feel it.
In the background, Munch's friends are walking away; they do not appear to hear the scream causing his distress.

Atmospheric depression

Munch's vision could also be due to a climatic phenomenon: in 1883, an eruption of the Krakatoa volcano in the Indian Ocean caused sunsets to turn red as far as Europe for several months. While this theory, which emerged in the 2000s, is taken seriously, it cannot be confirmed.

A most precious stone

Munch produced four versions of *The Scream*, in painting, pastel and pencil; prints were also made from a stone engraved by Munch, which was destroyed after some thirty copies were made.

Digital turnaround

Famous throughout the world, this work has acquired a certain posterity in pop culture, and was even turned into an emoji. In 2012, the 1895 pastel version went on sale and, for a time, became the most expensive work of art in the world.

RECORDS AND TORMENTS

Throughout his career, Munch reproduced the same motifs, whether portraits of his sister, melancholic figures by the sea or vampires. The Scream *was no exception to this. It is presented in different versions (1, 4 and 5) in the Munch Museum in Oslo, which keeps some 28,000 works by the artist.*

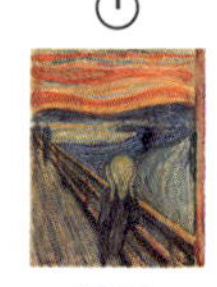

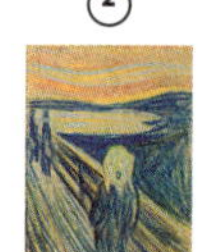

① **1893** Tempera — Stolen in February 1994, found three months later.

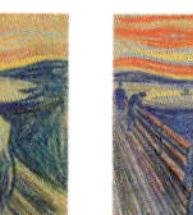

② **1893** Pastel

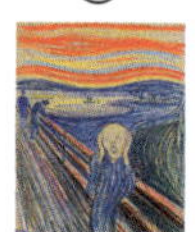

③ **1895** Pastel — Sold for 91 million euros in 2012.

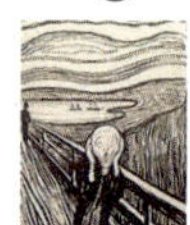

④ **1895** Lithography

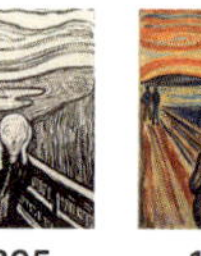

⑤ **1910** Tempera — Stolen in August 2004, found in 2006.

EXPRESSIONISM IN A NUTSHELL

- An artistic movement that originated in Germany and the Nordic countries in the 1910s, before spreading throughout Europe.
- Artists who rejected the social and political structures of their time, amidst the profound disruption caused by the Industrial Revolution.
- Bright colours that allowed painters to express a subjective reality, a representation of their feelings.

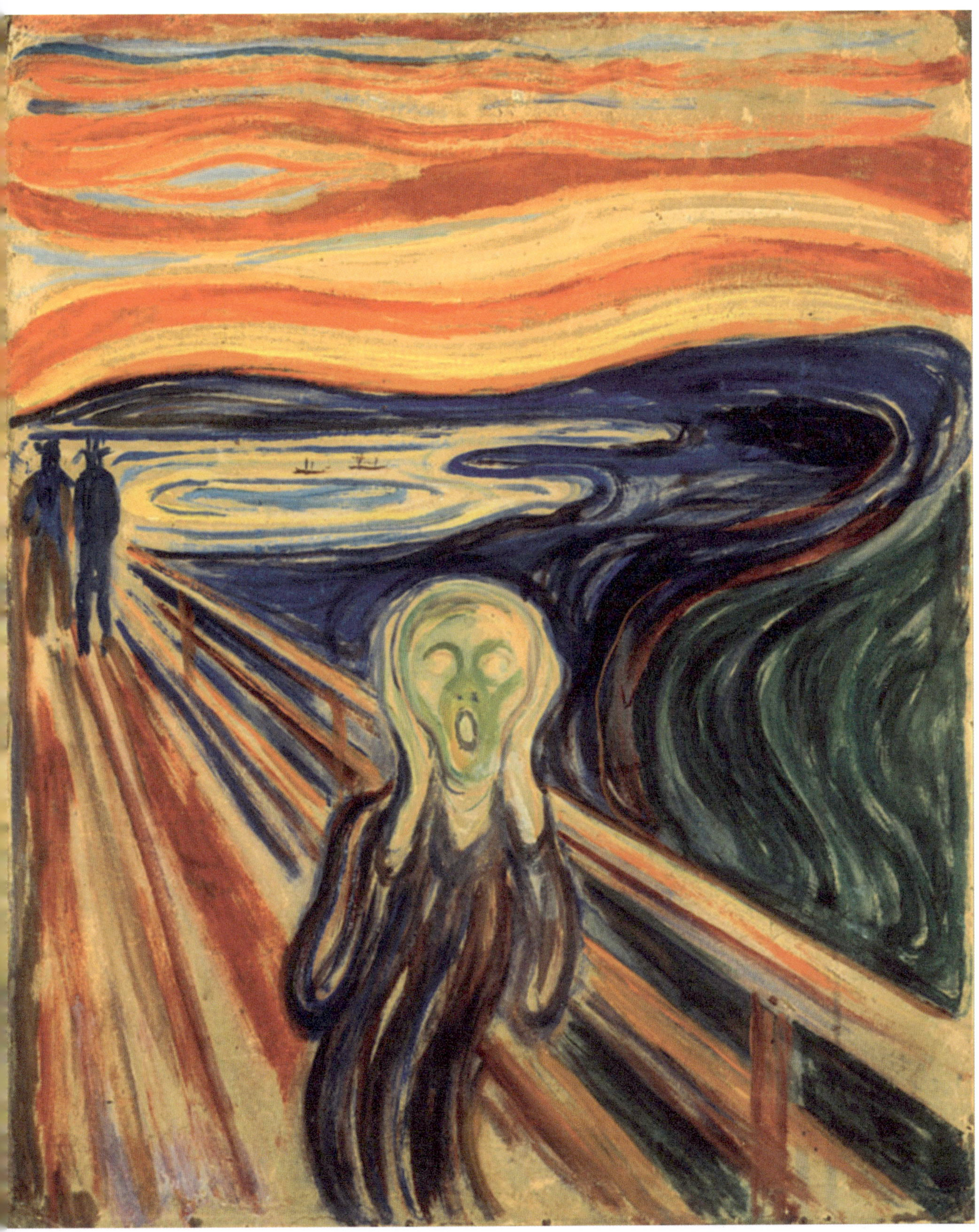

Gustav Klimt

A golden brush

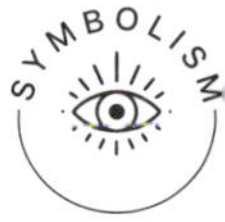

Klimt's highly decorative art has made him one of the best known and most appreciated artists in the history of art; in his time, however, he embodied a modern break with the past and was rejected by conservative viewers.

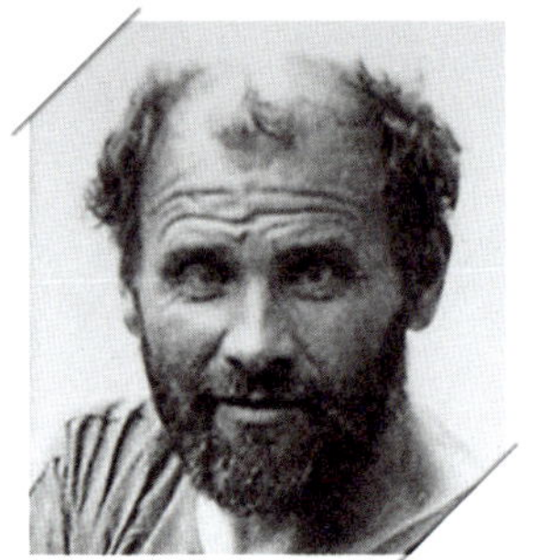

And yet, it started well

Klimt entered the University of Applied Arts in Vienna at the age of 14. Together with his brother, he opened a studio that designed large sets for theatres and museums. He was awarded multiple medals and prizes, but this success was overshadowed by the passing of his father and brother.

The end of tradition

A recognised artist, he broke with academic art by participating in the Vienna Secession, which advocated a new, modern and symbolist form of art. Despite the scandals and the censorships that ensued, Klimt benefited from the support of his patrons and sponsors.

The Klimt complex

In Klimt's time, Freud's theories were spreading. They appear in his works, in the form of women who are in turn emasculating and maternal. Although he tried his hand at other colours, the painter is best known for his golden works, which still inspire artists today.

IT WAS SAID OF HIM

"One can acknowledge that Klimt is Viennese by the fact that he is praised worldwide, and attacked only in Vienna." Felix Salten, Austrian author of the novel *Bambi, a Life in the Woods*, adapted by the Disney studios in 1942.

Edvard Munch
Page 252

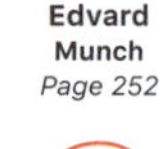

1862
Born in Vienna

1870
Jules Verne immersed his readers "Twenty Thousand Leagues Under the Sea"

1885
Pasteur developed the rabies vaccine

1908
Painted *The Kiss*

1912
The Qing imperial dynasty came to an end, and China became a republic

1918
Died in Vienna

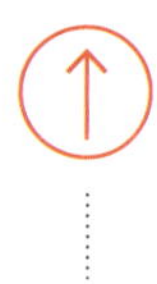

Henri Matisse
Page 262

THE KISS ↗

1908
Oil on canvas and gold leaf on enamel-covered brass background
180 × 180 cm
Belvedere Palace, Vienna

WHAT ARE WE LOOKING AT?

This masterpiece by Klimt was met with immediate success. It is, without doubt, one of the most universal representations of love ever produced, which would explain its fame.

Cuddle lover

The embrace of love is a recurring feature in Klimt's work, among others in the *Beethoven Frieze*, a nude work dominated by man, and the dining room of the Stoclet Palace in Brussels.

A kiss, a kiss!

Klimt brings the motif to its climax by turning the embrace into a real kiss for the first time. The couple, depicted in a cocoon of drapery, is engaging in an intense embrace, with their hands joined.

In fine fettle

The protruding limbs suggest that the couple is naked, giving the painting a more carnal colouration and resonating with the phallic form that enshrouds them. On this form, round motifs can be seen, reminiscent of the background of *The Kiss*, painted by Munch in 1897, which may have inspired Klimt's composition.

Sentimental precariousness

However, the lovers' happiness seems fragile. They are lost in a world without landmarks, symbolised by the golden background. The carpet of flowers that welcomes them disappears, forming a precipice.

All the gold in the world

The use of gold graces this work with a highly decorative quality: the painting becomes an object. Klimt was influenced by the work of his father, a goldsmith, and by the discoveries of archaeological treasures that were recounted in the news. His interest for the golden colour was further intensified after his trip to Italy, where he discovered the mosaics of Ravenna.

MODERNISM IN EUROPE

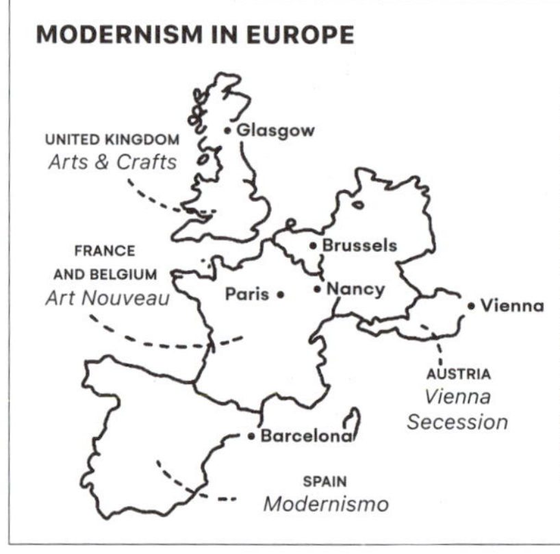

At the end of the 19th century, a wind of artistic modernity blew across Europe. It permeated the classical and applied arts with flowing, decorative lines inherited from nature. This modernity was given different names in different countries.

OTHER LEADING FIGURES OF THE VIENNA SECESSION

- Egon Schiele (1890–1918), Alfred Roller (1864–1935) and Koloman Moser (1868–1918), painters.
- Josef Hoffmann (1870–1956), Josef Maria Olbrich (1867–1908) and Otto Wagner (1841–1918), architects.

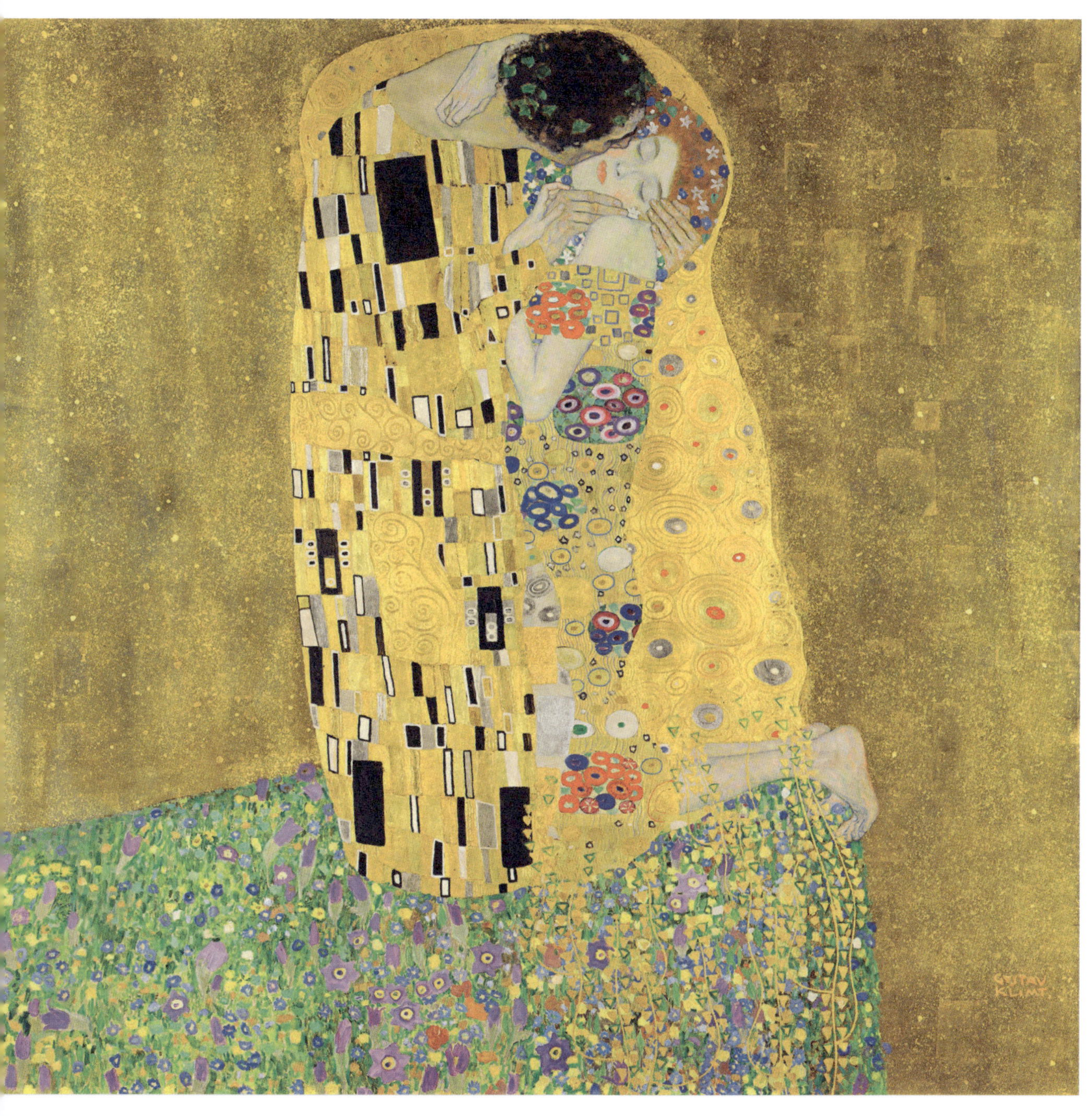
GUSTAV
KLIMT

A gallery of frames

Essential features that we forget to look at

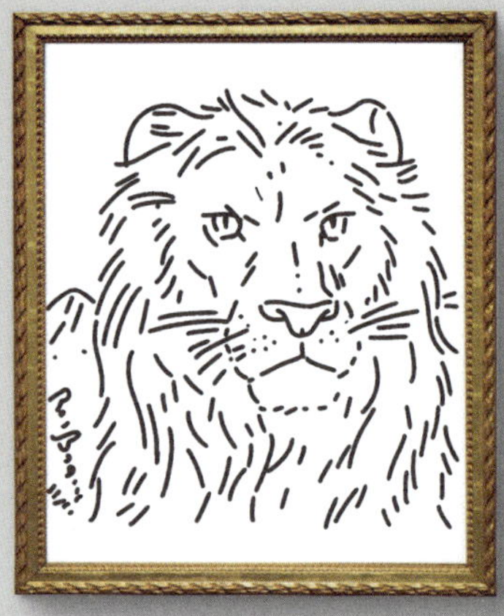

ROSA BONHEUR
El Cid
1879
95 × 76 cm
Prado Museum, Madrid

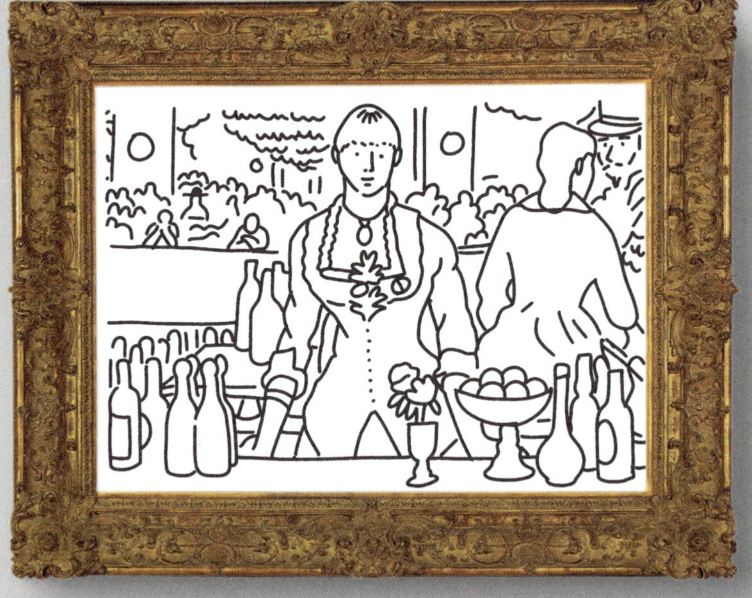

ÉDOUARD MANET
A Bar at the Folies-Bergères
1882
96 × 130 cm
The Courtauld Institute of Art, London

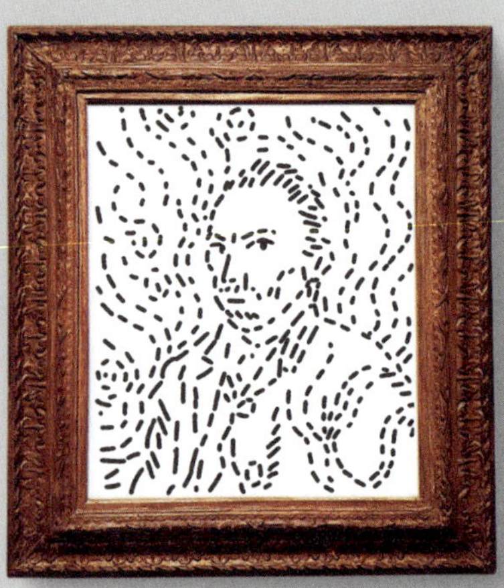

VINCENT VAN GOGH
Self-Portrait
1889
65 × 54.2 cm
Musée d'Orsay, Paris

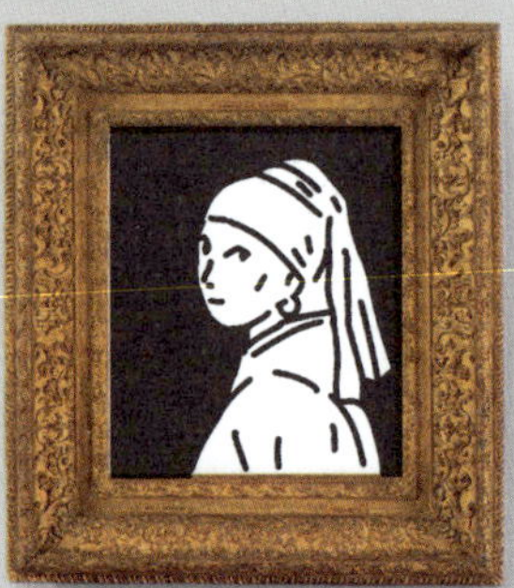

JOHANNES VERMEER
Girl with a Pearl Earring
1665
39 × 44.5 cm
Mauristhuis, The Hague

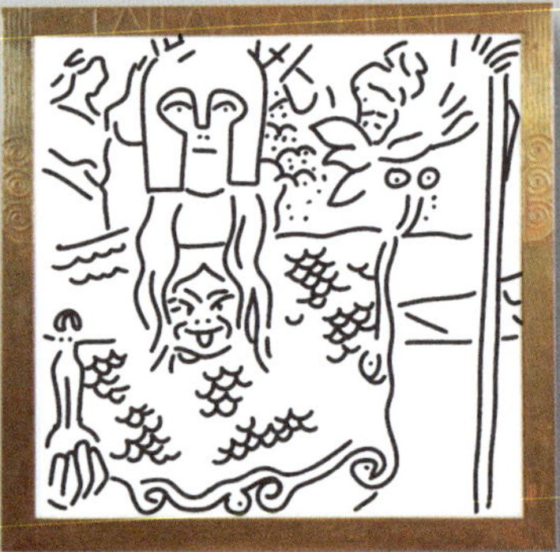

GUSTAV KLIMT
Pallas
1898
75 × 75 cm
Wien Museum, Vienna

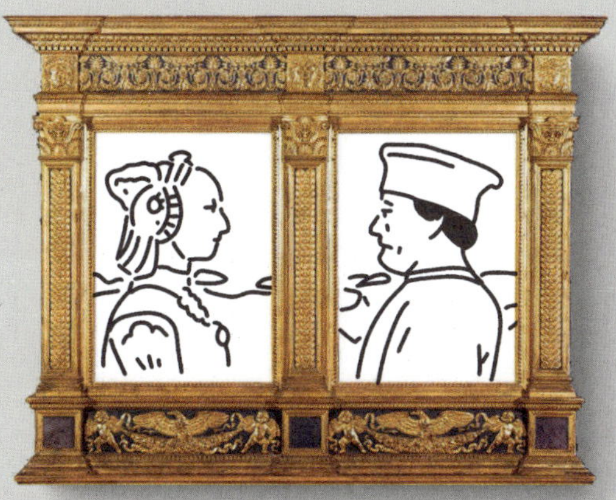

PIERO DELLA FRANCESCA
Diptych of Federico da Montefeltro and Battista Sforza
1473–1475
47 × 33 cm (each)
Uffizi Gallery, Florence

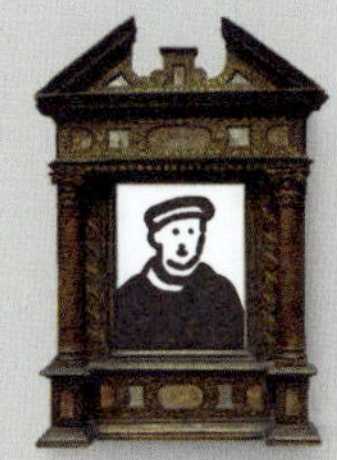

CORNEILLE DE LYON
Portrait of a Man
1563–1540
16.5 × 14.3 cm
National Gallery of Art, Washington

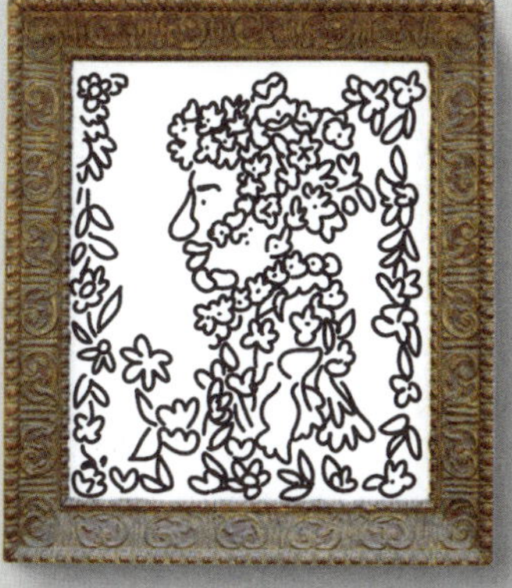

GIUSEPPE ARCIMBOLDO
Spring
1573
76 × 63.5 cm
Musée du Louvre, Paris

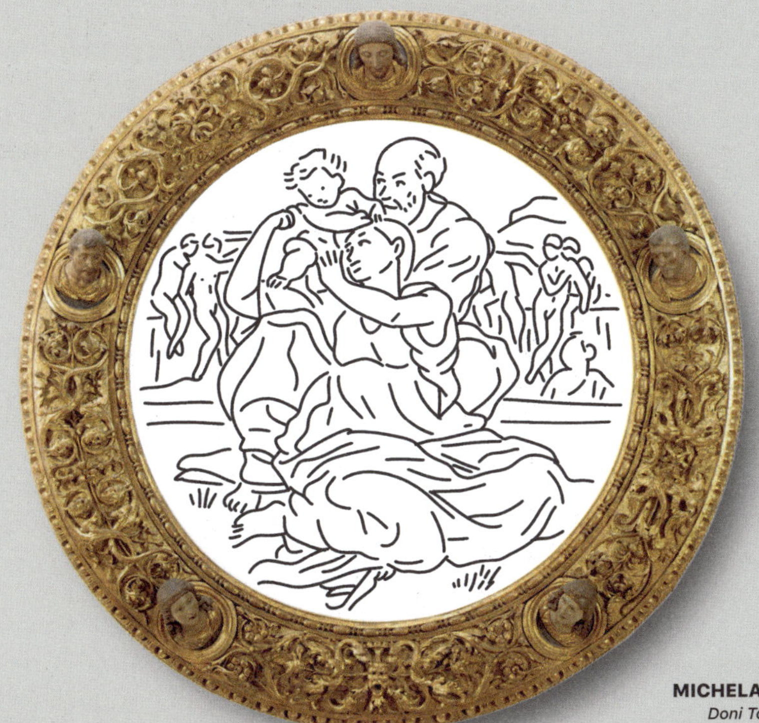

LEONARDO DA VINCI
The Mona Lisa
1503–1506 or 1513–1519
77 × 53 cm
Louvre Museum, Paris

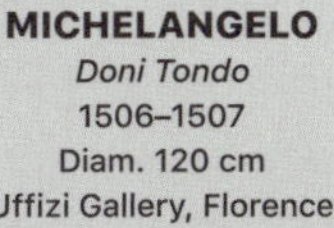

MICHELANGELO
Doni Tondo
1506–1507
Diam. 120 cm
Uffizi Gallery, Florence

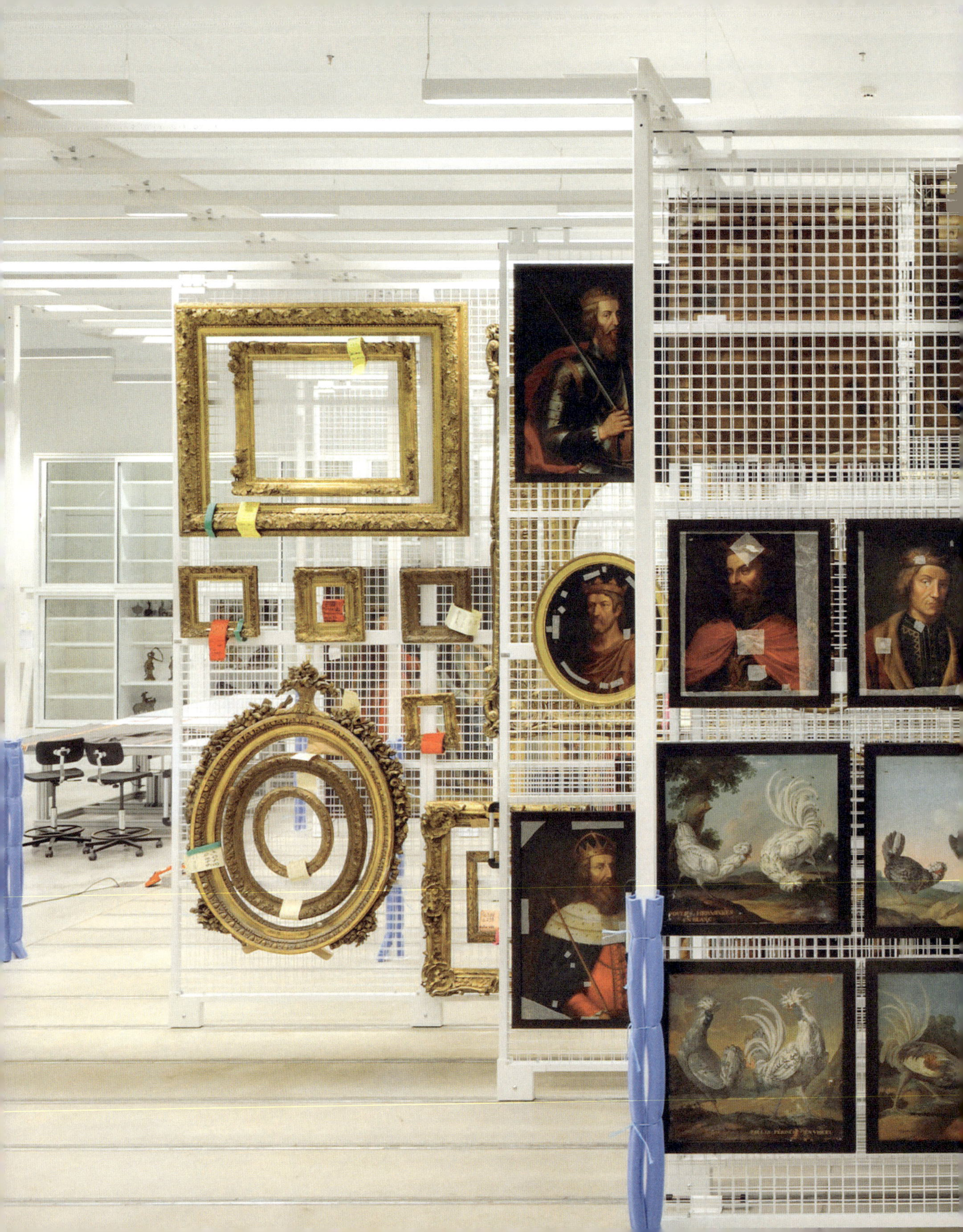

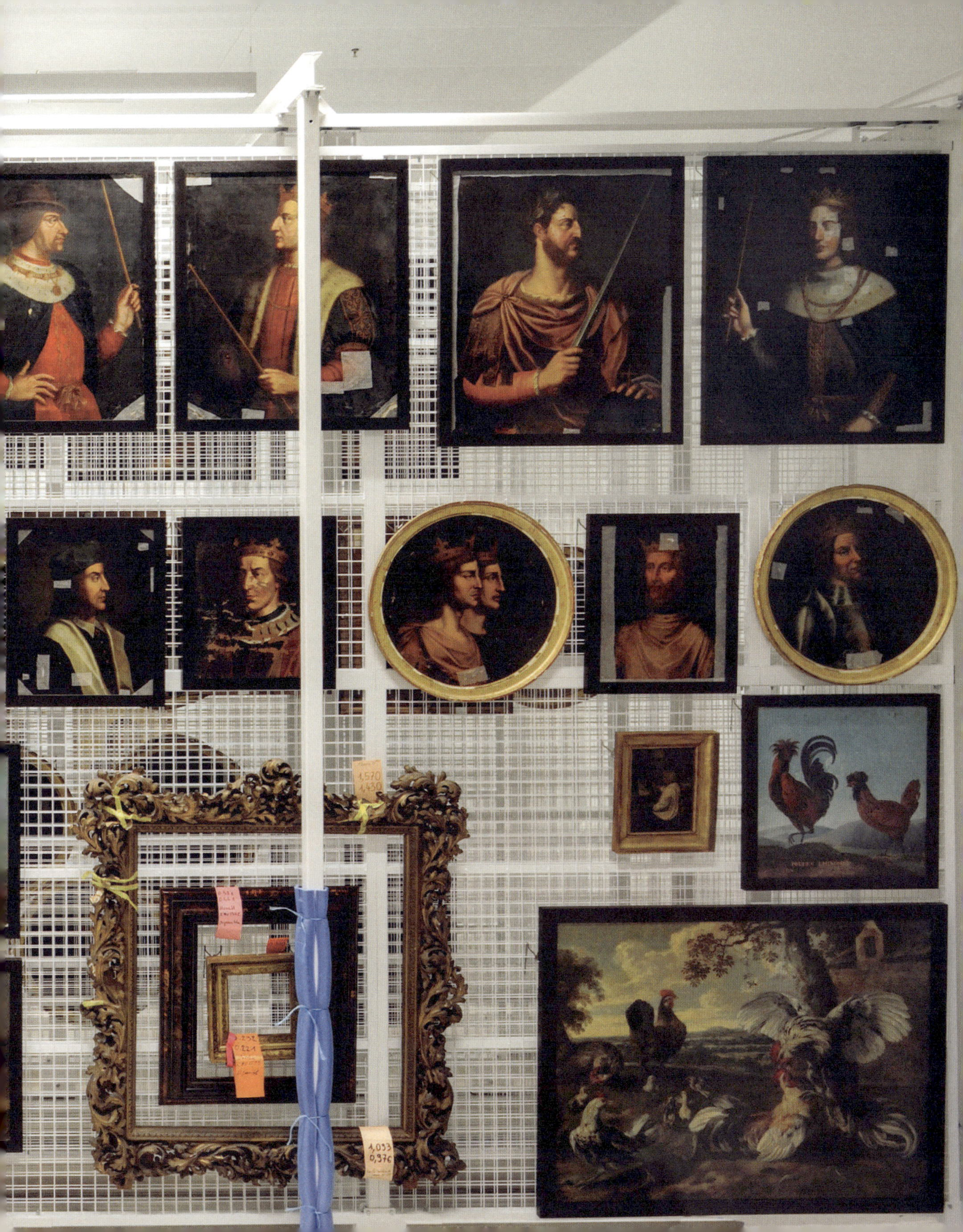
1,570
1,430
1,033
0,976

The Avant-Garde

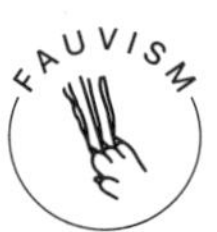

Term coined in 1905

Bright colours, simplified volumes and shapes

Henri Matisse *p. 262*

Gustave Courbet *p. 198*

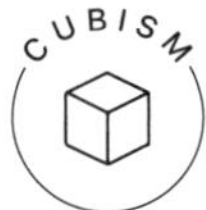

Circa 1908–1914

Multiple dimensions rendered on one plane, geometric shapes

Pablo Picasso *p. 264*

Georges Braque *p. 272*

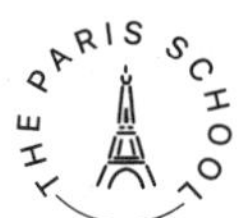

First half of the 20th century

A name that designated foreign artists living in Paris

Amedeo Modigliani *p. 268*

Marc Chagall *p. 270*

Tamara de Lempicka *p. 290*

The new explorers

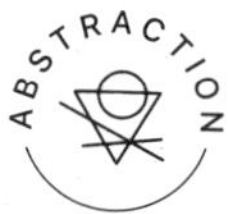

from the 1910s

Absence of figurative subjects and search for formal purity

Hilma af Klint *p. 274*

Vassily Kandinsky *p. 276*

Piet Mondrian *p. 278*

Kazimir Malevich *p. 280*

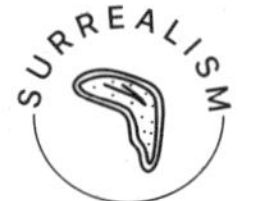

Theorised in 1924

Rejection of the world's rationality, interest in dreams, the subconscious and psychoanalysis

René Magritte *p. 292*

Salvador Dalí *p. 296*

Georgia O'Keeffe *p. 304*

Frida Kahlo *p. 306*

Francis Bacon *p. 314*

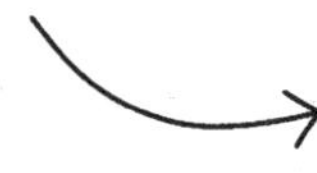

In reaction to these radical expressions, artists of the United States persisted in figurative art

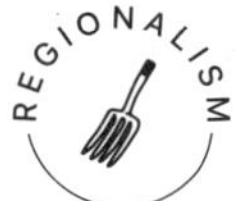

Edward Hopper *p. 302*

Grant Wood *p. 288*

The pre-eminence of the new New York scene

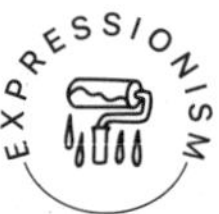

from the 1940s

Large formats, coloured flat tints and the artist's brushwork

Mark Rothko *p. 308*

Jackson Pollock *p. 310*

Joan Mitchell *p. 312*

from the 1950s

"A popular art destined to the masses, ephemeral, short term, consumable, easily forgettable, produced in series, inexpensive…"

Roy Lichtenstein *p. 320*

Andy Warhol *p. 322*

The new stars

In a context of diversification of supports and disciplines, of internationalisation and of a growing art market

David Hockney *p. 324*

Gerhard Richter *p. 330*

Jean-Michel Basquiat *p. 332*

Yayoi Kusama *p. 334*

Chéri Samba *p. 336*

Banksy *p. 338*

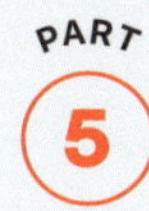

From Henri Matisse to Banksy

Radical painting

The most audacious experimentations are allowed

Nourished by the experiences of their predecessors, the artists of the 20th century took things further and further, reaching absolute abstraction. The art scene also grew internationally, with the emergence of American painting and artists from all walks of life, who were valued by the art market.

Henri Matisse

Colours that rub off on the future

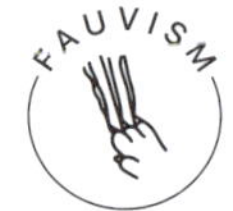

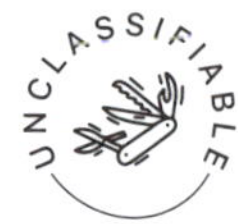

Known for his famous *Dance*, which reflects his taste for colour, Matisse was known for sensual and radical painting that marked the 20th century by its frankness. He experienced both scandal and fame during his lifetime.

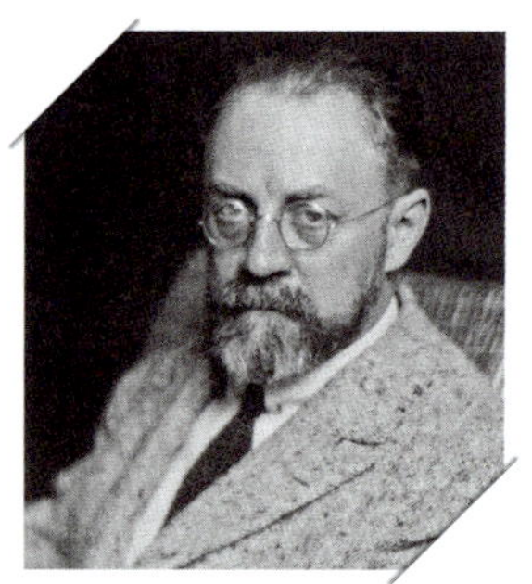

Revelation

A notary's clerk by training, Matisse began drawing at the age of 20. He truly began honing his skills during a convalescence, which revealed his true calling to him. He then trained with Gustave Moreau, copied the masters exhibited at the Louvre Museum, and discovered the works of Paul Cézanne.

The advent of the Fauvists

In 1905, Matisse discovered a world of colour in the South, with André Derain. The artists would exhibit alongside others at the Salon d'Automne. Their colours were bold, conveying a sensitive radicalism that caused a scandal. This was enough for the art critic Louis Vauxcelles to call them "les fauves" (the wild animals).

It's an eyeful

From odalisques to interiors and his famous gouache-painted paper cut-outs, Matisse's trademark remained colour. It evolved with his travels and the lights of the Mediterranean, from Morocco to Nice via Vence.

HENRI MATISSE SAID

"Beautiful blues, beautiful reds, beautiful yellows – matter to stir the sensual depths in men. This is the starting point of Fauvism."

Gustav Klimt
Page 254

1869
Born in Cateau-Cambrésis

1894
Beginning of the Dreyfus Affair, which would divide France

1911
Henri Matisse painted *The Red Studio*

1950s
Rock music reached France

1954
Died in Nice

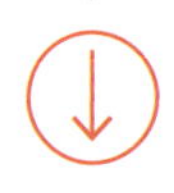

Pablo Picasso
Page 264

THE RED STUDIO

1911
Oil on canvas,
181 × 219.1 cm
The Museum of Modern Art, New York

WHAT ARE WE LOOKING AT?

Having recently moved to Issy-les-Moulineaux, the painter revealed the interior of his studio, where the colour red is both alluring and destabilising, by its intensity and omnipresence.

The sound of happiness

In 1910, at the Salon d'Automne, Matisse exhibited *The Dance* and *Music*, whose strident colours once again caused a scandal. In 1911, his art grew more peaceful. He revealed new harmonies based on forms and colours in his "Symphonic Interiors". Within this series, however, *The Red Studio* stood out with its radical nature.

Inception

Matisse created copies of his works within themselves, producing works within works. One can recognise his *Decorative Figure*, cast in bronze, above which the hangs the painting *Luxury II*. On the left, on a pink background, appears his work *Grand Nu à la Colle*, which he later destroyed. Higher up, *Nude with a White Scarf* extends beyond the frame and to its right, *Young Sailor* appears. Matisse rendered these last two paintings with a less intense palette than in reality, in order to preserve the work's overall harmony.

Lost in space

By dressing his work in a monochromatic red atmosphere, Matisse blurred reference points. This impression is reinforced by the absence of any edge defining the left-hand corner of the room, which can be deduced from the orientation of the work *Grand Nu à la Colle*. The ghostly appearance of the furniture, of which only the outline remains, adds to the confusion – particularly the large clock whose handless dial is the only identifiable element: spectators not only lose the notion of space, but also that of time.

ARTIST, A PROFESSION OF FAITH

In 1943, Matisse moved to Vence. There, the sisters of the religious community convinced him to create their chapel. From stained glass to the furniture, he imagined all aspects of the project, in collaboration with the architect Auguste Perret and the master glassmaker Paul Bony.

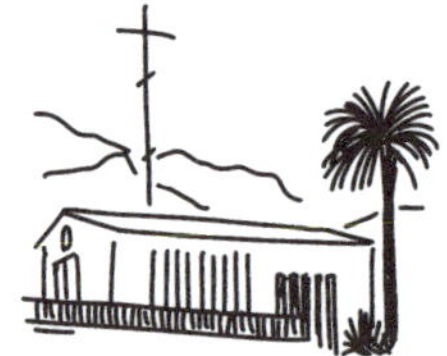

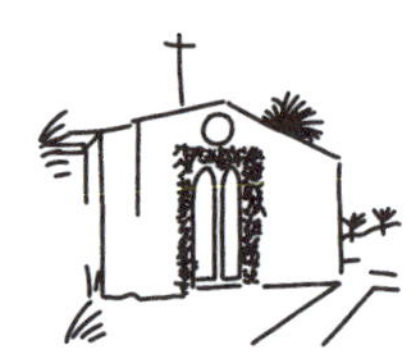

The Chapelle du Rosaire, 1949–1951, Vence

FAUVISM IN A NUTSHELL

- A dazzling artistic movement that lasted only a few years.
- A rendering of volume through colour and simplified shapes.
- A bright palette, perceived as aggressive at the time.
- Subjective colours that do not reflect reality.

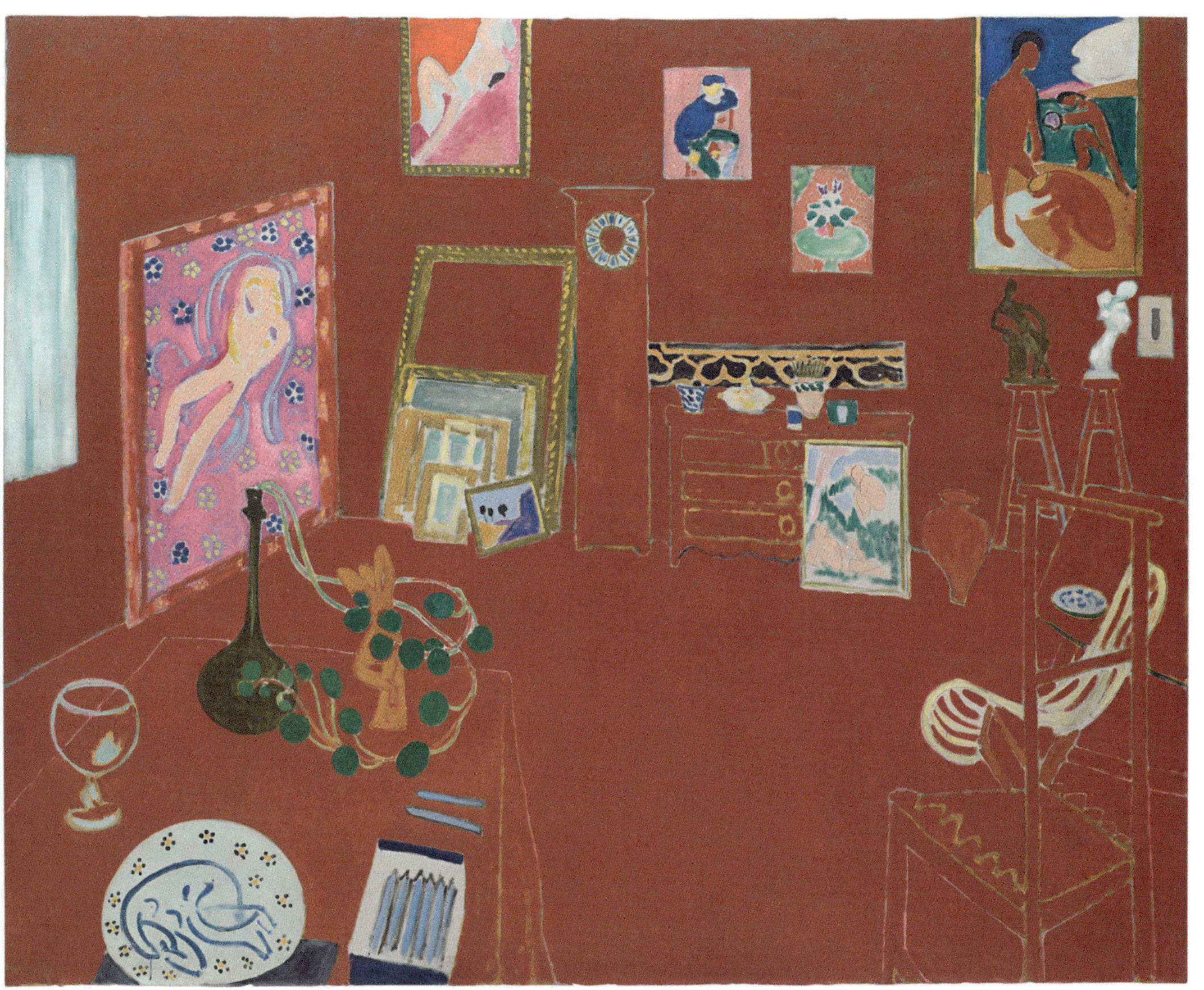

A quality christening

The "Symphonic Interiors" series was named by Alfred Barr, an art historian and the first director of the MoMA in New York. Four of these paintings were produced for the Russian collector Sergei Shchukin. The other three paintings are entitled: *The Painter's Family*, *Intérieur aux Aubergines* and *The Pink Studio*.

Pablo Picasso

The cubic root of art

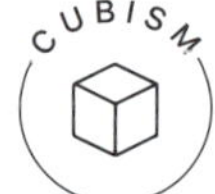

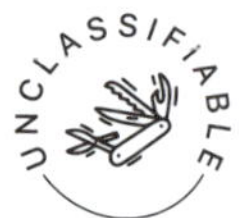

Picasso is known as the leader of cubism, with Georges Braque; however, his art evolved greatly over the course of his long career. A prolific artist, he was inspired by both Diego Velázquez and Paul Cézanne.

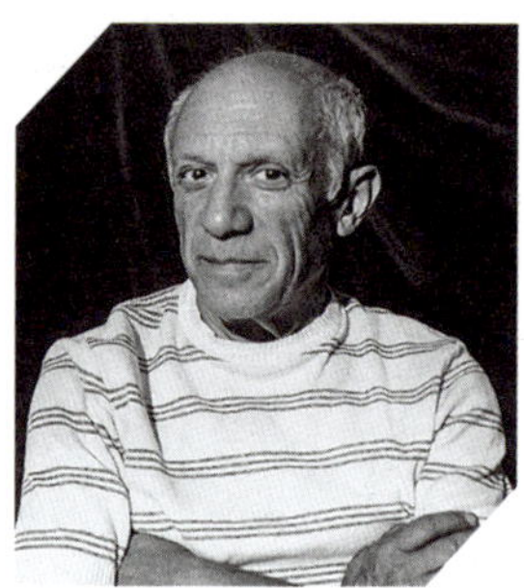

Arrived at the right place

At the age of 20, he moved to Paris, and settled in the legendary Bateau-Lavoir studio. There, he met Max Jacob, Guillaume Apollinaire, Henri Matisse and André Derain. Cubism, of which he and Georges Braque (p. 272) became the leading representatives, was born in this context.

The movement that hides the career

Picasso is best known for his blue and pink periods. The first is melancholic, while the second is marked by the circus. However, these phases and the exploration of cubism are but a brief moment in the artist's long career, as he tried his hand at many different practices: painting, engraving and sculpture, among others.

He dances with the times

After cubism, Picasso became interested in ballet, designing sets and costumes. He flirted with Surrealism, without ever yielding to abstraction. His work was inspired by the old masters, mythology, the dramas of his time and other subjects.

WEEPING WOMEN

Picasso was known for his many female companions. In the 21st century, greater attention is being paid to the abuses that they suffered.

Henri Matisse
Page 262

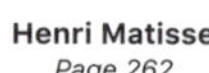
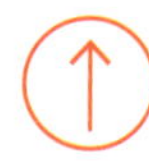

1881
Born in Málaga

1903
First edition of the Tour de France

1907
Painted *Les Demoiselles d'Avignon*

1910
The croque-monsieur appeared in Paris

1973
Died in Mougins

Amedeo Modigliani
Page 268

LES DEMOISELLES D'AVIGNON

1907
Oil on canvas
243.9 × 233.7 cm
MoMA, New York

WHAT ARE WE LOOKING AT?

This painting features a group of unstructured female nudes.
It established a revolutionary aesthetic breakthrough that favoured the rise of the cubist movement.

Working ladies

Initially entitled *Bordel d'Avignon* (Brothel at Avignon), the painting evaded censorship under the title of *Les Demoiselles d'Avignon* (The Ladies of Avignon), but it indeed refers to the neighbourhood of the Rue d'Avignon in Barcelona, which was renowned for its licentious activities.

A change in plans

These women are therefore prostitutes. The painter places us in the uncomfortable position of a voyeur.

The initial project also included two male figures: a sailor and a medical student. Supposedly embodying clients potentially infected with venereal diseases, they evoked Eros and Thanatos, gods of Love and Death.

Cubism loading

The painting exudes an aggressiveness that shocked audiences. In an image devoid of depth, bodies featuring sharp angles stand out, appearing to be dislocated. The seated nude figure is showing viewers her back and face at the same time.

Sources from here and elsewhere

The female nudes' raised arms are borrowed from the painting *The Turkish Bath* by Ingres, who, even in his time, began to disarticulate women's bodies. The three figures on the left are inspired by Iberian masks, while the two faces on the right have been replaced by African masks. In this colonial period at the beginning of the century, Picasso was influenced by sub-Saharan art.

THE THREE PHASES OF CUBISM

1908 to 1909	1910 to 1912	1912 to 1914
Cezanian cubism	**Analytic or hermetic cubism**	**Synthetic cubism**
Shapes become increasingly geometric.	Motifs that are difficult to identify. Palettes based on greys and browns.	A return to colour. Nested objects. Additions of collages and various materials.

CUBISM IN A NUTSHELL

- Volumes represented as flat surfaces on the painting.
- The absence of perspective and depth.
- Angular and geometric shapes.

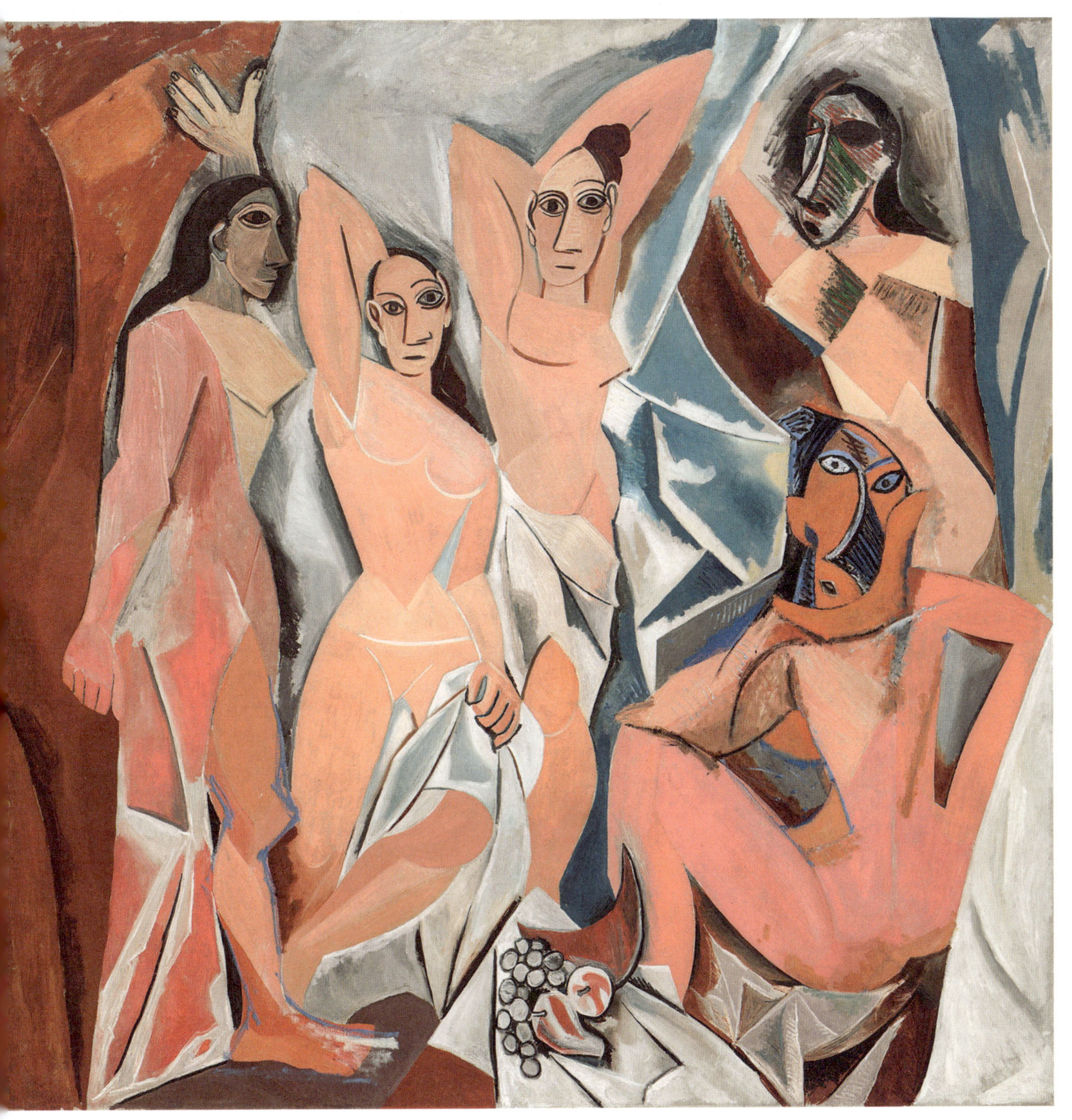

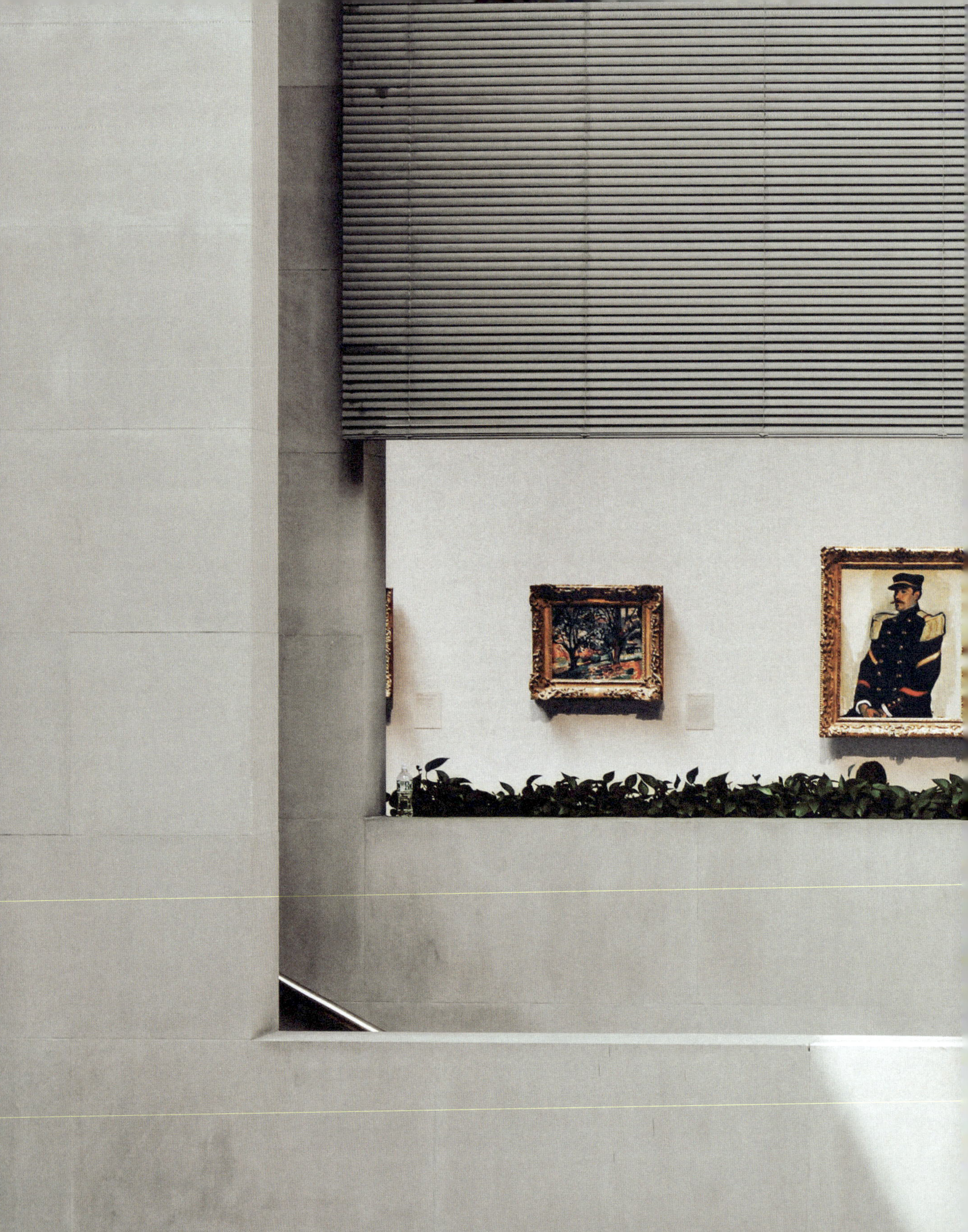

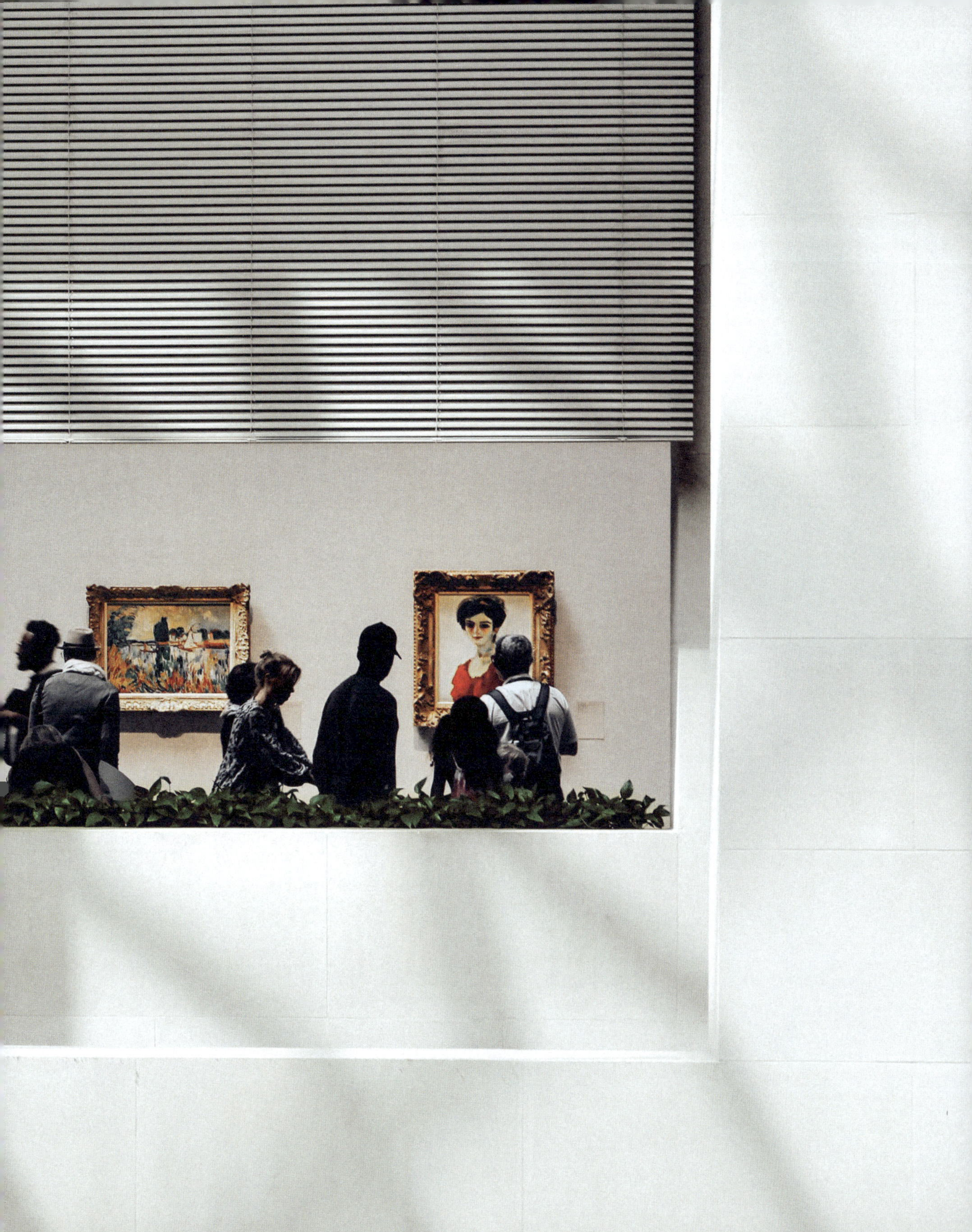

Amedeo Modigliani

Portraits worth a neck and an arm

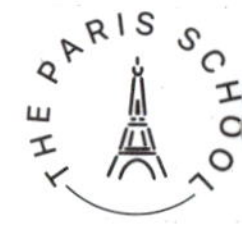

From the audacity of his very carnal nudes to his strangely beautiful portraits, Modigliani sought to invent an ideal that synthesised his influences. His work often remains overshadowed by his tragic life.

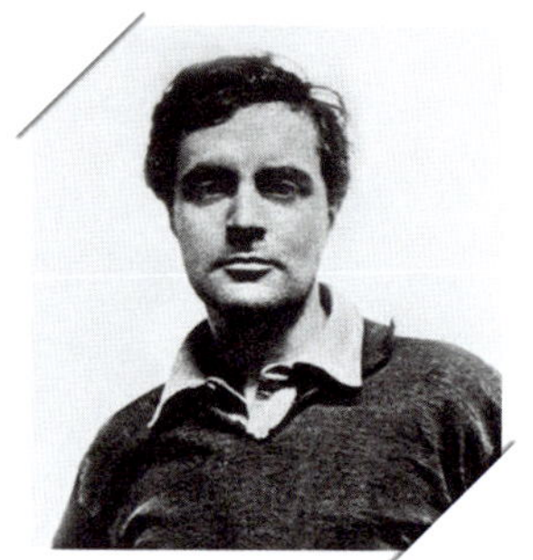

A stubborn portraitist

Modigliani studied in Florence and Venice, then moved to Paris, where he met Guillaume Apollinaire and Pablo Picasso (p. 264). A figurative painter in an increasingly abstract artistic context, he combined Italian tradition, antiquity and non-Western arts as he sought to achieve an expression of universal beauty.

Nudes and necks

The artist is known for his mask-like portraits, featuring empty eyes and stretched necks, but also for his provocative nudes. He produced a masterful series of portraits between 1916 and 1919: 35 paintings that were inspired by Paul Gauguin (p. 248) as much as by the Renaissance, but were devoid of any mythological pretext.

A sulphurous reputation

Modigliani's art is overshadowed by his legend. He was the archetype of the cursed, alcoholic artist: he died of illness at the age of 25, and in despair, his pregnant partner committed suicide. Even today, his name remains associated with forgery, and his works sell for stratospheric amounts at auction houses.

ANTI-DATE

During his years in Paris, Modigliani produced 420 paintings, but only dated 14 of these.

Pablo Picasso
Page 264

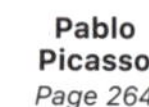

1884
Born in Livorno

1885
Maupassant published *Bel-Ami*

1890
Birth of Charles de Gaulle

1919
Painted *Jeanne Hébuterne*

1920
Died in Paris

Marc Chagall
Page 270

JEANNE HÉBUTERNE

1919
Oil on canvas
91.4 × 73 cm
Metropolitan Museum of Art, New York

WHAT ARE WE LOOKING AT?

This is one of the many portraits that Modigliani painted of Jeanne Hébuterne, his muse and companion. Always an elegant figure, here, she is presented in simpler clothing, highlighting the couple's intimacy.

Love at first sight in Montparnasse

Jeanne Hébuterne, a talented young artist and model, fascinated Modigliani with her singular beauty, her pale complexion, her long dark hair and her intense gaze. She had a passionate relationship with him, which she hid from her parents until she became pregnant and gave birth to a baby, also named Jeanne.

In the privacy of their home

Modigliani painted 25 portraits of his muse, in which the young woman was always elegantly dressed. Here, she appears in more casual clothing, and her loose shirt hints at another pregnancy.

Crossroads of influence

This portrait is typical of Modigliani's art: a stretched morphology, simplified lines, and blue eyes. Modigliani was inspired by Italian Mannerism, with its slender bodies, as much as he was by the pure sculptures of Brancusi, a Romanian sculptor whom the artist frequented in Paris, when he himself tried his hand at sculpture.

A tragedy in two acts

The two lovers' passion came to a heartbreaking end, completing Modigliani's artistic myth. When he fell ill, he promised Jeanne to marry her, but he died before he was able to keep his word. The fragile young woman committed suicide on the following day; she leapt from the building where her parents lived, while she was expecting her second child.

ARTISTS' STUDIOS IN MONTPARNASSE

① **Gauguin's, Modigliani's and Jeanne Hébuterne's studio:** 8, rue de la Grande Chaumière
② **Picasso's studio:** 242, boulevard Raspail
③ **Matisse's studio:** 33, boulevard des Invalides
④ **Van Dongen's studio:** 33, rue Denfert-Rochereau

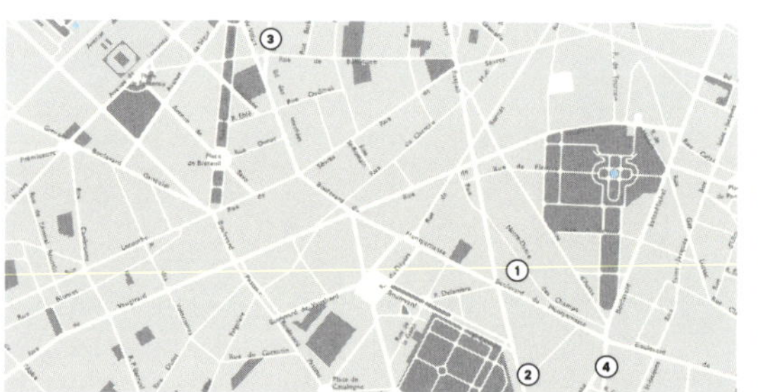

NOT-SO-EXPERT EXPERTISE

Modigliani was said to have thrown three of his sculptures into the *Fosso Reale* in Livorno, Tuscany. In 1984, they were found at the bottom of the canal. Some curators attributed them to the artist, but the expert Carlo Pepi claimed that this was a deception. His doubts were confirmed by the students responsible for the hoax, and the curators were removed from their positions.

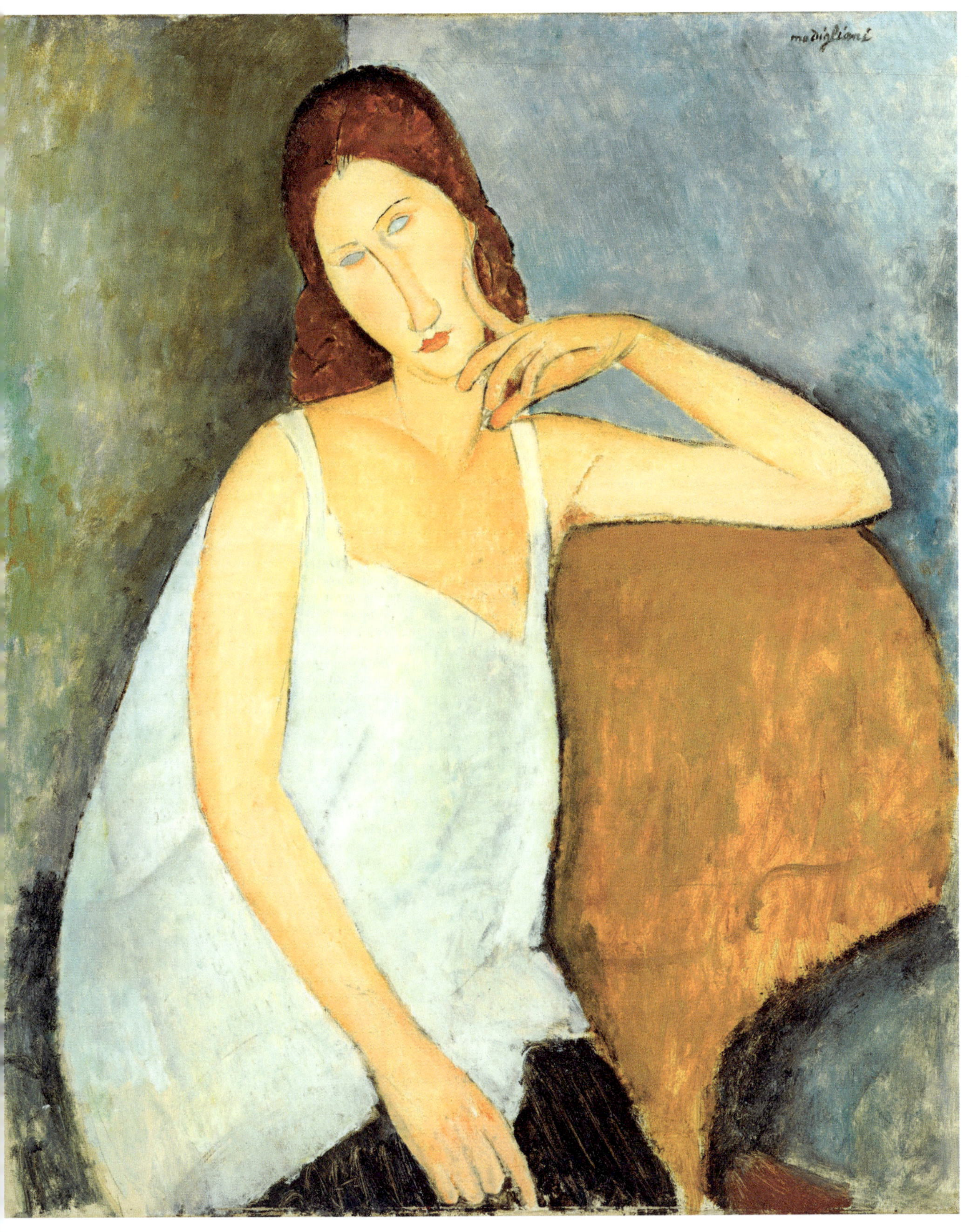
modigliani

Marc Chagall

Poetry at work

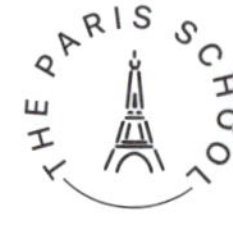

Chagall's colourful and dreamlike art produced seductive and accessible works. Forced to travel for many years, after the Second World War, he settled in the south of France, where his creativity flourished once again.

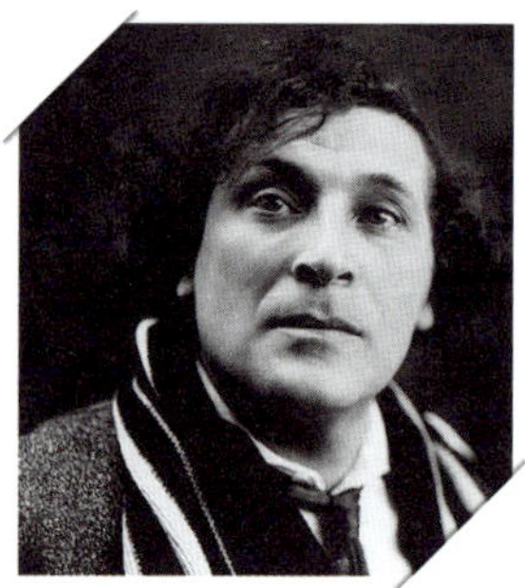

A happy busy bee

Chagall trained by taking various drawing and painting courses, while at the same time earning a living with small advertising jobs. He was awarded a grant, which enabled him to go and study in Paris. There, he set up shop at La Ruche, an emblematic studio located in the Montparnasse District.

In the spotlight

The artist was closely linked to the world of show business. Throughout his career, he produced costumes, sets and murals for theatres around the world. In 1964, he unveiled the famous ceiling of the Opéra Garnier in Paris, commissioned by André Malraux.

Tailor-made cocktails

Chagall's art is a joyful mixture of the painter's experiences. Between Judaism and Christianity, Russian tradition and French Avant-Garde, rural villages of his childhood and modern Parisian horizons, his universe was pervaded with poetry and colours, inviting spectators to dream.

MARC CHAGALL SAID

"[Painting] appeared to me like a window through which I could take flight towards another world."

Amedeo Modigliani
Page 268

1887
Born in Liozna, Russia

1903
The first Goncourt Prize was awarded

1911
Painted *I and the Village*

1929
Edwin Hubble demonstrated the expansion of the Universe

1985
Died in New York

Georges Braque
Page 272

I AND THE VILLAGE

1911
Oil on canvas
192.1 × 151.4 cm
MoMA, New York

WHAT ARE WE LOOKING AT?

In this work, Chagall combines his attachment to his childhood village in Russia with the modern influences that he discovered in Paris.

Russia in France

When Chagall painted this picture, he had arrived in Paris a year earlier. In his luggage, he carried the influences of Russian Neo-Primitivism, a movement based on popular culture. In the French capital, he met Slavic artists such as his friend Ossip Zadkine, who also stayed at La Ruche.

A blazing friendship with Blaise

At the same time, he developed friendships with French artists, in particular a very strong relationship with the poet Blaise Cendrars, who introduced him to everybody who was anybody in the artistic world of Paris. Chagall was impressed by the effervescence of the French Avant-Garde.

New decor

It is in this context that he painted *I and the Village*, which was named by Blaise Cendrars. This work lies at the crossroads of Chagall's worlds: on the one hand, his home village and the rural atmosphere of his childhood, and on the other, the influence of cubism, which can be seen on the ears of the goat, on the left, which are positioned at different angles.

Equal in dignity

In this village scene painted from his memories, the artist tends towards abstraction and defies the laws of reality, proportion and gravity, imbuing his work with a fantasy atmosphere of nostalgia.
The connection with his native land is expressed in the intense exchange of glances between the goat and his representation, materialised by the thin line connecting them both.

THE PARIS SCHOOL

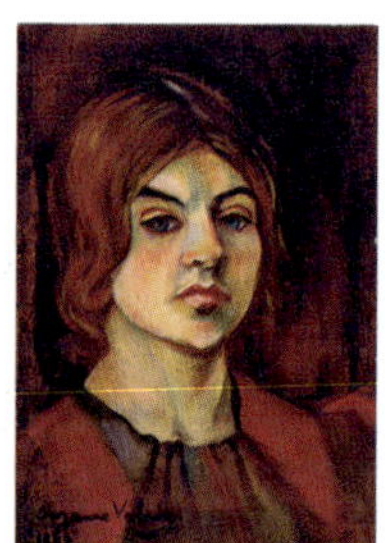

The Paris School became renowned for gathering the communities of foreign artists who moved to the French capital during the first half of the 20th century: Marc Chagall, Modigliani (p. 268), Soutine and others.
The name is also associated with French artists such as Valadon, Utrillo and Laurencin.

Suzanne Valadon
Self-Portrait
1898, The Museum of Fine Arts, Houston

ABUSE OF POWER

Fascism and Nazism considered art as a territory for conquest. The Nazis favoured tradition, and labelled works of art that were contrary to their ideology as "degenerate art". The regime held Chagall, a Jewish artist producing free and innovative works, in its sights, and would burn several of his works.

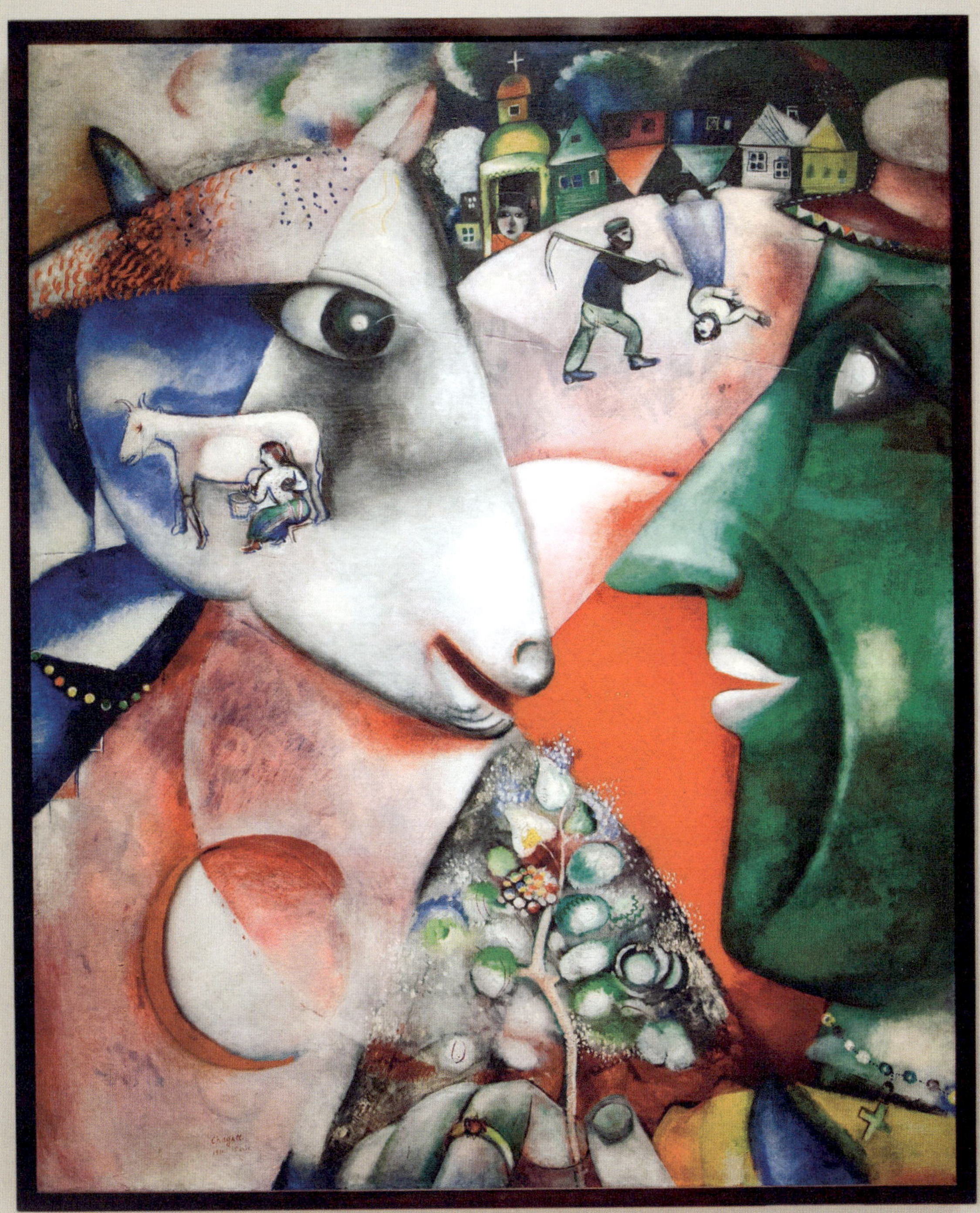

Georges Braque

The hidden side of the cube

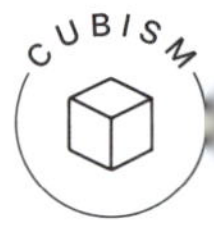

Alongside Picasso, Braque was a leading figure in cubism. His independent career resisted classification. His paintings are imbued with a poetry that blurs the line between his works and the worlds of literature and music.

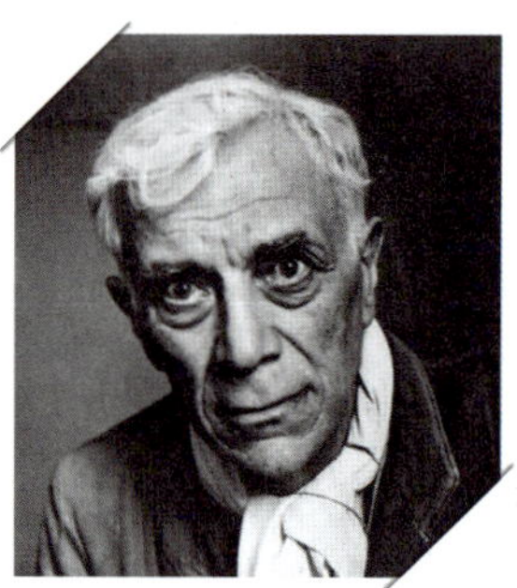

An unruly student

Braque followed in his father's footsteps, becoming a painter-decorator, before opting for an artistic career. He attended academies, but did not accept their teachings, preferring to learn directly in museums, in contact with the works.

A cubic master

Like all cubists, he suffered from Picasso's overwhelming popularity; however, the two men worked closely together. Braque's work was an essential contribution to the movement with, in 1908, the founding landscapes of l'Estaque and the invention of the "Papier collé" technique.

Unclassifiable

The artist followed his own path, producing still lifes, landscapes and interiors in grey and ochre tones. He mixed techniques, engraved, sculpted, and imagined costumes and ballet sets. His bold modernity absorbed classical tradition. Towards the end of his life, he earned recognition from New York to Venice.

GEORGES BRAQUE SAID

"It is worth remembering, however, that the word *Cubist* was first uttered by someone presented with my oil paintings, at the jury of the Salon d'Automne."

Marc Chagall
Page 270

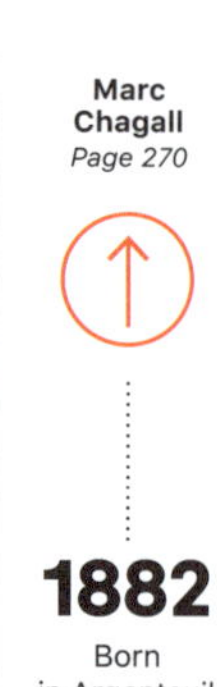

1882
Born in Argenteuil

1905
In France, the law for the separation of church and state was passed

1960
Painted *Black Bird and White Bird*

1961
Yuri Gagarin became the first man to travel in space

1963
Died in Paris

Hilma af Klint
Page 274

BLACK BIRD AND WHITE BIRD ↗

1960
Oil on canvas
134 × 167.5 cm
Private collection

WHAT ARE WE LOOKING AT?

The painter depicted one of his favourite motifs: a bird. Present until the end of his career, it perfectly symbolises the vitality of his creativity and the poetic and spiritual dimension of his art.

A two-winged symbol

Inspired by a flight of birds in the region of Camargue, Braque would elect them as one of his favourite subjects towards the end of his career; they are considered to be one of the artist's most iconic motifs. They appeared early in his work, but it was from the 1950s onwards that he consistently devoted himself to painting them.

Pots and birds

Braque was commissioned to paint a ceiling for the Louvre Museum. For this work, he was inspired by drawings found on Etruscan pottery. This institutional mission allowed him to become the first artist to be exhibited in his lifetime in the largest French museum.

A lingering mystery

Over the years, the artist gave the birds an increasingly abstract form. He sought to detach himself from their reality, in order to better translate them in his paintings. The painter does not claim any symbolism: the bird simply allows him to depict space and movement. Its suspended presence, however, inspires viewers with the idea of a more spiritual overcoming.

They fly high

These two birds are coloured flat tints, devoid of any details. The painter has created an organised set of forms that appear to be floating. The rounded shapes in the background may evoke a celestial universe, planets or moments of the day. The pink and yellow tones are reminiscent of dawn or dusk, with their processions of animals, depicted in black and white, which are only shadows and highlights.

PAPIER COLLÉ

The technique of "Papier collé", invented by Braque and adopted by Picasso, consisted in integrating fragments of wallpaper or newspapers into compositions. Braque would produce 57 works using this technique, while Picasso would produce 300.

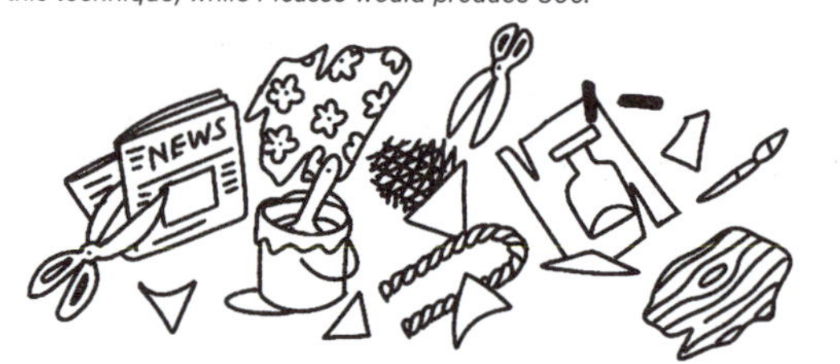

LEADING FIGURES OF CUBISM

- Georges Braque
- Pablo Picasso (p. 264)
- Juan Gris (1887–1927)
- Fernand Léger (1881–1955)
- Jean Metzinger (1883–1956)
- André Lhote (1885–1962)

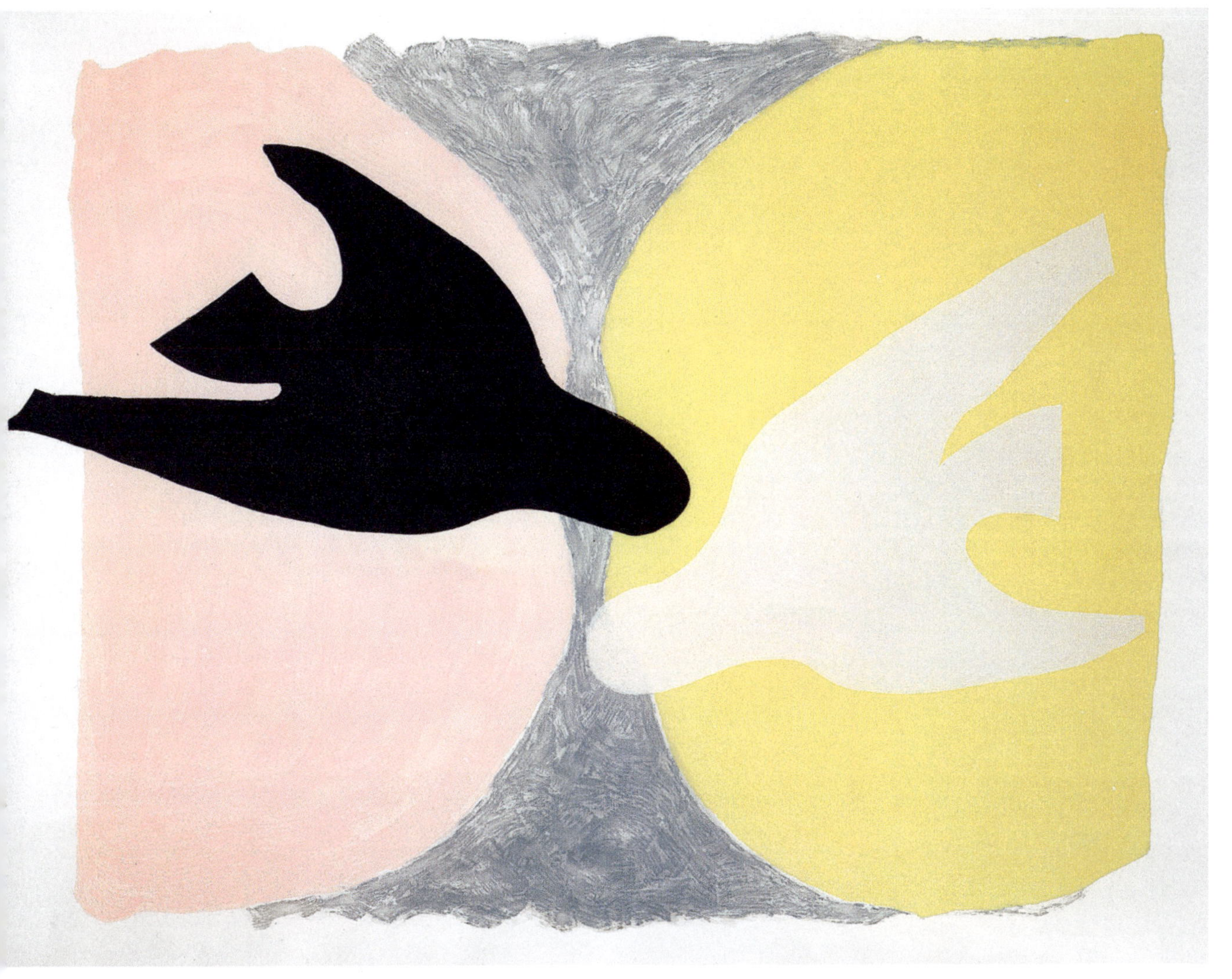

Night-time birds

This easel-scale work evokes the colours of the day; however, *The Birds*, displayed in the Louvre, are painted in monumental dimensions, in black on a dark blue background. The nocturnal impression is reinforced by the stars and the crescent moon featured in this work. The three paintings are set in gold panelling.

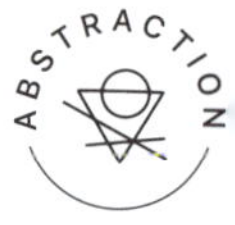

Hilma af Klint

A painting full of spirits

Hilma af Klint led a strange double life. An apparently classical painter, she worked in secret on a revolutionary abstract production, inspired by nature and esotericism, which she would only reveal later in her career.

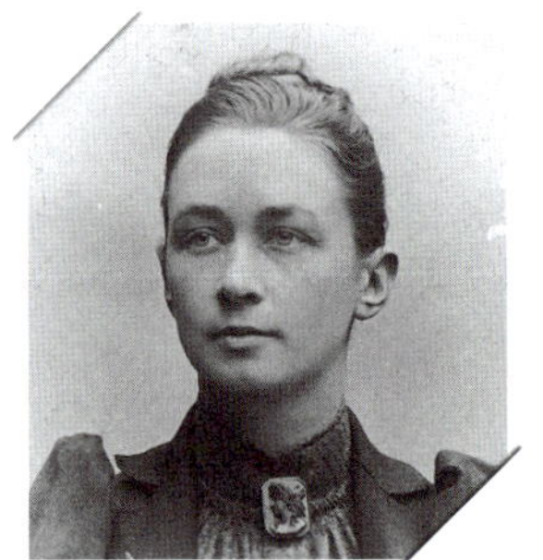

"The Five"

Hilma af Klint would be one of the first women to enter the Royal Academy of Fine Arts in Sweden. She became interested in esotericism and, with others, founded a group called "The Five". They practised automatic writing and drawing, methods later explored by the Surrealists.

A complex language

Her work was inspired by spirituality and natural sciences, which she evoked through organic forms. Her message remains difficult to analyse, even though she left notes enabling spectators to decode elements.

Better late than never ...

Hilma af Klint preceded Malevich (p. 280) and Kandinsky (p. 276) in the realms of abstraction, but remained a lesser-known artist. In accordance with her will, her works would be kept secret for twenty years after her death. Their disclosure, in the 1960s, went unnoticed, and the artist would only become renowned some twenty years later.

HILMA AF KLINT SAID

"I had no idea what the paintings were supposed to depict; nevertheless, I worked swiftly and surely, without changing a single brushstroke."

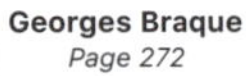

Georges Braque
Page 272

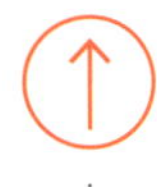

1862
Born in Stockholm

1895
First edition of the Venice Biennale

1915
Painted *Svanen, nr 17, Grupp IX/SUW, Series SUW/UW*

1922
The British government recognised the independence of Egypt

1944
Died in Danderyd

Vassily Kandinsky
Page 276

SVANEN, NR 17, GRUPP IX/SUW, SERIE SUW/UW ↗

1915
Oil on canvas
150.5 × 151 cm
Moderna Museet, Stockholm

WHAT ARE WE LOOKING AT?

This painting is part of the Swan series, in which af Klint depicts this animal in an increasingly abstract fashion, evoking the duality of the world.

Otherworldly commission

In 1906, during a séance, af Klint declared that she had received a commission from a higher spiritual entity, named Amaliel, to produce a set of abstract paintings.

Maximum productivity

Despite her colleagues' reluctance, she accepted the commission, which resulted in the production of 193 paintings between 1906 and 1915. Collectively named the "Paintings for the Temple", these were divided into letter-coded subgroups.

Swans and signs

As part of this extensive project, between 1914 and 1915, af Klint began work on the *Svanen* series, in which she created variations on the figures of two swans, which were gradually replaced by abstract geometric forms.

Not so pleasing

This series is linked to af Klint's interest in theosophical thought. Theosophy was a spiritual movement that appealed to many personalities at the time of the artist, but was later denounced as a cult.

According to the movement's founder, the swan is a symbol of the majesty of the spirit. In many myths, this animal is also an emblem of the celestial world.

Two sides of the same coin

Within this sub-series, the artist extended her spiritual thinking and depicted variations of her favourite themes inspired by duality (black and white, male and female, life and death), which end up intertwining and forming a congruent whole.

OTHER LEADING FIGURES OF ABSTRACTION

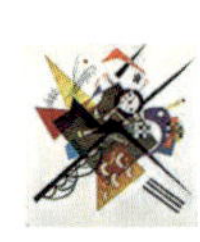

Vassily Kandinsky
On White II
1923
Centre Pompidou, Paris

Kasimir Malevitch
Black Square
1915
The State Tretyakov Gallery, Moscow

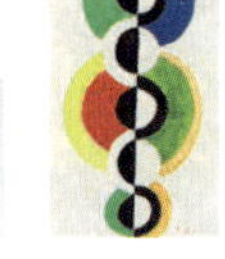

Robert Delaunay
Rhythms
Circa 1932
Private collection

Piet Mondrian
New York City 1942
Centre Pompidou, Paris

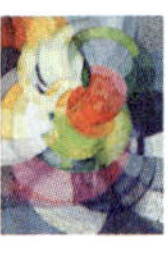

František Kupka
Disks of Newton 1912
Philadelphia Museum of Art

CHEAT SHEET

Today, the spiritual message contained within Hilma af Klint's avant-garde works remains difficult to decipher, but the artist left behind numerous notebooks providing insights into her work. For example, it is known at that the letter W stands for the material, and the letter U for the spiritual.

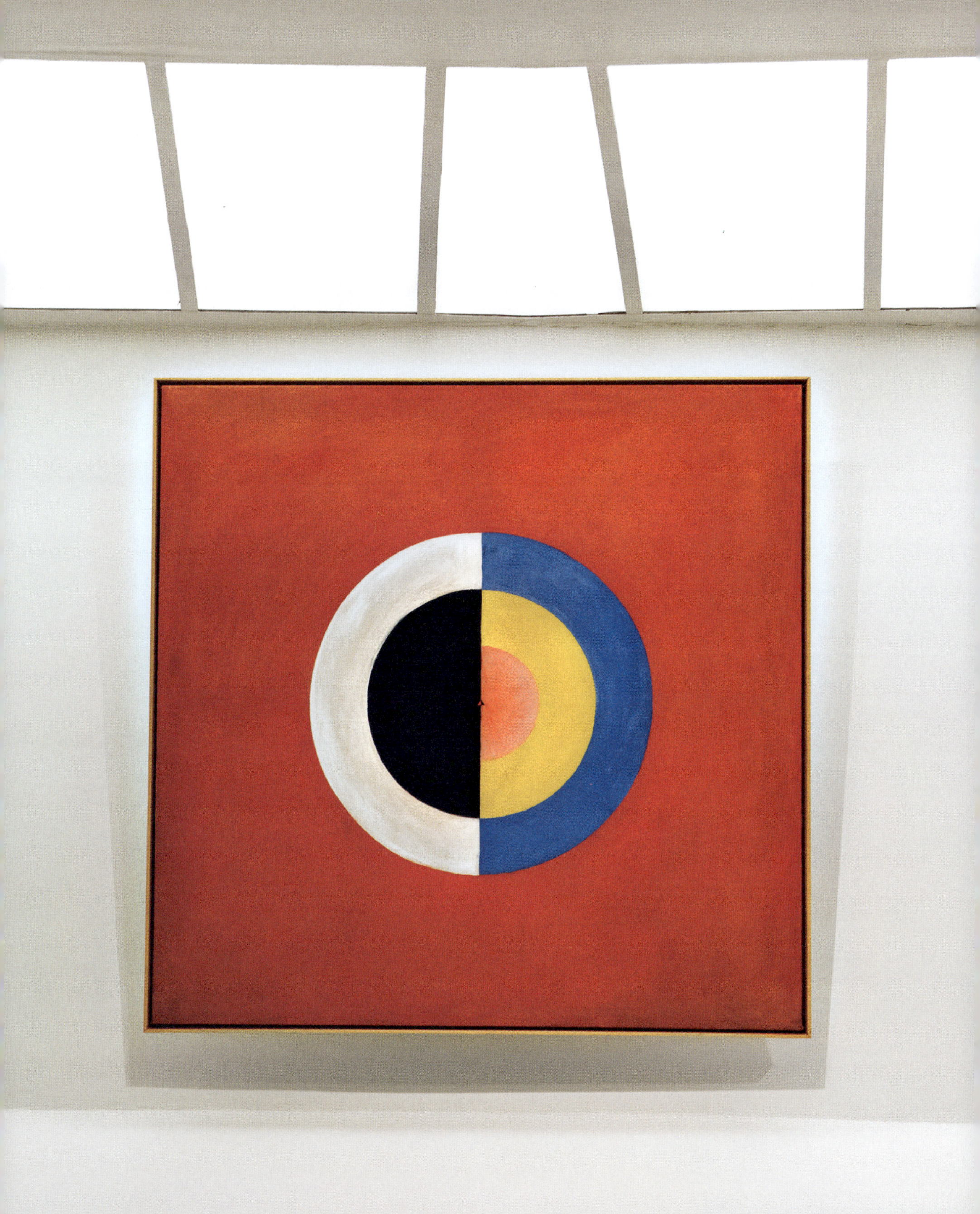

Vassily Kandinsky

Colours finding their shapes

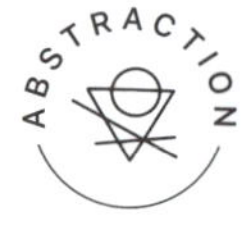

Known as one of the greatest precursors of abstraction, Kandinsky was also an intellectual, and wrote extensively to theorise his practice. He nevertheless sought to produce art that was accessible to all, perceived immediately through the senses.

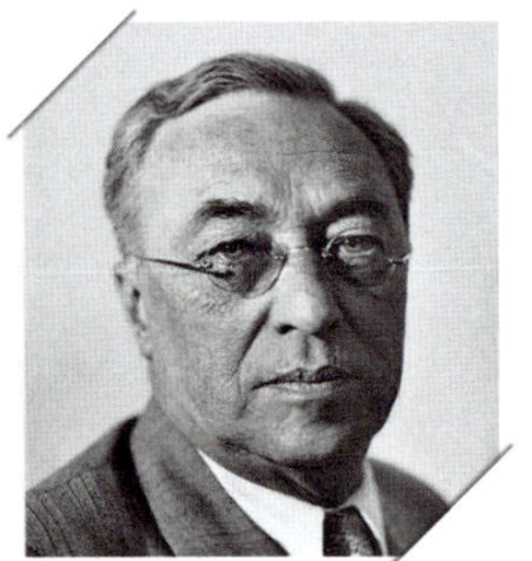

Quite a fuss

Born into a wealthy family, Kandinsky studied law, ethnography, economics, and began writing a thesis. At the age of 30, he experienced a real aesthetic shock discovering Monet's haystacks, whose abstract aspect he admired. He then began studying painting in Munich.

The truth is out there

Kandinsky's work was influenced by the idea of a new perception of reality and by scientific discoveries such as X-rays or the theory of relativity, which promote the idea of an invisible or subjective world. This would lead him to embrace abstract art.

Democratisation before its time

For the artist, it was a way of reaching a universal language. He aspired to produce art that was accessible to all. Kandinsky often connected music and painting, seeking immediacy in perception through the senses.

IT ALL BECOMES CLEARER IN WRITING

Throughout his life, the artist wrote to theorise his practice. His essay, *Concerning the Spiritual in Art*, marked the history of modern art.

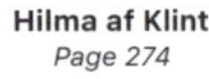

Hilma af Klint
Page 274

1866
Born in Moscow

1910
The Mexican Revolution began

1923
King Kong beat his chest in movie theatres

1925
Painted *Gelb-Rot-Blau (Yellow-Red-Blue)*

1944
Died in Neuilly-sur-Seine

Piet Mondrian
Page 278

GELB-ROT-BLAU ↗
(YELLOW-RED-BLUE)

1925
Oil on canvas
128 × 201.5 cm
Musée National d'Art Moderne, Centre Pompidou, Paris

WHAT ARE WE LOOKING AT?

Kandinsky materialised his theories about the relationship between shapes and colours as paintings, granting access to a spiritual perception of the world.

In the right place

When Kandinsky painted this picture, he was teaching colour theory and analytical drawing at the Staatliches Bauhaus school. He carefully followed the seminar on colour given by the painter Ludwig Hirschfeld Mack and, at the same time, wrote a new essay entitled *Point and Line to Plane*. This work is the translation of Kandinsky's thought process: shapes and colours match.

Blowing hot and cold

The painter has organised his composition in two parts. On the left, a warm world, tinted with yellow and criss-crossed with geometric lines; on the right, another, colder world, marked by blues and greens, where free forms are expressed. The composition produces an impression of movement and imbalance, but the complementary nature of the colours and shapes creates a feeling of harmony.

Smoothly

The arrangement of the three basic colours, which give the painting its name, is not organised randomly. Yellow and blue symbolise the two ends of a spatial boundary: yellow for proximity, blue for distance. The painter deliberately placed red in the centre, as he considered it to be an active colour that can pull towards yellow or blue. It provides a smooth transition between two contrasting worlds.

IN ALL DIRECTIONS

Synaesthesia is the ability to feel the effects of one sense on another (hearing colours, seeing sounds, etc.). Kandinsky possessed this rare ability, and often associated his paintings with music.

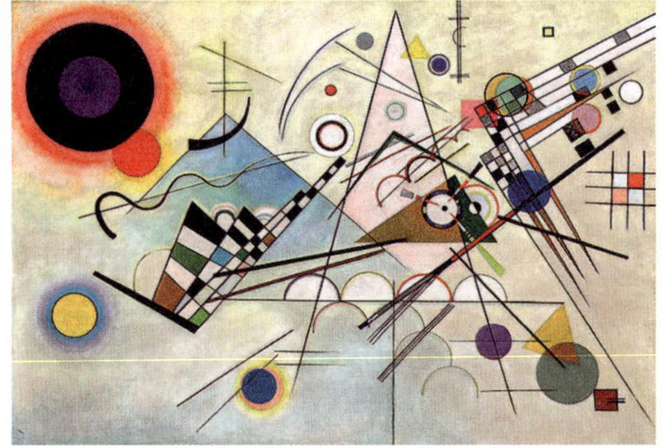

Composition 8, 1923, Solomon R. Guggenheim Museum, New York.

BAUHAUS IN A NUTSHELL

- A school founded by the German architect Walter Gropius.
- An artistic movement that flourished in architecture and design.
- A functional aesthetic that struck a chord with modernity.
- The desire to master techniques and materials with the aspiration of being consistent with the industrial era.

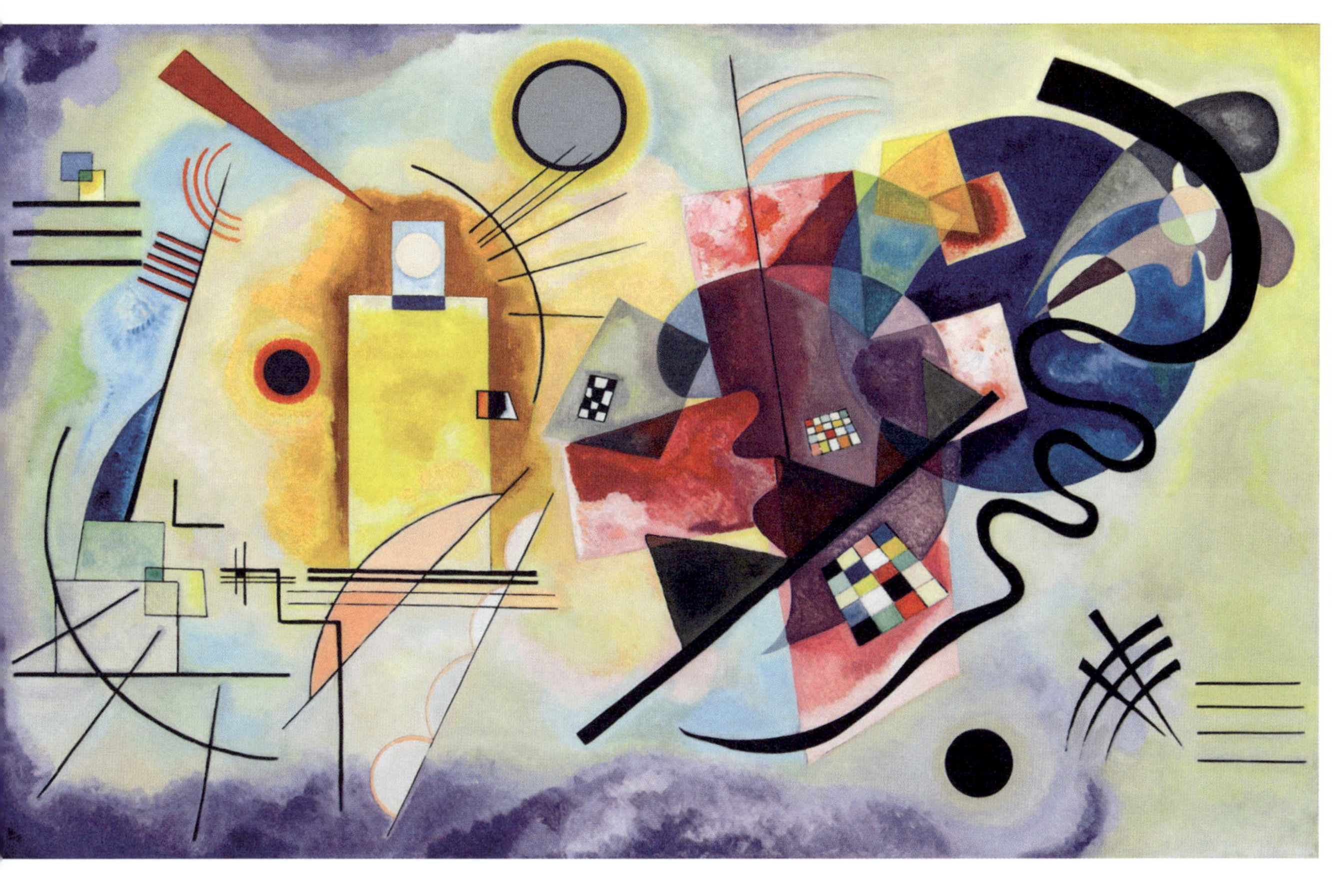

Inflexible about freedom

Long before he joined the Bauhaus school, Kandinsky, with painter Franz Marc, created an almanac that remained famous in the history of art: the *Blue Rider* (*Der Blaue Reiter*, in German). Published in 1912, it testified to the willingness of the participating artists to break away from artistic conformism and allowed Kandinsky to clarify his path towards abstraction.

Piet Mondrian

A very square job

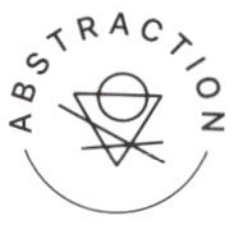

With his minimalist paintings, who owe their accessibility to the simplicity of the palette and motifs used, Pieter Cornelis Mondriaan became one of the greatest names of geometric abstraction. He sought to express a universal truth through a plastic medium.

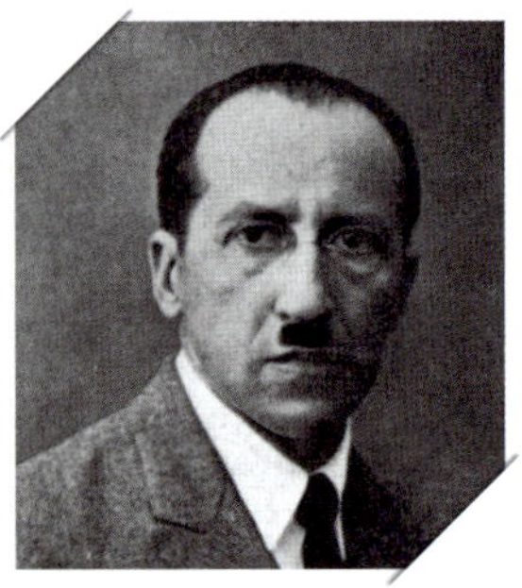

A change in plans

Mondrian studied to become a drawing teacher, then joined the Rijksakademie van Beeldende Kunsten, in Amsterdam. He earned a living by producing portraits and giving art lessons to women of good society.

Holy matters and idols

His interest in theosophy (p. 274) imparted his works with symbolist overtones, and his brushwork became more luminous and expressive. In 1912, he moved to Paris. He admired Braque (p. 272) and Picasso (p. 264), and began producing cubist works. Five years later, he embraced abstraction, and joined the Dutch De Stijl movement.

Getting to the point

He developed a mode of expression that would make him famous, which he called "Neoplasticism". He reduced his palette to primary colours, and his motifs to vertical and horizontal lines. Studying the relationship of the former to the latter, he sought to attain a pure and orderly truth that allowed him to depict the very essence of things.

GOLDEN HEALTH

In Amsterdam, at the beginning of his career, Mondrian was not very wealthy. As was often the case for artists in need, he paid his doctors with works of art.

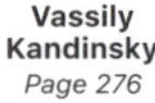
Vassily Kandinsky
Page 276

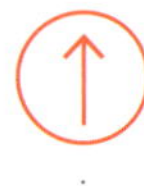

1872
Born in Amersfoort, the Netherlands

1888
Van Gogh cut off his ear

1930
Painted *Composition with Red Blue and Yellow*

1930
The Chrysler Building opened in New York

1944
Died in New York

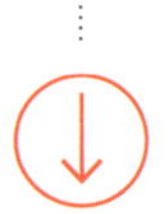
Kasimir Malevitch
Page 280

COMPOSITION WITH RED BLUE AND YELLOW

1930
Oil on canvas
45 × 45 cm
Kunsthaus, Zürich

WHAT ARE WE LOOKING AT?

In this composition, typical of Mondrian's art, the colour red dominates the canvas, imbuing the work with a strong material presence.

Don't fix something that isn't broken

Mondrian remained true to his style. Over the years, he produced variations, painting double lines, highlighting colours, making them disappear, replacing them with shades of grey, then reverting to lines and coloured dots to produce rhythmic effects, under the influence of the New York blues scene of the 1940s.

Making a dream come true

Between 1929 and 1931, Mondrian worked on compositions in which red was given the most space. It was at this time that architect Alfred Roth sent him this request: "The delightful moment when I can fulfil my greatest desire has come: to commission a painting from you."

A politeness competition

Mondrian offered his client the choice: "Tell me in writing if you prefer blue and yellow, white and grey, or red, little blue and yellow and white and grey. The latter works (with red) are more 'reëel' [*sic*]." Following exchanges revealed that Roth let him decide.

Well summarised

While Mondrian usually sold his paintings for 3,000 francs, he only asked Roth for half that amount, even though he was experiencing financial difficulties. On the back of the work, a note seems to sum up his work: "To count only with relations, while creating them and seeking their balance in art and in life, is the beautiful work of today: it is preparing for the future."

PRIMARY AND SECONDARY

The primary colours are blue, red and yellow. They each have a complementary (or secondary) colour. The combination of these primary and secondary colours is a fantastic playground for artists to experiment with.

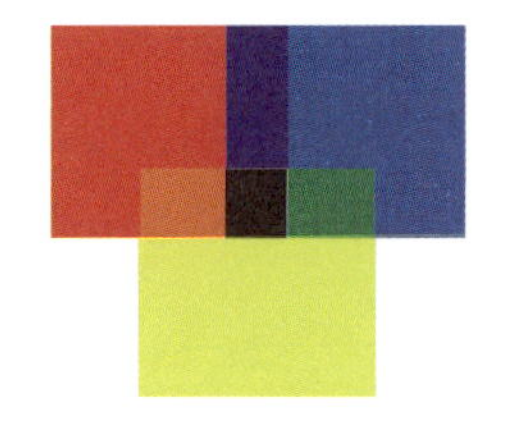

primary colours:	secondary colours:
blue	orange
red	green
yellow	purple

DE STIJL IN A NUTSHELL

- A magazine founded in 1917 by Theo Van Doesburg, which led to the publication of a manifesto in 1918.
- A movement based on the manifesto of the Dutch abstract artists.
- The gathering of all the arts: painting, sculpture, design and more.

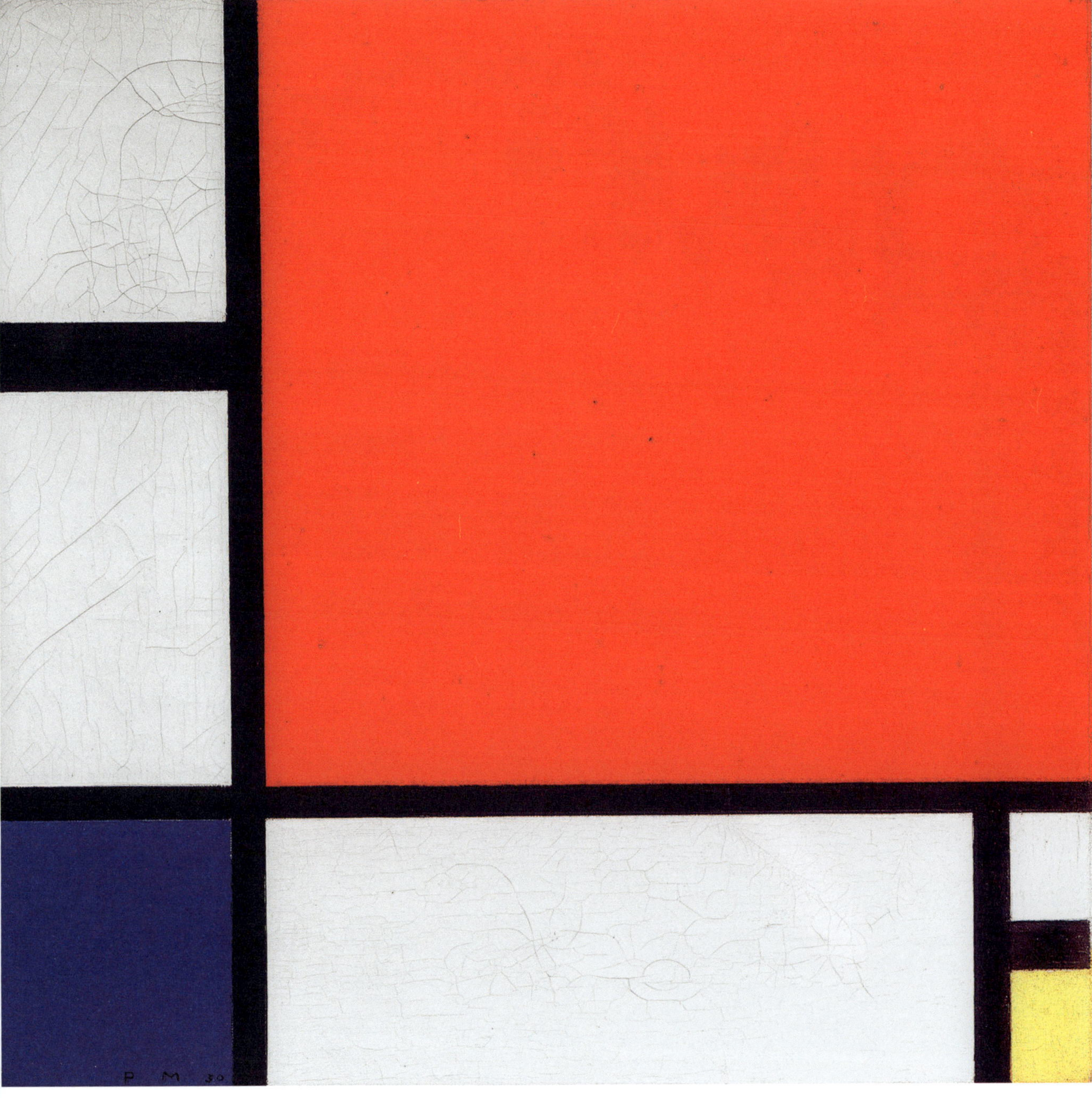
P M 30

Kasimir Malevitch

Nothing is already a lot

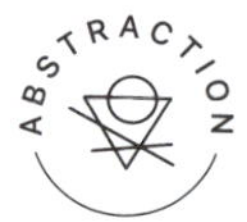

While assimilating the Russian and Western influences that surrounded him, Malevich created art that was free from the constraints of representation. This radicalism, which he named "Suprematism", marked the history of painting.

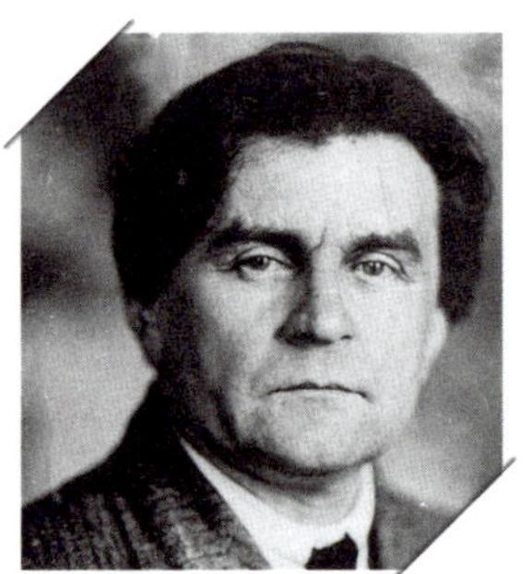

Impressed

A Ukrainian citizen of Polish origin, Malevich grew up among workers and peasants. In 1904, embracing painting, he went to study in Moscow, where he was overwhelmed by the works of Monet (p. 224), whose light and colour he admired.

The subject becomes a complement

In the capital, rich with Russian and Western avant-garde influences, Malevich learned from Cézanne (p. 242) and the cubists, among others. He produced dynamic compositions, preferring form and colour to the subject, whose importance disappeared.

Goodbye real world

Following a few years of meteoric progress, Malevich achieved a state of total abstraction, which he named "Suprematism". Malevich conceived a system to represent nothingness, devoid of any reference to reality, founded on a set of geometric shapes and colours.

MALEVICH ON STAGE

Victory over the Sun:
This name, which sounds like a yoga pose, is the title of the surrealist opera for which Malevich designed sets and costumes in 1913.

Piet Mondrian
Page 278

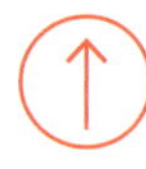

1878
Born in Kiev

1905
Norway became independent from Sweden

1915
Painted *Black Cross*

1925
First edition of Roland Garros

1935
Died in Leningrad

Grant Wood
Page 288

BLACK CROSS

1915
Oil on canvas
80 × 80 cm
Musée National d'Art Moderne, Centre Pompidou, Paris

WHAT ARE WE LOOKING AT?

Also named *Two Suprematist Planes in Orthogonal Relations*, it is one of the painter's first Suprematist works, in which he introduced one of the key motifs of his repertoire: the cross.

Baptism of fire

In 1915, in Saint Petersburg, Malevich became one of the leading figures of the "0,10 Exhibition", which would remain in the annals of painting. The artist presented dozens of abstract and radical works that marked the birth of his Suprematist art.

Like playing tic-tac-toe

With Suprematism, Malevich represented nothingness. He arranged shapes and colours, usually on a white background, according to a repertoire that had created. Three shapes form the main basis of Malevich's art: the quadrilateral, the circle and the cross.

Squared principle

The circle and the cross are variations of the square. The circle is a quadrilateral that would have spun on itself, while the cross would represent the intersection of two rectangular planes.

Work in progress

The motif's irregular contours soften the radical nature of this black motif, depicted on a white background. They are also a possible indications of movement, just as the circle is a movement of the square.

Here, the cross – made up of two halves of a square – is maybe still being constructed.

Slightly flummoxed

With this cross, nevertheless, Malevich cleverly played on a religious symbol and a marker of authority. This ambiguous provocation left more conservative spectators in doubt; unable to clearly express a rejection, they reproached the artist for his approach based on nothingness.

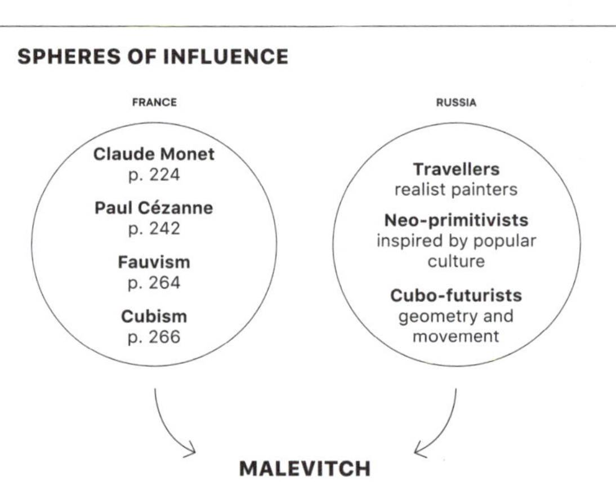

LEADING FIGURES OF THE RUSSIAN AVANT-GARDE

- Kasimir Malevitch
- Mikhail Larionov (1881–1964)
- Natalia Gontcharova (1881–1962)
- Lioubov Popova (1889–1924)
- Piotr Kontchalovski (1876–1956)
- Marc Chagall (p. 270)
- Vassily Kandinksy (p. 276)

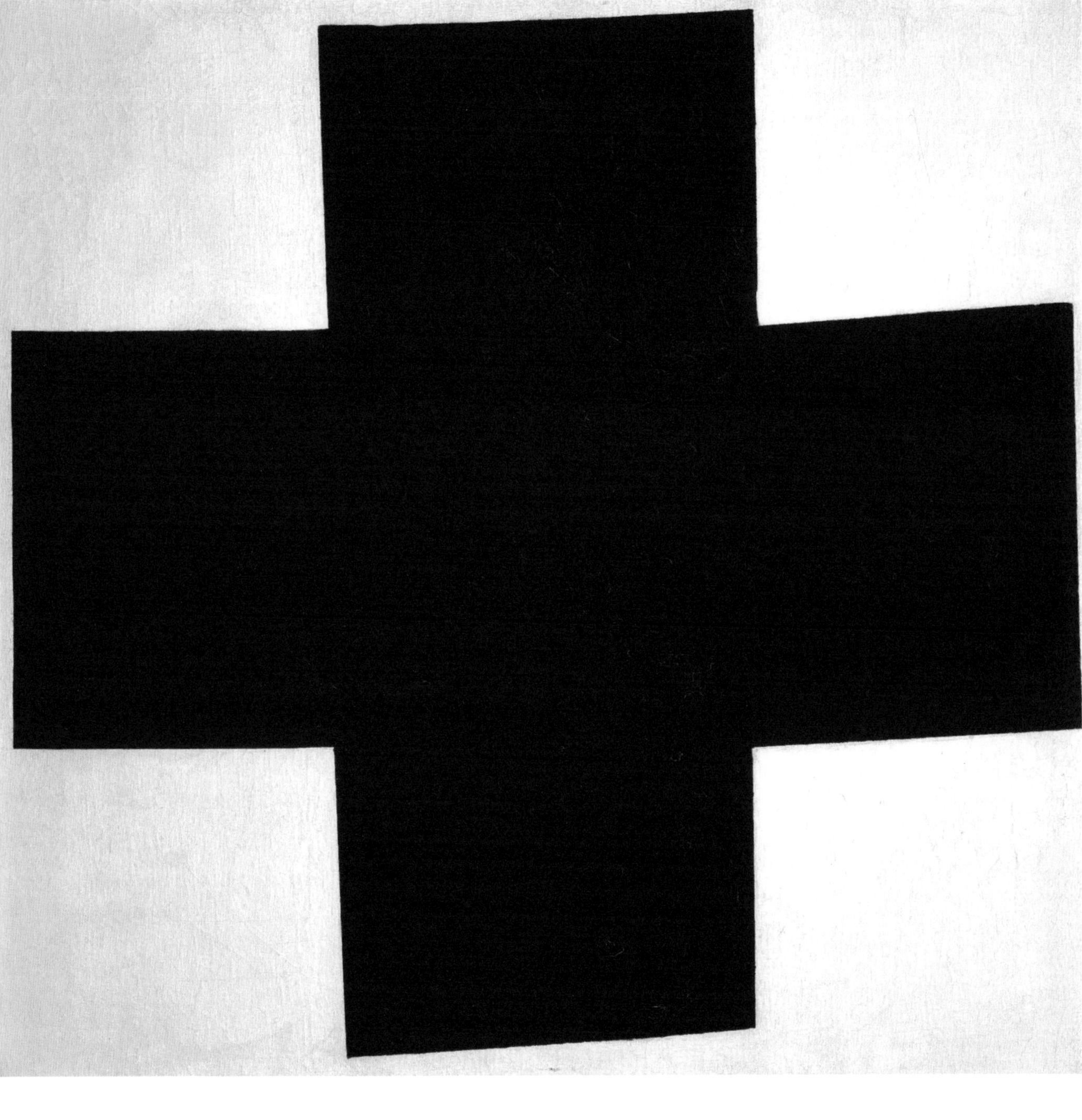

Malevich and Klein

Like floating in the air

Monochrome is a genre in its own right. While the end result is the same, a work based on a single colour, the path to reach it differs from one artist to another. Here, Malevich and Klein sought to render the idea of levitation.

WHITE ON WHITE **BY KASIMIR MALEVICH**
1918

Inspired by aerial photography, Malevich sought to produce the sensation of floating, to render an infinite purity extending beyond reality and nature. His artistic personality is apparent in the visible touch, the dynamism of the off-centre square and the shades of white.

Oil on canvas, 79.4 × 79.4 cm
MoMA, New York

***IKB 3, MONOCHROME BLEU* BY YVES KLEIN**
1960

Klein also printed the monochrome of his personality with his "Klein Blue", also known as IKB, for "International Klein Blue". This work offers the viewer an experience of colour. It features rounded edges that detach the work from the wall, producing an impression of levitation.

Pure pigment and synthetic resin on canvas mounted on wood, 199 × 153 cm
Musée National d'Art Moderne, Centre Pompidou, Paris

Transporting a painting

The “nail to nail” method

It is not unusual for works to travel from one museum to another. However, moving a work of art is no easy task; in fact, it is quite a gauntlet to run. As the saying goes, transport is ensured "from nail to nail", even though other means have been used to hang paintings for a long time.

HOW DOES ONE VALUE SOMETHING PRICELESS?

The value of the insurance can range from a few thousand euros to several tens of millions euros. However, museum works are priceless: firstly, because they are unique and irreplaceable, and secondly, because they were often added to a museum’s collections a long time ago, and therefore have no actual market value. Therefore, the amount is calculated on the basis of the loss that the museum would incur if the work was damaged, stolen or destroyed.

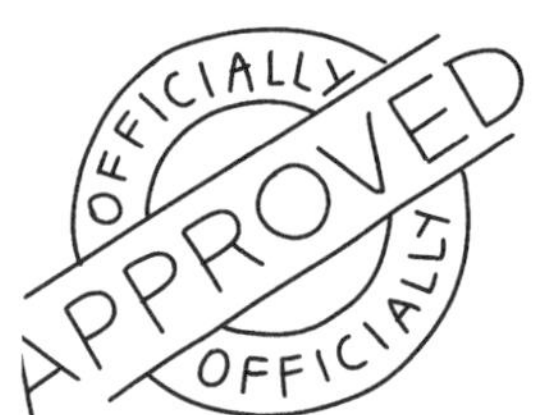

Contracts may feature highly specific clauses, such as prohibiting the carrier from driving on cobblestone roads.

① **Authorisation**

A request for a loan, complete with justifications, is sent to the museum that holds the desired work. This request is issued several years in advance.

② **Contract and insurance**

The contract defines the value of the insurance premium and specifies the exact conditions of transport, in order to assess the risks involved (shocks or vibrations, for instance). By law, loans are offered free of charge.

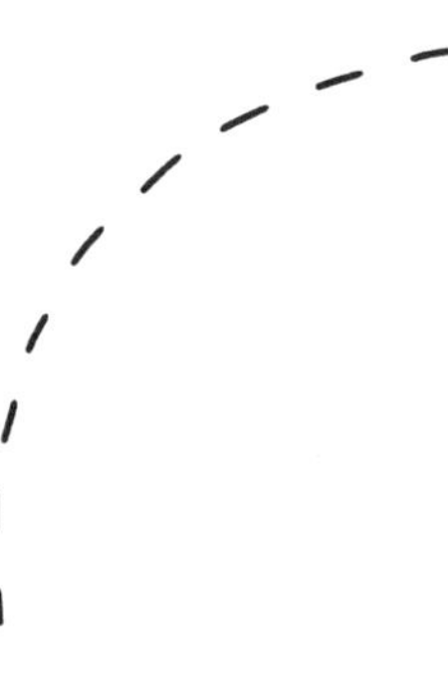

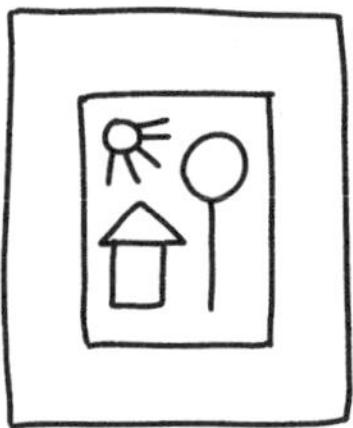

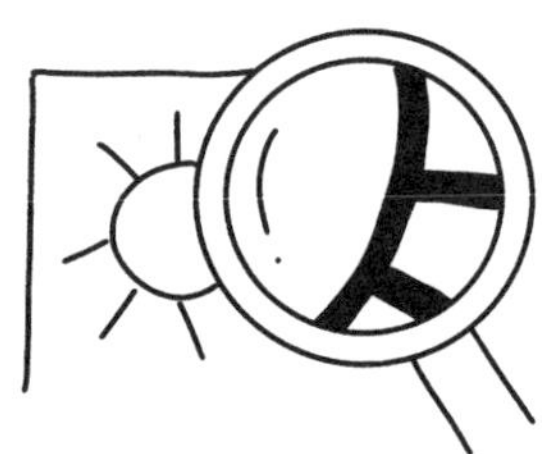

⑨ **Return**

For the return journey, all these operations are repeated.

⑧ **Exhibition**

The work can then be hung and exhibited in accordance with the terms and conditions and the duration established by the loan contract.

⑦ **Condition report on arrival**

The work is unpacked and checked to ensure that it is in the same condition as when it was shipped. Observation in a different light can reveal details that were already present, but were previously unseen.

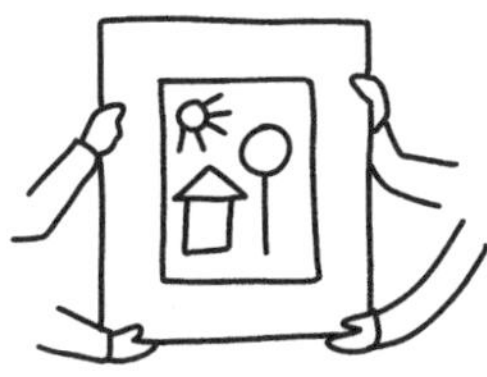

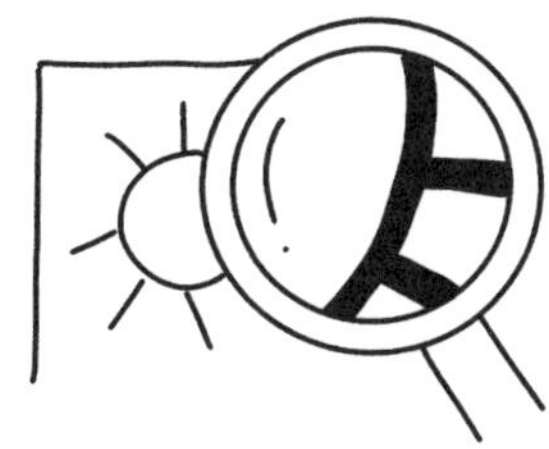

MORE RESPONSIBLE SOLUTIONS ...

Practices are evolving to ensure greener transport (for instance, pooled means of transport and less polluting packaging materials), with the aim of reducing the carbon footprint of exhibitions.

③

Unhanging

This is a technical procedure, as works are secured: they are hung using specific fixings, preventing them from being taken away. This is particularly the case for small formats, which can easily be slipped into a handbag.

④

Condition report on departure

This is the work's "medical record". As for an apartment, an inventory of fixtures is drawn up on departure and on arrival, on the way out and on the way back.
This procedure aims to establish liabilities in case the work is damaged.

⑤

Packing

The paintings are vibration-isolated and packed in unmarked, single-use crates. When fragile works or works that are sensitive to temperature variations must be transported, secure devices such as climate-controlled enclosures or special suspensions are provided.

The pilot may refuse to transport the work of art if they fear that adverse weather conditions will expose it to shocks.

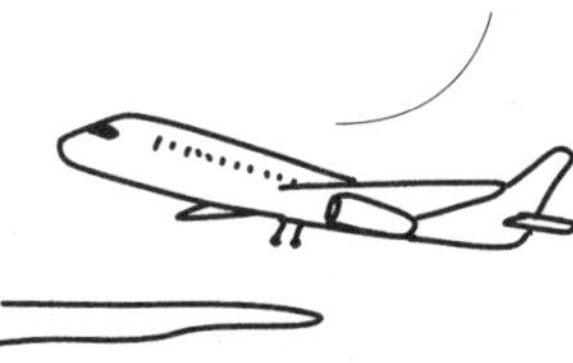

⑥

Transport

The route followed by the truck or the plane is held secret. A representative of the museum, a member of the transport company's team and, sometimes, armed security guards accompany the work. In France, convoys are discreet and unmarked. In other countries, they may include a patrol, with flashing lights and sirens.

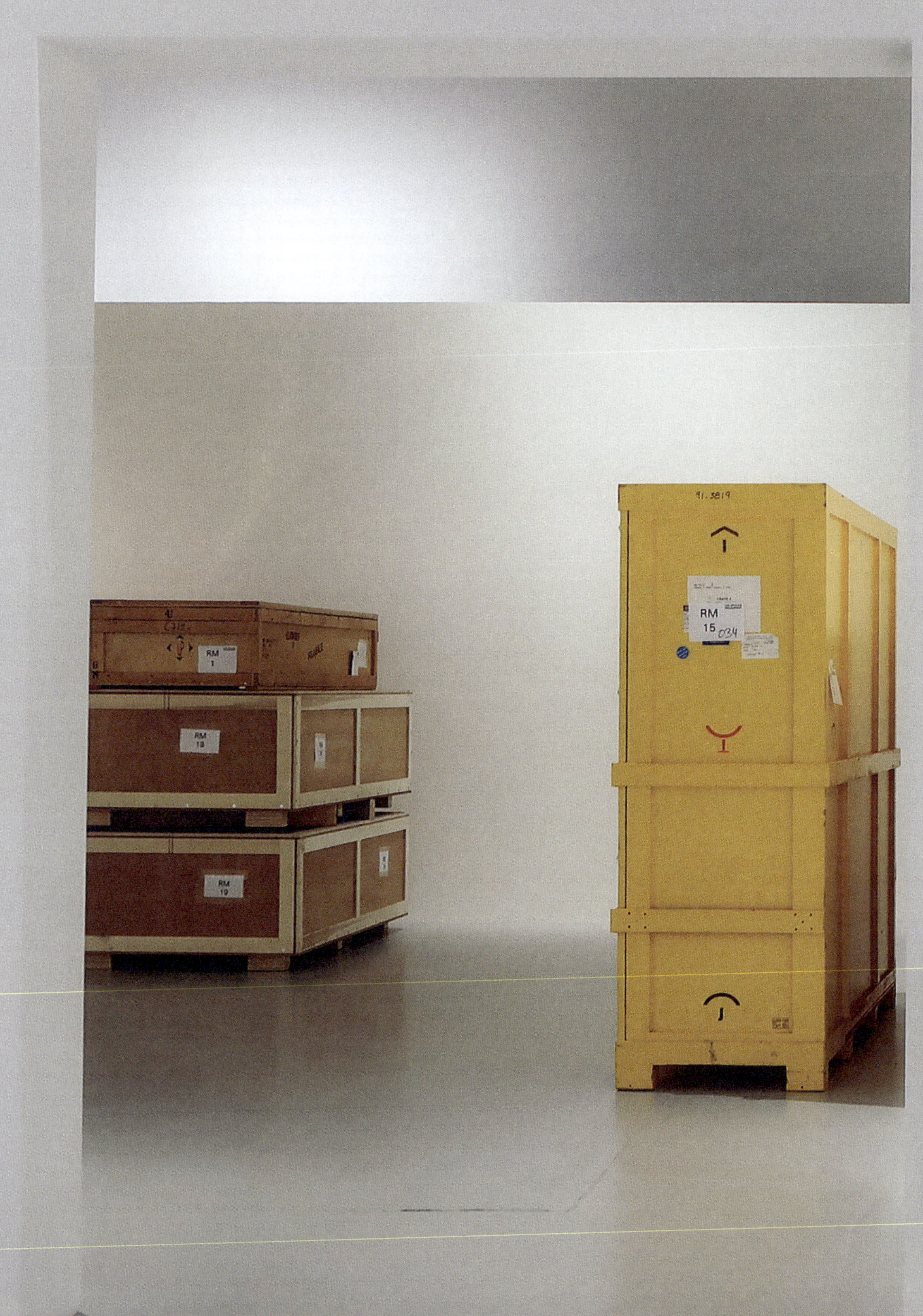
RM
1
RM
18
RM
19
91.3819
RM
15
034

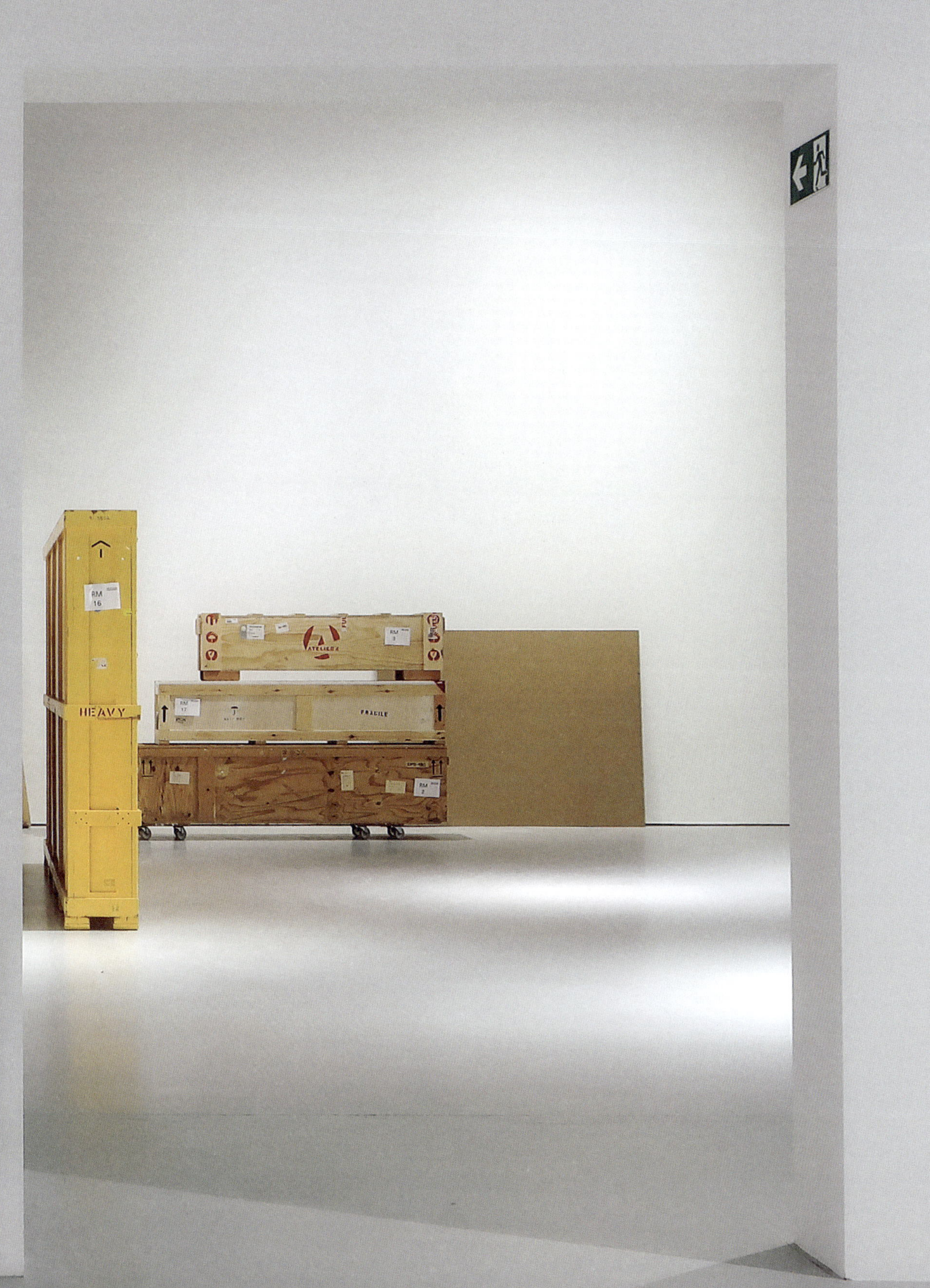
RM
16
HEAVY
FRAGILE

Grant Wood

"Country" painting

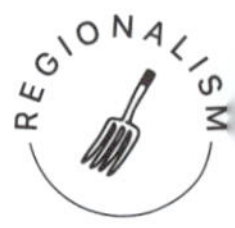

Grant Wood was born in rural Iowa. Defining his identity was a difficult process for him, caught between his personal aspirations and the farmer society into which he was born. His paintings convey a kind of naive and anxious strangeness.

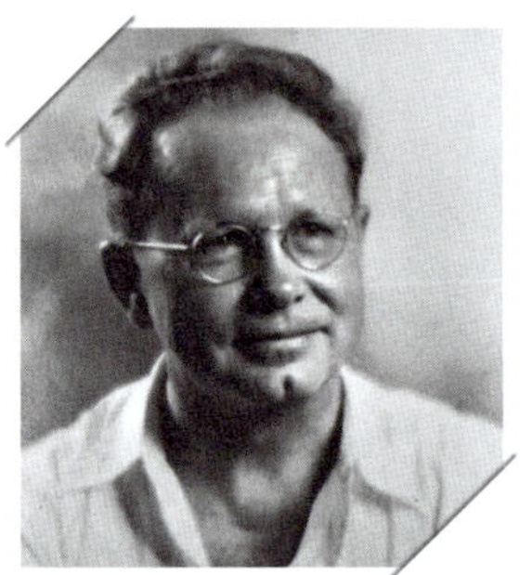

Warm-up tour

Before he became a painter, Grant Wood's worked in the field of decorative arts. His jewellery and metalwork creations are presented in prestigious exhibitions in Chicago. From his beginnings, he retained a taste for decorative motifs and sinuous, organic lines.

Back to the roots

When he embraced fine arts, Grant Wood was influenced by European art, particularly Impressionism, which he discovered in Paris. He later became aware that everyday rural America was a source of artistic material that he could draw from.

Accuracy or nothing

The painter was also influenced by the Flemish Primitives, whose precision he admired; accuracy would become an obsession for him. He knew how to simplify reality; however, every detail needed to be accurate and authentic.

THE AMERICAN *MONA LISA*

American Gothic became a global icon that was subverted many times in shows such as The Simpsons and *Desperate Housewives*, or on the front cover of *Time* magazine.

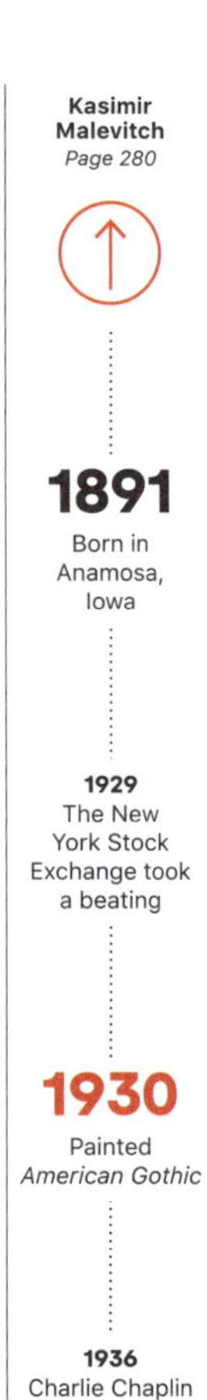

Kasimir Malevitch
Page 280

1891
Born in Anamosa, Iowa

1929
The New York Stock Exchange took a beating

1930
Painted *American Gothic*

1936
Charlie Chaplin directed *Modern Times*

1942
Died in Iowa City

Tamara de Lempicka
Page 290

AMERICAN GOTHIC

1930
Oil on soft Masonite
78 × 65.3 cm
Art Institute, Chicago

WHAT ARE WE LOOKING AT?

A highlight of American regionalism, this painting is the "American *Mona Lisa*", inspired by the painter's experience of rural life. However, an ambiguity remains, between essential values and rigid conformity.

① An uptight atmosphere

The cameo is an emblem of the Victorian style in the previous century. This couple is cut off from modernity, out of step with their times.

② A timeless style

The work owes its title to the window. Indeed, its pointed arch is reminiscent of the Carpenter Gothic architectural style, inspired by the 17th-century Gothic revival in England, which was itself inspired by the Middle Ages.

③ Sunday best

The farmer, with a pitchfork in hand, is wearing his jacket over his work overalls.
He is the perfect embodiment of rural America at the time, hardworking and traditionalist.

④ Tradition and modernity

The realism of the faces is inspired by the Flemish Primitives, such as Hans Memling, but the figures' frontal stance also recalls Henri Rousseau.

⑤ Slightly repressed

From the features of the faces to the posture of the figures and the verticality of the painting, everything appears to be very rigid, translating the couple's conformism … which was, in fact, invented from scratch: Wood indeed asked his sister and his dentist to pose for him.

⑥ Who's looking after the chickens?

Grant highlights conformity by means of gendered associations. The man is standing in front of the farmhouse, while the woman, standing in front of the house, is wearing an apron that matches the curtains.

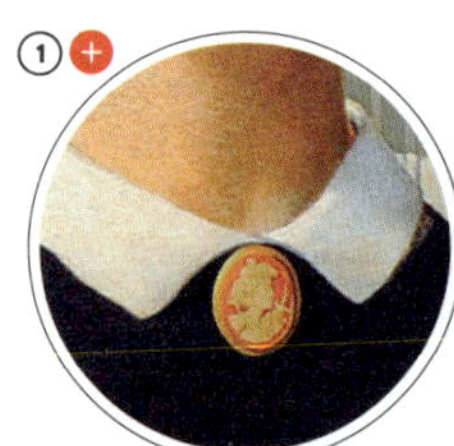

AMERICAN REGIONALISM IN A NUTSHELL

- A movement founded in reaction to the Avant-Garde and the Great Depression.
- A celebration of authentic American values.
- A realistic style.

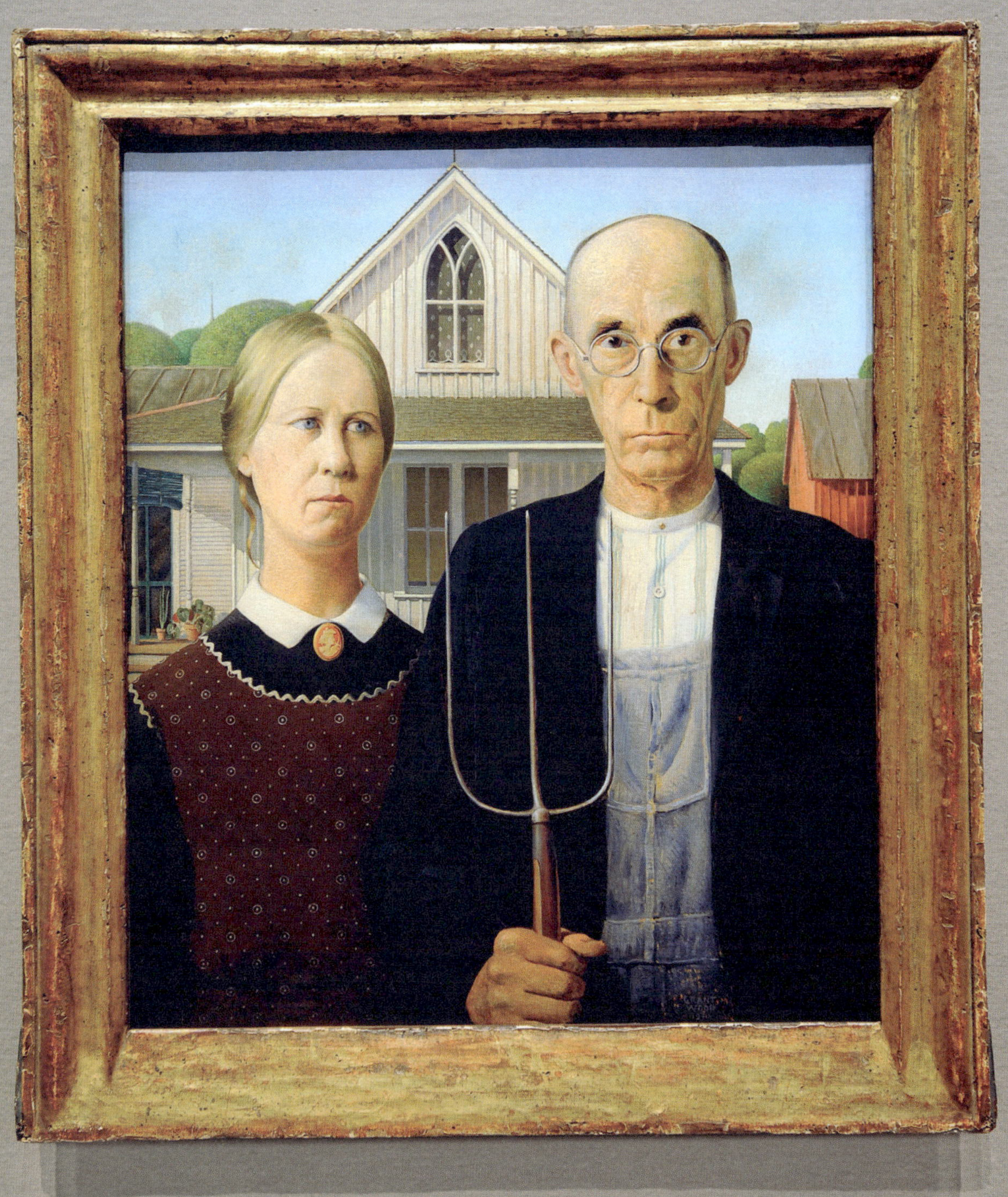

Tamara de Lempicka

At the forefront of art deco

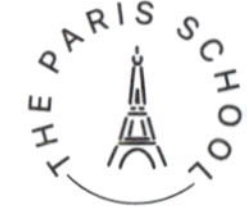

At the height of the multidisciplinary Art Deco movement, Tamara de Lempicka's erotic and worldly paintings expressed a modernity tinged with industrial progress. In spite of depressive episodes that hindered her career, her work was widely recognised.

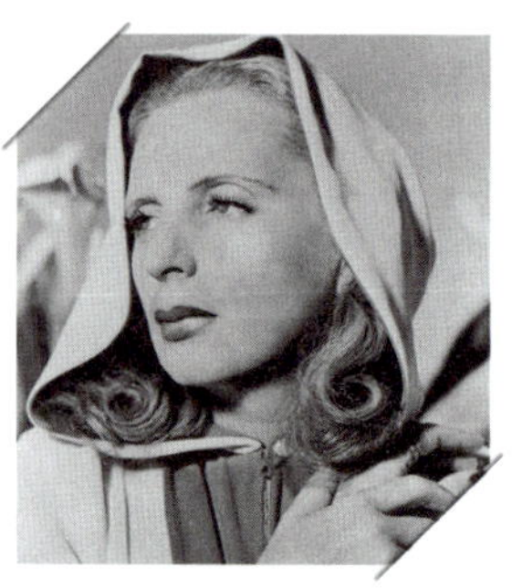

An ideal little girl

Lempicka first discovered painting when she posed for a portrait as a child, and again, during a trip to Italy, during which she discovered the works of the Renaissance. In 1918, she fled the Bolshevik Revolution to Paris, where she studied with Maurice Denis and André Lhote.

The party is over

She made a name for herself in the 1920s, from Milan to Berlin, and received numerous commissions for portraits. The financial and political crisis of the 1930s plunged her into a depression that she struggled to overcome, despite moving to the United States.

Made of hardened steel

Flouting the rules of propriety, Lempicka had many affairs with men and women. Her sensual painting evokes the works of Ingres (p. 180), while conveying the Art Deco spirit. The bodies are firm, angular, featuring metallic reflections borrowed from the industrial world.

A VOLCANIC CONCLUSION

After her death, the artist's ashes were scattered over the Popocatepetl volcano in Mexico, where she settled towards the end of her life.

Grant Wood
Page 288

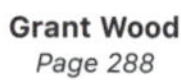

1898
Born in Warsaw

1922
Howard Carter discovered the tomb of Tutankhamun

1925
Fitzgerald published *The Great Gatsby*

1927 to **1930**
Painted *Young Lady with Gloves (Girl in a Green Dress)*

1943
Antoine de Saint-Exupéry published *The Little Prince*

1980
Died in Cuernavaca

René Magritte
Page 292

YOUNG LADY WITH GLOVES (GIRL IN A GREEN DRESS) ↗

1927–1930
Oil on plywood
61.5 × 45.5 cm
Musée National d'Art Moderne, Centre Pompidou, Paris

WHAT ARE WE LOOKING AT?

Between sensuality, modern accents and inspiration from the old masters, this masterpiece embodies de Lempicka's art at its best.

Validated

Tamara de Lempicka presented this portrait at the Salon des Indépendants in 1932. At the peak of the artist's career, this work was purchased by the state – an acquisition that came as a consecration for her.

Now you don't see it, now you do

The artist has portrayed an attractive young woman, with the appearance of a glamorous icon, but she has done her best to reveal what is hidden: the woman's visible nipples and navel. They are apparent under her dress, which appears to be pressed against her body by a wind coming from the side. To protect herself, the young woman is pulling down her hat, whose shadow intensifies her gaze, while her red mouth contrasts with the dominant green.

Back to the roots

Beyond the erotic play, this sensuality of draperies, alternately clinging to the woman's body or floating in the air, seems to be inspired by the Italian statuary and mannerism, which marked the painter's youth. Tamara de Lempicka's work features the smooth, icy texture and distance already present in the works of artists such as Agnolo Bronzino (p. 70).

Shapes and curves

The play of fabrics and shadows creates a set of geometric shapes that connect this work to modernity; the hat thus becomes a stylised white disc, while the neck is shaded with a rectangular triangle. The fabric of the dress takes flight, describing angular frills typical of art deco, a style that is also echoed in Georgia O'Keeffe's (p. 304) paintings.

THREE ICONIC ART DECO CREATIONS

Art Deco is inspired by nature, which it geometrises. It draws its name from the International Exhibition of Modern Decorative and Industrial Arts, which was held in Paris in 1925. It is expressed in all the arts, from painting and sculpture to glassware, fashion and architecture, even extending to the skyscrapers of New York.

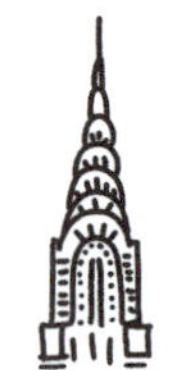

Architecture
William Van Alen
Chrysler Building
1930

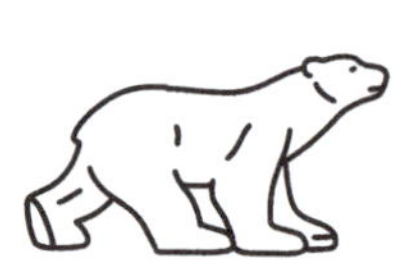

Sculpture
François Pompon
White Bear
1927

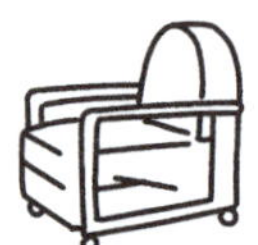

Furniture
Jacques-Émile Ruhlmann
Club armchair
Circa 1925

OTHER LEADING FIGURES OF ART DECO

- Jacques-Émile Ruhlmann (1879–1933), interior architect and designer.
- Paul Poiret (1879–1944) and Jeanne Lanvin (1867–1946), fashion designers.
- René Lalique (1860–1945), glass and jewellery maker.
- Chana Orloff (1888–1968), sculptor.
- Paul Iribe (1883–1935), illustrator.

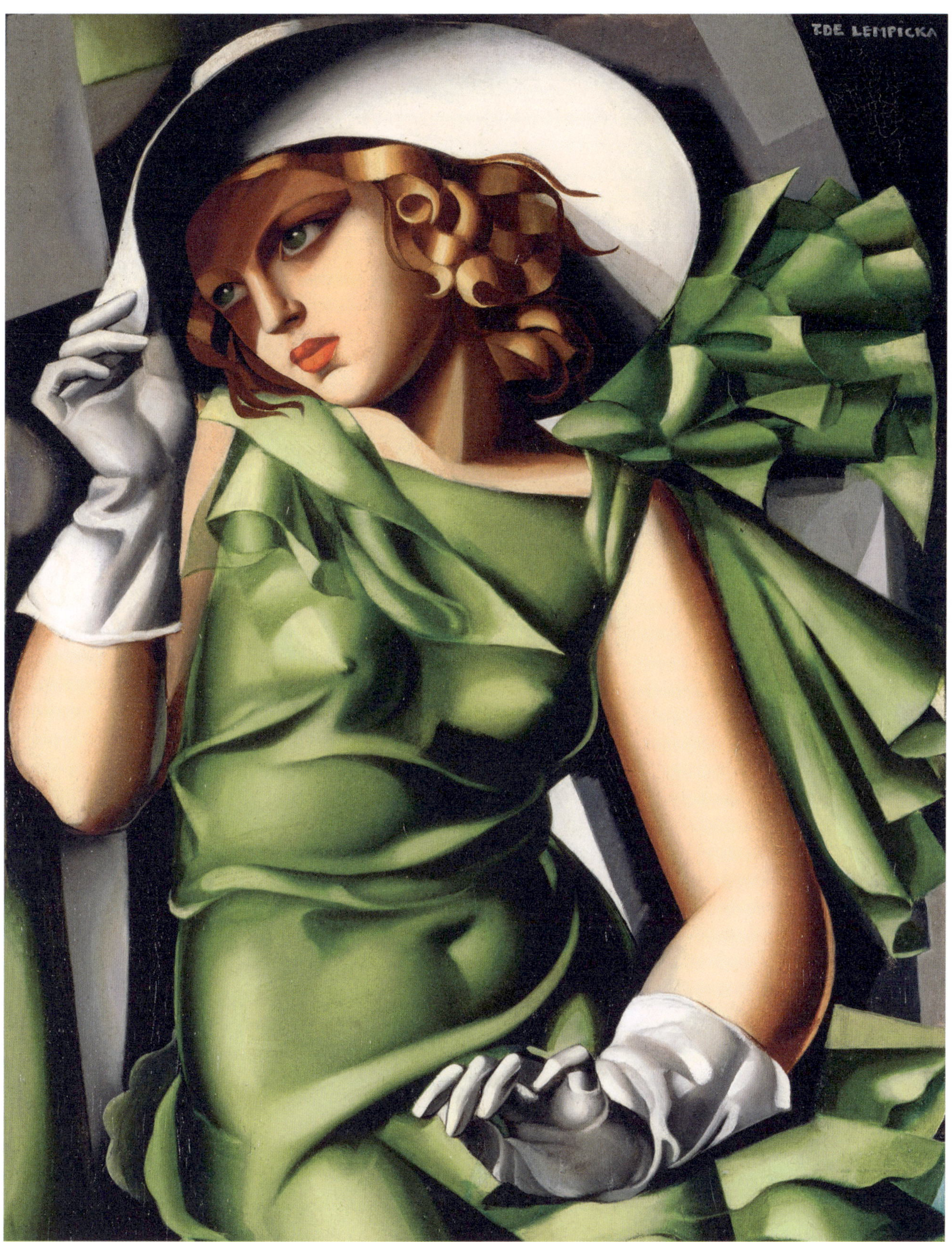
T.DE LEMPICKA

René Magritte

The art of presenting apples

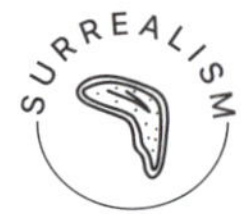

An enigmatic artist, Magritte delivered deeply intellectual works, but also produced more immediate creations that resonated with every viewer. His apples and bowler hats are renowned worldwide.

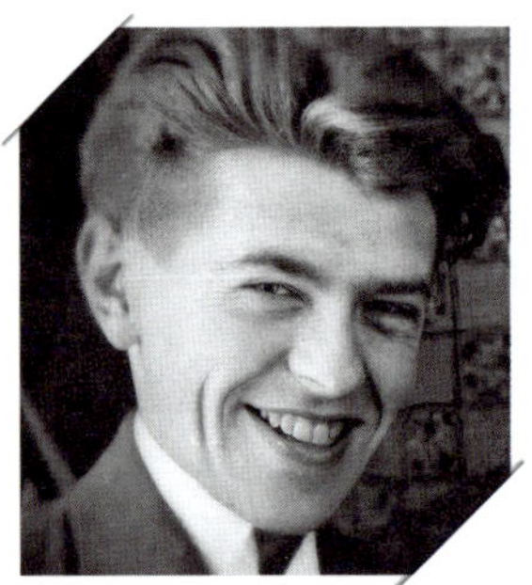

Hostile to ads

Magritte learned to paint as a teenager. In his youth, he immersed himself in the works of the Impressionists and the cubist productions of the French Avant-Garde. He initially earned a living by creating posters and advertising designs, which he described as "imbecile work".

A genre of his own

While he sought to define his style in the world of abstraction, his art blossomed through contact with the Dadaists and the French, then the Belgian Surrealists. However, he replaced the arbitrary associations of objects imagined by the Surrealists with logical and poetic connections.

The gesture and the word

Through his works, Magritte produced art that was singular, illusionist and enigmatic, sometimes also amusing, borrowing from the rebus technique. As a philosopher, he questioned the very idea of painting and representations. He intertwined words and images, questioning the relationship between the two.

RENÉ MAGRITTE SAID

"I finally can see, in the appearance of the real world itself, the same abstraction as in paintings."

Tamara de Lempicka
Page 290

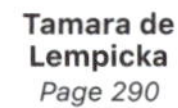

1898
Born in Lessines

1903
Marie Curie became the first woman to win the Nobel Prize

1938
Painted *Not to Be Reproduced*

1940
The Lascaux cave was discovered

1967
Died in Brussels

Salvador Dalí
Page 296

NOT TO BE REPRODUCED

1938
Oil on canvas
81 × 65.5 cm
Museum Boijmans Van Beuningen, Rotterdam

WHAT ARE WE LOOKING AT?

This strange image was commissioned by the collector and patron Edward James. True to form, the artist mischievously diverted the initial function of the portrait.

Last-minute masterpiece

The British artist Edward James, an admirer of Magritte's work, had already worked with the artist in the past, commissioning a triptych from him to decorate his ballroom. On the location, the patron would request two additional commissions from him, including his portrait. The painting was inspired by a photograph of Edward James, seen from behind, contemplating another of Magritte's works, titled *On the Threshold of Liberty*.

A two-way one-way mirror

Magritte's proposal is fantastic, but familiar: it is based on the principle of the mirror, which he has cleverly diverted.
He offers us a reflection of what is visible – what is visible to viewers, that is, by duplicating the image as it appears to them, creating a situation that is both accurate and impossible.

Selective reflection

The impression of strangeness is reinforced by the realism of Magritte's drawing and the artist's attempt at illusionism.

The mirror's frame and the book – which is correctly oriented, placed on the edge of the fireplace – are both depicted with precision and accuracy.

It's all about Poe

Deepening his reflection on reality and appearances, Magritte chose a book by Edgar Allan Poe, a master of the fantasy genre. It is *The Narrative of Arthur Gordon Pym of Nantucket*, the only complete novel produced by the writer, which he presented as an authentic story, although it was full of implausibilities.

IN MAGRITTE'S PAINTINGS, ONE CAN SEE …

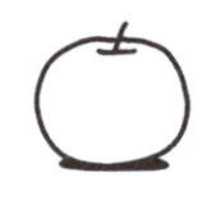

Apples

Birds
(sometimes depicted as eggs!)

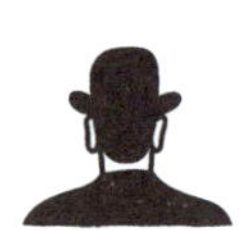

Men with bowler hats

Clouds

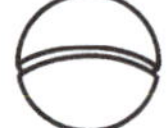

Bells

WHO WERE THE FIRST SURREAL-ISTS?

The movement, born in France at the instigation of André Breton, brought together painters and poets, including:

- Louis Aragon (1897–1982), Robert Desnos (1900–1945), Paul Éluard (1895–1952), Jacques Prévert (1900–1977)
- René Magritte, Giorgio De Chirico (1888–1978), Marcel Duchamp (1887–1968), Salvador Dalí (p. 296)

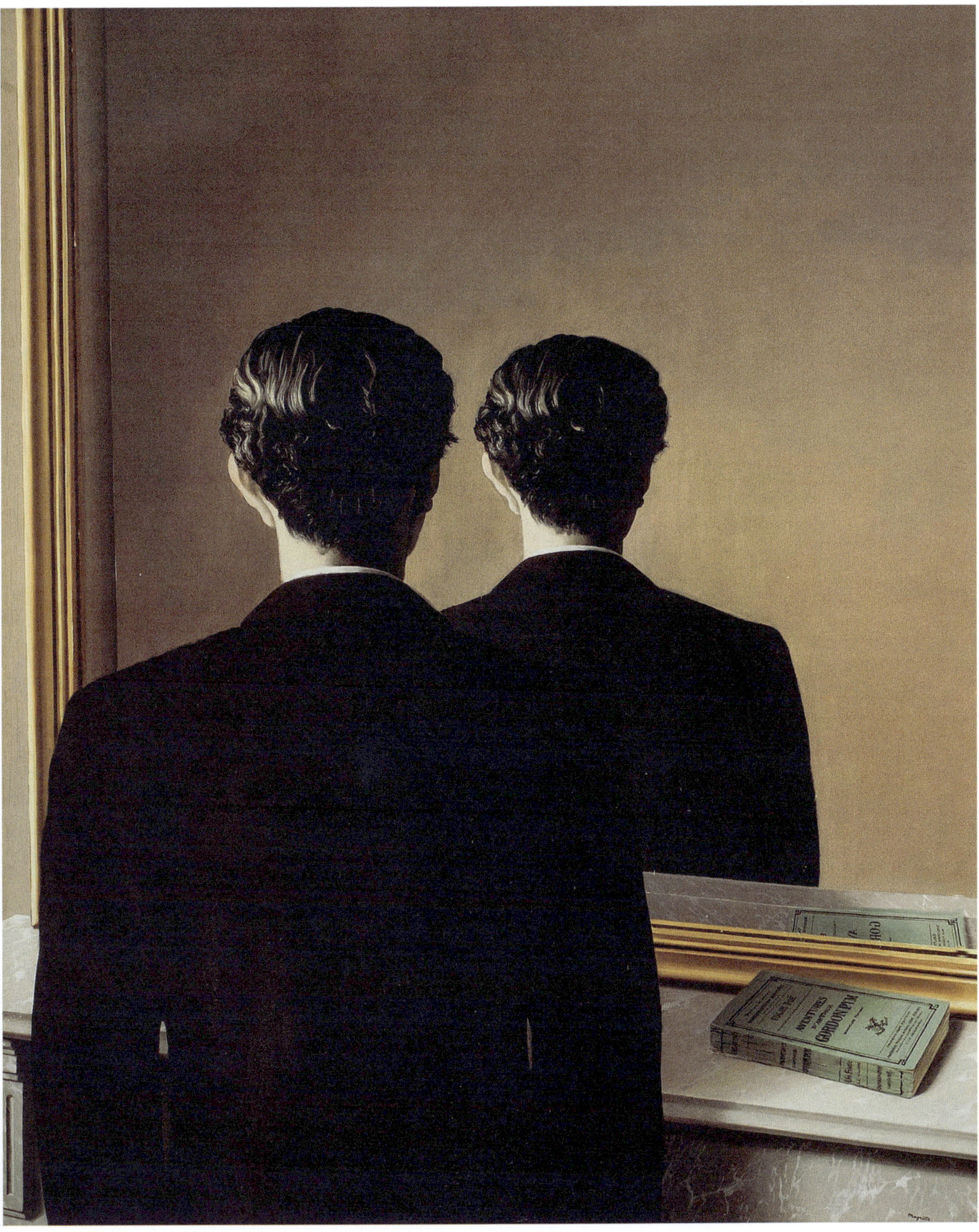
EDGAR POE
AVENTURES
GORDON PYM

Magritte and Botticelli

Horses galore!

Magritte did not fail to pay tribute to Sandro Botticelli in his works. While the two artists may appear to be far removed, one should note that the Renaissance cultivated an art of enigmas and messages that would have appealed to the Belgian painter.

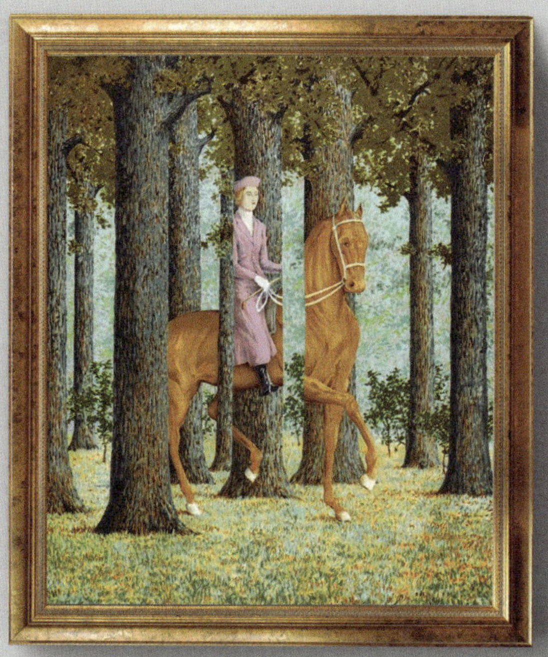

***THE BLANK SIGNATURE* BY RENÉ MAGRITTE**
1965

Magritte has diverted the visual illusion used by Botticelli in the work opposite, and questions our perception: the horse alternately appears and disappears amidst the landscape, in an incoherent and incomplete manner that is inconsistent with the layering of the painting's planes.

Oil on canvas, 81.3 × 65.1 cm
National Gallery of Art, Washington DC

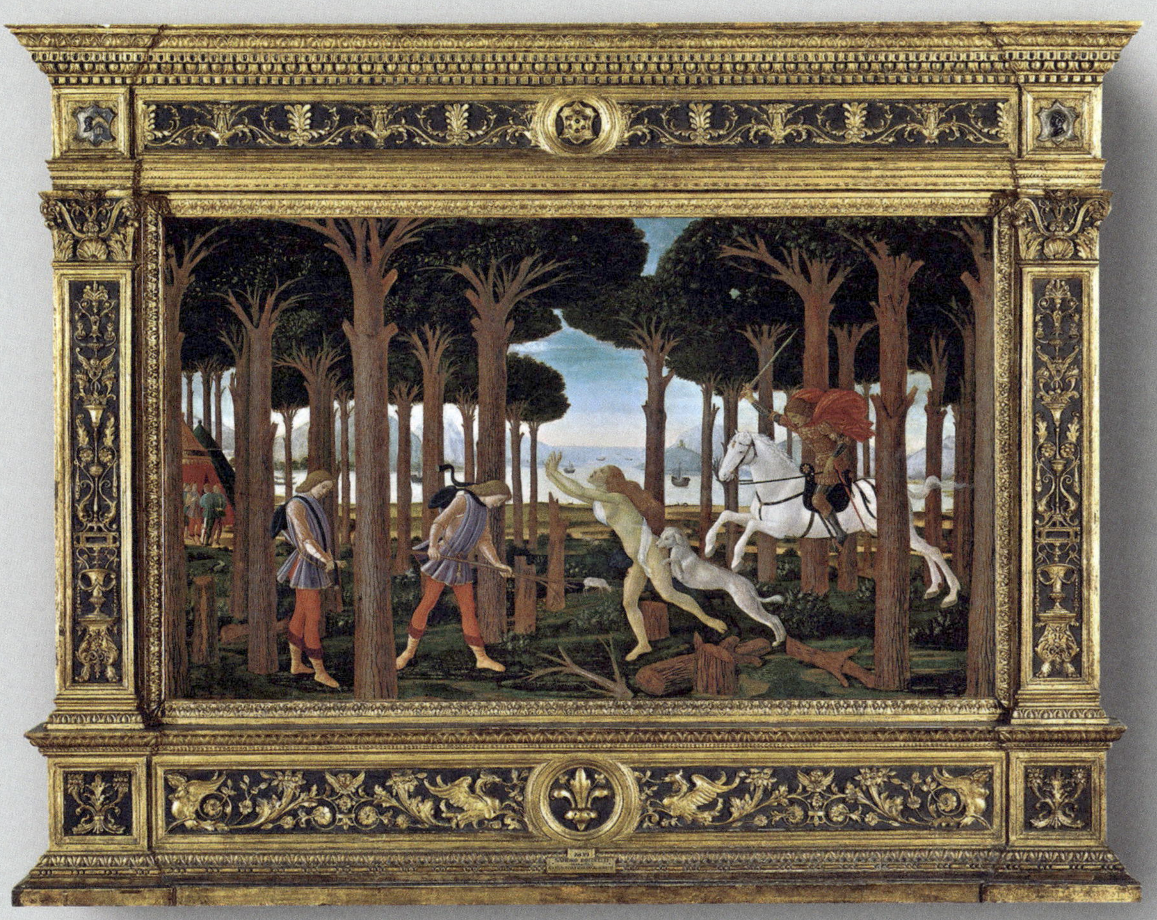

***THE STORY OF NASTAGIO DEGLI ONESTI, PART ONE* BY SANDRO BOTTICELLI**
1483

In this scene from Boccaccio's *Decameron*, the trees produce an impression of depth and create several temporalities. The rider appears to be further away than the figure in the blue tunic, depicted twice in the foreground and a third time in the background, on the left.

Mixed media on wood panel, 82.3 × 139 cm
Prado Museum, Madrid

Salvador Dalí

Eccentric challenger

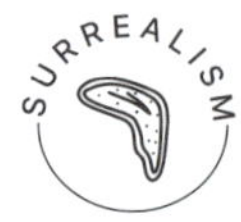

Dalí was as renowned for his unconventional attitudes as he was for his finely finished works. His artistic universe lies halfway between classical inspirations and the Avant-Garde movement, tinged with science fiction.

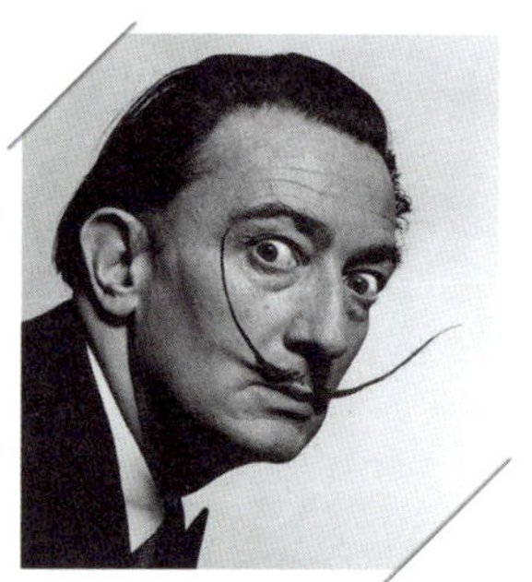

A rebel at heart

With little interest in studies, Dalí quickly turned to drawing. At his father's request, he enrolled in the Royal Academy of Fine Arts of San Fernando, in Madrid, but was expelled for his nonconformist and anti-establishment behaviour. This, however, did not prevent him from exhibiting and achieving his first successes.

In a world of his own

In Paris, he joined the Surrealists and collaborated with the filmmaker Luis Buñuel. Spending time with these artists, he found his style and developed his paranoiac critical method, in which he transformed the exploration of delirium into a driving force for creativity.

At the forefront

He theorised his curiosity about religious and scientific issues in his *Mystic Manifesto*, and explored innovations such as the representation of the third dimension. He created holograms and stereoscopic works.

THE LIFE OF GALA

Dalí's name is inseparable from that of his wife, Gala. Far from merely being a muse on a pedestal, she was also his agent and the organiser of her husband's career.

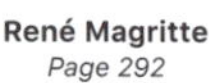
René Magritte
Page 292

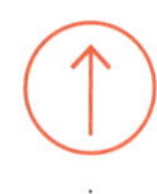

1904
Born in Figueras

1922
James Joyce granted Ulysses a second life

1931
Painted *The Persistence of Memory*

1967
First edition of the Super Bowl

1989
Died in Figueras

Edward Hopper
Page 302

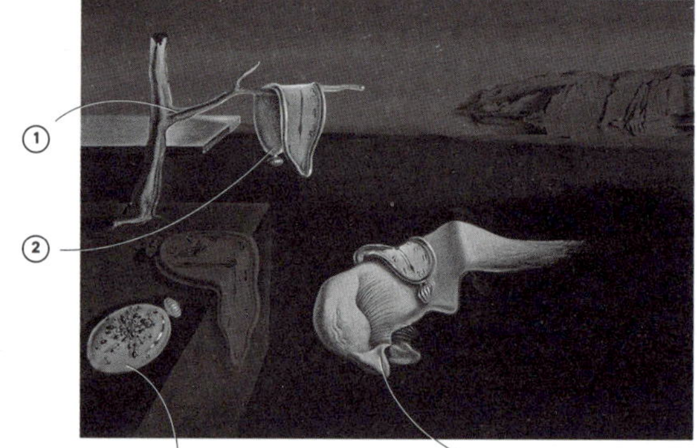

THE PERSISTENCE OF MEMORY

1931
Oil on canvas
24.1 × 33 cm
MoMA, New York

WHAT ARE WE LOOKING AT?

This masterpiece by Dalí is both immediate and enigmatic. It offers a reflection on time from a spiritual, scientific and ideological perspective.

① An erratic landscape

On the horizon, the water and rocks are realistic; however, this impression is countered by the geometric elements that anchor the scene in a dreamlike context. Despite the apparent sterility of the cubic structure, a tree has grown, even though only its dead trunk remains.

② All in good time

The artist is said to have visualised these "soft watches" when looking at a pie chart. Beyond the anecdote, these objects symbolise the measurement of time, an objective and scientific fact, related to the division of labour in the modern world. Here, the deliquescence of these timepieces can be perceived as a form of resistance. By interpreting time as a subjective notion, Dalí may also be echoing Einstein's theories on relativity.

③ Meticulous work

In the foreground, the metal case of a watch, turned face down, attracts insects like rotting flesh. This motif can be compared to that of a vanitas (p. 110): it conveys the idea of time being counted and the impermanence of all things on Earth.

④ Soft in the knee

On the floor, the embryonic, almost extraterrestrial form is likely a self-portrait of the artist, already featured in previous works.
He has reduced himself to a face with oversized eyelashes and a nose, from which a tongue may be protruding. Draped over a rock, it appears to be melting into the ground, where it is fading.

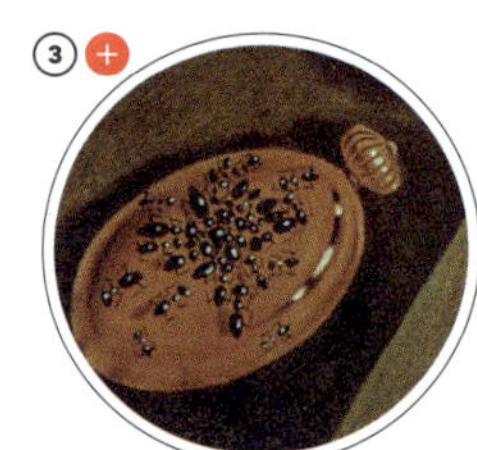

SURREALISM IN A NUTSHELL

- A movement that found its origins in Dadaism and revolted against the rationality of the world.
- An interest in the subconscious, psychoanalysis, automatic writing and dreams.
- A manifesto written by André Breton in 1924.
- An interdisciplinary movement, from literature to cinema to painting.

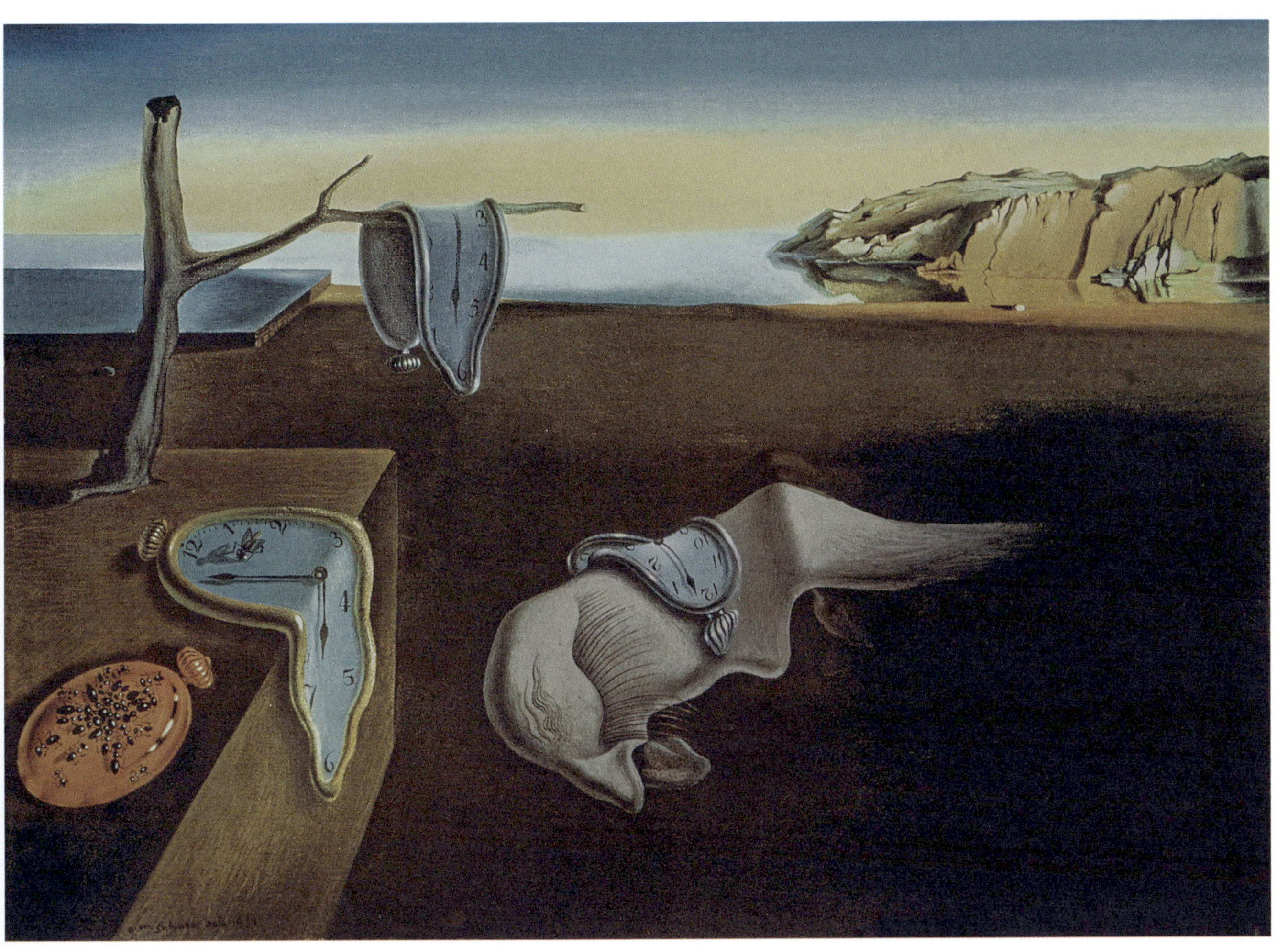

Very precious art

While Dalí painted watches with talent, he also distinguished himself in the art of jewellery. His taste for precise drawing enabled him to produce highly detailed designs of jewels on paper. These were then crafted in New York, under his supervision. After passing through the hands of various collectors, these precious items are now kept by the Dalí Foundation.

The secret youth of a painting
Future-proof

Oil paints take a long time to dry, but they are a good preservative. This is why some ancient paintings are sometimes better preserved than modern paintings, produced using more contemporary techniques such as acrylics. However, some crucial rules must be observed to ensure the proper conservation of works of art over time, regardless of their age.

Conservation

Conservation includes actions carried out on the works and their environment, in order to prolong their life as much as possible. There are two approaches.

• Preventive conservation

This approach consists in acting on the possible causes of a degradation.

• Curative conservation

In this case, an intervention is carried out on existing damage. Sometimes, this process overlaps with restoration actions.

RISKS RELATED TO THE ENVIRONMENT OF THE WORKS

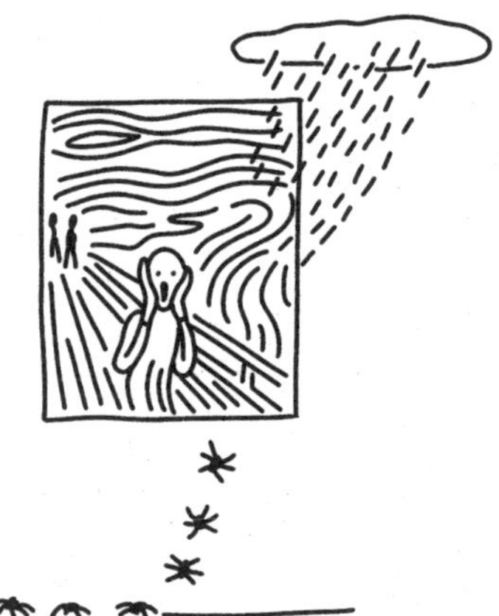

How to act?

Never open the windows, even to ventilate the room.

Control light and humidity.

Inspect the work regularly, in order to prevent mould or infestation by pests.

NATURAL DISASTERS AND DAMAGE

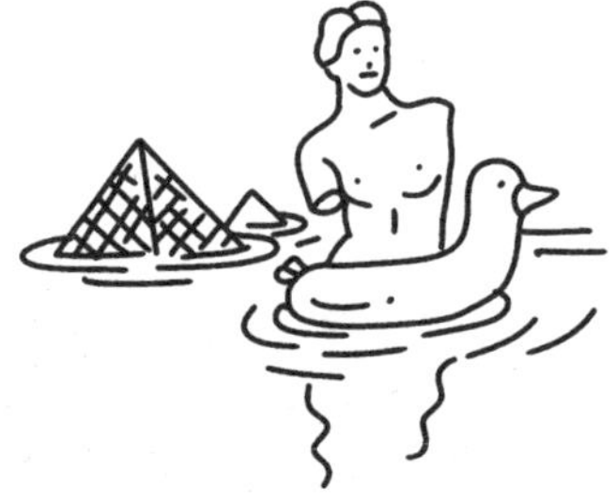

How to act?

Avoid locating the museum's storerooms underground, near a river or in an earthquake zone.

Maintain and equip the building to limit the spread of hazards, such as fire or flooding.

HUMAN BEINGS

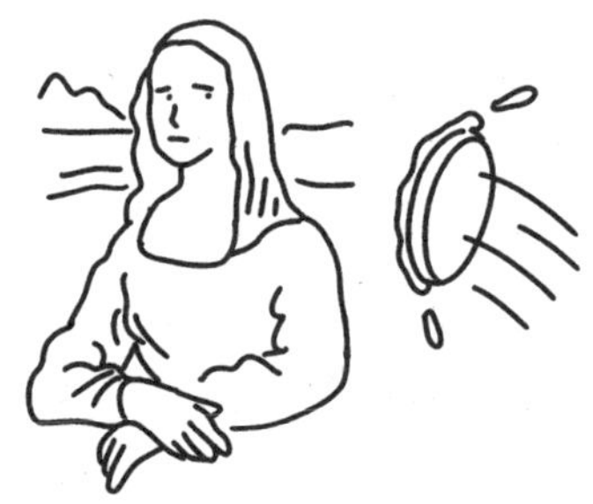

How to act?

Train museum staff in the conservation, maintenance and moving of works.

Inform visitors and impose rules, the most common being: do not touch!

Restoration

As in the case of transport (p. 284), the restoration of a work begins with a condition report, which supports a diagnosis and the assessment of actions to be taken. While there is no systematic approach, and each restoration process is tailored to the work and its condition, three main steps must be followed to ensure a complete restoration. Here are some examples of actions to be taken.

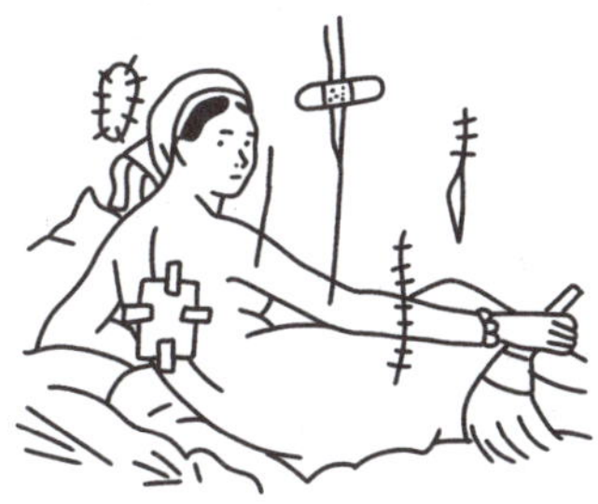

STABILISING

When a work of art is seriously damaged, the ongoing process of degradation must be interrupted:

- Gluing back any loose scales of paint,
- Sewing a torn canvas,
- Treating mould.

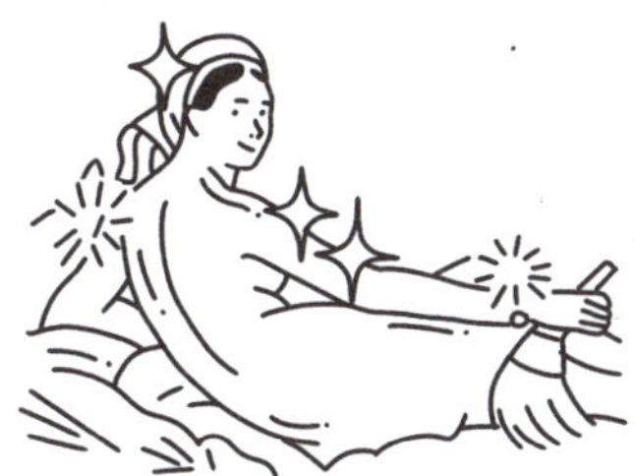

REVIVING

Once it has been ensured that the work will not deteriorate further, its appearance can be improved, and its aesthetic qualities restored:

- Cleaning the work,
- Lightening yellowed varnishes,
- Removing restoration repaints,
- Filling in areas where the paint layer has disappeared, by applying putty, before painting.

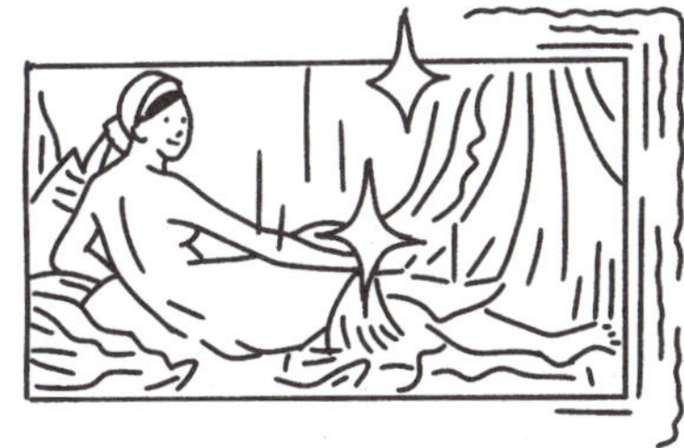

PRESERVATION

This process is also part of the principle of conservation, i.e. taking all necessary measures to ensure that the condition of the work is maintained over time:

- Applying a new coat of varnish to protect the work and revealing its colours,
- Protecting the reverse face,
- Framing the work.

A WELL-PERFORMED RESTORATION IS ...

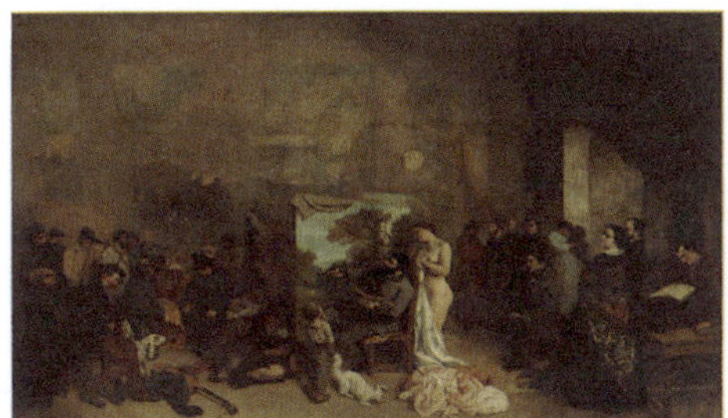

Before

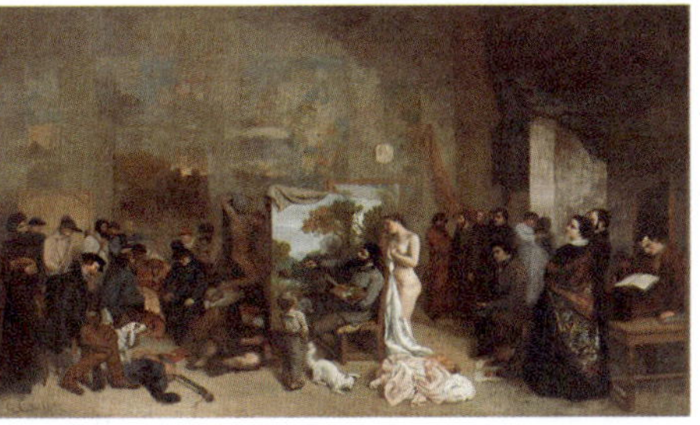

After

- Minimalist: interventions are made only where necessary.
- Reversible: it must be possible to revert the work to its previous state during a subsequent restoration.
- Performed with legibility in mind: it must allow the work to be better viewed and understood.

← *The Painter's Studio* by Gustave Courbet was restored in 2014, in the Musée d'Orsay itself; indeed, its six-metre length made it somewhat difficult to move!

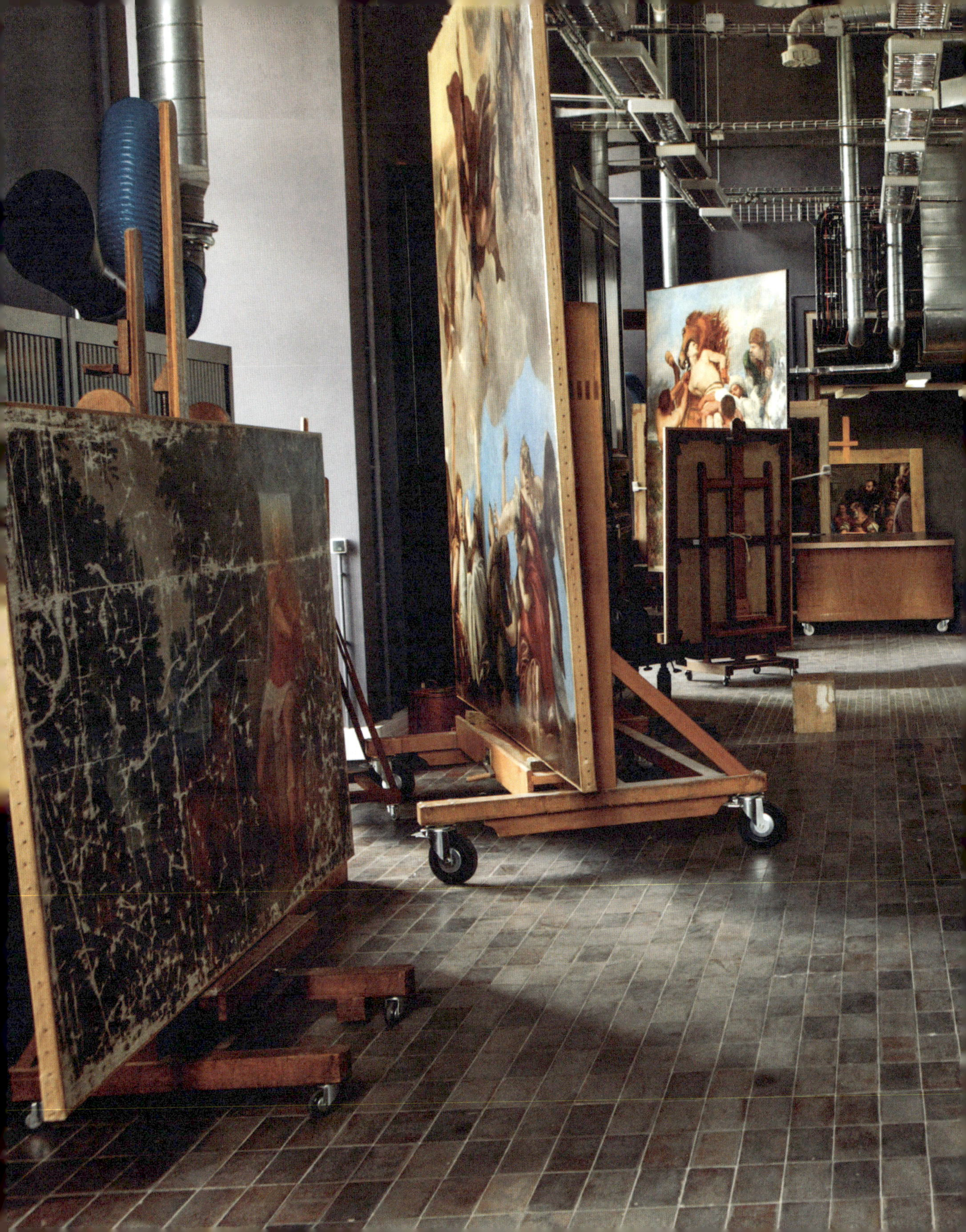

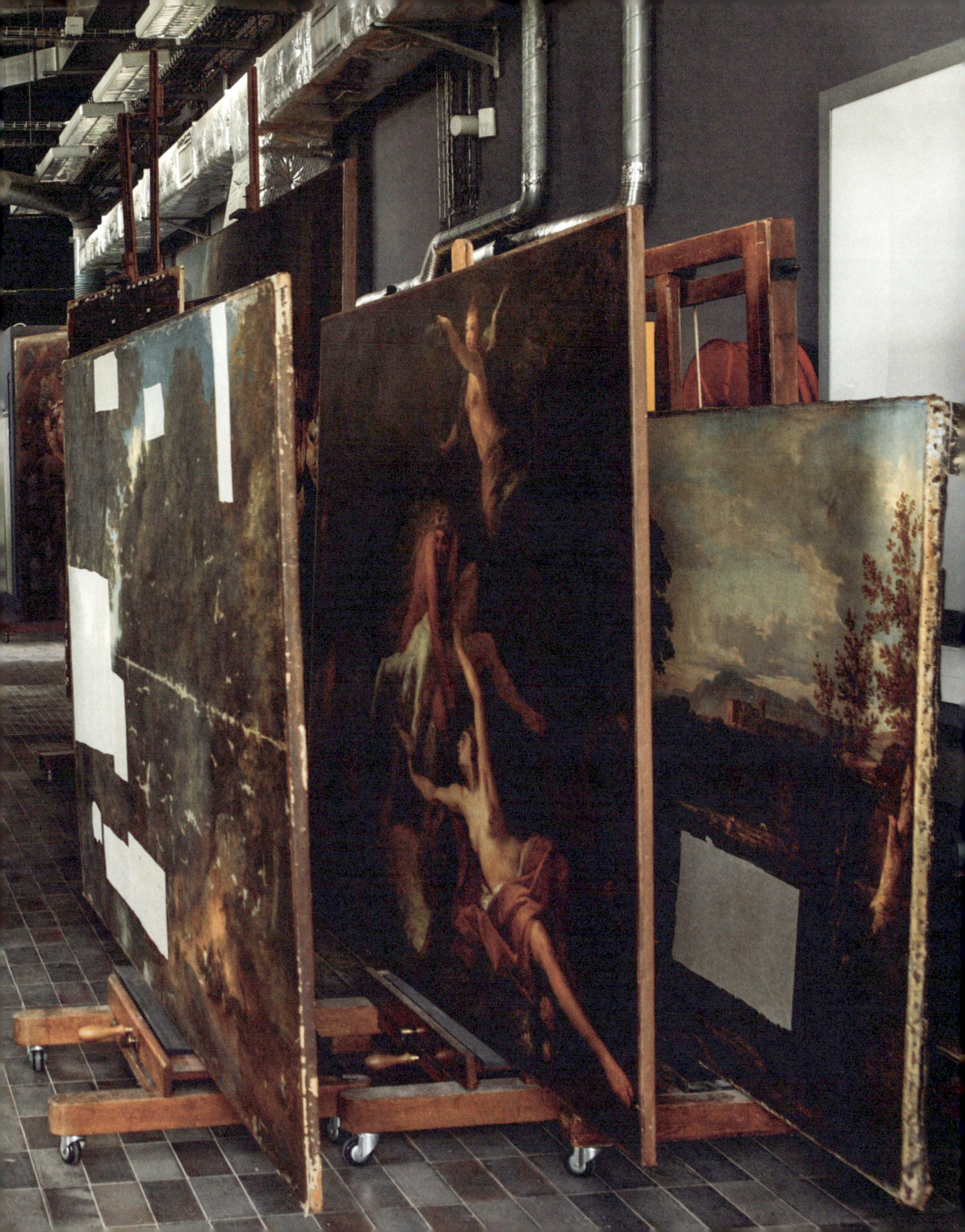

Edward Hopper

A touch of American class

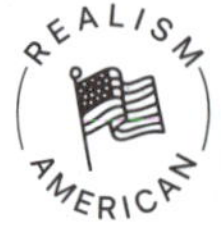

Edward Hopper is one of the greatest names in American realist painting. His work reflects the influence of the European Avant-Garde and Surrealism movements. He was the painter of atmospheres par excellence.

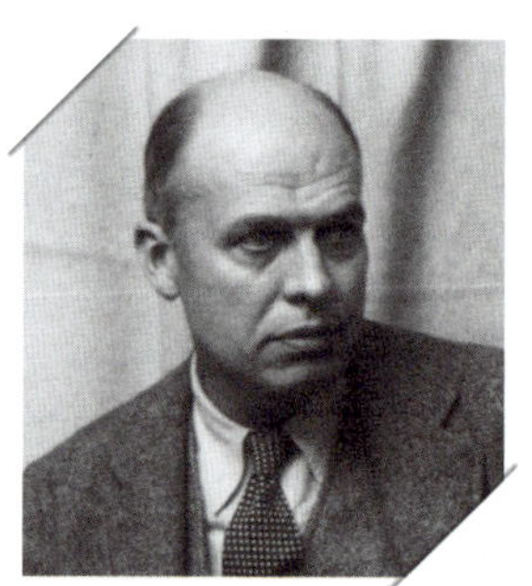

Transatlantic realism

Hopper trained with the American realists such as Chase, Millet and Robert Henri, in particular, through whom he discovered Thomas Eakins and Édouard Manet (p. 216). He experienced European painting by himself, by staying several times in Paris, where he confronted himself with Impressionism.

A diplomat

Amidst the artistic upheaval of the 20th century, Hopper admired the Surrealists, evolving towards a realistic and sensitive art that embodied a new form of American modernity. However, he would not become a recognised painter until he was in his forties.

A window open to all perspectives

He was known for his unique atmospheres, represented in an eerie light. The characters, sitting alone or in small groups, are immersed in deep meditation. The windows allow them to escape, while also placing the spectator in the position of a voyeur.

EDWARD HOPPER SAID

"Great art is the outward expression of an inner life in the artist, and this inner life will result in his personal vision of the world."

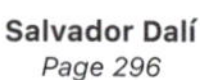
Salvador Dalí
Page 296

1882
Born in Nyack, New York State

1927
First edition of the Winter Olympics in Chamonix

1942
Painted *Nighthawks*

1953
Invention of pocket edition books

1967
Died in New York

Georgia O'Keeffe
Page 304

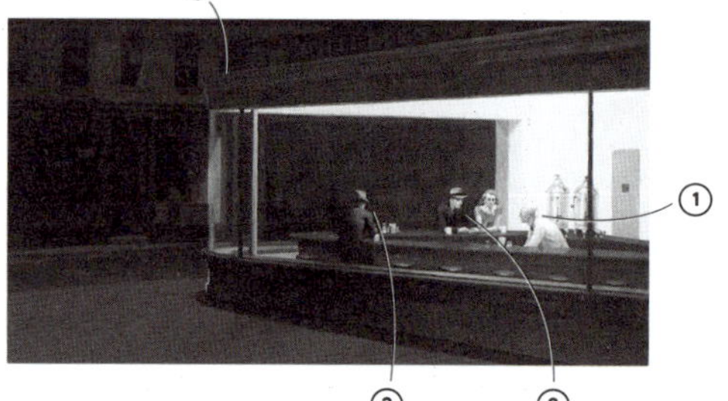

NIGHTHAWKS

1942
Oil on canvas
84.1 × 152.4 cm
Art Institute, Chicago

WHAT ARE WE LOOKING AT?

***Nighthawks* is one of the great icons of American painting. Here, Hopper demonstrates his talent for rendering atmospheres that carry a powerful meaning. In this work, he successfully captured the essence of individualism and loneliness.**

① Alone together

The protagonists appear to be deep in thought. Only the waiter seems to be talking, however, with no one to talk to. Hopper is depicting the loneliness and anonymity of big cities. The atmosphere is quiet, but filled with meaning.

② An equivocal perspective

With her red hair and pink dress, the young woman sits in the limelight, while the man's dark suit gives us the impression that he is fading into the night. While they are not looking at each other, a palpable ambiguity can be felt. The perspective suggests that they are touching hands.

③ Hands up

Through engraving, Hopper was able to define his style, consisting in the representation of vast urban settings. This work also conveys the atmosphere of the American Film Noir, featuring gangsters and private detectives in felt hats.

② +

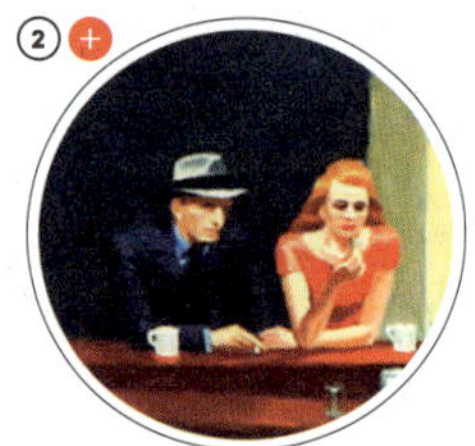

④ Like an aquarium

Hopper borrowed the theme of modernity and cafés from the Impressionists; here, however, the French hustle and bustle has given way to solitude. The influence of Surrealism is also perceptible: although the scene is perfectly realistic, it evokes a feeling of strangeness; no door appears to lead to the outside world.

OTHER RENOWNED AMERICAN REALIST PAINTERS

- Winslow Homer (1836–1910)
- Robert Henri (1865–1929)
- George Bellows (1882–1925)
- William Glackens (1870–1938)
- John Sloan (1871–1951)

OH, MY GOD!

In 1913, the first Armory Show took place. For the first time, the revolutionary works of the European Avant-Garde were exhibited in the United States. The event was part triumph and part scandal, and became a milestone in the country's cultural history. Hopper would sell his first work there.

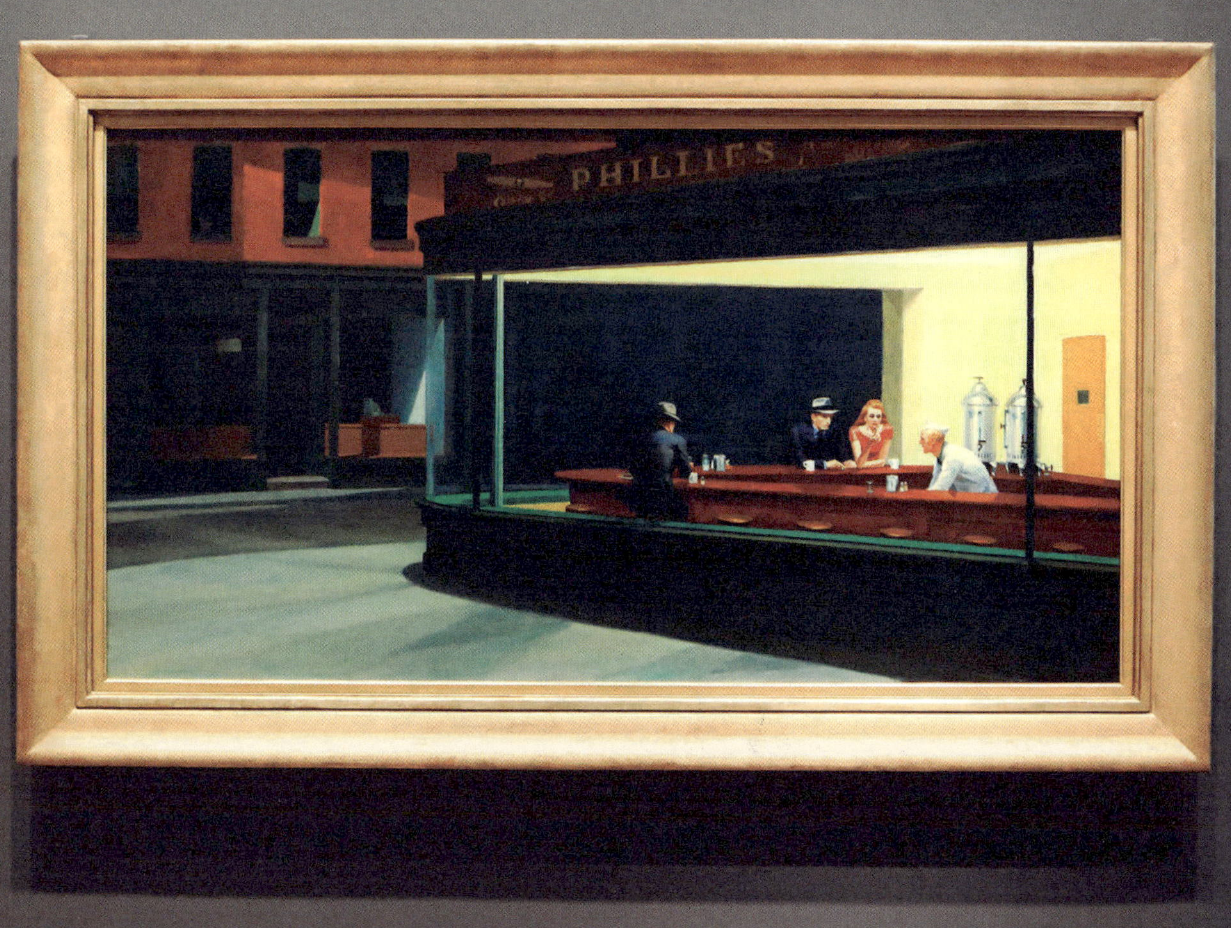
PHILLIES

Georgia O'Keeffe

Passionate to the bone

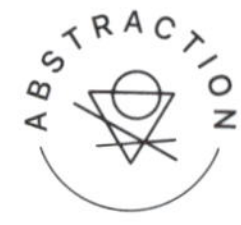

She is one of the most popular artists in the United States. Her luminous and colourful painting borrows organic forms from nature, to which she added a spiritual dimension. Her landscapes are amplified by a cosmic aura.

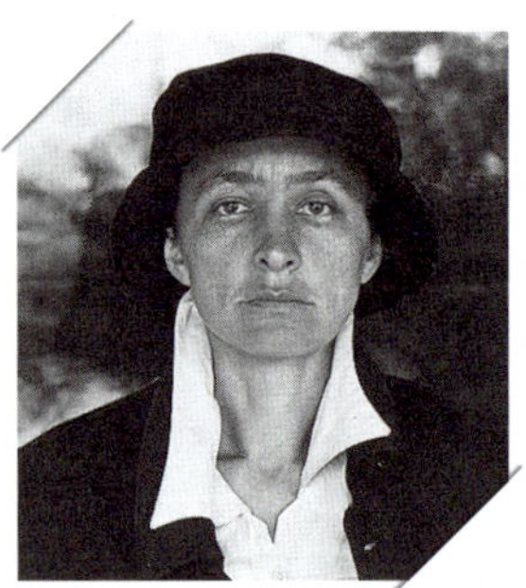

Business and feelings

O'Keeffe trained in Chicago and New York, and then at Columbia University. Her work caught the eye of Alfred Stieglitz, a gallery owner and photographer, who exhibited them at Gallery 291. He would become her companion in life. The couple divided their time between the hustle and bustle of New York and the quiet of the vast open spaces, far from the city.

Fertile ground

O'Keeffe's art was influenced by nature. From nature, she drew a spirituality that can be found in the works of the German Romantics (p. 178) or Kandinsky (p. 276). She produced cosmic landscapes and symbolist still lifes, which went so far as to extrapolate flowers and clouds into luminous abstractions.

You freaks!

Although the painter's works sometimes bore an unquestionable erotic charge, she firmly rejected any systematically sexual interpretation of her works. She would repeatedly protest against the art critics in this regard.

POO POO PEE DOO

Georgia O'Keefe was so well known in the United States that she became the second most photographed woman in the country, after Marilyn Monroe.

Edward Hopper
Page 302

1887
Born in Sun Prairie, Wisconsin

1900
Women were allowed to participate in the Olympic Games

1935
Painted *Ram's Head, White Hollyhock-Hills*

1972
The First Earth Summit was held in Stockholm

1986
Died in Santa Fe, New Mexico

Frida Kahlo
Page 306

RAM'S HEAD, WHITE HOLLYHOCK-HILLS

1935
Oil on canvas
76.2 × 91.4 cm
Brooklyn Museum, New York

WHAT ARE WE LOOKING AT?

The artist presents the characteristic components of her work: a mineral and cosmic landscape, a skull and a flower, the spiritual evocation of life and her passion for New Mexico.

New Mexico, new life

O'Keeffe discovered New Mexico at the age of 30, during a holiday with her sister. Instantly captivated, she would return to the state several times, finally settling there permanently in 1949, after Alfred Stieglitz's death – with, at last, the feeling of having found a place of her own.

Hilly curves

In 1935, the artist spent several extremely prolific months in New Mexico, as she wrote to Stieglitz. She was fascinated by the state's landscape and colours. Her paintings draw parallels between the hills' ochre reliefs and the human body.

Down to the bone

O'Keeffe collected bones that she found in the desert; some witnesses recounted seeing her dragging them behind her. She boiled them to remove any remaining flesh, then brought them back to New York. They are the symbol of the desert: arid and harsh, yet alive.

Not completely dead

The artist did not associate the skull to the notion of death, but rather to that of the cycle of life. She admitted to finding these bones more alive than the animals themselves. The skull is depicted by a white rose, which evokes Hispanic funeral rites and introduces the idea of continuity after death.

IN O'KEEFE'S PAINTINGS, ONE CAN SEE ...

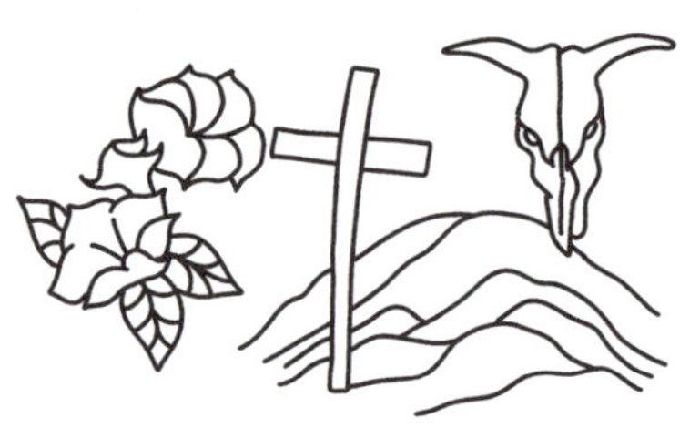

Organic forms *and* **abstract patterns** *extrapolated beyond reality,* **spiritual signs, cosmic representations** *and* **mountain landscapes**.

A STAR DURING HER LIFETIME

Georgia O'Keeffe became famous in the press as early as the 1920s. Three major, prestigious retrospectives would mark her career during her lifetime.
The first took place in 1943 in Chicago (The Art Institute), and the following ones took place in New York in 1946 and 1970 (Museum of Modern Art then Whitney Museum of American Art).

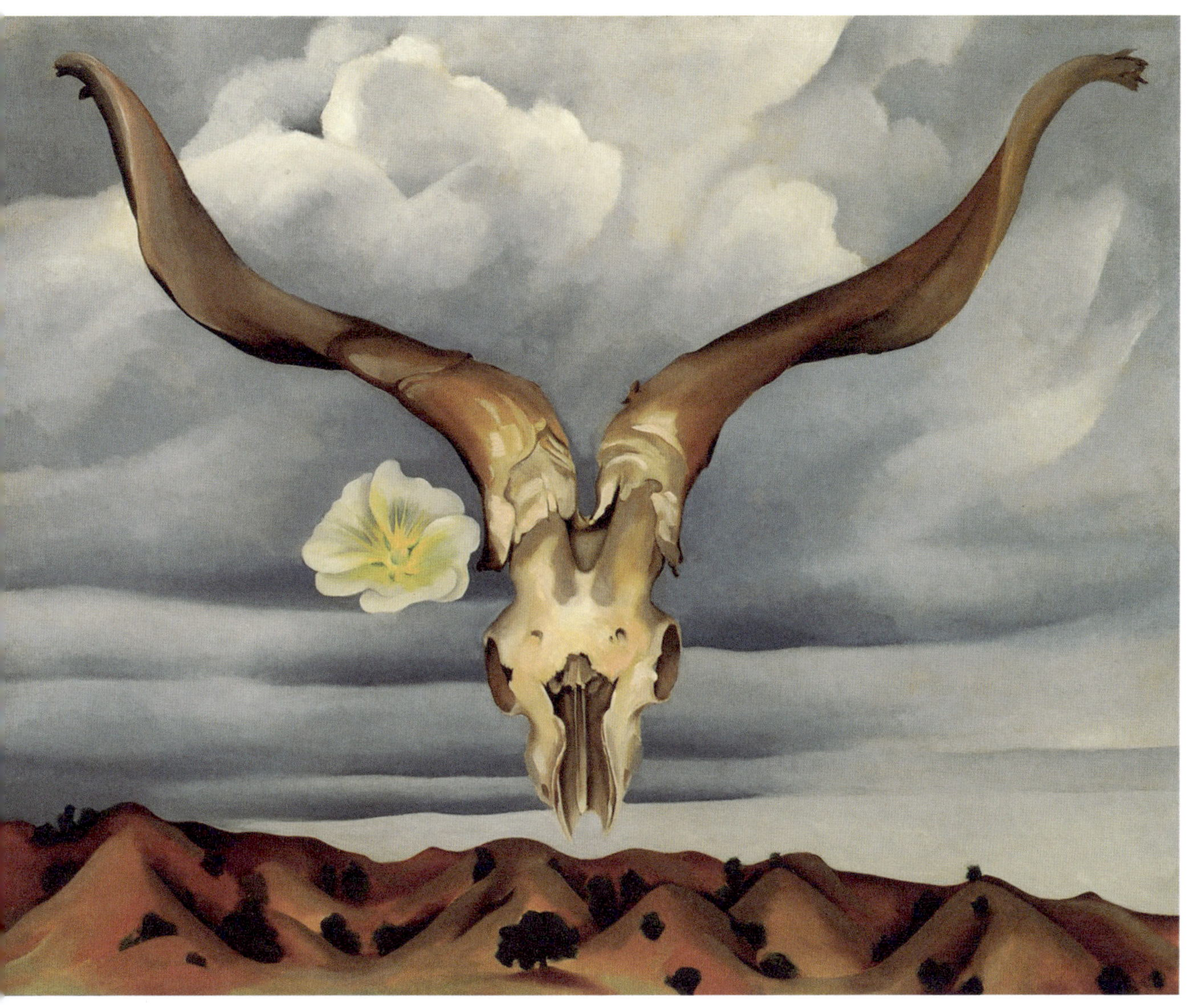

Well-assured posterity

New Mexico was a land of inspiration for the painter. Today, the state is home to the Georgia O'Keeffe Museum, to the north of Santa Fe, where many of her works are on display. In the same state, one can also visit one of the artist's homes and her studio.

Frida Kahlo

Painting pain

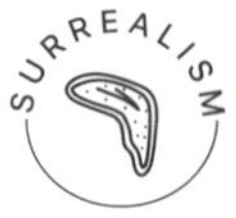

Frida Kahlo enjoyed international fame and a glamorous marketing aura, which tended to mask her surrealist works; rife with symbols and largely autobiographical, they were inspired by her suffering and her political commitments.

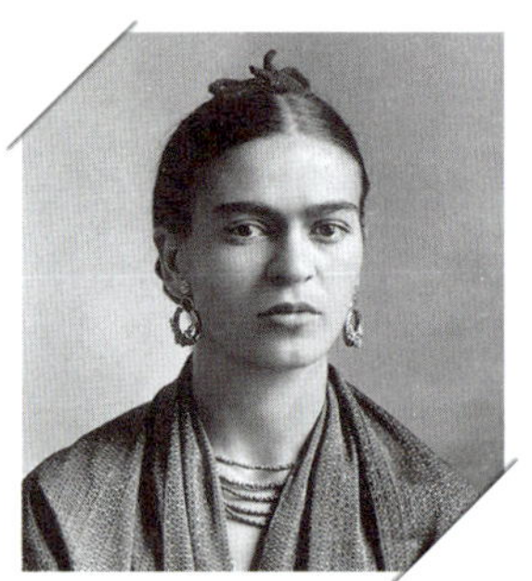

A tough life

From her childhood, Kahlo suffered from a malformation of the spine, and a bus accident when she was 18 would leave her with severe injuries. She took up painting during her convalescence. Wearing a corset and prosthetics, she would undergo numerous surgeries and interrupted pregnancies throughout her lifetime.

Commitment without obligation

The artist had a tumultuous relationship with the painter Diego Rivera, with infidelities occurring on both sides. Both were members of the Communist Party, until Rivera was ousted. They were then drawn to Trotsky and his anti-Stalinist communism.

Telling the story of her life

Frida Kahlo's art and life are closely connected. Often painting while lying down, she drew on her suffering to feed her surrealist paintings, impregnated with Mexicanidad and references to classical European art. Her art immerses viewers in a melancholic and mysterious world.

HER EARLIEST FANS

In 1942, Frida Kahlo was a teacher at the art school La Esmeralda. She was surrounded by a small group of faithful students, who named themselves "Los Fridos".

Georgia O'Keeffe
Page 304

1907
Born in Mexico City

1927
Monet's Water Lilies were exhibited at the Musée de l'Orangerie

1940
Painted *Self-Portrait with Thorn Necklace and Hummingbird*

1946
Edith Piaf sang *La Vie en Rose*

1954
Died in Mexico City

Mark Rothko
Page 308

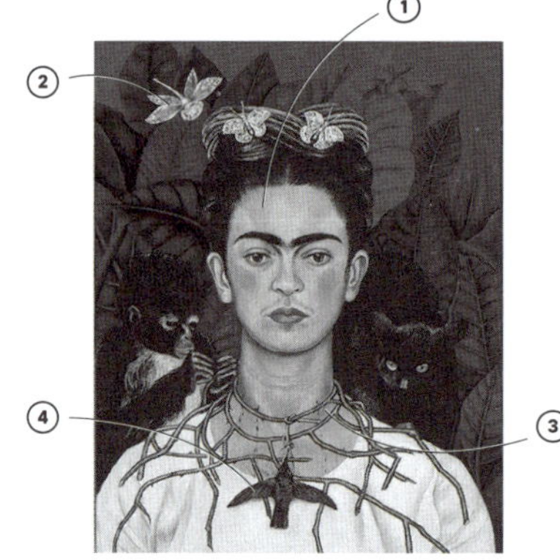

SELF-PORTRAIT WITH THORN NECKLACE AND HUMMINGBIRD

1940
Oil on canvas
61.3 × 47 cm
University of Texas, Austin

WHAT ARE WE LOOKING AT?

This is one of the painter's most emblematic self-portraits, produced at an ambiguous moment when, having just divorced Rivera, she was at the pinnacle of her artistic glory.

① Saint Frida

Of Kahlo's 150 existing works, more than a third are self-portraits, contributing to her *post mortem* stardom. Here, Kahlo portrayed herself as a Christian icon. Her frontal pose, the symmetry and the impassivity of her features are reminiscent of Byzantine icons; however, the image's realism counteracts this divine impression.

② Blooming passion

As the weight of her divorce bore down on her, she was inspired by the surrealist Roland Penrose, who portrayed his wife in *Winged Domino*, after they had just separated. She has depicted herself with flowers and butterflies above her head, but the poetic representation of the blooming bramble around her neck has become an instrument of torture.

③ A thorn in her back

This "necklace" evokes Christ's crown of thorns, an allusion to Kahlo's suffering.

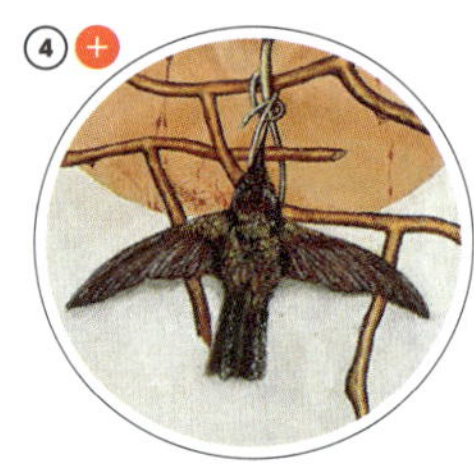

Her rigid posture and the way she is ensconced are also reminiscent of the corset that she wore and the pain that she has to endure, while the butterflies, which may symbolise resurrection in Christian art, seem petrified forever.

④ Lucky charm

The bird may suggest the Holy Spirit, but here, the artist drew on references from secular traditions. Half-saint, half-witch, accompanied by her black cat, Kahlo wears this hummingbird as an amulet against the folly of love, represented by the monkey.

OTHER RENOWNED MEXICAN PAINTERS OF THE 20TH CENTURY

- Diego Rivera (1886–1957)
- Rufino Tamayo (1899–1991)
- Juan O'Gorman (1905–1982)
- José Clemente Orozco (1883–1949)
- David Alfaro Siqueiros (1896–1974)
- Leonora Carrington (1917–2011)
- Fanny Rabel (1922–2008)

A HOUSE AND A MUSEUM

La *Casa Azul*, or the "blue house", where Kahlo and Riviera resided in Mexico City from 1937 until the painter's death, has been transformed into a museum to her glory.

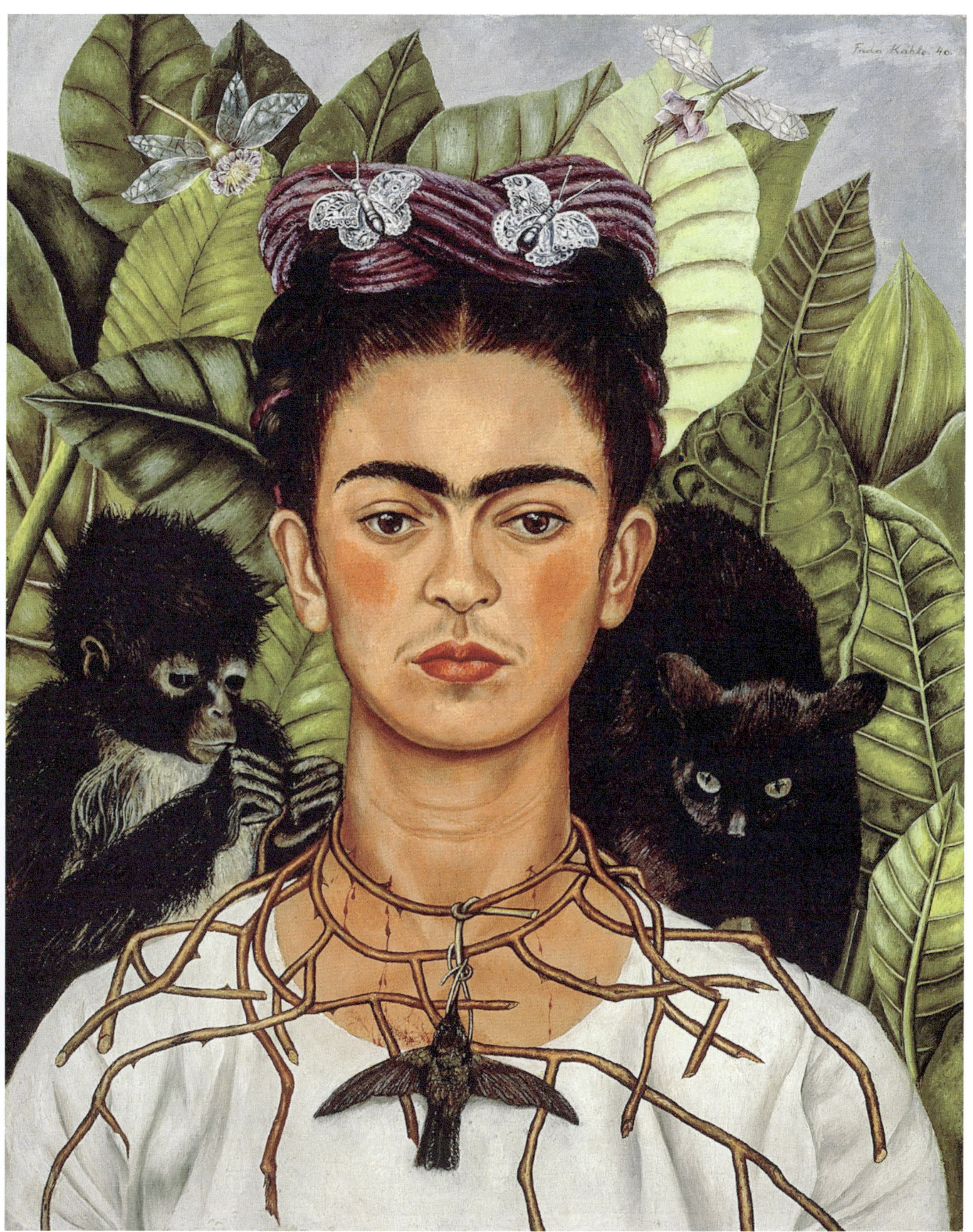
Frida Kahlo. 40.

Mark Rothko

Emotions into colours

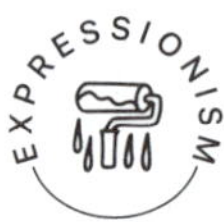

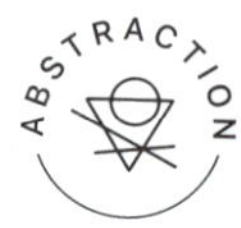

A Russian painter who became an American citizen, Markus Rothkowitz, known as Mark Rothko, followed the trend of American abstract expressionism. This movement was born as a reaction to patriotism, which went out of fashion when the United States entered World War II.

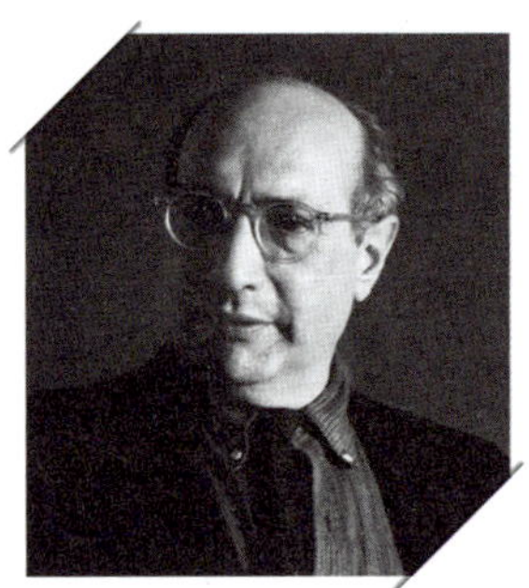

The long road of an artist

In the 1930s, Mark Rothko painted landscapes, nudes and scenes of everyday life; after, his works bore the influence of Greek mythology, which he depicted in increasingly abstract paintings. Towards the end of the 1940s, he crystallised his emblematic motif: large rectangles of colour, featuring diffuse outlines, in which viewers could immerse themselves.

Straight to the point

The artist rejected the notion of abstraction to qualify his work. To him, removing the figurative elements of his works was a way of suppressing the obstacles between the artist and the idea, and then between the idea and the viewer.

Not for decoration

Rothko feared that his paintings would be perceived as decorative items. He often recommended dimming the lights, so that the audience could appreciate them as he had intended.

Frida Kahlo
Page 306

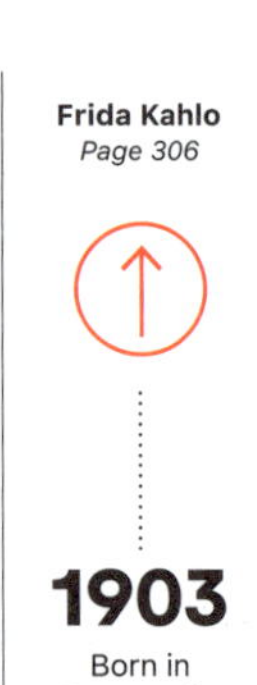

1903
Born in Daugavpils

1930
Joséphine Baker performed *J'ai Deux Amours*, her first great success

1936
In France, the Popular Front's victory led to the introduction of paid holidays

1962
Painted *Red, Orange, Orange on Red*

1970
Died in New York

Jackson Pollock
Page 310

RED, ORANGE, ORANGE ON RED

1962
Oil on canvas
233 × 204.5 cm
Saint Louis Art Museum

WHAT ARE WE LOOKING AT?

This work is a painting in the pure Rothko style – a monumental creation featuring intense flat colours, with indistinct boundaries.

Straight to the heart

Rothko removed figurative forms from his works, as he was interested in the representation of human emotions. The artist did not dwell on the relationship between forms and colours.

Large works

For him, small paintings did not allow viewers to penetrate them. The artist therefore favoured large formats, welcoming observers to enjoy a most intimate experience possible by immersing themselves in his works.

The old-fashioned way

Rothko claimed a traditional heritage. He ground his pigments himself, and used egg as a binder. Even though he did not consider himself to be colourist, his masters were Titian (p. 62) and Henri Matisse (p. 262). He admired the light that emanated from Titian's colours and the completeness of Matisse's palette.

Art gave him faith

The artist's quest was also a spiritual one: his paintings transcend the sensible world, especially his dark works, featuring red, brown and black tones, which would even lead to the creation of a chapel.

A picture worth 1,000 words

Rothko generally refused to name his works; most titles were assigned to his paintings after his death. The painter believed that the meaning of the work should be carried by the work itself, and that any text would corrupt the viewer's perception of the painting.

WORTH A PRETTY PENNY

If the record for the most expensive work is held by the unrivalled Salvator Mundi*, attributed to Leonardo da Vinci, which sold for $450 million, paintings by American abstract expressionist artists are not to be outdone.*

$ 300M
Willem de Kooning
Interchange
sold in 2015

$ 200M
Jackson Pollock
17A
sold in 2015

$ 186M
Mark Rothko
No. 6 (Violet, Green and Red)
sold in 2014

$ 140M
Jackson Pollock
No. 5
sold in 2006

ABSTRACT EXPRESSIONISM IN A NUTSHELL

- The first great American art movement.
- Monumental formats.
- The absence of figurative subjects.
- Flat works, without depth.
- Paintings depicting emotions.

MARK ROTHKO SAID

"A painting is not a picture of an experience, but is the experience."

Jackson Pollock

The drop of paint that makes creativity overflow

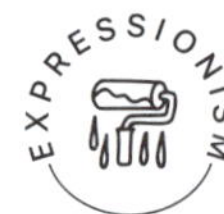

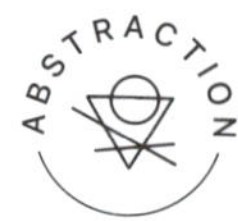

Pollock benefited from the influence of the New York scene, which dominated from the 1950s onwards. With his *dripping* technique, he created a unique style, somewhere between chance and mastery, which made him one of the greatest names in Abstract Expressionism.

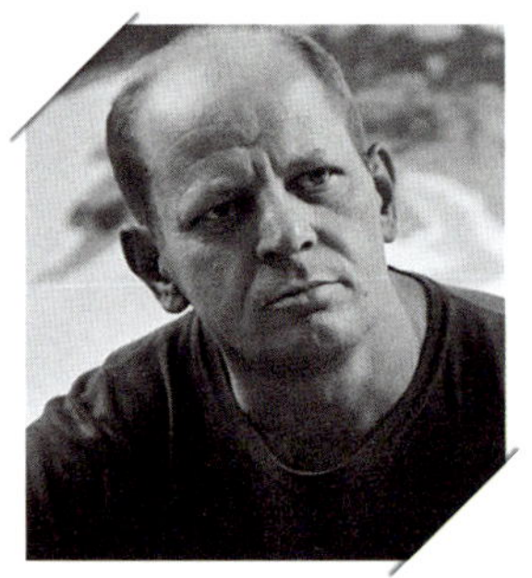

Chauvinistic

Pollock was introduced to art by his mother. Expelled from his first school in Los Angeles, he went to study in New York, where he was influenced by Thomas Hart Benton, who defended American regionalism (p. 288) against European modernism.

New Deal, good deal

After his training, Pollock was supported for a few years by American government funding and the collector Peggy Guggenheim. He developed a style influenced by the Mexican muralists, Picasso (p. 264), the Surrealists (p. 296), but also by the Navajo Native Americans.

It's trippy when it's drippy

After Pollock married the artist Lee Krasner, the couple moved to Long Island, where Pollock developed his *dripping* technique. Pollock's great artistic fulfilment, however, did not prevent him from suffering from psychological instability and alcoholism. He died prematurely in a car accident.

AN INNOVATOR

"Jackson broke the ice." With these words, the artist Willem De Kooning expressed the extent to which Pollock's pioneering aesthetic research fostered the emergence of a new form of art.

Mark Rothko
Page 308

1912
Born in Cody, Wyoming

1923
Foundation of what would become the Walt Disney Company

1932
Flowers and Trees became the first animated film in colour

1947
Painted *Watery Paths*

1956
Died in Springs, Long Island

Joan Mitchell
Page 312

WATERY PATHS ↗

1947
Oil on canvas
114 × 86 cm
National Gallery of Modern and Contemporary Art, Rome

WHAT ARE WE LOOKING AT?

This painting dates from the early years of Pollock's experiments with *dripping*. In full apprehension of his discovery, the painter performed his work in a state of mind between automatism and awareness.

He caused a stir

In 1947, Pollock developed his *dripping* technique. It would keep him busy for only a few years; however, the works that he produced using this technique made his reputation, with some becoming instant classics.

An old recipe

This flowing technique was not of his invention; he had already had the opportunity to observe it with André Masson, Max Ernst or in the studio of the muralist Siqueiros, for whom he worked. He would use this method himself from the early 1940s, but until then the technique was used as a means to execute a painting.

Drop by drop

From 1947 onwards, with Pollock, the process and the result become one and the same: the process was the work, revealing the gestures and the rhythm given by the artist, standing above the canvas. Through this strictly abstract work, Pollock expressed his inner vibrations, seeking to impose order on chaos.

In control

As time went by, Pollock's technique evolved. At the beginning, Pollock's gesture was automated, to an extent; this trait would, however, disappear as the artist became aware of his work. Later in his career, even if the splashes were random, Pollock adopted a more controlled approach, projecting an expected result from the outset.

THE CREATION OF THE LEGEND

Pollock's dripping *technique became legendary thanks to the photographer Hans Namuth. In 1950, he immortalised the artist at work in his studio, through photographs and videos that attained cult status.*

TWO CURRENTS OF ABSTRACT EXPRESSIONISM

Two styles rubbed shoulders, even clashing at times:

- *Action painting:* Painting based on gestures (see Mitchell, p. 312).
- *Colour field painting:* Coloured flat tints (see Rothko, p. 308).

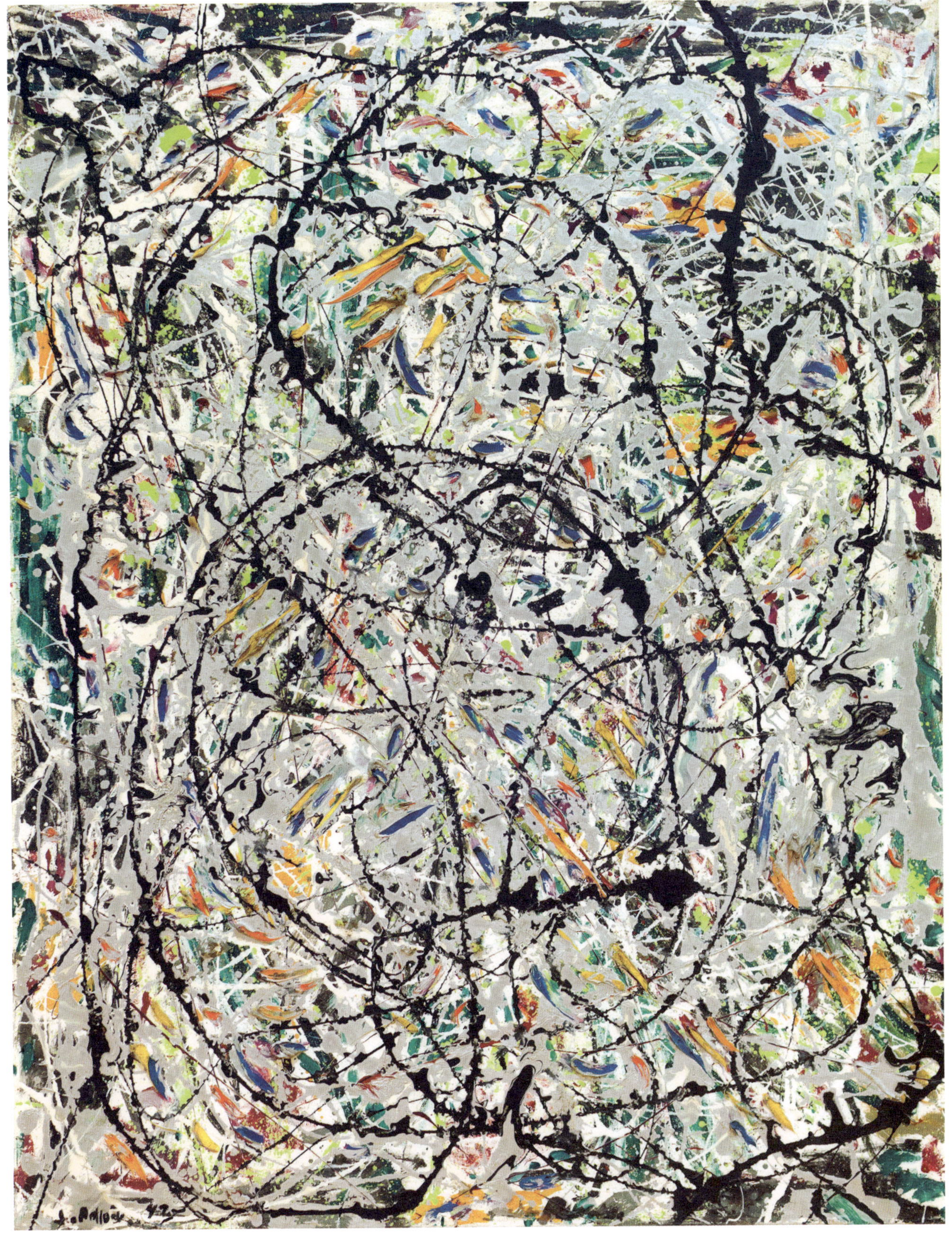

Joan Mitchell

Striking brushwork

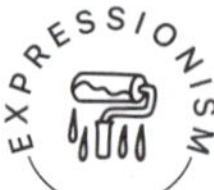

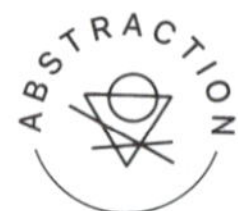

Joan Mitchell is one of the great names in Abstract Expressionist painting. Her works, whether produced on individual panels or polyptychs, feature a dynamic touch. She took a lyrical approach to art, between perception and feeling.

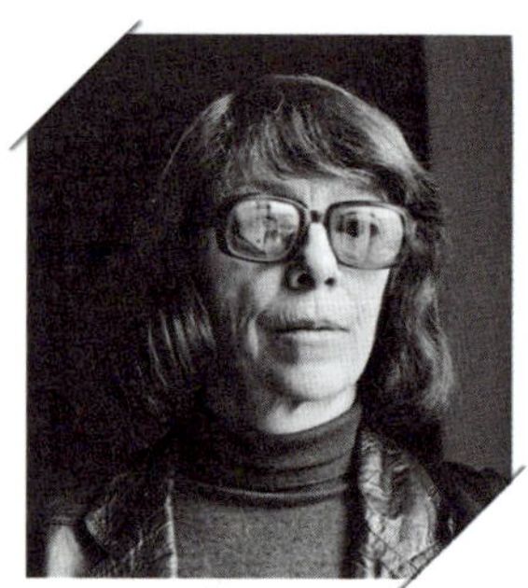

In the swing of things

Mitchell grew up in Chicago, where she developed an interest for the Impressionists and Post-Impressionists. She studied at the Art Institute, where she was influenced by the Avant-Gardes, then discovered the works of Jackson Pollock (p. 310) in New York in 1947, before spending a little over a year in France, in Paris and then in Le Lavandou.

The call of the Big Apple

She moved to New York at the end of 1949. Asserting her Abstract Expressionist style, she acquired a reputation on the local art scene, where women still received little consideration. She would stay many times in Paris, before settling there in 1959.

Energy in spades

The painter moved to Vétheuil, where Monet lived (p. 224), even though she denied any connection with him. Immersed in nature, with her brutal touch and her explosive colours, she expressed the feelings of her external perceptions.

JOAN MITCHELL SAID

"What excites me when I'm painting is what one colour does to another and what they do to each other in terms of space and interaction."

Jackson Pollock
Page 310

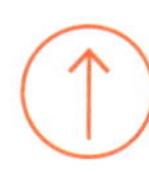

1925
Born in Chicago

1962
John Steinbeck was awarded the Nobel Prize for Literature

1980
Painted *Two Sunflowers*

1986
Buren installed his "Columns" in the main courtyard of the Palais-Royal in Paris

1992
Died in Paris

Francis Bacon
Page 314

TWO SUNFLOWERS ↗

1980
Oil on canvas
279.4 × 360.7 cm
Fondation Louis Vuitton, Paris

WHAT ARE WE LOOKING AT?

Mitchell painted sunflowers on several occasions. Here, she adopted a palette that translates blossoming, in an intense and solar expressionist manner, depicting the artist's interiority.

In life and in death

Fascinated by flowers, she observed sunflowers from every angle, from blooming to decomposition. Here, the painting's atmosphere is particularly warm, representing both sunflowers in full bloom and the sun that they are soaking up. The yellow evoked the works of Van Gogh (p. 246), by whom she was fascinated since her childhood.

Rorschach test

Mitchell did not seek to reproduce a motif inspired by the observation of reality. In her studio, she adopted a lyrical approach to painting, in which she expressed her perceptions. She would only name the work once it was finished, according to whatever emotions the result evoked in her.

Colours studied

The artist's brushstrokes are particularly dynamic; the green and yellow tones produce rhythm, while pink provides an acidic contrast, and the colour brown imbues the composition with depth, giving it roots.

Decomposed composition

The work is composed of two panels, a common practice among abstract expressionists, and one that Mitchell experimented with as early as 1956. She produced polyptychs comprising two or four panels, often separately, which she then combined into a single work. This approach broke the immediacy of the gaze, inviting viewers to a deeper form of observation.

THE NEW YORK SCHOOL

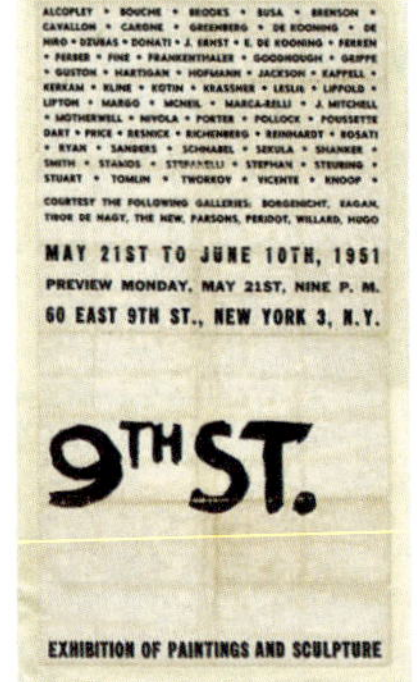

In 1951, the New York artists came together under the banner of the New York School, whose name echoes the Paris School (p. 270). They gathered for the first time at the famous *9th Street Art Exhibition of Paintings and Sculpture*, which established American Abstract Expressionism. Joan Mitchell featured among the exhibitors, alongside other well-known artists such as Willem and Elaine De Kooning, Jackson Pollock and his wife, Lee Krasner – whose name is spelled "Krassner" on the exhibition poster.

LEADING FIGURES OF ABSTRACT EXPRESSIONISM

- Joan Mitchell
- Jackson Pollock (p. 310)
- Lee Krasner (1908–1984)
- Willem De Kooning (1904–1997)
- Franz Kline (1910–1962)
- Clyfford Still (1904–1980)
- Mark Rothko (p. 308)

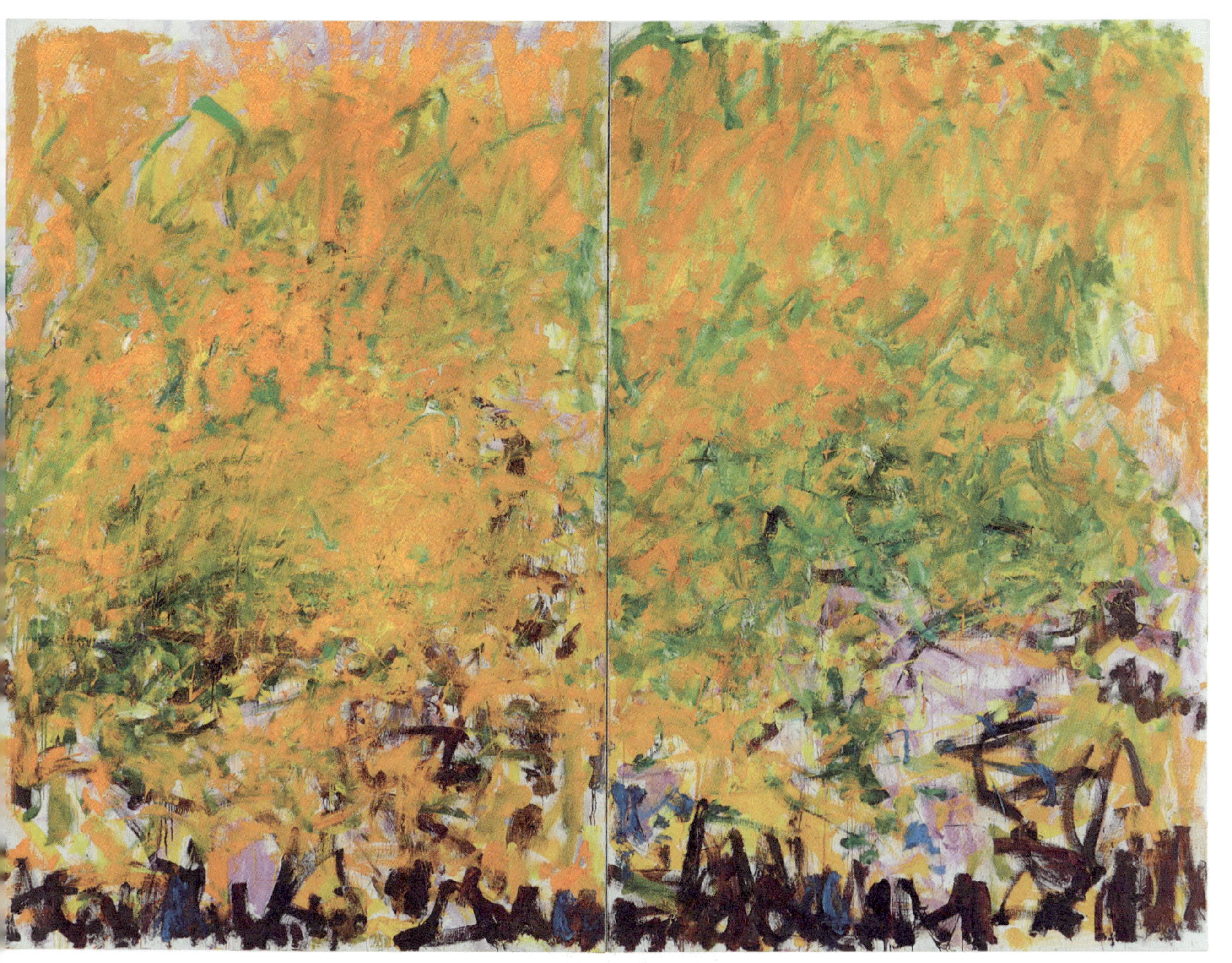

An international talent

At the end of her career, Joan Mitchell's work and her essential contribution to abstract expressionism were rewarded with numerous distinctions in both her home countries. In France, she was awarded the Grand Prix National de Peinture; in the United States, she was awarded an Honorary Doctorate from the prestigious School of the Art Institute of Chicago.

Francis Bacon

Anxiety laid on canvas

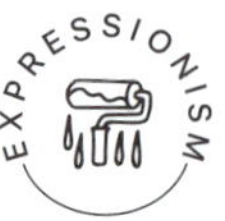

An atheist, Bacon produced art teeming with religious and classical references. He was one of the greatest painters of the 20th century. His expressionist paintings fascinate audiences, in spite of their anguished atmosphere.

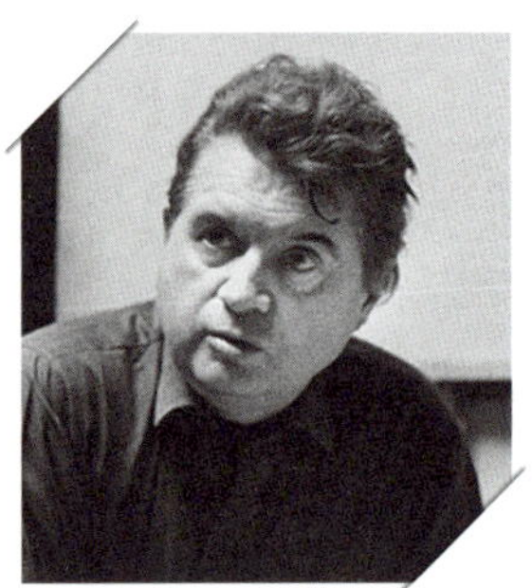

Initiatory journey

The young Francis Bacon was in conflict with his father. He was entrusted to a tutor, with whom he discovered his sexuality, touring the gay bars of Berlin. He then travelled to Paris, where he was fascinated by the works of Pablo Picasso (p. 264), and decided to become an artist.

Unfiltered

In London, Bacon earned a living as a decorator. In 1933, he began to establish the codes of his art. The violent frankness of his works fascinated critics. Over the years, he achieved international fame.

In the flesh

Bacon painted distorted bodies and faces within suggested geometric spaces. Colours are laid down in flat tints, featuring striking contrasts. Between triptychs and crucifixions, the artist played with classical codes, ranging from Rembrandt (p. 118) to Velázquez (p. 112).

FRANCIS BACON SAID

"We nearly always live through screens – a screened existence. And I always think, when people say my work looks violent, that perhaps I have from time to time been able to clear away one of those screens or veils."

Joan Mitchell
Page 312

1909
Born in Dublin

1917
The bronze trial casts of Rodin's sculpture *The Gates of Hell* were melted down

1932
Louis-Ferdinand Céline published *Voyage au bout de la nuit*

1953
Painted *Study after Velázquez's Portrait of Pope Innocent X*

1992
Died in Madrid

Roy Lichtenstein
Page 320

STUDY AFTER VELÁZQUEZ'S PORTRAIT OF POPE INNOCENT X

1953
Oil on canvas
152.1 × 117.8 cm
Des Moines Art Center

WHAT ARE WE LOOKING AT?

**Between 1949 and 1971, Bacon produced about 50 portraits of popes, most of them inspired by Velázquez's portrait of Innocent X.
Beyond the Spanish master, Bacon drew on various influences.**

Popes galore

Bacon was obsessed with the works of the Spanish master, to the point that he collected books depicting them. These reproductions stimulated Bacon's creativity, who introduced a distortion of the colours and removed the material relationship to the works.

Shy

Bacon refused to go and see Velázquez's painting in Rome, even though he was presented with the opportunity to do so.
This reaction is reminiscent of the artist's later attitude towards his models: he preferred to paint from a photograph, rather than tolerate an interloper in his studio.

Feeling breathless

With his mouth open, the pope appears to be suffocating – a situation that Bacon, who suffered from anxiety and asthma, was certainly familiar with. Accentuating this sense of oppression, the man is encased in a kind of transparent cage – a recurring item in Bacon's art, which he used to reframe the image and focus the viewers' attention.

Say "Aaaaah"!

By his own admission, the painter sought to represent a scream. It was inspired by a scene from *Battleship Potemkin*, a movie by the filmmaker Eisenstein, presenting a nurse filled with fear.
His fascination with open mouths also stems from a book on oral diseases, enriched with hand-coloured illustrations.

THE CANONICAL POPE

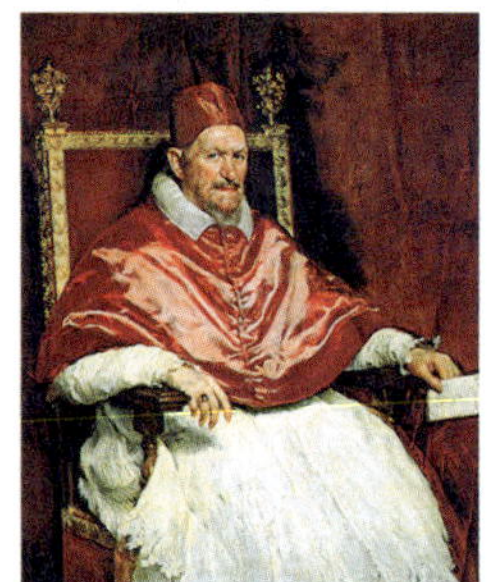

This masterly portrait by Velázquez is a milestone in the history of painting. The artist rendered the pope's physiognomy so realistically that the pope is said to have exclaimed, when viewing the work: *Troppo vero!* (It's too real!).

Diego Velázquez
Portrait of Innocent X
1650, Doria Pamphilj Gallery, Rome

A RADICAL CHOICE

Bacon made a habit of destroying works that he was unhappy with. After his death, some one hundred paintings, which had been torn apart or otherwise damaged, were found in his studio.

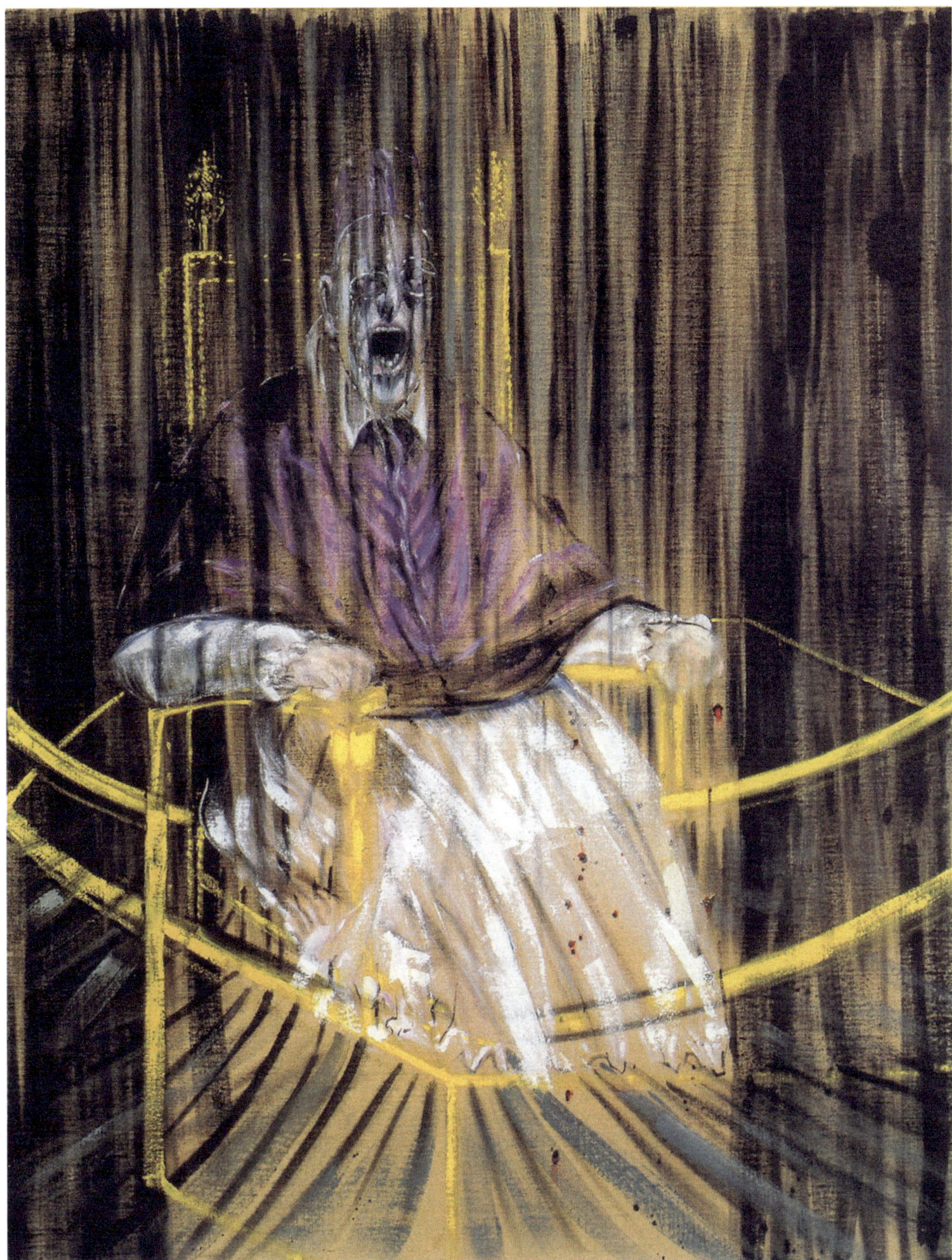

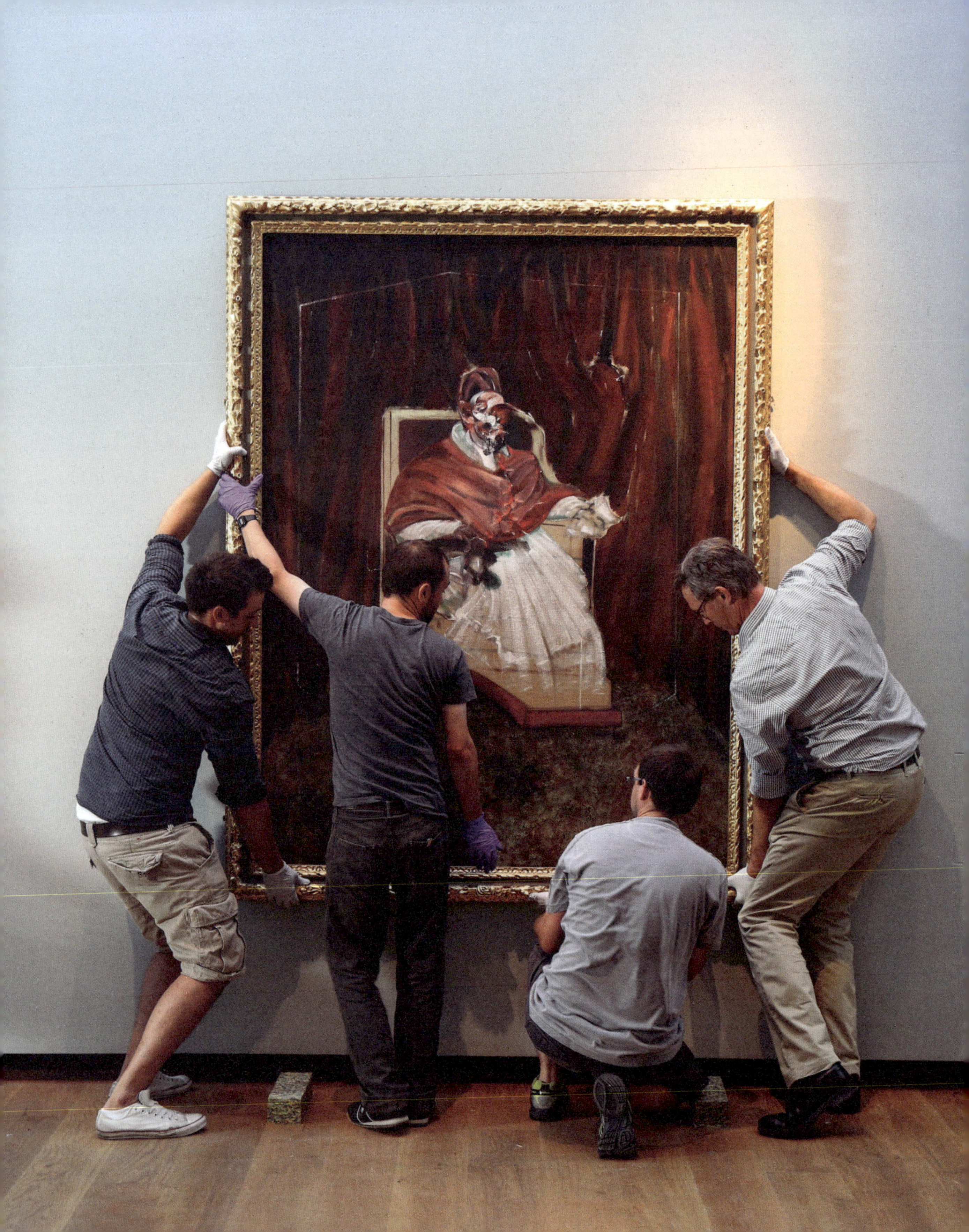

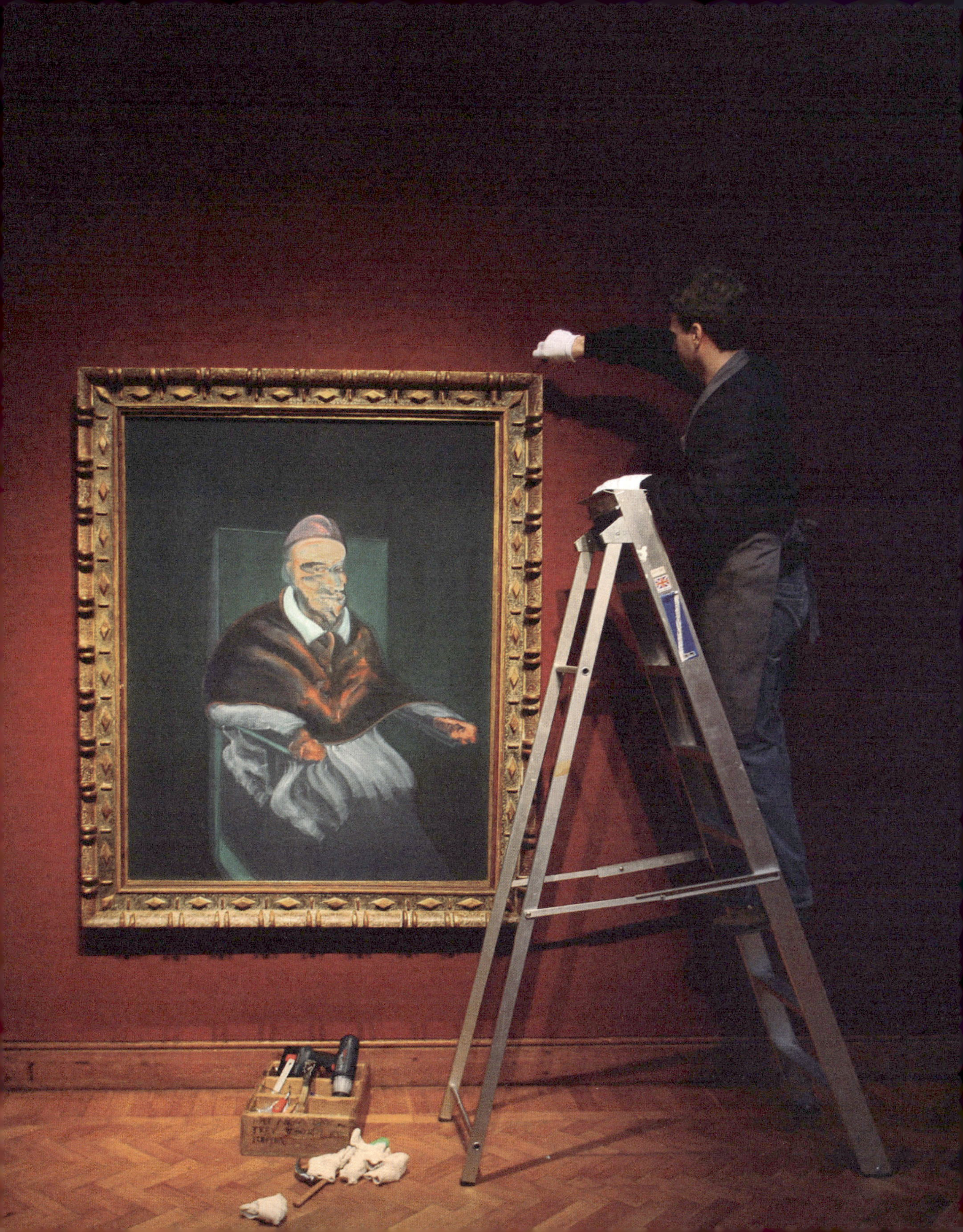

Meanwhile in Australia ...

Meanwhile in Australia: David Malangi makes money — or doesn't

In the 1960s, the artist and ethnologist Karel Kupka travelled to Australia to further his knowledge of Aboriginal art. He discovered an organised production system of paintings on bark that, beyond serving a traditional ceremonial purpose, was designed to satisfy a growing Western demand.

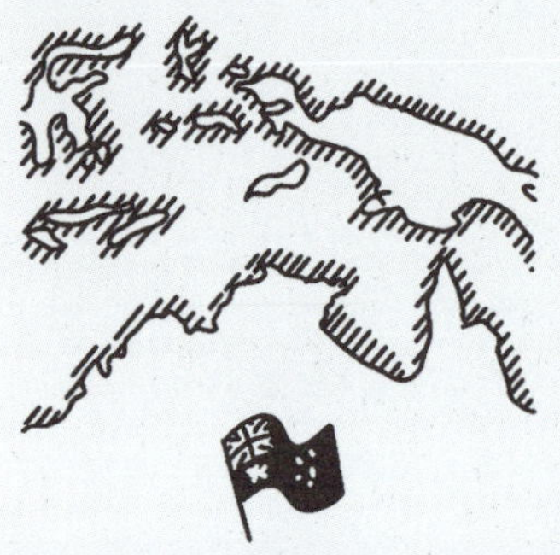

Setting the scene

In 1966, the Australian government created its first $1 note. To illustrate it, a graphic designer chose three Aboriginal works from three different regions. By placing them side by side, however, he deprived them of their context and obscured their meaning – but above all, in a context of Western domination, no-one even considered that these works could be the work of artists, whose permission should have been requested. Among these artists was David Malangi.

The masterpiece

- During his stays in Australia, Karel Kupka collected Aboriginal works, including the *Funerary Rites of Gurrmirringu* by David Malangi, which would be featured on the famous one-dollar note. It was through the efforts of missionary Alan Fidock that Malangi was identified, paid, and awarded a medal.
- The painting illustrates a burial ceremony that was recounted to David Malangi by his father. The deceased man is depicted at the bottom, in the centre. His name is Gurrmirringu, ancestor of the Manarrngu group, to which Malangi belonged. He was bitten by a Mulga snake, perhaps depicted next to him, unless this is the animal form of the deceased. In this guise, he becomes a Mokoi – a spirit of the Manarrngu.
- Two men are guarding his remains and playing music sticks, while a third man, returning from the hunt, is skinning a kangaroo. At the top, a fourth is accompanying the percussion with a melody played on the didgeridoo.

THE YOLNGU SOCIETY

"Yolngu" is the generic term for the people of central and eastern Arnhem Land, an Aboriginal reserve in north-eastern Australia. This name includes different groups, including the Manarrngu of Malangi. In Yolngu mythology, the country was founded by animal and human heroes. These ancestors continue to shape the world and its future, and are often represented in Yolgnu paintings.

WHO WAS DAVID MALANGI?

Born in 1927 in the Ramingining region, he learned to paint from his father. He produced his first works using coloured sands, and later created paintings on bark.

While works designed for ceremonial purposes were abandoned at the location, the Aborigines began to produce new works for Western clients. Malangi participated in this production, and also worked on canvas or paper.

The $1 note incident made him famous in 1967. From the 1970s onwards, he was featured in American museums, and became one of the first groups of Aboriginal artists to exhibit at the Sydney Biennale in 1979.

Having received numerous honours and awards, he died in 1999 in Yathalamarra, in the heart of Arnhem Land.

AN ANCESTRAL ART

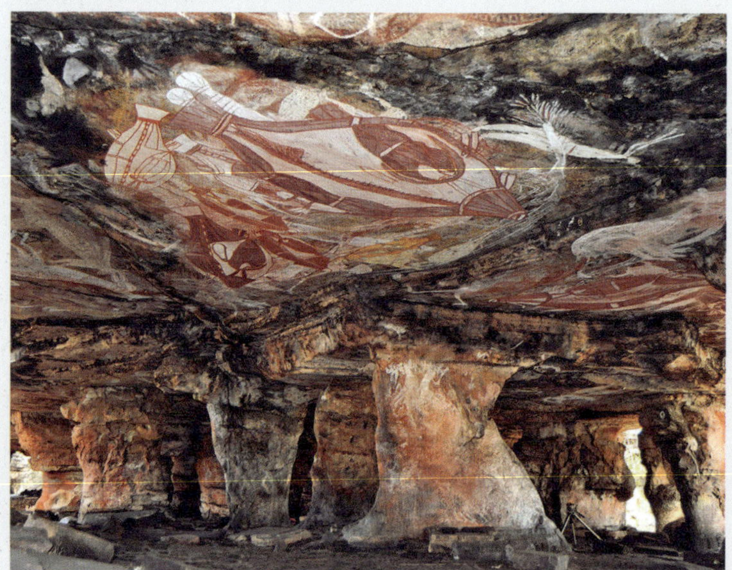

In Arnhem Land lies the archaeological site of Nawarla Gabarnmang. The ceilings of this rock shelter are extensively covered with decorative art, which first began some 26,000 years ago and is estimated to have continued until the turn of the 20th century. A piece of painted stone dating from 28,000 BC was also found; it is the oldest known Australian painting to date.

Decorative art at Nawarla Gabarnmang, Australia, Circa 28,000 BC

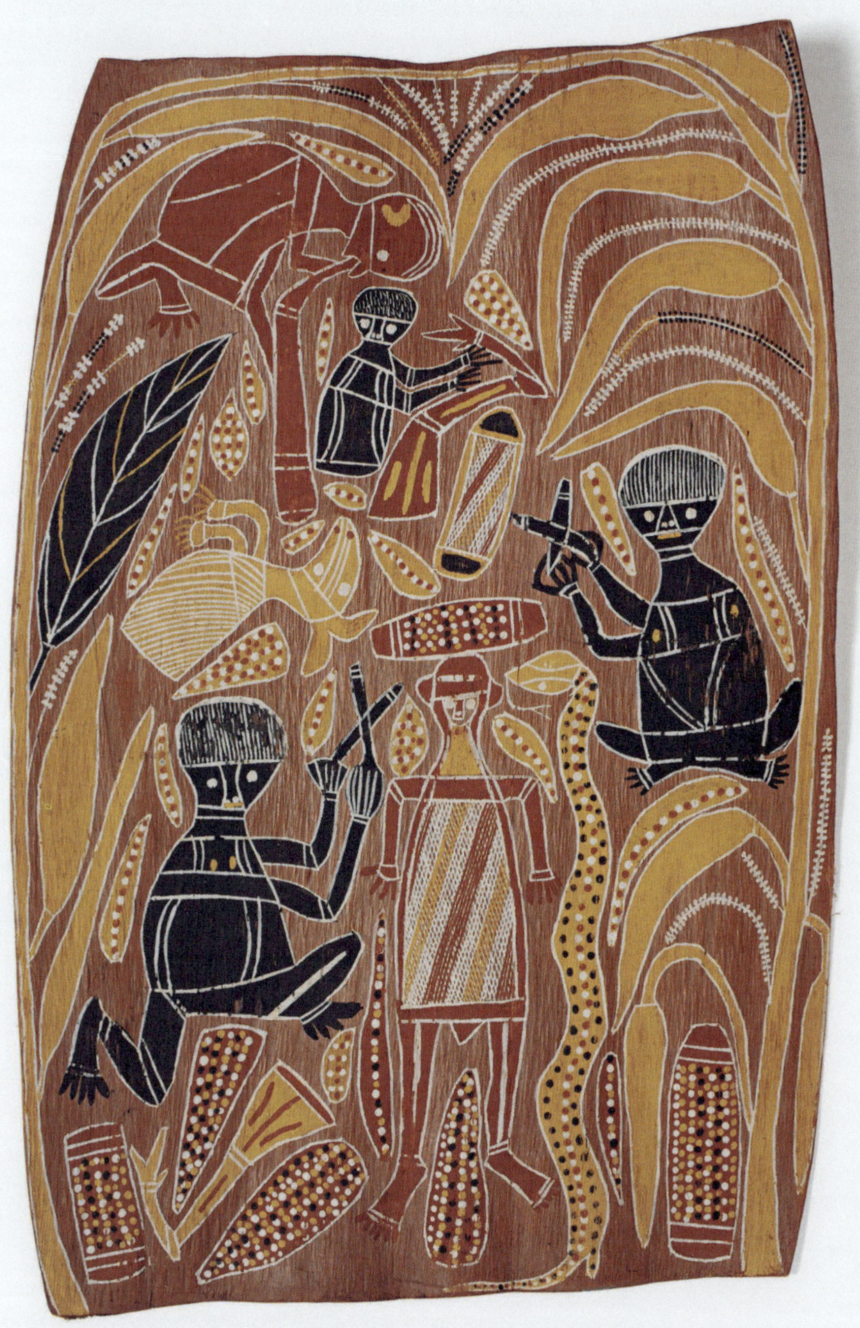

David Malangi
FUNERARY RITES OF GURRMIRRINGU
Collected in 1963 by Karel Kupka
Paint on bark
73.5 × 48 cm
Musée du Quai Branly

Roy Lichtenstein

An enticing screen

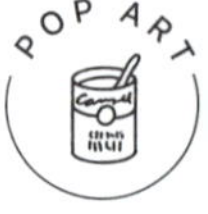

Lichtenstein, a great name of the pop art trend, alongside Andy Warhol, became known worldwide for his comic book imagery. The artist reclaimed and enlarged motifs from the consumer society, which he observed with distance and irony.

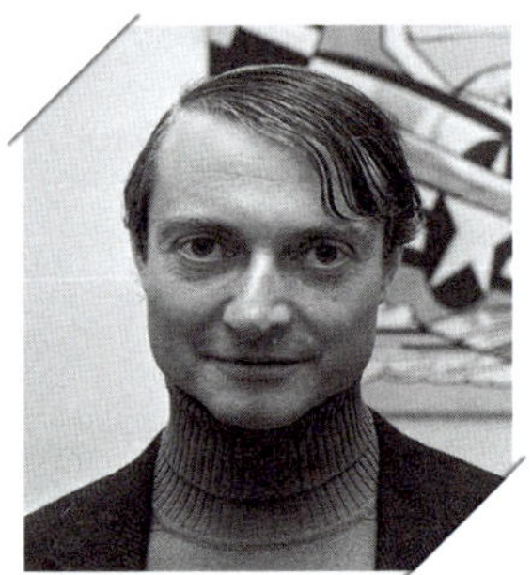

Making the best of a bad job

Lichtenstein was passionate about drawing since his childhood. He began studying in the hopes of embracing an artistic career, but was interrupted by the war. Conscripted by the American army, then transferred to Europe, he used this opportunity to discover the Louvre Museum and French art.

Deliberately cliché

He was inspired by images from everyday life and from comics. He simplified them with the aim of creating unified and stereotyped patterns, by manually reproducing the dots normally associated with mechanical printing processes. With humour and distance, Lichtenstein was more interested in the representation of the subject than in the subject itself.

Out of the box

The artist was a jack-of-all-trades; he devoted himself to ceramics and to sculpture, while also trying his hand at different genres, including landscapes, by reinterpreting classical Chinese art. His works evoke Pablo Picasso, Fernand Léger, Henri Matisse and others.

POINTILLISM 2.0

Lichtenstein was inspired by the "Ben-Day" printing technique invented by Benjamin Henry Day, in which a pattern is reproduced by mixing red, yellow, blue and black dot patterns.

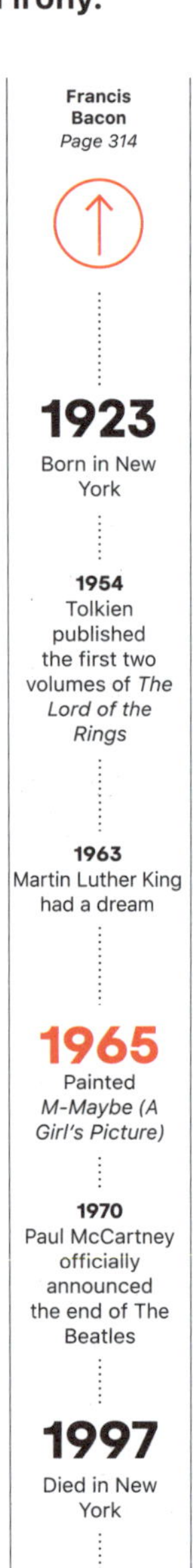

M-MAYBE (A GIRL'S PICTURE)

1965
Oil and acrylic on canvas
152 × 152 cm
Museum Ludwig, Cologne

WHAT ARE WE LOOKING AT?

Lichtenstein recreates the stereotype of the young blonde woman, as promoted by consumer society. Under an enviable appearance, she is a victim, above all.

To each their own

Between 1963 and 1965, Lichtenstein produced works taken from enlarged comic book panels, which can be divided into two main themes: on the one hand, images of a sentimental nature, featuring seductive blonde women, on the other, war-related motifs, conveying a model of masculinity.

The "housewife under 50" demographic

Inspired by consumerism, the painter reinforces the clichés of an advertising ideal designed to seduce potential customers targeted by these communications. Lichtenstein portrayed these women as victims, in situations of passive suffering and distress caused by the absence of a man. They are observed in personal, domestic contexts, situations pertaining to the private world.

Stood up

M-Maybe presents us with an attractive young woman who appears to be waiting for a man; she has been waiting long enough to worry about him and to formulate assumptions about his lateness. Viewers are left with the vague feeling that he will not be joining her.

Telling herself a story

The artist creates a tension between the young woman's archetype and the authenticity of her intimate thoughts and her hesitation. He invites the viewer to create a story leading to the current situation.

POP ART IN A NUTSHELL

The term "pop art" was coined in 1955 by art critic Lawrence Alloway, but it was the artist Richard Hamilton who best defined it in describing his own work. According to him, pop art is…

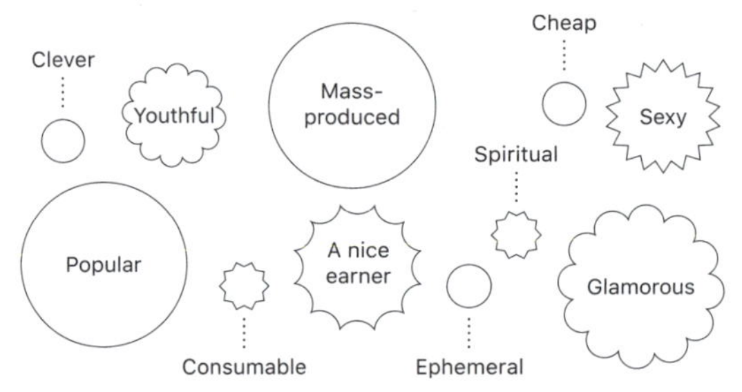

LEADING FIGURES OF POP ART

- Roy Lichtenstein
- Richard Hamilton (1922–2011)
- Andy Warhol (p. 322)
- Jasper Johns (né en 1930)
- James Rosenquist (1933–2017)
- Evelyne Axell (1935–1972)
- Pauline Boty (1938–1966)

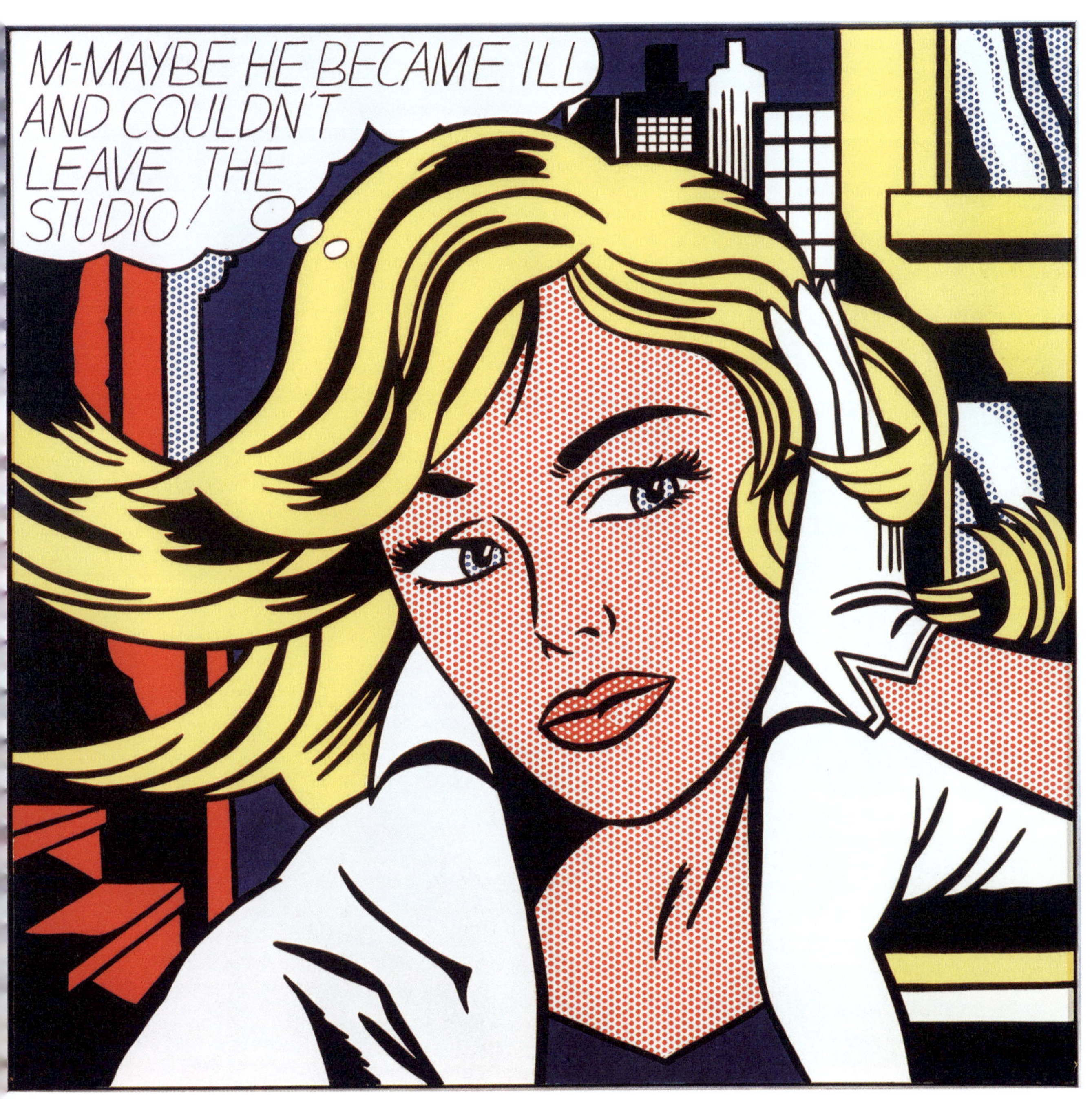
M-MAYBE HE BECAME ILL AND COULDN'T LEAVE THE STUDIO!

Andy Warhol

Rehearsal in the spotlight

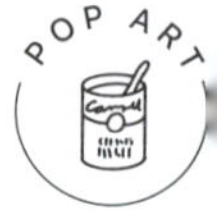

A publicist by trade, Andrew Warhola, the son of Czechoslovakian immigrants, became Andy Warhol, the king of pop art. From his New York Factory, he was as fascinated by celebrity as he was by mass consumption, and cultivated the art of repetition.

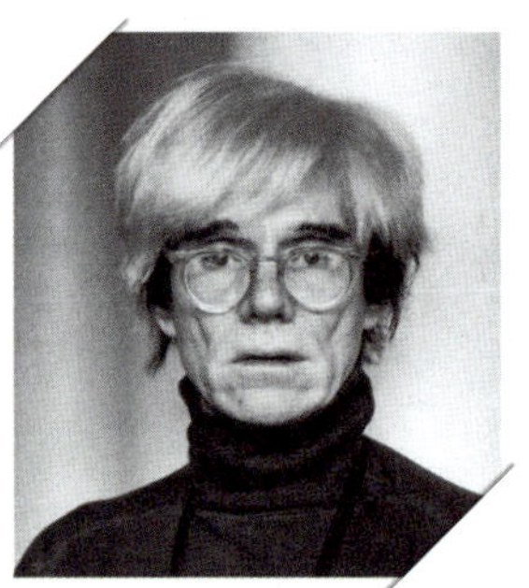

Thanks, mum!

As a sick child, Warhol was forced to stay at home. His mother gave him art supplies, as well as comics and magazines, already forming the basis for his art. He continued in this direction and graduated as a graphic designer.

A well-fitting shoe

Aged 21, he moved to New York. He worked for the fashion and advertising industry, producing illustrations of shoes, among others. He accumulated a visual repertoire, which he used to create works with an ambiguous status, between artistic creation and commercial production.

Welcome to the factory

He was met with success in the early 1960s, with his Campbell's Soup cans, which introduced an art of repetition that would become his trademark. His studio, which he named The Factory, became a mecca for the underground culture, and was frequented by many artists.

A MOST FAMOUS BANANA

When I say "pop", you say "rock"! In 1967, Warhol produced the mythical studio album *The Velvet Underground and Nico*, and illustrated the cover of the album with his famous banana, featuring the indication "Peel slowly and see".

Roy Lichtenstein
Page 320

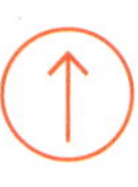

1928
Born in Pittsburgh

1938
Volkswagen's best-seller, the Beetle, was born

1964
Painted *Shot Sage Blue Marilyn*

1970
First celebration of Earth Day

1987
Died in New York

David Hockney
Page 324

SHOT SAGE BLUE MARILYN

1964
Acrylic and screen printing on linen canvas
101.6 × 101.6 cm
Private collection

WHAT ARE WE LOOKING AT?

As Warhol discovered screen printing, he repeatedly portrayed unfortunate stars, reflecting his fascination with glamour and tragedy.

An icon in a square

With its multiple variations, this portrait of Marilyn Monroe is one of the most famous works of the pop art trend. It embodies the essence of a movement, but above all, of a country and an era. In 2022, it confirmed its status as an ineffable work, reaching no less than $195 million at an auction sale.

Drama queens

Underneath their cheerful colours, Warhol's screen printing portraits of celebrities are tragic. Warhol painted Elizabeth Taylor while she was hospitalised, Jackie Kennedy after her husband had just been assassinated, and Marilyn Monroe after she had just committed suicide, as if he aimed to question the media's morbid appetite for these dramas.

Consumer product

Warhol himself was fascinated by what Marilyn Monroe embodied: fame and drama.
He reproduced her portrait in dozens of copies, a metaphor for the actress's over-exposure, as she was merchandised and perceived as a sexual object. Warhol used a promotional photograph for *Niagara*, a film in which the actress played an unfaithful seductress.

Camouflage

The photograph has been expeditiously coloured with paint: the actress becomes a cliché of herself, constantly reproduced, artificial and distant, behind these flat tints that act as a mask. The repetition removes any meaning from this image. What remains of this overexposure?

SCREEN PRINTING

Screen printing, which allows users to print designs on a wide range of materials, is a popular technique in industrial circles, and therefore among pop artists. The principle is similar to that of the stencil.

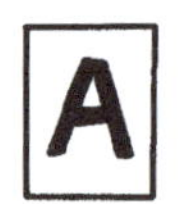

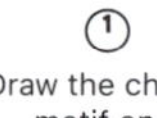

① Draw the chosen motif on a transparent sheet (plastic, Rhodoid, etc.).

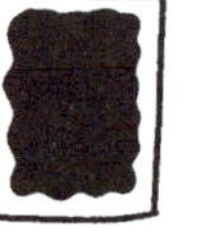

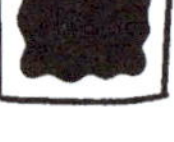

② Coat the substrate with a photosensitive emulsion. When exposed to UV light, it will harden in the areas that haven't been drawn on.

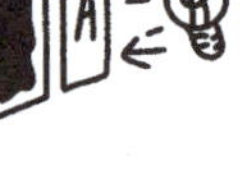

③ Place the transparent sheet onto the frame and expose it to the light.

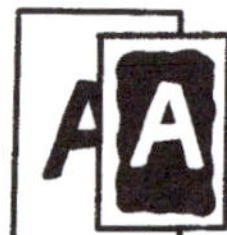

④ Rinse the frame. The unexposed ink surface, protected from the light by the motif, will be removed.

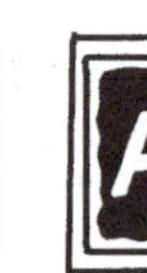

⑤ Apply the ink using a squeegee, then allow it to dry.

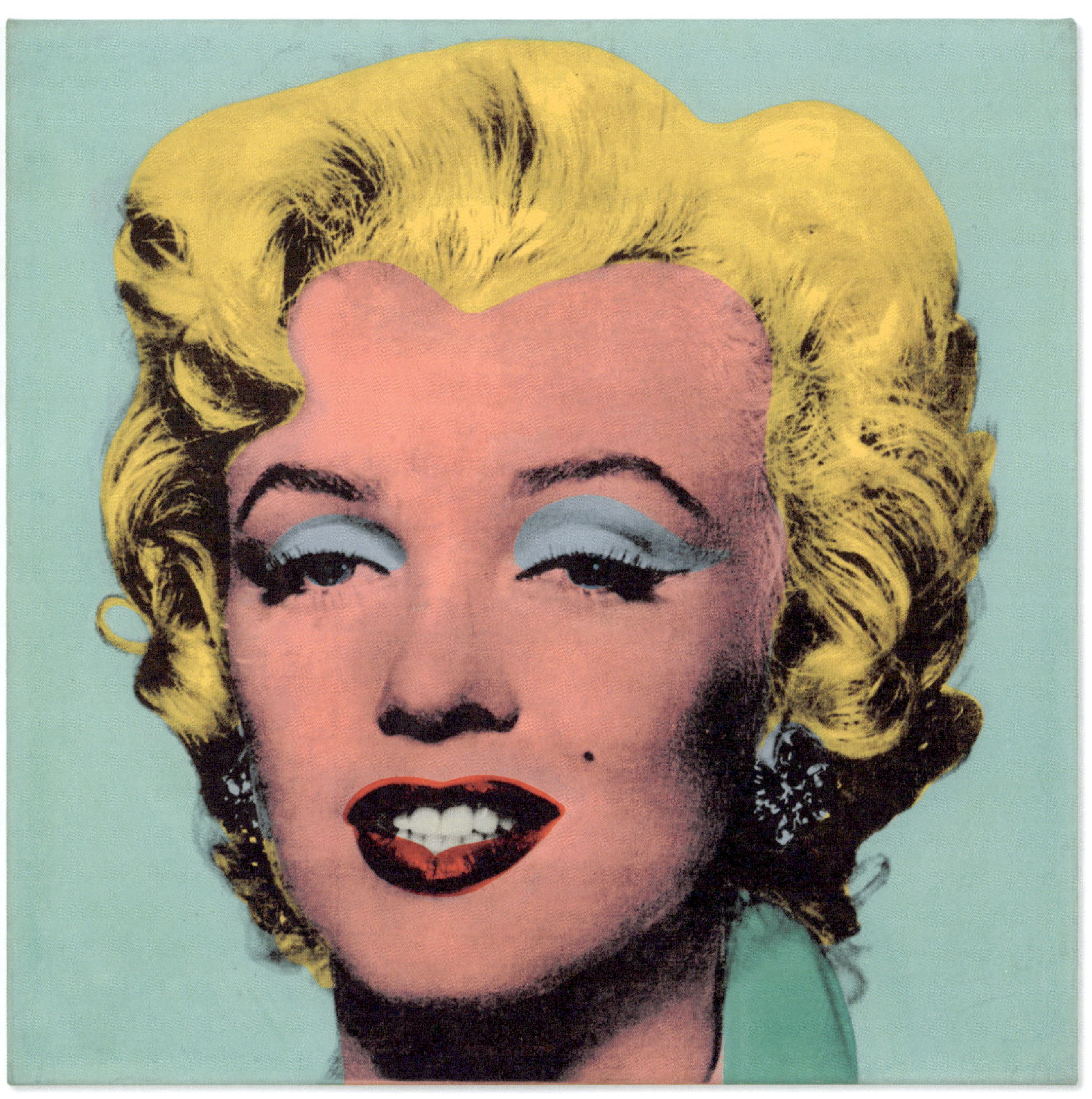

David Hockney

Making a splash the pool

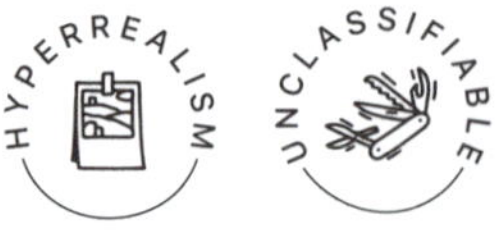

**He is the most popular contemporary artist in the UK. His painting, simple in appearance and featuring joyful accents, reveals a complex use of colour and perspective.
Hockney disconcerted viewers using the variations of his style.**

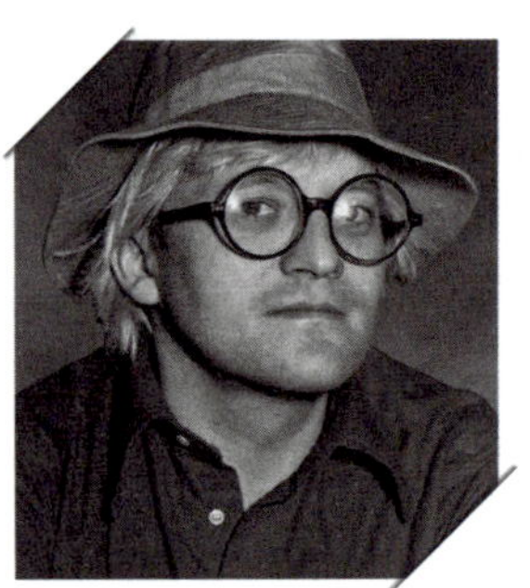

Coming out

Hockney trained at the Royal College of Art, in London, and was tempted by social realism. He then turned to abstract painting, but soon reintroduced figurative elements in his works, affirming his homosexuality in his paintings at a time when it was still an offence, in 1960s England.

The good life

After his studies, he moved to Los Angeles. Influenced by the sweetness of life, his hedonistic painting gained in light and colour. He would later embrace an even more lively approach with his vivid landscapes. Hockney cheated with perspectives to involve viewers in his paintings.

Borrowing pays off

Hockney incorporated many references in his works, ranging from Henri Matisse (p. 262) to Francis Bacon (p. 314) to the Italian Renaissance, but Pablo Picasso (p. 264) would have a determining influence on him. Observing the cubist's work, Hockney understood that he was not bound to a single style.

TECHNOPHILE

The artist was also interested in photography and new technologies. Today, he produces his works directly on a digital tablet.

Andy Warhol
Page 322

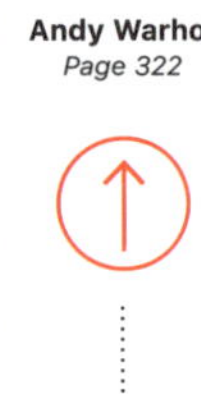

1937
Born in Bradford

1944
French women were allowed to vote

1960
Fellini immortalised the Trevi fountain in *La Dolce Vita*

1967
Painted *A Bigger Splash*

1974
Roland Moreno invented the smart card

Gerhard Richter
Page 330

A BIGGER SPLASH

1967
Acrylic on canvas
242.5 × 243.9 cm
Tate Modern, London

WHAT ARE WE LOOKING AT?

This is one of the painter's most famous works. He celebrates the sweetness of Californian life, while freezing for eternity a moment so fleeting that it becomes invisible.

Arrest me, I'm a splasher!

This painting is part of a suite of three works, *The Splash*, *A Little Splash* and *A Bigger Splash*. The artist represents the same motif of a pool from which a splash of water rises, facing modern-looking houses. Hockney, inspired by California, created many variations of the now-iconic pool motif, in which he sought to capture the movement of water.

A heterogeneous construct

Here, the pool is taken from a magazine photograph, while the architecture in the background was drawn beforehand. The composition is structured in broad horizontal bands, disrupted by the splash. The diving board intersects these horizontal lines, creating an impression of depth.

Life in blue

The bright colours celebrate Californian life. The blue tones of the water and the sky contrast sharply with the yellow diving board and the orange architecture. Maliciously, the only human presence that might enjoy this idyllic setting is obscured by the splash.

Taking the time for speed

Here, Hockney has captured a snapshot that is usually not seen, because it is so ephemeral. Rather than succumbing to the temptation of splashing the canvas using dynamic brushstrokes, in the manner of expressionist artists, the painter chose to meticulously paint the water rising from the pool, using variations in colour and transparency.

SUCCESSFUL AUCTIONS

the artist was favoured by the contemporary art scene, and his popularity would be matched only by his value on the art market.

$44.7M	*Henry Geldzahler and Christopher Scott*	1969	sold in 2019
$ 79.5M	*Portrait of an Artist*	1972	sold in 2018
$27.4M	*The Splash*	(1966)	sold in 2020

WHAT IS THE "KITCHEN SINK"?

The social realist movement to which Hockney belonged at the beginning of his career was called "the Kitchen Sink" – a symbolic item of everyday life in the working classes. These artists magnify ordinary life, while offering a social and political reading of the world.

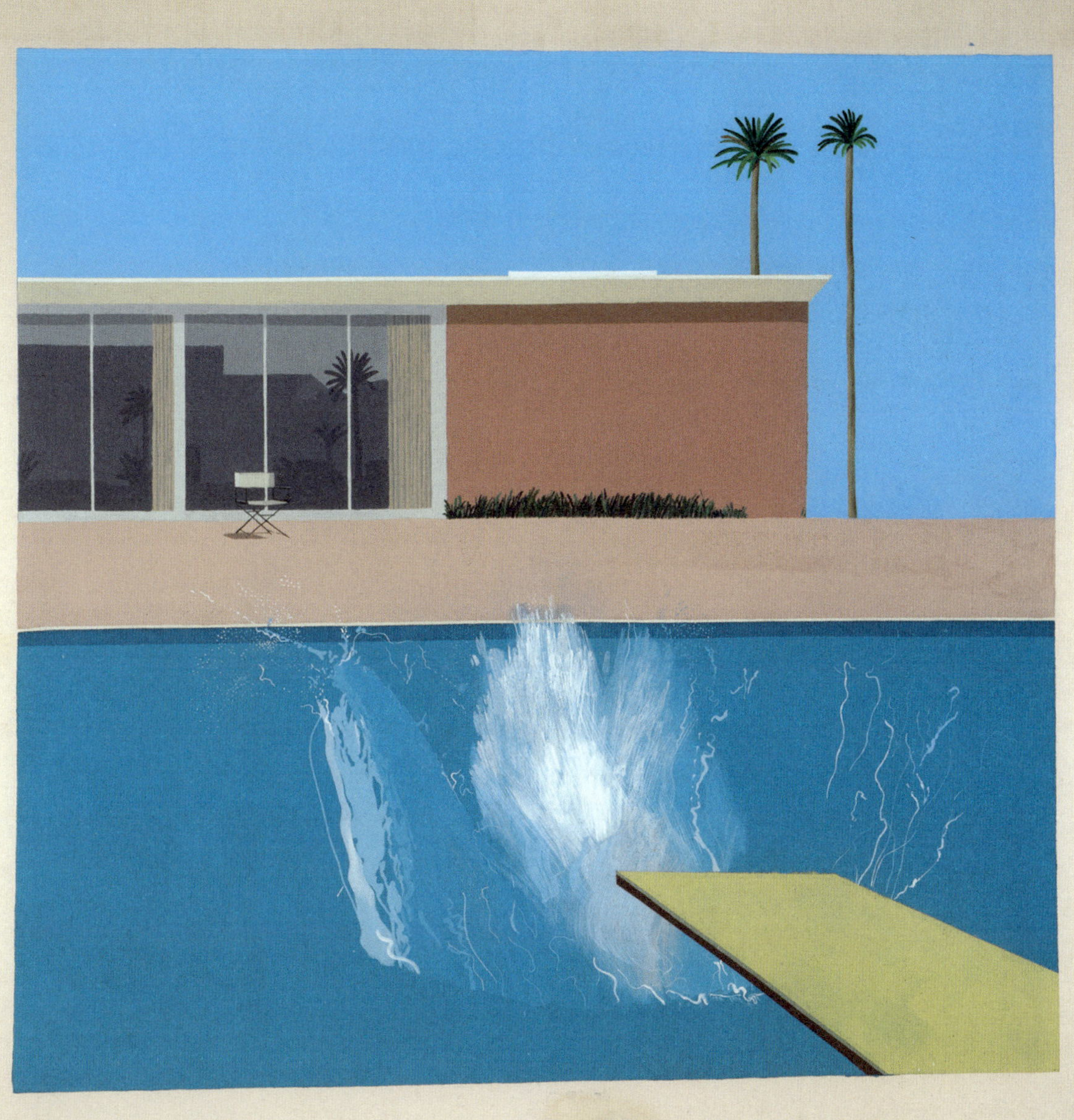

X–rays, infrared and ultraviolet

Masterpieces dissected by experts

It is possible to perform a "check-up" of a painting by subjecting it to a series of tests. Each technique can reveal key information for analysing and understanding the work. Reading and interpreting the results requires good eyesight ... and more.

A work in the spotlight

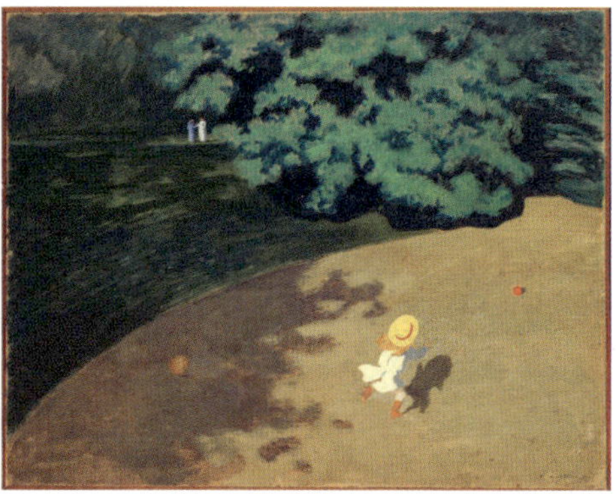

Félix Vallotton
The Balloon
1899,
Musée d'Orsay, Paris

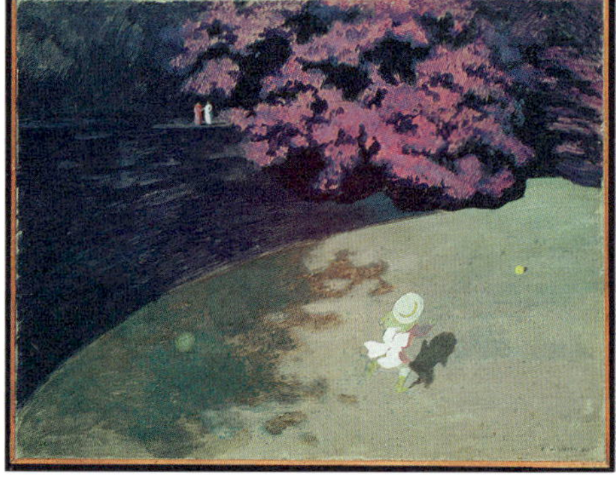

Infrared reflectography
This technique allows experts to identify preparatory drawings under the paint or changes in composition during the execution of the work.

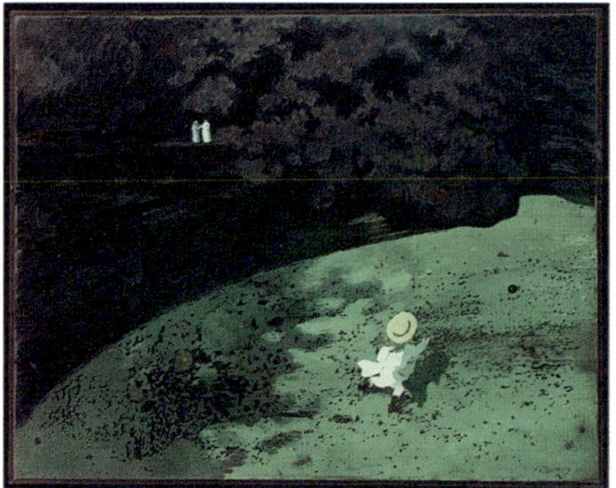

Ultraviolet imaging
This technique can be used to identify varnishes and their thickness, highlighting any irregularities or thinning that may have occurred during restoration. It also reveals repaints, i.e. additions made after the painting was completed, performed by the artist or a third party.

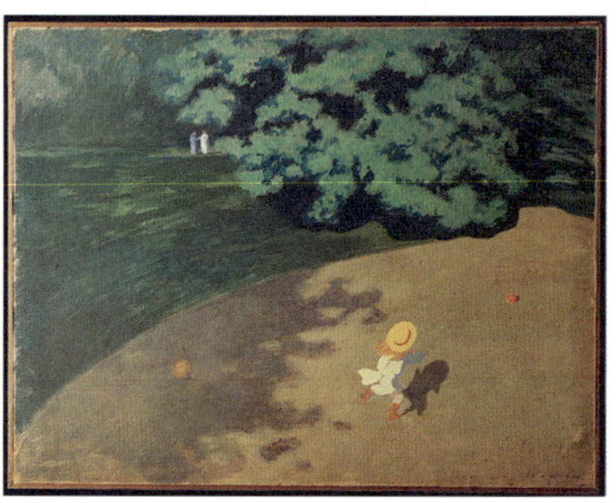

Incident light photography
This technique consists in taking a photograph with lighting at 15 degrees, to reveal any irregularities, cracks, dents or lifting. The general state of the paint layer also allows experts to appraise the artist's technique from a different angle.

In the depths of the works

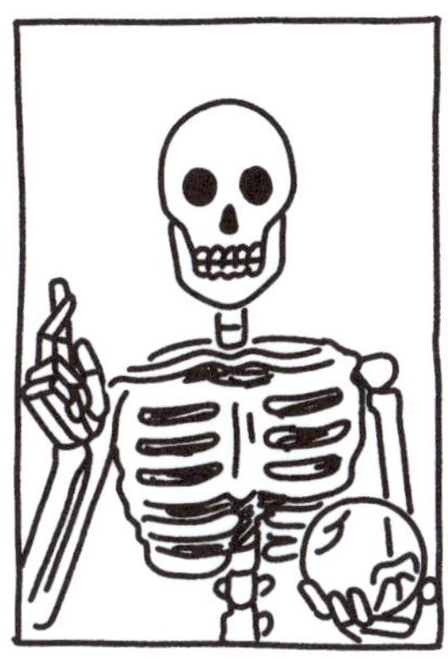

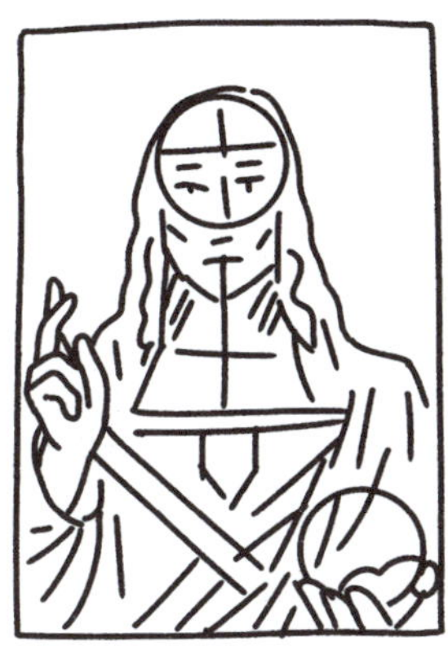

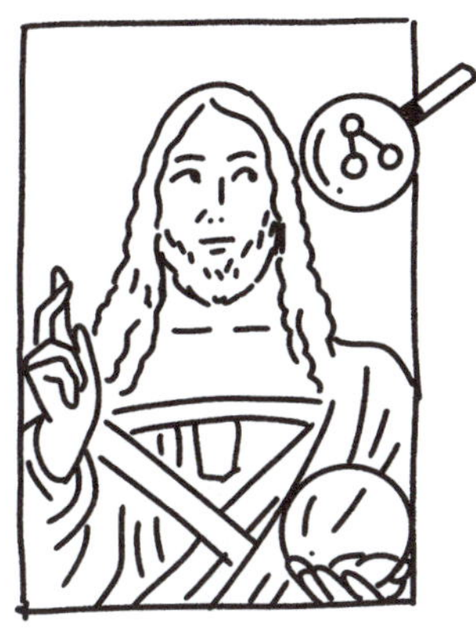

X-ray

This technique allows experts to observe the work's "skeleton", as it pierces the paint layer. They can then observe the support (wooden panel, or canvas and stretcher, p. 240), which reveals repairs, enlargements or cut-outs. Underlying compositions also become visible, sometimes revealing that the artist has painted over another creation.

X-ray fluorescence

This technique analyses the chemical composition of certain elements, without requiring the removal of any material. The sample is bombarded with particles and X-rays. This process enables experts to identify even the pigments used in an underlying composition, even if it is invisible and inaccessible.

Hyperspectral imaging

This technique complements X-ray fluorescence by providing information on the chemical nature of the materials used, and in particular certain dyes.
This data is invaluable for understanding the artist's technique, analysing their brushstrokes or detecting underlying drawings or pentimenti.

CUTTING-EDGE TECHNOLOGY UNDER THE PYRAMID

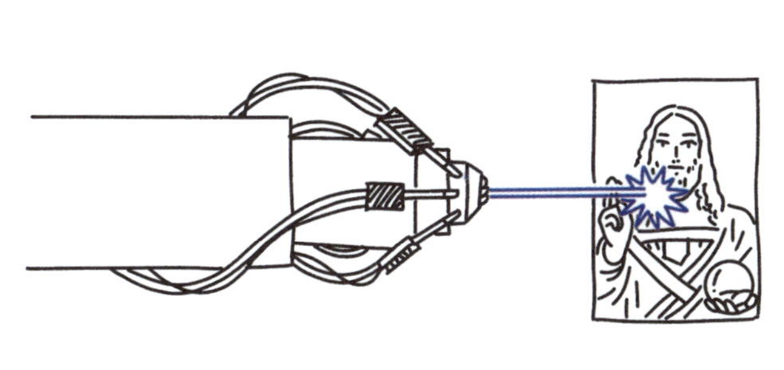

- The basement of the Louvre Museum is home to a unique scientific laboratory, the Centre de Recherche et de Restauration des Musées de France (or C2RMF). On its examination tables, every pigment of the most precious masterpieces is analysed.
- The laboratory houses a jewel of innovation named AGLAÉ, for "Accélérateur Grand Louvre d'Analyses Élémentaires" – the only particle accelerator of its size worldwide dedicated solely to analysing works of art.
- In addition to its unique performance, AGLAÉ enables experts to perform non-destructive analyses, i.e. analyses that do not require samples to be taken from the works.

WHY ANALYSE A WORK?

- **To ensure its conservation:** being aware of the general condition of a work of art helps to prevent deterioration or repair any damage.
- **For research:** studying the technical characteristics of a work provides a better understanding of an artist's work.
- **Authentication:** analysing a work can help confirm its attribution to an artist or, on the contrary, cause it to be reassessed.

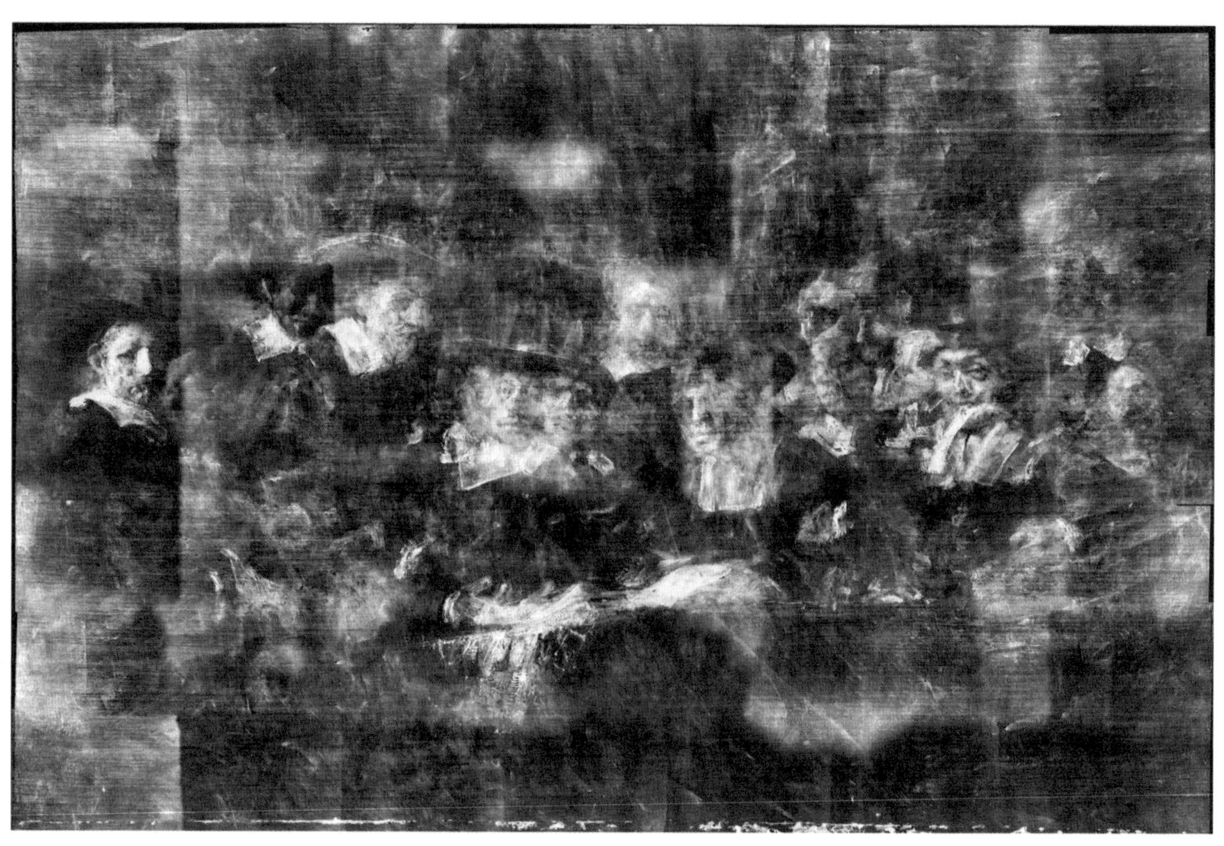

X-ray

On the right, *The Sampling Officials* (also known as Syndics of the Drapers' Guild), painted by Rembrandt in 1662 and exhibited at the Rijksmuseum in Amsterdam. Above, the work photographed using X-ray technique, revealing the changes made by the painter as he worked.

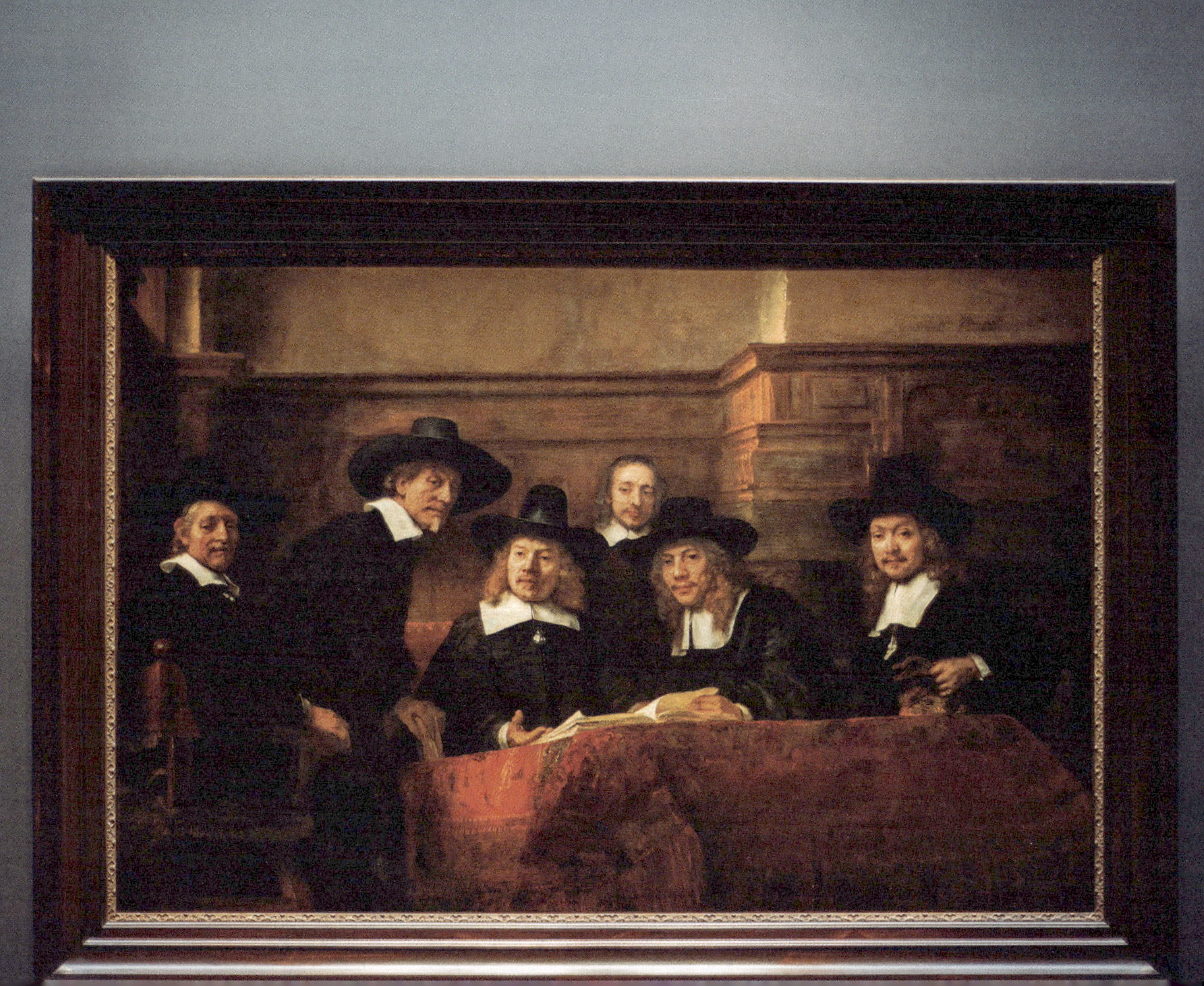

Gerhard Richter

It's all an artistic blur

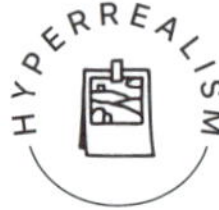

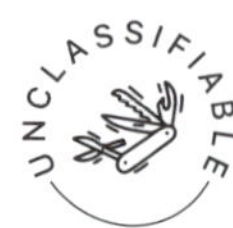

A major artist on the German scene, Richter destabilises observers by the diversity of his work, blending figuration and abstraction, between the melancholy of grey skies and the dynamic energy of the green rays that sometimes streak his paintings.

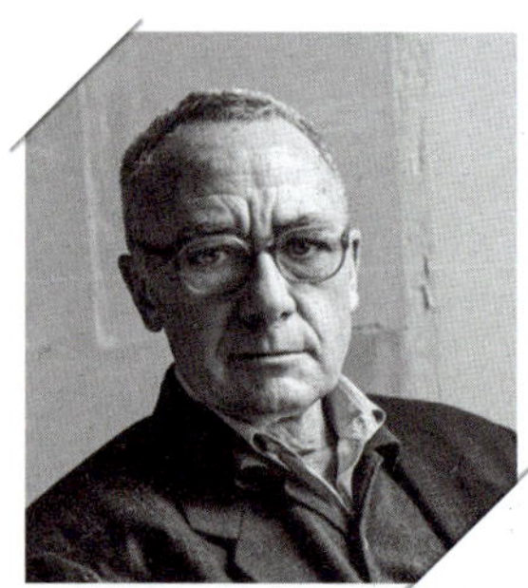

A promising start

As a teenager, Richter discovered photography. He began his career by painting signs and theatre sets, and then decided to embrace art, enrolling at the Academy of Arts. After completing his studies, he received enough commissions to be financially independent.

A clever mix

The artist constantly mixed photography and painting. He painted on photographs or, on the contrary, uses them as models, thus imagining photo-paintings, hyper-realistic and blurred renditions of his photographs.

Something for everyone

Richter is the author of both photo-paintings and rigorous geometric works, which passed through an Abstract Expressionism expressing his vitality through colour and brushwork. Like the German Romantics who preceded him, he was also influenced by nature and landscapes.

PREFERRED TOOL

Richter used a scraper, a tool that enabled him to crush colours on the support. He thus acknowledged the absence of complete control and a measure of chance in the final result of his works.

David Hockney
Page 324

1932
Born in Dresden

1957
Launch of the first artificial satellite

1970
Painted *Wolken (Clouds)*

1986
Chernobyl nuclear disaster

Jean-Michel Basquiat
Page 332

WOLKEN (CLOUDS)

1970
Oil on canvas
200 × 300 cm
Folkwang Museum, Essen

WHAT ARE WE LOOKING AT?

Clouds are an emblematic feature of Richter's works. They lie between the heritage of ancient painting and the modernity of an approach liberated from spirituality. They embody a motif that bridges the gap between figuration and abstraction.

Worthy heir

Richter's work falls within the long tradition of old masters. Clouds evoke the mystical character of great church paintings, the atmospheric effects of English landscape art works and the romanticism of 19th century artists.

No mystery

With these sky paintings, Richter sets new boundaries in the landscape painting genre. However, the painting conceals no spiritual message, even if it invites viewers to contemplation and introspection. Richter's clouds synthesise abstraction, figuration and photography.

Hanging clouds

Richter also solved a technical problem: nothing is more difficult than capturing, from life, the shape of an ever-changing cloud. He avoided this problem by using photography, painting his studies from low-angle shots of the sky.

Beta test

His series of paintings of clouds began at the end of the 1960s and continued until 1979, enabling him to perfect his blurred hyperrealism, which he later applied to other motifs.

Halftone

In his paintings of clouds, Richter worked with shades of grey, his favourite colour. Melancholic and gentle, it is also the nuance of moods and uncertainties; a "non-colour", a visual solution for the uncertain. It also reflected his artistic hesitations.

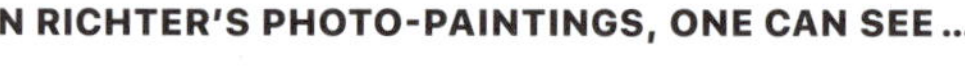

IN RICHTER'S PHOTO-PAINTINGS, ONE CAN SEE ...

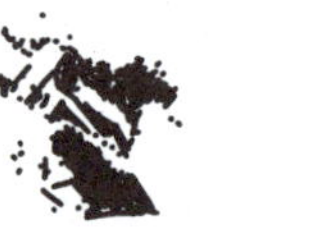

The Alps (23)

Candles (28)

Marine scenes (25)

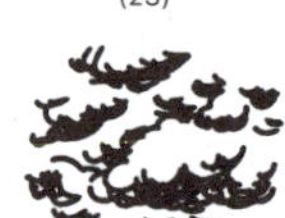

Clouds (30)

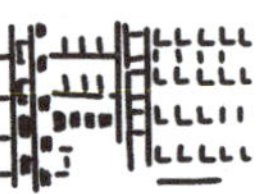

Buildings (31)

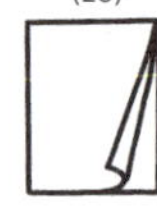

Pages turned over (20)

RICHTER'S ART IN A NUTSHELL

- Works produced using a scraper.
- Room left to chance.
- Photorealism.
- Painted photographs.
- The colour grey.
- A dynamic green ray.

Jean-Michel Basquiat

From graffiti to autograph

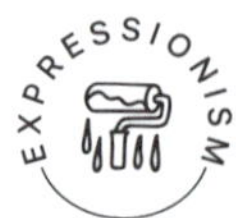

A young prodigy, Basquiat went from being a rising figure of street culture to an international celebrity. His black heroes highlight the lack of diversity in contemporary art.

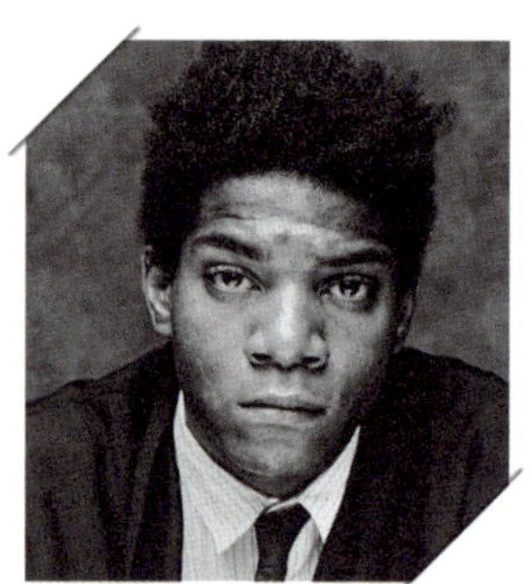

Gray's Anatomy

At the age of 8, Basquiat was hit by a car. He began drawing during his convalescence, when his mother bought him the famous manual *"Gray's Anatomy (Anatomy, Descriptive and Surgical)"*. The illustrations in this treatise would leave their mark on his work, rife with skulls and skeletons.

Yo!

Confronted with street life in his teenage years, the artist developed a culture steeped in graffiti and hip-hop. He became known as a street artist under the name SAMO, short for "same old shit", and soon became an influential figure of New York's East Village district.

Ambassador

As a black artist in America in the 1980s, Basquiat defended a form of art that was rebellious, heroic and anti-establishment, populated by kings and heroes. Promoting black American culture, he also railed against racism and exclusion.

MAGIC FORMULA

"Royalty, heroism and the streets." With these now-legendary words, Basquiat replied to curator and art critic Henry Geldzahler, who asked him to define his art during an interview in 1983.

Gerhard Richter
Page 330

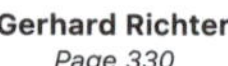
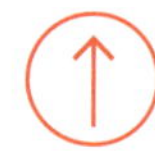

1960
Born in New York

1974
The skeleton named Lucy was discovered in Ethiopia

1981
Painted *Untitled*

1982
Release of *E.T., the Extra-Terrestrial* by Spielberg

1988
Died in New York

Yayoi Kusama
Page 334

UNTITLED

1981
Acrylic and oil pastel on canvas
206 × 176 cm
Board Collection, Los Angeles

WHAT ARE WE LOOKING AT?

Revealing numerous artistic influences, this is Basquiat's first "head" – very likely a self-portrait. Often described as a skull, it is actually very much alive.

Brainboxes galore

This painting is regularly interpreted as a vanitas (p. 110). The iconography indeed depicts a skull, suggested by the visible teeth, a feature associated with the anatomical studies that Basquiat observed during his youth, and perhaps also to the voodoo culture passed on to him by his Haitian father. Reality, however, is more complex.

Grey matter

This head is very much alive, with sensitive functions (eyes, nose and ears) and features revealing intense, visible brain activity. In place of the brain, one can see cubes and graffiti, revealing a bubbling psychic environment.

A well-formed head

Basquiat followed in the footsteps of the abstractionists, who sought to represent immaterial truths, but nevertheless opted for a figurative approach. The trepanned skull, which connects the sensory and intellectual worlds, is reminiscent of Leonardo da Vinci (p. 44). The references don't stop there: this head evokes an African mask, denouncing the appropriation of non-Western cultures by the modernists.

Under pressure

Basquiat worked fast; nonetheless, he would need several months to produce this powerful painting, featuring a bold palette. He had reached a pivotal moment in his career, and was on his way to becoming the new face of the New York scene. This painting would be displayed at his first solo exhibition.

CLASH OF THE TITANS

The young prodigy worked with the master of pop art, Andy Warhol. Their duo was prolific, but their works were subject to harsh criticism and their relationship turned sour. Their bond would be tenuous, but unbreakable.

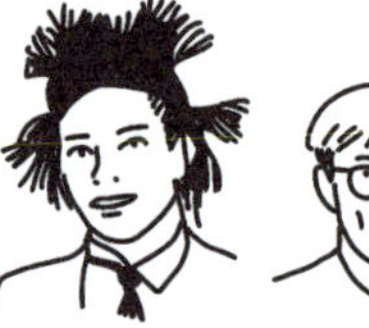

FORCED, BUT PRODUCTIVE REST

Immobilisation of the body appears to be a source of inspiration. The biographical theme of artists finding their path during convalescence is recurrent throughout history.
Examples include Edvard Munch (p. 252), Henri Matisse (p. 262), Frida Kahlo (p. 306), or Andy Warhol (p. 322).

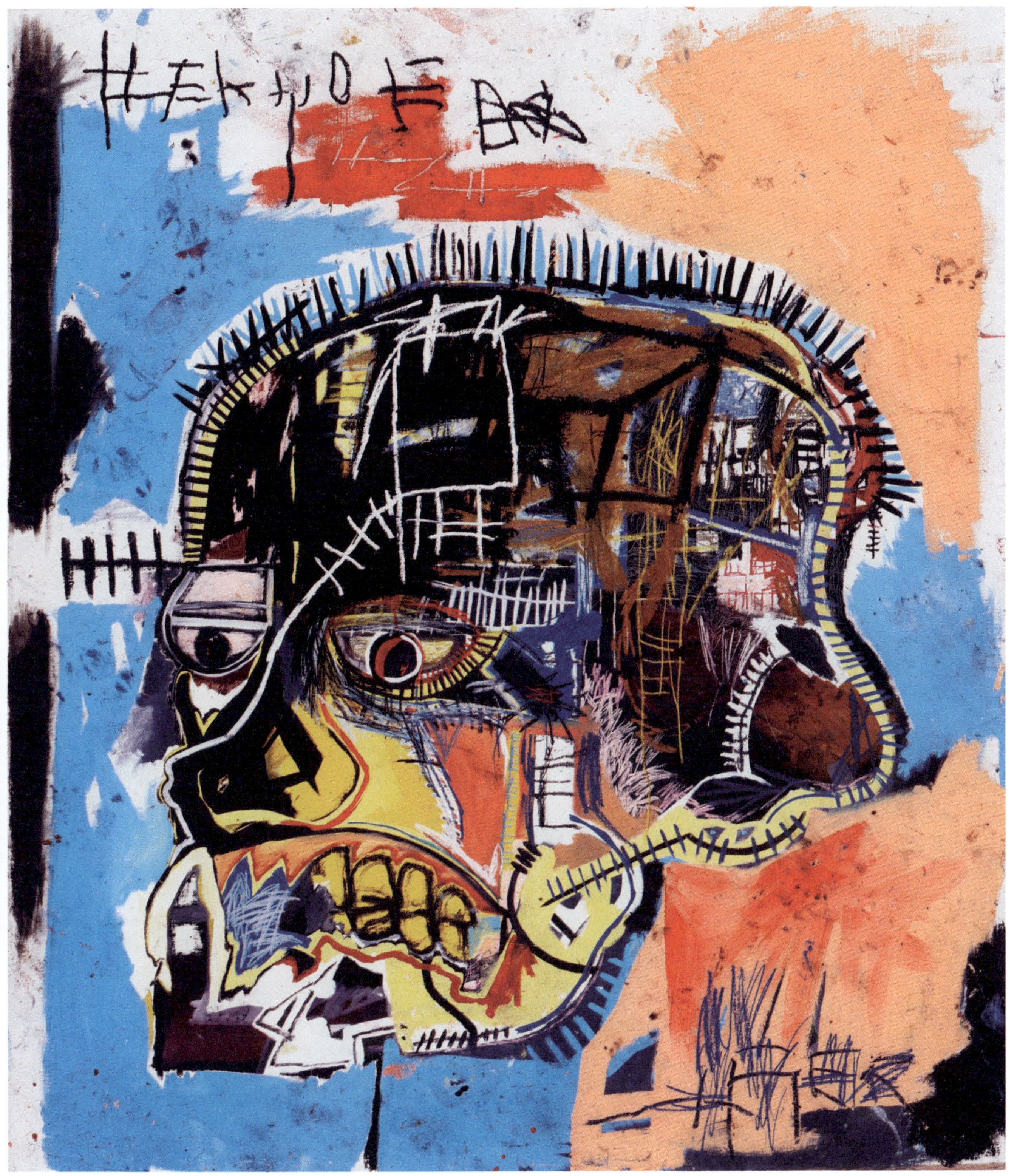

Yayoi Kusama

Dotty for dots

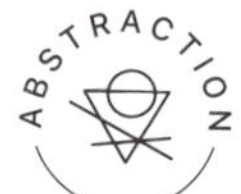

More than an artist, Yayoi Kusama is a phenomenon. Profoundly atypical, rather unconcerned by celebrity, she lives and works beyond the codes of art. Large crowds gather to contemplate her varied and prolific works, marked by polka dots and repetition.

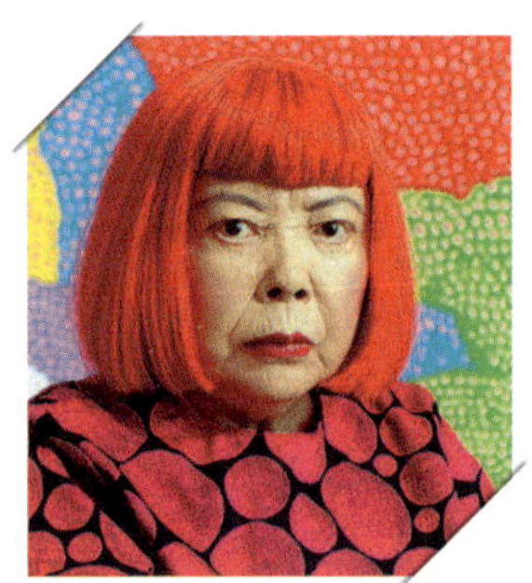

East to West

Yayoi Kusama became known in New York in the 1960s, and in the 1980s, her art conquered the West once again. The artist, who began painting in her teens, expresses herself in many ways, ranging from sculptures to installations.

Healing evil through good

Struggling with anxieties and obsessions since childhood, Kusama used her art as a means of overcoming her difficulties. This concept, which she named "Self-Obliteration", took form in the 1960s, in the guise of performances and videos.

The same old thing

Her work is marked by repetitions, which she initially formulates by painting minimalist networks of lines. Then, in negative, she creates the main markers of repetition, in the shape of polka dots and elongated shapes symbolising phalluses, covering objects, furniture items and even entire rooms.

YAYOI KUSAMA SAID

"People are confused and don't know how to understand me. Regardless, some want to call me a Surrealist, trying to pull me to their side, others want me in the camp of Minimal art, pushing me in the other direction."

Jean-Michel Basquiat
Page 332

1929
Born in Matsumoto

1989
Painted *Midnight Pumpkin*

1993
Jane Campion became the first woman to win the Palme d'Or at Cannes

2004
Facebook was created, and the world left a "Like"

Chéri Samba
Page 336

MIDNIGHT PUMPKIN

1989
Acrylic on canvas
45.5 × 38 cm
Private collection

WHAT ARE WE LOOKING AT?

The pumpkin is one of the artist's key motifs, which became the subject of many of her works, on a variety of media.

Variations galore

The artist would use this motif in her paintings, but also in her sculptures or her Mirror Rooms. In 1993, she installed *Mirror Room (Pumpkin)* at the Venice Biennale, one of the most important contemporary art events in the world; visitors attending the event were given pumpkins.

In her own style

The motif appeared very early in her career, in 1946. She depicted a squash in a painting in the *Nihonga* style, a movement that emerged in Japan at the end of the 19th century. The term describes a painting, on silk or paper, that combines traditional Japanese techniques and materials with the naturalistic subjects of Western painting, using oil or watercolour.

Made-to-measure polka dots

Although the artist most often worked in an unconventional register, her pumpkins follow a naturalist vein, which at first appears to be Academism. Over the years, Kusama surrounded her pumpkins with her favourite motifs: networks of lines and repetitions of polka dots, as seen here.

WHERE CAN ONE SEE KUSAMA'S WORKS?

Since 1994, the artist has produced monumental works, exhibited in Japan and Circa the world.

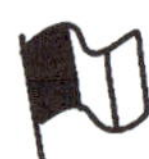

France
Lille

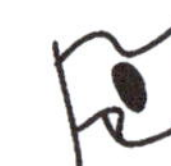

Japan
Fukuoka
Kagoshima
Nagano
Niigata

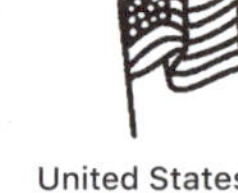

United States
Beverly Hills

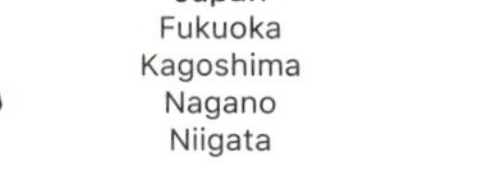

Portugal
Lisbon

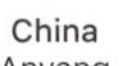

China
Anyang

TRENDY BEFORE THE TREND

The artist created the concept of the *Infinity Mirror Rooms* – entire rooms composed of mirrors, plunging visitors into unlimited, dizzying spaces. In this age of social networking and selfies, these works of art generate endless queues; however, the first version of this installation dates back to the mid-1960s.

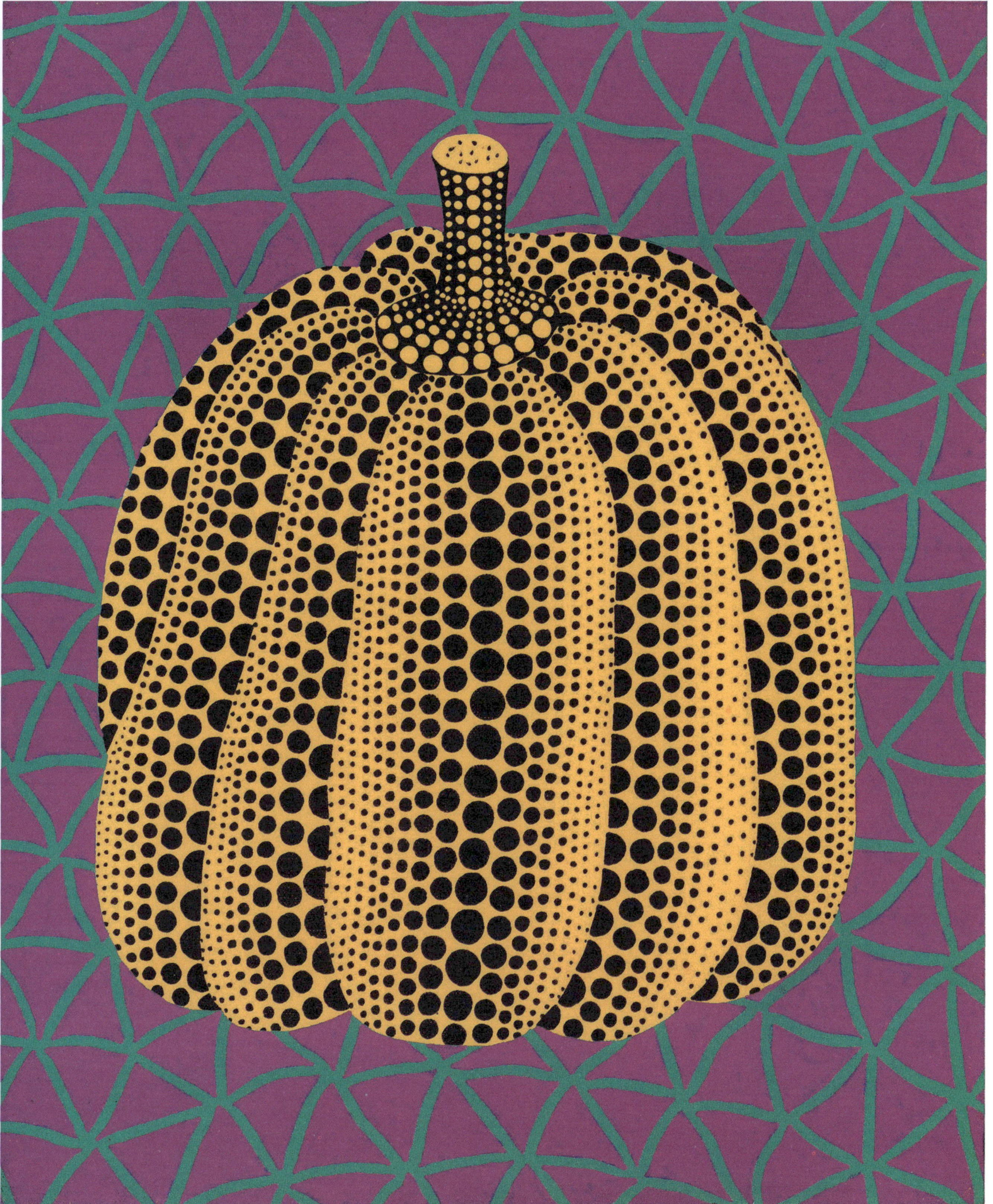

Chéri Samba

In plain text

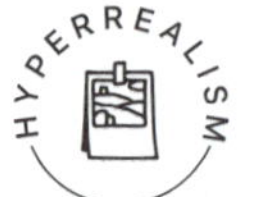

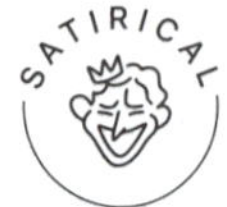

Samba wa Mbimba, known as Chéri Samba, is one of the great names in African contemporary art. He defines his painting as popular, in the truest sense of the word – accessible, and produced for the people.

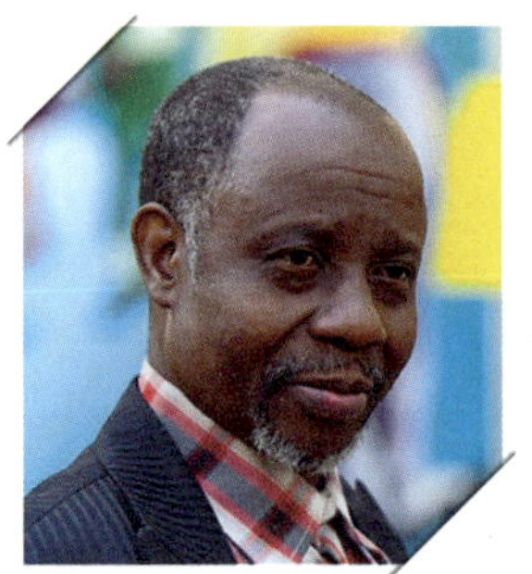

Playing with pencils

Born in Kinto M'Vuila in the Democratic Republic of Congo, in a rural environment where toys were in short supply, Samba spent his childhood drawing. At the age of 16, he ran away from his father, who wanted him to become a blacksmith, and fled to Kinshasa.

24 hours a day

In the capital, he worked for two advertising agencies, and observed the works of painters Bodo and Mass, which he practised reproducing at night. He went on to become renowned as a cartoonist, gradually becoming a national star. Today, Samba is famous worldwide.

Accessible art

He acquired his style by adding messages to his works, inspired by comics and advertising. He then took the name Chéri Samba. His approach of painting is immediate, and he himself describes it as "popular".

CHÉRI SAMBA SAID

"It was I who gave it the name of *popular painting*. Because it comes from the people, concerns the people and is addressed to the people."

Yayoi Kusama
Page 334

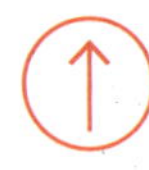

1956
Born in Kinto M'Vuila

1991
Nirvana released the album *Nevermind*

2011
Painted *The Real Map of the World*

2013
France legalised marriage for all

Banksy
Page 338

THE REAL MAP OF THE WORLD ↗

2011
Acrylic and glitter on canvas
200 × 300 cm
Fondation Cartier pour l'Art Contemporain, Paris

WHAT ARE WE LOOKING AT?

Chéri Samba seeks to raise awareness by showing how the supposedly objective representation of the world is, in reality, skewed by the Western prism.

The world turned upside down

Based on a text by Lilian Thuram, Samba questions the universal reference points of high and low, North and South, which automatically place Western populations above others. By turning the map of the world upside down, he demonstrates how populations of the South can claim a dominant position.

A matter of perspective

The painter also questioned Mercator's map projection, the universally accepted planisphere. While this map is reliable for distances, it distorts the surface of continents. Here, Samba uses the Peters projection, which distorts distances, but presents proportionate surfaces, illustrating the importance of the African continent.

Rancorous?

Here, Samba represents himself dominating the world. Both serious and amused, he appears to challenge viewers, inviting them to question themselves, should they dare to do so. He depicts himself in a strikingly realistic self-portrait, in response to art critic Bogumil Jewsiewicki who, in the book *Chéri Samba: the Hybridity of Art*, published in 1995, accused the artist being unable to represent himself. After a first painting named *Chéri Samba Corrige l'Historien Bogumil Jewsiewicki*, in which Samba appears twice, he continued the exercise in this work.

THE MEANING OF WORDS

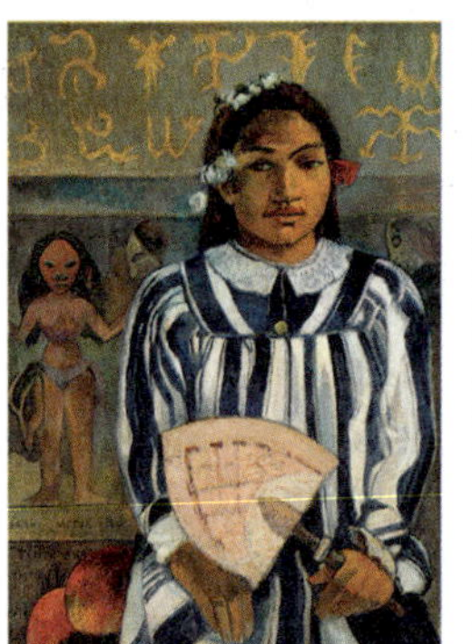

At the beginning of the 20th century, the European avant-garde was inspired by non-Western art, and this influence came to be known as "primitivism". The term was popularised in 1984, during a major exhibition devoted to it at MoMA. The word is still in use today, but is often questioned; indeed, it implies that these civilisations' arts are considered primitive, and is associated with a colonialist view of the world.

Paul Gauguin
Merahi metua no Tehamana (Tehamana Has Many Parents, or The Ancestors of Tehamana) 1893.
Art Institute of Chicago.

LEADING FIGURES OF CONTEMPORARY CONGOLESE PAINTING

- Bodo (1953–2015)
- Chéri Chérin (born in 1955)
- The Mbuecky twins
- Moké (1950–2001)
- Sim Simaro (born in 1949)
- Maître Syms (born in 1957)
- Vuza-Ntoko (born in 1954)

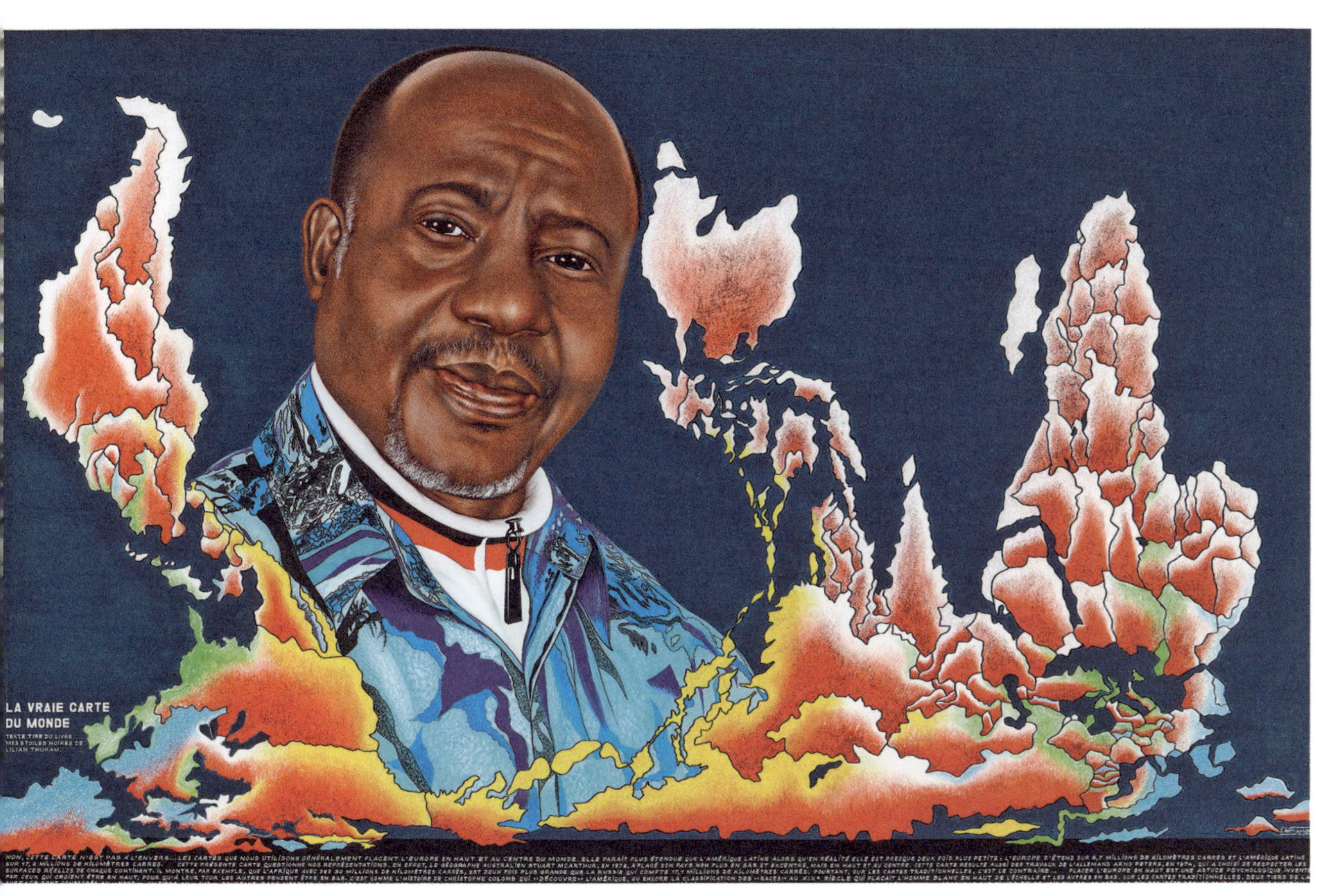
LA VRAIE CARTE DU MONDE
TEXTE TIRÉ DU LIVRE MES ÉTOILES NOIRES DE LILIAN THURAM.

Banksy

Spray-on fame

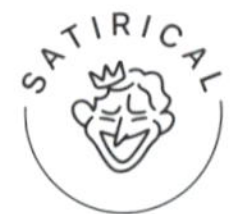

Banksy is an anonymous artist, whose identity is a regular topic of discussion, and whose stencilled works are instantly recognisable. The artist has made irony their trademark.

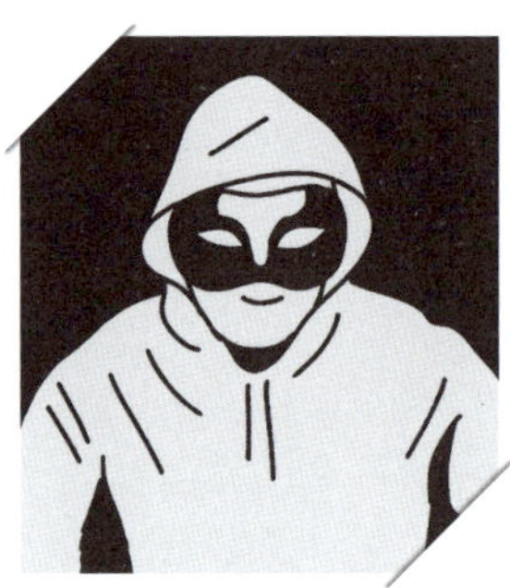

Crikey, it's the rozzers!

Originally from Bristol, Banksy made a name for himself in the 1990s, with works produced in the UK and North America. At first, he worked with spray paint, freehand, then switched to stencils, a faster technique that enabled him to escape the police.

Sold in spite of himself

The artist achieved international renown with a highly acclaimed exhibition and show in Los Angeles in 2006, followed by his first appearance at an auction the following year. He himself would be stunned to see his work institutionalised by the art market.

Masked vigilante

Banksy is renowned for his corrosive irony, pinpointing the shortcomings of modern society and pointing the finger at social injustice, sometimes using his favourite animal: the rat. He is also known for his hoaxes, which bring his art closer to performance art.

MYSTERY MAN

Who is he? Banksy's film *Exit Through the Gift Shop* offers several hypotheses: Robin Gunningham, a Bristol graffiti artist, or Robert Del Naja, singer for Massive Attack ...but the movie may also simply be another way of sowing doubt.

Chéri Samba
Page 336

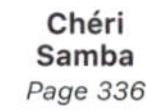
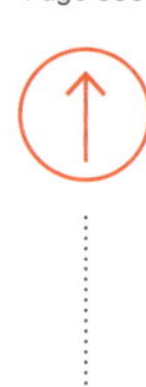

1990s
The beginnings of Banksy, whose date of birth is unknown

1998
France won its first World Cup

2018
Painted *Liberté, Égalité, Cable TV*

2020
The world went into lockdown

LIBERTÉ, ÉGALITÉ, CABLE TV

2018
Aerosol stencil paint

WHAT ARE WE LOOKING AT?

Around 20 June 2018, World Refugee Day, works by Banksy were discovered in the streets of Paris. Among them, a parody of a painting by Jacques-Louis David provided a bitter take on current events.

An affirmed position

On the Avenue de Flandre, the artist produced a rereading of the famous painting by Jacques-Louis David (p. 170), representing Napoleon at the Great St. Bernard.
The correlation between the scene and the date of 20 June 2018, suggests that the artist was outraged at the surveillance carried out at the Italian border.

Lack of vision

Unlike the original, the rider is blinded by their cape, which is turned inside out by the wind. The work may denounce the lack of discernment of a leader who, perched on a rearing horse, is heading for disaster. It may also refer to the French political debates, at the time, about the hijab.

Bread and circuses

The evocation of Napoleon, who came to power through a coup and exploited art for the purpose of propaganda, is also a symbol of abusive power; indeed, on social networks, the artist captioned this work *"Liberté, Égalité, Cable TV"*. The blindness is no longer that of the powers that be, but that of the people, whose minds are dulled by mass consumerism and entertainment.

Takes one to known one

Since Banksy had already subverted *The Raft of the Medusa* by Géricault (p. 184) to alert the public to the conditions of the refugees in Calais, he ironically seems to be turning the history and cultural heritage of France against itself.

THREE MAJOR TRENDS IN URBAN ART

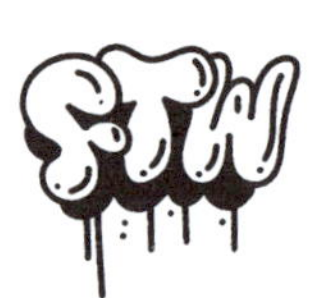

Graffiti
Graffiti is the free and often competitive practice of stylised writing. Born from a protest movement, it rejects society, institutions and the art market.

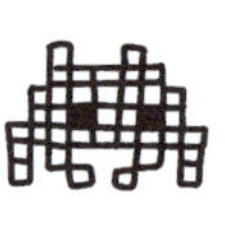

Street art
A broad term that encompasses artists who use the street as a means of expression, with the possible aim of gaining notoriety and accessing art galleries.

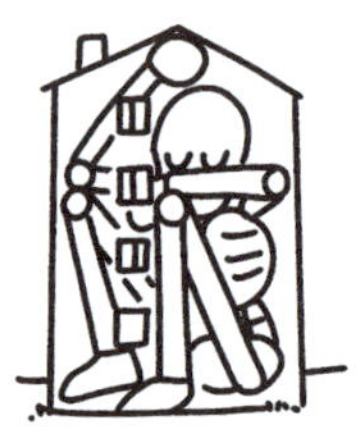

Muralism
Institutionalised art, in which artists produce officially commissioned works.

OTHER WELL-KNOWN URBAN ARTISTS

- JR (born in 1983)
- Blek le Rat (born in 1951)
- Shepard Fairey (born in 1970)
- Lady Pink (born in 1964)
- Jef Aerosol (born in 1957)
- Miss.Tic (1956–2022)
- Invader (born in 1969)
- Faith47 (born in 1979)
- Ernest Pignon-Ernest (born in 1942)

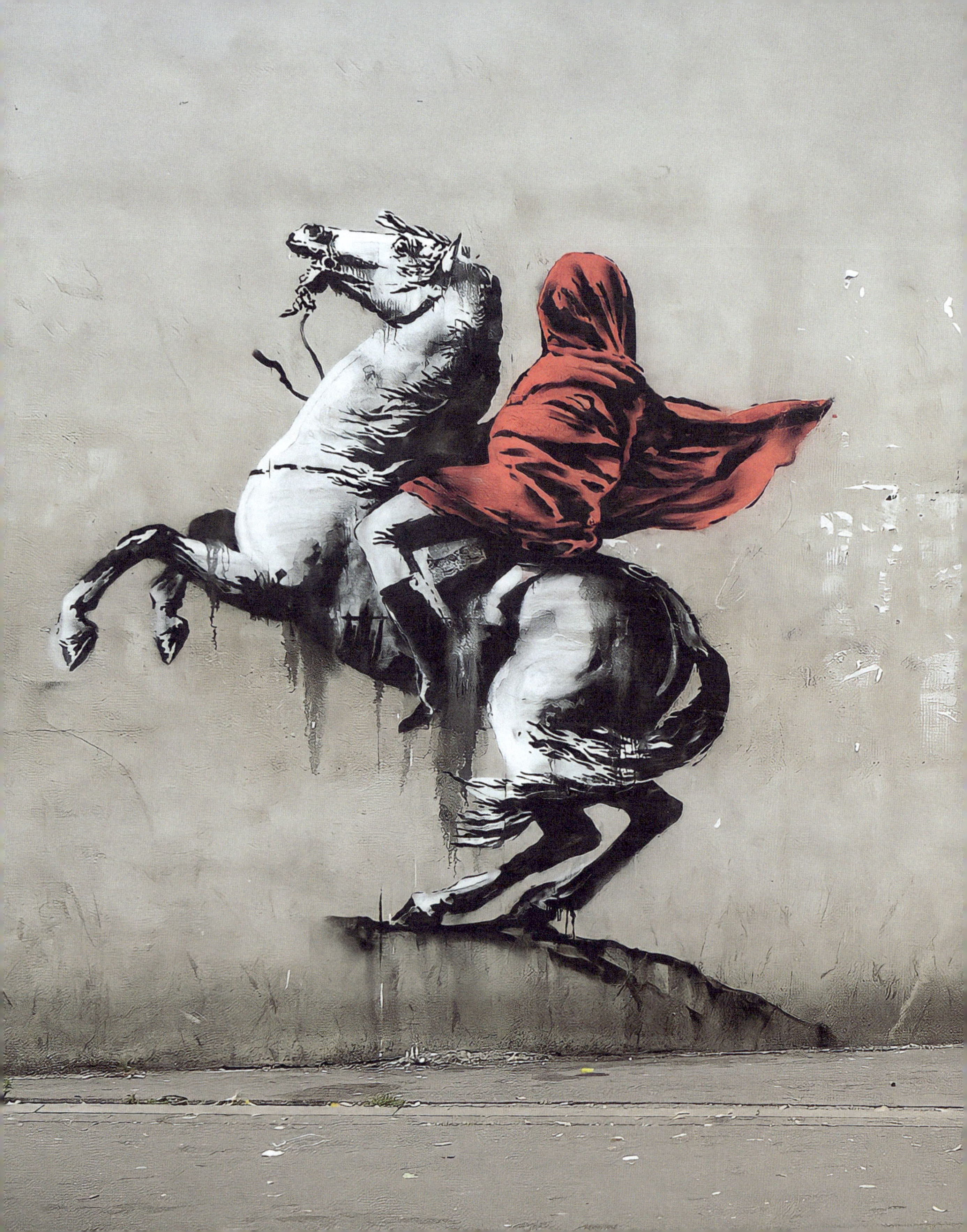

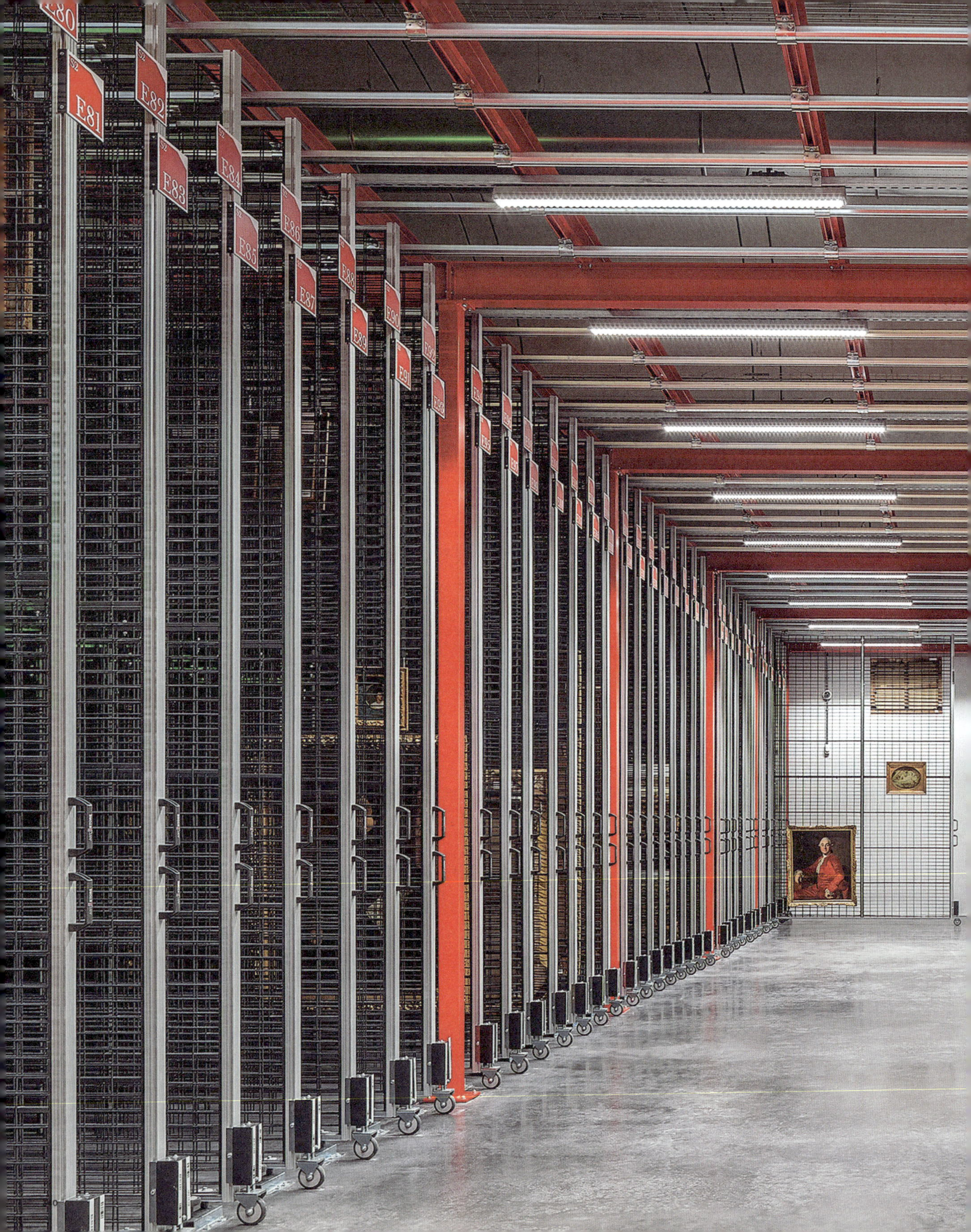
E81
E82
E83
E84
E85
E86
E87
E89
E91

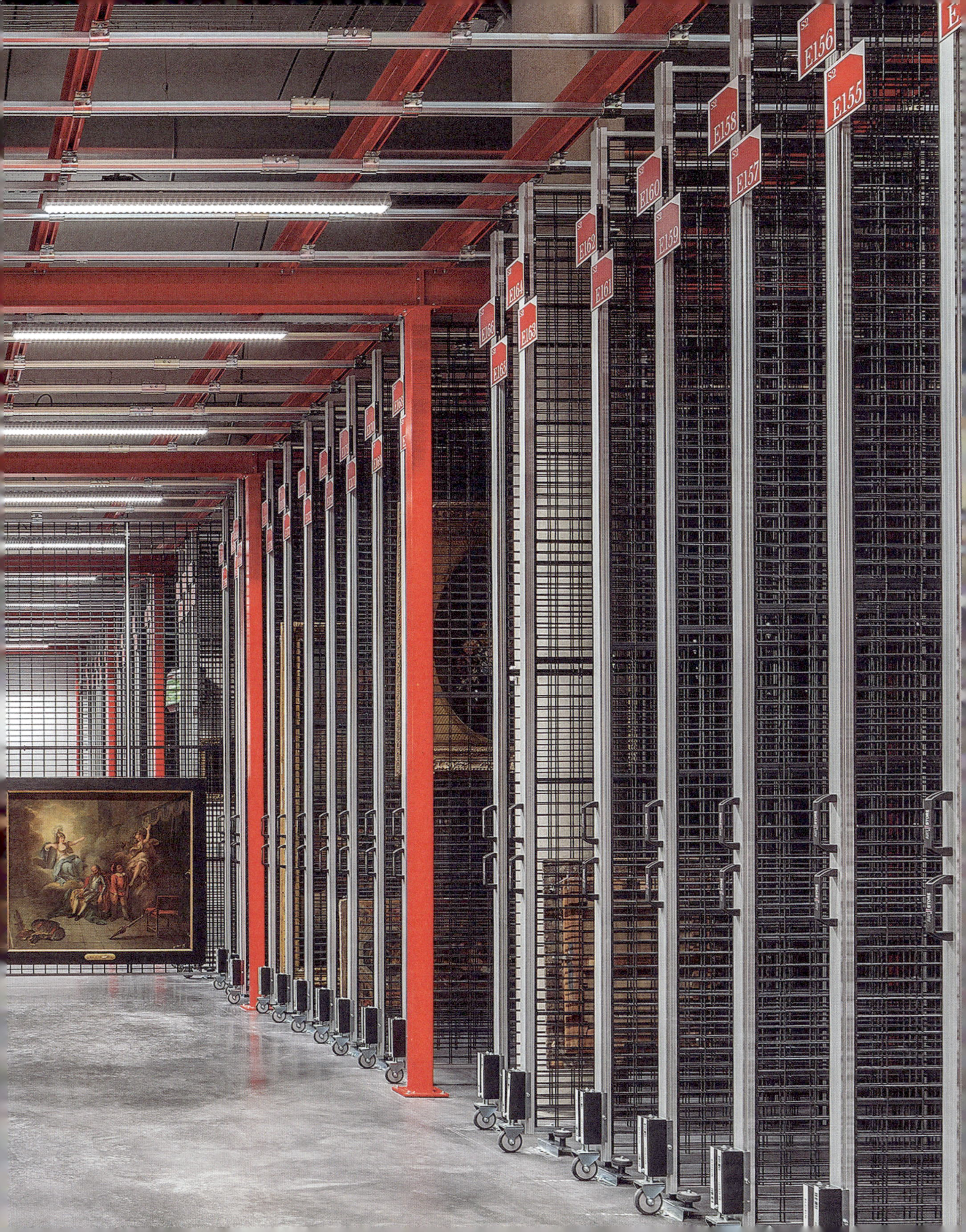
E156
E155
E158
E157
E160
E159
E162
E161
E164
E163
E166
E165

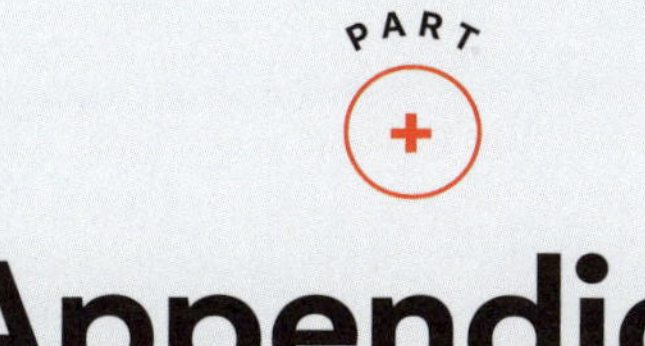

Appendices

Table of works

- p. 73: Lavinia Fontana
Portrait of Bianca degli Utili Maselli
1613, Oil on canvas
99 × 133.5 cm
Private collection
- p. 74l: Mir Sayyid Ali
Emissaries bring news from the provinces of Khaybar and Chin to Anoshirvan, page from the album Hamzanama
16th century
Textile, paper, 70 × 55 cm
MAK - Museum of Applied Arts, Vienna
- p. 74r: Abd al-Samad
Hunters in a Forest, folio from the album Golšan
Mid-16th century-early 17th century
Drawing, ink
42.23 × 26.67 cm
LACMA, Los Angeles
- p. 75: Possibly attributed to Miskin, Mughal school
Zal pleads with the Simurgh to save his son Rustam, folio 30
Circa 1595–1605
Gouache and gold on paper
40.3 × 27.3 cm
Bibliothèque Nationale de France, Paris
- p. 78: Ottavio Leoni
Chalk portrait of Caravaggio
Circa 1621, chalk on paper
Marucelliana Library, Florence
- p. 79: Caravaggio
The Entombment
Circa 1600–1604, oil on canvas
300 × 203 cm
Vatican Museums, Rome
- p. 80l: Andrea Mantegna
Saint Sebastian
Circa 1480, tempera on canvas
255 × 140 cm
Louvre Museum, Paris
- p. 80 centre: El Greco
Saint Sebastian
Circa 1577, oil on canvas
191 × 152 cm
Catedral de San Antolín, Palencia
- p. 80r: Peter Paul Rubens
Saint Sebastian
1614, oil on canvas
200 × 120 cm
Gemäldegalerie der Staatlichen Museen zu Berlin
- p. 81: Luca Giordano
The Fall of the Rebel Angels
1660–1665, oil on canvas
420 × 280 cm
Kunsthistorisches Museum, Vienna
- p. 82: Annibale Carracci
Self-Portrait
1590–1600, oil on canvas
45.4 × 37.9 cm
Uffizi Gallery, Florence
- p. 83: Annibale Carracci
The Choice of Hercules
1595–1596, oil on canvas, 167 × 223 cm
Museo Nazionale di Capodimonte, Naples
- p. 84: Annibale Carracci
The Bean Eater
1584–1585, oil on canvas
57 × 68 cm
Palazzo Colonna, Rome
- p. 85: Paul Cézanne
Man with a Pipe
1890–1892, oil on canvas
82.5 × 73.5 cm
State Hermitage Museum, Saint Petersburg
- p. 86: Guido Reni
Self-Portrait
1602–1603, oil on canvas
Barberini Palace, Rome
- p. 87: Guido Reni
Massacre of the Innocents
Circa 1611, oil on canvas, 268 × 170 cm
National Art Gallery, Bologna
- p. 88t: Artemisia Gentileschi
Self-Portrait as the Allegory of Painting
1638–1639, oil on canvas
98.6 × 75.2 cm
Windsor Castle, London
- p. 88bl: Artemisia Gentileschi
Cleopatra
1630, oil on canvas
97 × 71 cm
Private collection
- p. 88b centre: Artemisia Gentileschi
Lucretia
1630–1635, oil on canvas, 96.5 × 75 cm
Private collection
- p. 88br: Artemisia Gentileschi
Susanna and the Elders
Circa 1610, oil on canvas, 170 × 119 cm
Schloss Weißenstein, Pommersfelden
- p. 89: Artemisia Gentileschi
Penitent Magdalene
1625–1626, oil on canvas
122 × 97 cm
Seville Cathedral
- p. 90: *Caravaggio*
Judith Beheading Holofernes
Circa 1598, Oil on canvas, 145 × 195 cm
National Gallery of Ancient Art, Rome
- p. 91: Artemisia Gentileschi
Judith Slaying Holofernes
Circa 1614–1620, oil on canvas, 199 × 162.5 cm
Uffizi Gallery, Florence
- p. 95: Georges de La Tour
The Card Sharp with the Ace of Diamonds
Circa 1636–1640, oil on canvas
106 × 146 cm
Louvre Museum, Paris
- p. 98: Studio of Peter Paul Rubens
Peter Paul Rubens
Circa 1620, oil on canvas, 41.3 × 33.7 cm
National Gallery of Art, London
- p. 99: Peter Paul Rubens
The Descent from the Cross
1612–1614, oil painting
420 × 310 cm
Cathedral of Our Lady, Antwerp
- p. 102: Jan Brueghel the Elder and Peter Paul Rubens
The Garden of Eden
1615, oil on wood
174.3 × 14.7 cm
Mauristhuis, The Hague
- p. 103: Henri Rousseau
The Dream
1910, oil on canvas
204.5 × 298.5 cm
New York, MoMA
- p. 104: Judith Leyster
Self-Portrait
Circa 1630, oil on canvas
74.6 × 65.1 cm
National Gallery of Art, Washington
- p. 104: Judith Leyster
The Last Drop (or the Gay Cavalier)
Circa 1629, oil on canvas,
89.1 × 73.5 cm
Philadelphia Museum of Art
- p. 106: Johannes Vermeer
The Procuress (detail)
1656, oil on canvas
143 × 130 cm
Staatliche Kunstsammlungen, Dresden
- p. 107, 240l: Johannes Vermeer
The Milkmaid
Circa 1660, oil on canvas, 45.5 × 41 cm
Rijksmuseum, Amsterdam
- p. 108: Godfried Schalcken
Portrait of Rachel Ruysch
Before 1706, oil on canvas
71.8 × 28.2 cm
The Wilson, Cheltenham
- p. 109: Rachel Ruysch
Still-Life with Fruit, Flowers, and Insects
1711, oil on canvas, 87 × 69.5 cm
Private collection
- p. 110l: Mathias Huss
Death Taking the Printers and a Bookseller
Coloured engraving from La Grant Danse Macabre
1499
Private collection
- p. 110r: Philippe de Champaigne
Vanitas
17th century, oil on canvas
28.4 × 37.4 cm
Museum of Tessé, Le Mans
- p. 112: Diego Velázquez
Self-Portrait
Circa 1650, oil on canvas
45 × 38 cm
Museum of Fine Arts, Valencia
- p. 113: Diego Velázquez
Las Meninas
1656, Oil on canvas, 320.5 × 281.5 cm
Prado Museum, Madrid
- p. 114t: Antony Van Dyck
Self-Portrait
1620–1627, oil on canvas
81.5 × 69.5 cm
Alte Pinacothek, Munich
- p. 114t: Anthony Van Dyck
Charles I in Three Positions
1635–1636, oil on canvas
84.4 × 99.4 cm
Windsor Castle, England
- p. 115: Anthony Van Dyck
Charles Iat the Hunt
1636, oil on canvas
266 × 207 cm
Louvre Museum, Paris
- p. 118: Rembrandt Van Rijn
Self-Portrait with Two Circles
1665–1669, oil on canvas
114.3 × 94 cm
Kenwood House, London
- p. 119: Rembrandt Van Rijn
The Night Watch or the Shooting Company of Frans Banning Cocq and Willem van Ruytenburch
1642, oil on canvas
379.5 × 453.5 cm
Rijksmuseum, Amsterdam
- p. 120: Rembrandt Van Rijn
Slaughtered Ox
1655, oil on wood
94 × 69 cm
Louvre Museum, Paris
- p. 121: Diego Velázquez
Le Christ crucifié
Circa 1632, oil on canvas, 248 × 169 cm
Prado Museum, Madrid
- p. 122: Simon Vouet
Self-Portrait
1626–1627, oil on canvas
45 × 36.5 cm
Musée des Beaux-Arts, Lyon
- p. 123: Simon Vouet
Allegory of Faith and Contempt for Wealth
1638–1640, oil on canvas
170 × 124 cm
Louvre Museum, Paris
- p. 124t: Nicolas Poussin
Self-Portrait
1650, oil on canvas
98 × 74 cm
Louvre Museum, Paris
- p. 124b: Giovanni Francesco Barbieri, known as Guercino
Et in Arcadia Ego
Circa 1618, oil on canvas
81 × 91 cm
National Gallery of Ancient Art, Rome
- p. 125: Nicolas Poussin
Et in Arcadia Ego
Circa 1638, oil on canvas
85 × 121 cm
Louvre Museum, Paris
- p. 126: Nicolas Poussin
The Empire of Flora
1631, oil on canvas, 132 × 181.4 cm
Gemäldegalerie, Dresden
- p. 127: Cy Twombly
Empire of Flora
1961, mixed media
101.2 × 148 cm
Cy Twombly Foundation
- p. 128–129, 131: Charles Le Brun
Entry of Alexander into Babylon
Circa 1664–1665, oil on canvas
450 × 707 cm Louvre Museum, Paris
- p. 130: Nicolas de Largillierre
Portrait of Charles Le Brun
1683–1684, oil on canvas
80 × 63 cm
Uffizi Gallery, Florence
- p. 133l: Jacques-Louis David
Andromache Mourning Hector
1783, oil on canvas
275 × 247 cm
Louvre Museum, Paris
- p. 133 centre: Jean Siméon Chardin
The Buffet
1728, oil on canvas
194 × 129 cm
Louvre Museum, Paris
- p. 133r: Jean-Marc Nattier
Perseus, under the Protection of Minerva, Turns Phineus to Stone by Brandishing the Head of Medusa
1718, oil on canvas
113.5 × 146 cm
Musée des Beaux-Arts, Tours
- p. 134t: Gu Kaizhi
Nymph of the Luo River
345–406, ink and colour on silk
27.1 × 572.8 cm
The Palace Museum, Beijing

- p. 134 centre: Han Huang
  Five Bulls, 723–787
  Ink on paper, 20.8 × 139.8 cm, The Palace Museum, Beijing
- p. 134b: Zhou Fang
  Court Ladies Adorning Their Hair with Flowers
  8th-9th century, colour on silk
  45.5 × 175.5 cm
  Provincial Museum, Liaoning
- p. 135: Shitao
  Jingting Mountains in Autumn
  1671, ink on paper
  86 × 41.7 cm
  Musée Guimet, Paris
- p. 138t: Rosalba Carriera
  Portrait of Antoine Watteau
  1721, pastel on paper
  55 × 43 cm
  The Luigi Bailo Museum, Treviso
- p. 138b: ***The Map of Tendre***
  1856, Bibliothèque Nationale de France, Paris
- p. 139: Antoine Watteau
  Pilgrimage to Cythera
  1717, oil on canvas
  129 × 194 cm
  Louvre Museum, Paris
- p. 140tl: Giorgione
  The Tempest
  1506–1508, oil on canvas
  82 × 73 cm
  Galleria dell'Accademia, Venice
- p. 140t centre: El Greco
  View of Toledo
  1596–1600, oil on canvas
  121 × 106 cm
  Metropolitan Museum of Art, New York
- p. 140b centre: Claude Gellée
  The Embarkation of the Queen of Sheba
  1648, oil on canvas
  149.1 × 193.7 cm
  National Gallery, London
- p. 140bl: Albrecht Altdorfer
  The Battle of Alexander at Issus
  1529, oil on wood panel
  158.4 × 120.3 cm
  Alte Pinakothek, Munich
- p. 140tr: Canaletto
  The Entrance to the Grand Canal, Venice
  Circa 1730, oil on canvas
  49.6 × 73.6 cm
  The Museum of Fine Arts, Houston
- p. 141bl: Albert Bierstadt
  Yosemite Valley
  1868, oil on canvas
  91.4 × 137.1 cm
  The Oakland Museum of California, California
- p. 140br: Hubert Robert
  Fountain of Minerva, Rome
  1772, oil on canvas
  50 × 60 cm
  Musée des Beaux-Arts, Angers
- p. 141t centre: Claude Monet
  Impression, Sunrise
  1872, oil on canvas
  48 × 63 cm
  Musée Marmottan Monet, Paris
- p. 141tr: André Derain
  L'Estaque
  1906, oil on canvas
  Musée des Beaux-Arts, Chaux-de-Fonds
- p. 141tl: Caspar David Friedrich
  The Monk by the Sea
  1808–1810, oil on canvas
  110 × 171.5 cm
  Alte Nationalgalerie, Berlin
- p. 141b centre: Paul Signac
  Entrance to the Grand Canal, Venice
  1905, oil on canvas
  73.5 × 92.1 cm
  Museum of Art, Toledo (Ohio)
- p. 141br: Zao Wou-ki
  The Wind Pushes the Sea
  2004, oil on canvas
  194.5 × 390 cm
  Private collection
- p. 144: Jean Siméon Chardin
  Self-Portrait
  1771, pastel on paper
  46 × 38 cm
  Louvre Museum, Paris
- p. 145: Jean Siméon Chardin
  Basket with Wild Strawberries
  1761, oil on canvas
  38 × 46 cm
  Under acquisition by the Louvre Museum
- p. 146: Joseph Ducreux
  Self-portrait in the Guise of a Mockingbird
  1783, oil on canvas
  55.4 × 46.3 cm
  Musée National des Châteaux de Versailles et de Trianon
- p. 147: Jean Siméon Chardin
  The Ray
  1728, oil on canvas
  114 × 146 cm
  Louvre Museum, Paris
- p. 148: William Hogarth
  Self-Portrait
  Circa 1735, oil on canvas
  54.6 × 50.8 cm
  Yale Center for British Art, New Haven
- p. 149: William Hogarth
  Marriage à-la-Mode: The Tête à Tête
  1743–1745, oil on canvas
  69.9 × 90.8 cm
  National Gallery, London
- p. 150: Giambattista Tiepolo
  Fresco in the staircase of the Würzburg Residence (detail)
  1750–1753, fresco
  Würzburg Residence
- p. 151: Giambattista Tiepolo
  The Banquet of Cleopatra
  1743–1744, oil on canvas
  250.3 × 357 cm
  National Gallery of Victoria, Melbourne
- p. 154: Gustaf Lundberg
  Portrait of François Boucher
  1741, pastel on blue paper
  65 × 50 cm
  Louvre Museum, Paris
- p. 155: François Boucher
  Venus at Vulcan's Forge
  1769, oil on canvas
  273.5 × 204.7 cm
  Kimbell Art Museum, Fort Worth
- p. 158: Jean Honoré Fragonard
  Self-portrait
  1800–1806, oil on canvas
  Louvre Museum, Paris – On deposit at the Villa-Musée Fragonard, Grasse
- p. 159: Jean Honoré Fragonard
  The Happy Accidents of the Swing
  Circa 1767–1768, oil on canvas
  81.8 × 64.8 cm
  Wallace Collection, London
- p. 160: Jean Honoré Fragonard and Marguerite Gérard
  Le Bouquet
  1783–1784, oil on canvas
  Dimensions unknown
  Private collection
- p. 161: Gerard Ter Borch
  The Messenger ("The Unwelcome News")
  1650–1660, oil on canvas
  70 × 54 cm
  State Hermitage Museum, Saint Petersburg
- p. 162l: Nakkach Osman
  The Carrying-in of a Model of Süleymaniye Mosque
  (detail from Surname-i Hümayun)
  1582–1588
  Topkapı Palace, Istanbul
- p. 162 centre: Ahmed Karahisari,
  Calligraphy Exercise
  16th century, ink and paper
  35 × 26.3 cm
  Sakıp Sabancı Museum, Istanbul
- p. 162r: Kara Memi
  ***Divan-i Muhibbi**, 1566*
  Istanbul University Library
- p. 163: ***"Saz"-Style Drawing of a Dragon Amid Foliage***
  1540–1550. Ink, watercolour and gold on paper
  27.2 × 40.6 cm
  Metropolitan Museum of Art, New York
- p. 164: Adélaïde Labille-Guiard
  Self-Portrait
  Circa 1774, watercolour and gouache on ivory
  10.3 × 8.4 cm
  Bomann-Museum, Celle
- p. 165: Adélaïde Labille-Guiard
  Self-Portrait with Two Pupils
  Circa 1785, oil on canvas
  210.8 × 151.1 cm
  Metropolitan Museum of Art, New York
- p. 168: Élisabeth Vigée Le Brun
  Self-Portrait with a Straw Hat
  After 1782, oil on canvas
  97.3 × 70.5 cm
  National Gallery, London
- p. 169: Élisabeth Vigée Le Brun
  Marie-Antoinette and Her Children
  1787, oil on canvas
  275 × 215 cm
  Musée National des Châteaux de Versailles et de Trianon
- p. 170: Jacques-Louis David
  Self-Portrait
  1794, oil on canvas
  81 × 64 cm
  Louvre Museum, Paris
- p. 171: Jacques-Louis David
  Oath of the Horatii
  1784, oil on canvas
  330 × 425 cm
  Louvre Museum, Paris
- p. 172t: Marie-Guillemine Benoist
  Self-Portrait Painting David's Belisarius Begging for Alms
  1786, oil on canvas
  95.7 × 78.5 cm
  Staatliche Kunsthalle, Karlsruhe
- p. 172b: Jacques-Louis David
  Portrait of Madame Récamier
  1800, oil on canvas
  174 × 244 cm
  Louvre Museum, Paris
- p. 173: Marie-Guillemine Benoist
  Portrait of Madeleine
  1800, oil on canvas
  81 × 107 cm
  Louvre Museum, Paris
- p. 174t: Vicente López Portaña
  El Pintor Francisco de Goya
  1826, oil on canvas
  94 × 78 cm
  Prado Museum, Madrid
- p. 174b: Francisco de Goya
  The Old Women or Time
  1808–1812, oil on canvas,
  181 × 125 cm
  Palais des Beaux-Arts, Lille
- p. 175: Francisco de Goya
  The Letter, known as "The Young"
  Circa 1813–1820, oil on wood
  181 × 125 cm
  Palais des Beaux-Arts, Lille
- p. 176t: Gerhard von Kügelgen
  Portrait of Caspar David Friedrich
  Circa 1808, oil on canvas
  53.3 × 41.5 cm
  Kunsthalle, Hamburg
- p. 176b: Caspar David Friedrich
  The Abbey in the Oakwood
  1809–1810, oil on canvas
  110 × 171 cm
  Alte Nationalgalerie, Berlin
- p. 177: Caspar David Friedrich
  Wanderer above the Sea of Fog
  Circa 1818, oil on canvas
  94.8 × 74.8 cm
  Kunsthalle, Hamburg
- p. 178: Joseph Mallord William Turner
  Self-Portrait
  Circa 1799, oil on canvas
  74.3 × 58.4 cm
  Tate Britain, London
- p. 179: Joseph Mallord William Turner
  Rain, Steam and Speed
  1844, oil on canvas
  91 × 121.8 cm
  National Gallery, London
- p. 180: Camille Dolard
  Portrait de Jean-Auguste-Dominique Ingres à la Fenêtre
  1856–1858, photograph
  24 × 18 cm
  Musée d'Orsay, Paris
- p. 181: Jean-Auguste-Dominique Ingres
  Louise de Broglie, Countess d'Haussonville
  1845, oil on canvas
  131.8 × 92.1 cm
  The Frick Collection, New York
- p. 182: Jean-Auguste-Dominique Ingres
  La Grande Odalisque
  1814, oil on canvas
  91 × 162 cm
  Louvre Museum, Paris
- p. 183: Suzanne Valadon
  The Blue Room
  1923, oil on canvas
  90 × 116 cm
  Musée des Beaux-Arts, Limoges (on deposit with the Musée National d'Art Moderne, Paris)

- p. 184: Horace Vernet
Jean-Louis-André-Théodore Géricault
1822–1823, oil on canvas
47.3 × 38.4 cm
Metropolitan Museum of Art, New York
- p. 185: Theodore Géricault
The Raft of the Medusa
1818–1819, oil on canvas
491 × 716 cm
Louvre Museum, Paris
- p. 186tl: Peter Paul Rubens
Achilles Discovered by Ulysses Among the Daughters of Lycomedes
1630–1635, oil on canvas
107.5 × 145.5 cm
Prado Museum, Madrid
- p. 186tr, 191: Eugène Delacroix
Liberty Leading the People
1830, oil on wood
260 × 325 cm
Louvre Museum, Paris
- p. 186bl: Titian
Venus with a Mirror
Circa 1555, oil on canvas
124.5 × 105.4 cm
National Gallery of Art, Washington
- p. 186br: Peter Paul Rubens
Venus, Mars and Cupid
Circa 1635, oil on canvas
195.2 × 133 cm
Dulwich Picture Gallery, Dulwich
- p. 187tl: Nicolas Coypel
Apollo Crowned by Minerva
1667–1668, oil on canvas
214 × 235 cm
Louvre Museum, Paris
- p. 187tr: Jonas Åkerström
Venus, Adonis and Cupid
18th century, oil on canvas
173 × 130 cm
Nationalmuseum, Stockholm
- p. 187bl: Raphael
The Three Graces
1503–1505, oil on canvas
17 × 17 cm
Chantilly Castle
- p. 187br: Peter Paul Rubens
The Three Graces
1630–1635, oil on canvas, 220.5 × 182 cm
Prado Museum, Madrid
- p. 190: Félix Nadar
Eugène Delacroix
1858, photograph
- p. 192: Eugène Delacroix
The Death of Sardanapalus
1827, oil on canvas
392 × 496 cm
Louvre Museum, Paris
- p. 193: Peter Paul Rubens
The Tiger Hunt
1615–1617, oil on canvas
248.2 × 318.3 cm
Musée des Beaux-Arts, Rennes
- p. 194–195: Hokusai
Mount Fuji on a Clear Day,
Thunderstorm Beneath the Summit,
Morning after a Snowfall at Koishikawa,
Dawn at Isawa in Kai Province,
The Great Wave off Kanagawa,
In *Thirty-Six Views of Mount Fuji*
Circa 1829–1833
36 prints with a dark blue border and 10 additional plates with a black outline
24.8 × 36.9 cm
Bibliothèque Nationale de France, Paris
- p. 198t: Atelier Nadar
Gustave Courbet
19th century, photograph
8.5 × 5.8 cm
Bibliothèque Nationale de France, Paris
- p. 198b1: Gustave Courbet
Red Apples
1872, oil on canvas
34 × 23 cm
Private collection
- p. 198b2: Gustave Courbet
The Cliffs at Étretat
1870s, oil on canvas
32 × 81.3 cm
Private collection
- p. 198b3: Gustave Courbet
Reclining Nude
1862–1863, oil on canvas
75 × 97 cm
Private collection
- p. 198b4: Gustave Courbet
Poor Woman of the Village
1866, oil on canvas
86.2 × 127.1 cm
Private collection
- p. 199: Gustave Courbet
The Desperate Man
1844–1845, oil on canvas
45 × 54 cm
Private collection
- p. 200: Gustave Courbet
L'Origine du Monde
1866, oil on canvas
46.3 × 55.4 cm
Musée d'Orsay, Paris
- p. 201: Orlan
L'Origine de la Guerre
2011, Cibachrome pasted on aluminium
88 × 105 cm
Artist's collection
- p. 202: Atelier Nadar
Jean-François Millet
1856–1858, photograph
- p. 203: Jean-François Millet
The Angelus
1857–1859, oil on canvas
55.5 × 66 cm
Musée d'Orsay, Paris
- p. 204–205, 207: Rosa Bonheur
Ploughing in the Nivernais
1849, oil on canvas
133 × 260 cm
Musée d'Orsay, Paris
- p. 206: André-Adolphe Eugène Disdéri
Rosa Bonheur
1861–1864, albumen print on cardboard
8.4 × 5.2 cm
Getty Center, Los Angeles
- p. 208tl: Jacob Cornelisz Van Oostzanen
Portrait of an Ox Won in a Parrot Shooting Contest
1564, oil on canvas
126 × 149.5 cm
Amsterdam Museum
- p. 208b centre: Jean-Honoré Fragonard (school of)
The White Bull in the Stable
1661–1665, oil on canvas
72.5 × 91 cm
Louvre Museum, Paris
- p. 208tr: William Merritt Chase
The Family Cow (Calf's Head)
1869, oil on canvas
50.8 × 40.6 cm
Indianapolis Museum of Art
- p. 208bl: Jan Asselijn
Head of a Lowing Ox
1634–1652, oil on canvas
100 × 80.5 cm
Staatliches Museum, Schwerin
- p. 208t centre: Paulus Potter
The Young Bull
1647, oil on canvas
339 × 235.5 cm
Mauritshuis, The Hague
- p. 208br: Jean-François Millet
Calling the Cows Home
Circa 1872, oil on canvas
94.6 × 64.8 cm
Metropolitan Museum of Art, New York
- p. 209tl: Vincent Van Gogh
The Cows
1890, oil on canvas
55 × 65 cm
Palais des Beaux-Arts, Lille
- p. 209t centre: Paul Sérusier
White Cow
Circa 1895, oil on canvas
60 × 73 cm
National Museum, Warsaw
- p. 209tr: Jean Dubuffet, *Cow*
1966, ink marker on paper
25.1 × 16.5 cm
Metropolitan Museum of Art, New York
- p. 209bl: Léon Barillot
La Vache brune
1891, oil on canvas
130.6 × 98.5 cm
Musée des Beaux-Arts, Pau
- p. 209b centre: Franz Marc
Cows, Red, Green, Yellow
1911, oil on canvas
62 × 87.5 cm
Städtische Galerie im Lenbachhaus und Kunstbau, Munich
- p. 209br: Edward Saidi Tingatinga
The Buffalo
Circa 1970, enamel on wood panel
60 × 60 cm
Red Hill Art Gallery, Kenya
- p. 210t: William Bouguereau
Circa 1880, photograph
11.4 × 8.89 cm
LACMA, Los Angeles
- p. 210b1: Amaury-Duval
Marie-Anne Detourbay
1862, oil on canvas
100 × 83 cm
Musée d'Orsay, Paris
- p. 210b2: Jean-Léon Gérôme
Pollice Verso
1872, oil on canvas
100.3 × 148.9 cm
Phoenix Art Museum, Phoenix
- p. 210b3, 219: Alexandre Cabanel
The Birth of Venus
1863, oil on canvas
130 × 225 cm
Musée d'Orsay, Paris
- p. 210b4: Hippolyte Flandrin
Study (Young Male Nude Seated Beside the Sea)
1837, oil on canvas
98 × 124 cm
Louvre Museum, Paris
- p. 211: William Bouguereau
Dante and Virgil
1850, oil on canvas
280.5 × 225.3 cm
Musée d'Orsay, Paris
- *p. 212t: Portrait in profile of Gustave Moreau*
Circa 1880, photograph
Gustave Moreau Museum, Paris
- p. 212b1: Gustave Moreau
Salome at the Prison
1873–1876, oil on canvas
40 × 32 cm
National Museum of Western Art, Tokyo
- p. 212b2: Gustave Moreau
Salome Dancing before Herod
1876, oil on canvas
143.5 × 104.3 cm
Hammer Museum, Los Angeles
- p. 212b3: Gustave Moreau
The Apparition
1876, watercolour
106 × 72 cm
Musée d'Orsay, Paris
- p. 212b4: Gustave Moreau
Salome in the Garden
1878, watercolour
72 × 43 cm
Private collection
- p. 213: Gustave Moreau
The Apparition
Circa 1876, oil on canvas
142 × 103 cm
Musée Gustave Moreau, Paris
- p. 214t: Frédéric Hollyer
Edward Burne-Jones
Circa 1882, photograph
- p. 214bl: Dante Gabriel Rossetti
Lady Lilith
1866, oil on canvas
96.5 × 85.1 cm
Delaware Art Museum
- p. 214b centre: John Everett Millais
Mariana
1851, oil on wood
59.7 x 49.5 cm
Tate Britain, London
- p. 214br: Frederic Leighton
Flaming June
Circa 1895, oil on canvas
120.6 × 120.6 cm
Museo de Arte de Ponce, Puerto Rico
- p. 215: Edward Burne-Jones
The Wheel of Fortune
Between 1875 and 1883, oil on canvas
200 × 100 cm
Musée d'Orsay, Paris
- p. 216t: Atelier Nadar
Édouard Manet
Before 1870, photograph
39.6 × 29.8 cm
Bibliothèque Nationale de France, Paris
- p. 216b: Claude Monet
Luncheon on the Grass
1865, oil on canvas
248 × 217 cm
Musée d'Orsay, Paris
- p. 217: Édouard Manet
The Luncheon on the Grass
1863, oil on canvas
207 × 265 cm (before two size reductions: 214 × 270 cm)
Musée d'Orsay, Paris
- p. 218: Édouard Manet
Olympia
1863, oil on canvas, 130.5 × 191 cm
Musée d'Orsay, Paris
- p. 220l: *Claude-Marie Dubufe*
Édouard and Juliette Dubufe
1846, oil on canvas
131 × 98 cm
Château de Compiègne

- *p. 220r: Gustave Courbet*
  Self-Portrait (The Man with a Pipe)
  1846, oil on canvas
  45 × 37 cm
  Musée Fabre, Montpellier
- p. 222–223: **Henri Gervex**
  A Session of the Painting Jury
  Before 1885, oil on canvas
  300 × 419 cm
  Musée d'Orsay, Paris
- p. 224: **Atelier Nadar**
  Claude Monet
  1899, photograph
- p. 225: **Claude Monet**
  The Stroll
  1875, oil on canvas
  100 × 81 cm
  National Gallery of Art, Washington DC
- p. 226: **Claude Monet**
  Blue Water Lilies
  1916–1919, oil on canvas
  204 × 200 cm
  Musée d'Orsay, Paris
- p. 227: **Joan Mitchell**
  La Grande Vallée IX
  1983–1984, oil on canvas
  260 × 260 cm
  Collection of FRAC Normandie, Rouen
- p. 230: **Edgar Degas**
  Circa 1855–1860, photograph
- p. 231: **Edgar Degas**
  In a Café, also known as L'Absinthe
  Between 1875 and 1876, oil on canvas
  92 × 68.5 cm
  Musée d'Orsay, Paris
- p. 232: **Auguste Renoir**
  Circa 1910, photograph
- p. 233: **Auguste Renoir**
  Bal du Moulin de la Galette
  1876, oil on canvas
  131.5 × 176.5 cm
  Musée d'Orsay, Paris
- p. 234: **Berthe Morisot**
  19th century, photograph
- p. 235: **Berthe Morisot**
  The Cradle
  1872, oil on canvas
  56 × 46.5
  Musée d'Orsay, Paris
- p. 236: **Martial Caillebotte**
  Gustave Caillebotte
  1878, photograph
- p. 237: **Gustave Caillebotte**
  Paris Street; Rainy Day
  1877, oil on canvas
  212.2 × 276.2 cm
  Art Institute, Chicago
- p. 238t: **Georges Seurat**
  1888, photograph
- p. 238b1: **Camille Pissarro**
  Apple Picking at Éragny-sur-Epte
  1888, oil on canvas
  60.9 × 73.9 cm
  Museum of Art, Dallas
- p. 238b2: **Paul Signac**
  Saint-Tropez, Fontaine des Lices
  1895, oil on canvas
  65 × 81 cm
  Guggenheim Museum, Bilbao
- p. 238b3: **Henri-Edmond Cross**
  Pines on the Coastline
  1896, oil on canvas
  54 × 65.4 cm
  Private collection
- p. 238b4: **Maximilien Luce**
  Notre-Dame de Paris
  1900, oil on canvas, 116 × 81.3 cm
  Private collection
- p. 238b5: **Lucie Cousturier**
  Self-Portrait
  1905–1910, oil on canvas
  34 × 26 cm
  Museum of Art, Indianapolis
- p. 239: **Georges Seurat**
  The Channel at Gravelines, Evening
  1890, oil on canvas
  65.4 × 81.9 cm
  MoMA, New York
- p. 240l: **Johannes Vermeer**
  The Milkmaid
  1660, oil on canvas, 45.5 × 41 cm
  Rijksmuseum, Amsterdam
- p. 240 centre: **Leonardo Da Vinci**
  Saint John the Baptist
  1508–1519, Oil on wood, 69 × 57 cm
  Louvre Museum, Paris
- p. 240r: **Jan Brueghel the Elder**
  Earth or the Earthly Paradise
  1607–1608, oil on copper
  45 × 63.7 cm
  Louvre Museum, Paris
- p. 242: *Paul Cézanne in front of* **The Bathers**
  1904, photograph
- p. 243: **Paul Cézanne**
  Kitchen Table, or Still Life with Basket
  Between 1888 and 1890, oil on canvas
  65 × 81.5 cm
  Musée d'Orsay, Paris
- p. 244tl: **Caravaggio**
  Basket of Fruit
  1594–1602, Oil on canvas
  46 × 64.5 cm
  Pinacoteca Ambrosiana, Milan
- p. 244t centre: **John F. Francis**
  Still Life, Apples and Chestnuts
  1859, oil on panel
  43.82 × 52.07 cm,
  LACMA, Los Angeles
- p. 244tr: **Paul Cézanne**
  Green Apples
  1873, oil on canvas
  26 × 32 cm
  Musée d'Orsay, Paris
- p. 244bl: **Raphaelle Peale**
  Still Life with Cake
  1818, oil on wood, 27.3 × 38.7 cm
  Metropolitan Museum of Art, New York.
- p. 244br: **Gustave Courbet**
  Still Life with Apples and a Pear
  1871, oil on canvas, 24.1 × 31.3 cm
  Philadelphia Museum of Art, Philadelphia
- p. 245tl: **Vincent Van Gogh**
  Still Life with Apples
  1887, oil on canvas
  45.7 × 60.4 cm
  Van Gogh Museum, Amsterdam
- p. 245t centre: **Zinaida Serebriakova**
  Apples on the Branches
  1910s, oil on canvas
  55 × 78.5 cm
  Private collection
- p. 245tr: **Juan Gris**
  Apples
  1924, oil on canvas, 24 × 35 cm
  Private collection
- p. 245bl: **Paul Gauguin**
  Still Life with Apples, a Pear, and a Ceramic Portrait Jug
  1889, oil on canvas
  28.6 × 36.2 cm
  Fogg Art Museum, Cambridge (USA)
- p. 245br: **Félix Vallotton**
  Still Life with Apples
  1910, oil on canvas
  38 × 46 cm
  MuMa, Le Havre
- p. 246: ***One of the presumed portraits of Vincent Van Gogh.***
- p. 247: **Vincent Van Gogh**
  The Starry Night
  1889, oil on canvas, 73.7 × 92.1 cm
  MoMA, New York
- p. 248t: **Paul Gauguin**
  Late 19th century, photograph
- p. 248b: **Paul Gauguin**
  The Vision after the Sermon
  1888, oil on canvas
  73 × 92 cm
  National Gallery of Scotland, Edinburgh
- p. 249: **Paul Gauguin**
  Tahitian Women on the Beach
  1891, oil on canvas
  69 × 91.5 cm
  Musée d'Orsay, Paris
- p. 250: **A. Nathanson**
  Félix Vallotton
  1897, photograph
- p. 251: **Félix Vallotton**
  Box Seats at the Theatre, the Gentleman and the Lady
  1909, oil on canvas
  46 × 38 cm
  Private collection
- p. 252t: **Edvard Munch**
  1892, photograph
- p. 252b1: **Edvard Munch**
  The Scream
  1893, tempera on cardboard
  91 × 373.5 cm
  National Museum of Art, Architecture and Design, Oslo
- p. 252b2: **Edvard Munch**
  The Scream
  1893, pastel on cardboard
  79 × 55.9 cm
  Munch Museet, Oslo
- p. 252b3: **Edvard Munch**
  The Scream
  1895, pastel on cardboard
  Private collection
- p. 252b4:**Edvard Munch**
  The Scream
  1895, lithography
  44.8 × 40.4 cm
  Munch Museet, Oslo
- p. 252b5, 253: **Edvard Munch**
  The Scream
  1910, tempera and oil on cardboard
  83.5 × 66 cm
  Munch Museet, Oslo
- p. 254: **Gustav Klimt with a cat**
  1911, photograph
- p. 255: **Gustav Klimt**
  The Kiss
  1908, oil on canvas and gold leaf on enamel-covered brass background
  180 × 180 cm
  Belvedere Palace, Vienna
- p. 262: **Henri Matisse**
  Undated photograph
- p. 263: **Henri Matisse**
  The Red Studio
  1911, oil on canvas
  181 x 219.1 cm
  The Museum of Modern Art, New York
- p. 264: **Pablo Picasso**
  1946, photograph
- p. 265: **Pablo Picasso**
  Les Demoiselles d'Avignon
  1907, oil on canvas
  243.9 × 233.7 cm
  MoMA, New York
- p. 268: **Amedeo Modigliani**
  Circa 1919, photograph
- p. 269: **Amedeo Modigliani**
  Jeanne Hébuterne
  1919, oil on canvas, 91.4 × 73 cm
  Metropolitan Museum of Art, New York
- p. 270: **Pierre Choumoff**
  Marc Chagall
  1920s, photograph
- p. 271: **Mark Chagall**
  I and the Village
  1911, oil on canvas, 192.1 × 151.4 cm
  MoMA, New York
- p. 272: **Georges Braque**
  photograph
- p. 273: **Georges Braque**
  Black Bird and White Bird
  1960, oil on canvas
  134 × 167.5 cm
  Private collection
- p. 274t: **Hilma af Klint**
  photograph
- p. 274b1: **Vassily Kandinsky**
  On White II
  1923, oil on canvas
  105 × 98 cm
  Musée National d'Art Moderne, Centre Pompidou, Paris
- p. 274b2: **Kasimir Malevich**
  Black Square
  1915, oil on canvas
  80 × 80 cm
  The State Tretyakov Gallery, Moscow
- p. 274b3: **Robert Delaunay**
  Rhythms
  Circa 1932, gouache, watercolour, brush and ink on pearlescent Japanese paper
  19 × 22 cm
  Private collection
- p. 274b4: **Piet Mondrian**
  New York City
  1942, oil on canvas
  119.3 × 114.2 cm
  Musée National d'Art Moderne, Centre Pompidou, Paris
- p. 274b5: **František Kupka**
  Disks of Newton
  1912, oil on canvas
  100.3 × 73.7 cm
  Philadelphia Museum of Art
- p. 275: **Hilma af Klint**
  Svanen, nr 17, Grupp IX/SUW, series SUW/UW
  1915, oil on canvas
  150.5 × 151 cm
  Moderna Museet, Stockholm
- p. 276t: **Vassily Kandinksy**
  photograph

- p. 276b: **Vassily Kandinsky**
  Composition 8
  1923, oil on canvas
  140 × 201 cm
  Solomon R. Guggenheim Museum, New York
- p. 277: **Vassily Kandinsky**
  Gelb-Rot-Blau (Yellow-Red-Blue)
  1925, oil on canvas
  128 × 201.5 cm
  Musée National d'Art Moderne, Centre Pompidou, Paris
- p. 278: **Piet Mondrian**
  Circa 1922, photograph
- p. 279: **Piet Mondrian**
  Composition with Red Blue and Yellow
  1930, oil on canvas
  45 × 45 cm
  Kunsthaus, Zürich
- p. 280: **Kasimir Malevich**
  Before 1935, photograph
- p. 281: **Kasimir Malevich**
  Black Cross
  1915, oil on canvas
  80 × 80 cm
  Musée National d'Art Moderne, Centre Pompidou, Paris
- p. 282: **Kasimir Malevich**
  White on White
  1918, oil on canvas
  79.4 × 79.4 cm
  MoMA, New York
- p. 283: **Yves Klein**
  IKB 3, Monochrome bleu
  1960, pure pigment and synthetic resin on canvas mounted on wood
  199 × 153 cm
  Musée National d'Art Moderne, Centre Pompidou, Paris
- p. 288: ***Grant Wood***
  1941, gelatin silver print
  Figge Art Museum, Davenport
- p. 289: **Grant Wood**
  American Gothic
  1930, oil on soft Masonite
  78 × 65.3 cm
  Art Institute, Chicago
- p. 290: **Tamara de Lempicka**
  1941, photograph
- p. 291: **Tamara de Lempicka**
  Young Lady with Gloves (Girl in a Green Dress)
  1927–1930, oil on plywood
  61.5 × 45.5 cm
  Musée National d'Art Moderne, Centre Pompidou, Paris
- p. 292: **René Magritte**
  June 1922, photograph
- p. 293: **René Magritte**
  Not to Be Reproduced
  1938, oil on canvas
  81 × 65.5 cm
  Museum Boijmans Van Beuningen, Rotterdam
- p. 294: **René Magritte**
  The Blank Signature
  1965, oil on canvas
  81.3 × 65.1 cm
  National Gallery of Art, Washington
- p. 295: **Sandro Botticelli**
  The Story of Nastagio Degli Onesti, Part One
  1483, mixed media on panel
  82.3 × 139 cm
  Prado Museum, Madrid
- p. 296: **Philippe Halsman,**
  Salvador Dalí
  1954, photograph
- p. 297: **Salvador Dalí**
  The Persistence of Memory
  1931, oil on canvas
  24.1 × 33 cm
  MoMA, New York
- p. 299: **Gustave Courbet**
  The Painter's Studio: A Real Allegory
  1855, oil on canvas
  361 × 598 cm
  Musée d'Orsay, Paris
- p. 302: **Edward Hopper**
  Date unspecified, photograph
- p. 303: **Edward Hopper**
  Nighthawks
  1942, oil on canvas
  84.1 × 152.4 cm
  Art Institute, Chicago
- p. 304: **Alfred Stieglitz**
  Georgia O'Keeffe
  1921, platinum-palladium print
  23.5 × 18.1 cm
  Metropolitan Museum of Art, New York
- p. 305: **Georgia O'Keeffe**
  Ram's Head, White Hollyhock-Hills
  1935, oil on canvas
  76.2 × 91.4 cm
  Brooklyn Museum, New York
- p. 306: **Guillermo Kahlo**
  Frida Kahlo
  1932, gelatin silver print
- p. 307: **Frida Kahlo**
  Self-Portrait with Thorn Necklace and Hummingbird
  1940, oil on canvas
  61.3 × 47 cm
  University of Texas, Austin
- p. 308: **Mark Rothko**
  Photograph
- p. 309: **Mark Rothko**
  Red, Orange, Orange on Red
  1962, oil on canvas
  233 × 204.5 cm
  Saint Louis Art Museum
- p. 310: ***Jackson Pollock***
  1953, photograph
- p. 311: **Jackson Pollock**
  Watery Paths
  1947, oil on canvas
  114 × 86 cm
  National Gallery of Modern and Contemporary Art, Rome
- p. 312t: **Marion Kalter**
  Joan Mitchell
  1978, photograph
- p. 312b: **Franz Kline**
  Poster for "The 9th Street Art Exhibition of Paintings and Sculpture", *1951*
- p. 313: **Joan Mitchell**
  Two Sunflowers
  1980, oil on canvas
  279.4 × 360.7 cm
  Fondation Louis Vuitton, Paris
- p. 314t: ***Francis Bacon in his studio in London***
  1966, photograph
- p. 314b: **Diego Velázquez**
  Portrait of Innocent X
  1650, oil on canvas
  140 × 120 cm
  Doria Pamphilj Gallery, Rome
- p. 315: **Francis Bacon**
  Study after Velázquez's Portrait of Pope Innocent X
  1953, oil on canvas
  152.1 × 117.8 cm
  Des Moines Art Center
- p. 318: ***Decorative art at Nawarla Gabarnmang***, *Australia, circa 28,000 BC*
- p. 319: **David Malangi**
  Funerary rites of Gurrmirringu
  Collected in 1963 by Karel Kupka bark painting
  73.5 × 48 cm
  Musée du Quai Branly
- p. 320: **Eric Koch**
  Roy Lichtenstein
  1967, photograph
  Tate Britain, London
- p. 321: **Roy Lichtenstein**

  1965, oil and acrylic on canvas
  152 × 152 cm
  Museum Ludwig, Cologne
- p. 322: ***Andy Warhol in London***
  1984, photograph
- p. 323: **Andy Warhol**
  Shot Sage Blue Marilyn
  1964, acrylic and silkscreen on linen canvas
  101.6 × 101.6 cm
  Private collection
- p. 324: **Michel Viard**
  David Hockney
  1973, photograph
- p. 325: **David Hockney**
  A Bigger Splash
  1967, acrylic on canvas
  242.5 × 243.9 cm
  Tate Modern, London
- p. 326: **Félix Vallotton**
  The Ball
  1899, oil on cardboard pasted on wood
  49.2 × 62 cm
  Musée d'Orsay, Paris
- p. 330: **Gerhard Richter**
  1999, photograph by Jacqueline Salmon
- p. 331: **Gerhard Richter**
  Wolken (Clouds)
  1970, oil on canvas
  200 × 300 cm
  Museum Folkwang, Essen
- p. 332: **Jean-Michel Basquiat**
  1984, photograph
- p. 333: **Jean-Michel Basquiat**
  Untitled
  1981, acrylic and oil pastel on canvas, 206 × 176 cm
  Board Collection, Los Angeles
- *p. 334: Yayoi Kusama*
  Date not specified, photograph
- p. 335: **Yayoi Kusama**
  Pumpkin (T. Wa)
  1989, acrylic on canvas
  38 × 45.5 cm
  Private collection
- p. 336t: **Chéri Samba**
  Date not specified, photograph
- p. 336b: **Paul Gauguin**
  Merahi metua no Tehamana (Tehamana Has Many Parents, or The Ancestors of Tehamana)
  1893, oil on rough cloth
  75 × 53 cm
  Art Institute, Chicago
- p. 337: **Chéri Samba**
  The Real Map of the World
  2011, acrylic and glitter on canvas
  200 × 300 cm
  Fondation Cartier pour l'Art Contemporain, Paris
- p. 339: *Banksy*
  Liberté, Égalité, Cable TV
  2018
  Aerosol stencil paint

Table of photos

Table of thematic focuses

Table of face-to-face works

Index by keyword

Index by artist

Selected bibliography

GENERAL WORKS

- BARTER, Judith A., KELLY Sarah E., MAHONEY, Denise *et al.*, *American Modernism at the Art Institute of Chicago: From World War I to 1955*, Art Institute of Chicago, 2009
- BÉGUIN, André, *Dictionnaire technique de la peinture pour les arts, le bâtiment et l'industrie*, M.Y.G/Béguin, 2009
- BLOOM, Jonathan M., BLAIR, Sheila S., *The Grove Encyclopedia of Islamic Art and Architecture*, Oxford University Press, 2009
- GOMBRICH, Ernst, *The Story of Art (16th edition)*, Phaidon, 2001
- HUREL, Roselyne, *Miniatures & peintures indiennes, vol. I*, Bibliothèque Nationale de France, 2010
- KUPKA, Karel, *Dawn of Art; Painting and Sculpture of Australian Aborigines*, Angus and Robertson, 1965
- MICHEL, Christian, *The Académie Royale de Peinture et de Sculpture – The Birth of the French School*, Getty Publications, 2018
- RECHT, Roland (ed.), *De la puissance de l'image : les artistes du Nord face à la Réforme*, Éditions du Musée du Louvre, 2002
- RIOUT, Denys (ed.), *Un texte, une œuvre, quatorze œuvres du Musée national d'art moderne, commentées*, Gallimard, 2020
- SALE, Marie-Pierre, *Watercolor: A History*, Abbeville Publishing Group, 2020
- TAYLOR, Paul, *Dutch Flower Painting 1600–1720*, Yale University Press, 1995
- TILMAN, Osterwold, *Pop Art*, Taschen, 2013

MONOGRAPHS

- ANDERSON, Jaynie, *Tiepolo's Cleopatra*, MacMillan, 2003
- AURICCHIO, Laura, *Adélaïde Labille-Guiard: Artist in the Age of Revolution*, Getty Publications, 2009
- BADE, Patrick, *Tamara de Lempicka*, Parkstone Press International, 2006
- BÄTSCHMANN, Oskar, GRIENER, Pascal, *Hans Holbein*, Reaktion Books, 2014
- BLUMENFELD, Carole, *Marguerite Gérard 1761–1837*, Gourcuff, 2019
- BUSSAGLI, Marco, *Jheronimus Bosch*, La Martinière, 2020
- CHENG, François, *Shitao, 1642–1707 : la saveur du monde*, Phébus, 1998
- COMTE-SPONVILLE, André, *La Matière heureuse, réflexions sur la peinture de Chardin*, Hermann, 2006
- DISTEL, Anne, *Renoir*, Abbeville Press, 2021
- DUROZOI, Gérard, *Matisse*, Studio Editions, 1993
- *Eugène Delacroix / choix de textes par Yves Florenne*, Mercure de France, 1963
- FOHR, Robert, *Georges de La Tour : le maître des nuits*, Cohen & Cohen, 2018
- FRIEDEL, Helmut, HOBERG, Annegret (ed.), *Vassily Kandinsky*, Prestel, 2008
- GAGE, John, *J.M.W. Turner: A Wonderful Range of Mind*, Yale University Press, 1987
- GLORIEUX, Guillaume, *Watteau*, Citadelles & Mazenod, 2011
- HALL, Marcia B., *Michelangelo: The Frescoes of the Sistine Chapel*, Harry N. Abrams, Inc, 2002
- HOFMANN, Werner, *Degas: A Dialogue of Difference*, Thames & Hudson, 2007
- HOPTMAN, Laura, KULTERMANN, Udo, TATEHATA, Akira, *Yayoi Kusama*, Phaidon, 2000
- HUMFREY, Peter, *Titien*, Phaidon Press, 2007
- INGLIS, Erik, *Jean Fouquet and the Invention of France: Art and Nation After the Hundred Years War*, Yale University Press, 2011
- ITZHACK, Goldberg, *Chagall*, Citadelles & Mazenod, 2019
- JOBERT, Barthélémy, *Delacroix*, Princeton University Press, 1998
- LE MEN, Ségolène, *Courbet*, Abbeville Press, 2008
- LE MEN, Ségolène, *Monet*, Citadelles & Mazenod, 2010
- LEE, Simon, *Delacroix*, Phaidon, 2015
- LEVY, Marianne, *Marie-Guillemine Laville-Leroulx et les siens : une femme peintre de l'Ancien Régime à la Restauration (1768–1826)*, L'Harmattan, 2018
- LOPEZ-REY, José, *Velázquez. The Complete Works*, Taschen, 2022
- MATHIEU, Pierre-Louis, *Gustave Moreau: Complete Edition of the Finished Paintings, Watercolours and Drawings*, Phaidon Press, 1977
- MURPHY, Caroline P., *Lavinia Fontana: A Painter and Her Patrons in Sixteenth-century Bologna*, Yale University Press, 2002
- OBERHUBER, Konrad, *Raphael: The Paintings*, Prestel, 2000
- PASSEZ, Anne-Marie, *Adélaïde Labille-Guiard : 1749–1803, biographie et catalogue raisonné de son œuvre*, Arts et Métiers graphiques, 1973
- PEDROCCO, Filippo, *Titien*, Rizzoli International Publications, 2001
- PIOT, Cyril, *Les Ménines de Velázquez. Une théologie de la peinture*, Thalia, 2011
- RAUTMANN, Peter, *Delacroix*, Citadelles & Mazenod, 1997
- ROBERTSON, Clare, *The Invention of Annibale Carracci*, Silvana Editoriale, 2008
- ROSAND, David, *Véronèse*, Citadelles & Mazenod, 2012
- ROSENBERG, Pierre, TEMPERINI, Renaud, *Chardin*, Flammarion, 1999
- ROSS, Frederick C., ROSS, Kara Lysandra, *William Bouguereau: The Essential Works*, ACC Art Books, 2022
- SALVY, Gérard-Julien, *Guido Reni*, Gallimard, 2001
- SCHÜTZE, Sebastian, *Caravaggio. The Complete Works*, Taschen, 2015
- SCHWARTZ, Gary, *Vermeer in Detail*, Harry N. Abrams Inc., 2017
- SELZ, Jean, *Edvard Munch*, Éditions Flammarion, 1974
- SERS, Philippe, *Kandinsky: The Elements of Art*, Thames and Hudson Ltd, 2016
- TERRASA, Jacques, *Déesses et paillassons Les grands nus de Picasso*, Presses universitaires de Vincennes, 2010
- VELLEKOOP, Marije, *et al.*, *Van Gogh at Work*, Yale University Press, 2013
- WELU, James A., BIESBOER, Pieter (ed.), *Judith Leyster: a Dutch Master and Her World*, Yale University Press, 1993
- WHITE, Christopher, *Anthony Van Dyck and the Art of Portraiture*, Modern Art Press, 2021

EXHIBITION CATALOGUES

- MUNHALL, Edgar, *Ingres and the Comtesse d'Haussonville*, The Frick Collection, 1985
- THUILLIER, Jacques (ed.), *Vouet*, Réunion des musées nationaux, 1990
- HERBERT, Robert L., *Seurat*, Réunion des musées nationaux, 1991

- STORR, Robert, MICHAUD, Yves, *Joan Mitchell,* Réunion des musées nationaux, 1994
- MARTIN, Jean Hubert, PELTIER, Philippe, *David Malangi,* Réunion des musées nationaux, 1995
- HERGOTT, Fabrice, SYLVESTER, David (ed.), *Francis Bacon,* Éditions du Centre Pompidou, 1996
- Chéri Samba, *Musée national des Arts d'Afrique et d'Océanie,* Hazan, 1997
- WEISS, Jeffrey, *Mark Rothko,* National Gallery of Art, Washington, 1998
- CHRISTIANSEN, Keith, MANN, Judith W., *Orazio and Artemisia Gentileschi,* Met Publications, 2001
- LIVINGSTON, Jane, *The Paintings of Joan Mitchell,* University of California Press, 2002
- POMAREDE, Vincent, WALLENS, Gérard de, *L'École de Barbizon,* Réunion des musées nationaux, 2002
- AVRIL, François (ed.), *Jean Fouquet : peintre et enlumineur du xve siècle,* Bibliothèque nationale de France / Hazan, 2003
- BRUGEROLLES, Emmanuelle (ed.), *François Boucher et l'art rocaille : dans les collections de l'École des beaux-arts,* Éditions de l'École nationale supérieure des beaux-arts, 2003
- JENKINS, Susan, *No Ordinary Place: The Art of David Malangi, Canberra,* National Gallery of Australia, 2004
- MAGNIN, André (ed.), *J'aime Chéri Samba,* Éditions de la Fondation Cartier pour l'art contemporain, 2004
- SOLIS, Felipe *et al.*, *The Aztec Empire,* Guggenheim Museum Publications, 2004
- SAINTE FARE GARNOT, Nicolas, *Jacques-Louis David (1748–1825),* Culturespaces / N. Chaudun, 2005
- SCHNEIDER, Eckhard et al., *Roy Lichtenstein: Classic of the New,* Walther König, 2005
- GUEGAN, Stéphane, POMAREDE, Vincent, PRAT, Louis-Antoine *et al.*, *Ingres, 1780–1867,* Gallimard, 2006
- HALLET, Mark, RIDING, Christine (ed.), *William Hogarth,* Éditions du musée du Louvre, 2006
- CUZIN, Jean-Pierre, SALMON, Dimitri, *Fragonard, regards croisés,* Mengès, 2007
- SELEZNEVA, Ekaterina L. (ed.), *Chagall entre ciel et terre,* Fondation Pierre Gianadda, 2007
- MERLE DU BOURG, Alexis, *Antoon Van Dyck : portraits,* Fonds Mercator, 2008
- PRIGNITZ-PODA, Helga, *Frida Kahlo Retrospective,* Prestel, 2010
- BERET, Chantal (ed.), *Yayoi Kusama,* Éditions du Centre Pompidou, 2011
- CHEROUX, Clément, LAMPE, Angela (ed.), *Edvard Munch, l'œil moderne,* Éditions du Centre Pompidou, 2011
- GUÉGAN, Stéphane (ed.) *Manet : inventeur du moderne,* Gallimard / musée d'Orsay, 2011
- CONTINI, Roberto, SOLINAS Francesco (ed.), *Artemisia : pouvoir, gloire, et passions d'une femme peintre,* Gallimard, 2012
- DEBRAY, Cécile (ed.), *Matisse : paires et séries,* Éditions du Centre Pompidou, 2012
- GODFREY, Mark, SEROTA, Nicholas (ed.), *Gerhard Richter : panorama* Éditions du Centre Pompidou, 2012
- MARTIN, Jean-Hubert (*et al.*), *Dalí,* Éditions du Centre Pompidou / Museo nacional centro de arte Reina Sofia, 2012
- BORMAND, Marc, (ed.), *Le Printemps de la Renaissance, la sculpture et les arts à Florence, 1400–1460,* Éditions du musée du Louvre / Officina Libraria, 2013
- CAHN, Isabelle, DUCREY, Marina, POLETTI, Katia, *Vallotton,* Réunion des musées nationaux, 2013
- OTTINGER, Didier, *Hopper,* Réunion des musées nationaux, 2013
- THIÉBAUT, Dominique, *Giotto e compagni,* Éditions du musée du Louvre / Officina Libraria, 2013
- COLLANGE, Adeline, KAZEROUNI, Guillaume (ed.), *Georges de La Tour : trois « nuits » pour une Renaissance,* Les beaux jours, 2014
- COUSSEAU, Henry-Claude *et al.*, *Georges Braque (1882–1963),* Réunion des musées nationaux, 2014
- BAILLIO, Joseph, SALMON, Xavier (ed.), *Élisabeth Louise Vigée Le Brun,* Réunion des musées nationaux, 2015
- FAROULT, Guillaume (ed.), *Fragonard amoureux : galant et libertin,* Réunion des musées nationaux, 2015
- BALDASSARI, Anne (ed.), Fondation Louis Vuitton, *Icônes de l'art moderne : la collection Chtchoukine,* Gallimard / Fondation Louis Vuitton, 2016
- GADY, Bénédicte, MILOVANOVIC, Nicolas (ed.), *Charles Le Brun, 1619–1690,* Lienart, 2016
- OTTINGER, Didier (ed.), *Magritte, la trahison des images,* Éditions du Centre Pompidou, 2016
- SCHATBORN, Peter (ed.), *Rembrandt intime,* Fonds Mercator, 2016
- BERNARDI, Claire, FERLIER, Ophélie (ed.), *Gauguin : l'alchimiste,* Réunion des musées nationaux, 2017
- GEORGEL, Chantal, GIRVEAU, Bruno, SCOTTEZ-DE WAMBRECHIES, Annie, *Millet,* Réunion des musées nationaux / Palais des beaux-arts de Lille, 2017
- BASHKOFF, Tracey R, *et al.*, *Hilma af Klint: Paintings for the Future,* Guggenheim Museum Publications, 2018
- *Edward Burne-Jones,* Tate Publishing, 2018
- HASKELL, Barbara (ed.), *Grant Wood: American Gothic and Other Fables,* Whitney Museum of American Art, 2018
- DELIEUVIN, Vincent, FRANK, Louis (ed.), *Léonard de Vinci,* Éditions du Louvre / Hazan, 2019
- BROWN, David Blayney, CURIE, Pierre (ed.), *Turner : peintures et aquarelles, collections de la Tate,* Paris, Fonds Mercator, 2020
- MARTENS, Maximiliaan P. J. (ed.), *Van Eyck, une révolution optique,* Hannibal Publishing / MSK Gent, 2020
- COTENTIN, Régis, DUJARDIN, Donatienne, (ed.), *Expérience Goya,* Réunion des musées nationaux, 2021
- DEBENEDETTI, Ana, *Botticelli, artiste et designer,* Fonds Mercator, 2021
- La Collection Morozov. *Icônes de l'Art moderne,* éditions Fondation Louis Vuitton / Gallimard, 2021
- VIRASSAMYNAÏKEN, Ludmila (ed.), *À la mort, à la vie ! Vanités d'hier et d'aujourd'hui,* Éditions Bernard Chauveau, 2022

DIGITAL SOURCES

- Suzy Lévy, *"Les cafés montmartrois au xixe siècle, lieux de communication"* Published in *Communication & Langages*, 1995
- Fred Hoffmann, Jean-Michel Basquiat Head Imagery, 2019: https://fredhoffmanfineart.com/
- L'Art en question, Canal Éducatif à la Demande: https://www.canal-educatif.fr/
- L'Histoire par l'Image: https://histoire-image.org/
- Bibliothèque Nationale de France: https://www.bnf.fr
- Louvre Museum: https://www.louvre.fr
- Musée d'Orsay: https://www.musee-orsay.fr/
- Centre Pompidou: https://www.centrepompidou.fr/
- The National Gallery: https://www.nationalgallery.org.uk/
- The National Gallery of Art: https://www.nga.gov/
- The Metropolitan Museum of Art: https://www.metmuseum.org/

CREDITS

Illustrations: © Jean André: p. 12–13, 17, 18, 27, 42–43, 48–49, 54, 74, 76, 96–97, 108, 111, 132, 134, 136, 144, 156–157, 162, 166–167, 186–187, 194, 196, 206, 220–221, 224, 242, 256–257, 260, 262, 270, 284–285, 290, 292, 298–299, 304, 310, 322, 330, 332, 334, 338

Centre credits: © 2010 RMN-Grand Palais
(Louvre Museum) / René-Gabriel Ojéda: p. 133 centre, 154, 158
© Abaca Press / Alamy Banque d'Images / ADAGP, Paris, 2022: p. 201
© Adam Eastland Art + Architecture / Alamy Stock Photo: p. 64
© agefotostock / Alamy Banque d'Images: p. 218
© Archivah / Alamy Banque d'Images: p. 134t
© Archive PL / Alamy Banque d'Images: p. 245t centre
© ART Collection / Alamy Banque d'Images: p. 56bl
© Art Collection 2 / Alamy Banque d'Images: p. 57
© Artepics / Alamy Banque d'Images / © The Estate of Francis Bacon / All rights reserved / ADAGP, Paris and DACS, London 2022: p. 315
© Artvee: p. 226
© Azoor Photo / Alamy Banque d'Images: p. 237
© bordeauxphotopassion.fr: p. 175
© Bridgeman Images: p. 28–29, 31, 52–53, 55, 62, 81, 87, 99, 103, 110l, 113, 115, 133 r, 139, 141tl, 169, 177, 185, 215, 217, 220l, 228–229, 231, 249, 268, 269, 297, 322, 328
© Bridgeman Images / © 2022 Banco de México Diego Rivera Frida Kahlo Museums Trust, Mexico, D.F. / ADAGP, Paris: p. 307
© CC0 / BnF: p. 75
© CC0 / Figge Art Museum: p. 288
© CC0 / Flicker / Steven Zucker: p. 50
© CC0 / LACMA: p. 74r, 210t
© CC0 / MAK, Vienne: p. 74l
© CC0 / Mauritshuis: p. 102, 208b centre
© CC0 / MET: p. 140t centre, 163, 165, 184, 208br, 304
© CC0 / The National Gallery of Art, London: p. 61
© CC0 / National Gallery of Art, Washington: p. 225
© CC0 / Philadelphia Museum of Art: p. 104
© CC0 / Rijksmuseum: p. 107, 119, 240l
© CC0 / RoyalCollins: p. 134b
© CC0 / Wichita Art Museum: p. 41
© CC0 / Wikimedia: p. 20, 22, 24, 26h, 26bl, 26br, 27tl, 27tr, 27bl, 27br, 30, 32, 34, 35tl, 35tr, 35bl, 35br, 36–37, 38, 40, 44, 45, 46t, 46b, 54, 56tr, 56br, 58, 60, 62, 68, 70, 72h, 72b, 78, 80l, 80 centre, 80r, 82, 84, 85, 86, 88t, 88bl, 88b centre, 88br, 90, 95, 98, 104, 106, 108, 110r, 112, 114t, 114b, 118, 122, 124t, 124b, 130, 134 centre, 138t, 138b, 140tl, 140tr, 140bl, 140b centre, 140br, 141t centre, 141tr, 141bl, 141b centre, 144, 148, 150, 160, 161, 162l, 162 centre, 162d, 164, 168, 170, 171, 172h, 172b, 174h, 174b, 176h, 176b, 178, 179, 180, 183, 186tr, 186bl, 186br, 187tl, 187tr, 187bl, 187br, 190, 194, 195, 198h, 198b1, 198b2, 198b3, 198b4, 199, 202, 206, 208tl, 208h centre, 208tr, 208bl, 209tl, 209h centre, 209bl, 209b centre, 210t, 210b1, 210b2, 210b3, 210b4, 211, 212h, 212b1, 212b2, 212b3, 212b4, 214h, 214bl, 214b centre, 214br, 216h, 216b, 219, 220d, 222–223, 224, 230, 232, 233, 236, 238h, 238b1, 238b2, 238b3, 238b4, 238b5, 239, 240 centre, 240r, 242, 244tl, 244h centre, 224tr, 244bl, 244br, 245tl, 245tr, 245bl, 245br, 246, 248t, 248b, 250, 252b1, 252b2, 252b3, 252b4, 252b5, 253, 254, 255, 270, 274h, 274b1, 274b2, 274b3, 274b4, 274b5, 276h, 276b, 277, 278, 280, 282, 290, 292, 295, 299, 302, 306, 308, 314b, 318, 328, 336b
© CC0/ JuzaPhoto: p. 91
© Centre Pompidou, MNAM-CCI, Dist. RMN-Grand Palais / image Centre Pompidou, MNAM-CCI / © Tamara de Lempicka Estate, LLC / ADAGP, Paris, 2022: p. 291
© Centre Pompidou, MNAM-CCI, Dist. RMN-Grand Palais / Philippe Migeat / © Succession Yves Klein c/o ADAGP, Paris, 2022: p. 283
© Chéri Samba / Courtesy Galerie MAGNIN-A Paris: p. 337
© Christie's Images / Bridgeman Images: p. 109
© CNMages / Alamy Stock Photo / © 2022 Heirs of Josephine N. Hopper / ADAGP, Paris: p. 303
© Collection KMSKA / CC0: p. 10, 11
© Collection Zao Wou-ki / ADAGP, Paris, 2022: p. 141bd
© Courtesy of Artcurial: p. 142, 143, 145
© Courtesy of Pest Control Office, Banksy, Paris, 2018: p. 339
© Cy Twombly Foundation: p. 127
© Danica O. Kus: p. 340–341
© David Grossman / Alamy Stock Photo / © Georgia O'Keeffe Museum / ADAGP, Paris, 2022: p. 305
© David Hockney / Tate Modern: p. 325
© David Lichtneker / Alamy Stock Photo: p. 329
© DCarreño / Alamy Stock Photo: p. 203
© DCarreño / Alamy Stock Photo: p. 65, 121
© Éric Jouvenaux: p. 173
© Éric Koch: p. 320
© Fine Art Images / Bridgeman Images: p. 73, 133l, 181, 293
© Flickr Eddie C3: p. 33
© Fondation Félix Vallotton, Lausanne: p. 251
© Franck Legros / Alamy Stock Photo: p. 120
© Galerie Red Hill Art, Kenya: p. 209br
© George Etheredge: p. 275
© Gerhard Richter 2022 (0165): p. 331
© Getty Images / Bloomberg / Contributor / © The Estate of Francis Bacon / All rights reserved / ADAGP, Paris and DACS, London 2022: p. 317
© Getty Images / Chalkie Davies: p. 332
© Getty Images / Oli Scarff / Employee / © The Estate of Francis Bacon / All rights reserved / ADAGP, Paris and DACS, London 2022: p. 316
© Getty Images / picture alliance / Contributor: p. 100–101
© Getty Images/picture alliance / Raphael GAILLARDE: p. 300–301
© Giorgio Morara / Alamy Stock Photo: p. 39
© Philippe Halsman / Magnum Photos: p. 296
© Hugo Maertens, Collection KMSKA - Flemish Community (CC0): p. 25
© ideelart: p. 312b
© incamerastock / Alamy Stock Photo: p. 89
© Isabella Stewart Gardner Museum / Bridgeman Images: p. 63
© Jacqueline Salmon/Artedia / Bridgeman Images: p. 330
© Joan Mitchell Foundation: p. 227, 313
© Kimbell Art Museum, Fort Worth, Texas: p. 92–93, 152–153, 155
© Luc Boegly/Artedia / Bridgeman Images p. 191
© Luisa Ricciarini / Bridgeman Images: p. 21, 79, 83
© Malcolm Park / Alamy Stock Photo: p. 71, 149
© Malcolm Park editorial / Alamy Stock Photo: p. 23
© Mario Dondero. All rights reserved 2022 / Bridgeman Images: p. 314t
© Marion Kalter. All rights reserved 2022 / Bridgeman Images: p. 312t
© MasterBliss / Alamy Banque d'Images: p. 243
© mccool / Alamy Banque d'Images: p. 262
© Michael Ventura / Alamy Banque d'Images: p. 289
© Michel Sima / Bridgeman Images: p. 264
© Michel Viard / Horizon Features. All rights reserved 2022 / Bridgeman Images: p. 324
© Mondrian / Holtzman Trust / Bridgeman Images: p. 279
© Musée d'Art Moderne et Contemporain de Saint-Etienne Métropole:

p. 286–287
© Musée du Louvre, Dist. RMN-Grand Palais / Angèle Dequier: p. 51, 125, 146, 192
© Musée du Quai Branly – Jacques Chirac, Dist. RMN-Grand Palais / Patrick Gries / Bula'bula Art Center: p. 319
© National Gallery of Art, Washington / ADAGP, Paris, 2022: p. 294
© National Gallery of Victoria, Melbourne / Felton Bequest / Bridgeman Images: p. 151
© National Trust Photographic Library / Bridgeman Images: p. 186tl
© Odyssey-Images / Alamy Banque d'Images: p. 247,
© Odyssey-Images / Alamy Banque d'Images / ADAGP, Paris, 2022: p. 271
© Peter Willi / Bridgeman Images: p. 128–129, 131
© Photo 194892636 © Maria Rzeszotarska | Dreamstime.com: p. 207
© Photo Josse / Bridgeman Images: p. 66–67, 69, 123, 147, 182, 204–205, 213, 235
© PVDE / Bridgeman Images: p. 252t
© Rheinisches Bildarchiv Köln, Wolfgang Meier, rba_d013160 /
© Estate of Roy Lichtenstein New York / ADAGP, Paris, 2022: p. 321
© Richard Soberka / Hemis.fr: p. 258–259
© RMN-Grand Palais (MNAAG, Paris) / Daniel Arnaudet: p. 135
© RMN-Grand Palais (Musée d'Orsay) / Hervé Lewandowski: p. 200
© RMN-Grand Palais / image of the MMA / ADAGP, Paris, 2022: p. 209tr
© Roman Milert / Alamy Stock Photo: p. 59
© Saint Louis Art Museum / Funds given by the Shoenberg Foundation, Inc. / Bridgeman Images / © 1998 Kate Rothko Prizel & Christopher Rothko / ADAGP, Paris, 2022: p. 309
© Salvador Dalí, Fundació Gala-Salvador Dali / ADAGP, Paris, 2022: p. 297
© SLUB / Dresde: p. 56tl
© Staatliche Kunstsammlungen Dresden / © Staatliche Kunstsammlungen Dresden / Bridgeman Images: p. 126
© Stefano Baldini / Bridgeman Images: p. 47
© Stefano Baldini / Bridgeman Images / ADAGP, Paris, 2022: p. 311
© Succession H. Matisse 2023/ photo: The Museum of Modern Art / Scala: p. 263
© Succession Picasso 2022 / ADAGP, Paris, 2022: p. 265
© Superstock/UIG / Bridgeman Images: p. 281
© The Andy Warhol Foundation for the Visual Arts, Inc. / Licensed by ADAGP, Paris, 2022: p. 323
© The Eli and Edythe L. Broad Collection / The Estate of Jean-Michel Basquiat / ADAGP, Paris, 2022: p. 333
© The Picture Art Collection / Alamy Banque d'Images : p. 193
© The Stapleton Collection / Bridgeman Images / ADAGP, Paris, 2022: p. 273
© Unsplash / Abbie Bernet: p. 266–267
© Unsplash / redcharlie: p. 14–15
© Unsplash / Václav Pluhař: p. 116–117
© Unsplash / Wesley Mc Lachlan: p. 16
© Wallace Collection, London, UK / Bridgeman Images: p. 159
© YAYOI KUSAMA: p. 334
© YAYOI KUSAMA / Christie's Images / Bridgeman Images: p. 335

On the cover, for the detail of the painting by Frida Kahlo, *Itzcuintli Dog with Me* (1938, oil on canvas, private collection): © 2022 Banco de México Diego Rivera Frida Kahlo Museums Trust, Mexico, D.F. / Adagp, Paris / Fine Art Images / Bridgeman Images photography

THANKS

As I am writing these words, I am looking back on all the work that I accomplished – with pride, but also with a certainty: I could never have achieved this without guidance from Les Éditions du Chêne, who cared to entrust me with this beautiful project – and, I would even say, followed their intuition, as in a way, the idea of this book began to hatch in me a long time ago, without my even noticing it.

I would therefore like to thank the entire team, who worked with passion on this book. I am particularly grateful to Emmanuel Le Vallois, publishing house director, for his reassuring confidence and amazing vision; and to my editor, Hélène Sevin, for her patience and her attentiveness, for her ideas, which only helped better define the final form of this book, and for all our energising and intellectually nourishing conversations, which made me feel that I was right there where I was meant to be.

Thanks to Sabine Houplain, the artistic director, and to Bureau Berger for their well thought-out layout, and also to Jean André, whose drawings add an innovative and warm touch to this work.
Thanks also to Clothilde Bollard-Duval, Magali Brénon and Joanne Dasoul for their meticulous and valuable corrections.

I am also very grateful to Florence Raymond, head of the documentary resources, digital and prospective innovation department at the Palais des Beaux-Arts in Lille, who generously shared her experience with me, and whose fascinating explanations were so helpful to me.

Thanks also to Augustin Lepage, who welcomed me to the backstage of the Atelier de Luynes, and to Arthur Bessaud, founder of the Démasqués gallery, for his insights into urban art.

I would also like to express my profound affection to my family and friends (they know who they are), who have shown interest and support while I was working on this project. Lord knows they have patiently tolerated my absences.

Finally, I would like to symbolically express my gratitude to all the teachers who, since my childhood, passed their taste for art on to me, before I was bold enough to call it my own:
to Pascale, teacher at the Clémenceau school, for Mondrian, Cézanne's still lifes and *The Newborn Child* by Georges de La Tour; to Madame Le Fol and Madame Steib, at the Chalais secondary school, for the stained glass windows by Chagall in Mainz, Germany; to Madame Mallet, in my first year of secondary school at Bréquigny, for Malevitch, to Madame Delarue, in my second year, for Nadja and Breton, and to Madame Fraisse-Marbot, in my final year, for the "Magritte" exhibition at Le Jeu de Paume; to Monsieur Charlie Pommier, to Bertrand d'Argentré, for his courses in visual creation, Willy Ronis, symbolism and Gustave Moreau; to Monsieur Michel Marques, at the ISTC, for Eisenstein, for his courses in the semiology of still images and moving images. Finally, thanks to Madame Lecourt and Monsieur Neiva for their passion; maybe they are reading these words over my shoulder from where they are.

A member of Penguin Random House Verlagsgruppe GmbH,
Neumarkter Strasse 28, 81673 München

First published in French
Léonard, Frida et les autres

A CIP catalogue record for this book is available from
the British Library

Art direction: Sabine Houplain & Bureau Berger

Layout: Bureau Berger

Translation: David Rocher

Copy-editing: John Stilwell

Production: Cilly Klotz

Typesetting: Weiß-Freiburg GmbH — Grafik und Buchgestaltung

Lithography: Hyphen Group

Printing and binding: Toppan Lefung

Printed in China
ISBN 978-3-7913-7718-6
www.prestel.com